Principles of
Cybersecurity

G-W PUBLISHER

Linda K. Lavender

Be prepared with the skills
needed in the field of cybersecurity

Guided Tour

- **Reading Prep** literacy integration activities at the beginning of each lesson encourage your development of confidence and skill in literacy and learning.
- **Check Your Cybersecurity IQ** pretest will help you evaluate your prior knowledge of the chapter content and identify areas of the chapter on which to focus study.
- **Certification Objectives** list the CompTIA Security+ and Microsoft MTA Security Fundamentals objectives covered in the chapter to help you prepare for taking certification exams.

- **Essential Question** at the beginning of each chapter will engage you as you uncover the important points presented in the content.
- **Learning Goals** identify the knowledge and skills you will gain by studying the chapter.
- **Key Terms** lists the important words so you can focus on learning the technical terms in each lesson.

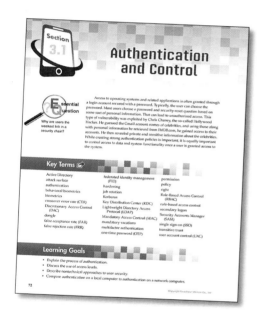

- **Quick Look** allows you to immediately apply the knowledge you just learned for reinforcement.
- **Certification objective callouts** enable you to focus learning on skills related to industry-recognized certification.

Guided Tour

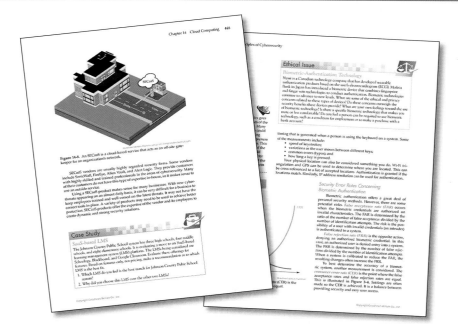

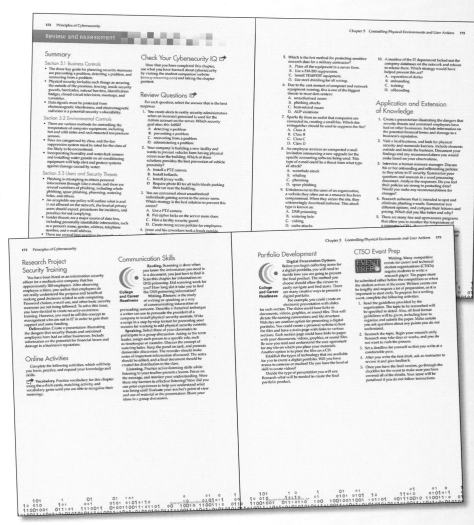

- **Case Study** presents you with a scenario and asks you what should be done to connect your learning to real-life situations.
- **Ethical Issue** illustrates a situation for you in which an ethical or moral judgment is needed.

- **Check Your Cybersecurity IQ** posttest will help you evaluate what you have learned after studying the chapter and areas in which additional study may be needed.
- **Review Questions** cover the concepts presented in the chapter and allow you to evaluate your understanding of the material.
- **Application and Extension of Knowledge** activities challenge you to relate what you learned in the chapter to your own ideas and projects.
- **Research Project** provides you with an opportunity to apply your research skills by investigating a topic in greater detail.
- **Online Activities** present an opportunity for you to practice the key terms presented in each chapter.

Textbook

Principles of Cybersecurity is an exciting, full-color, and highly illustrated learning resource that prepares students with skills needed in the field of cybersecurity. This text will also help prepare students for industry-recognized certification.

By studying this text, students will learn about security threats and vulnerabilities. The textbook begins with an introduction to the field of cybersecurity and the fundamentals of security. From there, it covers how to manage user security, control the physical environment, and protect host systems. Nontraditional hosts are also covered, as is network infrastructure, services, wireless network security, and web and cloud security. Penetration testing is discussed along with risk management, disaster recovery, and incident response. The textbook concludes with a chapter on employability skills.

Laboratory Manual

The student laboratory manual provides hands-on practice with questions and lab activities. Each chapter corresponds to the text lessons and reinforces key concepts and applied knowledge.

G-W Learning Companion Website

The G-W Learning companion website is a study reference that contains e-flash cards, vocabulary exercises, interactive quizzes, and more! Accessible from any digital device, the G-W Learning companion website complements the textbook and is available to you at no charge. Visit www.g-wlearning.com.

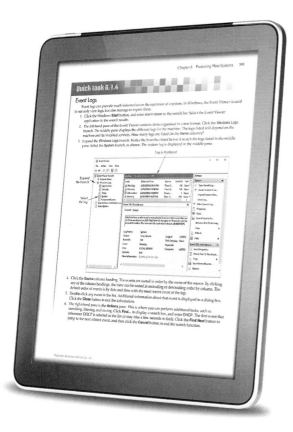

Instructor Resources

LMS Integration

Integrate Goodheart-Willcox content within your Learning Management System for a seamless user experience for both you and your students. LMS-ready content in Common Cartridge format facilitates single sign-on integration and gives you control of student enrollment and data. With a Common Cartridge integration, you can access the LMS features and tools you are accustomed to using and G-W course resources in one convenient location—your LMS.

In order to provide a complete learning package for you and your students, G-W Common Cartridge includes the Online Textbook and Online Instructor Resources. When you incorporate G-W content into your courses via Common Cartridge, you have the flexibility to customize and structure the content to meet the educational needs of your students. You may also choose to add your own content to the course.

QTI® assessment files are available within the Online Instructor Resources for import into your LMS. These pre-built assessments help you measure student knowledge and track results in your LMS gradebook. Questions and tests can be customized to meet your assessment needs.

Online Instructor Resources (OIR)

Online Instructor Resources provide all the support needed to make preparation and classroom instruction easier than ever. Available in one accessible location, the OIR includes instructor's resources and instructor's presentations for PowerPoint®. These resources are available as a subscription and can be accessed at school, at home, or on the go.

Instructor Resources

One resource provides instructors with time-saving preparation tools such as answer keys, lesson plans, chapter reviews and quizzes, pretests, posttests, and other teaching aids.

Instructor Presentations for PowerPoint®

Instructor's Presentations for PowerPoint® provide a useful teaching tool when presenting the lessons. These fully customizable slides help you teach and visually reinforce the key concepts from each chapter. Slides include the list of Learning Goals and Key Terms from each chapter, definitions for each Key Term, talking points for important concepts, and selected Review Questions.

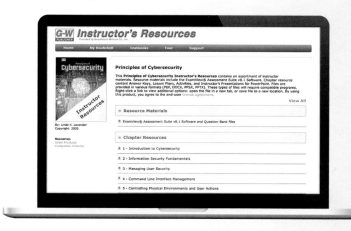

ExamView® Assessment Suite

ExamView® Assessment Suite enables you to create and print tests quickly and easily from a test bank of hundreds of questions. The components include the ExamView® Test Generator, ExamView® Test Manager, and ExamView® Test Player. You can have the software generate a test for you with randomly selected questions. You may also choose specific questions from the question banks and, if you wish, add your own questions to create customized tests to meet your classroom needs.

G-W Integrated Learning Solution

The G-W Integrated Learning Solution offers easy-to-use resources for both students and instructors. Digital and blended learning content can be accessed through any Internet-enabled device, such as a computer, smartphone, or tablet. Students spend more time learning, and instructors spend less time administering.

G-W Learning Companion Website/Student Textbook

The G-W Learning companion website is a study reference that contains e-flash cards, vocabulary exercises, interactive quizzes, and more! Accessible from any digital device, the G-W Learning companion website complements the textbook and is available to the student at no charge. Visit www.g-wlearning.com.

Cybersecurity

by

Linda K. Lavender

Publisher

The Goodheart-Willcox Company, Inc.

Tinley Park, Illinois

www.g-w.com

The Goodheart-Willcox Company, Inc. Brand Disclaimer: Brand names, company names, and illustrations for products and services included in this text are provided for educational purposes only and do not represent or imply endorsement or recommendation by the author or the publisher.

The Goodheart-Willcox Company, Inc. Safety Notice: The reader is expressly advised to carefully read, understand, and apply all safety precautions and warnings described in this book or that might also be indicated in undertaking the activities and exercises described herein to minimize risk of personal injury or injury to others. Common sense and good judgment should also be exercised and applied to help avoid all potential hazards. The reader should always refer to the appropriate manufacturer's technical information, directions, and recommendations; then proceed with care to follow specific equipment operating instructions. The reader should understand these notices and cautions are not exhaustive.

The publisher makes no warranty or representation whatsoever, either expressed or implied, including but not limited to equipment, procedures, and applications described or referred to herein, their quality, performance, merchantability, or fitness for a particular purpose. The publisher assumes no responsibility for any changes, errors, or omissions in this book. The publisher specifically disclaims any liability whatsoever, including any direct, indirect, incidental, consequential, special, or exemplary damages resulting, in whole or in part, from the reader's use or reliance upon the information, instructions, procedures, warnings, cautions, applications, or other matter contained in this book. The publisher assumes no responsibility for the activities of the reader.

The Goodheart-Willcox Company, Inc. Internet Disclaimer: The Internet resources and listings in this Goodheart-Willcox Publisher product are provided solely as a convenience to you. These resources and listings were reviewed at the time of publication to provide you with accurate, safe, and appropriate information. Goodheart-Willcox Publisher has no control over the referenced websites and, due to the dynamic nature of the Internet, is not responsible or liable for the content, products, or performance of links to other websites or resources. Goodheart-Willcox Publisher makes no representation, either expressed or implied, regarding the content of these websites, and such references do not constitute an endorsement or recommendation of the information or content presented. It is your responsibility to take all protective measures to guard against inappropriate content, viruses, or other destructive elements.

Cover illustration: deepadesigns/Shutterstock.com
Interior design elements: Mictoon/Shutterstock.com
Chapter opener spy: NatBasil/Shutterstock.com

Introduction

Cybersecurity is the field of computer science related to protecting digital assets and computer systems against unauthorized or criminal access and use. The BLS reports there are roughly 83 thousand jobs in this area with a median salary of nearly $90,000. It projects a growth of 37 percent through 2024. Demand for individuals with cybersecurity skills is expected to be very high. The Council on Cybersecurity has reported an unprecedented demand for highly skilled cybersecurity practitioners. These individuals are needed to building security into new and existing networks. They also need to be capable of assessing security on a real-time basis. These individuals are the front-line defenders against cybersecurity threats across industries and governmental agencies.

Principles of Cybersecurity will prepare you with skills needed in the field of cybersecurity. By studying this text, you will learn about security threats and vulnerabilities. You will learn how to identify these issues and how to combat them. This text also helps prepare you for certification in CompTIA Security+ and Microsoft MTA Security Fundamentals.

Cybersecurity is an advanced topic. To be successful, you should have completed courses in basic computer hardware as well as networking. Many students will have obtained CompTIA A+ and CompTIA Networking+ certification prior to taking a cybersecurity class.

About the Author

Linda K. Lavender is a cybersecurity and network administration teacher for Virginia Beach City Public Schools, Advanced Technology Center. She is also an adjunct instructor in information technology for Tidewater Community College in Virginia Beach. She holds a Master of Science in cybersecurity and a Bachelor of Science in computer information systems from Saint Leo University, Florida. She has been named teacher of the year by several organizations, including ACTE. She is certified in CompTIA Security+, Network+, A+, CySA+, and CTT+; Microsoft MCTS, MCTIP, MCP, MOS, and MTA; and CIW Foundations.

Reviewers

Goodheart-Willcox Publisher would like to thank the following teachers and administrators who reviewed selected chapters and contributed valuable input to this edition of *Principles of Cybersecurity*.

Charles W. Brown, Jr.
CATE Instructor
Central High School
Pageland, SC

Lisa-Marie Burns
Business Education Department
 Chair
Washington High School Fremont
 Unified School District
Fremont, CA

Kristin A. Burr
Business Teacher
Merritt Island High School
Merritt Island, FL

Norma Johnson Cancel
Business Marketing and Career
 Education Instructor
Daleville High School
Daleville, AL

Jason T. Clark
Computer Systems Technology
 Instructor
Appomattox County High School
Appomattox, VA

Florence Lynn Copeland
CTE Instructor
Chula Vista High School
San Diego, CA

Jason Cordes
Career and Technology Education
 Teacher
Bryan Independent School District
Bryan, TX

Susan Crane
Business Education Teacher
Southern Alamance High School
Graham, NC

Paula F. Dana
Business Education Instructor
Darlington High School
Darlington, SC

Phyllis Bullock Eppes
Business Education Teacher
Powhatan High School
Powhatan, VA

Sharon Flanagan
Business Education Teacher
Sipsey Valley High School
Buhl, AL

Michael P. Harlen
Educator
Brookland-Cayce High School
Columbia, SC

Madison Holloman
Business Education Teacher
Irmo High School
Columbia, SC

Sharon Lambert
Business/Technology Teacher
Dunnellon High School (Marion
 County Public Schools)
Dunnellon, FL

Shannon Lynch
Career & Technical Education
 Teacher, Computer Technology
Southern Alamance High School
Graham, NC

Teri H. Mitchell
Career Tech Instructor—STEM,
 Cyber, Computer Science
Challenger Middle School
Huntsville, AL

Renee Monteith
Business Teacher
Clover High School
Clover, SC

Stephen Morisani, Jr.
Mathematics and Computer
 Science Instructor
Fairhope High School
Fairhope, AL

Darius Powell
Business Education Teacher
Sycamore High School
Cincinnati, OH

Sharon Ray, Ed.S.
Business Education and
 Technology Teacher
Holly Pond High School
Holly Pond, AL

Javier Rios
Career and Technical Education
 Instructor
JHF Polytechnic High School
Sun Valley, CA

Tracy C. Smith
Business Teacher–Career and
 Technical Education
Fuquay-Varina High School
Fuquay-Varina, NC

Jessica Tibbs
Business and Information
 Technology Teacher
Prince Edward County Public
 Schools
Farmville, VA

Kathy Van Vleet
Technology Instructor
West Port High School
Ocala, FL

Melanie Weser
Teacher/Network Administrator
Peninsula Catholic High School
Newport News, VA

John Williams
CATE Computer Science and IT
 Instructor
Whale Branch Early College
 High School
Seabrook, SC

Brief Contents

Contents

Quick Look

Special Features

Research Project

Case Study

Ethical Issue

Chapter 1

Introduction to Cybersecurity

It seems every day there is a story in the news about computer hacking, cybersecurity, or even cyberterrorism. There have been some prominent hacking events that have affected aspects of many of our lives. These include hacks against retail organizations, stolen Social Security numbers, and hacks against the US political system in the form of attacks against the Democratic National Party and campaign officials. Even US governmental agencies tasked with keeping the nation safe are not immune to hacks. In March 2017, a hacker provided WikiLeaks with enormous amounts of confidential material taken directly from the CIA networks.

A career in cybersecurity can be a rewarding and fulfilling profession. Cybersecurity professionals are committed to providing service to their companies, organizations, or government against threats and attacks. Although they often work behind the scenes, their work is valued and critical to the security and success of their organizations. Jobs in the cybersecurity field are in high demand. While earnings vary by organization and area, in general professionals can expect higher-than-average salaries. This career field will constantly evolve. It offers endless opportunities for lifelong learning and skill development. Every business and organization can be affected by cyberthreats, so cybersecurity professionals enjoy the flexibility of job opportunities around the world and across diverse employers.

Chapter Preview

While studying, look for the activity icon for:

- Pretests and posttests
- Vocabulary terms with e-flash cards and matching activities
- Self-assessment

G-WLEARNING.com

Reading Prep

To skim is to glance quickly through material to get an overview. It is also known as *prereading*. Before reading this chapter, skim the material by reading the first sentence of each paragraph. Use this information to create an outline for the chapter before you read it.

College and Career Readiness

Check Your Cybersecurity IQ ➭

Before you begin this chapter, see what you already know about cybersecurity by visiting the student companion website (www.g-wlearning.com) and taking the chapter pretest.

Certification Objectives

CompTIA Security+

1.3 Explain threat actor types and attributes.
3.2 Given a scenario, implement secure network architecture concepts.
3.4 Explain the importance of secure staging deployment concepts.
3.7 Summarize cloud and virtualization concepts.
5.6 Explain disaster recovery and continuity of operation concepts.

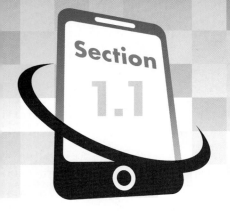

Introduction to Cybersecurity

Essential Question

How do computer hackers provide a benefit to society?

It seems like not a week goes by without news of some sort of computer hacking or security breach. Are there more risks now than ever? The answer to that is, yes. Society is moving more into a digital- and Internet-based world. However, security breaches are not new. Data security has been an issue since the early days of computers. There are many reasons a person may try to hack into data, and there are many ways to prevent this.

Key Terms ☛

attack vector
black-hat hacker
bug-bounty program
cyberattack
cybersecurity
darknet

deep web
gray-hat hacker
hacker
hacking
hacktivisim
onion network

phreaking
script kiddie
Tor browser
virus
white-hat hacker
worm

Learning Goals

- Examine historical context of cybersecurity in modern computing systems.
- Explain cybersecurity and information assurance.
- Identify motivations for hacking.
- List common defenses against cyberattacks.

History of Cybersecurity Attacks and Issues

Consider your school's learning environment. Many classes now are using cloud-based portals for online classrooms. Examples of these portals are Blackboard and Google Classroom. Medical offices and hospitals are tracking patient records in a purely digital form. Online portals offer patients personal access to their information. Homes are more connected to the Internet than ever. Garage-door openers to televisions, kitchen appliances, doorbells, and even light bulbs may be connected to the Internet, as shown in **Figure 1-1.**

All of this connectivity provides conveniences not available just a few years ago. However, in exchange for this convenience, being connected to the Internet provides the physical means for hackers to attack. Devices and software have become targets, and security breaches allow hackers access to these resources. *Hacking* is the act of circumventing or breaking past security boundaries. A *hacker* is a person who engages in hacking. An *attack vector* is the avenue or path the hacker uses to commit the attack.

Hackers are commonly referred to as white-, black-, or gray-hat hackers. Typically, a *white-hat hacker* is generally ethical and law-abiding. These hackers are examples of why the word hacker does not always mean something bad. The *black-hat hacker* usually operates outside the law. The *gray-hat hacker* falls somewhere between the other two. Gray hats do no harm, but do not ask permission.

Hacking has also become more common, in part, due to the abundance of free tools that hackers can use. These tools can be used to infiltrate systems, spy on users, plant malware, or worse.

Macrovector/Shutterstock.com

Figure 1-1. Many devices in the modern home are Internet-enabled and may present cybersecurity risks.

The issues related to cybersecurity have been around for quite some time. *Cybersecurity* is the process of protecting a system against unintended or malicious changes or use. A *cyberattack* is an attempt to steal, damage, or destroy data or a computer system. Cybersecurity issues include attacks on phone systems, computer viruses, and computer hacks. Other issues include tricking someone to reveal sensitive information, data theft, social engineering, and various forms of malware.

There are many costs associated with cybercrime. The cost of financial cybercrimes is expected to reach $6 trillion a year by the year 2021. Other costs include actual damage to a system, theft of confidential and intellectual property, lost productivity, and harm to an organization's reputation. A company cannot afford to ignore the impacts that cyberattacks can have on its business.

Businesses commonly have an information technology department. This department manages the electronic aspects of using computers to store, send, receive, and transmit data. There are many ways in which data can be accessed. A cybersecurity professional must be knowledgeable and skilled in protecting the data, regardless of location or system. He or she must be trained to protect and defend all avenues of access. Areas that can be compromised are known as *attack surfaces*.

Quick Look 1.1.1

Hacking Tools

In recent years, hacking has become easier due to free hacking tools that can be found on the Internet. The increase in cyberattacks is due, in part, to the availability of these tools. In this exercise, you will explore how easy it is to find hacking tools online and identify what potential destruction they may cause if used in an attack.

1. Launch a web browser, and navigate to a search engine, such as Google.
2. In the search box, enter the phrase free hacking tools.

Quick Look 1.1.1 Continued

3. How many results were returned in the search?
4. Choose a link or two, and review the information and tools you see. Consider the damage a user can do by using these tools without understanding their full intent. Did any of the pages you viewed discuss laws or ethical behavior regarding these tools? Be prepared to discuss your findings with the class.
5. Navigate to the website www.hackmageddon.com. This website provides information on cybersecurity attacks, including statistics and recent news.
6. Choose the most recent time line that is posted. Do you recognize any hacks from news stories or personal experience?
7. Review other features on this site, such as the statistics or graphs from the previous month, as shown. Look at the industries affected. Are there any industries listed that you find surprising? Be prepared to discuss your findings with the class.

Phone Hacks

Some of the earliest cyberattacks were phreaking incidents. *Phreaking* is hacking into a phone system. Individuals would hack into phone lines to make free phone calls. John Draper, also known as Cap'n Crunch, was one of the first well-known phreakers. In 1971, he figured out a toy whistle from Cap'n Crunch cereal, shown in **Figure 1-2,** emitted a frequency at 2600 hertz. This was the same tone that AT & T used to reset its trunk lines. By blowing the whistle into the phone lines, he could place long distance calls for free! Draper was eventually charged with toll fraud and sentenced to five years probation.

©1971markus@wikipedia.de

Figure 1-2. The whistle that hacked a phone company.

Viruses

A *virus* is malicious software code that is unleashed and attempts to perform its destructive content. A virus that is "in the wild" exists outside of the lab or computer where it was created. The Internet has played an important role in the spread of viruses. Since devices are interconnected, malware such as viruses can spread farther and faster than through simple sharing of disks or other storage media.

One of the first well-known viruses in the wild for IBM PC computers was the Brain boot sector virus. It was developed in 1986 by two computer programmers from Pakistan. This virus is sometimes referred to as the Pakistani flu. It could replace the executable code found on floppy disks.

Another well-known virus is the Melissa virus that was unleashed in 1999. It became a household name as it spread via e-mail. This virus spread through an infected Microsoft Word document attached to an e-mail message. The document contained an embedded macro that was the actual virus. When a user opened the document, the virus was activated. The virus caused an increase in e-mail traffic that impacted businesses and their ability to send and receive e-mail. It resulted in an estimated $80 million in damages.

Frederic Cohen first used the term *virus* in 1983 in his explanation on how a computer program could infect other programs since it could replicate itself.

Computer Hacks

Probably one of the most famous computer hackers of our time is Kevin Mitnick, **Figure 1-3.** Eventually, he was arrested and jailed for his actions. Mitnick has since become a popular security consultant, speaker, and the author of many popular hacking books, such as *The Art of Deception*. He runs his own business and security firm.

Mitnick started his hacking using nontechnical means, such as dumpster diving. *Dumpster diving* is digging through trash for useful information. He also used social engineering. *Social engineering* involves manipulating people to get information that can be used to hack computer systems. Mitnick's first hacking used both techniques to ride the Los Angeles bus system for free. By age 16, he had hacked his first computer system, Ark. Ark was a computer system owned by Digital Equipment Corporation (DEC). This led to subsequent attacks against other companies, such as Pacific Bell.

Kevin Mitnick

Figure 1-3. Kevin Mitnick is a reformed hacker who now runs a cybersecurity business and is a public speaker on cybersecurity issues.

Quick Look 1.1.2

Time Line of Early Cyberattacks

Viruses and other malware often play a significant role in cyberattacks. Even the earliest cyberattacks involved viruses. In this exercise, you will explore some of the early cyberattacks and how malware played a role in those attacks.

1. Launch a web browser, and navigate to the NATO website (www.nato.int).

Quick Look 1.1.2 Continued

2. Use the site's search function, and enter the search phrase: nato review history of cyber attacks timeline. In the search results, select the article titled The History of Cyber Attacks— A Timeline, as shown.

Enter the search phrase →

Select this article →

3. Review the highlights of cyberattacks. In which year were both the Democratic and Republican campaign databases hacked?
4. What made the attack shown in October 2010 unusual from some of the previous attacks?
5. When did NATO promote the concept of cyberdefense to protect the networks of its Alliances?
6. Navigate to a search engine, and enter the search phrase: sean spencer timeline of computer viruses. Select the link for the article Timeline of Computer Viruses from www.mapcon.com.
7. What was the first virus to attack Apple computer systems and when did it occur?
8. In 1989, the first virus demanding ransom appeared. What was this virus called?
9. Look through the time line. What was the name of the first virus to target children?

Darknet

The *darknet,* sometimes called the *dark web,* is part of the Internet that is not easily accessible to the average user. It represents the underground of the Internet. It is thought much of the darknet is used for criminal activity. However, many people use the darknet because of the anonymity it offers. Users of the darknet who are not hackers include:

- dissidents in foreign countries;
- political activists; and
- users who want to reach news and information that is blocked by their country's firewalls and filters.

For example, China blocks content that is freely accessible in most countries. The darknet may allow access to this blocked content by bypassing China's firewalls and filters.

The darknet should not be confused with the deep web. The *deep web* includes resources that are not found with a typical search engine, such as Google or Bing. **Figure 1-4** illustrates the differences between the Internet, deep web, and darknet.

FYI
The concept of the darknet was developed by the United States military to provide a high level of security that protected the location and information of its users.

The Internet	Deep Web	Darknet
Includes websites and resources that can be located and accessed using a standard web browser, like Internet Explorer or Chrome.	Includes resources located on the Internet, such as governmental databases, member-only sites, etc., that are not found with a typical search engine.	Includes websites that are intentionally hidden and only accessible through a special browser called the Tor browser.

Goodheart-Willcox Publisher

Figure 1-4.   The deep web and the darknet both use the Internet, but they are not the same thing.

Keywords on websites are indexed to allow the sites to be found via search engines such as Google. Someone can use a standard web browser, such as Microsoft Edge, to access most websites. The darknet also consists of websites, but these sites are cloaked with anonymity. A special web browser is needed to access these anonymous sites.

Anonymity on the darknet is done through a process called the onion network. Unlike access to a normal website, accessing a URL through the *onion network* involves data being rerouted through many computers before you are delivered to your destination. Access to the anonymous websites on the darknet is through a *Tor browser,* as shown in **Figure 1-5.** Tor stands for "the onion router" browser. The Tor browser was built using the open-concept tools used to create the Firefox web browser.

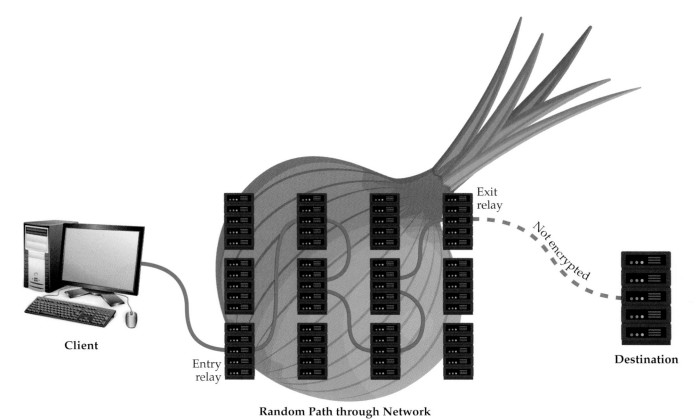

Goodheart-Willcox Publisher; servers: Sujith RS/Shutterstock.com; computer: Romvo/Shutterstock.com; onion: DRogatnev/Shutterstock.com

Figure 1-5.   The Tor browser is used to access the anonymous darknet by routing traffic through multiple random servers.

Quick look 1.1.3

Exploring Tor Traffic

To get a better understanding of how much traffic is sent through onion-routing transmissions, you can explore an interactive data visualization of Tor traffic. The data-visualization company Uncharted has created a map detailing Tor traffic. This map shows the flow of traffic along with nodes in the network.

1. Launch a web browser, and navigate to this site: torflow.uncharted.software. It may take a few seconds for the map to populate with data.
2. Explore the settings on the lower, left-hand corner of the screen to customize the view.
3. Use the mouse to zoom in on specific areas of the map.
4. Change the date-range slider at the bottom of the screen to view how Tor traffic has changed over time.

CompTIA Security+
1.3

Cybersecurity and Information Assurance

When most people think about the term *cybersecurity*, the image that comes to mind is an unknown person attacking a business or individual. This is reinforced by the numerous reports on the news of hacking attacks involving an "unknown hacker." However, when it comes to protecting businesses, governmental systems, or even personal data, there is much more to consider. This is where the concept of information assurance comes into play. Information assurance is discussed in detail in Chapter 2. It deals with the broader category of protecting data. This includes data that is stored on systems, data in transit, the processing of data, and even the physical access to data and information in its printed form.

Information assurance involves five key areas, as shown in **Figure 1-6.** These are discussed in detail in Chapter 2. Each area presents tasks, policies, and procedures that must be undertaken to protect an organization's data. They are non-sequential processes. These are interconnected systems that illustrate the core principles followed by the security professionals in an organization's information technology department.

Natural Disasters

Hackers are not the only threat to the information used by businesses. Data can be lost or destroyed through physical and natural disasters such as floods, fires, or unexpected catastrophes. What if a sinkhole opens outside of a business, as shown in **Figure 1-7**?

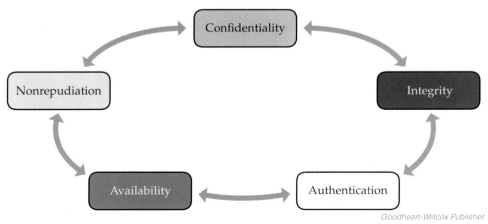

Goodheart-Willcox Publisher

Figure 1-6. The five areas of information assurance.

This happened to the tenants of Corporate Plaza in Allentown, Pennsylvania. In the middle of the night on February 24, 1994, a water main broke underneath a major thoroughfare next to the office building. Within a very short time, a massive sinkhole developed and partially collapsed the building. The building was ultimately condemned and demolished. Some tenants never gained access to the building and their files. In interviews with the local newspaper, a vice president of an investment firm lamented about the years of records that were in the office and lost. However, the director of the Parking Authority assured those who had received parking tickets that she had stored the computer records on a backup disk located outside of the building.

a katz/Shutterstock.com

Figure 1-7.   Threats to information security include natural disasters, such as this sinkhole that opened in New York City, as well as hackers and malware.

Insider Threats

Another threat faced by businesses is more common than most people realize. This threat comes from inside the organization from one of the employees. Two very prominent examples of insider threats are Edward Snowden and Terry Childs.

Edward Snowden has become an infamous information whistle-blower. He was a contractor from Booz Allen Hamilton working for the United States Central Intelligence Agency (CIA). During his employment, he downloaded a multitude of sensitive and classified files from the National Security Agency (NSA) to his personal laptop and fled the country. Ultimately, he leaked this information to journalists sparking one of the most intense debates over the use of governmental surveillance programs, national security, and individual privacy. As of 2017, Edward Snowden has remained in hiding in Russia where he was granted temporary asylum.

The case of Terry Childs reveals a different type of damage an employee can cause to an organization without stealing and releasing confidential information. In 2008, Childs managed the network for the City of San Francisco, specifically its Fibre WAN. This network runs the critical city system services such as e-mail, website, payroll, law enforcement records, call center, and more. He had unlimited access to the systems and changed all administrative passwords on the switches and routers. When this was discovered, he refused to hand over the new passwords for twelve days. Ultimately, he handed over the information to the mayor. He was charged and convicted of hacking under California laws and sentenced to four years in prison.

Motivations for Black-Hat Hackers

Hackers strike for many reasons. It is important for security professionals to understand the motivation behind hacking attacks and threats. By evaluating why hackers attack, security technicians are better able to identify potential risks their organization might face. Generally, black-hat hacker motivations fall into these categories:

CompTIA Security+
1.3

- criminal intent
- hacktivism
- state-sponsored hacking and cyberwarfare
- challenge and thrills
- revenge
- competition

Criminal Intent

The main reason black-hat hackers commit their acts is for criminal intent. This type of attack is seen in some of the major credit card breaches. During the holiday season in 2013, Target was the victim of a massive security breach. Hackers gained access to the credit and debit card data of over 110 million Target customers.

Another example of criminal intent occurred in 2016. Ukrainian hackers targeted law firms in Chicago. The hackers wanted to gain information that could be used for insider training.

In the summer of 2017, the credit-reporting agency Equifax was hacked. Hackers stole the personal information of 143 million Americans. This was nearly 60 percent of the adult population of the United States at that time. Canadians and Britons were also affected. The hackers gained access to Social Security numbers, birth dates, addresses, driver's license numbers, credit card numbers, and legal documents.

REDPIXEL.PL/Shutterstock.com

Figure 1-8. The hacktivist group Anonymous often uses the Guy Fawkes mask as a public symbol for its members.

FYI

A denial of service attack is when the hacker's motivation is to prevent legitimate access to a company's website. It is not used to steal or destroy any information.

Hacktivism

Some individuals are motivated to hack based on ideals or personal beliefs. Their aim is to target and harm companies or individuals with whom they have a fundamental disagreement. This type of action is called *hacktivisim.* This term is a play on the words *hacker* and *activism.*

One of the most familiar hacktivist groups is known as Anonymous, as shown in **Figure 1-8.** Anonymous is a leaderless group in which individuals can associate with other like-minded individuals. Its members often target organizations or businesses viewed as hindering free speech and Internet use. The attacks may include defacement of web pages, denial of service attacks, and theft and release of information.

Anonymous was behind the 2011 attack of the security-consulting firm HBGary Federal. Its CEO, Aaron Barr, thought he had unmasked key members of Anonymous. He was preparing to meet with the Federal Bureau of Investigation (FBI) and publicly announced his intentions. Anonymous hacked the company and determined he did not have their identities. During the attack, hackers discovered numerous system flaws and poor security practices. They ultimately took over the company's servers and social media platforms. Hackers also destroyed data. The credibility of the company and its executives was ruined as a result of the cyberattack.

State-Sponsored Hacking and Cyberwarfare

Governments have found themselves defending their systems from hackers over political decisions. For example, in 2007, the country of Estonia was hit with one of the early known denial of service attacks by foreign individuals. The attack was prompted by Estonia's decision to remove a war memorial. This move angered officials in Russia. Estonia accused Russia of the attack. However, no direct connection has been proven between the hackers and the Russian government.

Emerging threats are now seen from hackers conducting attacks and intelligence gathering as agents of governments. Nations are training their citizens in the technical expertise to become cyberwarriors. The US Department of Homeland Security states that cyberwar programs from nation states pose a significant risk. The goal of these programs is "to weaken, disrupt, or destroy the United States." Foreign cyberwarriors conduct espionage to gain advanced technological knowledge. They also conduct attacks to acquire data to conduct further attacks against our infrastructure. High-value targets include the electrical grid systems, financial markets, and transportation networks.

There is a very famous cyberwarfare attack that was launched against Iran in 2010. In June of that year, a computer worm affected software in at least 14 industrial sites. One of these sites was a uranium-enrichment plant. A *worm* is malicious software that spreads on its own through computer networks. The worm was named Stuxnet. It was very sophisticated and only targeted computers running Windows 7 *and* Siemens Step7 software. The Step7 software was used to control the centrifuges used in enriching uranium. Once finding its target, the worm masked its intentions and proceeded to instruct the centrifuges to spin too fast, as shown in **Figure 1-9.** This resulted in the destruction of the equipment. The infection did considerable damage to Iran's nuclear program at this facility. Iran was forced to replace every damaged centrifuge.

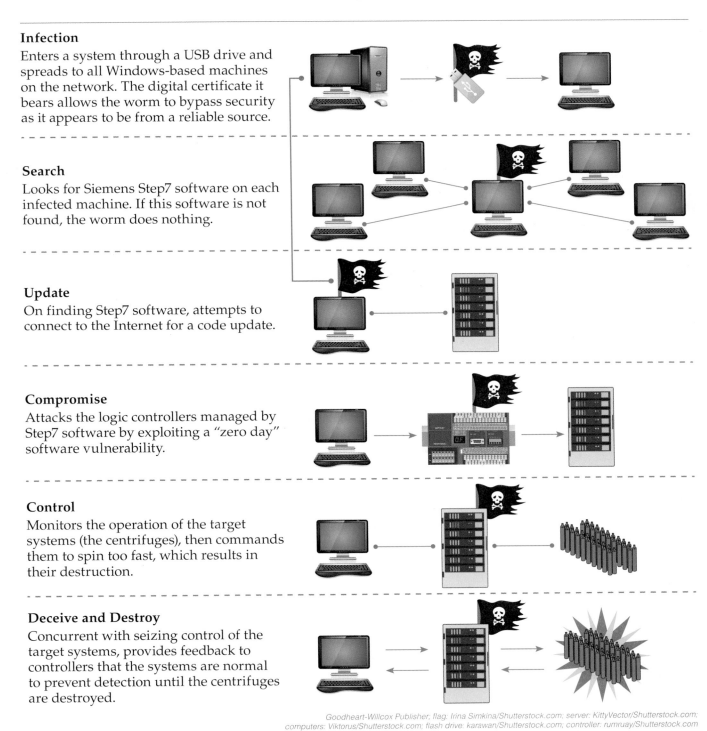

Infection

Enters a system through a USB drive and spreads to all Windows-based machines on the network. The digital certificate it bears allows the worm to bypass security as it appears to be from a reliable source.

Search

Looks for Siemens Step7 software on each infected machine. If this software is not found, the worm does nothing.

Update

On finding Step7 software, attempts to connect to the Internet for a code update.

Compromise

Attacks the logic controllers managed by Step7 software by exploiting a "zero day" software vulnerability.

Control

Monitors the operation of the target systems (the centrifuges), then commands them to spin too fast, which results in their destruction.

Deceive and Destroy

Concurrent with seizing control of the target systems, provides feedback to controllers that the systems are normal to prevent detection until the centrifuges are destroyed.

Goodheart-Willcox Publisher; flag: Irina Simkina/Shutterstock.com; server: KittyVector/Shutterstock.com; computers: Viktorus/Shutterstock.com; flash drive: karawan/Shutterstock.com; controller: rumruay/Shutterstock.com

Figure 1-9. The Stuxnet worm was used to conduct a cyberwarfare attack against Iran's nuclear program.

Stuxnet is generally considered to be the first cyberweapon. To date, no hacker or country has claimed credit for this attack. However, most industry experts believe its sophistication could only have been created by a nation-sponsored attacker. Clues revealed from the virus point to Israel and the United States, but this has never been publicly confirmed.

Quick Look 1.1.5

Report on Cyberwarfare

TED-Ed is a youth and education initiative sponsored by the TED organization. It offers instructional videos and lessons on a variety of subjects. In this exercise, you will take a closer look at some of the issues regarding cyberwarfare. Navigate to its website (ed.ted.com). Using the site's search function, enter the phrase defining cyberwarfare. Select the video in the returned results to view it. Then, answer the following questions.

1. How many international treaties cover cyberwarfare?
2. Are acts committed by cybercriminals defined as acts of war?
3. Do you think laws and treaties will help curb possible cyberattacks?
4. How do you feel the United States should respond to these emerging and potential threats?
5. Discuss your answers with your classmates.

Challenges and Thrills

In many cases, hackers launch attacks to challenge their skills or just for the thrill of breaking into a computer system. These attacks can be more difficult to predict, since the hacker has probably not chosen the victim for any specific reason. One type of attacker that falls into this category is known as a script kiddie. *Script kiddie* is a slang term used to describe an individual who uses premade tools to perform their attacks. Once thought of as novice hackers, users of these tools today can cause significant damage to their victims.

An example of an attack carried out for the challenge or thrill involved the Hong Kong toy manufacturer Vtech. A hacker broke into its systems in 2015. The hacker spoke anonymously to a tech reporter and revealed the purpose behind his attack. He spoke about being in a chat board and was curious about a web service Vtech used to manage its products. He began exploring the site and found it vulnerable to many types of attacks. The hacker told the reporter he has no intention of releasing the data he uncovered. Rather, he wanted to expose the security flaws in the system. Because there were images of children involved, the hacker provided the evidence to the reporter as he did not feel Vtech would believe or respond to his actions. Ultimately, Vtech publicly admitted the hacking attack. To date, the hacker has not been identified.

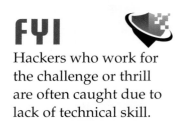

FYI

Hackers who work for the challenge or thrill are often caught due to lack of technical skill.

Revenge

Revenge hacking is an attack against a person or company the hacker believes has wronged him or her in some manner. This type of hack is becoming more common. These attacks are frustrating to their victims. It also takes time for law enforcement to adequately investigate the attacks.

More and more companies are attempting to "hack back" against the hackers. They are choosing to quietly fight back by hacking those they believe to have committed the attack. This type of revenge hacking is also referred to as *active defense.* According to private security research firms, this is an open secret in the security

Ethical Issue

WikiLeaks

WikiLeaks is a website that posts information submitted by individuals that has been otherwise censored or restricted. It is controversial. The information may be obtained legally or as a result of hacking actions. Edward Snowden is an American citizen who was a contractor for the National Security Agency. He downloaded data and gave it to WikiLeaks to post. Research his actions and those of WikiLeaks. Do you believe these actions were ethical and responsible from both parties? Be prepared to defend your answer. Submit a one- to two-page summary, and defend your choice.

community. Although active defense may provide some satisfaction or recovery of information, it is likely illegal in the United States as a violation of the Computer Fraud and Abuse Act.

In October of 2017, a congressman from Georgia proposed to make active defense legal. He submitted a bill for consideration known as the Active Cyber Defense Certainty Act (ACDC). The law would define active defense and declare it is legal. However, it would not prevent civil action against anyone engaging in active defense.

Competition

Another motivation for hacking is competition. Businesses compete against other businesses. Some businesses engage in the unethical activity of stealing information from their competitors. This may be done to damage the competing business or use proprietary information for its own gain. Such an attack was committed by David W. Kent, the founder of OilPro.com, a professional networking site. Kent was convicted of hacking into a competitor's site to steal information and use it to boost the value of his own company. He then tried to sell his own company to the competitor. He was ultimately sentenced to one year in jail for his actions.

Overview of Attack Defenses

There is no perfect defense against threats to networks and data. In fact, network defense is a multifaceted approach. It involves software developers, skilled security professionals, solid policies and procedures, and educated users. All elements must work together to provide protection.

Many security problems come from design flaws in software. Flaws can be found in commercial off-the-shelf applications, such as web browsers or office applications, as well as custom software. One way developers are attempting to find threats before they are exploited is through a bug-bounty program. A *bug-bounty program* offers rewards for flaws and vulnerabilities found in their program. When a bug is reported, it can be patched before it is discovered and exploited by hackers. Companies such as Facebook, Google, and Microsoft have bug-bounty programs, as shown in **Figure 1-10**.

In addition to the policies and procedures, a penetration test can be used to uncover issues. *Penetration testing*, commonly called *pen testing*, is a process in which white-hat hackers will attempt to penetrate a network to locate vulnerabilities. Penetration testing will be conducted under one of the following conditions.

- no previous knowledge of the system
- some knowledge of the system
- overview of the system provided before testing

FYI

Many who participate in bug-bounty programs are gray-hat hackers.

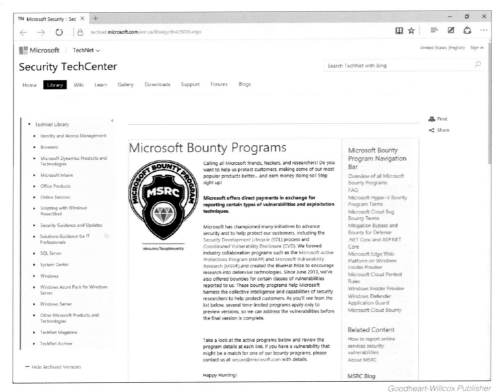

Figure 1-10. Many software developers, including Microsoft, have bug-bounty programs that pay for security vulnerabilities found by users.

Security administrators should conduct their own vulnerability tests. However, often they will also use penetration testers. Pen testers are usually security consultants hired to test the defenses of an organization. In security circles, these penetration testers are sometimes known as *red teams.* They sign contracts outlining the type of testing to be conducted. This may consist of physical defenses, application penetration, and social engineering.

Quick Look 1.1.6

Bug-Bounty Program

A company called Bugcrowd has developed an innovative approach to bug-bounty programs. Its business plan brings together top security professionals and software developers to analyze and identify software programs for vulnerabilities. In this exercise, you will explore how the program works and the benefits it provides to companies and penetration testers.

1. Launch a web browser, and navigate to the Bugcrowd website (www.bugcrowd.com).
2. Locate the How It Works link, and click it to view an overview of the service.
3. Look for statistics on vulnerabilities found. What do they describe?
4. Explore the site further, and investigate the programs they offer. Do they outline bounties paid for found bugs?

SECTION REVIEW 1.1

Check Your Understanding

1. What is an attack surface?
2. A hacker that uses premade tools to conduct attacks is known as which type of hacker?
3. When you want to remain anonymous on the Internet, what manages the traffic flow?
4. A hacker motived by personal beliefs is practicing what type of hacking?
5. What is the team called that is hired or used to assess the security of a company?

Build Your Key Terms Vocabulary

As you progress through this course, develop a personal cybersecurity glossary. This will help you build your vocabulary and prepare you for a career. Write a definition for each of the following terms, and add it to your cybersecurity glossary.

attack vector

black-hat hacker

bug-bounty program

cyberattack

cybersecurity

darknet

deep web

gray-hat hacker

hacker

hacking

hacktivisim

onion network

phreaking

script kiddie

Tor browser

virus

white-hat hacker

worm

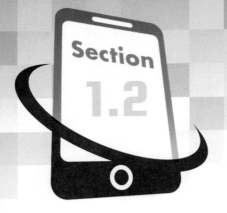

Section 1.2

Virtualized Machines

Essential Question

What benefits does virtualization offer in a business environment?

Virtualization technology has revolutionized the computing environment. It offers considerable benefits. A single physical computer can host many virtual machines. This reduces the need for additional computers. In turn, the need for electrical power and space for physical machines is reduced. In addition to reducing costs, companies that use virtual machines can respond quickly to business and organizational needs. Efficiency of IT management can be increased. Downtime can be minimized or eliminated.

Key Terms 🖋

application cell
container
host operating system
Hyper-V
hypervisor
provisioning

sandbox
snapshot
Type 1 hypervisor
Type 2 hypervisor
VirtualBox

virtual machine (VM)
virtual machine escape
virtual machine monitor (VMM)
virtual machine (VM) sprawl
VMWare

Learning Goals

- Identify the concepts of virtualizing operating systems.
- Install and configure a virtual machine.

Virtualization and Its Benefits

In computing environments, the term *virtualization* refers to running a simulation of an operating system instead of the actual operating system. In this setting, a *virtual machine (VM)* runs on the actual operating system of a physical computer. The virtual machine looks and functions like an actual computer operating system. However, it is separated from the operating system running on the machine, as shown in **Figure 1-11.** In order for a machine to be virtualized, special software must be installed on the host computer. This software manages the virtualized environment.

Security administrators can run virtual machines as any other integrated device on the network. VMs can also be fully or partially isolated from other systems. This provides a great deal of flexibility and security. Systems can be tested or preconfigured before they are deployed. Additional hardware resources, such as memory, disk space, and processing power, can easily be configured to accommodate additional demands. An administrator can also move a virtual system from one physical machine to another. This allows for fast recovery of system failures.

Virtualization technology has been available to the PC computing environment since the 1990s. When a VM is created, the virtualization software makes the physical hardware on the machine available to any virtualized or guest virtual machine. In order for the virtual machine to work, the virtualization software must be able to bridge the communication from the virtual machines to either the host operating system or the physical hardware. The specific software that handles this responsibility is known as a *hypervisor* or *virtual machine monitor (VMM).*

There are several popular choices for virtualization software. *VMWare* is a line of virtualization products that includes the desktop workstation and player versions. *VirtualBox* is an open-source virtualization platform from Oracle. *Hyper-V* is a virtualization platform developed by Microsoft for its servers and desktops.

Each virtual machine runs its own operating system. This is known as the *guest operating system.* Each individual VM is sometimes referred to as a *container* or *application cell.* Each VM allows for isolation of the processes and hardware, such as memory, disk, and CPU, from other containers.

There are two types of hypervisors: Type 1 and Type 2. Each of these interfaces differently with the operating system and hardware. A *Type 1 hypervisor* does not interface with the host operating system. Instead, it interacts directly with the hardware, as shown in **Figure 1-12.** The *host operating system* is the operating system located on the physical machine. Often, Type 1 hypervisors are called *native* or *bare metal* hypervisors. Type 1 hypervisors are more popular for servers. They run more efficiently since they do not have to communicate through the operating system. A *Type 2 hypervisor* runs on the host operating system.

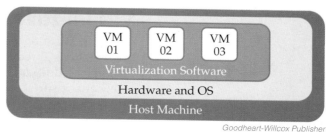

Goodheart-Willcox Publisher

Figure 1-11. A virtual machine looks and acts like an actual operating system, but it is separated from the operating system on the host machine by special software.

CompTIA Security+
3.2

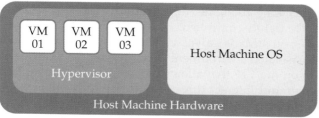

Type 1 Virtualization

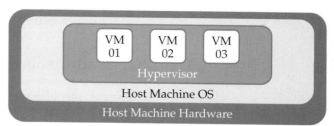

Type 2 Virtualization

Goodheart-Willcox Publisher

Figure 1-12. A Type 1 hypervisor interacts directly with the host hardware, not the host operating system, whereas a Type 2 hypervisor runs on the host operating system.

Virtualization and Cybersecurity

Virtualization can provide a tremendous cost savings to businesses and organizations. It reduces the need to purchase, support, and power many physical machines. Additionally, it can provide security benefits. However, it also provides a new attack surface for hackers.

Security Advantages

CompTIA Security+

3.4

A security advantage of using virtualized systems is the ability to run them in isolated environments. This reduces a hacker's ability to gain access to the servers. Another advantage is being able to easily and securely test patches and system deployments before rolling them out to networks. This concept is known as a sandbox. As a child, you may have played in a sandbox. You could move the sand all around and build with it while the sand remained inside the sandbox. A *sandbox* in computing is an isolated place to test and deploy applications and configurations. The changes remain within the VM until you choose to move them outside the VM.

CompTIA Security+

5.6

Many virtual platforms offer the ability to create snapshots. A *snapshot* is a saved version of the system in its current state. The system can be quickly returned to a saved state at any time by restoring the snapshot. In effect, this allows you to undo changes that have been made. Many IT administrators maintain a library of snapshots that can be rapidly restored as needs dictate.

Another key benefit is the concept of provisioning. In virtual computing, *provisioning* is the ability to quickly deploy resources when needed. For example, suppose a virtual machine needs additional resources. This may be memory, disk space, or even an additional network interface card. The virtualization software allows you to allocate these resources immediately to a system.

Security Concerns

There are security concerns to consider with virtualization. The hypervisor could be attacked. This could allow a hacker to take control over all virtual systems running on the physical host machine. In many cases, virtual servers need to communicate with other virtual or physical machines. This provides an avenue for attack. Security administrators must ensure that virtual controls, such as virtual firewalls, are configured and tested to counter this.

CompTIA Security+

3.7

VM sprawl is another concern. *Virtual machine (VM) sprawl* occurs with the continuous deployment of virtual machines. VMs are relatively easy to create and deploy. Often, many systems are created for special purposes or additional power. In a system that is not well managed, it is possible for administrators to forget about these VMs. This can drain system resources.

It is common for many VMs to run from a single physical host machine. It is critical this system is locked down as much as possible to prevent unwanted access from malware or other hacking attempts. Administrator access to the physical host machine should also be tightly controlled.

A unique security exploit on VMs is called virtual machine escape. Normally each VM runs in its own isolated environment. In a *virtual machine escape* exploit, malicious code is run on the VM that allows the guest operating system to break out of its environment and interact directly with the hypervisor. This then allows direct access to the host operating system. VM escape is a very serious threat to virtualized platforms. Worms are also a security concern.

Quick Look 1.2.1

Installing VirtualBox

It is important to get an understanding how to install and configure virtual machines. In this exercise, you will create the shell for an operating system in a VM. However, at this time, you will not install a guest operating system. You must have the permissions needed to install software to complete this exercise.

1. Launch a web browser, and navigate to the VirtualBox website (www.virtualbox.org).
2. Navigate to the downloads page, and download the latest version of VirtualBox for your host platform. For example, if your host computer is running a Windows operating system, download the version for Windows hosts.
3. Once the installer is downloaded, install the VirtualBox software on your host machine. Use the default settings for the installation.
4. Launch VirtualBox.

New

5. On the opening screen, click the **New** button on the toolbar to begin. A wizard will guide you through the steps of creating a virtual machine.
6. On the first page of the wizard, click in the **Name:** text box, and enter My Test OS, as shown. This will be the name of the virtual machine. Click the **Next** button.

Name the VM →

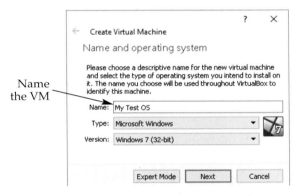

7. The next page of the wizard asks you to set the amount of memory for the virtual machine. Click the **Next** button to accept the default setting.
8. The next page of the wizard asks if you wish to create a virtual hard disk for the VM. Click the **Create a virtual hard disk now** radio button, and then click the **Create** button.
9. You must now set up the virtual hard disk. On the next page of the wizard, click the **VDI (VirtualBox Disk Image)** radio button. Then, click the **Next** button.
10. On the remaining pages of the wizard, accept the default settings. When the wizard is finished, the main VirtualBox screen appears, and your VM is listed on the left, as shown.

Toolbar →

Virtual machine →

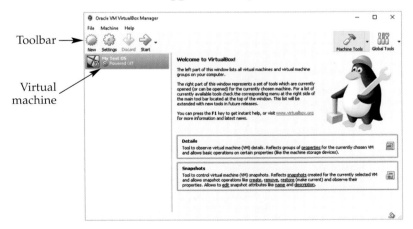

Quick Look 1.2.1 Continued

Settings

11. With your VM selected in the list, click the **Settings** button on the toolbar. The **Settings** dialog box is displayed for your VM.
12. Click **General** on the left of the dialog box, and click the **Advanced** tab on the right. Notice the path to the VM is listed. You can also change settings such as sharing the clipboard and dragging and dropping between the host operating system and the VM.
13. Click **User Interface** on the left, and then the drop-down arrow next to the **Machine** button. The option for a snapshot is located here.
14. Click **Storage** on the left, and then click disk image branch under **Storage Devices**. This branch has an icon that looks like a CD/DVD. The name of this branch should be Empty because you have not yet loaded an operating system.
15. In this exercise, you will not be loading an operating system. If you were, the next step would be to click the CD/DVD icon to the right of the **Optical Drive:** drop-down list, click **Virtual Optical Disk File…** in the drop-down menu, browse to the location of the ISO installation disk, and open the disk image. To load the operating system from a DVD, click **Host Drive** in the drop-down menu instead of the **Virtual Optical Disk File…** option.
15. Click the **Cancel** button to exit the **Settings** dialog box without making any changes. Then, close VirtualBox.

SECTION REVIEW 1.2

Check Your Understanding

1. What is the name of the software that controls the communication between the VM and the physical host?
2. A native or bare metal hypervisor does not communicate with which element(s) of the physical host?
3. What is the name of Microsoft's software implementation of a hypervisor?
4. Briefly describe VM sprawl.
5. To create an image of a VM in its current state, what would you do?

Build Your Key Terms Vocabulary

As you progress through this course, develop a personal cybersecurity glossary. This will help you build your vocabulary and prepare you for a career. Write a definition for each of the following terms, and add it to your cybersecurity glossary.

application cell	Type 1 hypervisor
container	Type 2 hypervisor
host operating system	VirtualBox
Hyper-V	virtual machine (VM)
hypervisor	virtual machine escape
provisioning	virtual machine monitor (VMM)
sandbox	virtual machine (VM) sprawl
snapshot	VMWare

Skills Needed by Cybersecurity Professionals

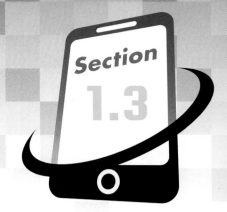

Cybersecurity professionals must interact with many different people. These may be people within the company or people outside the company. In order to be successful, it is important to have the skills needed to communicate and collaborate. It is also important to have the technical skills needed to complete the tasks. Obtaining certifications is one way to demonstrate you have the required technical skills.

Essential Question

What are the critical skill sets employers are looking for in cybersecurity professionals?

Key Terms

Certified Information Systems Security Professional (CISSP)
CompTIA Advanced Security Practitioner (CASP)

CompTIA Cybersecurity Analyst (CySA+)
CompTIA Security+
soft skills

Learning Goals

- Identify skills needed for a successful career in cybersecurity.
- Compare industry certifications offered in cybersecurity.

Skill Sets

What skills are necessary to begin a successful career in the world of cybersecurity? It is obvious that technical skills are critical. A cybersecurity professional must know how to recognize, prevent, and fix security issues. However, he or she must also have the soft skills to work with people.

Technical Skills

To be successful, it is important to learn specific security technical skills. These are the skills that will be covered in detail throughout this text. There are other areas where technical expertise will be beneficial:
- operating systems
- networking

Kjetil Kolbjørnsrud/Shutterstock.com

Figure 1-13. Having the technical skill to work with routers, switches, and servers is beneficial to a cybersecurity professional.

GaudiLab/Shutterstock.com

Figure 1-14. Soft skills, such as the ability to work with others and to communicate effectively, are needed to be successful in any career.

- databases
- spreadsheets
- HTML
- coding

Knowledge of Microsoft desktop and server operating systems as well as the Linux operating system will help to improve your security skills. Knowing networking protocols, including TCP/IP, and understanding switches and router management will also help improve your security skills, as shown in **Figure 1-13.** The ability to code, including scripting, is also valuable, as is having basic understanding in the use of databases, spreadsheets, and HTML.

Soft Skills

In addition to learning and mastering technical skills, it is the soft skills that are so important to IT professionals. *Soft skills* are those skills necessary to communicate and work with others. They are called soft skills because there is no exact science to measure true success. When you create a custom formula in a spreadsheet, you show you have the technical ability to use the software. This is a hard skill. Technical skills are hard skills. On the other hand, the ability to communicate with others is harder to measure. This is a soft skill. Here are some examples of soft skills:

- collaboration
- effective communication (written and oral)
- leadership
- problem solving
- respect
- reliability

Soft skills are covered in more detail in Chapter 18.

Cybersecurity professionals will interact with many people. This may be other team members working to solve a problem, as shown in **Figure 1-14.** You may need to speak with the CEO of an organization or the most junior employee. No matter who you are interacting with, you must be able to communicate effectively. This includes writing memos, creating tutorials, and preparing a presentation. You will need to provide information so others can make effective decisions and problem solve. Often, the situation will be critical and time-sensitive. You will be expected to excel in communicating the needed information. Here are some tips to improve your skills:

- Take opportunities to speak in front of small groups or to guests who might be visiting your classroom or home.
- Create custom tutorials on how to perform a task, and ask others to critique your work.
- Practice time-management skills by arriving to class, work, or other activities at least a few minutes before they begin.
- Play strategy games that require problem-solving techniques, which will help to sharpen your critical-thinking skills.

Quick Look 1.3.1

Soft Skills Self-Assessment

Soft skills are critical to success in any career, including cybersecurity. The place to start in improving your soft skills is to evaluate your current skills. In this exercise, you will evaluate your own soft skills.

1. Launch a web browser, and navigate to the Mind Tools website (www.mindtools.com).
2. Using the site's search function, enter the search phrase test your skills.
3. In the search results, click the link for the article titled Test Your Skills. This article includes a quiz to evaluate your current skill set, as shown.

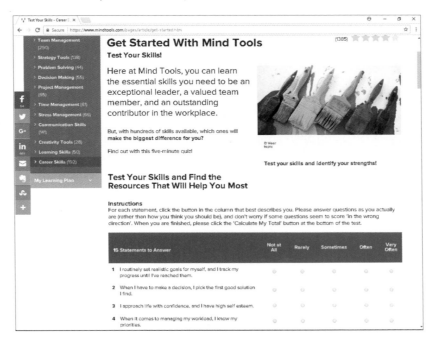

4. Answer the questions in the quiz. Be honest with your answers. Do not answer them trying to get the best score.
5. Calculate your score. You may be prompted to sign in or create an account, but this is not required. You can choose to skip signing in.
6. Review the evaluation of your score. Do you agree with the assessment?
7. Think of ways you could improve your skills in these areas. Be prepared to participate in a class discussion.

Security Certifications

Industry certifications are a critical tool to help employees prove their skills to employers. These certifications focus on in-demand skills needed by industry professionals. These tests are written by industry experts and are designed to evaluate your mastery of critical subject matter. A cybersecurity certification proves you have the skills needed to manage the many aspects of system security. Areas covered include a technical focus, risk management, forensic analysis, and more. There are many security certifications available. You can be certified in varying levels of skill and mastery. Popular certifications in the cybersecurity field are offered by CompTIA and by Microsoft. The cybersecurity field typically offers good wages, as shown in **Figure 1-15.** Certification is a way to prove your skills for this field.

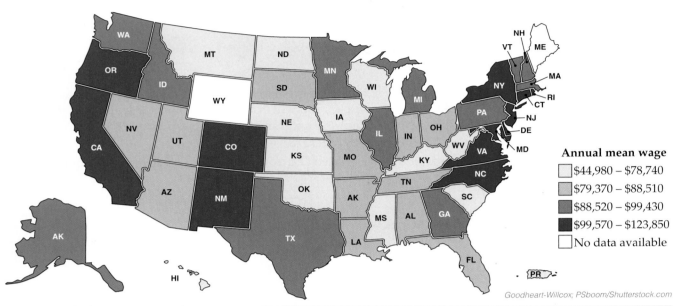

Goodheart-Willcox; PSboom/Shutterstock.com

Annual mean wage
- $44,980 – $78,740
- $79,370 – $88,510
- $88,520 – $99,430
- $99,570 – $123,850
- No data available

Top-Paying Locations for Cybersecurity Jobs				
State	Employment	Employment per Thousand Jobs	Hourly Mean Wage	Annual Mean Wage
District of Columbia	850	1.21	$59.54	$123,850
New York	5,170	0.57	$55.62	$115,690
New Jersey	2,180	0.55	$54.80	$113,990
California	7,990	0.50	$52.30	$108,780
New Mexico	670	0.83	$51.88	$107,900

Source: Bureau of Labor Statistics

Figure 1-15. Cybersecurity positions typically offer good wages throughout the country. In some areas, wages are very high.

CompTIA

CompTIA is an organization that promotes technical excellence through certification. It is well-known, and its certifications are highly regarded. The certifications are vendor neutral. This means they do not cover any one specific manufacturer or computer system. CompTIA offers three levels of certification in the cybersecurity area:

- Security+
- CSA+
- CASP

Case Study

Cybersecurity Podcasts

Technology and security threats are constantly evolving. As a cybersecurity professional, it is important to stay abreast of threats, emerging technologies, and resources. One such way is to listen to cybersecurity podcasts. Use a search engine to locate two podcasts from different sources. Listen to each podcast. Write a one-page summary of each podcast. Do you believe this format is beneficial to you? Would you recommend them to others in the security field?

CompTIA Security+ is the entry-level certification for computer security. It focuses on the major aspects of security in a business. These aspects include vulnerabilities, threats, risk, and the steps to secure systems and data. The objectives for this certification are covered in this text.

CompTIA Cybersecurity Analyst (CySA+) certification focuses on the skills to assess, combat, and prevent security threats. CySA+ was introduced in February 2017. It is the newest security certification.

CompTIA Advanced Security Practitioner (CASP) focuses on critical thinking, incident response, risk management, and technical integration throughout business. CASP is a mastery-level certification. As you complete additional coursework in cybersecurity, you may become qualified to pass this certification exam.

Microsoft MTA Security Fundamentals

Microsoft offers the Microsoft Technology Associate (MTA) certification for many areas. These are entry-level certifications. They introduce the high-level concepts of issues facing businesses. The MTA Security Fundamentals certification covers topics from vulnerabilities and threats, to user management, risk, and best practices. The objectives for the MTA Security Fundamentals certification are covered in this text.

Other Relevant Certifications

There are other industry certifications for cybersecurity. The Certified Ethical Hacker (CEH) certification tests your ability to conduct, analyze, and assess the security of a system. This is discussed in more detail in Chapter 13. The *Certified Information Systems Security Professional (CISSP)* is a professional certification for those with strong managerial background and technical expertise. It is offered by (ISC)². This is an international association of cybersecurity professionals. CISSP certification is highly regarded throughout the world. It requires at least five years of full-time employment in two of eight areas. You can take the exam without the work experience. If you pass and fulfill the work requirement within six years, you will receive certification. Also, Cisco offers the Cisco CyberOps certification.

SECTION REVIEW 1.3

Check Your Understanding

1. Skills that are necessary for communication are called _____.
2. Which organization provides certifications such as Security+ and CySA+?
3. Microsoft offers MTA certification, which is an entry-level certification in security fundamentals. What does MTA stand for?
4. Which certification is used by penetration testers as evidence of their knowledge of preventative hacking?
5. Which certification requires a minimum of five years of full-time employment in cybersecurity-related fields?

Build Your Key Terms Vocabulary

As you progress through this course, develop a personal cybersecurity glossary. This will help you build your vocabulary and prepare you for a career. Write a definition for each of the following terms, and add it to your cybersecurity glossary.

Certified Information Systems Security
  Professional (CISSP)

CompTIA Advanced Security
  Practitioner (CASP)

CompTIA Cybersecurity Analyst
  (CySA+)

CompTIA Security+

soft skills

Review and Assessment

Summary

Section 1.1 Introduction to Cybersecurity

- History has shown that cyberattacks come from many avenues, from phone hacks to viruses and computer hacks. The darknet is the underground of the Internet and used by cybercriminals as well as individuals seeking anonymity.
- Cybersecurity threats come not only from hackers, but from natural disasters and insiders. Information assurance looks at the broad scope of keeping data safe.
- There are many motivations for why hackers conduct their attacks. These include criminal intent, hacktivism, state-sponsored hacking and cyberwarfare, challenge and thrills, and revenge.
- There is no perfect defense against cyberattacks, rather a multifaceted approach is needed. This includes identifying design flaws in software as well as conducting penetration testing.

Section 1.2 Virtualized Machines

- Virtualized systems are fast becoming the most common implementation of network services as they provide huge cost-savings and security benefits by reducing the need for physical machines.
- Virtual machines use special software called a hypervisor to facilitate communication between physical machines and guest operating systems.
- As with any technological solution, virtual machines provide security benefits such as isolation, but bring new methods of access for hackers to penetrate.

Section 1.3 Skills Needed by Cybersecurity Professionals

- Strong technical skills, or hard skills, are critical to prepare for a career in defending computer systems against cyberthreats. Soft skills are also needed for a cybersecurity professional to be successful in a career.
- Industry certifications help prove technical skills in cybersecurity. Several industry certifications are available from CompTIA, Microsoft, EC-Council, and (ISC)^2.

Check Your Cybersecurity IQ

Now that you have completed this chapter, see what you have learned about cybersecurity by visiting the student companion website (www.g-wlearning.com) and taking the chapter posttest.

Review Questions

For each question, select the answer that is the best response.

1. There is a database that a company wants to allow preregistered, selected customers to access. It does not want the database publicly advertised. Which is the best solution for the location of the database?
   A. In a hidden folder on the company's normal web server.
   B. On the darknet.
   C. On a web server that is not indexed by search engines.
   D. On a company server that is not a web server.

2. What makes the Tor browser more secure?
   A. It is open source.
   B. It was developed by the US military.
   C. It is based on Firefox.
   D. It routes traffic through a multitude of networks.

3. Information assurance primarily deals with _____.
   A. laws associated with computer hacking
   B. management of the security of a network
   C. protecting the data and assets of an organization
   D. securing web servers from unknown hackers

4. A company has a poor environmental record. It is hit with a cyberattack that reveals its poor practices along with employee names and their salaries. Which is the most likely motivation of the hacker?
   A. hacktivism
   B. thrill of the attack
   C. revenge
   D. cyberwarfare

5. A cyberattack against a country's water system infrastructure would most likely be the actions of which type of hacker motivation?
   A. cyberwarfare
   B. money (criminal)
   C. thrill of hacking
   D. hacktivism

6. Which is a true statement about a worm?
   A. It is launched from removable media.
   B. It affects Windows-based operating systems more than Linux-based systems.
   C. It only needs a network port to infect other computers.
   D. All of these are true about worms.

7. A company develops software for the insurance industry. It wants to ensure that bugs are found prior to being hit with an attack exploiting an unknown flaw in the code. Which of the following is the best option to implement?
   A. An information assurance program.
   B. A bug-bounty program.
   C. Hire a script kiddie.
   D. Have the network administrator earn an industry certification in security.

8. Malware that causes a virtual machine to interact directly with the physical host machine is called:
   A. VM sprawl
   B. VM escape
   C. VM exploit
   D. VM expose

9. Which of the following is not considered a soft skill for cybersecurity professionals?
   A. Configuring a firewall to protect web servers.
   B. Writing a report to management about a cyberincident.
   C. Teaching coworkers about security awareness.
   D. Taking charge of a cyberincident.

10. This certification tests your ability to evaluate attacks and perform penetration tests.
    A. Security+
    B. CSA+
    C. CISSP
    D. CEH

Application and Extension of Knowledge

1. Interview someone who works in the cybersecurity field. What skills does he or she identify as most needed? What are some of the favorite and least favorite aspects of the job? Ask other questions related to his or her job. Summarize your answers in a class discussion.

2. The CyberPatriot challenge is an international competition that allows teams of middle and high school students to find and fix vulnerabilities. Explore this challenge on its website (www.uscyberpatriot.org). Review the contest, possible fees, and challenges. Create a presentation to encourage your school's participation in this event.

3. Identify a recent data security breach that occurred. How many users were affected? What were the details of the breach? Create a brief slideshow using software such as PowerPoint or Google Slides that highlights the key aspects of the breach.

4. Create a one- to two-page paper detailing why you are interested in a cybersecurity career. Highlight your interests, background, and goals. What are your plans to continue your education?

5. NOVALabs from PBS has created a CyberSecurity Lab in game form. Using a search engine, enter the search phrase **NOVALabs cybersecurity**, and select the link from the PBS website. Play the game! When you are done, summarize how you did and what new topics you learned. Describe your experience in a one-page paper. Do you feel this game is a good introduction to cybersecurity?

Research Project
White Hat vs. Black Hat

Society has been shaped by those individuals who call themselves a hacker. Some are notorious for their bad deeds and criminal acts, while others fight against hacking attempts. Your task is to investigate one of the hackers in the list as assigned to you by your teacher. Develop a thorough background on the individual, and describe whether they are white or black hat. Why is he or she famous, or notorious, in the world of cybersecurity? What is his or her background, and what is he or she doing today? What lessons can be learned from this person and his or her actions?

White-Hat Hackers	Black-Hat Hackers
Paul Syverson	Ross Ulbright
Danny O'Brien	Adrain Lamo
Mike Dahn	Kevin Mitnick
Andy Ellis	Julian Assange
Roger Schell	Max Butler
Dorothy Denning	Loyd Blankenship
Ronald Rivest	Michael Calce
Kevin Poulson	Sven Jaschan
Robert Morris	Kevin Poulson
Tim Berners Lee	Albert Gonzalez
John Gilmore	George Hotz
Amir Taaki	Gary McKinnon

Deliverables. Write a one- to two-page report. Your summary should include a title page and should be formatted following your school's style guidelines. You must cite multiple references (no Wikipedia references are allowed). Include a summary that focuses on the good elements or bad deeds of the hacker.

Online Activities

Complete the following activities, which will help you learn, practice, and expand your knowledge and skills.

Vocabulary. Practice vocabulary for this chapter using the e-flash cards, matching activity, and vocabulary game until you are able to recognize their meanings.

Communication Skills

College and Career Readiness

Reading. Review the vocabulary list at the beginning of this chapter. Sight words are those words you automatically recognize. Identify the sight words with which you are familiar. For those words that are unfamiliar, write contextual clues that will help you decode the meanings of the words.

Writing. A writing style is the way in which a writer uses language to convey an idea. Select a page or a couple of pages of notes you have taken during class. Evaluate your writing style and the relevance, quality, and depth of the information. Once you have done so, write a one-page paper synthesizing your notes into complete sentences and thoughts. Organize your material so it is logical to the reader. Describe what you have learned to the class.

Speaking. An introduction is making a person known to someone else by sharing the person's name and other relevant information. Introduce yourself to a person in the class whom you do not know well. What will you tell this person about yourself?

Listening. Hearing is a physical process. Listening combines hearing with evaluation. Effective leaders learn how to listen to their team members. Carefully listen to your instructor as the virtualized machines material of this chapter is presented. Take notes about the main points. Organize the key information you heard. Was the presentation effective in relating the information about this material? What points would you reiterate if you were presenting the chapter? Were there any barriers preventing you from listening?

Portfolio Development

College and Career Readiness

Portfolio Overview. When you apply for a job, community service, or college, you will need to tell others why you are qualified for the position. A portfolio can be used to support your qualifications. A *portfolio* is a selection of related materials that you collect and organize to show your qualifications, skills, and talents to support a career or personal goal. For example, a certificate that shows you have completed lifeguard and first-aid training could help you get a job at a local pool as a lifeguard. An essay you wrote about protecting native plants could show that you are serious about ecofriendly efforts and help you to get a volunteer position at a park. A transcript of your school grades could help show that you are qualified for college. A portfolio is a *living document*, which means it should be reviewed and updated on a regular basis. Two types of portfolios commonly used are print portfolios and digital portfolios. A digital portfolio may also be called an *e-portfolio*.

Artists and other communication professionals have historically presented portfolios of their creative work when seeking jobs or admission to educational institutions. However, portfolios are now used in many professions, including cybersecurity.

1. Use the Internet to search for print portfolio and digital portfolio. Read articles about each type of portfolio.
2. In your own words, compare and contrast a print portfolio with a digital one.

CTSO Event Prep

Student Organizations. Career and technical student organizations (CTSOs) are a valuable asset to any educational program. These organizations support student learning and the application of the skills learned in real-world situations. Competitive events may be written, oral, performance based, or a combination. There is a variety of organizations from which to select, depending on the goals of your educational program. To prepare for any competitive event, complete the following activities.

1. Go to the website of your organization to find specific information for the events. Visit the site often as information changes quickly. If the organization has an app, download it to your digital device.
2. Closely read all of the organization's guidelines. These rules and regulations must be strictly followed, or disqualification can occur.
3. Communication plays a role in all the competitive events, so read which communication skills are covered in the event you select. Research and preparation are important keys to a successful competition.
4. Select one or two events that are of interest to you. Print the information for the events and discuss your interest with your instructor.

Chapter 2

Information Security Fundamentals

In Chapter 1, you learned that information assurance is the comprehensive approach to protecting data and assets. There are several core principles that professionals apply to decisions and solutions in order to meet these goals. Security professionals must analyze all areas of a business to protect against security threats. This chapter explains how a business can be divided into security domains. Each domain has specific security situations.

Differences between vulnerabilities and threats are also explored. A significant threat to data and systems comes from malware. There are many variants to malware. It is important to understand the specific threats posed by the different software threats. "Human hacking" is also discussed. This security hack exploits vulnerabilities people unwittingly expose primarily through interactions with people, social media, and websites. Another essential responsibility of security administrators is being aware of governmental and industry regulations. These regulations must be followed in order to protect data confidentiality and integrity.

Chapter Preview

Section 2.1   Security Principles
Section 2.2   Vulnerabilities and Threats
Section 2.3   Legal Requirements

While studying, look for the activity icon for:

- Pretests and posttests
- Vocabulary terms with e-flash cards and matching activities
- Self-assessment

G-WLEARNING.com

College and Career Readiness

Reading Prep

A textbook generally provides a preview of the book and how the material is presented. Before reading this chapter, review the introductory material preceding Section 2.1. Does this material help you understand how to use this text?

Check Your Cybersecurity IQ 🡒

Before you begin this chapter, see what you already know about cybersecurity by visiting the student companion website (www.g-wlearning.com) and taking the chapter pretest.

Certification Objectives

CompTIA Security+

1.1   Given a scenario, analyze indicators of compromise and determine the type of malware.
1.2   Compare and contrast types of attacks.
1.6   Explain the impact associated with types of vulnerabilities.
2.5   Given a scenario, deploy mobile devices securely.
3.1   Explain use cases and purpose for frameworks, best practices and secure configuration guides.
5.8   Given a scenario, carry out data security and privacy policies.

Microsoft MTA Security Fundamentals

1.1   Understand core security principles.
1.2   Understand physical security.
1.3   Understand Internet security.
2.6   Understand malware.

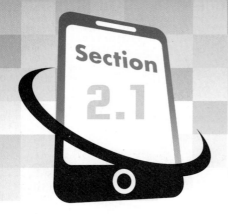

Security Principles

Essential Question

What is the best balance between protecting data and allowing access?

As it is with most projects, planning for cybersecurity incidents and protection is a critical component of a solid security plan. As a security professional, you are responsible for protecting data against a wide range of threats. In the process, you must make sure data remain confidential, the integrity of the data is maintained, and the data are available when needed. There are key security principles that guide security professionals in their choices and decisions.

Attacks can occur from many sources, so it is important to design layered solutions that assist with prevention and protection. Additionally, it is important to analyze all areas that are impacted by technology and cyberattacks. Security domains help to manage the task of protecting data by dividing an organization's operations into separate areas. There are many domains that can be used. Frameworks act as lists or guides to identify and manage the tasks needed to secure each domain.

Key Terms 📤

attack surface
CIA triad
confidentiality

defense in depth
frameworks
integrity

Internet of Things (IoT)
nonrepudiation process

Learning Goals

- Explain each of the three main security principles.
- Identify business security domains.

MTA Security Fundamentals
1.1

CIA Triad

A fundamental guiding principal among cybersecurity professionals is the CIA triad, as shown in **Figure 2-1.** In this case, CIA does not stand for the clandestine governmental spy agency. Rather, the *CIA triad* is the three underlying principles of data protection: confidentiality, integrity, and availability.

Confidentiality

Confidentiality is the condition of being private or secret. Providing confidentiality is the practice of ensuring users only have access to the data they need. The data are protected against unauthorized or unintentional access. Often, *need to know* is used to determine the level of access a user has to data, if at all. If a worker does not "need to know" the information to do his or her job, then access is not granted to the data.

Confidentiality is implemented by the rights and privileges granted to the individual computer users. For example, an employee who edits a company's social media accounts probably does not need access to corporate payroll information. It is not simply a matter of not trusting an employee. Consider what would happen if that user's password is stolen. A hacker could login as the user and access whatever data the employee has rights to view or manage. It could even be another employee who steals the password.

Another way to incorporate confidentiality is through encryption. Encryption converts the data into a format that can only be read by the holder of the decryption key. Encryption is covered in detail in Chapter 11.

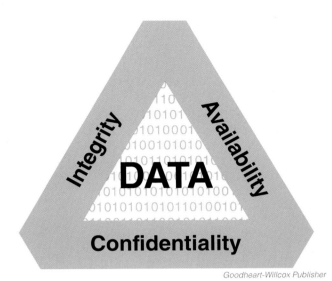

Goodheart-Willcox Publisher

Figure 2-1. The CIA triad provides three basic principles guiding cybersecurity professionals.

Integrity

Integrity is the state of being complete or uncorrupted. This core principle ensures the data are not changed or altered without permission to do so. For example, an employee in the payroll department should not be able to change his or her own wage. Nor should such an employee be able to delete a bad performance review for a friend. In both cases, doing so would lower the integrity of the data.

A practical example of ensuring integrity can be handled using folder and file permissions. **Figure 2-2** shows the permissions settings for a user. Edward Johnson has been given the Windows file permissions to the payroll folder to view *and* read data. However, he cannot make changes to files in this folder. In this way, he cannot affect the integrity of the data in the folder. You will learn how to view and grant permissions in Chapter 3.

Another key aspect of ensuring integrity is a process known as nonrepudiation. In a *nonrepudiation process,* changes are tracked by which user account made them. The user is unable to refuse to accept changes that he or she made. Through the nonrepudiation process, a historical reference shows which accounts made which changes. The nonrepudiation process also is important in legal issues. The historical record may be used to prove a user's actions in criminal or civil cases.

Availability

The third principle in the CIA triad is availability. This means the data can be accessed when needed. A problem such as a hardware failure or a hacking attack might prevent access to data. Security professionals must have solutions to ensure data can be accessed when a problem such as one of these occurs.

Security Domains

When looking at a business or organization, it can be overwhelming to consider the many areas that must be secured. The goal is to protect data and assets. To make this a more manageable process, security teams often break down the

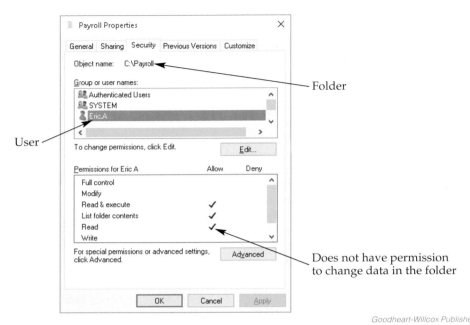

Goodheart-Willcox Publisher

Figure 2-2. This user has been granted permission to read the files in the Payroll folder. However, the user cannot write (save) to the folder. This means he or she cannot make changes to the data in the folder.

areas of a business or organization into information technology security domains. The commonly referenced IT domains are:

- users;
- workstation;
- LAN;
- WAN;
- remote access; and
- system.

These sections are based primarily on network infrastructure with the exception of the users.

When considering security domains, you must identify the attack surface. The *attack surface* is all of the locations and methods that could constitute a security risk. These are the areas you need to recognize in order to develop prevention and detection strategies. As part of the planning, create multiple levels of protection. Having multiple levels of protection is known as *defense in depth.* Consider an analogy from medieval times: the defense of castles, as shown in **Figure 2-3.** Castles were often placed on hills so defenders could scan below them for attacking forces. Trees were cleared to provide clear lines of sight around the castles. Moats were added for additional protection. Turrets provided cover for defenders who could attack incoming forces. Access to the castle was limited to entrances protected with iron gates. Each of these defensive measures is unique and separate from each other.

To liken this to a business, defense in depth might include security guards to access the building. Then, employees might have to use a code to access a door

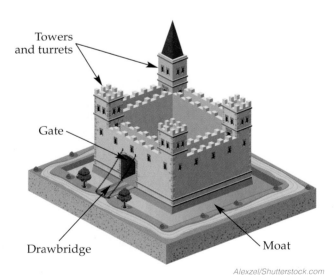

Alexzel/Shutterstock.com

Figure 2-3. Medieval castles practiced the concept of defense in depth. Multiple layers of security must be overcome to breach the castle.

lock. To log in to the computer network, a fingerprint might be required. So, for an intruder to gain access to the network, he or she would need to:

1. Slip past the security guards;
2. Know or hack the door-lock code; and
3. Hack the fingerprint lock on the network.

Another defense in depth best practice is to diversify equipment and vendors. For example, if you are using only Cisco routers and there is a vulnerability that is exploited by hackers, it would affect all of your routers. If you had a diversity of routers from different manufacturers, you would still have the ability to continue limited operations and not suffer a complete failure. This is known as *systems resilience.*

CompTIA Security+
3.1

In order to organize protection against cybersecurity threats, many companies use frameworks. *Frameworks* help break down the aspects of a business and security domains into manageable task areas and tasks. In turn, this helps create plans and actions to defend against cyberthreats. The Center for Internet Security (CIS) provides controls for frameworks. These are just one example of a security framework that can be used as a baseline for an organization to develop their own specific documentation and security planning.

Users

The users domain is all about people. This domain includes the staff at the business. However, it could also include vendors or contractors who use the network. It also includes guests who have been provided Wi-Fi access.

Users represent the weakest link in the security chain. They provide specific vulnerabilities and threats. For example, users might reveal confidential data, have weak passwords, leave confidential papers on desks, or lose flash drives containing important data. It is critical to create a domain to deal with these issues. Simple measures such as proper trash disposal, not using sticky-notes on monitors, and locking computers when not near them can go far in securing systems. Another strategy is a screen saver that locks the computer so that unauthorized users cannot access the system.

Workstation

The workstation domain deals with the issues surrounding workstations or other devices used by people. Workstations are computers such as desktop or laptop units. Other devices include tablets, smartphones, and Internet of Things devices.

What is the Internet of Things? *Internet of Things (IoT)* describes the connection of nontraditional computing devices to the Internet, as shown in **Figure 2-4.** Computer technology is moving at a fast pace. Internet connectivity is being added to nontraditional devices such as home appliances, wearable devices, trash cans, lightbulbs, and much more! This phenomenon is the Internet of Things.

Zapp2Photo/Shutterstock.com

Figure 2-4. The Internet of Things describes the connection of devices to the Internet.

LAN

The local area network (LAN) is the network infrastructure within a small area. This area is usually a single building. Issues related to the LAN may be related to servers, switches, routers, and media. The LAN domain covers these issues.

WAN

A wide area network (WAN) is the network infrastructure for more than one geographic location. The Internet is an example of a WAN. There are distinct threats and vulnerabilities that could occur in this part of the network infrastructure. The WAN domain covers these issues. Important considerations in this security domain include ensuring firewalls are correctly configured and routers are properly secured, patched, and updated. Threats to Supervisory Control and Data Acquisition (SCADA) can threaten critical systems.

Remote Access

More and more, businesses are allowing employees or other users to remotely connect to the computer network. The remote access domain addresses challenges presented by remote access. These challenges include securing data in transit over the Internet, verification of the authorized users and locations, and the security of the remote system.

System

System domain is a generic term. The system domain includes the services and software used to provide access to data and other resources. This domain covers web servers, database servers, and any server operating system or feature used to support data access.

Quick Look 2.1.1

Frameworks

Frameworks are guides that can be used to help plan security defenses. These frameworks can be detailed and can be used in many digital formats. Frameworks have often been collaboratively developed by many organizations and individuals and are available at no charge for security professionals to use and adapt to their own security decisions. In this exercise, you will take a brief look at an example of some frameworks.

1. Launch a web browser, and navigate to the Center for Internet Security website (www.cisecurity.org).
2. Locate the About us link, which is likely at the bottom of the page, and click it. Review the information about this group, including its goals and mission. What do you think the benefits of using a volunteer method to create these controls offers over a for-profit organization?
3. Click on the CIS Controls link at the top of the page, as shown.

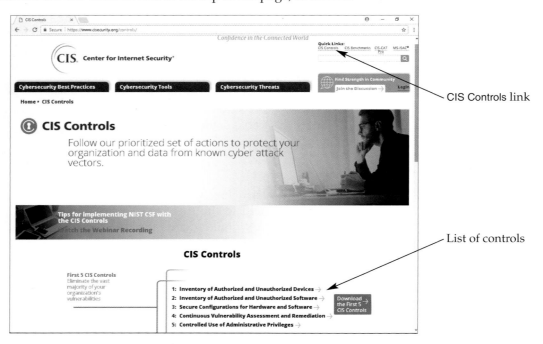

Quick Look 2.1.1 Continued

4. How many controls are offered?
5. Review the first five controls. Click the name of each control to display detailed information about the control.
6. Discuss with your classmates why control 5 is an important control to implement.
7. Review the complete list of the 20 controls. Discuss with your class how these controls can help plan your cybersecurity defenses.

SECTION REVIEW 2.1

Check Your Understanding

1. Which security principle relates to protecting data against unauthorized changes?
2. What is the practice of having multiple layers of security to protect against intruders?
3. Briefly describe frameworks.
4. Nontraditional computing devices with Internet access describes _____.
5. What is the weakest link in an organization's security policy and plan?

Build Your Key Terms Vocabulary

As you progress through this course, develop a personal cybersecurity glossary. This will help you build your vocabulary and prepare you for a career. Write a definition for each of the following terms, and add it to your cybersecurity glossary.

attack surface

CIA triad

confidentiality

defense in depth

frameworks

integrity

Internet of Things (IoT)

nonrepudiation process

Vulnerabilities and Threats

A person's social media account could be a threat to a business network. Should a business be allowed to tell an employee what can or cannot be posted?

With the key security areas of a business or organization identified, the next steps are to analyze the types of situations and hacks that could affect the security of data that could be impacted. This needs to be done in each of the six security domains. One place to start is to consider the vulnerabilities and threats that could occur.

Vulnerability or threat? These two terms are often used interchangeably, but they have different meanings. A *vulnerability* is a flaw or potential for harm, while a *threat* is something that takes the vulnerability to a level that the flaws can be exploited. Malware represents an ongoing threat to an organization due to user actions and the constant threat and variations of malware that exist.

Key Terms 🔗

adware	keylogger	rootkit
armored virus	logic bomb	secure cookie
backdoor	macro virus	session cookie
cookie policy	malware	social engineering
cryptomalware	payload	third-party cookie
digital footprint	persistent cookie	threat
drive-by-download	polymorphic virus	time bomb
dumpster diving	pretexting	Trojan horse
firmware	ransomware	vulnerability
heuristic methodology	remote access Trojan (RAT)	zero-day vulnerability

Learning Goals

- Compare and contrast forms of malware.
- Explain vulnerabilities that exist in software.
- Identify cybersecurity threats outside of malware.

Copyright Goodheart-Willcox Co., Inc.

Malware

Malware, or malicious software, is computer code intentionally written to cause some form of harm, from stealing or destroying data to collecting information or allowing remote access to a system. It exploits vulnerabilities in a computer system. A *vulnerability* is a flaw or potential for harm. Malware is a significant source of threats to computers and systems. A *threat* is something that takes a vulnerability to a level where the flaws can be exploited.

There are many reasons a hacker may create malware. The purpose of malware is found in its payload. The *payload* is the actions of the malicious code.

Most people hear the term malware and think "computer virus." Computer viruses are a form of malware. However, there are many other types of malware. Some of the most common forms of malware are:

- Trojan horse;
- worm;
- time or logic bomb;
- armored virus;
- ransomware;
- polymorphic;
- rootkit;
- backdoor; and
- macro virus.

CompTIA Security+
1.1

MTA Security Fundamentals
2.6

Trojan horse

A *Trojan horse* is malware hidden inside other software that appears to be harmless. This type of malware takes its name from the ancient story of Greek soldiers hiding inside a wooden horse so they could invade the city of Troy, as shown in **Figure 2-5.** In computing, a Trojan horse represents the same type of threat: malicious or dangerous code hidden inside something that appears innocent. It may be inside a screen saver, game, or other type of file. As with the residents of Troy, a user is unaware of this threat lurking in the file. Once someone downloads, executes, or installs the program, he or she has put the computer system at risk.

A *remote access Trojan (RAT)* is a form of malware that allows the hacker to use an embedded backdoor to gain administrative control of the victim's computer. It is a Trojan horse in that the victim is infected by downloading a seemingly normal file containing the malware. In addition to administrative access, some RAT programs may monitor the system to obtain keystrokes.

Malchev/Shutterstock.com

Figure 2-5. In the legend of the Trojan horse, Greek soldiers hid inside a wooden horse that was then offered to the city of Troy as a gift. Once the horse was inside the city walls, the soldiers exited the horse and attacked the city.

Worm

As mentioned in Chapter 1, a worm is a form of malware that infects systems with its payload. Unlike many other forms of malware, a worm moves or spreads from one computer to another through open network connections. Worms can be very destructive. They can also be difficult to remove. Some examples of this threat include the Sasser and MyDoom worms.

The Sasser worm did not have a destructive payload in terms of destroying or stealing data. It attempted to run code that exploited a vulnerability in Windows causing these computers to slow or shut down, as shown in **Figure 2-6.** However, even this payload caused an estimated 18 billion dollars in damages.

The MyDoom worm holds the dubious distinction as the quickest-spreading worm via e-mail. This malware went through e-mail contact lists and continued

Goodheart-Willcox Publisher

Figure 2-6. This is the shutdown message users received due to the Sasser worm.

this process on each new system. The MyDoom worm slowed down Internet access by 10 percent and caused roughly 38 billion dollars in damages.

Time or Logic Bomb

A time bomb or logic bomb is malicious software that does not launch immediately when a system is infected. Instead, it relies on some type of trigger, which can be a date, time, or condition. The malware remains dormant looking for the trigger. When the trigger occurs, the payload is unleashed.

A *time bomb* deploys its payload when a date or time occurs. An early example of a time bomb is a virus called Michelangelo. This virus delivered its payload only on the day of Michelangelo's birthday, which is March 6th. Once the payload was delivered, it reformatted the infected system's hard disk by overwriting data with random characters.

A *logic bomb* will deploy when conditions exist that the malware is seeking. The Stuxnet virus discussed in Chapter 1 illustrates this. Stuxnet did nothing to systems that did not have the Siemens software installed. It only delivered its payload when this software was present.

Armored Virus

An *armored virus* is designed to prevent security analysts from reading the source code. It does so by attempting to prevent access to or disassembly of the code itself. Armored viruses use special methods to attempt to ward off antivirus software, technicians, and ultimately detection.

Bitcoin is an electronic currency invented in 2008 and released as an open-source tool in 2009. It is a peer-to-peer system of transactions that does not involve banks, third-party organizations, or governments.

Ransomware

Ransomware is fast becoming a serious threat to users. *Ransomware* does not steal or destroy data, rather it encrypts data so the user cannot access it unless a fee is paid to the hacker. Usually, the ransom must be paid via Bitcoins, which makes it difficult to trace. This type of malware is referred to as *cryptomalware.*

Encryption is when data are converted into unreadable characters by applying a security key. To read the data, the correct key (or algorithm) must be used to convert the data back into readable data, as shown in **Figure 2-7.** With ransomware, hackers hold your data hostage until a ransom is paid to receive the decryption key.

A computer system is usually infected with ransomware when a user opens an infected e-mail attachment. Ransomware can also be spread when a user visits a web page that is infected. The ransomware is automatically downloaded. This action is known as a *drive-by-download.*

An example of ransomware occurred with Hollywood Presbyterian Hospital. Computer systems needed for pharmaceutical orders, lab work, and the emergency room were locked until a ransom of 17,000 bitcoins, or roughly 3 million dollars, was paid. The hospital paid the ransom. It was fortunate the hackers

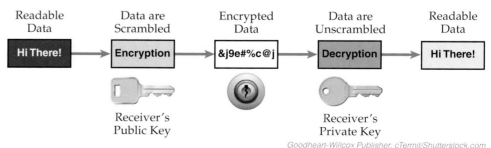

Goodheart-Willcox Publisher; cTermit/Shutterstock.com

Figure 2-7. Encryption makes data unreadable without the proper key to unlock the encryption.

actually provided the decryption key. Not all hackers follow through after receiving payment.

Polymorphic

If you ever watched the Mighty Morphin Power Rangers cartoon, you will remember how the characters changed or morphed from humans into rangers. Polymorphic viruses work in the same manner. A *polymorphic virus* changes its characteristics in attempts to avoid detection from antivirus programs.

Rootkit

A *rootkit* is a virus that infects a computer before the operating system loads. This makes it difficult to remove. The computer must be booted with a repair and recovery disk or flash drive. Rootkits often deliver serious payloads. This may include the ability to remotely access a computer without needing or knowing the credentials on the system.

The term rootkit comes from the words *root* and *kit*. Root is the term for administrator in Linux/Unix systems. Kit refers to the malicious programs within the virus.

Backdoor

A *backdoor* is a secret or unknown access point into a system. This is not always a virus; it could be a user you are not aware of that has administrative privileges. It can take the form of a hidden program, embedded in the firmware of a computer, or an account can be hardcoded in an operating system or program.

A popular movie reference to the use of backdoors was in the 1983 movie War Games starring Matthew Broderick. Broderick played a teenage hacker who stumbled across a system he thought was from a game developer. He found a backdoor and used it to access some games, one of which was a war-game simulation. In trying to play the game, he nearly started World War III.

Macro Virus

Macros are little scripts users often create to perform repetitive tasks. In Microsoft Office programs, macros are created using the programming language Visual Basic for Applications (VBA). These "mini programs" can be inserted into files created with Word, PowerPoint, Excel, and Access. A *macro virus* is a macro that has been programmed to carry out a malicious intent.

Quick Look 2.2.1

Macro Programming

Creating a macro in Microsoft Office is very easy. Microsoft Word has a record function that stores the actions of the user. When the macro is used, those actions are replicated.

1. Launch Microsoft Word, and begin a new, blank document.

Macros

2. Click the **View** tab on the ribbon, and locate the **Macros** button. Click the arrow below the button to display a drop-down menu, and click **Record Macro...** in the menu. The **Record Macro** dialog box is displayed. Here is where you name the macro before recording it.

3. Click in the **Macro name:** text box, and enter your name. Spaces are not allowed in the macro name, so leave them out when entering your name.

Quick Look 2.2.1 Continued

4. Click in the **Description:** text box, and enter A macro to insert my name, as shown.

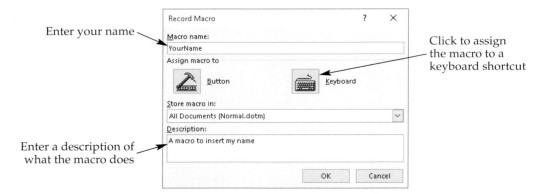

Enter your name

Click to assign the macro to a keyboard shortcut

Enter a description of what the macro does

5. Click the **Keyboard** button in the dialog box. The **Customize Keyboard** dialog box is displayed. This is used to assign the macro to a keyboard shortcut.

6. Click in the **Press new shortcut key:** text box, and then press the [Alt] and [N] keys on the keyboard at the same time. Look near the bottom of the dialog box, and verify the Currently assigned to: label reads [unassigned]. If this key combination is currently assigned to a command, choose a different key combination.

7. Click the **Assign** button in the dialog box to set the keyboard shortcut for the macro, and then click the **Close** button. The dialog box closes, and you are now in record mode. Anything you do in Word will be included as an action in the macro.

8. To the document, add your name, press the [Enter] key, and add your class and section.

9. Click the arrow below the **Macros** button on the ribbon, and click **Stop Recording** in the drop-down menu. The macro is now complete and ready for use. You can also view the computer code that was created.

10. Click **View>Macros>Macros** on the ribbon. The **Macros** dialog box is displayed. Any existing macros will be listed in this dialog box.

11. Select the macro named with your name, and click the **Edit** button in the dialog box. The Microsoft Visual Basic editor is opened, and the code for the macro is displayed in a window, as shown. There are many ways a hacker could edit this code to insert malicious actions.

Macro name

Code for recorded actions

Defending Against Malware

How do you get malware infections? There are many ways malware can make its way into computer systems. These are the most common examples:

- downloading software from the Internet
- opening infected attachments from e-mail or other social media platforms
- using infected media, such as a flash drive

Preventing malware infections is the best defense. However, sometimes malware slips past all precautions and defenses. Using an antimalware software program is critical to catch threats that may have been installed without your knowledge.

It is important to keep the operating system fully patched. A *patch* is an update provided by the vendor to correct errors or bugs. Many viruses exploit vulnerabilities left in place due to uninstalled patches.

Be careful of any program downloaded from the Internet. Never download anything from a website that appears to be suspicious or unreliable. Ensure the URL displayed in the browser matches the site. For example, www.microsoft.com is the correct URL. However, a hacker may set up a website to *look* like the official site, but the URL may be www.micr0s0ft.com. Notice the zeros where there should be the letter O.

Companies should also consider an equipment policy that prohibits the use of removable media, such as flash drives. A system should also be in place to scan e-mail messages and attachments as they are received by the company's e-mail system. Many malware infections are transmitted via e-mail.

Antimalware security companies maintain a database of known threats. Often, antimalware software also uses heuristic methodology. *Heuristic methodology* is an approach to finding previously undetected unwanted programs or variants of known viruses. Antivirus companies have designed several heuristic methods to search for potentially malicious software. Some of the approaches include deep inspection of files, such as determining intent or looking for key words or phrases in the file. Others include running the code in an isolated environment to test it before determining if it is safe. Looking at file signatures is another method. Basically, this is looking for files that are variations of known virus files. Heuristic scanning can be successful, but can also result in a lot of false positives. A *false positive* occurs when the software incorrectly flags a valid file as a threat.

FYI

Did you know, *heuristic* comes from the ancient Greek word *heuriskein,* which means to find or discover!

Quick Look 2.2.2

Antimalware Software

There are many antimalware programs on the market. Some are free, and others offer paid subscriptions. With so many choices, it can be difficult to make the best decision on which to pick.

1. Launch a web browser, and navigate to a search engine. Enter the search phrase best paid antimalware software.
2. In the search results, select an article from a source you believe to be reliable. Which program is recommended as the top choice? What were some of the highest-rated features of this product? Browse through the list of all products. Which one do you like best, and why?
3. Return to the search engine, and enter the search phrase best free antimalware software.
4. In the search results, select an article from a source you believe to be reliable. Which free antimalware programs would you recommend and why?
5. Discuss your conclusions with your class.

Software Vulnerabilities

Malware often exploits vulnerabilities in software. Hackers use uncorrected vulnerabilities to cause harm or steal private information. It is important to understand software vulnerabilities.

CompTIA Security+
1.6

Zero-Day Vulnerability

A *zero-day vulnerability* exists in software when it was released and remains unknown until it is exploited by hackers. Because it is unknown to the developer, there is no immediate fix or patch usually available. It is difficult to protect against an unknown vulnerability. The best defense is to keep the system and software patched. Also, monitor forums and support logs for announcements about zero-day attacks so immediate action can be taken. Many software developers have bug-bounty programs in place to try to identify zero-day vulnerabilities.

An example of a zero-day attack occurred in March of 2017. Cisco discovered that 318 types of its devices had a zero-day vulnerability in the firmware. This allowed the possibility of a remote attacker accessing a device without having login credentials and being able to take full control of the device.

CompTIA Security+
2.5

Firmware

Firmware is essentially software that is embedded in hardware. An example of this is the wireless router software used to configure and manage wireless networks. Manufacturers occasionally release patches for firmware. Cybersecurity technicians should not forget about updates on devices with embedded firmware. Routers, switches, computers, and many IoT devices are only updated through their firmware. Failure to update these devices can cause serious harm. For example, the Food and Drug Administration (FDA) issued a safety communication on certain models of cardiac pacemakers. The firmware addressed the vulnerabilities of cyber-attacks that could interrupt the functionality of some pacemakers. If the pacemakers were to be hacked, the safety of individuals wearing them would be at risk.

Other Security Threats

There are many security threats beyond malware. These include keyloggers, adware, cookies, and social engineering. It is important to understand each of these threats.

CompTIA Security+
1.1

MTA Security Fundamentals
1.2

Keyloggers

A *keylogger* is technology that tracks a user's keystrokes on the keyboard. In some cases, screenshots of the screen can be recorded. Keyloggers can be hardware or software based. A hardware keylogger is a small device that plugs into the computer, as shown in **Figure 2-8.** The keyboard is plugged into the back of the device. A software keylogger is a program that runs in the memory of an operating system.

Keyloggers run in stealth mode. Often, they will not appear as a running application or process on the system. This is a challenge for cybersecurity technicians to detect the intrusion.

Adware

Adware is software installed on a computer that collects data on the user, such as what sites he or she visits, and then redirects advertising sites to the web browser. Adware is not always considered malware. Some adware is advertised when you install a program or visit a site. However, many adware programs are installed without your permission or knowledge. Adware can cause problems with the multiple pop-up windows on browsers. It also raises security and privacy concerns about your web surfing.

Figure 2-8. Hardware keyloggers are widely available. They can be used to record every keystroke on the keyboard.

Cookies

MTA Security Fundamentals
1.3

Cookies are small text files that are saved on the computer for use with web browsers and websites. If a website uses a cookie, the cookie contains information about your visit to the site. It can be used to store preferences so, when you return to the site, you do not have to provide this information again.

The idea behind cookies is simple. They make your web surfing personalized to your browsing. Unfortunately, cookies can be used maliciously. There are different types of cookies to be aware of:

- session cookies
- persistent cookies
- secure cookies
- third-party cookies

Most reputable companies will publish a cookie policy. A *cookie policy* should state if the site uses cookies. If cookies are used, the policy should explain how. In some cases, the user may be able to opt out. Most web browsers also have a setting to prevent cookies from being saved.

Quick Look 2.2.3

Cookie Policy

It is a good practice for a company to have a cookie policy if its website uses cookies. This provides an openness to the users. Some sites even have a pop-up window to alert the user that cookies are being used.

1. Launch a web browser, and navigate to a search engine.
2. Enter the search phrase CNN privacy policies. In the list of results, select the article entitled Privacy Policy—CNN.com (it will likely be the first article listed).

Quick Look 2.2.3 Continued

3. On the CNN Privacy Statement page, scroll down to the section entitled Cookies and Other User and Ad-Targeting Technologies. They categorize cookie use as performance and advertising. What is the difference between these cookie types?

4. What control does CNN have over third-party cookies that may be issued from its site?

5. Navigate to the About Cookies website (www.aboutcookies.org), and click the **Cookie Law** link. This site provides information on the "cookie law" in the United Kingdom. Because CNN can attract users from countries outside the United States, it must follow laws in those countries. What rules exist in the United Kingdom that apply to cookie use?

Session Cookies

A *session cookie* exists only as long as the web browser is open. This type of cookie is intended to exist only while you are visiting the website. When the browser is closed, session cookies are deleted.

Persistent Cookies

A *persistent cookie* stays on your computer until an expiration date is met, as shown in **Figure 2-9.** Because they remain after your browser is closed, they are sometimes referred to as *tracking* cookies. They are called that because adware or other programs will read the cookies on your computer to record information about your browsing history and your habits.

Secure Cookies

A *secure cookie* can only be sent using an encrypted session. The data in the cookie are sent using the secure Hypertext Transfer Protocol (HTTPS).

Third-Party Cookies

A *third-party cookie* originates from a visit to a website, but references a different website. For example, suppose you visit the news.com website. This site may create a session or persistent cookie. The page you visited on news.com displayed an ad from the computers.com website. The computers.com website may create a cookie on your computer despite the fact you never visited that site. The cookie from computers.com is a third-party cookie in this example.

FYI

Super cookie! A new type of cookie was used by AT&T and Verizon Wireless against customers on their smartphones. This cookie tracks and monitors users' browsing habits and activity, and users are unable to delete or evade them. After public outcry, AT&T revealed it will stop using super cookies, and Verizon Wireless added an opt-out option.

Case Study

Cookies

Develop a brief presentation for faculty and staff about the purpose and potential issues of browser cookies. This presentation should describe what cookies are and how they invade privacy. Also, discuss how cookies can be used in hacking attempts. Explain how to remove cookies and how to make browser settings relevant to controlling cookies. This presentation will be given to staff that may not be computer savvy, so make sure you are writing to your intended audience. It should be informative and engaging.

Date cookie
was created

Date when
cookie will
be renewed

Figure 2-9. A persistent cookie will remain on the computer until a date has passed. The persistent cookie shown here will remain on this computer for six months.

Quick Look 2.2.4

Cookies with Google Chrome

Many, if not most, websites use some type of cookie. Most web browsers have settings for managing cookies. In Google Chrome, you can search for cookies by a particular website.

1. Launch the Google Chrome web browser, and navigate to the AOL web page (www.aol.com).

**Customize
and Control
Google
Chrome**

2. Click the **Customize and Control Google Chrome** button, and click **Settings** in the drop-down menu. A new tab is opened that contains the Chrome settings.
3. Click the Advanced or Advanced Settings link at the bottom of the page.
4. In the Privacy area, click the Content settings link, and then click the Cookies link (this link may be labeled All cookies and site data).
5. Review the settings for cookies. Notice there are options to keep cookies and block third-party cookies.
6. Scroll down until the Search cookies text box is displayed, and enter aol in the text box, as shown. All of the cookies stored by Chrome are filtered to show only those set by AOL.

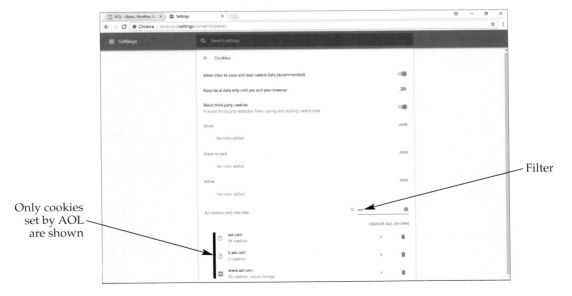

Filter

Only cookies
set by AOL
are shown

Quick Look 2.2.4 Continued

7. Click on a set of cookies to see the individual cookies. Click an individual cookie to see data about it, including when it will expire. For some cookies, you will not be able to read the content as some content is written in JavaScript.

8. Close Chrome, and then relaunch it.

9. Display the cookies, and filter for AOL cookies. Are there any cookies still present from AOL? Explain why or why not.

Ethical Issue

Third-Party Cookies

The Wall Street Journal website has a short video that covers the use of cookies, specifically third-party cookies and behavioral tracking. Use a search engine, and search for **wall street journal how advertisers use internet cookies to track you.** Then, select and view the video from www.wsj.com entitled How Advertisers Use Internet Cookies to Track You.

Behavioral tracking is monitoring what you do online. This is done site-to-site through third-party cookies. Advertisers often use third-party cookies to develop a trail of sites you have visited. Some companies are even using flash cookies to store information that is not deleted when or if you delete cookies.

Is it ethical for companies to engage in behavioral tracking? Should it be regulated by the government? Defend your thoughts.

CompTIA Security+
1.2

MTA Security Fundamentals
1.1

Social Engineering

Social engineering is a hacker using social tools and techniques to obtain information. Social tools include methods that provide personal information on individuals. This could be through searching social media platforms such as Facebook and Instagram, publicly accessible websites, or falling prey to conversational techniques in which the victim unknowingly reveals personal information. Once data about a person are collected, the hacker can use that information to impersonate or target the individual. By impersonating the individual, that hacker can gain access to systems. What is interesting about this type of attack is it is often indirectly applied. The victim is not always the one to whom social engineering is applied. For example, a hacker could target Jason in order to obtain information about his boss. The boss is the victim, but social engineering is applied to Jason.

An excellent case of social engineering involves the attack against technology journalist Mat Honan, who writes for Wired magazine. A hacker wanted his Twitter handle @Mat. Due to some vulnerabilities in how Honan created and used passwords and poor identity practices at Apple and Amazon, Honan lost more than his Twitter account. He also lost all data on his MacBook, iPhone, and iCloud backup. This included personal files and irreplaceable photos. Through vulnerabilities, the hacker obtained Honan's e-mail address, billing address, and the last four numbers of the credit card on file. Using this information, the hacker essentially took digital possession of Honan's accounts. Through iCloud, the hacker also took control of Honan's Apple devices. All of this took place within minutes.

You can read Honan's story on the Wired website (www.wired.com). Use a search engine, and enter the search phrase mat honan apple amazon hack. Then, choose the article on the Wired website from the returned results.

When an individual goes online, he or she often leaves personal information behind. This may happen despite precautions taken by the individual. A *digital footprint* is information about a person left behind by his or her actions on the Internet, as shown in **Figure 2-10.** Data may be left behind in many ways:

- review left on Yelp
- question on a support forum
- account on a gaming site
- online console gaming
- video uploaded to YouTube
- e-mail
- online searches
- social media posts
- governmental databases

A hacker will use these sources and many others to obtain information about a person. The hacker wants to find out as much about a target as possible to prepare for an attack.

Hackers who use social engineering have several techniques to find information. One is known as pretexting. *Pretexting* is using a lie or scam to obtain private information. Other techniques include:

- convincing people to reveal information;
- looking through social media sites for information;
- using public records stored online or available via public-library searches;
- using advanced web-search techniques; and
- dumpster diving.

Convincing People

One of the easiest ways to get information is to simply ask for it! Of course, going to an employee and asking for an account number is not likely going to

Want to see some old archived sites? Check out this cool site: www.waybackmachine.org. Try it, and see if some of your information appears on sites that have been archived!

Goodheart-Willcox Publisher

Figure 2-10. Social media posts contribute greatly to a person's digital footprint. This is not limited to posts on the individual's own pages. When a person posts on a business's page, he or she has added to his or her digital footprint.

work. However, if the hacker has credible information to support the request, he or she will appear as if entitled to the information.

In his book *The Art of Deception*, Kevin Mitnick describes how easy it is to get individuals to tell you things. He uses inquiries such as:

"I am writing a book and want to make sure I am using the correct terminology. Can you tell me if BankCU is the correct name of the ATM software company?"

Most people want to be helpful and will provide information. He then takes that information, and calls another department and asks questions such as:

"This is Chris from BankCU. I am doing a quality assurance check. Can I confirm you are using our correct new support number of 1-800-555-1111?"

This user will likely say, "No, we are using a different number," since the hacker is providing an invalid number. Over time, the hacker will have enough credible information to call a company and pretend to be an employee from the bank. Then, he or she can obtain the specific information being targeted.

Another convincing scheme is simple friendliness. A hacker can strike up a conversation with a target. The scheme could work like this: after chatting with a person, the hacker might say, "Didn't you go to elementary school with my mom? Your name seems so familiar!" The victim might say, "Where did your mom go to school? My mom went to Kennedy Primary in Houston." This may seem like innocent information, but many websites often ask security questions that in theory only the authorized person should know. The schools a user attended or the streets he or she lived on as a child are often on those preconfigured lists. **Figure 2-11** shows an example of a website with a security question for log in.

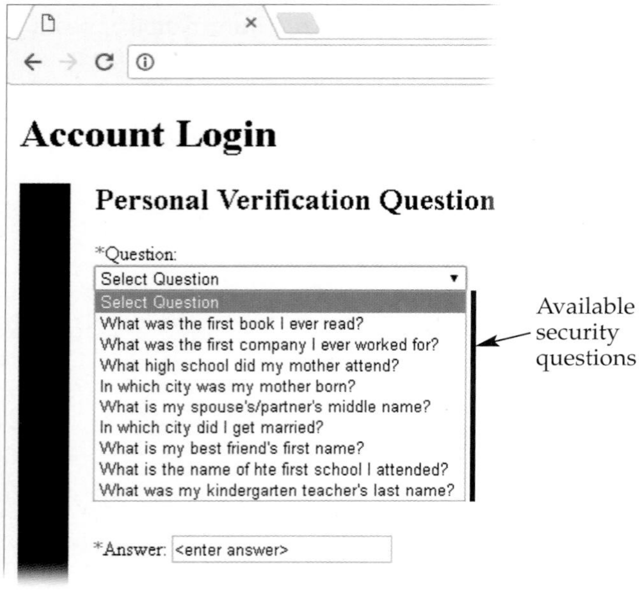

Available security questions

Figure 2-11. This website offers the user several security questions from which to choose. When the user created the account, he or she selected one of these questions and provided the correct answer.

Social Media

Social media sites, such as Facebook, Twitter, Instagram, and LinkedIn, are a treasure trove of information for hackers. Many users do not realize some of their information is not fully private. Other users simply are not too concerned. Users also make the mistake of accepting friend requests or followers from people they do not know. Once a user has access to your social media site, the information you post or your profile data can be read by anyone.

A common mistake some people do not realize when using Facebook, if they share a post that was originally public, or comment on a public post, that could be accessible to users that are not your friends. Social media platforms are like breadcrumbs that hackers can follow. For example, suppose a hacker wants to find out information about a user named JaMarques Owens. He or she may first try to friend JaMarques. If he does not respond, the hacker would then start looking at JaMarques's friends and see if he has identified any family members. The hacker would start looking through those profiles and search as well. Over time, it is quite likely the hacker can find out a great deal about JaMarques, including his family, friends, location, schools attended, and personal likes and dislikes. All of this even if JaMarques never accepts the friend request! The hacker can then search through other social media platforms and compile a great deal of information about JaMarques.

Public Records

City and state governments are putting more and more information online. Public records can contain much information about an individual. This includes information about property ownership. Hackers can use information in public records to obtain more information about a person.

Here is an example of using public records to find information about a person. A property for sale in Boston is located on Zillow.com. This is an online real estate website. Next, the hacker takes the address and visits the official website of the city of Boston (www.boston.gov). This website has a link Search Property Info with Assessing online. Clicking this link, the hacker enters the address in the Real Estate Assessments and Taxes search box. By displaying the details for the property, a great deal of information is available, as shown in **Figure 2-12.** This includes the owner's name and mailing address.

Some cities and counties have created free public records directories. There are also websites that collect public records and provide a centralized search engine. Collecting data from various sources is called *aggregating* data. In some cases, the information provided includes obituaries that reference families and places of birth. This can be valuable information to a hacker.

Court records are also in public databases. Most states offer this access for free. In some states, such as California, a small fee may be required to access the records. **Figure 2-13** shows an example of a court record from Arlington, VA, that is available online. On this site, you can search for a hearing by date, name, type of hearing, or other criteria.

Goodheart-Willcox Publisher

Figure 2-12. Public records, including real estate records, can provide much information about a person.

Figure 2-13. Often, court records can be located online. This is an example from Alexandria, Virginia.

Quick Look 2.2.5

Personal Data Online

There are many websites that aggregate data from other sources. Many of the sites charge a fee, but there are some that will give you some information for free.

1. Launch a web browser, and navigate to the Spokeo website (www.spokeo.com).
2. In the search box, enter your name or a parent's name, and click the Search button. All matches will be returned. Depending on how common the name is, there could be quite a few selections.
3. If needed, use the tools to filter the results by location. Notice relatives are connected to each result. This may help in identifying the correct person.
4. Click the link corresponding to the correct person. A map of the current address is displayed along with some basic information. The other information on Spokeo is fee-based.
5. Navigate to the Zaba Search website (www.zabasearch.com). This site will give an address for a person you enter.
6. Search for the same person as on the Spokeo website. Did you get different information or was it identical?
7. Navigate to the Pipl website (www.pipl.com). This is another site for locating people.
8. Search for the same person as on the other two sites. Did this site provide any additional information?

Advanced Internet Searches

Internet searches are often used to find personal information and other data on a target's digital footprint. Most Internet search engines have advanced methods to help find data. **Figure 2-14** shows five tips for conducting advanced searches. Most average users are not aware of these methods. For purposes of this discussion, the search engine Google will be used. However, the tools often work in any search engine.

Tip #1	Enclose specific keywords in quotation marks.
Tip #2	Use a hyphen (-) to exclude words or a plus sign (+) to ensure words are included.
Tip #3	Conduct the search on a specific website.
Tip #4	Limit searches to specific dates or a range of dates.
Tip #5	Search for only specific file types.

Goodheart-Willcox Publisher

Figure 2-14. Tips for conducting advanced searches on the Internet.

Enclosing specific keywords within quotation marks tells the search engine all of those words must be present in the results. For example, entering "John Smith New York NY" into Google will only return results that contain *all* of those words. By contrast, entering the same words without the quotation marks will return results that contain *any* of those words.

A hyphen (-) can be used to exclude words from the search. For example, entering eagles -football -Philadelphia into Google will search for anything that contains the word *eagles*. However, of those found, any that include the word *football* or *Philadelphia* will not be included in the list of results. In effect, this search will be focused away from the popular NFL team. Similarly, a plus sign (+) can be used to ensure certain words are included in the results.

A search can be conducted on a specific site. For example, entering site:Microsoft.com Bill Gates into Google will only return results from sites within Microsoft.com. This search could be further refined by enclosing Bill Gates in quotation marks. That would limit the results to only items within Microsoft.com that include both Bill and Gates.

Searches can be limited to a specific numeric value, such as date or range of dates. For example, to information about PlayStation in only the current year, enter Playstation..2018 into Google (assuming the current year is 2018). The two periods (dots) tell Google not to display any results before this year. To specify a range of dates, separate the dates with two periods. **Figure 2-15** shows an example of

There are many commands that can be used with search engines to conduct an advanced Internet search. A quick search of the Internet should result in several sites that list the commands for your preferred search engine.

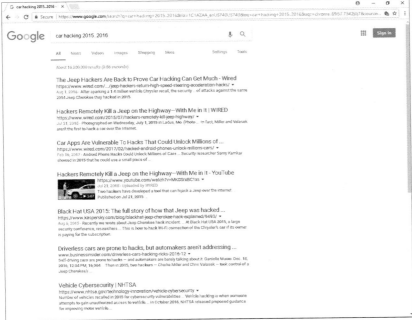

Goodheart-Willcox Publisher

Figure 2-15. Entering the search phrase car hacking 2015..2016 will display results only from those years.

searching for information on car hacking, but only from 2015 through 2016. This can also be used to limit searches to a specific year. For example, cybersecurity 2015..2015 will display results only from the year 2015.

A search can be limited to a specific file type. For example, the file type for a Microsoft Excel spreadsheet is XLS or XLSX. To limit a search to only the XLS file type, enter filetype:xls and a keyword into Google. To search for an Excel file that contains the word password, enter filetype:xls password into Google. Since there are two native file formats for Excel, you may want to do this search twice, once for each file type.

Quick Look 2.2.6

Advanced Internet Search

Advanced Internet searches can be useful in refining the results to more closely match the information being sought. Hackers may also use advanced Internet searches to gather information about potential victims.

1. Launch a web browser, and navigate to the Google website (www.google.com).
2. In the search box, enter cyber hacks 2014..2015, and press the [Enter] key to conduct the search. Google looks for information on hacks that occurred in the years 2014 and 2015.
3. Conduct a new search by entering filetype:pdf "computer hackers". This search looks for any PDF file that contains the phrase *computer hackers.*
4. Conduct a new search by entering allintitle:computer hackers. This command ensures the words *computer* and *hackers* appears in the title of the search results. Notice, however, that the words can appear in any order and do not even need to be next to each other in the title.
5. Conduct a new search by entering cache:http://lifehacker.com. The result is not a search, but rather a cached version of the website is displayed. A cached version is a saved version, which may not be the most current version.

CompTIA Security+
1.2

MTA Security Fundamentals
1.2

FYI

In the movie *Argo*, the Iranians successfully reassembled strip-cut shredded documents to gain information. This was accurate; they used the term *carpet weavers* to describe the individuals who reassembled the paper strips.

Dumpster Diving

Have you ever watched an old movie where students sneak into a teacher's office or workroom looking through the trash to find carbon copies of an upcoming test? *Dumpster diving* is digging through trash for useful information. Stealing information from trash is not a new technique. It can still be used to gain valuable information to commit a hack. Business documents could reveal contacts, such as vendors or partners. Drafts of projects often end up in the trash. Old or unneeded business cards and other seemingly innocent information may be similarly discarded.

To help protect against dumpster diving, shred documents when they are no longer needed. Confidential papers or any other papers that could reveal sensitive information should be shredded. There are generally three types of cuts made to the paper with shredders, as shown in **Figure 2-16.** The type selected depends on the level of protection needed.

- Strip-cut shredders slice the paper into long strips.
- Crosscut shredders slice the paper into short strips.
- Micro-cut shredders slice the paper into small bits similar to confetti; provides the most secure shredding.

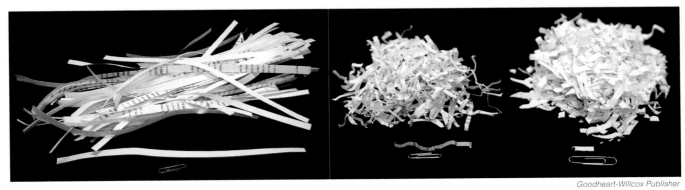

Figure 2-16. There are different types of paper shredders. The most secure shredding is achieved with a micro-cut shredder.

SECTION REVIEW 2.2

Check Your Understanding

1. What is a Trojan or Trojan horse?
2. Software that is preinstalled or embedded in hardware is known as _____.
3. Which type of cookie remains on the computer after the browser is closed until it reaches its expiration date?
4. What is the social engineering technique in which the hacker lies to get information?
5. If you are digging through a trash can for information, what is this hacking technique called?

Build Your Key Terms Vocabulary

As you progress through this course, develop a personal cybersecurity glossary. This will help you build your vocabulary and prepare you for a career. Write a definition for each of the following terms, and add it to your cybersecurity glossary.

adware	persistent cookie
armored virus	polymorphic virus
backdoor	pretexting
cookie policy	ransomware
cryptomalware	remote access Trojan (RAT)
digital footprint	rootkit
drive-by-download	secure cookie
dumpster diving	session cookie
firmware	social engineering
heuristic methodology	third-party cookie
keylogger	threat
logic bomb	time bomb
macro virus	Trojan horse
malware	vulnerability
payload	zero-day vulnerability

Legal Requirements

ssential uestion

When should governmental regulation be applied to digital security?

As you plan security measures, it is important to understand that in a business you can set policies the information technology department and management team put into place. These security measures are optional. Every company can set policies, such as how long a password must be or what data users can access, and decide levels of permissions for users. However, there are some laws that you may have to follow. Doing so is not optional.

Some laws are generic in nature and apply to all systems. Some laws apply only to certain types of businesses. Failure to abide by laws could result in criminal or civil penalties. The business may also lose the ability of providing a service, such as processing credit cards.

Key Terms 🖙

compliance
Computer Fraud and Abuse Act (CFAA)
Electronic Communication Privacy Act (ECPA)
electronic health record (EHR)
Gramm-Leach-Bliley Act (GLBA)

Health Insurance Portability and Accounting Act (HIPAA)
Payment Card Industry Data Security Standard (PCI DSS)
protected health information (PHI)
Sarbanes-Oxley Act (SOX)

Learning Goals

- Define compliance.
- Identify laws and standards related to digital security.

Compliance

When the requirement is a legal or regulatory directive, you are responsible for ensuring compliance with the terms. *Compliance* means you are following the rules or standards that have been established. Since technology is key to data storage and access, many laws have been established to ensure that data and privacy are protected. While most of the laws are enacted at a federal level, states may also have their own laws. Companies that work with other businesses or customers located outside the United States may also have to comply with legal regulations set by those countries. For example, the European Union (EU) adopted strong data privacy rules, the General Data Protection Regulation (GDPR) act. The GDPR act was adopted in April 2016. Enforcement began in May 2018. Any company with business or customer interests in the EU must be compliant with this act.

Some of the major federal US laws that apply to cybersecurity measures include:

- Computer Fraud and Abuse Act (CFAA);
- Electronic Communication Privacy Act (ECPA);
- Gramm-Leach-Bliley Act (GLBA);
- Sarbanes-Oxley Act (SOX); and
- Health Insurance Portability and Accountability Act (HIPAA).

The Payment Card Industry Data Security Standard (PCI DSS) is a set of rules that also apply to businesses who accept credit cards. In addition to federal law and compliance regulations, many states have their own computer security laws. These must be followed if a company conducts business within the state that enacted the law.

Laws and Standards

Laws are enacted by the government. Federal laws are passed by Congress, as shown in **Figure 2-17.** They apply everywhere throughout the country. State laws are passed by individual state legislatures. They apply only within the state. Standards are different from laws. An industry standard is a set of rules adopted by a particular industry. Businesses in that industry agree to follow the rules in the standard.

Computer Fraud and Abuse Act

The *Computer Fraud and Abuse Act (CFAA)* deals with unauthorized access of computers. It covers primarily *protected* computers located on US governmental systems, financial institutions, and interstate or foreign communication. In theory, most computers and

Bulent Demir/Shutterstock.com

Figure 2-17. Congress passes federal laws that apply throughout the United States.

cell phones are probably covered under this law. The law was originally enacted in 1986. It has been updated several times since it first took effect. While there are many specific aspects to the law, some of its main points deal with individuals who knowingly access computers for which they are not authorized to do so.

The law covers both criminal and civil litigation. Many computer hackers have found themselves prosecuted under this law. Criminal penalties include fines and imprisonment. Fines could also be assessed for civil litigation.

There are many critics of the law. Much of the criticism is based in part due to the very broad nature of the law. This has resulted in some controversial prosecutions.

One of the most debated prosecutions was of Aaron Swartz. He connected his computer to the MIT network and downloaded 2.7 million academic papers. These papers were freely available to anyone on campus, including visitors, by using the JSTOR service. JSTOR (pronounced *jay-store*) is a nonprofit organization that maintains a large digital library and collaborates with academic institutions. In Swartz's case, JSTOR did not file a complaint over the downloads, but the Justice Department ultimately charged him with 13 felony counts. The possible penalties included jail time of 50 years and fines of up to a million dollars.

The CFAA has been used to prosecute unauthorized access, such as the case of Matthew Keys, a former Social Media Editor for Reuters. After being fired from his job, Keys gave hackers the account names and passwords for Tribune company websites. In other cases, however, judges have ruled that prosecutors have over-reached on charges. One such case involves Lori Drew. She faked a social media profile on MySpace. The profile was used to engage in cyberbullying of a 13-year-old girl, who believed the profile was for a boy from school. Ultimately, it was ruled that Drew's actions did not represent unauthorized access.

Electronic Communication Privacy Act

FYI

The ECPA was originally enacted to address interception of conversations on "hard" telephone lines, or landlines. It has since been updated to consider other technologies and methods of access.

The *Electronic Communication Privacy Act (ECPA)* protects wire and electronic transmissions of data. This law covers communication such as e-mail, telephone conversations, and data stored electronically. Essentially, the law protects electronic communication whether made orally (by voice) or digital data transmissions. Protection starts at the beginning of the transmission, through the data in transit, and the data stored on computers, as shown in **Figure 2-18.** The ECPA has three titles:

* Wiretap Act;
* Stored Communications Act (SCA); and
* Pen Register Act.

The Wiretap Act prohibits the intentional interception, use, disclosure, or procurement of any communication. Even attempting this is prohibited. Additionally, data collected by any such method cannot be used as evidence in court.

The Stored Communications Act (SCA) protects the privacy of the content of files stored by service providers. It also protects records including subscriber names, billing records, and IP addresses.

FYI

The USA PATRIOT Act also covers electronic communication.

The Pen Register Act requires governmental entities obtain a court order on these devices. A pen register is a device that captures the numbers and related information of outgoing calls. A trap and trace captures numbers and information on incoming calls.

There are many issues with the ECPA, and there are exceptions that have been made through the USA PATRIOT Act. There are also issues of conflict with the Fourth Amendment rights to protect individuals from unreasonable search and seizure. Currently, stored data older than 180 days are considered to be abandoned, and thus not subject to a warrant. This applies to e-mail and data stored in the cloud. Proposals have been made in Congress to address these conflicts and privacy issues.

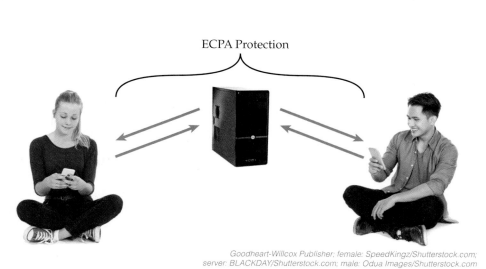

ECPA Protection

Goodheart-Willcox Publisher; female: SpeedKingz/Shutterstock.com; server: BLACKDAY/Shutterstock.com; male: Odua Images/Shutterstock.com

Figure 2-18. ECPA protection begins at the start of the transmission and continues to the end, including the data stored on computers.

Gramm-Leach-Bliley Act

The *Gramm-Leach-Bliley Act (GLBA)* ensures that financial businesses are protecting your private data. It was enacted in 1999 and is also known as the Financial Services Modernization Act of 1999. This act applies to companies of all sizes that provide financial services and products. Financial services can include loans, insurance, and financial and investment advice. Any business that provides these services is subject to its provisions, such as a bank. It also covers other businesses such as a retail store if the company offers financing or credit cards, check cashing companies, tax-preparation services, and even real estate appraisers.

To implement the GLBA, the Federal Trade Commission (FTC), shown in **Figure 2-19,** issued the Safeguards Rule. Businesses must develop, implement, and maintain a comprehensive information security program to comply with the Safeguards Rule. This program needs to contain administrative, technical, and physical safeguards that are appropriate to the size and complexity of an organization. Companies must anticipate likely threats and hazards that could affect the security and integrity of the data. This not only includes potential security threats to IT systems, but the employees who have access to customer information. It also includes potential system failures.

The other key provision of the GLBA is the Financial Privacy Rule. This regulates the collection and disclosure of a consumer's nonpublic personal information (NPI). Under this rule, businesses must provide customers with written notice describing their privacy policies and practices. Consumers should be given the opportunity to opt out of the sharing of some of their personal financial information.

A third protection under this act is for pretexting protection. Pretexting may include requests from phishing e-mail, phony telephone calls, or direct mail. Companies must train their employees and implement practices to reduce the success of a pretexting act.

There are some criticisms of this act. Some privacy advocates believe too great of a burden is placed on the individual consumer to protect his or her data. These advocates believe consumers should have the right to opt in and decide for themselves what data, if any, can be shared. Also, there are no standards on notices required by the GLBA. This can create confusion to consumers, especially in regards to confusing legal terminology.

Mark Van Scyoc/Shutterstock.com

Figure 2-19. The Federal Trade Commission (FTC) issued the Safeguards Rule to implement the Gramm-Leach-Bliley Act.

Sarbanes-Oxley Act

The *Sarbanes-Oxley Act (SOX)* prevents company executives from hiding or destroying electronic records for a minimum of five years. In the early 2000s, there were a few large corporations including Enron and WorldCom, who engaged in deceptive and fraudulent financial and accounting practices. When these issues were discovered, some of the companies closed. This cost investors, stockholders, and employees millions of dollars, retirement pensions, and jobs.

Sarbanes-Oxley was named after the two sponsors in Congress: Senator Paul Sarbanes of Maryland and Representative Michael Oxley of Ohio. It became law in 2002. Enforcement of this law is done through the Securities and Exchange Commission (SEC).

Figure 2-20. The Enron Complex in Houston was the headquarters of Enron when the company was involved in fraudulent practices that led in part to the Sarbanes-Oxley Act. This building is now owned by Chevron Corporation and no longer called the Enron Complex.

This law is designed to crack down on corporate fraud. Some of its provisions included creating a Public Company Accounting Oversight Board to oversee the accounting industry. Company loans to its executives were banned. Rules were instituted to protect whistleblowers who came forward to report fraudulent practices.

Some of the key provisions require executives to personally certify the accuracy of financial information and statements. Violators could be penalized with up to 20 years in prison. Internal control structure and procedures have to be maintained. It is here that the IT department has a significant role in protecting the information. For example, data, including files and e-mail, must be retained. One of the contributing companies that prompted the legislation was the deeds of Arthur Andersen. This was a prominent accounting firm. In an effort to hide actions of fraudulent work for the company Enron, employees deleted relevant files and shredded paper copies of the files and e-mail. Enron was an energy company headquartered in Houston, Texas, as shown in **Figure 2-20.**

There have been many cases prosecuted under SOX. One of the first cases involved an auditor from Ernst & Young in San Francisco. He pled guilty to destroying documents in an effort to impede an investigation from the SEC. In this case, he did not physically dispose of the documents, but altered their contents. While there have been many successful prosecutions of fraud resulting from this law, there was the strange case of John Yates. Yates was a commercial fisherman seeking red grouper off the coast of Florida. During the outing, the boat was boarded by a state Fish and Wildlife officer who discovered that 72 of the fish were undersized. On the vessel's return to port, an examination only found 69 fish. Yates was charged with violating the Sarbanes-Oxley Act by destroying tangible evidence and convicted. Yates appealed his conviction, arguing the law applied to documents, not fish. After three years, the Supreme Court agreed and reversed the case against Yates.

Health Insurance Portability and Accountability Act

CompTIA Security+
5.8

The *Health Insurance Portability and Accounting Act (HIPAA)* protects electronic medical records and personal health information. Any company that handles medical records or insurance information must comply with the requirements of this legislation. It applies to medical practices and hospitals, as shown in **Figure 2-21.** In addition, it covers pharmacies and other businesses that handle personal health-care information. It even applies health-care-related employee information within a business.

Health-care information can reveal much about a person. It can be exploited and used improperly. It can even be used as a form of identity theft in which a criminal can impersonate a victim to obtain medical care. Stolen medical records can result in fraudulent billing. Consider the case of Helene Michel of Medical Solutions Management, Inc. Over a four-year period, she used her position to enter nursing homes where she accessed and stole patient records. She then used this information to submit $10 million in false billings to Medicare. She was convicted of health-care fraud and HIPAA identity-theft crimes and sentenced to 12 years in federal prison.

HIPAA is managed by the Department of Health and Human Services (HHS). It provides two key rules that are important to consumers: the Privacy Rule and the Security Rule. There are other rules and regulations with HIPAA as well.

The Privacy Rule establishes a set of national standards for the protection of all "individually identifiable health information." This information is also known as *protected health information (PHI)*. PHI could be in the form of electronic data, paper records, or even spoken conversation. Not complying with the Privacy Rule could result in civil fines. For "willful actions," criminal charges could be filed.

Most medical practices use some form of digital or electronic platform for health records. A record in this form is called an *electronic health record (EHR)*. The Security Rule establishes a set of national standards to protect personal health information in elec-

Monkey Business Images/Shutterstock.com

Figure 2-21. Anyone who handles health-care information, such as a doctor's office, must follow the rules outlined in HIPAA.

tronic form. These standards help organizations understand the safeguards they must undertake to ensure the confidentiality, integrity, and security of information. Safeguards may be physical, administrative, or technical in nature. Failure to maintain the standards set by the Security Rule could be costly. Consider the case against an Indiana Walgreens pharmacy. A pharmacist accessed a customer's prescription history and shared it with others. The information was used to harass and intimidate the customer. A jury awarded a verdict of $1.44 million to the customer for the violations of the standard of care required by HIPAA compliance.

Payment Card Industry Data Security Standard

The *Payment Card Industry Data Security Standard (PCI DSS)* is a set of regulations from credit card vendors that apply to businesses using their services. This is an industry standard, not a law. A council was founded in 2006 by American Express, Discover, JCB International, MasterCard, and Visa. The PCI council developed 12 different requirements that businesses who process credit card payments must follow to protect credit card and user information. The 12 standards are based on the six goals shown in **Figure 2-22.**

Credit card data has long been sought by criminals. There have been many examples of stolen credit card data. Companies such as J.C. Penney, Home Depot, Target, Dairy Queen, and Jimmy Johns have seen breaches, and the list goes on. In 2016, Business Insider revealed that more money is stolen through credit card fraud in the United States than in the rest of the world. Most stolen credit card numbers are sold on the dark web to other criminals. These criminals then create phony cards from the numbers and sell them. It is a lucrative market. Any organization that processes credit cards must do its part in protecting the data. The PCI DSS provides the tools to understand what must be done. It provides the framework to implement data protection.

The key aspect of the PCI DSS is that it applies to *any* organization, regardless of the size or number of transactions. If it accepts, transmits, or stores any cardholder data, PCI DSS applies. For example, suppose you sell crafts and use a tool such as Square on your iPhone or Android device to process the credit card transaction, as shown in **Figure 2-23.** You must comply with the mandates in the PCI DSS.

The PCI DSS has four levels of compliance based on a merchant level. The merchant level is determined by the number of transactions per year. Your small business selling crafts would likely be level 4. However, a company that processes

FYI

When you go to a doctor or hospital, you or your parents may be asked to sign a form that states you received a notice of the provider's privacy practices. This is related to the HIPAA Privacy Rule.

Goals	PCI DSS Standard
Build and Maintain a Secure Network	1. Install and maintain a firewall to protect cardholder data.
	2. Do not use vendor-supplied defaults for system passwords and other security parameters.
Protect Cardholder Data	3. Protect stored cardholder data.
	4. Encrypt transmission of cardholder data across open, public networks.
Maintain a Vulnerability Management Program	5. Use and regularly update antivirus software or programs.
	6. Develop and maintain secure systems and applications.
Implement Strong Access Control Measures	7. Restrict access to cardholder data by business need-to-know.
	8. Assign a unique ID to each person with computer access.
	9. Restrict physical access to cardholder data.
Regularly Monitor and Test Networks	10. Track and monitor all access to network resources and cardholder data.
	11. Regularly test security systems and processes.
Maintain an Information Security Policy	12. Maintain a policy that addresses information security for employees and contractors.

Goodheart-Willcox Publisher

Figure 2-22. The PCI DSS contains 12 standards based on six goals.

Square, Inc.

Figure 2-23. A device such as this one from Square can be used with a smartphone to accept and process credit card payments as well as payments from smartphone apps.

over six million transactions per year would be at level 1. Some of the requirements differ depending on the level assignment.

There are potential penalties for noncompliance. Fines could run as high as $5,000 to $100,000 per month on the acquiring bank. The credit card bank may choose to pass the cost to the merchant or terminate the payment relationship with the merchant. This would be in addition to any possible civil litigation from cardholders.

Quick Look 2.3.1

State Security Laws

You must be familiar with the laws of any state in which your company does business. This includes any interstate commerce the company may engage in. As a cybersecurity professional, it is your responsibility to ensure compliance.

1. Launch a web browser, and navigate to the National Conference of State Legislatures website (www.ncsl.org). This site provides information related to state legislatures, including cybersecurity laws for each state.
2. Use the site's search function, and search for **security breach notification laws**. In the results, click the link for the article of the same name.
3. Find your state on the list. Does your state have more than one law?
4. Click the link to the laws in your state. Read the text or description of the laws.
5. Open the laws for another state. How do they compare to the laws in your state?
6. Discuss with your classmates some of the laws and penalties you see on these pages.

SECTION REVIEW 2.3

Check Your Understanding

1. What is meant by compliance?
2. Which law covers unauthorized access to computers?
3. What is the basic purpose of the Gramm-Leach-Bliley Act (GLBA)?
4. What governmental agency monitors issues related to the SOX rules?
5. What is the minimum number of credit card transactions for the PCI DSS regulations to apply?

Build Your Key Terms Vocabulary

As you progress through this course, develop a personal cybersecurity glossary. This will help you build your vocabulary and prepare you for a career. Write a definition for each of the following terms, and add it to your cybersecurity glossary.

compliance

Computer Fraud and Abuse Act (CFAA)

Electronic Communication Privacy Act (ECPA)

electronic health record (EHR)

Gramm-Leach-Bliley Act (GLBA)

Health Insurance Portability and Accounting Act (HIPAA)

Payment Card Industry Data Security Standard (PCI DSS)

protected health information (PHI)

Sarbanes-Oxley Act (SOX)

Review and Assessment

Chapter Summary

Section 2.1 Security Principles

- The CIA triad describes the three underlying principles of data protection. These principles are confidentiality, integrity, and availability.
- The areas of a business can be broken down into six security domains to help manage the process of protecting data and assets: users, workstation, LAN, WAN, remote access, and system. Users represent the weakest link in the security chain.

Section 2.2 Vulnerabilities and Threats

- Malware is computer code intentionally written to cause some form of harm. The action it performs is called its payload.
- Software and firmware may include vulnerabilities when it is released. Patches are issued to fix these issues when they are discovered.
- Security threats beyond malware include keyloggers, adware, cookies, and social engineering. Even innocent information posted on public websites or social media can provide a means for a hacker to find a way into an account or business website.

Section 2.3 Legal Requirements

- Security professionals are responsible for ensuring compliance with the terms of laws and regulations that have been enacted to protect data. There are many federal and state laws that apply to cybersecurity as well as industry standards.
- Some of the laws that apply to cybersecurity measures include the Computer Fraud and Abuse Act (CFAA), Electronic Communication Privacy Act (ECPA), Gramm-Leach-Bliley Act (GLBA), Sarbanes-Oxley Act (SOX), and Health Insurance Portability and Accountability Act (HIPAA). The Payment Card Industry Data Security Standard (PCI DSS) is a set of regulations that also applies.

Check Your Cybersecurity IQ 📲

Now that you have completed this chapter, see what you have learned about cybersecurity by visiting the student companion website (www.g-wlearning.com) and taking the chapter posttest.

Review Questions 📲

For each question, select the answer that is the best response.

1. A guessed password affects which basic principle of a company's security?
   A. Confidentiality
   B. Safety
   C. Availability
   D. Integrity

2. A Windows 7 machine used by the receptionist did not get the latest security patches, and a known vulnerability was exploited. Which business security domain should have addressed this issue?
   A. Workstation
   B. LAN
   C. Server
   D. WAN

3. Which of the following presents a threat to the network?
   A. An unpatched computer.
   B. A computer infected with a root kit.
   C. The sales manager's use of a weak password.
   D. Files are not protected with a password.

4. The data on a server is encrypted from a _____ threat. This affects the _____ principle.
   A. ransomware; confidentiality
   B. worm; availability
   C. ransomware; availability
   D. root kit; integrity

5. This type of malware spreads through an open network port.
   A. Trojan horse
   B. Worm
   C. Root kit
   D. Polymorphic

6. Which situation leaves you *most* vulnerable to malware infections?
   A. Installing purchased software from a DVD.
   B. Surfing the Internet on mobile devices.
   C. Exchanging messages through a social media app.
   D. Using a flash drive on multiple machines.

7. Bug-bounty programs are especially useful against which of the following?
   A. Ransomware attacks
   B. Zero-day vulnerabilities
   C. Keyloggers
   D. Malicious cookies

8. Which of the following is true of adware?
   A. It is always considered malware.
   B. It spreads from computer to computer through network ports.
   C. It can cause problems with multiple browser pop-up windows.
   D. It will encrypt the data on your hard drive.

9. This type of cookie is only used when a website is displayed in the browser. It is removed when the browser is closed.
   A. Session cookie
   B. Persistent cookie
   C. Term cookie
   D. Third-party cookie

10. Companies that handle money, such as a credit union, are subject to which law?
    A. SOX
    B. PCI DSS
    C. HIPAA
    D. GLBA

Application and Extension of Knowledge

1. Research how IoT is expected to present challenges for cybersecurity. Spotlight some nontraditional devices that have already caused some incidents. Be prepared to present your findings in a class discussion.

2. Interview a small business owner in your community. Discuss his or her understanding of security concerns related to customer credit card data. Is he or she aware of the policies required by the PCI DSS? Summarize your interview in a one-page written report. Format the report according to your school's guidelines.

3. Locate the HIPAA privacy practices for your doctor's office, a local hospital, or a medical center. Develop a brief presentation to summarize the type of information they can share and which information you have some say in its disclosure. Identify some situations where they can disclose and share your PHI.

4. Research the scandal and fraud committed by the companies Enron and Arthur Andersen. Write a one- to two-page summary on some of the fraudulent practices that they used. Describe how these cases factored into the development of the Sarbanes-Oxley Act.

5. Investigate the digital footprint for a parent, grandparent, or guardian using advanced Internet searches and tools you found online. Present your findings to the person you investigated. Write a one- to two-page summary of how he or she reacted to the data you found. Include an explanation of whether or not you feel the data could present any security threats to the person.

Research Project Asset-Tracking Software

The Center for Internet Security website (www.cisecurity.org) provides controls, and one of the top responsibilities is tracking authorized and unauthorized assets on a computer. To assist with this responsibility, there are software programs that can scan networks and report on devices found and software installed on the machines. Research available products. Consider which products are best suited for a company that has around 100 desktop computers, five servers, and four networked printers.

Deliverables. Write a memo to your chief information officer (CIO) that recommends a software product to scan the network for devices and software. Include in the memo your analysis on the features offered by the software and why you think it is the best option for the company. Be sure to discuss the cost, including any annual renewal fees.

Online Activities

Complete the following activities, which will help you learn, practice, and expand your knowledge and skills.

Vocabulary. Practice vocabulary for this chapter using the e-flash cards, matching activity, and vocabulary game until you are able to recognize their meanings.

Communication Skills

College and Career Readiness

Reading. Skimming means quickly glancing through an entire document. This reading technique will give you a preview of the material to help your comprehension when you read a chapter. You should notice headings, key words and phrases, and visual elements. The goal is to get the main idea of the content. Skim this chapter. Identify the main ideas of the content. Provide an overview of what you read.

Writing. It is important to use critical-thinking skills to make sense of challenges you will face as a cybersecurity professional. Make a list of data breaches about which you have heard or read. Describe options presented for dealing with each incident and the pros and cons of the options.

Speaking. Developing effective communication skills requires individuals to be able to participate in and contribute to discussions. As your instructor lectures on this chapter, contribute thoughtful, relevant comments when participation is invited. Ask questions when necessary to help determine or clarify the meanings of the topics discussed during the lesson.

Listening. Active listening is fully participating as you process what a person says. Active listeners know when to comment and when to remain silent. Use active-listening skills while your instructor presents this chapter. Participate in the discussion by making relevant comments when appropriate, and build on the instructor's ideas by asking related questions. Respond appropriately to the presentation.

Portfolio Development

College and Career Readiness

Objective. Before you begin collecting information for your portfolio, write an objective for the finished product. An *objective* is a complete sentence or two that states what you want to accomplish. The language in your objective should be clear and specific. Include enough details so you can easily judge when it is accomplished. Consider this objective: I will try to get into college. Such an objective is too general. A better, more detailed objective might read: I will be accepted into the cybersecurity program at one of my top three college choices. Creating a clear objective is a good starting point for beginning to work on your portfolio.

1. Decide the purpose of the portfolio you are creating, such as short-term employment, career, community service, or college application.
2. Set a timeline to finish the final product.
3. Write an objective for your portfolio.

CTSO Event Prep

Performance. Some competitive events for career and technical student organizations (CTSOs) have a performance component. The activity could potentially be a decision-making scenario for which your team will provide a solution and present it to the judges. To prepare for the performance component of a presentation, complete the following activities.

1. On your CTSO's website, locate a rubric or scoring sheet for the event.
2. Confirm whether visual aids may be used in the presentation and the amount of setup time permitted.
3. Review the rules to confirm whether questions will be asked or if the team will need to defend a case or situation.
4. Make notes on index cards about important points to remember. Use these notes to study. You may also be able to use these notes during the event.
5. Practice the performance. You should introduce yourself, review the topic that is being presented, defend the topic being presented, and conclude with a summary.
6. After the performance is complete, ask for feedback from your instructor. You may also consider having a student audience listen and give feedback.

Chapter 3

Managing User Security

It is often said that the user is the weakest link in the security chain. When an individual signs in to a network, he or she has essentially been given the key to access various elements of the network. This includes hardware, software, and, of course, the data. If a user makes a poor decision, such as having a weak password, or leaves the workstation unattended, it could have a serious effect on network security. Since humans cannot be automated, security administrators must put in place policies and configurations to reduce the risks associated with users.

In this chapter, you will explore technologies and procedures that can be implemented to assist in protecting networks from threats associated with users. One of the important areas that must be protected is the login process. Authentication, or verifying user identity, is one of the most important tasks in a security plan. Weak policies or poor decisions often lead to vulnerability in system security. Once a user is authenticated, controlling where he or she can go, what files can be read or changed, and what tasks can be performed is another critical management aspect of a security plan.

Chapter Preview

While studying, look for the activity icon for:
- Pretests and posttests
- Vocabulary terms with e-flash cards and matching activities
- Self-assessment

G-WLEARNING.com

Reading Prep

Before reading this chapter, review the table of contents for this text. Create a graphic organizer tracing the content from simple to complex ideas.

College and Career Readiness

Check Your Cybersecurity IQ ↗

Before you begin this chapter, see what you already know about cybersecurity by visiting the student companion website (www.g-wlearning.com) and taking the chapter pretest.

Certification Objectives

CompTIA Security+

Microsoft MTA Security Fundamentals

Authentication and Control

Essential **Q**uestion

Why are users the weakest link in a security chain?

Access to operating systems and related applications is often granted through a login account secured with a password. Typically, the user can choose the password. Most users choose a password and security-reset question based on some sort of personal information. That can lead to unauthorized access. This type of vulnerability was exploited by Chris Chaney, the so-called Hollywood Hacker. He guessed the Gmail account names of celebrities, and using those along with personal information he retrieved from IMDB.com, he gained access to their accounts. He then revealed private and sensitive information about the celebrities. While creating strong authentication policies is important, it is equally important to control access to data and system functionality once a user is granted access to the system.

Key Terms 📤

Active Directory
attack surface
authentication
behavioral biometrics
biometrics
crossover error rate (CER)
Discretionary Access Control (DAC)
dongle
false acceptance rate (FAR)
false rejection rate (FRR)
federated identity management (FID)

hardening
job rotation
Kerberos
Key Distribution Center (KDC)
LDAPS
Lightweight Directory Access Protocol (LDAP)
Mandatory Access Control (MAC)
mandatory vacations
multifactor authentication
one-time password (OTP)
permission
policy

right
Role-Based Access Control (RBAC)
rule-based access control
secondary logon
Security Accounts Manager (SAM)
Security Assertion Markup Language (SAML)
Shibboleth
single sign-on (SSO)
transitive trust
user account control (UAC)

Learning Goals

- Explain the process of authentication.
- Discuss the use of access levels.
- Describe nontechnical approaches to user security.
- Compare authentication on a local computer to authentication on a network computer.

User Authentication

User security starts with validating users. *Authentication* is the process of validating a user. This helps ensure that only authorized users are accessing the network and its resources.

MTA Security Fundamentals
2.1

Passwords

The most common type of authentication is a password. Before the user is granted access, he or she must enter the correct password for the user account. This is also one of the least-secure methods of authentication. Some of the problems associated with password authentication include:

CompTIA Security+
1.2

- weak passwords;
- reuse of passwords on multiple sites;
- poor password policies; and
- password-cracking tools.

Weak passwords are those that can be guessed or easily seen by someone shoulder surfing, as shown in **Figure 3-1.** *Shoulder surfing* is watching someone as he or she is entering a password.

Many people will use the same password for many sites. For example, a user may have the same password for his or her network access, bank account, and social media. If this user's password is stolen or cracked, the hacker has access to all of these other sites. Always use a different password for each system where you must log in.

If not forced to change their passwords, many users will continue to use the same password indefinitely. It is a poor password policy that allows this to happen. A technical setting can be made to force users to change passwords at an interval, such as once a month or once a year.

There are many password-cracking tools. These can often be found on the Internet for free. Hackers can use these tools to breach the password level of defense.

Goodheart-Willcox Publisher

Figure 3-1. A good or strong password is key to how effective password protection is. Here, the password 123ABC is identified as a very poor password.

Quick Look 3.1.1

Passwords

Password protection is not a very reliable method of securing a system. Despite this, it is still important for users to have good passwords. Do you have a good password?

1. Launch a web browser, and navigate to this website: www.howsecureismypassword.net.
2. Enter your password. How secure is your password? Compare your results with others in your class.
3. Add a number and a symbol, such as the percent sign (%), to the end of your password. What impact did this have on the strength of your password?

CompTIA Security+
4.1, 4.3

Multifactor Authentication

Passwords alone are not a solid defense for systems. There are other methods that can be used as well. Each method is called a factor, and factors can be combined to make the authentication process more secure. When different forms of authentication are combined, it is called *multifactor authentication.* There are several factors that can be used with authentication, including:

- what you know;
- what you have;
- what you are; and
- what you do.

What You Know

A password is an example of "what you know." Some programs and websites might ask you to provide the answer to an additional security answer. This is *not* an example of multifactor authentication. It is one-factor or single-factor authentication. The only factor here is your knowledge of an answer. Asking a security question provides a stronger authentication than a password alone, but it does not provide a second factor.

What You Have

In the "what you have" factor, the user must possess a device that contains security information. The most common types of devices are common access cards (CACs) and tokens. These devices are not used to replace the password. Rather, the user must insert the card into a reader or hold the token near the receiver and then enter his or her username and password. This is an example of using two factors for authentication: 1) password, and 2) CAC or token.

CACs are common in military facilities, as shown in **Figure 3-2.** A CAC contains security information for the user stored on a microchip. This is similar to the new microchipped credit cards. In fact, CACs are generally the size of most credit cards. A CAC reader is a device that senses the microchip in the CAC and determines if it contains the correct information to allow access. These readers can be installed on computers or computerized devices, embedded into keyboards, or attached to a computer as a USB device.

A token may be a small device that can be attached to a key chain. More commonly, though, it is an app running on a smartphone. Smartphones are being used more frequently now than actual physical tokens. The user has an app on his or her phone that represents the token. This app is used to obtain the password.

Regardless if the token is a device or phone app, it has numbers that change, and it is considered a one-time password (OTP). A *one-time password (OTP)* is

Goodheart-Willcox Publisher

Figure 3-2. The US military uses common access cards as its standard identification for service personnel.

valid for only one login or transaction, and it is often valid for only a short period. The token service produces a series of numbers and characters that are automatically generated and sent to the token. In most cases, the user must enter the characters. However, some systems require a physical connection by inserting the token into the computer's USB port. This type of token is usually called a *dongle.*

Tokens offer a great deal of security. If a token is lost or stolen, it cannot be used for authentication. The user's name and password are needed as well as the token.

What You Are

The third factor is "what you are." This refers to a biological feature of the user. The measurement and analysis of a biological feature is called *biometrics.* In this method, along with the user's name and password, the user must provide some physical characteristic, as shown in **Figure 3-3.** Some of the most common methods of biometric authentication include fingerprints and retina or iris scans. In recent years, biometric authentication methods have expanded to include palm prints, facial recognition, and voice analysis.

What You Do

Keystroke biometrics is a new category. This category is referred to as *behavioral biometrics.* Instead of "what you are," this factor is better described as "what you do." This authentication method refers to identifying measurable patterns in human activities. Keystroke dynamics is an example of this factor. *Keystroke dynamics* measures the patterns of rhythm and

CompTIA Security+
3.9

Pixza Studio/Shutterstock.com

Figure 3-3. A fingerprint scanner provides a level of security to this server room that is not offered by a password or CAC.

Ethical Issue

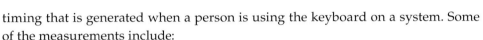

Biometric-Authentication Technology

Nymi is a Canadian technology company that has developed wearable authentication products based on the user's electrocardiogram (ECG). Mofiria Bank in Japan has introduced a biometric device that combines fingerprint and finger vein technologies to conduct authentication. Biometric technologies continue to advance to new levels. What are some of the ethical and privacy concerns related to these types of devices? Do these concerns outweigh the security benefits these devices provide? What are your own feelings toward the use of biometric technology? Is there a specific biometric technology that makes you more or less comfortable? Do you feel a person can be required to use biometric technology, such as a condition for employment or to make a purchase with a bank account?

FYI

Keystroke dynamics goes back to the first uses of the telegraph machine. Many telegraph operators could recognize the sending operator by the uniqueness of the keying rhythm. This was known as "Fist of the Sender." During World War II, Fist of the Sender was used to help tell if the communication was from friend or foe.

- - - - - - - - - - - - - - -

CompTIA Security+
4.3

timing that is generated when a person is using the keyboard on a system. Some of the measurements include:

- speed of keystrokes;
- variations as the user moves between different keys;
- common errors (typos); and
- how long a key is pressed.

Your physical location can also be considered something you do. Wi-Fi triangulation and GPS can be used to determine where you are located. This can be cross-referenced to a list of accepted locations. Authentication is granted if the locations match. Similarly, IP address resolution can be used for authentication.

Security Error Rates Concerning Biometric Authentication

Biometric authentication offers a great deal of personal security methods. However, there are some potential risks. *False acceptance rate (FAR)* occurs when the biometric credentials are authorized on invalid characteristics. The FAR is determined by the ratio of the number of false *acceptances* divided by the number of identification attempts. The risk is the possibility of a user with invalid credentials (an intruder) is authenticated to a system.

False rejection rate (FRR) is the opposite action, denying an authorized biometric credential. In this case, an authorized user is denied entry into a system. The FRR is determined by the number of false *rejections* divided by the number of identification attempts. When a system is calibrated to reduce the FAR, the resulting changes often increase the FRR.

To best determine the accuracy of a biometric system, another measurement is considered. The *crossover error rate (CER)* is the point where the false acceptance rates and false rejection rates are equal. This is illustrated in **Figure 3-4.** Settings are often made so the CER is achieved. It is a balance between providing security and easy user access.

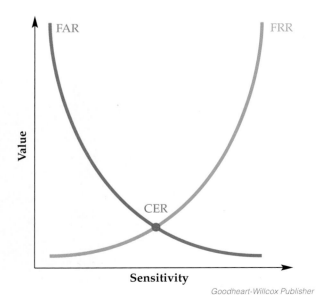

Goodheart-Willcox Publisher

Figure 3-4. The crossover error rate (CER) is the point where the FAR and FRR are equal.

Quick Look 3.1.2

Emerging Authentication Methods

The one-time password is a quickly emerging technology with many potential practical applications. Consider what is happening in Iowa. It is testing and developing a replacement to hardcopy driver's licenses using smartphones.

1. Launch a web browser, and navigate to the ABC News website (www.abcnews.com). Using the site's search function, enter the search phrase "digital drivers licenses Iowa tests high tech" (including the quotation marks).
2. Select the article titled The Problem with Digital Drivers Licenses: Iowa Tests High Tech IDs. Watch the video, and read the article. There is no sound in this video.
3. What do you think of this method of providing licenses?
4. Discuss with your class the pros and cons of using this method.
5. Research further some new uses and applications of OTP technology. Can you think of situations where OTP would be beneficial? Discuss your findings with your class.

Access Levels

Another security decision deals with how to give users access to resources and data on a network. Imagine a company with several hundred employees. What if you had to give each user access rights individually! This would be a tedious process, but, more important, the probability for error is high. It would also be difficult to determine instantly a user's access. To make this process easier and potentially more secure, access-control methods can be used.

The first access control used most often with the military or supporting organizations is MAC. *Mandatory Access Control (MAC)* is a security strategy that sets a strict level of access to resources based on criteria set by the network administrator. In a military setting, this is commonly implemented with classifications such as confidential, secret, and top secret. These levels form a hierarchy of access, as shown in **Figure 3-5.** When data or resources are identified and configured with a category, then only users with the matching credential can have access. Because it is mandatory, exceptions are not allowed. Administrators are not allowed to make changes, such as allowing someone with a credential for secret to read data categorized as top secret.

The next access control is known as DAC. With *Discretionary Access Control (DAC)*, a user can be granted additional rights to data beyond what is allowed by his or her assigned access level. The user who owns the data can grant permissions to another user. For example, suppose a teacher wants to share a folder with some of her students. If she owns the data (folder), she can decide who else has rights to access the folder.

A very common access control is RBAC. With *Role-Based Access Control (RBAC)*, rights are assigned to a role instead of manually to each individual user. Users are associated as a member of a role or group, as shown in **Figure 3-6.** When permissions are set or changed, this is done to the role. Then, each member of the role is automatically assigned the new or updated permissions. If a user is removed

Goodheart-Willcox Publisher

Figure 3-5. The US government uses three levels of access. A user with confidential-level access can only use data at that level. A user with top-secret-level access can use data at any level.

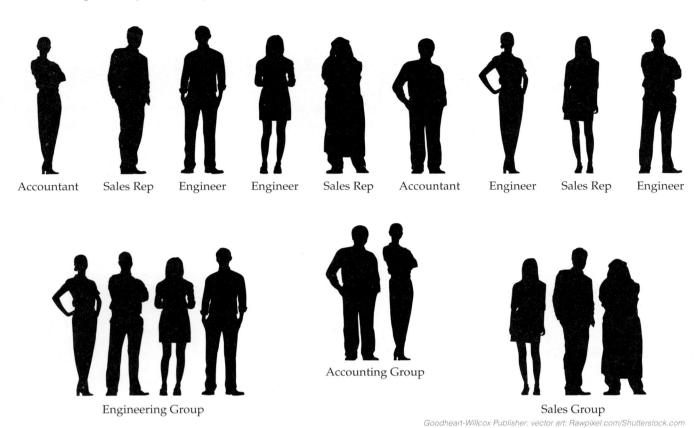

Accountant   Sales Rep   Engineer   Engineer   Sales Rep   Accountant   Engineer   Sales Rep   Engineer

Engineering Group

Accounting Group

Sales Group

Figure 3-6. By using roles, or groups, permissions can be assigned to many users in a single step.

from the role, his or her access to the role's resources are instantly revoked. This helps eliminate mistakes and provides a higher level of security.

If a role is not used in the example shown in **Figure 3-6,** permissions would need to be assigned to each engineer one at a time. However, by creating a role, or group, the engineers can be assigned to the group. If a new engineer is hired, assigning the correct permissions is as simple as adding him or her to the group.

Rule-based access control is similar to the other controls except rules are established for various situations. A common example of a rule-based control is that users may only be permitted to log in to the network during specific hours.

Access-control methods assist in helping businesses with another security measure called *separation of duties,* which refers to splitting up duties of one job so multiple people are required to complete it. This keeps any one person from compromising the job. By using one of the above methods, you can clearly define what a user can and cannot have access to use or view. Limiting the scope of what a user can perform allows for stronger security. A user cannot access or use what he or she cannot see.

Figure 3-7 shows the default user groups on a Windows 10 computer. These groups allow an administrator to set up privileges for users and limit the scope of what they can do. For example, to prevent a user from using the Remote Desktop program to access another computer on the network, simply do not add the user's account to that group.

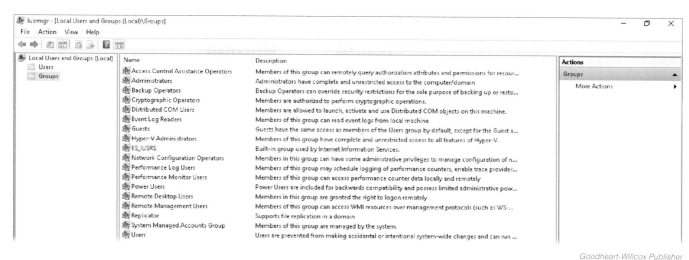

Figure 3-7. These are the default user groups in Windows 10.

Security Options Related to Existing Employees

Often, businesses will underestimate the threats that existing employees can pose to data and systems. These threats may be either from malicious or inadvertent actions. In a 2017 Insider Threat Report, 74 percent of the respondents felt they were vulnerable to insider threats. Some of the reasons include:

- insider threats can go on for years without detection;
- it is not easy to determine if an employee is doing regular work from harmful actions;
- employees find it easy to cover their actions; and
- it is hard to prove guilt or malicious intent.

In Chapter 1, you discovered that the City of San Francisco had been locked out of access to its infrastructure by an insider. Edward Snowden is also a clear example of insider theft of data. Implementing some administrative controls might have assisted in these issues.

A nontechnical control that can be implemented is mandatory vacations. With *mandatory vacations,* users are forced to take vacations where they are not on the premises or using the systems. By enforcing this control, their access to the network and its resources is removed. A user who is not following security policies or committing data theft would be reluctant to leave for vacation in the fear his or her actions would be discovered in the absence. During the user's vacation, it is much easier to audit what a user has been working on, test passwords and other access levels, and compare network traffic levels to those when the user was present. For example, if traffic loads drop, this may indicate the user has been uploading or downloading a great deal of data. This may, in turn, indicate a theft of data or data vandalism.

The second nontechnical control is job rotation. With *job rotation,* users cycle through different roles. If mandatory vacations are implemented, other users must step in to complete the role during the vacation. There are some clear benefits to rotating users. Multiple individuals are capable of performing job duties. When a user rotates into a position, he or she can check and verify settings, data, and other aspects of the position.

Quick Look 3.1.3

Mandatory Vacations

Some security techniques are not technical in nature. One nontechnical approach is the mandatory vacation. It may not be appropriate to apply this technique to all positions.

1. Look at the following job positions. Research them, if needed, to find out what each position typically does. Which positions do you think should be a candidate for mandatory vacations? Discuss with your classmates.
   - Accounting Manager
   - Receptionist
   - Salesperson
   - Network Administrator
   - Chief Information Security Officer (CISO)
2. For the positions you identified, for how many *consecutive* days should the employee remain out of the office?
3. How should the employee's remote access to the network be handled?

User Access to Resources

It is critical that employees have only the privileges needed to perform their job responsibilities. This concept is known as *least privilege.* It is always easier to grant additional privileges than it is to take them away. Removing privileges may cause resentment when an employee finds he or she cannot do something previously possible. There are several important areas to consider when it comes to user access, including:
- local computer access (including software, operating system features, and so on);
- access to files and folders; and
- physical access to areas in your building.

Local computer access is discussed here. Access to files and folders is discussed in Section 3.2. Concerns related to physical access are discussed in Chapter 5.

Local Computer Access

An employee must have access to the resources needed to perform his or her job tasks. Access should be granted only to the software and folders needed. However, there are some other resources on the local computer the user should be allowed to access. This includes changing the personal-preferences configuration, such as changing the desktop background or the clock. Microsoft Windows breaks these privileges into two areas: rights and permissions.

A *right* is the ability to perform a type of action on the computer. This includes the right to log in or the right to install or remove software. A *permission* deals with the specific abilities within a right or with files and folders. Examples of permissions include the ability to delete or create a file and the ability to submit a job for printing.

When a user logs on a computer in a Windows environment, he or she is accessing the computer in one of two ways:
- The computer is a workstation on a network located in an organizational domain, which is the database that stores all the resources on the network.
- The computer is a standalone computer that operates independently from the rest of the computers on the network.

Workstation on a Network

Figure 3-8 shows an example of a security database (domain) on a network. In this model, the user provides his or her login name and password. If multifactor authentication is used, the other credentials must also be entered. This information is passed to the server's security database where it is compared with what has been set up for the user. If they match, the user is authenticated. If not, authentication fails, and the user is denied access.

CompTIA Security+
4.2

Microsoft creates security domains by using the Active Directory. The *Active Directory* is essentially a database of the network resources and includes objects such as user and group accounts, computers, servers, and printers. Businesses assign names to their directories and often refer to this as the domain. Directories are based on the LDAP standard. The *Lightweight Directory Access Protocol (LDAP)* provides standards and ensures that directories or directory services are constructed and used in the same manner. This allows a user on a Microsoft directory to access resources on a directory on another platform, such as Apple's directory.

LDAPS is the secure form of LDAP, where LDAP is used with SSL to send directory communications encrypted. The default port for LDAPS is 636.

CompTIA Security+
2.6

Directories are needed to help us locate objects in the database. For example, when you print to a network printer, you do not have to identify its location in the directory. The LDAP will perform that function.

All directories are constructed in a hierarchical manner. This is commonly referred to as the *tree approach*. Network administrators define the objects in the structure, but they follow the same format. The database can be further organized using objects called *organizational units*. These can be customized to the company's needs. Geographic locations are another way in which organizational units may be created. Multiple levels of organizational units can be created if needed. Objects that represent resources, such as users or printers, are called *leaf objects*.

Consider the example shown in **Figure 3-9.** The network administrator has named the domain Wagner Accounting. In this example, Wagner Accounting chose to organize resources by department. There is an organizational unit for IT, accounting, and support staff. Within each of these organizational units are the leaf objects.

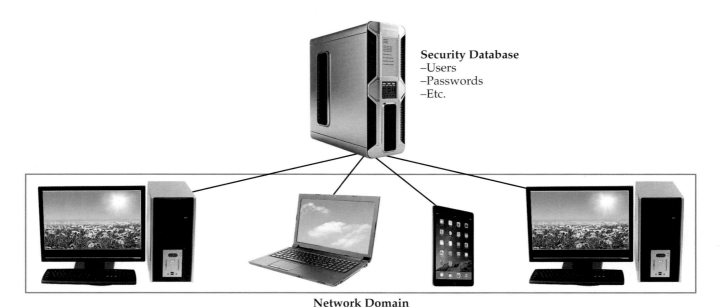

Security Database
–Users
–Passwords
–Etc.

Network Domain

Figure 3-8. When logging into a network security domain, the user's credentials are checked against the security database.

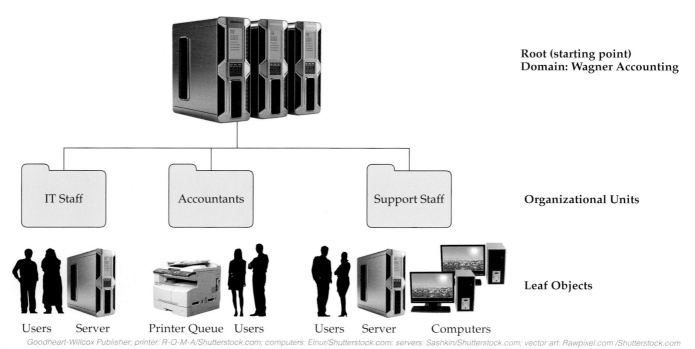

Root (starting point)
Domain: Wagner Accounting

Organizational Units

Leaf Objects

Users   Server   Printer Queue   Users   Users   Server   Computers

Figure 3-9. The directory structure can be created as a hierarchy.

LDAP compliance ensures that all objects follow specific rules. For example, suppose that Kari Johnson is a customer service representative for Wagner Accounting. Her user object's complete name includes all levels of the tree. This name is called the *distinguished name.* Each level has a prefix that identifies the level. So Kari's distinguished name is:

cn=kJohnson.ou=supportstaff.dc=WagnerAccounting.dc=com

Notice the prefixes. They identify the levels:

cn = common name
ou = organizational unit
dc = domain controller (domain components)

In Microsoft server operating systems, the authentication model used is called Kerberos (pronounced *ker-bear-us). Kerberos* is the standard authentication protocol on all versions of Microsoft Server when using the Active Directory. This is an advanced protocol and offers several key characteristics to provide security. In it, two key main functions comprise the role of the *Key Distribution Center (KDC):*

* Authentication Service (AS) exchange
* Ticket Granting Service (TGS) exchange

The KDC is a service running on a server that has a copy of the Active Directory. Its job is to manage the main functions listed above. **Figure 3-10** illustrates the communication between the KDC and devices. This process occurs whenever a user requests *any* type of network resource. In this way, there are constant security checks during a user's session.

Additional Access Levels

Single sign-on (SSO) is an authentication service that allows a user to use one login and password combination to access a set of services. For example, after logging into a network, the user does not have to provide credentials to access his or her e-mail. In many Microsoft-enabled services, Kerberos is used to facilitate the SSO requests. SSO is not without risks, however. A hacker obtaining the SSO credentials can access all other services configured with that SSO authentication.

CompTIA Security+
4.2

Kerberos is named after the Greek character Cerberus, the three-headed dog that guards the gates of Hades!

CompTIA Security+
4.1

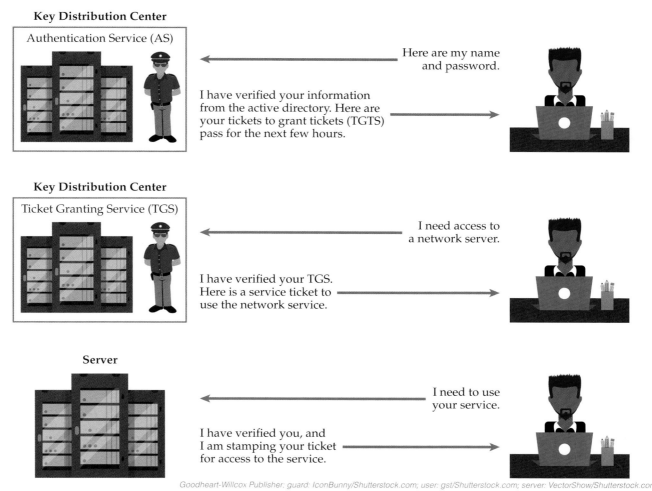

Figure 3-10. The KDC processes the exchange of ticket to provide authorization whenever the user requests any type of network resource.

Single sign-on is implemented with many products, including Shibboleth and SAML. *Shibboleth* is an open-source project. *Security Assertion Markup Language (SAML)* is an open standard used by parties, including Shibboleth and others, that allows the exchange of authentication and authorization information.

Another access level is called federated identity management. *Federated identity management (FID)* allows semi-independent systems to work together. The goal of a federated system is to allow users of one system to access resources from another system. Most social media and web users are familiar with options to "Log in with Facebook" or "Log in with Google." In these instances, the requesting app looks to Facebook or Google for user authentication. This eliminates the need to have its own way to create and manage user accounts. Using FID also provides a form of SSO.

The other access level that security managers need to be aware of is called a transitive trust. There are many ways a trust relationship can be configured between domains. *Transitive trust* occurs when the trust relationship is considered two-way. Once a user is authenticated in one security domain, he or she is authenticated into the other security domain. It is important to be aware of trust relationships and their potential impact on authentication of users throughout the organizations.

One example of the use of a transitive trust is Microsoft's Active Directory. Suppose you configure an Active Directory domain called ACME.com.

CompTIA Security+
4.2

Federated basically means a collection of smaller units or organizations.

ACME.com is considered the highest or parent domain. Another domain called NYC.Acme.com is created. NYC is a child domain located under the ACME.com domain. In this Microsoft relationship, child domains and their parent domains automatically establish transitive trust.

Standalone Computer

When a user is connected to a server running an Active Directory, the user logs into the network using his or her account located in the Active Directory. When a computer is not connected to a network, it is a standalone machine. The logon accounts must be stored on that machine. Every Microsoft Windows computer maintains a local database of user accounts. A local account can be used in the event the Active Directory database is not available. A local account can also be used to perform any diagnostics or troubleshooting on the local machine.

Microsoft calls the local database the *Security Account Manager (SAM)*. It is a nonhierarchical database. In addition to the local users, the passwords are stored in a hashed format, which makes it unreadable. A *hash* is a computed value that uniquely identifies data. The security database is stored in C:\%systemroot%\system32\config\SAM. It is important to be aware of the local accounts, especially those with administrative access. These accounts are prime targets for hackers.

FYI

The notation %systemroot% is a variable. Its value depends on where the Windows operating system is installed. The **set** command can be used at the command prompt to show the value of the %system% and other variables.

Quick Look 3.1.4

Local User Accounts

A computer that is not connected to a network does not have access to the network's Active Directory. However, it still has a local database of user accounts.

1. On a Windows computer, click **Start>All Apps>Windows System>Command Prompt** in Windows 10 (**Start>All programs>Accessories>Command Prompt** in Windows 7) or enter command prompt into the search bar to open the local command prompt window.

2. At the command prompt, enter net users. When the [Enter] key is pressed to execute the command, all local users in the SAM file are displayed, as shown.

3. Enter the **set** command. This shows the local variables. Look through all the variables stored on the machine. Which variable do you believe represents the logged-in user?

Quick Look 3.1.4 Continued

4. Enter the **net localgroup** command. The local security groups on the system are displayed, as shown.

```
Administrator: Command Prompt                                    —    □    ×

Microsoft Windows [Version 10.0.10586]
(c) 2016 Microsoft Corporation. All rights reserved.

C:\Windows\system32>net localgroup

Aliases for \\LAPTOPEA

-------------------------------------------------------------------
*Access Control Assistance Operators
*Administrators
*Backup Operators
*Cryptographic Operators
*Distributed COM Users
*Event Log Readers
*Guests
*Hyper-V Administrators
*IIS_IUSRS
*Network Configuration Operators
*Performance Log Users
*Performance Monitor Users
*Power Users
*Remote Desktop Users
*Remote Management Users
*Replicator
*System Managed Accounts Group
*Users
The command completed successfully.

C:\Windows\system32>_
```

Secondary Logon

Users with administrative rights can access and configure all aspects of a computer. Therefore, they need to be especially careful with their logon information. A hacker who gains access through an administrator account can make any changes the administrator can make. Security and network administrators should consider using a secondary logon. A *secondary logon* allows you to be logged in as a standard user, but run specific programs as an administrator. The secondary logon can be accessed two ways. It can be accessed from the graphical interface. It can also be accessed from the command line.

For routine work, the administrator logs on to the system without administrative rights. Many tasks can be completed without the need for administrative rights. Then, when higher-level tasks must be completed, the secondary logon that has administrative rights needed to perform those tasks. Limiting the initial login to a standard user reduces the potential exposure to hackers.

MTA Security Fundamentals
2.1

Quick Look 3.1.5

Secondary Logon

A secondary logon can help reduce the exposure of an administrative logon to hackers. The secondary logon can be accessed through the graphical interface or on the command line.

1. In Windows, click the **Start** button.

Quick Look 3.1.5 Continued

2. Find any program on the menu, and right-click on its icon to display the shortcut menu. Look for the menu item **Run as administrator**, as shown. If this menu item does not appear, choose a different program.

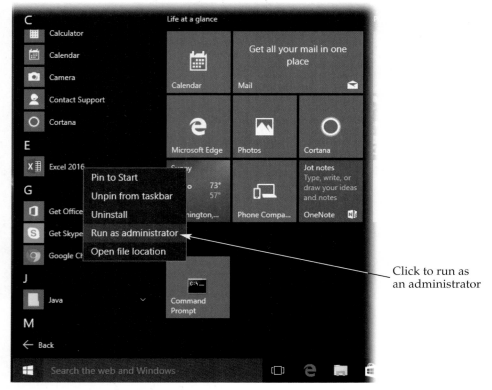

Click to run as an administrator

3. Click **Run as administrator** in the shortcut menu. If you do not have administrator rights, you will be prompted for credentials. You may also be asked if you wish to allow the program to make changes to the computer. Answer yes. The program will launch and be running under administrator rights.
4. Close the program you launched.
5. Click **Start>All Apps>Windows System>Command Prompt** in Windows 10 (**Start>All programs>Accessories>Command Prompt** in Windows 7) or enter command prompt into the search bar to open the local command prompt window.
6. At the command prompt, enter runas /user:*accountname* calc using a valid account name, as shown. You will be prompted to enter the password for the user account.

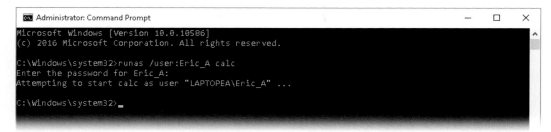

7. Enter the correct password. The calculator app is launched and running under administrator rights.
8. Close the calculator app and the command prompt window.

Password-Protected Screen Savers

A simple and effective way to limit access to a local computer is to set a password-protected screen saver. After a period of inactivity, the screen saver will turn on. To turn off the screen saver and gain access to the computer, a password must be entered. The option for requiring a password is part of the basic screen saver settings, as shown in **Figure 3-11.** Check the **On resume, display logon screen** check box. Also, enter the number of minutes of inactivity for the screen saver to turn on.

Similarly, a password can be required when the computer "sleeps." This is part of the power settings. To conserve electricity, the computer can be set to enter sleep mode after a period of inactivity. A password can be required to wake the computer from sleep mode. In the power options, choose **Require a password on wakeup**, and then click the **Require a password (recommended)** radio button.

User Rights

As you learned earlier, users are granted rights. This allows them to or prevents them from performing tasks. For example, a user may not be allowed to install software or change Windows settings. Most of these settings are configured in policies. In computers, a *policy* is a set of rules that can automatically control access to resources.

Policies are typically defined on local computers or in the Active Directory. Policy management on the local computer is called a *local policy.* Policies that are configured on the server are called *group policies.* There are more options available with group policies. This is because they apply to potentially a great deal of users and services. Policies at the local level, only apply to users who sign in on that machine.

As a security administrator, it is important to ensure that your systems are protected from unwanted access. This is commonly called *locked down* and is part of a process known as hardening the system. *Hardening* refers to the process of reducing or eliminating the vulnerabilities on a system. This, in turn, reduces the attack surface

FYI

On a Windows system, the computer can be manually locked by pressing the [Windows key][L] key combination.

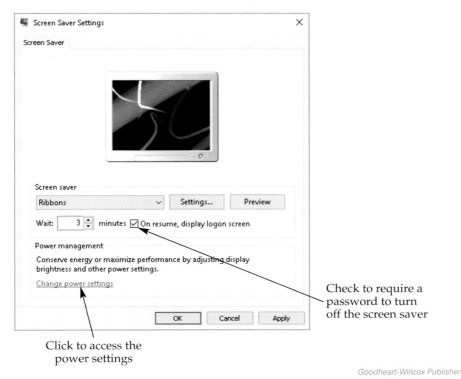

Goodheart-Willcox Publisher

Figure 3-11. Adding a password to the screen saver is an easy way to add simple protection to a computer system.

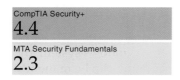

CompTIA Security+
4.4

MTA Security Fundamentals
2.3

of the system. The *attack surface* is the many areas that could give a hacker access to a system. The smaller the surface, the more protected the system is against intrusion.

There are many policies to choose from, especially at the network level. One of the most important policies that can be configured is the password policy. A preferred *password policy* provides rules that must be followed when a password is created or changed. It helps ensure that users are providing strong passwords. This can help prevent someone from trying to hack into a user's account by trying to guess the user's password. **Figure 3-12** shows the available options for a password policy.

Other password policies that should be set deal with logon attempts with incorrect passwords, as shown in **Figure 3-13.** When a hacker tries to guess a user's password, each incorrect guess is an invalid logon attempt. Invalid logon attempts need to be monitored and stopped to prevent a hacker from gaining access.

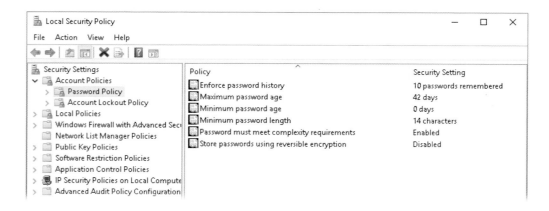

Policy	Description
Enforce password history	The user password cannot match a password used within this numerical range of previous passwords.
Maximum password age	Once a password has been used for the number of days set in this policy, the user will be forced to change the password.
Minimum password age	A password must be used for the number of days in this policy before it can be changed. This helps prevent the user from changing the password back to the previous one after being forced to change the password when it expires.
Minimum password length	The password must contain at least this number of characters. To help prevent password hacks, this number should be set no lower than eight.
Password must meet complexity requirements	Enabling this option forces the user to create a password at least six characters in length and containing at least three of these four criteria: • an uppercase letter • a lowercase letter • a number • a special character (such as #, %, @, etc.)
Store password using reversible encryption	Enabling this option stores passwords in plain text. Unless specifically needed by an authentication protocol, this setting should be disabled as enabling it makes the system much more vulnerable.

Figure 3-12. Password policies allow a system administrator to enforce rules for passwords.

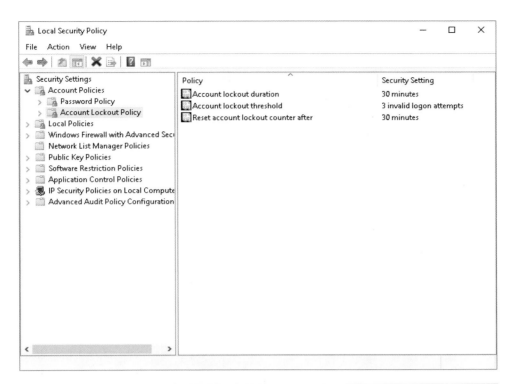

Policy	Description
Account lockout duration	This setting identifies how long an account will be disabled after the account lockout threshold is reached.
Account lockout threshold	This setting identifies the number of incorrect logon attempts before the account will be locked out.
Reset account lockout counter after	Incorrect logons will be only tracked for the time duration set here.

Goodheart-Willcox Publisher

Figure 3-13. Password policies should be set to handle invalid logon attempts.

Quick Look 3.1.6

Local Password Policies

Password policies are an important part of securing not only the local computer, but also the network. These policies can be viewed on the local machine.

1. Log in to Microsoft Windows as a local user with administrator rights.
2. Click the **Start** button, enter administrative tools in the search box, and click **Administrative Tools** in the list.
3. In the window that is displayed, double-click the **Local Security Policy** shortcut. The **Local Security Policy** window is displayed.
4. Click the arrow next to Account Policies to expand the tree, and then select the Password Policy branch.

Quick Look 3.1.6 Continued

5. Double-click the Enforce Password History setting to display details, as shown. Click the **Explain** tab in the dialog box to view information about the policy. What is the maximum number of new unique passwords that can be remembered?

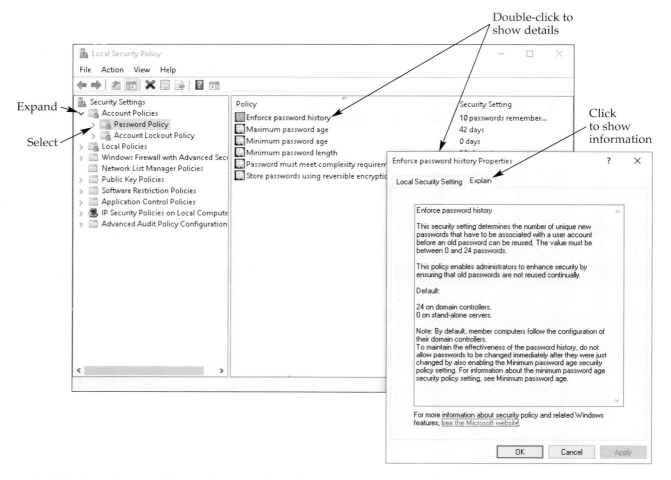

6. Which setting would you choose to have the maximum password option never expire?
7. Click the **Cancel** button to close the details window.
8. In the **Local Security Policy** window, expand the Local Policies branch, and select the User Rights Assignment branch.
9. By default, which accounts can change the system time?
10. Close the **Local Security Policy** window. Be sure you have not made changes to any of the local policies.

User Account Control (UAC)

MTA Security Fundamentals
4.1

Another way to limit a user's ability to make changes is with the user account control setting. The *user account control (UAC)* is a technology used to govern security by limiting what a standard user is able to do on a system. Additional privileges require a higher UAC setting or administrative rights. For example, a user with a low UAC setting would be prompted to provide credentials before changing settings or installing software. Setting an appropriate level of the UAC is important since changes to configurations can be made by software programs and scripts (small programs) without the user's knowledge or interaction. The setting in the UAC helps prevent unknown or potentially dangerous settings being made without knowledge of the user who is logged in.

Quick Look 3.1.7

User Account Control Settings

The UAC will display an alert whenever software or a script attempts to make changes to the computer. The user must allow the program to continue.

1. Log in to Microsoft Windows as a local user with administrator rights.
2. Click the **Start** button, enter user account control in the search box, and click **Change User Account Control settings** in the list. The **User Account Control Settings** dialog box is displayed, as shown.

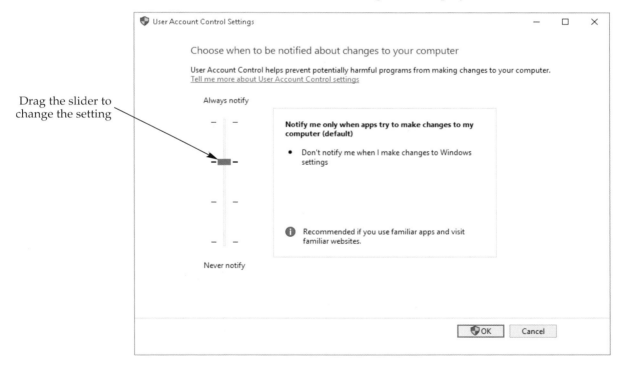

3. Click and drag the scroll bar to view a description of the four different settings. Always notify may be the most intrusive. It will always prompt for confirmation and, in some cases, a logon for a user with appropriate privileges. However, this is the most-secure setting possible.
4. Click the Cancel button to close the dialog box without changing the UAC setting.

SECTION REVIEW 3.1

Check Your Understanding

1. What is the vulnerability that allows a person to see what a user is entering, such as a password?

2. Directories should be based on which protocol to allow use with multiple systems?

3. A security technique that requires the user not to be using the computer system is known as what strategy?

4. What allows you to log in one time and access multiple services without having to reenter login credentials?

5. What system configuration should you set to require administrative credentials for installing software?

Build Your Key Terms Vocabulary

As you progress through this course, develop a personal cybersecurity glossary. This will help you build your vocabulary and prepare you for a career. Write a definition for each of the following terms, and add it to your cybersecurity glossary.

Active Directory

attack surface

authentication

behavioral biometrics

biometrics

crossover error rate (CER)

Discretionary Access Control (DAC)

dongle

false acceptance rate (FAR)

false rejection rate (FRR)

federated identity management (FID)

hardening

job rotation

Kerberos

Key Distribution Center (KDC)

LDAPS

Lightweight Directory Access Protocol (LDAP)

Mandatory Access Control (MAC)

mandatory vacations

multifactor authentication

one-time password (OTP)

permission

policy

right

Role-Based Access Control (RBAC)

rule-based access control

secondary logon

Security Accounts Manager (SAM)

Security Assertion Markup Language (SAML)

Shibboleth

single sign-on (SSO)

transitive trust

user account control (UAC)

Access to files and Folders

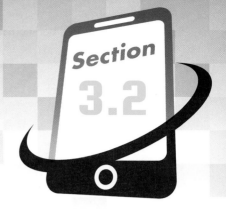

Data and information are some of the biggest assets of any company or organization. It is important to allow individuals to access the data they need. However, they should not have more privileges than necessary. In a Microsoft Windows environment, there are two types of access permissions that apply to the file system: share permissions and NFTS permissions. Protecting data access (confidentiality) and preventing unwanted changes (integrity) are high priorities for security administrators. It may be difficult to determine how a user obtained his or her abilities if poorly planned file-system structure and permission assignments are implemented.

Essential Question

Why should a user's local access to files and folders be limited?

Key Terms ☛

explicit permissions
implicit permissions
inherited permissions

New Technology File System (NTFS) permissions
share permissions

Learning Goals

- Explain how to set permissions on a shared folder.
- Differentiate between share and NTFS permissions.

Share Permissions

Sharing a file or folder is allowing another user access to it. *Share permissions* allow you to share folders. Anyone connecting to the folder from a remote connection can access to the files in a shared folder. Share permissions have no effect on user access when logging in directly at the machine. Following the concept of least privilege, only allow users to have the shares needed to perform their tasks.

Consider the example shown in **Figure 3-14.** Valeria needs to use the notes in the Marketing Campaign folder on Damien's computer. Since the folder and files are on Damien's computer, he has *discretionary access control*. This means he is the one

MTA Security Fundamentals
2.2

Goodheart-Willcox Publisher; vector art: Studio_G, Gst/Shutterstock.com

Figure 3-14. These users need to share files that are stored on one of their computers.

FYI

In a centralized networking environment, this is typically the responsibility of the network administrator to share folders located on servers.

who can choose to share the folder. He can give Valeria the permissions needed for her to access the folder and files from her computer.

Sharing a Folder in Windows

Before a folder can be shared in Windows, sharing must be enabled. This is configured in Control Panel under **Network and Internet>Network and Sharing Center**. Select **Change advanced sharing** settings, and then click the **Turn on file and printer sharing** radio button.

The user who owns the folder has full-control permissions. This user is able to share the folder to selected individuals. When a folder is shared, the owner selects the individuals who are being granted access. Then, the owner gives these users the appropriate permissions.

There are only three permissions available when sharing a folder: read, change, and full control. These are described in **Figure 3-15.** The setting for a permission is either allow or deny. Allow explicitly grants the user the permission. Deny explicitly excludes the user from the permission. This is an important distinction. A user can receive permissions from multiple sources, such as a group he or she is a member of or directly on the user's account. Unless a deny selection is present, the permissions *combine.*

Example 1

Rashad is given the read permission to the Sales folder (allow). He is in a group called SalesStaff. This group is given read and change permissions (allow) to the same folder. In this case, Rashad receives the combination of the allow permissions. The net result is Rashad's *effective* permission to Sales of read *and*

Share Permission	Description
Read	Allows a user to see the files and read their contents, but changes are not allowed.
Change	Allows a user to see and read files and to make changes to files as well as rename files, delete files, and create new files.
Full Control	Allows a user to see, read, and change files and give other users permissions.

Goodheart-Willcox Publisher

Figure 3-15. These are the permissions that can be assigned when sharing files and folders.

change. Rashad is able to create files, delete them, and make modifications along with reading and viewing the files.

Example 2

Rashad is given the read permission to the Sales folder (allow). The change permission to the sales folder is set to deny for him. Because the change permission includes the read permission, he is *also* denied read permission to the folder. However, he is in a group called SalesStaff. This group is given read and change permissions (allow) to the same folder. In this case, Rashad receives the combination of the allow permissions, but the deny permission is also considered. The net result is Rashad's *effective* permission to Sales will be deny for read and change. Whenever deny and allow conflict, deny *always* prevails.

Quick Look 3.2.1

Share Permissions

It is easy to share folders. When doing so, it is important to consider which permissions are allowed and which are denied.

1. Launch Windows File Explorer, and navigate to your Users folder. This is the folder under Users named with your login name.
2. Right-click on your folder, and click **New>Folder** in the shortcut menu. Name the new folder Classnotes.
3. Right-click on the Classnotes folder, and click **Properties** in the shortcut menu.
4. In the **Properties** dialog box, click the **Sharing** tab. There are two ways to share the folder, using the **Share...** button or the **Advanced Sharing...** button.
5. Click the **Share...** button. A new window is displayed in which users are selected, as shown.

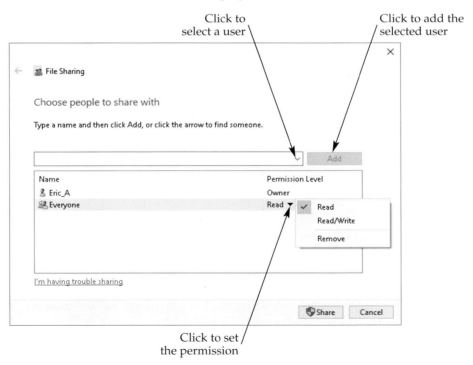

Click to select a user

Click to add the selected user

Click to set the permission

6. Click the drop-down list, and click **Everyone** in this list. Then, click the **Add** button. Note: this is for practice only; selecting **Everyone** allows *every* user on the network access to this folder!

Quick Look 3.2.1 Continued

7. Click the permission setting for the Everyone user, which is currently Read. Notice the three options available in the shortcut menu.

8. Leave the settings as the default Read. Then, click the **Share** button at the bottom of the window. When the system finishes sharing the folder, a link for user access is provided, as shown.

Link to shared folder

9. Click the **Done** button, and return to the **Properties** window.

10. Click the **Advanced Sharing...** button in the **Properties** window to display the **Advanced Sharing** dialog box, as shown. This option allows additional settings, such as changing the share name and assigning the full control permission.

Uncheck to stop sharing folder

Click to add a share name

Add a comment

Click to change sharing permissions

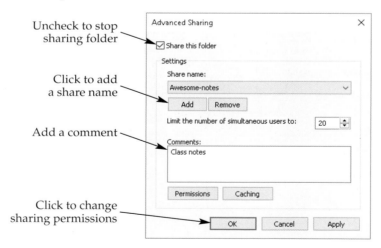

11. Click the **Add** button below the **Share name:** drop-down list, and enter the name Awesome-notes in the **New Share** dialog box that appears. Click the **OK** button to return to the **Advanced Sharing** dialog box.

12. Click in the **Comments:** text box, and enter Class notes.

Quick Look 3.2.1 Continued

13. Click the **Permissions** button. The **Permissions** dialog box is displayed, as shown. Notice how there are settings for each of the permissions.

14. Check the check box in the **Deny** column for the change permission. What happens to the read permission? Why did that happen?
15. Click the **Cancel** button so as not to change the permissions.
16. Click the **OK** button in the **Advanced Sharing** dialog box to save the new share.
17. Click the **Close** button in the **Properties** dialog box.

Security Considerations of Sharing Folders

Folders can be shared by any user who has full control over a folder. Shares can be found by just searching the network. Users can also view all shares on a computer. A shared folder presents an access point for a hacker or employee to use as a portal. This may be to exploit other system vulnerabilities or to provide access to confidential data. Therefore, shared folders should be monitored for unnecessary access.

Shares can be created and hidden. There are some default administrative shares that are hidden. These include sharing of fixed and removable drives such as C: or D:, the folder containing the Windows operating system, and a special communication share called IPC. Administrators sometimes hide other shares for ease of use. However, hidden shares may also be used by a hacker in an attempt to hide what he or she is doing. A hidden share is only accessible if you know the correct name and path to the folder. A hidden share is made in the advanced settings by putting a dollar sign ($) at the end of the share name. For example, if the folder Notes is shared as Notes$, only users who know this name and the path to the folder will be able to access it.

Quick Look 3.2.2

Shared Folders on a System

Shared folders on a system can be viewed using the command prompt. This will show all shared folders, including hidden folders.

1. On a Windows computer, click **Start>All Apps>Windows System>Command Prompt** in Windows 10 (**Start>All programs>Accessories>Command Prompt** in Windows 7) or enter command prompt into the search bar to open the local command prompt window.

2. Enter net share on the command line. All shared folders are listed, as shown. How many *hidden* shares do you see? Which shared folders could be concerning? Discuss with your classmates.

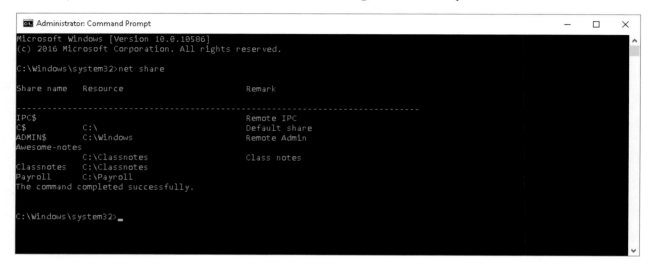

3. Close the command prompt.

4. Click the **Start** button, enter computer management in the search box, and click **Computer Management** in the list.

5. Expand the Shared Folders branch, and then select the Shares branch, as shown.

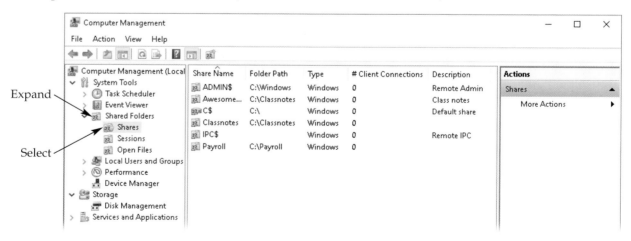

6. Based on what you see, are the shares for C$, IPC$, and ADMIN$ security concerns?

7. Notice the share you created named Awesome-notes. Click *once* on Awesome-notes to select it. Then, in the right-hand panel, click **More Actions** under the **Awesome-notes** heading (*not* the **Shares** heading). A shortcut menu is displayed.

8. Click **Stop Sharing** in the shortcut menu. When prompted, click the **Yes** button. This folder is no longer shared. Notice it is no longer listed as a shared folder.

NTFS Permissions

Sharing folders makes them available to users logged into another machine on the network. However, it has no impact on a user who logs in directly on the local machine. When a user logs into a local computer, by default he or she will have complete access to the files and folders within his or her Users folder. To secure the folders for users with local access, NTFS permissions need to be used. *New Technology File System (NTFS) permissions* allow rights to be set for users on the local machine.

NTFS provides more options for permissions as well. Share permissions were not very flexible. For example, suppose a user needs to be able to add files. With sharing, this user must be given change permission, which also allows files to be deleted. NTFS allows an administrator to be more specific, or *granular,* when assigning permissions. NTFS permissions also use allow and deny options when assigning permissions.

Figure 3-16 describes the different types of NTFS permissions. Notice that the full control permission allows the user to *take ownership* of the files. The owner of the file or folder is normally the person who created the object. As the owner, the user has discretionary control over the file or folder. In some cases, however, an administrator might need to take ownership of a file or folder. For example, if an employee has left the company and his or her user account is deleted, an administrator can take ownership of the files, and thus obtain full control access to the files.

NTFS Permission	Description
Full control	Gives the user the ability to take ownership; provides the ability to read, change, and give other people permissions.
Modify	The user can modify the properties of a file and create and delete files.
Read & execute	The user can read and run any executable files.
List folder contents	The user can see the files in the folder, but cannot view the contents of files; only applicable to folders, not files.
Read	The user can see files in the folder and read their contents.
Write	The user can edit contents of files.
Advanced	This button accesses more advanced options that are more granular, such as allowing files to be created, but denying the ability to delete files.

Goodheart-Willcox Publisher

Figure 3-16. Permission settings for NTFS.

Quick Look 3.2.3

NTFS Permission Settings

NTFS permissions allow more control and flexibility than shared folders. NTFS permissions can be viewed for folders and files.

1. Launch Windows File Explorer.
2. Navigate to the Classnotes folder you created earlier.
3. Right-click on the folder, and click **Properties** in the shortcut menu.

Quick Look 3.2.3 Continued

4. Click the **Security** tab in the **Properties** window, as shown.

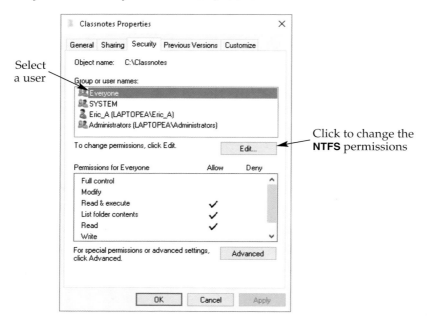

Select a user

Click to change the **NTFS** permissions

5. Select Everyone in the **Group or user names:** list, and click the **Edit...** button. A person or group can also be added using this button.
6. In the **Permissions** window that is open, make the setting needed to allow the modify permission. Notice the other NTFS permissions that can be set to allow or deny.
7. Click the **OK** button to close the **Permissions** window, and then click the **OK** button to close the **Properties** window.

Receiving Permissions

There are three ways a user receives permissions. These are explicit, inherited, and implicit assignments. It is important to understand each of these methods.

Explicit permissions are those a user is given at a specific location. The specific location may be a folder or a file.

Inherited permissions are those a user receives by default at a lower level. Suppose a user is assigned explicit permissions of read, list, and write for Folder1. He or she inherits the same permissions in all subfolders within Folder1.

Implicit permissions are those a user receives through another object, such as a group. Suppose a user is a member of the Engineers group. Whatever permissions the group has will be assigned implicitly to the user as well.

Implicit and explicit permissions factor into a user's effective permissions. There is a hierarchy of permission order:

1. Explicit deny
2. Explicit allow
3. Inherited deny
4. Inherited allow

Figure 3-17 illustrates three scenarios. The effective permissions for each scenario are explained.

Scenario	Effective Permissions	
Marissa is explicitly allowed read, list, and write permissions for the Marketing Campaign folder. She has no other explicit or implicit permissions.	Marissa can list, read, and write for both the Marketing Campaign folder and the Videos subfolder.	
Drew is explicitly allowed read, list, and explicitly denied write permissions for the Marketing Campaign folder. He is a member of the Marketing group, which is explicitly allowed read, list, and write permissions for the Marketing Campaign folder.	Drew's rights are read and list. The deny permission on write took away his allow write permission. These permissions are then inherited in the Videos subfolder.	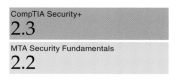
Carlos is a member of the SocialMedia group. This group is allowed list, read & execute, and write permissions for the Marketing Campaign folder. Carlos also is explicitly allowed modify permission for the Videos subfolder.	Carlos can list, read & execute, and write for the Marketing Campaign folder through his implicit permissions from the SocialMedia group. For the Videos subfolder, he inherits all of the above permissions and he also is allowed to modify the folder.	

Goodheart-Willcox Publisher

Figure 3-17. These scenarios illustrate how NTFS permissions are received by a user.

Combining NTFS and Share Permissions

In many cases, when a folder is shared, the permissions are not flexible or granular enough. In these situations, NTFS permissions are also given to the share. When the two permission sets are combined, the permissions are set by this rule: The more restrictive permission takes precedence.

Consider the following example. The marketing department has created the folder structure shown in **Figure 3-18.** These folders will be used to save the data for online research. The marketing manager shares the Research Data folder with the Marketing group and grants the group the *share* permission of read. The manager then assigns the Marketing group the NTFS permissions of read & execute, list, and write. This allows all users to add more data to the databases. However, in this scenario, the Marketing group will only have read permission assigned by the share since that is more restrictive than the NTFS permissions for the group. This applies to the Telephone Surveys and Online Surveys subfolders as well.

In many cases, it makes more sense to first share the folder with the target user or group with the full control permission. Then, assign the specific NTFS permissions you actually want the user or group to have. In this case, the most restrictive permissions will be the NTFS permissions.

Security Considerations of NTFS Permissions

NTFS permissions offer the ability to assign very specific permissions to users or groups. A user can have permissions from many areas, including share permissions and memberships in other groups. This can present security risks. Administrators should confirm each user's actual abilities by verifying effective permissions.

CompTIA Security+
2.3

MTA Security Fundamentals
2.2

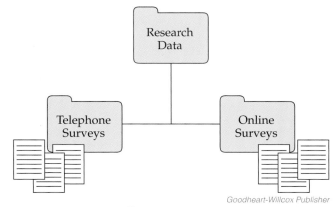

Goodheart-Willcox Publisher

Figure 3-18. The effective permissions for this folder structure depends on how the permissions were assigned.

Case Study

Permissions

Your English teacher has four different classes. He or she wants to have a common shared folder that students in all four classes can access and a shared folder created for each specific class. In the common folder, students should only be able to look at files and copy from the folder. In the class folder, each student within the class should be able to look at files, create files, but not delete any files. Students from other classes should not be able to access this folder.

1. What folder structure will you set up?
2. What share or NTFS permissions will you create for the common folder?
3. What share or NTFS permissions will you create for each class folder?

Quick Look 3.2.4

Effective User Rights

A user's effective rights can be difficult to keep track of, especially when combining share and NTFS permissions. There is an easy way to see the effective rights on a file or folder.

1. Launch Windows File Explorer.
2. Right-click on the Classnotes folder, and click **Properties** in the shortcut menu. In the **Properties** window, click the **Security** tab.
3. Click the **Advanced** button. The **Advanced Security Settings** dialog box is displayed.
4. Click the **Effective Permissions** tab, as shown.

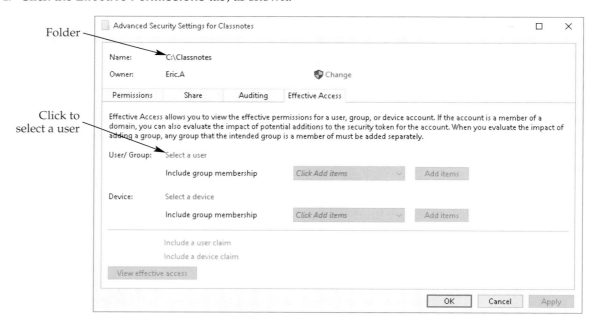

5. Click the Select a user link. In the dialog box that is displayed, click in the text box, and enter Everyone as the valid user name. You can also click the **Advanced** button to browse for the user.
6. Click the **OK** button to return to the **Advanced Security Settings** dialog box. The **View Effective Access** button at the bottom of the **Effective Access** tab should now be enabled.

Quick Look 3.2.4 Continued

7. Click the **View Effective Access** button, and scroll down in the window to see the permissions, as shown. Where there is a check mark, that permission is allowed. Where there is an X (or blank), the permission is denied.

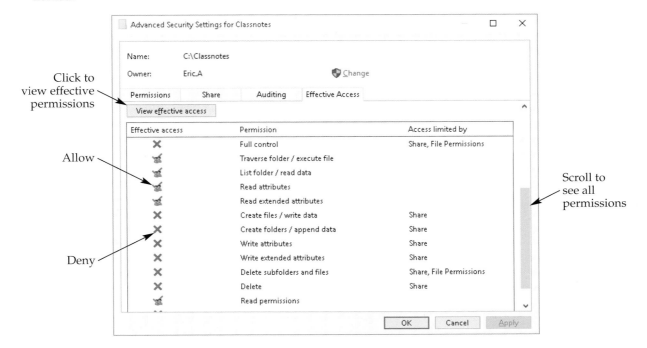

Click to view effective permissions

Allow

Deny

Scroll to see all permissions

SECTION REVIEW 3.2

Check Your Understanding

1. What are the permission options for shared folders?
2. Which NTFS permission allows the ability to rename a file?
3. How can a shared folder be set to hidden?
4. Permissions received from a higher folder are called what type of permissions?
5. The net result of all permission assignments results in what a user can do. This is called what type of permission?

Build Your Key Terms Vocabulary

As you progress through this course, develop a personal cybersecurity glossary. This will help you build your vocabulary and prepare you for a career. Write a definition for each of the following terms, and add it to your cybersecurity glossary.

explicit permissions

implicit permissions

inherited permissions

New Technology File System (NTFS) permissions

share permissions

Review and Assessment

Chapter Summary

Section 3.1 Authentication and Control

- User authentication involves proper planning and incorporation of solid policies that ensure a person should be accessing the system or data. Included in this is having and enforcing a password policy.
- There are several ways to establish access levels for security, such as TCSEC, MAC, DAC, RBAC, and rule-based access control. These can be used to manage user access to resources and data.
- There are nontechnical approaches to user security, such as mandatory vacations and job rotation, that can help ensure the security of data and systems.
- Users should only have access to the resources needed to do their job and no more. Access includes local computer, files and folders, and physical areas of the building.

Section 3.2 Access to Files and Folders

- Files and folders can be shared across a network. Share permissions are used to control how network users can access shared resources.
- NTFS permissions can be used to control access to the local computer. These permissions can be combined with shared permissions to offer more flexibility.

Check Your Cybersecurity IQ ➦

Now that you have completed this chapter, see what you have learned about cybersecurity by visiting the student companion website (www.g-wlearning.com) and taking the chapter posttest.

Review Questions ➦

For each question, select the answer that is the best response.

1. A user logs in and provides a password and a token ID value. This is an example of:
   A. biometric login
   B. hash value
   C. one-time password
   D. multifactor authentication

2. The accounting department supervisor made the decision to allow an employee more access to accounting data than the user previously had. What level of access does this represent?
   A. Mandatory Access Control (MAC)
   B. Discretionary Access Control (DAC)
   C. Role-Based Access Control (RBAC)
   D. rule-based access control

3. Which of the following best describes eliminating potential threats?
   A. attack surfacing
   B. policy implementation
   C. hardening a system
   D. hashing

4. A printer is considered which type of object in a directory tree?
   A. leaf
   B. LDAP
   C. OU
   D. CN

5. How does the Enforce Password History setting help create a strong password strategy?
   A. It prevents users from ever reusing a previous password.
   B. It prevents users from adding numbers to the end of a previous password.
   C. It prevents users from using a previous password for a specified number of changes.
   D. It prevents passwords that are already in from being used by others.

6. Which security strategy is most effective in preventing a normal user from automatically installing software on a computer?
   A. Grant the user only read and execute permissions to the computer.
   B. Set an appropriate UAC level.
   C. Join the computer to the network domain.
   D. Do not allow share permissions.

7. A portable hard drive is inserted into a computer and G: is assigned as the drive letter. What is the administrative share name for this device?
   A. G$
   B. G&
   C. $G
   D. G@

8. Which permission allows you to create a file?
   A. Write
   B. Modify
   C. Read
   D. Make

9. Savannah has list, read, and execute permissions allowed and write permission denied on a folder. The group Everyone has the read and change permissions allow on the folder. Which statement is true?
   A. Savannah is unaffected by the permissions given to the group.
   B. The allowed change permission takes precedence over the denied write permission.
   C. The change permission is not the same as the write permission so there is no conflict.
   D. The denied write permission takes precedence over the allowed change permission.

10. The final result of the permissions a user has on a file is known as what type of permissions?
    A. allowable permissions
    B. net permissions
    C. effective permissions
    D. usable permissions

Application and Extension of Knowledge

1. Survey classmates and other people you know who have Android and iPhone smartphones. Select people across a wide range of ages and both men and women. Ask if they use any biometrics on their phone, such as a fingerprint scanner. Who tends to use biometrics more, women or men? Are younger users more comfortable with biometric technology than older users? Create charts to summarize your results.

2. Password managers are online services that allow you to "lock" your passwords into an online "vault" and generate strong passwords for websites you use. Look into both paid and free password managers. Is there one you would recommend, or would you recommend not using a manager? Create a one-page summary with your recommendation.

3. On your home computer, review your security settings. Identify what areas you could change to harden or strengthen your system against potential vulnerabilities. Share and discuss these settings with your class.

4. Since employees are naturally given rights and permissions to use and view data, insider data theft is a growing concern to many businesses. Research and identify some strategies that businesses and organizations can use to prevent loss of data by employees.

5. Microsoft has many options for Windows 10 that can be configured using group policies. These are listed in an Excel spreadsheet located on the student companion website (www.g-wlearning.com). There are six domains, each on its own tab in the Excel file. Search through the policies. Identify ten specific policy settings that could help harden the Windows operating system. List the policies in order from 1 to 10 with 1 being the most beneficial. Compare your list with your classmates' lists.

Research Project
Biometric Privacy Laws

Biometric technologies are advancing at a fast rate. As with most any new technology, laws governing this technology are being developed as quickly as the technology. However, at least three states have already enacted privacy laws related to biometric technology: Illinois, Texas, and Washington. Other states are considering similar legislation. Research the laws in these and other states. Which states have already enacted laws? Which states have laws under consideration? Look into any controversies or criticisms of this legislation. Identify areas in which existing laws share common features or requirements. Which states have taken no action? Look for any grassroots organizations that are lobbying for greater protections.

Deliverables. Create a short slideshow to illustrate which states have enacted laws and the key elements of their laws. Have there been any prosecutions under these laws? Do you think any aspects of the law should be enacted in all states?

Online Activities

Complete the following activities, which will help you learn, practice, and expand your knowledge and skills.

Vocabulary. Practice vocabulary for this chapter using the e-flash cards, matching activity, and vocabulary game until you are able to recognize their meanings.

Communication Skills

College and Career Readiness

Reading. There are many cybersecurity terms shown in blue, bold-italic type in this chapter. These are key terms. Other terms are simply italicized. Make a list of the italicized terms, and add them to your personal glossary.

Writing. To follow standard English means your word choices, sentence structures, paragraphs, and narrative follow standard conventions used by those who speak English. Well-written paragraphs are usually the product of editing. Using standard English, write several paragraphs to describe a cybersecurity topic. Edit and revise your work until the ideas are refined and clear to the reader.

Speaking. *Impromptu speaking* is talking without advance notice to plan what will be said. Turn to the person next to you, and ask him or her to explain what shoulder surfing means in cybersecurity. Were you able to hold an impromptu conversation on this topic? What did you learn from speaking with the other person?

Listening. Practice active-listening skills by asking your friends or classmates about their plans for the weekend. Listen to their responses. Were there any sending barriers for the senders or receiving barriers for the receiver? How did you show you were listening?

Portfolio Development

College and Career Readiness

Checklist. Once you have written your portfolio objective, consider how you will achieve it. It is helpful to have a checklist of components that will be included in your portfolio. The checklist will be used to record ideas for documents and other items that you might include. Starting with a checklist will help you brainstorm ideas that you want to pursue.

The elements you select to include in your portfolio will reflect your portfolio's purpose. For example, if you are seeking acceptance into a computer security program, create a portfolio that includes your technical certifications and any awards or contests you have won related to computer security.

1. Ask your instructor for a checklist. If one is not provided, use the Internet and research Student Portfolio checklists. Find an example that works for your purpose.
2. Create a checklist. This will be your roadmap for your portfolio.

CTSO Event Prep

Objective Test. Some competitive events for career and technical student organizations (CTSOs) require entrants to complete an objective component of the event. This event will typically be an objective test that includes terminology and concepts related to a selected subject area. Participants are usually allowed one hour to complete the objective test component of the event. To prepare for an objective test, complete the following activities.

1. Read the guidelines provided by your organization.
2. Visit the organization's website and look for objective tests that were used in previous years. Many organizations post these tests for students to use as practice for future competitions.
3. Look for the evaluation criteria or rubric for the event. This will help you determine what the judge will be looking for in your presentation.
4. Create flash cards for each vocabulary term with its definition on the other side. Ask a friend to use these cards to review with you.
5. Ask your instructor to give you practice tests for this chapter of the text that would prepare you for the subject area of the event. It is important that you are familiar with answering multiple choice and true/false questions. Have someone time you as you take a practice test.

Chapter 4

Command Line Interface Management

All major operating systems provide the ability to manage their systems using a nongraphical interface. In Microsoft operating systems, there are two command line interfaces. The first is the shell, which is often referred to as the command prompt or command line. The second is a newer command-line interface called PowerShell. Linux also has its own shell. The most common Linux shell used is known as Bash.

Regardless of the interface type, managing systems from the command line interface offers more options and flexibility when running commands than when using a graphical interface. In many cases, using the shell is the only way to run a command. Consider the Windows command **IPCONFIG**. There is no equivalent command built into the Windows graphical interface. Becoming skilled at shell interfaces is an important skill to develop. Some Linux distributions have no graphical interface. Microsoft Server offers a version called Server Core that also has no graphical interface. Many of the advanced security and troubleshooting tools are performed in the shell.

Chapter Preview

Section 4.1   Windows Command Prompt
Section 4.2   Windows PowerShell
Section 4.3   Introduction to Linux

While studying, look for the activity icon for:

- Pretests and posttests
- Vocabulary terms with e-flash cards and matching activities
- Self-assessment

College and Career Readiness

Reading Prep

Before reading this chapter, read the opening pages and section titles for this chapter. These can help prepare you for the topics presented in the chapter. What do they tell you about what you will be learning?

Check Your Cybersecurity IQ ⤴

Before you begin this chapter, see what you already know about cybersecurity by visiting the student companion website (www.g-wlearning.com) and taking the chapter pretest.

Certification Objectives

CompTIA Security+

2.2 Given a scenario, use appropriate software tools to assess the security posture of an organization.

Windows Command Prompt

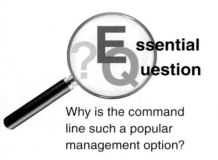

Essential Question

Why is the command line such a popular management option?

The Windows command prompt grew out of the original Microsoft computer operating system: Disk Operating System (DOS). PC computers used DOS, or MS DOS (Microsoft DOS), to run the computer until the release of Windows 95. Beginning with that release, the command-line interface acted as an application on the system. It was no longer the operating system; rather, Windows was the operating system and the command line, or command prompt, was one of its applications. Today, the command line still provides substantial commands for managing the computer system and its resources.

Key Terms 📇

append
batch file
command prompt

current directory
device driver
directory

switch
wildcard character

Learning Goals

- Navigate command line interface.
- Experiment with batch files to run command-line commands.
- Identify tips for working at the command prompt.

Working at the Command Prompt

The Windows *command prompt* is a command-line interface for manually entering commands. In Windows 10, the command prompt is located in the **Start** menu in **All Apps>Windows System>Command Prompt**. In Windows 7, it is located in **All Programs>Accessories>Command Prompt**. The actual program file is cmd.exe. When the application is launched, it appears in a window, as shown in **Figure 4-1.** All commands at the prompt must be entered with the keyboard and then executed by pressing the [Enter] key. Commands are *not* case sensitive. For example, entering DIR or dir is the same.

Multiple commands can be run by redirecting the output of the first command to a second command. Separate the commands with the pipe symbol (|).

For example, consider the dir | more entry. **DIR** is the first command. This is a directory listing. The pipe symbol sends the directory listing to the **MORE** command. The result is the screen output of the **DIR** command is paused until the user advances it so he or she can see one new line at a time.

Most commands have a built-in help to identify additional options or parameters of the command. A command option or parameter is called a *switch.* To access the help, add a forward slash (/) after the command and then a question mark (?). For example, dir /? provides additional options for the **DIR** command, as shown in **Figure 4-2.**

Some commands will work without a space between the command and the switch options. However, most commands will not. It is good practice to always put a space after every command you type.

Figure 4-1. The Windows command prompt is an application that runs in a window.

A command can be easily run from the Windows search bar by adding the /k option, such as cmd /k ipconfig.

```
Command Prompt                                      —    □    ×
C:\Users\Eric_A>dir /?
Displays a list of files and subdirectories in a directory.

DIR [drive:][path][filename] [/A[[:]attributes]] [/B] [/C] [/D] [/L] [/N]
  [/O[[:]sortorder]] [/P] [/Q] [/R] [/S] [/T[[:]timefield]] [/W] [/X] [/4]

  [drive:][path][filename]
              Specifies drive, directory, and/or files to list.

  /A          Displays files with specified attributes.
  attributes   D  Directories              R  Read-only files
               H  Hidden files             A  Files ready for archiving
               S  System files             I  Not content indexed files
               L  Reparse Points           -  Prefix meaning not
  /B          Uses bare format (no heading information or summary).
  /C          Display the thousand separator in file sizes.  This is the
              default.  Use /-C to disable display of separator.
  /D          Same as wide but files are list sorted by column.
  /L          Uses lowercase.
  /N          New long list format where filenames are on the far right.
  /O          List by files in sorted order.
  sortorder    N  By name (alphabetic)      S  By size (smallest first)
               E  By extension (alphabetic) D  By date/time (oldest first)
               G  Group directories first   -  Prefix to reverse order
  /P          Pauses after each screenful of information.
  /Q          Display the owner of the file.
  /R          Display alternate data streams of the file.
  /S          Displays files in specified directory and all subdirectories.
  /T          Controls which time field displayed or used for sorting
Press any key to continue . . .
```

Figure 4-2. The /? option can be used to display help for most commands, such as shown here for the **DIR** command.

Quick Look 4.1.1

Command Prompt Options

There are two modes to the command-line interface. It can be run in normal mode or as an administrator.

1. Click the Windows **Start** button, and enter cmd in the text box. This is perhaps the easiest way to launch the command prompt, but it is also located in the **Start** menu itself.

2. The command prompt is running in normal mode. In the command prompt window, enter exit. As soon as you press the [Enter] key, the window is closed.

3. Click **Start>All Apps>Windows System** (**Start>All Programs>Accessories** in Windows 7), and locate the **Command Prompt** icon.

Quick Look 4.1.1 Continued

4. To run the command prompt as an administrator, right-click on the **Command Prompt** icon, and click **Run as Administrator** in the shortcut menu.

5. If prompted, click the **Yes** button to continue, or enter appropriate credentials. Notice the title bar indicates the command prompt is being run as an administrator, as shown.

Command prompt is being run as an administrator

6. Enter dir. The **DIR** command lists files and folders in the current directory.

7. Enter dir /? to display help for the **DIR** command. Review the options available. Which switch would you use to perform a directory listing and include the subdirectories?

8. Enter dir /s /p. This combines two switches with the command. Describe the function performed by this entry. Note: the result of this command can be long. After you have viewed enough to determine the command's purpose, press the [Ctrl][C] key combination to exit the command. This key combination cancels any command prompt command (but does not exit the command prompt application).

9. Enter cls. The **CLS** command clears the screen. This command allows you to clean up the command prompt display.

10. Enter tasklist. This command is similar to running the task manager in the graphical interface.

11. The task list may be longer than one page (screen). To advance the page one line at a time, enter tasklist | more.

12. Press the [Enter] key to show each next line, or press the [Ctrl][C] key combination to exit the command.

13. Press the [F7] key. The commands previously used in this session of the command prompt are displayed in a pop-up box, as shown. You can navigate the list with the arrow keys. Press the [Enter] key to execute the highlighted command.

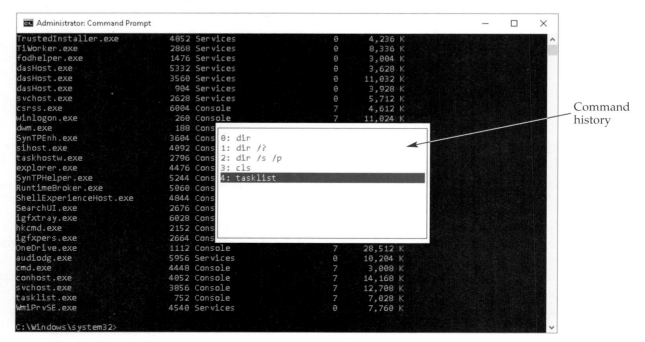

Command history

Quick Look 4.1.1 Continued

14. Press the [Esc] key to exit the history.
15. Enter **exit**. This closes the command prompt window.

Essential File and Directory Commands

A *directory* is a storage location for files and other directories. Some of the most used commands on the command prompt involve file and directory management and navigation. These commands include **MD**, **CD**, **DIR**, **DEL**, and **RD**.

The command to create a new directory or subdirectory is **MD**. This is short for make directory. For example, md Data will create a directory called Data. It will be located within the current directory. Notice that the case used when entering the name will be matched in the actual directory name. So, the directory name could be Data, data, or DATA, depending on how it is entered with the command.

Whenever a directory is created, two indicators are generated within it that appear as dots, as shown in **Figure 4-3**. These symbols are called markers, and the dots indicate the following:

- . is the marker for the current directory
- .. is the marker for the parent directory from which the current directory branches

Markers are found in every directory and subdirectory. They cannot be deleted.

The *current directory* is the directory that you are in, which is reflected in the command prompt. For example, in **Figure 4-3,** the current directory is Data. When a command is entered, Windows executes it based on the current directory. The **CD** command (change directory) allows you to make another directory the current directory. For example, cd Programs makes the Programs subdirectory the current directory. Entering cd \Programs\Apps changes to the Apps subdirectory located in the Programs directory off the root. The first backslash tells Windows to go to the root. From there, it looks for the Programs directory, and then for the Apps subdirectory. You can also use the backslash key (\) and parent directory marker (..) as shown in **Figure 4-4.**

Folders were originally called *directories*. Some commands still refer to folders as directories. For example, the **CD** command stands for *change directory.* Folder and directory are synonyms in computer terminology.

Remember, Windows ignores case when considering directory and file names, so there cannot be a Data directory and a DATA directory in the same location.

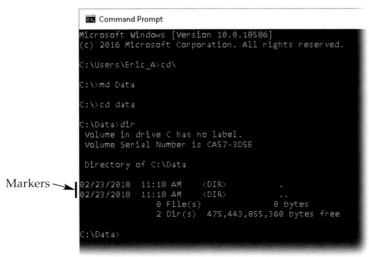

Figure 4-3. Markers exist in every directory and subdirectory.

| cd\ | Changes the current directory to the root directory of the drive. |
| cd.. | Moves up one directory (to the parent directory). For example, if the current directory is c:\data\Jan\budget and cd.. is entered, the new current directory would be the c:\data\Jan directory. |

Goodheart-Willcox Publisher

Figure 4-4. Options for the **CD** command to move to the drive's root directory or to the parent directory of the current directory.

Unlike when using Windows File Explorer, when you change to a directory using the command prompt, the contents are not immediately displayed. You must "ask" to see the files and subdirectories using the **DIR** command. This is short for directory listing. The **DIR** command is a very powerful command when combined with some of its switches. For example, the **/s** switch will tell the command to search not just the current directory, but all subdirectories it contains. Also, the view can be filtered to see just certain file types. Or, files can be displayed in different orders, such as by name, date created, file extension, or size.

Wildcard characters can be used with the **DIR** command. A *wildcard character* is used to represent one or more unknown characters in a string. The question mark wildcard (?) represents a single unknown character. The asterisk wildcard (*) represents any number of unknown characters. Wildcards can be used to help in searches and identifying specific files, programs, and features. Here are some examples:

- dir B*.* displays all files in the current directory with a file name that starts with the letter B, contains any other characters, and has any file extension
- dir *.pdf displays all files in the current directory with the .pdf file extension and can be any name
- dir Day0?.txt displays all files in the current directory with the .txt file extension that have a name beginning with Day0 and contain one other character, such as Day01.txt, Day02.txt, and Day03.txt, but not Day03A.txt
- del *.exe deletes all files in the current directory with the .exe file extension

The command to delete files is **DEL**. To delete a single file, enter del *filename. extension.* The file extension must be included. The command to delete a directory is **RD**. This is short for remove directory. For example, rd **data** will delete the directory named data. By default, the **RD** command will not allow you to remove a directory if it contains any files or subdirectories. The current directory also cannot be deleted.

Quick Look 4.1.2

Navigational Commands

Navigating directories using a command-line interface is much different from navigating folders using a graphical interface. It is important to understand how commands are used to navigate.

1. Applying what you have learned, launch the command prompt as a regular user.
2. The command prompt should indicate Users*YourUserName*. This means the current directory is your personal users folder. If not, enter cd\users*YourUserName* using your valid user name.
3. Enter md Practice. This creates a directory named Practice from your current location. It is a subdirectory of your personal users folder. However, you have simply created the folder, not navigated to it.

Quick Look 4.1.2 Continued

4. Enter cd practice. The command prompt should now reflect that you have moved to the Practice directory. Notice that even though the directory was named with an uppercase P, this is ignored by the **CD** command.

5. Enter copy c:\windows*.exe. This copies all executable files (with the .exe file extension) from the Windows directory to the current directory, which is your Practice directory.

6. Enter dir s*.*. This displays only the files in the current directory that start with the letter S.

7. Enter cd.. to return to the parent directory of Practice. This is your personal users folder.

8. Enter rd practice. You should receive an error. Why did this happen?

9. Enter rd /? to display the help for the **RD** command. Which switch allows a directory to be deleted even if it contains content?

10. Enter rd practice /s. When prompted, confirm yes or y to delete the Practice directory.

11. Enter cd practice. You should receive an error stating the path cannot be found. This is because the Practice directory no longer exists.

12. Enter exit to close the command prompt.

Commands to Manage Local and Remote Hosts

There are many commands that will assist you in managing a system or remote host from the command line. For example, in Quick Look 4.1.1, you used the **TASKLIST** command. This command gives you a snapshot of what is currently running on a host. Tasks represent an instance of a program that is running. For example, if you have the Chrome browser running, you will see an instance of it in the task list. This is a good command to use to determine if there is any malware or other suspicious software running. It has some options that are useful.

The /fi switch is used to filter the search of the tasks running. You can filter by memory usage, process status, what services use a process, and more. For example, entering tasklist /fi "memusage gt 20000" will filter all running tasks to show only those that are using more than 20 megabytes of memory.

The format of the results returned by the **TASKLIST** command can be changed. To see the results as a list, enter tasklist /fo list. When using this format, it may be best to combine it with the **MORE** command. This will allow you to manually control the scrolling of the list.

If you are searching for specific processes that are running, you can combine the **TASKLIST** command with the **FIND** command. For example, enter tasklist | find "MicrosoftEdge" to see if Microsoft Edge is running, as shown in **Figure 4-5.** The quotation marks are required around the name of the process.

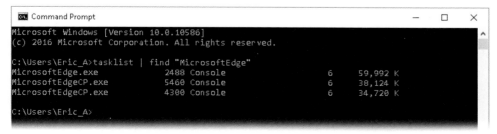

Figure 4-5. By combining the **TASKLIST** command with the **FIND** command, you can look for a specific process that is running, such as Microsoft Edge.

Stopping a task from running at the command prompt can be accomplished with the **TASKKILL** command. You can stop a process by its image name or by the processor identification (PID) number. The image name is the name of the process. The PID is a unique number assigned by the operating system to identify that specific process. Some processes run more than one time, so you may need to use the PID to be accurate.

Suppose you want to terminate the calculator program. You can do that by using the **TASKKILL** command with the /im (image name) or /pid switch. For example, enter taskkill /im notepad.exe to terminate the Notepad application by its image name.

Processes and services may be running on a computer. A *service* runs in the background of the operating system and does not interact with the desktop. It is different from a task. The **TASKLIST** command will not identify the running services. Enter net start to see the services that are started. By viewing these services, you can identify if there are any services that may make the host vulnerable to a hacking attempt. For example, you may find an unapproved virtual private network (VPN) client running. You can then take measures to disable or stop them from running. Enter net stop and the name of the service to end from running.

Another source of possible malware is device drivers. A *device driver* is a software program that instructs a piece of hardware how to operate. The **DRIVERQUERY** command is used to view installed drivers. The /si switch can be added to see which drivers are digitally signed by the manufacturer. The list of drivers can be exported to a comma separated value (CSV) file. This type of file can be open with a spreadsheet program. For example, enter driverquery /si /fo csv >drivers.csv to create a list of signed drivers and export it to a CSV file named drivers. Depending on how many drivers are installed, it may take a few seconds to generate the file. **Figure 4-6** shows an example of a driver list in a CSV file.

Automate Tasks with Batch Files

There are many times when a command or series of commands needs to be run more than once. A *batch file* is a single file in which a command, series of commands, or set of instructions to be processed in sequence is listed. Batch files are created with Notepad or any plain-text editor and saved with the .bat file extension. To run the batch file, simply enter the name of the file at the command prompt. The file extension does not need to be entered.

FYI

Be sure to test a batch file before implementing it. Do not assume you have correctly entered everything and there are no mistakes. When you run the batch file, you either must be in the same directory as the batch file or specify its path.

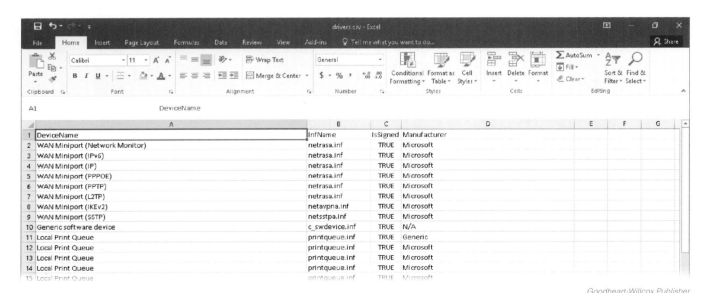

Figure 4-6. This spreadsheet is a CSV file generated to show all drivers that have been digitally signed.

Any command-line program can be included in a batch file. In addition, there are some specific commands that are primarily used in batch files. Consider the example illustrated in **Figure 4-7.** A batch file is created to issue the **ECHO** and **IPCONFIG** commands. The **ECHO** command is used to display two messages and the values of the computername and date system variables. The @echo off entry on the first line of the batch files suppresses the word echo from appearing when the **ECHO** command is used. Then, the **IPCONFIG** command is run.

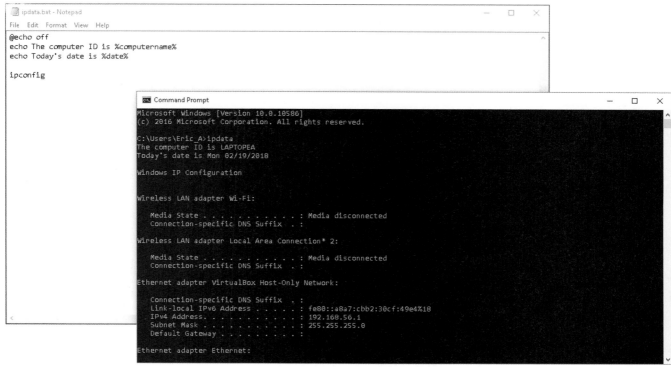

Goodheart-Willcox Publisher

Figure 4-7. Batch files can be used to automate tasks by combining several commands.

Quick Look 4.1.3

Commands in Batch Files

A batch file can be used to issue several commands in sequence. This is an effective means of simplifying several tasks.

1. Click **Start>All apps>Windows Accessories>Notepad (Start>All Programs>Accessories>Notepad** in Windows 7) to launch Notepad.
2. Add the following text to the file.
   @echo off

   Title: %computername% %date%
   echo Local users on %computer name%
   echo
   net user
3. Click **File>Save As...**, navigate to your personal Users folder, and save the file as localusers.bat. Be sure to enter .bat as the file extension, *not* the default .txt extension.

Quick Look 4.1.3 Continued

4. Applying what you have learned, launch the command prompt. If needed, navigate to your personal Users folder where the batch file is saved.

5. Enter localusers. The batch file is run, and the output should look similar to what is shown here.

Command Prompt Tips

There are some useful tips you can utilize when working at the command prompt. To redirect the output from the screen to a file, use the right chevron character (>). For example, dir > Files.txt will save the directory listing to a file named Files.txt in the current directory.

The data output from a command can be appended into the existing file by using two right chevrons (>>). To *append* data means to add it to an existing data set. For example, ipconfig >> pcdata.txt adds the output of the **IPCONFIG** command to the bottom of the existing pcdata.txt text file. If the file specified does not exist, it will be created.

There may be times when the output from a command needs to be used in something other than a plain text file. The **CLIP** command can be combined with another command to direct the output to the system clipboard. For example, ipconfig | clip will send the output of the **IPCONFIG** command to the clipboard. At first glance, it appears nothing has happened, but if you launch a word processor, you can see the data on the clipboard, as shown in **Figure 4-8.** The [Ctrl][V] key combination can be used to paste the data into the document.

You can use the **TITLE** command to change the title bar of the Windows command prompt. This can help document the machine being used. When taking a screenshot, the information is already included in the title bar. The title bar will reset for the next session of the command prompt. System variables can be used in the title. Entering title %computername% %date% will display the host's computer name and the current date in the title bar.

FYI

You can use the mouse to select text in the command prompt window and use the [Ctrl][C] key combination to place it on the system clipboard. The data can then be pasted into a document.

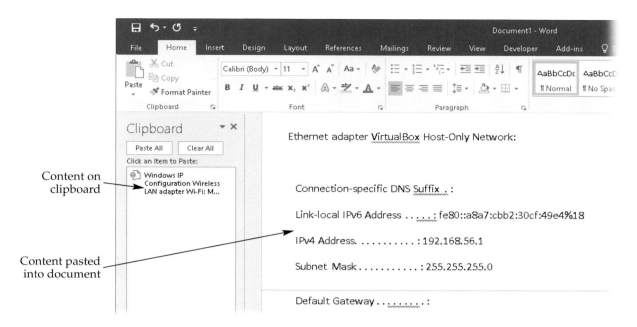

Figure 4-8. The output of a command-prompt command can be directed to the system clipboard and then used in a document.

Change the color of your command prompt for easier viewing. The color command uses two hex digits, as shown in **Figure 4-9.** The first digit specifies the background color. The second digit specifies the text color. For example, entering color 1F produces bright white text on a blue background. As with changing the title, the colors will reset for the next session of the command prompt.

To see the full list of system variables, use the **SET** command. If this command is entered without any arguments, it simply lists the system variables.

Hex Digit	Color	Hex Digit	Color	Hex Digit	Color	Hex Digit	Color
0	Black	4	Red	8	Gray	C	Light Red
1	Blue	5	Purple	9	Light Blue	D	Light Purple
2	Green	6	Yellow	A	Light Green	E	Light Yellow
3	Aqua	7	White	B	Light Aqua	F	Bright White

Figure 4-9. The color of the text and background for the command prompt can be changed using these hex digits.

SECTION REVIEW 4.1

Check Your Understanding

1. Which command would you enter at the command prompt to stop a task running?
2. What is the command entry to show all batch files that start with the letter S?
3. Which marker indicates the current directory?
4. Which command is placed in a batch file to display text on the screen?
5. What is the command entry to output the task list to a file called processes.txt?

Build Your Key Terms Vocabulary

As you progress through this course, develop a personal cybersecurity glossary. This will help you build your vocabulary and prepare you for a career. Write a definition for each of the following terms, and add it to your cybersecurity glossary.

append

batch file

command prompt

current directory

device driver

directory

switch

wildcard character

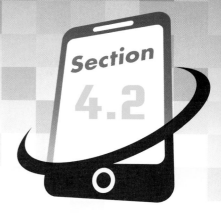

Windows PowerShell

Microsoft has signaled its intent to move toward a new shell environment: PowerShell. PowerShell was first available for Windows XP. Starting with Windows 7, it became integrated into the operating system. PowerShell can take the place of the command-line interface. Most command-line programs and options work equally well in the traditional shell and in PowerShell. Over time, PowerShell has gained in popularity. However, hackers have also discovered its power. They can create scripts to launch cyberattacks. Security administrators must be skilled in preventing attacks from this threat vector.

Essential Question

Why is PowerShell an ideal platform for script development?

Key Terms ✍

alias
cmdlets
object

piping
provider
script

Windows Management Instrumentation (WMI)

Learning Goals

- Describe how PowerShell uses the object model.
- Use advanced PowerShell commands.
- Create PowerShell scripts.

PowerShell Basics

PowerShell is a powerful command line shell that is integrated with Windows.NET technology. Windows.NET is a platform that developers use for building apps. PowerShell treats everything as objects. An *object* is a self-contained resource that stores information about itself in properties and provides program code that can be used to interact with it, as shown in **Figure 4-10.** For example, a file or folder is considered an object. Users, groups, servers, computers, etc., are also objects.

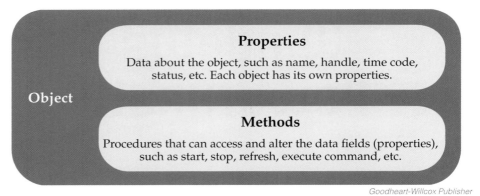

Figure 4-10. PowerShell treats everything as an object. Each object contains properties and methods.

FYI

Earlier, you learned about services. PowerShell also considers a service an object. Embedded in the service object are data, such as the service name. Each piece of data is called the *property*. The object also contains actions that can be performed on the data. Those actions are called *methods*. For example, the stop method can be used to end a service running.

Output from cmd.exe (the command prompt) is text. With PowerShell, the output from a command may *look* like text, but it is not. It is actually an object. This allows output results to be sent from one command into another. This process is called *piping.*

PowerShell was designed for network administrators. In addition to some very powerful command-line programs, PowerShell provides the ability to create your own variables and scripts. PowerShell does not just manage the file system or run commands, it can manage a wide array of systems, including:

- process;
- services;
- event logs;
- Windows Management Instrumentation (WMI);
- Active Directory; and
- Windows registry.

PowerShell Commands

Programs inside PowerShell are called *cmdlets* (pronounced *command-lets*). There are over one hundred cmdlets included in PowerShell. Commands are not case sensitive in PowerShell. Also, the commands you have used with the command prompt are in PowerShell, such as **CLS** and **MD**. However, they have been replaced with cmdlet equivalents. To make it easier, these commands have been established by creating an alias for the command. An *alias* is a replacement way to enter a command. PowerShell aliases include Linux commands along with command prompt commands. **Figure 4-11** shows keyboard keys used to navigate the PowerShell window.

PowerShell cmdlets use a specific syntax called *verb-noun syntax.* The command is a verb or action. What is being acted on is the noun. For example, get-childitem is a cmdlet. *Get* is the verb. This is the action. The noun is *childitem*. This is on what the verb will act.

Key	Function
[Page Up]	Jumps to the first command in the history buffer.
[Page Down]	Jumps to the last command in the history buffer.
Up arrow	Jumps back one command in the history buffer.
Down arrow	Jumps forward one command in the history buffer.
[Home]	Moves to the beginning of the command line.
[End]	Moves to the end of the command line.
[F7]	Shows the history buffer.

Goodheart-Willcox Publisher

Figure 4-11. Keys can be used to navigate the PowerShell window.

Quick Look 4.2.1

PowerShell Cmdlets and Aliases

PowerShell has many commands and aliases. It is easy to list all of the commands and aliases in PowerShell for quick reference.

1. Click **Start**>**All apps**>**Windows PowerShell**>**Windows PowerShell** (**Start**>**All Programs**>**Accessories**> **Windows PowerShell**>**Windows PowerShell** in Windows 7). The PowerShell window is displayed. There are visual cues that allow you to differentiate this from the command prompt. The default background is blue, the title bar states PowerShell, and there is a **PS** on the prompt.

2. Enter alias. Common command-prompt commands along with Linux commands are displayed with their new PowerShell cmdlet, as shown. Look for some of the commands you have used at the command prompt and find their PowerShell equivalents.

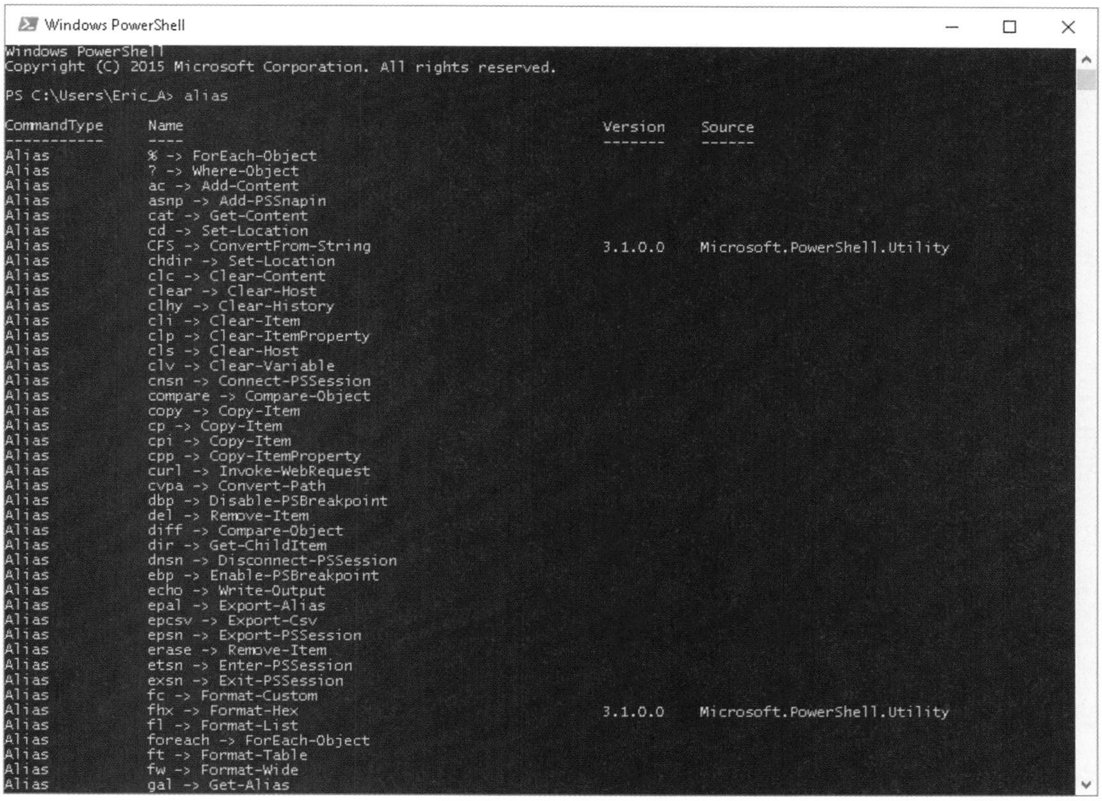

```
Windows PowerShell                                                    —   □   ×
Windows PowerShell
Copyright (C) 2015 Microsoft Corporation. All rights reserved.

PS C:\Users\Eric_A> alias

CommandType     Name                                Version    Source
-----------     ----                                -------    ------
Alias           % -> ForEach-Object
Alias           ? -> Where-Object
Alias           ac -> Add-Content
Alias           asnp -> Add-PSSnapin
Alias           cat -> Get-Content
Alias           cd -> Set-Location
Alias           CFS -> ConvertFrom-String           3.1.0.0    Microsoft.PowerShell.Utility
Alias           chdir -> Set-Location
Alias           clc -> Clear-Content
Alias           clear -> Clear-Host
Alias           clhy -> Clear-History
Alias           cli -> Clear-Item
Alias           clp -> Clear-ItemProperty
Alias           cls -> Clear-Host
Alias           clv -> Clear-Variable
Alias           cnsn -> Connect-PSSession
Alias           compare -> Compare-Object
Alias           copy -> Copy-Item
Alias           cp -> Copy-Item
Alias           cpi -> Copy-Item
Alias           cpp -> Copy-ItemProperty
Alias           curl -> Invoke-WebRequest
Alias           cvpa -> Convert-Path
Alias           dbp -> Disable-PSBreakpoint
Alias           del -> Remove-Item
Alias           diff -> Compare-Object
Alias           dir -> Get-ChildItem
Alias           dnsn -> Disconnect-PSSession
Alias           ebp -> Enable-PSBreakpoint
Alias           echo -> Write-Output
Alias           epal -> Export-Alias
Alias           epcsv -> Export-Csv
Alias           epsn -> Export-PSSession
Alias           erase -> Remove-Item
Alias           etsn -> Enter-PSSession
Alias           exsn -> Exit-PSSession
Alias           fc -> Format-Custom
Alias           fhx -> Format-Hex                    3.1.0.0    Microsoft.PowerShell.Utility
Alias           fl -> Format-List
Alias           foreach -> ForEach-Object
Alias           ft -> Format-Table
Alias           fw -> Format-Wide
Alias           gal -> Get-Alias
```

Quick Look 4.2.1 Continued

3. To view the cmdlets, enter get-command | more. Remember, the **MORE** command allows you to advance the list one line at a time and the [Ctrl][C] key combination cancels the command.

4. To narrow the search, the list can be filtered by verb or noun choices. Try these options:
   get-command -verb get
   get-command -noun disk
   get-command -noun network*

5. Enter 7*3. What happens?

6. Enter get-se and press the [Tab] instead of the [Enter] key. You can continue pressing the [Tab] key until the command you want appears. Then, press the [Enter] key to execute the command.

7. Enter get-service | sort-object status. This will run the **get-service** cmdlet, and then that output is sorted by the status column.

PowerShell Help

With the command prompt, the /? switch is used with a command to display help. In PowerShell, there is a separate cmdlet to get help. The **get-help** cmdlet is used to display help, and enter the name of the cmdlet. For example, entering get-help get-service will display help for the **get-service** cmdlet, as shown in **Figure 4-12.**

In recent versions of PowerShell, expanded help files are no longer included on the basic installation of PowerShell. Notice that this is indicated in **Figure 4-12.** The expanded help files can be accessed online using the -online switch. They can also be downloaded to the computer using the **update-help** cmdlet.

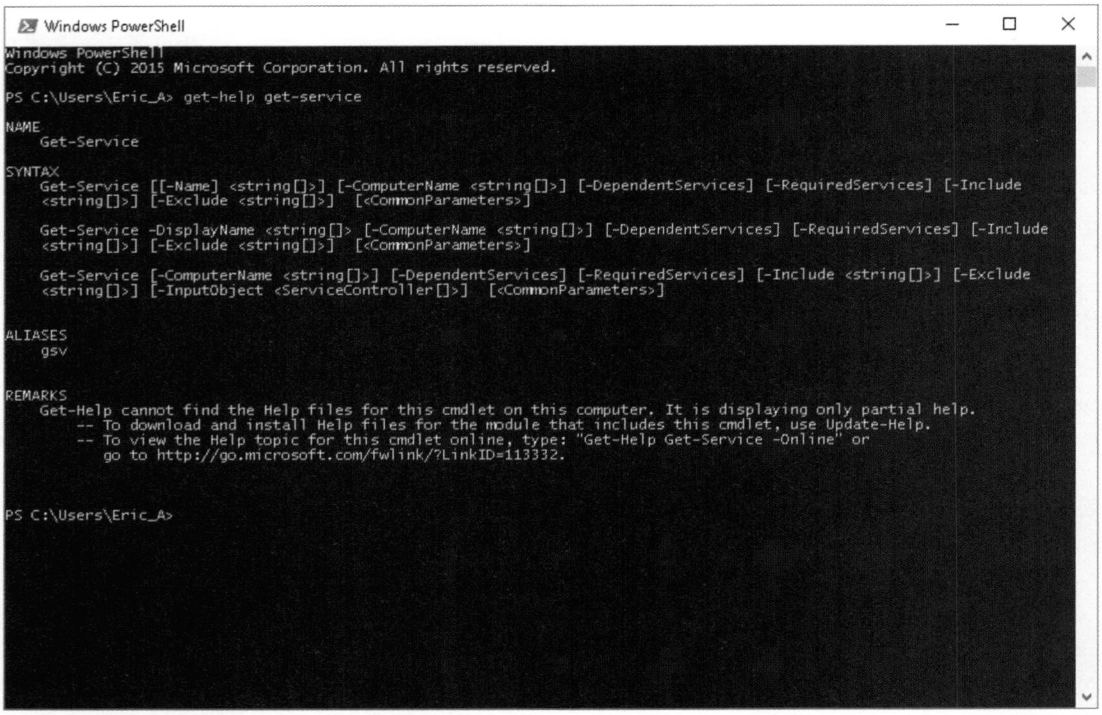

Goodheart-Willcox Publisher

Figure 4-12. Help is accessed in PowerShell with the **get-help** cmdlet.

Quick Look 4.2.2

Help for PowerShell Cmdlets

In PowerShell, a separate command is used to access help files. It is important to understand how to use help, including how to access expanded help online.

1. Click **Start>All apps>Windows PowerShell** (**Start>All Programs>Accessories>Windows PowerShell** in Windows 7), right-click on the **Windows PowerShell** icon, and click **Run as administrator** in the shortcut menu. When prompted, click the **Yes** button or enter the proper credentials to run the program.

2. Enter get-help get-service. Note: if you receive a message about downloading updated help files, enter N for no. What is the alias for this cmdlet?

3. Press the up arrow on the keyboard once to return to the previous command. At the end of the command, add the -online switch (get-help get-service -online). If you have an active Internet connection, the default web browser is launched and the online help options with more detail is displayed, as shown.

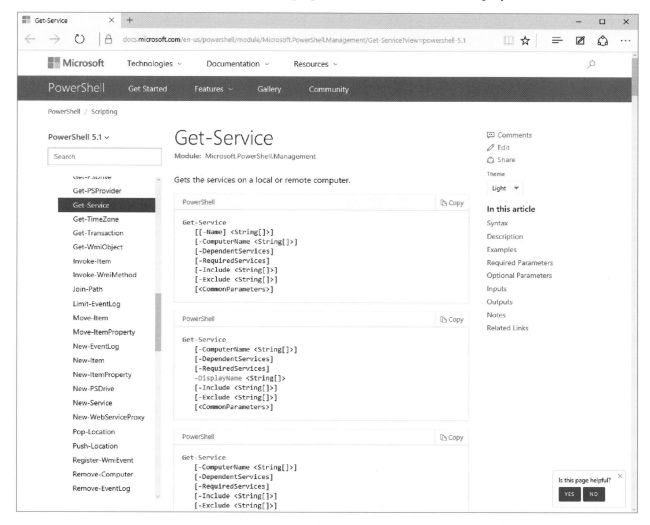

4. Read the information on the online help page. What would you enter to find all services that start with the letter S?

5. What would you enter to sort *all* services by status?

6. Close the web browser, and return to the PowerShell window.

Quick Look 4.2.2 Continued

7. Enter update-help. This cmdlet will install the expanded help files on the computer, as shown. It may take a few minutes to complete the download.

Help file download in process →

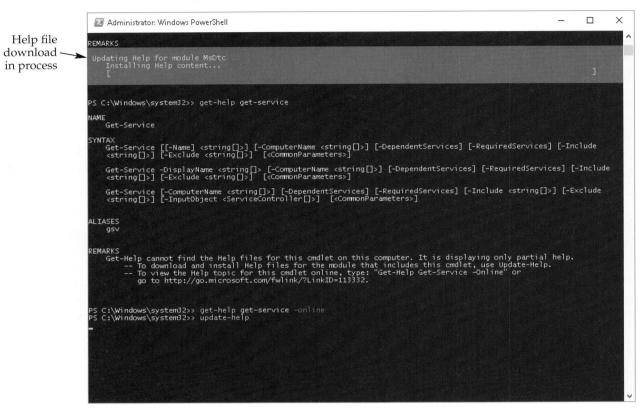

8. After it finishes, enter get-help get-service -examples. This will display the examples you saw in the online help.
9. Enter get-help get-service –detailed. This will display the full, expanded help that you saw in the online help.
10. Enter exit to close the PowerShell window.

Advanced PowerShell Command Options

PowerShell offers enormous abilities to manage local and remote systems. It includes many commands to aid in networking, security, Hyper-V virtualization, and Active Directory management for Microsoft servers. By adding additional parameters or piping multiple commands for a task, you can retrieve important information. Some helpful tools are introduced here so you can become comfortable with the PowerShell interface. There are so many more cmdlets to explore than those presented here. Future chapters will explore additional cmdlets to manage security and networks as well.

When in PowerShell, you are working in environments called providers. A *provider* can be thought of as a layer that allows you to focus on managing a specific data store using the same commands. By switching between the providers, you can exclusively manage other environments, such as the registry, file system, Active Directory, and more. For example, if you are working in the file system, running the **get-childitem** cmdlet displays files. However, if you are in the Active

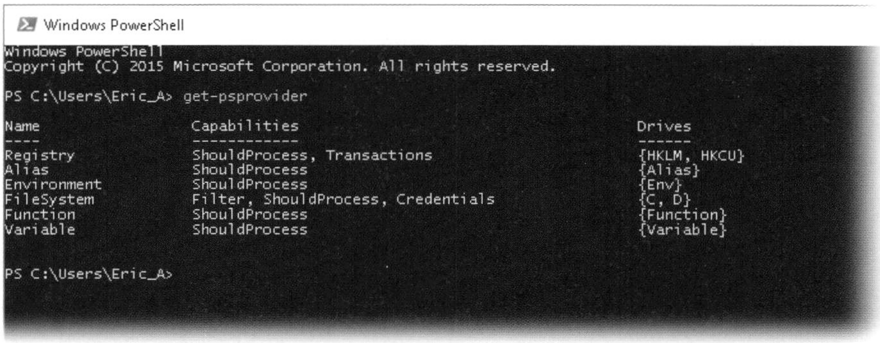

Goodheart-Willcox Publisher

Figure 4-13. The **get-psprovider** cmdlet lists providers available on the machine. The Drives column gives the shortcut for each provider.

Directory provider, the **get-childitem** cmdlet displays user objects. The different providers allow you to access different information stores. Use the **get-psprovider** cmdlet to see the providers installed on a system, as shown in **Figure 4-13.**

Each provider has a shortcut to access its environment. In the output for the **get-psprovider** cmdlet, the Drives column indicates the shortcut for each provider. For example, enter either cd hklm: or cd hkcu: to access the registry. Enter c: to access the file system, which is the default provider.

Regardless of provider, use the **get-childitem** cmdlet to list the items. This cmdlet is similar to the command prompt **DIR** command. Notice in the example in **Figure 4-14,** the date listed is the LastWriteTime. However, more data on each file are tracked than are displayed. To see additional properties, enter:

```
get-childitem | get-member
```

You can now query and view this information as well. For example, suppose you want to see the files in the order they were last accessed (opened). That date may be different from the last time the file was saved. Enter get-childitem | sort-object lastaccesstime to see this output. The results can be limited by using the -include switch. The -exclude switch removes items from the results.

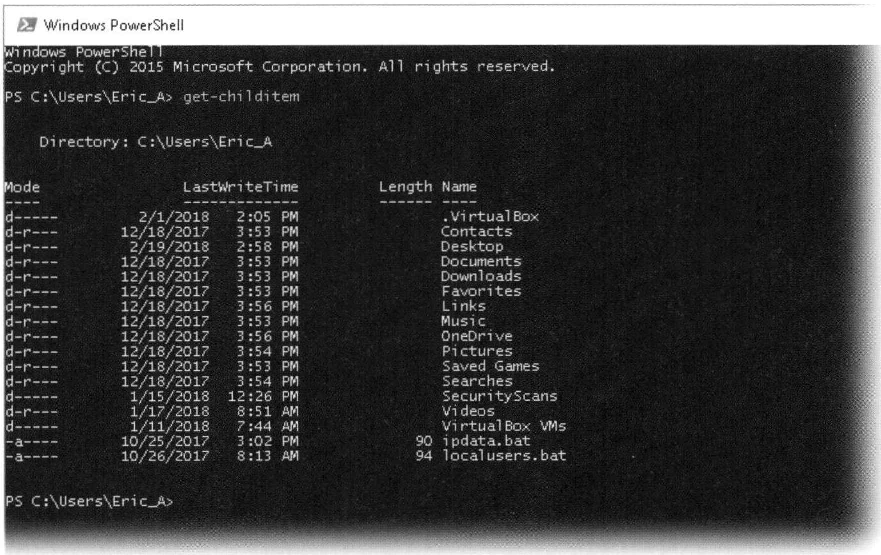

Goodheart-Willcox Publisher

Figure 4-14. Listing the items in the default environment using the **get-childitem** cmdlet.

Obtaining the computer's IP address from PowerShell is easy. The **get-netipaddress** cmdlet provides this information. To see the information presented in a column format, combine the cmdlet with the **format-table** cmdlet.

The **get-wmiobject** cmdlet provides information about hardware installed in the computer. *Windows Management Instrumentation (WMI)* is the infrastructure in Windows for managing data and operations. When using this cmdlet, a class must be specified for the search. WMI classes represent the resources that can be managed. For example, entering get-wmiobject win32_bios returns attributes of the system's basic input/output system (BIOS). **Figure 4-15** shows additional WMI object data.

Even with filtering, you may still retrieve more information than desired or needed. You can further filter objects according to specifications you set. For example, suppose you want to view only those services that are stopped. You can sort by stopped services, but it is easier to view only stopped services. This can be done with the **where_object** cmdlet. The **where_object** cmdlet analyzes each object in a list based on a condition. The specified condition must be enclosed in curly brackets. For example, enter get-service | where-object {$_.status -eq "stopped"} to show only services whose status equals stopped. In this command string, $_. is a variable representing the current object being processed. The variable is the property of that object. In this example, the property is status. **Figure 4-16** shows additional operators that can be used to test conditions.

Class	Meaning
win32_computersystem	Properties related to a computer running Windows
win32_environment	System environmental variables
win32_logicaldisk	Storage device on a system
win32_networkadapter	Network adapter installed
win32_networkadapterconfiguration	Configuration of a network adapter
get-help get-wmiobject –examples	Provides help examples for the cmdlet

Figure 4-15. These are some of the options for WMI object data that can be used with the **get-wmiobject** cmdlet.

Operator	Meaning
-contains	Contains
-eq	Equal to
-ge	Greater than or equal to
-gt	Greater than
-le	Less than or equal to
-lt	Less than
-match	Matches using regular expressions
-ne	Not equal to
-notcontains	Does not contain
-notmatch	Negated matching using regular expressions

Figure 4-16. These operators can be used to test conditions for the **where_object** cmdlet.

Suppose you need to find all Google services that are running. Enter the following.

get-service | where-object {$_.displayname –match "goog"}

The resulting list includes any service from Google that is currently running on the system. Notice you do not need to enter the full name for Google. This can help if a service happens to use an abbreviated name.

PowerShell also provides an easy way to send the data output to a file or HTML format. The data can be stored in comma separated value (CSV) format, converted to HTML, or saved in a plain text file. There are three different cmdlets to do this. For example, to send the output from the **get-service** cmdlet to a file:

- get-service | export-csv *filename*.csv
- get-service | convertto-html >*filename*.html
- get-service | out-file *filename*.txt

Quick Look 4.2.3

Advanced PowerShell Cmdlet Options

PowerShell has many useful commands, or cmdlets. Many of these cmdlets have options that can extend the usefulness of the command.

1. Click **Start>All apps>Windows PowerShell>Windows PowerShell** (**Start>All Programs>Accessories>Windows PowerShell>Windows PowerShell** in Windows 7).

2. Run the **get-childitem** cmdlet to see all files starting with T, but excluding those with a .dll file extension:

    get-childitem c:\windows\t*.* -exclude *.dll

3. View the items in the Windows folder in order by file size:

    get-childitem c:\windows*.* | sort-object length

4. View the installed printers in a column list:

    get-wmiobject win32_printer | format-table

5. Export the list of all processes to an HTML view:

    get-process | convertto-html >process.htm

6. Open the HTML file in the default web browser:

    invoke-item process.htm

7. List all files in the Windows folder greater than 20,000 bytes in size and sorted by name:

    get-childitem c:\windows | where-object {$_.length –gt 20000} | sort-object {$_.name}

Case Study

PowerShell ISE

Learning PowerShell can be challenging. Microsoft introduced the PowerShell Integrated Scripting Environment (ISE) to allow someone to work in and learn PowerShell using a graphical user environment. The Windows PowerShell ISE application is located in the **Start** menu in the same place as the Windows PowerShell application. Open the PowerShell ISE application, and look at the different modules. The prompt is at the bottom, and output appears in the middle. The top is used for writing a script. Practice running different commands. Write a one- to two-page summary on the features of the ISE. Describe the benefits of the ISE environment. Explain how it can be used to learn PowerShell, create scripts, and simply find and run commands. Include screenshots to illustrate any key points.

PowerShell Scripts

PowerShell does not use batch files. Instead, commands can be placed into scripts, which are similar to batch files. A *script* is a listing of PowerShell commands and options that will be processed in order. Scripts can be more powerful than batch files due to the advanced use of cmdlets and their methods. As with batch files, creating a script does not require knowledge of any special programming language. There are other commands that can be used as well to request input or provide output.

Scripts can be created using Notepad or any plain-text editor. Scripts in PowerShell have a .ps1 file extension. Make sure to change the file extension to this when saving the file. To run a script, enter ./ and the name of the script. If the script is not in the current directory, the complete path to the script file must be entered.

The PowerShell environment may need to be configured to allow running of scripts. To determine the current status, use the **get-executionpolicy** cmdlet. This cmdlet will report the current policy for the system. The four policies are:

- restricted (no scripts can be run);
- all signed (only scripts signed by a publisher can be run);
- remote signed (downloaded scripts must be signed by a trusted publisher); and
- unrestricted (no restrictions, all PowerShell scripts will run).

The **set-executionpolicy** cmdlet is used to change the policy. For example, set-executionpolicy allsigned will change to that policy. Before the policy is changed, you are prompted to accept or reject the change, as shown in **Figure 4-17.**

Figure 4-17. The policy may need to be changed to allow scripts to be run. You will be prompted to accept or reject the change.

Quick Look 4.2.4

PowerShell Scripts

PowerShell scripts are similar to batch files. They are created in a plain-text editor and saved with a .ps1 file extension.

1. Launch Notepad or any plain-text editor.
2. Save the file as RunningServices.ps1 in your personal Users folder.
3. Enter the following in the script file. The pound sign or hash tag (#) is used in a script file to indicate a comment. Anything after the pound sign is not executed.

   #This is my script -- *your name*
   #To insert some blank lines on the screen add empty quotation marks ""
   #To insert text on the screen, place the text between quotation marks
   ""

   "Open Running Services--Report generated on " + (get-date)
   ""

   get-service | where-object {$_.status -eq "running"}
4. Save the file, and exit Notepad.

Quick Look 4.2.4 Continued

5. Applying what you have learned, launch PowerShell and run it as an administrator.

6. Applying what you have learned, change to your personal Users folder where the RunningServices.ps1 script file is saved.

7. Enter .\runningservices to run the script, as shown. Note: if you receive an error that runningservices is not a recognized cmdlet, it is likely the policy needs to be changed to allow scripts to run.

8. Enter set-executionpolicy unrestricted, and confirm you want to change the policy.

9. Enter .\runningservices, and the script should now run.

10. Enter set-executionpolicy restricted, and confirm you want to change the policy. This returns the system to the safer policy for scripts.

SECTION REVIEW 4.2

Check Your Understanding

1. How is the syntax of a PowerShell cmdlet constructed?

2. When a command line or Linux command is run in PowerShell, what type of command is it?

3. How would you get additional help for the **get-process** cmdlet?

4. Which cmdlet displays the properties and methods of an object?

5. What is the file extension for saved PowerShell scripts?

Build Your Key Terms Vocabulary

As you progress through this course, develop a personal cybersecurity glossary. This will help you build your vocabulary and prepare you for a career. Write a definition for each of the following terms, and add it to your cybersecurity glossary.

alias	provider
cmdlets	script
object	Windows Management
piping	Instrumentation (WMI)

Introduction to Linux

Most desktop and laptop personal computers use either the Windows operating system or Mac OS. However, a great deal of network servers are actually running a Linux distribution, including many web servers. The Linux operating system is a very versatile and powerful operating system that is the choice of many IT departments. Linux is also open-source, which allows it to be freely modified. This offers a great deal of flexibility for customized Linux environments. It is important for security technicians to have a fundamental understanding of working with the Linux shell. Some versions of Linux were created with built-in hacking tools, and many hackers find that Linux is an easier platform for launching attacks.

Key Terms 🔗

command-language interpreter (CLI)

distro

forked

free and open source software (FOSS)

hard link

home directory

inode number

Linux

man page

symbolic link

Learning Goals

- Describe the Linux operating system.
- Compare and contrast the Linux shell to the Windows command line.
- Use Linux commands.
- Explain how to view command help in Linux.

Linux Overview

Linux is an open-source computer operating system that is derived from the UNIX operating system, as shown in **Figure 4-18.** UNIX was developed by AT&T Bell Labs in the 1970s. UNIX underwent changes and was forked. *Forked* means that people have modified a program to create a new development branch that is a separate program. Free and open-source software can be legally forked without

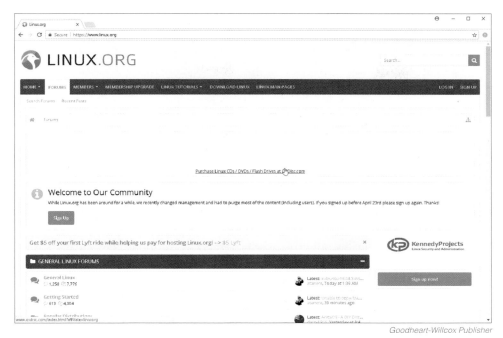

Figure 4-18. Linux is an open-source operating system. It is free to use and modify.

permission. *Free and open source software (FOSS)* is software whose source code is not locked and can be modified by anyone.

UNIX is a trademarked name and the software is proprietary. The Open Group holds the trademark and manages it for the industries that use UNIX. However, the source code has been forked into many branches. One of these branches is Linux.

Linux was originally created principally by Linus Torvalds. It is licensed under the GNU project. The GNU project, which is sponsored by the Free Software Foundation, was created to give computer users freedom in development and use of software. Users can freely run GNU software, share it, study and review its code, and even modify it. Releasing Linux under the GNU General Public License has allowed others to adapt it to their own versions or flavors of Linux.

A *distro,* or distribution, is a specific version of Linux. A distro typically includes a Linux kernel, which is the core operating system; tools and libraries licensed under GNU; and a package-management system. The package-management system is a collection of software tools for various functions. These functions include using, installing, configuring, and removing application programs on the Linux operating system.

There are hundreds of Linux distros available today. Some are commercial. Many are for special purposes, such for power users, home users, or by hardware or services. Hardware or service applications include distros for laptops, gaming, servers, routing, and hacking.

Linux Shell

With many distros available for Linux, the graphic user interface (GUI) can vary from one to another. However, the command line interface (CLI) provides a common interface. It offers an efficient way in which to manage the operating system.

In Linux, the command line environment is called the shell. The shell is a *command-language interpreter (CLI)* that executes the commands from direct keyboard entry or a program. Through the shell, a user can interact with the operating system. The Bash shell (Bourne-Again Shell) is the most popular shell.

FYI

In 1996, Linus Torvalds announced there would be a mascot for Linux. The mascot is a penguin named Tux. The name was suggested by a friend based on *Torvald's UNIX.*

FYI

The name Bash is a play on the name of the shell it replaced, which was called the Bourne shell.

```
login as: pi
pi@10.0.0.10's password:
Linux raspberrypi 4.9.41-v7+ #1023 SMP Tue Aug 8 16:00:15 BST 2017 armv7l

The programs included with the Debian GNU/Linux system are free software;
the exact distribution terms for each program are described in the
individual files in /usr/share/doc/*/copyright.

Debian GNU/Linux comes with ABSOLUTELY NO WARRANTY, to the extent
permitted by applicable law.
Last login: Sat Sep 30 13:58:19 2017 from 10.0.0.6

SSH is enabled and the default password for the 'pi' user has not been changed.
This is a security risk - please login as the 'pi' user and type 'passwd' to set
 a new password.

pi@raspberrypi:~ $
pi@raspberrypi:~ $ su
Password:
root@raspberrypi:/home/pi#
```

Regular user —
Super user —

Figure 4-19. The command-line prompt in Linux indicates how the user is logged in. A dollar sign means a regular user, while a pound sign means a super user.

To see what shell you are running, enter: echo $SHELL. The command returns a dollar sign or a pound sign, which indicates how you are logged in.

In Linux, directories are separated with the forward slash (/), not the backslash (\).

It is freeware developed by the Free Software Foundation and released under the GNU license. It is found in most Linux distros.

Typically, the command-line prompt reflects your login name and a symbol. The symbol be will either a pound sign (#) or a dollar sign ($). When the symbol is #, it reflects you are logged in as a super user with root privileges ({root}), as shown in **Figure 4-19.** Some commands may only be run in this mode. When the symbol is $, you are logged in as a regular user.

Linux Commands

When you first log in to Linux, the working directory is set to your home directory. A *home directory* is where you store your personal files. Most home directories will have the path /home/*UserName*. You can see this by entering the **pwd** command, as shown in **Figure 4-20.** Unlike the Windows shell, the shell interface in Linux *is* case-sensitive. The **pwd** command stands for print working directory. Despite the name looking similar to *password,* it has nothing to do with passwords!

The **cd** command (change directory) does just what it implies, changes the current directory where you are located. Do not forget about case sensitivity of commands, and put a space after the command and before the directory name.

```
login as: pi
pi@10.0.0.10's password:
Linux raspberrypi 4.9.41-v7+ #1023 SMP Tue Aug 8 16:00:15 BST 2017 armv7l

The programs included with the Debian GNU/Linux system are free software;
the exact distribution terms for each program are described in the
individual files in /usr/share/doc/*/copyright.

Debian GNU/Linux comes with ABSOLUTELY NO WARRANTY, to the extent
permitted by applicable law.
Last login: Fri Sep 15 14:42:11 2017 from 10.0.0.6

SSH is enabled and the default password for the 'pi' user has not been changed.
This is a security risk - please login as the 'pi' user and type 'passwd' to set
 a new password.

pi@raspberrypi:~ $ pwd
/home/pi
pi@raspberrypi:~ $
```

Figure 4-20. The home directory in Linux is usually /home/*UserName*.

Command	Description
cd ..	Navigates to the parent directory
cd /	Changes to the root folder
cd ~	Changes to the root of your home directory
rm	Removes files or directories
mkdir	Makes or creates a new directory
cp	Copies files from one location to another
mv	Moves or renames a file
echo	Sends information back to the screen
clear	Clears the screen of all information

Goodheart-Willcox Publisher

Figure 4-21. Options for using the **cd** command as well as other useful Linux commands.

For example, cd /Documents will change from the current directory to the subdirectory named Documents. Other examples of using the **cd** command as well as other basic commands are shown in **Figure 4-21.**

Viewing Files and Directories

To view the files in a directory, enter the **ls** command, as shown in **Figure 4-22.** The command **ls** is short for *list.* In this example, the directories are shown in blue. This makes it easier to distinguish directories from files. The real power of the **ls** command, as with many CLI commands, is adding switches to increase functionality.

When you run the **ls** command, it may not be obvious what the information represents, as shown in **Figure 4-23.** At the top of the list is the total number of files in this directory. The first character in an individual file or folder listing specifies the type of the file. A hyphen (-) means it is a normal file. A D means it is a directory. An S means it is a socket file. An L means it is a link file.

The next nine characters are Field 1. This specifies the file permissions. Permissions are discussed in detail later. The character after Field 1 is Field 2. This field indicates how many links to the file exist. After Field 2 is Field 3. This is the

```
login as: pi
pi@10.0.0.10's password:
Linux raspberrypi 4.9.41-v7+ #1023 SMP Tue Aug 8 16:00:15 BST 2017 armv7l

The programs included with the Debian GNU/Linux system are free software;
the exact distribution terms for each program are described in the
individual files in /usr/share/doc/*/copyright.

Debian GNU/Linux comes with ABSOLUTELY NO WARRANTY, to the extent
permitted by applicable law.
Last login: Fri Sep 15 15:09:26 2017 from 10.0.0.6

SSH is enabled and the default password for the 'pi' user has not been changed.
This is a security risk - please login as the 'pi' user and type 'passwd' to set
 a new password.

pi@raspberrypi:~ $ pwd
/home/pi
pi@raspberrypi:~ $ ls
Desktop    Downloads  Pictures  python_games  Videos
Documents  Music      Public    Templates
pi@raspberrypi:~ $
```

Goodheart-Willcox Publisher

Figure 4-22. The **ls** command in Linux lists the files and folders within a directory.

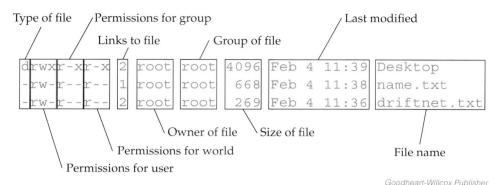

Type of file   Permissions for group   Links to file   Group of file   Last modified

Owner of file   Size of file   File name

Permissions for world

Permissions for user

Figure 4-23. The meaning of the information returned by the **ls** command.

owner of the file. In this example, the owner of the file is root. Field 4 specifies the group of the file. In the above example, the group is also called root. Field 5 is the size of the file. Field 6 is the date and time when the file was last modified. Field 7 is the last column. This is the actual name of the file.

Ethical Issue

Hacking Distro

There are many "hacking distros" of Linux, including Kali and Blackbox. Both of these distros are intended for security testing and maintenance. You have proposed to your IT manager that a hacking distro be installed on your computer in a virtual interface. The manager asks you to explain what the hacking distro would be used for and the tools it would contain. You must identify which hacking distro you would install and what capabilities it has. You must also justify why it is ethical for you to use this at work, even if it is running in an isolated environment. How will you convince the manager using a hacking distro is ethical and that it will not compromise the security of the company network?

Quick Look 4.3.1

Linux Commands and Switches

As with Windows command-line commands, many Linux commands have switches. To be proficient in using Linux, it is important to know how to use command switches.

1. As directed by your instructor, launch Linux and access the shell.
2. Are you logged in as a super user or regular user? How can you tell?

Quick Look 4.3.1 Continued

3. Enter the **pwd** command. What is your home directory?
4. Change to the etc directory by entering: cd /etc.
5. Enter ls -lh, as shown. The H stands for *human readable format*.

```
drwxr-xr-x   2 root root    4.0K Jan 18  2017 rsyslog.d
-rw-r--r--   1 root root     12K Aug 19  2015 RTIMULib.ini
drwxr-xr-x   2 root root    4.0K Sep  7 15:00 samba
-rw-r--r--   1 root root    4.1K May 17 11:59 securetty
drwxr-xr-x   4 root root    4.0K Sep  7 14:55 security
drwxr-xr-x   2 root root    4.0K Sep  7 14:46 selinux
-rw-r--r--   1 root root     11K Apr  5 20:07 sensors3.conf
drwxr-xr-x   2 root root    4.0K Sep  7 15:24 sensors.d
-rw-r--r--   1 root root     19K Dec 26  2016 services
drwxr-xr-x   2 root root    4.0K Sep  7 15:08 sgml
-rw-r-----   1 root shadow   940 Sep  7 15:37 shadow
-rw-r--r--   1 root root      73 Sep  7 14:47 shells
drwxr-xr-x   2 root root    4.0K Sep  7 14:59 skel
drwxr-xr-x   2 root root    4.0K Sep  7 16:12 ssh
drwxr-xr-x   4 root root    4.0K Sep  7 15:06 ssl
-rw-r--r--   1 root root     771 Jul 27 22:17 staff-group-for-usr-local
-rw-r--r--   1 root root      16 Sep  7 14:59 subgid
-rw-------   1 root root       0 Sep  7 14:47 subgid-
-rw-r--r--   1 root root      16 Sep  7 14:59 subuid
-rw-------   1 root root       0 Sep  7 14:47 subuid-
-r--r-----   1 root root     669 Jun  5 12:22 sudoers
drwxr-xr-x   2 root root    4.0K Sep  7 15:05 sudoers.d
-rw-r--r--   1 root root    2.7K Sep  7 15:05 sysctl.conf
drwxr-xr-x   2 root root    4.0K Sep  7 15:05 sysctl.d
drwxr-xr-x   5 root root    4.0K Sep  7 14:47 systemd
drwxr-xr-x   2 root root    4.0K Sep  7 14:46 terminfo
-rw-r--r--   1 root root       8 Sep  7 14:47 timezone
drwxr-xr-x   2 root root    4.0K Sep  7 15:30 timidity
drwxr-xr-x   2 root root    4.0K Jul  5 20:31 tmpfiles.d
drwxr-xr-x   3 root root    4.0K Sep  7 14:59 triggerhappy
-rw-r--r--   1 root root    1.3K Mar 16  2016 ucf.conf
drwxr-xr-x   4 root root    4.0K Sep  7 14:47 udev
drwxr-xr-x   2 root root    4.0K Nov 25  2016 udisks2
drwxr-xr-x   3 root root    4.0K Sep  7 15:02 ufw
drwxr-xr-x   2 root root    4.0K Sep  7 14:46 update-motd.d
-rw-r--r--   1 root root    1018 Jan 23  2017 usb_modeswitch.conf
drwxr-xr-x   2 root root    4.0K Jan 23  2017 usb_modeswitch.d
-rw-r--r--   1 root root      51 Jan 13  2017 vdpau_wrapper.cfg
drwxr-xr-x   2 root root    4.0K Sep  7 14:53 vim
drwxr-xr-x   3 root root    4.0K Sep  7 15:30 vnc
-rw-r--r--   1 root root    4.9K Mar 18 14:12 wgetrc
drwxr-xr-x   2 root root    4.0K Sep  7 15:24 wildmidi
drwxr-xr-x   2 root root    4.0K Sep  7 15:13 wpa_supplicant
drwxr-xr-x  11 root root    4.0K Sep  7 15:29 X11
drwxr-xr-x  10 root root    4.0K Sep  7 15:24 xdg
drwxr-xr-x   2 root root    4.0K Sep  7 15:08 xml
drwxr-xr-x   2 root root    4.0K Sep  7 15:24 xpdf
pi@raspberrypi:/etc $
```

6. Enter ls -lt. This lists the directory by modified time.
7. Enter ls -ltr. Adding r to the end of the switch reverses the order. Notice the differences in the directory listing.
8. Enter ls -R. Remember, commands are case sensitive, so be sure to enter an uppercase R. This command switch allows you to search the current directory and all others recursively. Recursively in this case means it will search the current directory and all subdirectories.

Links

When a file is created, you name it. At the same time, a unique number called an inode number is assigned by the operating system. An *inode number* corresponds to the location of the file's contents (the data in the file). The file name *links* to the inode number.

Links allow you to work with just a single file, but have access via different files. If you change the data in a file, the change will be reflected in both the original file and the linked file. There are two types of links: hard links and symbolic links, as shown in **Figure 4-24.** A *hard link* points directly to the original data. This allows you to point to a single file instead of creating multiple ones. A *symbolic link* is one made to *another* link, not directly to the original data. The primary difference between a hard link and soft link is that with a hard link, the data must be on the same file system and partition. A symbolic link does not have that restriction.

In Linux, the **ln** command is used to create both type of links. To create a hard link, simply enter ln *file1 file2*. To create a symbolic link, add the -s switch. The syntax for a symbolic link is ln -s *file1 file2*. Be aware, however, if you delete the original data file, the link is broken. If you try to view the contents via the symbolic link, you will receive an error. This is because the link is trying to reference the data in the originally linked file.

Linux Help and Command Execution Options

Most Linux commands can provide help on the command and its switches. Add the **--help** switch to display help. For example, ls --help will provide help on the **ls** command. This switch also provides the syntax or usage information of the command. Linux also contains some built-in commands. To view additional help on a shell's built-in commands, enter the **help** command followed by the name of the shell command.

Many executable programs also include a formal piece of documentation called a manual, or *man page.* You can view this documentation using the **man** command, as shown in **Figure 4-25.** In this example, the man page for the **ping** command is displayed. To exit or quit the man page, press the [Q] key.

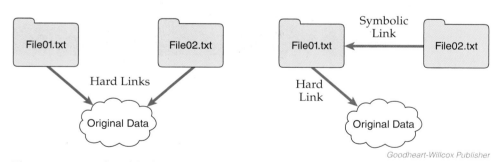

Goodheart-Willcox Publisher

Figure 4-24. A hard link is direct to the original data, while a symbolic link points to another link.

```
PING(8)              System Manager's Manual: iputils              PING(8)

NAME
      ping - send ICMP ECHO_REQUEST to network hosts

SYNOPSIS
      ping [-aAbBdDfhLnOqrRUvV46] [-c count] [-F flowlabel] [-i interval] [-I
      interface] [-l preload] [-m mark] [-M pmtudisc option] [-N node
      info option] [-w deadline] [-W timeout] [-p pattern] [-Q tos] [-s pack
      etsize] [-S sndbuf] [-t ttl] [-T timestamp option] [hop ...] destina
      tion

DESCRIPTION
      ping uses the ICMP protocol's mandatory ECHO_REQUEST datagram to elicit
      an ICMP ECHO_RESPONSE from a host or gateway.   ECHO_REQUEST datagrams
      (``pings'') have an IP and ICMP header, followed by a struct timeval
      and then an arbitrary number of ``pad'' bytes used to fill out the
      packet.

      ping works with both IPv4 and IPv6. Using only one of them explicitly
      can be enforced by specifying -4 or -6.

      ping can also send IPv6 Node Information Queries (RFC4620).  Intermedi
      ate hops may not be allowed, because IPv6 source routing was deprecated
      (RFC5095).

OPTIONS
      -4     Use IPv4 only.

      -6     Use IPv6 only.

      -a     Audible ping.

      -A     Adaptive ping. Interpacket interval adapts to round-trip time,
             so that effectively not more than one (or more, if preload is
             set) unanswered probe is present in the network. Minimal inter
             val is 200msec for not super-user.  On networks with low rtt
             this mode is essentially equivalent to flood mode.

      -b     Allow pinging a broadcast address.

      -B     Do not allow ping to change source address of probes.   The
             address is bound to one selected when ping starts.

      -c count
             Stop after sending count ECHO_REQUEST packets. With deadline
             option, ping waits for count ECHO_REPLY packets, until the time
Manual page ping(8) line 1 (press h for help or q to quit)
```

Figure 4-25. A man page is documentation on an executable program.

Quick Look 4.3.2

Linux Command Help

The help system in Linux can assist in learning how to use commands. Access help to see a description of the command and its available switches.

1. Launch Linux, and access the shell.
2. Enter the **clear** command to clean the screen display.
3. Enter cd / to navigate to the root directory.
4. Enter ls --help to view the help screen for the **ls** command.
5. Try running the **ls** command with the **-x** switch and then with the **-X** switch. What is the difference between the two switches? Look carefully at the output to see the difference.
6. Enter cd ~, and then enter pwd. What is the working directory?
7. Applying what you have learned, display help for the **rm** command. What is the command to use to remove empty directories?

Piping

The pipe symbol is used in Linux the same way as at the Windows command or PowerShell prompt. The symbol tells Linux to send the output of one command to another command. For example, entering ls | nl first creates a list using the **ls** command, and then sends the list to the **nl** command to create a numbered list.

The **head** and **tail** commands can be used to limit the view of the output. The **head** command displays the first part of a file. The **tail** command displays the last part of a file. The **-n** switch for either command is used to specify the number of lines to display. If you do not specify a number, the command will display ten lines. The **head** and **tail** commands are useful when a list is piped to them. This shortens the list display, as shown in **Figure 4-26.**

Output can be piped to multiple commands. Each subsequent command takes its output from the previously run command. For example, you can create a list of commands, shorten it to the first ten, and then number the list:

ls | head | nl

Grep

What is grep? The **grep** command is a utility for searching for plain-text data. It is useful for printing the lines from a file or input stream that match an expression. In this example, all files in the /passwd subdirectory in the /etc directory that contain the word Linda are listed:

grep Linda /etc/passwd

Data can also be piped to the **grep** command. The following example shows how to return specific information from the **ipconfig** command. Only the lines in the output of the **ifconfig** command that contain the string 192 will be returned:

ifconfig | grep 192

Viewing Running Processes

FYI

Just for fun: the **cal** command displays calendar information. Check out additional options with **cal -help**!

A process, or running program, can be viewed with the **ps** command. Each process has a unique identifier called a processor ID (PID), as shown in **Figure 4-27.** On a server, it is helpful to see who is running the processes. Add the **–u** switch to see that information. Also, remember, the **grep** command can be used to look for keywords. For example, ps | grep bash will look for any process that contains the string bash. The **top** command is even more detailed. It will run until you press the [Q] key to end the command.

Goodheart-Willcox Publisher

Figure 4-26. The **tail** command can be used to shorten a list to only a specified number of items at the end of the list.

Figure 4-27. Listing the processes that are running in Linux with the **ps** command.

SECTION REVIEW 4.3

Check Your Understanding

1. Different versions of Linux are referred to as what?
2. On a Linux system, how can you determine if you are logged in with super user rights?
3. What is the purpose of the **cd ~** command in Linux?
4. Creating a hard link to a file is done with which Linux command?
5. What you would enter in Linux to search the text output of the **ifconfig** command for the word "Link"?

Build Your Key Terms Vocabulary

As you progress through this course, develop a personal cybersecurity glossary. This will help you build your vocabulary and prepare you for a career. Write a definition for each of the following terms, and add it to your cybersecurity glossary.

command-language interpreter (CLI)   home directory

distro   inode number

forked   Linux

free and open source software (FOSS)   man page

hard link   symbolic link

Review and Assessment

Summary

Section 4.1 Windows Command Prompt

- Windows offers the command prompt for manually entering commands to manage files, processes, and many other aspects of the operating system.
- Batch files are a way to automate tasks using the Windows command prompt by combining several commands into a single script.
- Command output can be directed to a file or the system clipboard instead of the screen, and the command prompt window can be customized to suit your preferences.

Section 4.2 Windows PowerShell

- PowerShell is an object-based command line shell for Windows that can be used to manage the system.
- Advanced PowerShell command options can be used to manage networking, security, Hyper-V virtualization, and the Active Directory.
- PowerShell uses scripts to automate tasks, similar to batch files for the command prompt.

Section 4.3 Introduction to Linux

- Linux is an open-source operating system that was forked, or modified, from the Unix operating system and is available in many different distros.
- The Linux shell is the command line environment, and the Bash shell is the most popular version.
- Linux commands are case-sensitive, and most have switches to provide expanded options.
- Help is available for Linux commands through a command itself or on a man page displayed with the **man** command.

Check Your Cybersecurity IQ ↗

Now that you have completed this chapter, see what you have learned about cybersecurity by visiting the student companion website (www.g-wlearning.com) and taking the chapter posttest.

Review Questions ↗

For each question, select the answer that is the best response.

1. You are searching for a specific Excel file you believe contains proprietary company information. Which of the following Windows command prompt entries will assist in locating all Excel files on the computer?
   A. find *.xlsx /s
   B. dir *.xlsx /s
   C. locate *.xlsx /s
   D. dir *.xlsx /more

2. A directory contains a number of PDF files that need to be deleted. Which Windows command prompt entry will remove all PDF files from the current directory?
   A. remove *.pdf
   B. delete *.pdf
   C. erase *.pdf
   D. del *.pdf

3. When using the Windows command prompt, which of the following entries will direct the output to an existing file named results.txt?
   A. ipconfig /output results.txt
   B. ipconfig > results.txt
   C. ipconfig >>results.txt
   D. ipconfig /results.txt

4. Which of the following is a PowerShell cmdlet?
   A. getservice
   B. get-service
   C. get_service
   D. services-get

5. Using PowerShell, you need to create a list of all files in a directory with a name that begins with the letter D, and you want to save the list in a file named discovery.txt. What is the correct entry for doing this?
   A. get-childitem d*.*
   B. get-childitem d*.* > discovery.txt
   C. get-childitem d*.* | out-file discovery.txt
   D. get-childitem d*.* | export discovery.txt

6. The Linux shell entry ls | lh | nl returns an error. What is the correct command entry?
   A. ls -lh -nl
   B. ls -lh | nl
   C. ls -lh | Nl
   D. ls -Lh | Nl

7. To find additional syntax parameters for the Linux **mv** command, enter:
   A. mv --help
   B. mv /?
   C. help mv
   D. mv -h

8. You need to determine which program is using the majority of the CPU time on the computer. Which Linux command is best suited for this task?
   A. **grep**
   B. **cal**
   C. **echo**
   D. **ps**

9. Which of the following is a false statement?
   A. Linux commands are case sensitive.
   B. Windows command prompt commands are not case-sensitive, but PowerShell cmdlets are.
   C. PowerShell can be installed on Linux.
   D. PowerShell aliases include Linux commands along with command-prompt commands.

10. Which of the following is a true statement?
   A. PowerShell scripts can automate repetitive tasks.
   B. PowerShell scripts can only be run by administrators.
   C. Batch files run on the Windows command prompt can only contain one command.
   D. Linux commands are not case-sensitive.

Application and Extension of Knowledge

1. The command prompt **FINDSTR** command is similar to the Linux **grep** command. Use the help feature of the **FINDSTR** command to investigate how to use the command. Then, run the **IPCONFIG** command and pipe it to the **FINDSTR** command to view all IP addresses that start with 192. If you are not using a 192.168 IP address, change the first octet to match your configuration.

2. Research the **start-transcript** and **stop-transcript** cmdlets in PowerShell. Practice running these cmdlets while using other cmdlets. Write a one-page summary of the benefits of these cmdlets. Submit your summary to your teacher, and include the text file output generated by the transcript cmdlets.

3. Practice some of the features of the **get-random** cmdlet in PowerShell. Obtain a random number between 1 and 100; retrieve four random numbers between 10 and 50; input four of your friend's names and randomly select one. Summarize your commands in a document.

4. Investigate these system commands in Linux: **uptime**, **last**, **free**, and **du -h**. What information does each provide? Try each of the commands. Pipe the **du -h** command to the **more** command. Summarize how each command is used, one paragraph per command.

5. Ubuntu is a popular distro for Linux. Canonical, Ubuntu's parent company, has created other "flavors" of Ubuntu, such as Kbuntu. Research some of these flavors. Create a presentation illustrating two other flavors. Include why you might consider using them. Be prepared to give the presentation to the class.

Research Project
Linux Distros

There are hundreds of special-purpose Linux distros available. This project will let you become acquainted with some of them. Pick one of these categories to research:
- distros for laptops
- distros for gaming
- distros for novice Linux users
- distros for education
- distros for experienced Linux users

Identify the available distros for the selected category. Examine the purpose and benefits of each distro. Determine which distro you believe is the best in the category. Be sure to develop reasons for your recommendation.

Deliverables. Create a presentation summarizing three different distributions in the category you selected. Provide relevant details of the distro, including screenshots, features, logo, and where the distro can be downloaded. Identify the distro you recommend for the category. Provide your justification for choosing this distro. Include references to indicate the sources of the information used for your research. Ensure your presentation is professional, engaging, and free of grammatical and spelling errors.

Online Activities

Complete the following activities, which will help you learn, practice, and expand your knowledge and skills.

Vocabulary. Practice vocabulary for this chapter using the e-flash cards, matching activity, and vocabulary game until you are able to recognize their meanings.

Communication Skills

College and Career Readiness

Reading. When engaging in active reading, it is important to evaluate the material as you read it. Evaluation after reading often occurs naturally without the reader realizing it. Read this chapter, and evaluate the information as you read. Note the questions and comments you think about as you read.

Writing. Create a Venn diagram to show the relationship between the Windows command prompt and PowerShell. Where do the circles overlap? What do you think this overlap signifies? Write arguments to support your claims about what the overlap signifies. Use valid reasoning and sufficient evidence in your arguments.

Speaking. It is important to be prepared when you are speaking to an individual or a larger audience. Style and content influence how the listener understands your message. Create a short presentation about Windows PowerShell. Make use of visuals or demonstrations to enhance the presentation. Adjust your presentation length to fit the attention of the audience.

Listening. Formal listening situations, such as an audience member listening to a speech, require active listening. Attend a meeting where a speaker is making a formal presentation, such as your principal addressing the student body. Describe the line of reasoning, organization, development, and style the speaker used to prepare his or her information. Identify the target audience and purpose of the speech. Analyze the effectiveness of the presentation.

Portfolio Development

College and Career Readiness

Hard Copy Organization. As you collect material for your portfolio, you will need an effective strategy to keep the items clean, safe, and organized for assembly at the appropriate time. Structure and organization are important when working on an ongoing project that includes multiple pieces. A large manila envelope works well to keep hardcopies of documents, photos, awards, and other items. A three-ring binder with sleeves is another good way to store your materials.

Plan to keep similar items together and label the categories. For example, store sample documents that illustrate your writing or technology skills together. Use notes clipped to the documents to identify each item and state why it is included in the portfolio. For example, a note might say, "Newsletter with article about computer-skills contest."

1. Select a method for storing hardcopy items you will be collecting.

2. Create a master spreadsheet to use as a tracking tool for the components of your portfolio. You may list each document alphabetically, by category, by date, or use another convention that helps you keep track of each document that you are including.

3. Record the name of each item and the date that you stored it.

CTSO Event Prep

Teamwork. Some competitive events for career and technical student organizations (CTSOs) have a teamwork component. If it is a team event, it is important that the competing team prepare to operate as a cohesive unit. To prepare for teamwork activities, complete the following activities.

1. Review the rules to confirm whether questions will be asked or if the team will need to defend a case or situation.

2. Locate a rubric or scoring sheet for the event on your organization's website to see how the team will be judged.

3. Confirm whether visual aids may be used in the presentation and the amount of setup time permitted.

4. Make notes on index cards about important points to remember. Team members should exchange note cards so that each member evaluates the other person's notes. Use these notes to study. You may also be able to use these notes during the event.

5. Assign each team member a role for the presentation. Practice performing as a team. Each team member should introduce himself or herself, review the case, make suggestions for the case, and conclude with a summary.

6. Ask your instructor to play the role of competition judge as your team reviews the case. After the presentation is complete, ask for feedback from your instructor. You may also consider having a student audience to listen and give feedback.

Chapter 5

Controlling Physical Environments and User Actions

Hackers remotely accessing systems and targeting organizations are security threats. However, companies must also address the potential risks that come with individuals who can physically access equipment such as routers, switches, and servers. These risks come from a business's own employees, but also from other individuals, such as vendors, who have access to a business. Not all vulnerabilities to a business come from people. Many risks are environmental, such as heat, storms, fire, or floods. Regardless of the type of vulnerability, security professionals must ensure that data are protected. Following the principles of confidentiality, integrity, and availability remains the highest priority.

Technical and physical controls must be put in place to provide security. In addition, security-awareness training for employees is one of the most important elements to cybersecurity. A culture of cybersecurity awareness should be created. Most employees do not realize their actions can play a big role in cybersecurity incidents. According to the 2017 Verizon Data Breach Investigations Report (DBIR), 81 percent of hacking-related breaches involved passwords that were reused, stolen, weak, or able to be cracked. This is an area employees can control when given proper training. Creating a strong password strategy goes hand-in-hand with proper training.

Chapter Preview

While studying, look for the activity icon for:

- Pretests and posttests
- Vocabulary terms with e-flash cards and matching activities
- Self-assessment

*G-W*LEARNING.com

Reading Prep

Before reading this chapter, write the main heading for each section, leaving space under each. As you read the chapter, write three main points you learn related to each heading.

College and Career Readiness

Check Your Cybersecurity IQ ➦

Before you begin this chapter, see what you already know about cybersecurity by visiting the student companion website (www.g-wlearning.com) and taking the chapter pretest.

Certification Objectives

CompTIA Security+

1.2   Compare and contrast types of attacks.

1.6   Explain the impact associated with types of vulnerabilities.

2.3   Given a scenario, troubleshoot common security issues.

3.1   Explain use cases and purpose for frameworks, best practices and secure configuration guides.

3.9   Explain the importance of physical security controls.

5.1   Explain the importance of policies, plans and procedures related to organizational security.

5.7   Compare and contrast various types of controls.

Microsoft Technology Associate (MTA) – Windows Security

1.1   Understand core security principles.

1.2   Understand physical security.

4.2   Understand e-mail protection.

Section 5.1

Business Controls

Essential Question

Why are business controls important to data safety?

Data security extends beyond the 1s and 0s that make up the data. The physical equipment must be protected from damage and theft. There are many areas related to physical security, such as fencing, barricades, and closed-circuit television. Additionally, the signals transmitting the data are a potential source of hacking. Steps must be taken to protect these signals.

Key Terms ☛

bollards
closed-circuit television (CCTV)
electromagnetic radiation (EMR)

EMI shielding
Jersey walls
mantrap

tailgating
TEMPEST
turnstile

Learning Goals

- List the three key goals for planning security measures.
- Describe various measures related to physical security.
- Explain how electromagnetic interference and electromagnetic radiation are security risks.

Types of Controls

When planning security measures, safeguards should be designed that will help with three key goals in mind:
- preventing a problem
- detecting a problem
- recovering from a problem

It is obviously a lot easier to prevent a problem from occurring than to deal with the aftermath of an incident. Controls are the safeguards or countermeasures that can be implemented to detect or reduce the risk by slowing, minimizing, or even stopping a threat. Security controls allow you to organize the different methods and policies you need to create. There are different types of controls, as explained in **Figure 5-1.** As you explore the measures to protect data from physical and environmental access, each will be analyzed against these controls.

Physical Security Controls

There are a number of controls that help prevent physical user access to a facility or sensitive area. These include:

- securing the outside premises and parking areas;
- fencing;
- inside security guards;
- barricades;
- furnishings;
- identification badges;
- CCTV;
- mantraps; and
- turnstiles.

Keep in mind, not every approach can stop all intrusions. A solid strategy is to create a plan based on defense in depth, as discussed in Chapter 2. This plan calls for multiple layers of defensive strategies. If one plan fails to stop an intruder, subsequent layers may still stop the attack. Physical barriers should be only one layer of defense in depth.

Securing Outside Premises

The first layer of defense is controlling physical access to the business site. A common method to achieve this is a gated entrance to the parking lot. To pass through

CompTIA Security+
5.7

CompTIA Security+
3.1, 3.9

MTA Security Fundamentals
1.2

FYI

The concept of defense in depth has been around for thousands of years. Consider how medieval castles were defended. Moats, towers, outer and inner walls, and other measures helped soldiers defend their castle! Cybersecurity defenses can be layered as well.

Goal	Control Type	Description
Preventing	Physical Controls/ Deterrent Controls	These controls are used to prevent or deter an incident from occurring. An example is a gated parking lot.
Preventing	Technical Controls	These controls are usually software programs or policies that are implemented to protect systems. An example of a technical control is requiring a password of a specific length.
Preventing	Procedural Controls/ Administrative Controls	These controls are specified by policies or management to ensure something is done or not done. An example is to conduct annual training for all employees by a specific date.
Detecting	Detective Controls	These controls send notification to appropriate individuals when an incident is discovered so the threat can be addressed. An example is an alert that appears if malware is detected on a removable storage drive.
Preventing, detecting, or recovering (depends on specific control)	Legal/Regulatory Controls	Some controls are not optional. Legal or industry regulations may determine the level of control allowed. An example is a vendor that processes credit cards must conduct a vulnerability scan every 90 days.
Preventing, detecting, or recovering (depends on specific control)	Compensating Controls	Sometimes a control is not possible to implement. A compensating control, or an alternate control, is one in which a similar control can be conducted that meets the same criteria. An example is an administrative control that requires several employees to sign off on a task, which can be provided by a similar safeguard if there are not enough employees to perform that control.

Goodheart-Willcox Publisher

Figure 5-1. Controls help organize the various security methods and policies needed.

the gate, a security guard must approve the individual. The guard may be physically present in a guardhouse or the interaction may be through a remote camera.

In place of a security guard, proximity cards or transponders may be used. The card can be swiped like a credit card to open the gate. A transponder sends a radio signal to open the gate.

Fencing

Fencing can be placed around the property or around certain buildings or areas within a building. Fencing is not the most secure option. It can often be easily breached. However, it can help deter some people from accessing the facility.

Inside Security Guards

A security guard may be stationed at the entrance to a facility. To be allowed past the guard, an individual must present valid credentials. This method prevents unauthorized people from walking into the facility unchecked. Swipe cards may be used to supplement the security guard.

Barricades

Barricades are physical obstructions to passage. There are many different categories of barricades, and they may be permanent or temporary. Some are used to prevent vehicular traffic from getting too close to a building. An example of this is Jersey walls, as shown in **Figure 5-2A**. *Jersey walls* are tee-shaped walls usually made of concrete to prevent vehicles from passing. They can be moved into and out of place with heavy equipment. Sometimes they are permanently anchored. Another example is bollards. *Bollards* are vertical cylinders permanently installed to prevent vehicles from passing. They may be retractable to either allow or deny passage, as shown in **Figure 5-2B**. Bollards allow foot traffic to pass while preventing vehicular traffic.

Furnishings

Everyday office furniture can be used to act as barriers. Desks and countertops can be positioned to create a natural separation of visitors from employees. This is a common function of the reception desk. While it provides an inviting location for welcoming visitors, it also acts as a barrier to prevent unauthorized entry. Large potted trees or planters can also be used as barriers. They can be positioned to control the flow of foot traffic.

Identification Badges

Many organizations require all employees to wear company issued identification badges. These are just like the badges you may be required to wear in school. Often, ID badges include a photograph of the employee. In a large organization, it is unlikely any single person will know every other employee. Badges are a way to show that a person belongs in the building.

Even if employees are not required to wear badges, it is not uncommon for guests to be required to wear badges. Not only do guest badges indicate the person

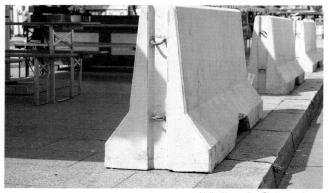

Heiko Kueverling/Shutterstock.com

A

Sanchai Khudpin/Shutterstock.com

B

Figure 5-2. Common physical security barriers include Jersey walls (A) and bollards (B).

has been approved to be there, they also serve to tell employees this is an outsider. Employees should be careful not to reveal confidential information to a guest. Monitor guest access to facilities. Clearly identify areas that are employee-only.

CCTV

Closed-circuit television (CCTV) is system in which video cameras transmit signals to a centralized monitoring location, but the signals are not publicly broadcast. This is also known as *video surveillance*. It allows for security guards or other employees to monitor key areas for unauthorized access or activity. There are many choices for CCTV depending on a business's needs. Some of the important elements include:

- movement; and
- housing.

CCTV cameras can be fixed or movable. Movable cameras may have the ability to pan, tilt, and zoom. This feature is known as PTZ. Some cameras allow for 360 degrees of viewing.

The housing of the camera should be considered. How will the camera be mounted? Common choices for mounting include domes and bullets, as shown in **Figure 5-3.** These cameras are visible. A discreet installation can be used if the camera should remain unseen. For example, the camera may be placed behind a two-way mirror.

There are additional features to consider with CCTV cameras. Does the camera need to provide an image at nighttime? If so, it will need to have infrared capability. Power requirements and network access are also important considerations. Will network access be wired or wireless? If used with a security guard, it may be important for the camera to have a zoom feature. Resolution is important to ensure the image quality is suitable. Especially consider light sources when evaluating resolution and image quality.

Bullet

Dome

Kodda/Shutterstock.com

Figure 5-3. This business has three CCTV cameras. The two bullet cameras provide targeted views, while the dome camera provides a broader 360-degree view.

Mantraps

Tailgating is an unauthorized person walking into a facility with or right behind authorized people to appear as if with them. Being seen with authorized people usually makes others believe the person is also an authorized individual. His or her presence is often not questioned. A method for stopping tailgating is to incorporate a physical defense called a mantrap.

A *mantrap* is a physical access control system that uses two sets of interlocking doors. Once a person enters an area, the first set of doors must close before the second set can be opened. Often, the second set of doors is controlled by a security guard who visually checks the people before opening the doors. A revolving door is a type of mantrap as it allows only one person to pass through at a time.

Turnstiles

Turnstiles are another method of controlling physical access. These can be seen at the entrances of many subways, amusement parks, and other public places. A *turnstile* is a device with bars or other obstruction to alternately block an entryway and allow only one person to pass at a time. There are different designs ranging from a single bar or panel to multiple bars that entirely block the entryway. The device can be set up to scan a security card so only those having the proper card can pass, as shown in **Figure 5-4.**

Stieber/Shutterstock.com

Figure 5-4. This turnstile has bars that fully cover the entryway, and it is set up so only those with the proper access card can pass through.

Quick Look 5.1.1

Physical Access Control

There are many approaches to physical access control. You may encounter several controls throughout a given day without realizing it.

1. Think about where you have seen physical access controls. In a class discussion, share the type of controls you saw and where they were. Did the controls seem appropriate for the locations?
2. Look around your school. Where are security cameras used? What types of cameras are installed?
3. As a class, discuss other locations where you recommend security cameras be installed and whether or not the existing cameras are the appropriate type.
4. Research prices for the security cameras the class has suggested. What would be the total cost for the additional cameras? If you have suggested existing cameras are the wrong type, include replacing these in the cost estimate.

Peter Wright revealed in his book *Spycatcher* that the British attempted to spy on the French in 1960 when the British were negotiating entry into the European Economic Community (EEC). They were unable to break the cipher, but found a secondary electrical signal and could reconstruct the plain text data that were sent.

Protecting Data Signals

Another area of physical security involves protecting the data signals as they travel along the network. Data transmissions must be reliable as well as secure. This is true for both wired and wireless transmissions.

One of the potential threats is electromagnetic interference (EMI). *EMI shielding* is a barrier placed around wires to block EMI from interfering with the electrical signals in the wires. Steel conduit is an example of EMI shielding. It also helps with temperature issues and will not burn or contribute to smoke volume in the case of a fire.

All electronic equipment gives off some type of electromagnetic signals. These signals, known as *electromagnetic radiation (EMR),* can be emitted from printers, computers, monitors, microwaves, transmission lines, and many other devices. Some are strong enough to interfere with other signals, resulting in data loss. These signals could also reveal data to hackers. *TEMPEST* is a specification developed by the National Security Agency (NSA) that deals with methods for spying using EMR and methods to prevent such activities. It is also issued as a NATO certification.

Companies that deal with sensitive and confidential data may choose to protect their data transmissions with approved TEMPEST products and specifications. Some TEMPEST protections are unclassified. The NSA and NATO list levels of protection that can be implemented. The following levels are three of them.

- NATO SDIP-27 Level A: The strictest standard, assumes a hacker is in immediate vicinity.
- NATO SDIP-27 Level B: Assumes a hacker is within a 20-meter radius of the transmissions.
- NATO SDIP-27 Level C: Assumes a hacker is within about 100 meters of free-space attenuation.

Quick Look 5.1.2

TEMPEST History

Much of TEMPEST is classified. However, the NSA has declassified some of its early documents detailing the discovery of compromising radiation from equipment. In this exercise, you will explore some of the first examples of how researchers discovered interception of data and their responses to protecting the data.

1. Launch a web browser, and navigate to the NSA website (www.nsa.gov).
2. Using the website's search function, enter the search phrase **tempest.pdf**, and select the file of the same name in the returned results. This is a scanned document titled *TEMPEST: A Signal Problem.* If you choose to browse the website for the article, it is located under Resources for Everyone>Freedom of Information Act>Frequently Requested Information>Declassification and Transparency Initiatives>Cryptologic Spectrum Articles.
3. Read the document. Make note of terms you are unfamiliar with, perhaps such as Yagi and dipole antennas.
4. Using a dictionary or other source, look up the meaning of the words you did not know.
5. According to the document, signals could travel around half a mile using free space. What type of conductors allowed the signals to travel further than just using the free space?
6. Bell researchers accidentally discovered they could read transmissions using an oscilloscope. What is an oscilloscope?
7. How did the United States Army Signal Corps handle the problem of RF emissions on the battlefield?

SECTION REVIEW 5.1

Check Your Understanding 📲

1. What threat is realized when an unauthorized person walks into a building behind authorized individuals?
2. A customer enters a bank foyer and is greeted by another set of doors. Employees "buzz" the doors open for customer access. What barrier did the bank install with this setup?
3. A firm is constructing a new building and would like to establish permanent barriers to control vehicle access. What should be used?
4. A gated entrance to a parking lot helps with which security goal?
5. What are the electrical signals that emanate from a printer called?

Build Your Key Terms Vocabulary 📲

As you progress through this course, develop a personal cybersecurity glossary. This will help you build your vocabulary and prepare you for a career. Write a definition for each of the following terms, and add it to your cybersecurity glossary.

bollards	mantrap
closed-circuit television (CCTV)	tailgating
electromagnetic radiation (EMR)	TEMPEST
EMI shielding	turnstile
Jersey walls	

Environmental Controls

?E ssential Q uestion

Which environmental factor poses the greatest risk to data security?

It is easy to think of cybersecurity plans only as protection against manmade threats, such as hackers and employees. However, a security plan must consider other threats to the data. A significant threat to data storage comes from environmental factors. These factors include heat (temperature), fire, and water. Heat is a by-product of electronic equipment. If the heat is not properly monitored and maintained, it often results in the shutdown or destruction of the equipment. Fire is a real threat to any business. Flooding can occur from natural disasters, but broken water pipes can also cause flooding. JFK airport in New York City experienced flooding in January of 2018 due to burst water pipes. Natural disasters can have a wide-ranging impact, such as when Hurricane Maria devastated Puerto Rico.

Key Terms ➦

data center
fire class

hot and cold aisles
server room

Learning Goals

- Plan a server room that incorporates hot and cold aisles.
- Compare and contrast fire classes and corresponding suppression methods.
- Describe measures that can be taken to control water around computer equipment.

Temperature Control

Heat is not a friend to electronic equipment. The materials can suffer a decreased life if exposed to high operating temperatures. Higher temperatures also increase the electrical resistance of the conductors. This in turn slows the speed of data and impacts performance. Temperature that varies a lot also can cause stress to systems. As materials heat up and cool down, they expand and contract. This can stress components. The design and purchase of equipment with proper cooling mechanisms is important. However, focus also needs to be placed on the physical locations of the equipment such as servers, switches, and routers.

In many businesses, servers and networking equipment are in a secured room called a *server room,* as shown in **Figure 5-5.** This centralized location also creates environmental concerns. The close proximity of all this equipment results in the output of a great deal of heat in an enclosed area. This heat, in turn, can damage the equipment running the network and the servers hosting data. A properly sized heating, ventilation, and air conditioning (HVAC) system needs to be incorporated into this area. Special considerations must be given to fire suppression.

A *data center* is a facility specifically designed to store and manage vast quantities of data. It is considerably larger than a server room. Data centers house a great deal of equipment to store and process data. They can either be located in their own facility or in a specially constructed room that is set up to handle the great needs for power, cabling, and environmental controls. Data centers run vast amounts of servers and other networking equipment. All of this equipment generates a great deal of heat that if not properly managed can cause malfunctions or shutdowns of systems. Heat is one of the biggest environmental threats to data centers.

One technique used to control temperature in a data center or server room is the use of hot and cold aisles. *Hot and cold aisles* is a technique in which server racks are placed in rows with cold air entering the room on one side and hot air exiting the room on the other side, as shown in **Figure 5-6.** The fronts of the server racks face the cold aisles. The HVAC outlets are located in the cold aisle. This allows the equipment to draw in the cold air through their fans. The hot air generated by the equipment is expelled through the back into the hot aisle. The HVAC return inlets are located in this aisle. Then hot air is removed from the room, cooled by the HVAC system, and returned to the room in the cold aisles.

The American Society of Heating, Refrigerating, and Air-Conditioning Engineers (ASHRAE) offers recommendations for maintaining and monitoring server rooms. Its recommendations include:

- ambient room temperatures should range between 64–80 degrees Fahrenheit;
- ambient humidity should be between 40–60 percent; and
- no fewer than six temperature sensors installed per rack.

Humidity control is important. If the air in the room is too dry, it can lead to a buildup of static electricity. If the air is too damp, it can cause corrosion on the equipment.

Monitoring temperature is critical. Racks holding equipment must be monitored, too. It is important to monitor the racks with the equipment separately from room temperature. When a notification is sent that the server room is overheating, it may already be too late for the servers and network equipment located in the racks. Therefore, rack-mounted sensors should be used in addition to the room sensors.

There are many temperature products on the market. Select one that uses simple network management protocol (SNMP). This protocol is designed for collecting and organizing data on managed network

Figure 5-5. A server room is a secured location in which the company's servers and other network devices are located.

Facebook has a data center in northern Sweden that uses artic air for cooling. Heat from data centers can be used to heat buildings in cold climates. A large data center can consume as much electricity as a small town in the United States.

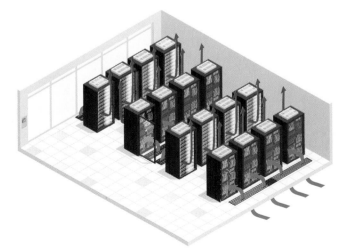

Figure 5-6. The use of hot and cold aisles is one method of managing temperature in a data center or server room.

devices by deploying SNMP agents on the remote devices. Agents communicate with devices called managers. One type of message sent by the agent is called a trap message. The temperature sensor collects traps and sends alerts to the manager when temperature levels are not at acceptable conditions. Security and network analysts use special software to monitor the activities reported by SNMP.

Quick Look 5.2.1

Data Centers

Data centers are fast becoming popular, especially due to increases in cloud computing. Security is critical for these facilities, from protection against hacking to physical safety of the equipment they contain.

1. Launch a web browser, and navigate to a search engine. Enter the search phrase inside google data centers.

2. In the search results, select the article from Google titled "Inside Our Data Centers." This page provides an overview of Google data centers and includes a short video that shows one of their highly secured data centers.

3. Select the video, as shown. As you watch the video, note the cooling methods and physical security measures put into place to secure the facility.

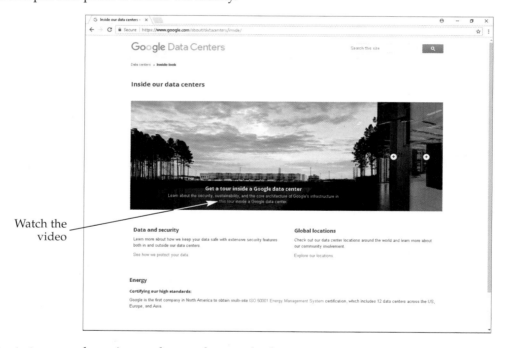

Watch the video

4. Navigate to a search engine, and enter the search phrase sap data center functionality.

5. In the search results, select the article on the SAP website (www.sapdatacenter.com) titled "How a Data Center Works—SAP Data Center."

6. Read the information on this page to see how a data center works. Note that the graphic at the top of the page contains ten hotspots marked by the plus symbol (+). These hotspots lead to photos and additional information. Observe the security level tier rating system developed by the American Standard Institute of Standards (ANSI), and the ten critical aspects of securing the data center.

Case Study

Server Room Environmental Controls

A small business named Graphic Designers, Inc., has recently expanded. It has created a server room to centralize all existing IT equipment, including servers located in racks, switches, routers, and equipment from the local telecommunication provider. Since this server room has been recently established, environmental controls need to be added to monitor temperature, humidity, and water leaks.

The American Society of Heating, Refrigerating, and Air-Conditioning Engineers (ASHRAE) offers recommendations for what type of equipment should be installed to help keep the server room operational. Research some of these recommendations. Then, prepare a memo to the CIO of Graphic Designers, Inc., with your suggestions and justifications for the equipment you recommend. Include any references to ASHRAE and specific vendors you select for your proposal. Include pricing information for the equipment.

Fire Control

Another serious threat to a business's data involves fire. Obviously, fires can be destructive. Quick action must be taken to put out any fire that may occur.

There are different types of fires based on the fuel that feeds the fire. The type of fire is referred to as a *fire class.* A Class A fire is fed by combustibles such as paper, wood, and many plastics. Anything that leaves an ash is considered a Class A fire. A Class B fire is fed by a flammable or combustible liquid, such as gasoline or oil. A Class C fire is an energized electrical fire. This includes fires caused by outlets, circuit breakers, appliances, and wiring. A Class D fire is fed by combustible metals, such as magnesium or titanium. This type of fire is more common in labs and industry than elsewhere. A Class K fire is fed by cooking oils, animal fat, and grease.

Fire extinguishers are rated by the fire class on which they should be used. Symbols on the extinguisher will indicate its rating, as shown in **Figure 5-7.** Be sure to have a fire extinguisher rated for the type of fire likely to be encountered.

It is critical that IT personnel understand fire types and proper use of extinguishers *before* an actual fire emergency occurs. The fire-suppression equipment located in a given area must be appropriate for the types of fire most likely to occur there. For example, electrical fires are more common in a server room than other types of fires. The fire-suppression equipment located in the server room must be appropriate for a Class C fire. IT personnel who will be working in that area also must receive the proper training on how to use the fire-suppression equipment.

Fire-suppression systems that use water, such as standard building sprinklers, may cause damage to computers and network equipment. An alternative to water-based systems is systems that use FM-200. This is an environmentally friendly, waterless product created by DuPont. It is the preferred solution for many organizations such as governmental buildings, museums, and most telecommunication facilities. FM-200 is suitable for protecting facilities in Class A, B and C fires.

FM-200 is a replacement for waterless fire-suppression systems that used Halon. Halon is a chemical that effectively extinguishes fire without damaging electrical systems. However, it is environmentally unfriendly. It is also potentially unhealthy for humans. The production and importation of Halon has been banned in the United States since 1994 when amendments to the Clean Air Act adopted in 1990 went into effect.

FYI

The United States Fire Administration (USFA) reports that almost 8 percent of all nonresidential fires were caused by electrical malfunctions.

- - - - - - - - - - - - - - - - -

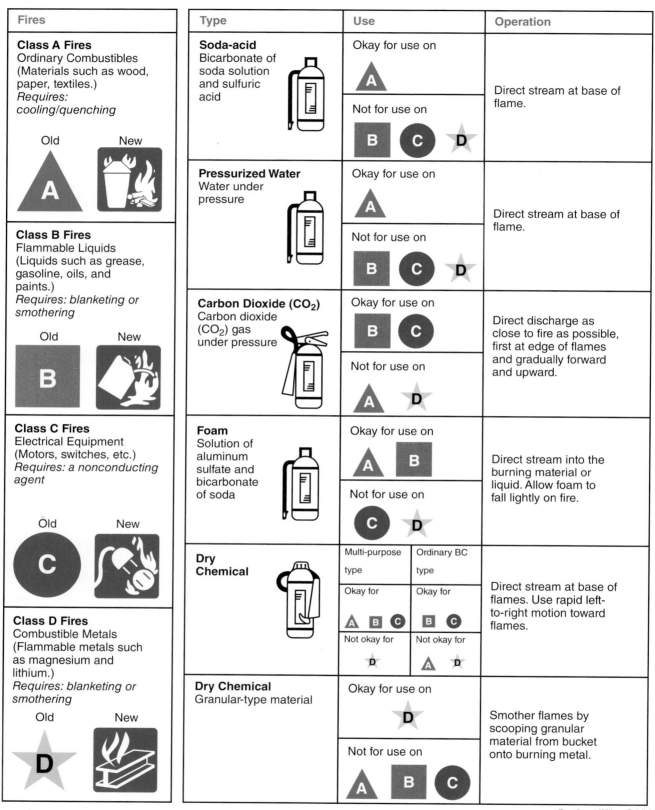

Figure 5-7. Fire extinguishers are rated by the type of fire on which they should be used. Be sure to have an appropriately rated fire extinguisher for the types of fires that may be potentially encountered.

Quick Look 5.2.2

Fire Safety

Fire prevention and safety is a concern for any business or organization. There are basic steps to take to help prevent a fire from happening. Knowing how to use a fire extinguisher is important should a fire happen.

1. Look around many homes or businesses and you will find many power strips in use. Launch a web browser, navigate to a search engine, and enter the search phrase **power strip safety**. Evaluate the results for reliable sources of information. What are some recommendations you find? Have you seen any bad practices implemented at your school or home?

2. In the search engine, enter the search phrase **using fire extinguishers 101**. In the search results, select the article How to Use a Fire Extinguisher from the website Fire Extinguisher 101. Read the information on the page. What is PASS?

3. In the search engine, enter the search phrase **FM-200 fire suppressant**. Evaluate the results for reliable sources of information. FM-200 is considered a waterless solution. Why would a company choose this solution instead of a water-based sprinkler system?

Water Control

Water and electrical equipment are not compatible. It is important to consider damage to systems from a water source. Most people think of the water damage caused by rainwater or river flooding, as shown in **Figure 5-8.** However, water can come from sprinklers, burst pipes, or even accidental spillage.

Pipes can burst without warning, and the water can quickly flood a room. In 2018, during a particularly cold week, a water pipe burst over the server room at the Virginia Beach, VA, SPCA. This water damaged a great deal of equipment. It also knocked out phone lines and electrical power. By the time an employee heard the dripping of water, the damage was already done.

The best way to prevent loss of data due to water is with preventative planning. Proper maintenance of buildings and equipment is usually the responsibility of facilities management. However, IT personnel should ensure routine maintenance checks are conducted in areas such as server rooms.

Additionally, moisture and humidity sensors should be used to monitor for leaks inside cooling equipment, leaks from nearby pipes, and water caused by a flood. There are even fluid-sensing cables that report to controllers regarding potential leaks. Another recommendation is installing water sensors at the lowest point on the floor where water would tend to puddle. If the server room has a raised floor, the sensors should be placed under the floor. Sensors should also be placed underneath any pipe junctions. The condensation trays in the air conditioning system should also be equipped with sensors to detect overflow.

FEMA/Rob Melendez

Figure 5-8. Water damage can be caused by excessive rain, burst pipes, or overflowing rivers. Water can cause severe damage.

SECTION REVIEW 5.2

Check Your Understanding

1. Humidity in a server room should not be any higher than what percentage?
2. What technique is used in rack placement in server rooms to help manage heat?
3. Temperature sensors use what networking protocol to report data?
4. Paper in a trash can catches fire. Which fire extinguisher class should be used to put out the fire?
5. Which environmental concern is potentially the biggest threat to data centers?

Build Your Key Terms Vocabulary

As you progress through this course, develop a personal cybersecurity glossary. This will help you build your vocabulary and prepare you for a career. Write a definition for each of the following terms, and add it to your cybersecurity glossary.

data center

fire class

hot and cold aisles

server room

Quick Look 5.3.2

Local DNS Cache

DNS poisoning at the local host is usually the result of manipulation of the local hosts file. The hosts file is used to prepopulate the local DNS cache when a computer is booted. This hosts file is an attractive target because it will add information to the DNS cache automatically when the computer starts.

1. On a Windows computer, launch file explorer.
2. Navigate to the C:\Windows\System32\Drivers\ETC folder.
3. Right-click on the file named hosts, and select **Open with** in the shortcut menu. Select to open it with Notepad. You may need to click **More Apps** before selecting Notepad.
4. In Notepad, scroll to the bottom of the file. Add a new line as shown: 129.4.3.2 bankofamerica.com. This is an example of where a hacker might change the file and add a deceptive entry. In most situations, the local hosts file is not modified from the default settings. Note: any changes to the hosts file will only take effect when the Windows operating system is restarted.

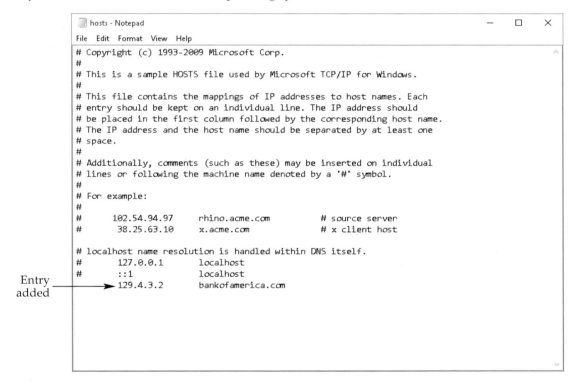

5. Close Notepad without saving any changes.
6. Applying what you have learned, open the command prompt. To view the local DNS cache, enter: ipconfig /displaydns. This command and switch displays any entries preset in the hosts file along with cached entries from local browsing. The entries returned by this command can be verified with another command.
7. To verify if an address in the cache is valid, enter nslookup and the address, such as nslookup 206.19.49.139. If the local DNS server agrees with the entry in the local host's cache, the entry is valid. Otherwise, the entry may be the result of a hack.
8. To remove all entries in the cache, enter: ipconfig /flushdns. This must be done as an administrator.

Watering Holes

Another method hackers use to target victims is a watering hole. In nature, a watering hole is a place where animals go to drink, as shown in **Figure 5-11.** Often, predators lurk by the watering hole waiting for prey. A watering hole attack is similar. In a *watering hole* attack, hackers discover which websites are often visited by specific individuals, departments, or all employees of a company. Once those sites are identified, the hackers search for vulnerabilities in the sites and attempt to embed malicious code. When the intended victim uses the legitimate site, he or she is not aware it has been compromised. This may result in stolen information or malware downloads. Many companies, including Twitter and Microsoft, have fallen victim to watering hole attacks.

Variations of Phishing

As phishing attacks evolve, they have become varied in execution. Some of these variations include follow-up phone calls to potential victims as a way to try to lend credibility to phished e-mails. Smishing is another variation. This term comes from the combination of short message service (SMS) and phishing. In *smishing,* hackers use SMS messages as the means of reaching victims instead of e-mail or other means.

Vishing is voice-based phishing in which the hacker calls the user while impersonating someone else. There are two very common examples of this. In one example, the hacker pretends to be from the IRS demanding payment. In the second example, the hacker tells the victim he or she has missed jury duty and will be arrested unless a fine is immediately paid.

Policies and Strategies for Security

Setting policies for an organization can provide guidelines so users understand what is and what is not allowed. These policies should be periodically

Andrzej Kubik/Shutterstock.com

Figure 5-11. Animals gather around a watering hole in nature. A watering hole attack involves looking for a common website a group of users visits, then hacking the site to install malware.

reviewed as technology and business processes change. At a minimum, an annual review is recommended.

Good computing habits will go far in protecting data and assets. There are several policies that will assist users with performing good computing habits. Two of these policies are an acceptable use policy and a clean desk policy.

An *acceptable use policy (AUP)* is a document created by the owner of the network containing information on proper usage of the network and related assets. It:

- sets such rules as what is not allowed with network assets;
- identifies the amount of privacy the user or employee should expect when using the network;
- identifies procedures for incidents; and
- explains what happens to individuals who do not comply with the terms in the policy.

Users should be asked to read, understand, and acknowledge their understanding of the terms within the AUP. Anyone who uses an organization's network is bound by the terms of the AUP, not just employees.

In some cases, employees can be fired for failing to abide by the AUP. This was the case for 23 employees of the New York Times who lost their jobs in December of 1999. These employees were terminated for sending inappropriate e-mail. The company said the firings were meant to maintain a professional and harassment-free workplace. The company cited its AUP in the firings.

A *clean-desk policy* is another important policy that businesses may use. This policy requires employees to remove sensitive documents from their desks when they are not present. A clean-desk policy also should cover computer access. It may require computers to be locked when not in use or shut down nightly. Many policies also cover paper copies of data. Locked file cabinets may be required. Proper trash disposal may be outlined.

Another way to help protect users from spam e-mail is to incorporate sender policy framework. *Sender policy framework (SPF)* is an e-mail protocol used to validate the legitimacy of the e-mail address. Most spammers and those sending phishing e-mail often spoof the e-mail address in use.

A company generates special records in the domain name system for authorized senders and their accompanying IP address. This is called an SPF record. By doing so, it is declaring the validity of the e-mail associated to that IP address.

CompTIA Security+
5.1

Ethical Issue

Keyloggers

A manager from the research and development department has approached the IT department with a concern that an employee may be stealing information from a current, highly sensitive project. After a normal scan of the employee's computer, there is no evidence of inappropriate files. However, the manager is sure the thefts are occurring. You consider putting a keylogger on the computer to capture screenshots and information from the keyboard. However, it does not state in the company's AUP that employees might be subject to this kind of search. On the other hand, this could be a major financial setback to the company if this employee is stealing information.

Write a memo to the chief information security officer (CISO) with your recommendation. The memo either should support placing the keylogger on the computer or present reasons why this should not be done. Be sure to justify your recommendation.

When e-mail arrives at the company, the e-mail provider software will verify the existence of an SPF record from DNS. If the address is there, the e-mail is allowed to be sent to the recipient. If the address is not there, the e-mail is not allowed entry to the system. SPF records are incorporated by the use of a TXT record in DNS.

Quick Look 5.3.3

School AUP

Most organizations will post the AUP on their website or direct users to its location at the login banner screen. A banner screen is displayed during the logon process and is often used for messages, announcements, or elements of the AUP. Locate your school's AUP, and fully read it. Then, answer the following questions.

1. Where did you find the AUP, and was it easy or difficult to locate?
2. Did you find the AUP easy to understand and follow?
3. What was something you read that you did not know before?
4. What changes would you make or recommend to this policy?
5. Share your reflections with your classmates.

Insider Threats

Many businesses do not consider their own employees when planning defensive and preventative systems against potential hackers. In 2014, the US Secret Service, CSO Magazine, and the Software Engineering Institute (SEI) conducted a cybercrime survey. For the previous year, 37 percent of respondents experienced an insider incident. Other survey results are shown in **Figure 5-12.**

Personally identifiable information (PII) is any data that can be used to pinpoint a specific person. As seen in this survey, not all insider threats are malicious in nature. Regardless of how private information is revealed, the damage is done. The loss of this information can result in substantial harm to businesses or individuals. For example, theft of PII may lead to identity theft.

PII is not always easy to classify. Which of these do you believe is PII?

- name
- gender
- address
- telephone number
- e-mail address

Did you say all of them? Most people consider all of these PII, but there is no US federal law that mandates this for general businesses. However, some federal laws, such as the Health Insurance Portability and Accountability Act (HIPAA), identify specific PII that is protected.

Insiders made up the highest percentage of the following incidents.	
• Private or sensitive information unintentionally exposed	82%
• Confidential records compromised or stolen	76%
• Customer records compromised or stolen	71%
• Employee records compromised or stolen	63%

Goodheart-Willcox Publisher

Figure 5-12. Some of the results from a survey conducted by the US Secret Service, CSO Magazine, and the Software Engineering Institute (SEI).

Quick Look 5.3.4

California Online Privacy Protection Act

One of the most definitive sources for defining PII is the California Online Privacy Protection Act (CalOPPA). A look at some of the specifics of this law can be informative to see how it applies to consumers.

1. Launch a web browser, and navigate to the Consumer Federation of California website (www.consumercal.org). This is a nonprofit advocacy organization for consumer rights.
2. Click the **About CFC** link in the menu at the top of the page, and then click the **CFC Educational Foundation** link in the menu on the left, as shown.

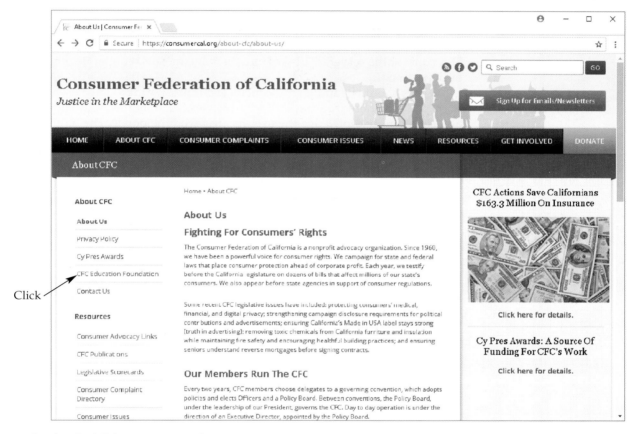

3. On the CFC Education Foundation Privacy Protection Consumer Guide page that is displayed, scroll down to the Online Privacy Protection section, and click **The California Online Privacy Protection Act (CalOPPA)** link. A new page is displayed that provides an overview of the act.
4. When does this law apply to businesses located in other states?
5. What happens if a website does not display the information required?
6. The recent amendment added tablets and other mobile device apps. If an app is not in compliance, what fine would the business pay?
7. What is AB370? Are you in favor of this?
8. Locate a website that you believe tracks PII. Does it abide by the CalOPPA?

Best Practices

CompTIA Security+
2.3

MTA Security Fundamentals
1.1

Best practices should be followed to help locate employees who may be using their access to steal data or deny access to it. In Chapter 1, you learned how Edward Snowden and Terry Childs demonstrated their ability to steal or damage information from their employers. In Chapter 3, you learned of two strategies that could help identify these behaviors: mandatory vacations and job rotation. Here are some other practices that could help safeguard company data if implemented correctly.

A key security practice related to personnel is separation of duty. With *separation of duty,* responsibilities are divided so no single individual has complete control over a process or task. More than one individual is required to complete a task. This acts as a barrier to prevent fraud or other security issues. For example, IT personnel may not have complete access to the entire network. A single person may have administrative access to routers, but not to the Active Directory or the servers. This is common in businesses with large or medium-size IT departments.

CompTIA Security+
1.6, 5.1

Users should be trained in security awareness. Additionally, user compliance with policies should be tracked. Key policies, such as the AUP, should be read and signed to acknowledge the user has received the policy. The human resource department often takes care of all of this with a technique called onboarding.

Onboarding is the process of providing a new employee with all information he or she needs on the company, business processes, security policies, and other related material. Security-awareness training is an essential part of onboarding. Annual follow-up training is also important. Frequent repetition and exposure to information helps employees understand and retain the information.

Offboarding is the process of closing an employee's accounts and records when he or she leaves the company. This is another critical aspect of managing users. The IT department must ensure that user accounts are disabled when the user leaves. The accounts should be scheduled for deletion as outlined in company policies. ID cards must be turned in. Company equipment, such as laptops or smartphones, must be returned. The employee needs to be removed from organizational charts and the e-mail system. Any data on the employee's work computer must be removed. In some cases, the data must be archived. In other cases, the data must be destroyed.

SECTION REVIEW 5.3

Check Your Understanding

1. A fake e-mail that is targeted to the chief financial officer of an organization is considered what type of attack?

2. A person receives a fake phone call from someone claiming to be from a software company. What type of attack is he or she experiencing?

3. A user enters a web address in a browser, but an incorrect page is displayed. What was modified on the user's computer that redirected the browser to the incorrect site?

4. The rules and guidelines for appropriate behavior with computer systems is outlined in what document?

5. Ensuring employees return keys and ID badges is part of which human resource practice?

Build Your Key Terms Vocabulary

As you progress through this course, develop a personal cybersecurity glossary. This will help you build your vocabulary and prepare you for a career. Write a definition for each of the following terms, and add it to your cybersecurity glossary.

acceptable use policy (AUP)

DNS poisoning

offboarding

onboarding

personally identifiable
    information (PII)

pharming

phishing

sender policy framework (SPF)

separation of duty

smishing

spear phishing

vishing

watering hole

whale phishing

Review and Assessment

Summary

Section 5.1 Business Controls

- The three key goals for planning security measures are preventing a problem, detecting a problem, and recovering from a problem.
- Physical security includes such things as securing the outside of the premises, fencing, inside security guards, barricades, natural barriers, identification badges, closed-circuit television, mantraps, and turnstiles.
- Data signals must be protected from electromagnetic interference, and electromagnetic radiation is a potential security vulnerability.

Section 5.2 Environmental Controls

- There are various methods for controlling the temperature of computer equipment, including hot and cold aisles and rack-mounted temperature sensors.
- Fires are categorized by class, and the fire suppression system must be rated for the class of fire likely to be encountered.
- Incorporating humidity and water-leak sensors and installing water guards on air conditioning equipment will help alert and protect systems against damage caused by water.

Section 5.3 Users and Security Threats

- Phishing is attempting to obtain personal information through fake e-mails, and there are several variations of phishing, including whale phishing, spear phishing, pharming, watering holes, and others.
- An acceptable use policy will outline what is and is not allowed on the network, the level of privacy users should expect, procedures for incidents, and penalties for not complying.
- Insider threats are a major source of data loss, including personally identifiable information, such as a person's name, gender, address, telephone number, and e-mail address.
- There are several best practices for security related to personnel, including separation of duty and providing good onboarding and offboarding of employees that incorporates proper cybersafety training.

Check Your Cybersecurity IQ

Now that you have completed this chapter, see what you have learned about cybersecurity by visiting the student companion website (www.g-wlearning.com) and taking the chapter posttest.

Review Questions

For each question, select the answer that is the best response.

1. You create alerts to notify security administrators when an incorrect password is used for the Admin account on the server. Which security goal does this fulfill?
   A. detecting a problem
   B. preventing a problem
   C. recovering from a problem
   D. administering a problem

2. Your company is building a new facility and wants to prevent vehicles from having physical access near the building. Which of these solutions provides the best prevention of vehicle proximity?
   A. Install a PTZ camera.
   B. Install bollards.
   C. Install Jersey walls.
   D. Require photo ID for all individuals parking their car near the building.

3. You are concerned about unauthorized individuals gaining access to the server room. Which strategy is the best solution to prevent this access?
   A. Use a PTZ camera.
   B. Put cipher locks on the server room door.
   C. Hire a facility security guard.
   D. Create strong access policies for employees.

4. Jason and his coworkers took a break outside during working hours. When they reentered the facility, they were joined by another, unknown individual. This could have been prevented with:
   A. tailgating
   B. proximity cards
   C. CCTV
   D. mantraps

5. Which is the *best* method for protecting sensitive research data for a military contractor?
   A. Place all the equipment in a server farm.
   B. Use a FM-200 suppression.
   C. Install TEMPEST equipment.
   D. Use steel shielding for all wiring.

6. Due to the vast amount of computer and network equipment running, this is one of the biggest threats to most data centers:
   A. unauthorized access
   B. phishing attacks
   C. heat-related issues
   D. AUP violations

7. Sparks fly from an outlet that computers are connected to, creating a small fire. Which fire extinguisher should be used to suppress the fire?
   A. Class A
   B. Class B
   C. Class C
   D. Class D

8. An employee receives an unexpected e-mail invitation announcing a new upgrade for the specific accounting software being used. This type of e-mail could be a threat from what type of attack?
   A. waterhole attack
   B. whaling
   C. pharming
   D. spear phishing

9. Unbeknownst to the users of an organization, a website they often use as a resource has been compromised. When they access the site, they unknowingly download malware. This attack type is known as:
   A. DNS poisoning
   B. watering hole
   C. vishing
   D. cache attacks

10. A member of the IT department locked out the company databases on the network and refuses to release them. Which strategy would have helped prevent this act?
    A. separation of duties
    B. onboarding
    C. training
    D. offboarding

Application and Extension of Knowledge

1. Create a presentation illustrating the dangers that security threats and untrained employees have had on other businesses. Include information on the potential financial losses and damage to a business's reputation.

2. Visit a local business, and look for physical security and manmade barriers. Include elements outside and inside the business. Document your findings and any recommendations you would make based on your observations.

3. Interview a human resource manager. Discuss his or her onboarding and offboarding policies as they relate to IT security. Summarize your questions and answers in a word processing document. Analyze the responses. Do you feel their policies are strong in protecting data? Would you make any recommendations for changes?

4. Research software that is intended to spot and eliminate phishing e-mails. Summarize two different options, and compare their features and pricing. Which did you like better and why?

5. There are many free and open-source programs that allow you to monitor the temperature of a computer's CPU. Research some of these choices. Download one, and test its effectiveness. Document your research. Include screenshots of the program you selected.

Research Project
Security Training

You have been hired as an information security officer for a medium-size company that has approximately 300 employees. After observing employee actions, you realize that employees do not really understand the purpose and benefit of making good decisions related to safe computing. Password choices, e-mail use, and other basic security measures are not being followed. To solve this issue, you have decided to create security-awareness training. However, you need to sell this concept to management who are not in IT in order to gain their support and some funding.

Deliverables. Create a presentation illustrating the dangers that security threats and untrained employees have had on other businesses. Include information on the potential for financial losses and damage to a business's reputation.

Online Activities

Complete the following activities, which will help you learn, practice, and expand your knowledge and skills.

Vocabulary. Practice vocabulary for this chapter using the e-flash cards, matching activity, and vocabulary game until you are able to recognize their meanings.

Communication Skills

College and Career Readiness

Reading. Scanning is done when you know the information you need is in a document, you just have to find it. Scan this chapter for information on DNS poisoning. Did scanning work for you? How long did it take you to find the DNS poisoning information?

Writing. Rhetoric is the study of writing or speaking as a way of communicating information or persuading someone. Describe a rhetorical technique a writer can use to persuade the president of a company to install physical security controls. Write a script in a step-by-step format for presenting your reasons for wanting to add physical security controls.

Speaking. Select three of your classmates to participate in a group discussion. Acting as the team leader, assign each person to a specific role, such as timekeeper or recorder. Discuss the concept of watering holes. Keep the panel on task, and promote democratic discussion. The recorder should make notes of important information discussed. The notes should be edited, and a final document should be created for distribution to the class.

Listening. Practice active-listening skills while listening to your teacher present a lesson. Focus on the message, and monitor your understanding. Were there any barriers to effective listening? How did you use prior experiences to help you understand what was being said? Evaluate your teacher's point of view and use of material in the presentation. Share your ideas in a group discussion.

Portfolio Development

College and Career Readiness

Digital Presentation Options. Before you begin collecting items for a digital portfolio, you will need to decide how you are going to present the final product. The method you choose should allow the viewer to easily navigate and find items. There are many creative ways to present a digital portfolio.

For example, you could create an electronic presentation with slides for each section. The slides could have links to documents, videos, graphics, or sound files. This will dictate file naming conventions and file structure. Websites are another option for presenting a digital portfolio. You could create a personal website to host the files and have a main page with links to various sections. Each section page could have links to pages with your documents, videos, graphics, or sound files. Be sure you read and understand the user agreement for any site on which you place your materials. Another option is to place the files on a CD.

Establish the types of technology that are available for you to create a digital portfolio. Will you have access to cameras or studios? Do you have the level of skill to create videos?

Decide the type of presentation you will use. Research what will be needed to create the final portfolio product.

CTSO Event Prep

Writing. Many competitive events for career and technical student organizations (CTSOs) require students to write a research paper. The paper must be submitted either before the competition or when the student arrives at the event. Written events can be lengthy and require a lot of preparation, so it is important to start early. To prepare for a writing event, complete the following activities.

1. Read the guidelines provided by the organization. The topic to be researched will be specified in detail. Also, all final format guidelines will be given, including how to organize and submit the paper. Make certain you ask questions about any points you do not understand.

2. Research the topic. Begin your research early. Research may take days or weeks, and you do not want to rush the process.

3. Set a deadline for yourself so that you write at a comfortable pace.

4. After you write the first draft, ask an instructor to review it and give feedback.

5. Once you have the final version, go through the checklist for the event to make sure you have covered all of the details. Your score will be penalized if you do not follow instructions.

Chapter 6

Protecting Host Systems

Every device on a network presents an entry point to the entire network whether it is a router, server, computer, or even printer. Threats to the network can originate from unpatched operating systems, insecure system settings, and intentional or inadvertent user actions. There are precautions IT administrators take to prevent security incidents. Administrators also review systems for unusual activity or errors and warnings that may indicate a potential failure or suspect activity.

A large ransomware attack occurred in May of 2017. The worm was called WannaCry. It infected over 230,000 systems worldwide in the first days of its release. Affected systems included those for FedEx, MIT, and hospitals in the United Kingdom's health-care network. WannaCry encrypted files on computers running outdated or unpatched Windows operating systems. Microsoft had issued a critical warning and patch in March of 2017, but two months later, systems that were yet to be patched were affected by the worm. This was a preventable security incident as Microsoft had even issued emergency security patches for older Windows operating systems such as Windows XP and Server 2003. This exploit clearly illustrates the importance in assessing, maintaining, and protecting host systems.

Chapter Preview

While studying, look for the activity icon for:

- Pretests and posttests
- Vocabulary terms with e-flash cards and matching activities
- Self-assessment

G-WLEARNING.com

College and Career Readiness

Reading Prep

Before you begin reading this chapter, consider how the author presents the information. As you read, consider how this chapter provides the foundation for the next chapter.

Check Your Cybersecurity IQ ➦

Before you begin this chapter, see what you already know about cybersecurity by visiting the student companion website (www.g-wlearning.com) and taking the chapter pretest.

Certification Objectives

CompTIA Security+

1.5 Explain vulnerability scanning concepts.
2.1 Install and configure network components, both hardware and software based, to support organizational security.
2.2 Given a scenario, use appropriate software tools to assess the security posture of an organization.
3.3 Given a scenario, implement secure systems design.
3.6 Summarize secure application development and deployment concepts.
4.4 Given a scenario, differentiate common account management practices.

Microsoft MTA Security Fundamentals

2.4 Understand audit policies.
3.1 Understand dedicated firewalls.
4.1 Understand client protection.
4.3 Understand server protection.

Operating System Services

Essential Question

What is the importance to security of establishing a baseline?

There are many areas where a network may be vulnerable to an attack from a hacker, configuration errors, or environmental issues. One of the areas that needs to be maintained are the hosts, or personal computing devices, that are used on the network. If these computers are not maintained and updated on a regular basis, they present avenues of attack. This is also true if they are running programs and services that are not necessary. Security professionals need to have a focus on host security, especially by implementing preventative measures. Along with preventative measures, analyzing event logs can help identify suspicious or concerning events that may indicate a breach in security.

Key Terms ➦

attack surface	daemon	hardening
auditing	event logging	service
baseline	group policy	

Learning Goals

- Describe operating system hardening.
- Create system baselines.
- Analyze system event logs.

CompTIA Security+
3.3

MTA Security Fundamentals
4.3

System Hardening

Hardening is closing or locking down any unnecessary paths on an operating system that can be used for unapproved access. This includes closing unused network ports, disabling services that do not need to be running, and removing programs and access that are not necessary. These paths present vulnerabilities. If exploited, they can lead to threats against the host and other systems on the network. By securing systems, the attack surface for vulnerabilities is reduced. An *attack surface* is a point or area in a system that could be used or compromised to allow hackers entry into the system.

Running programs such as applications and services could provide access to a system. If a program is running, it provides an entrance or attack vector into the system that could be exploited. The attack vector is the path the hacker uses to get into the system. The attack surface is the point of entry.

Services

A *service* is any program that is run in the background of an operating system to provide specific features and functionality. On a Linux host, a service is called a *daemon.* Some services are required by the operating system. In addition, services run for applications such as file transfer protocol (FTP) and dynamic host configuration protocol (DHCP).

In Windows, services can be managed from PowerShell or the graphical control manager, as shown in **Figure 6-1.** In Linux, the **systemctl** command is used to stop and start services. To manage a service in Windows, you can control its startup mode, status, and if it logs on automatically to the operating system. The graphical interface is accessed through Task Manager. Click the **Services** tab in Task Manager, and then click **Open Services** or the **Services...** button at the top of the tab.

The view in the graphical interface can be sorted by clicking the column title. For example, to sort by status, click the **Status** label at the top of the column. Click the heading a second time to reverse the order. Click a specific service in the list to view a description. Double-click the name to view its parameters or make changes to the service, as shown in **Figure 6-2.** There are four tabs with options: **General**, **Logon**, **Recovery**, and **Dependencies**.

The **General** tab contains some key information, including a description of the service and its startup type. The *startup type* either instructs the operating system to load the service automatically on boot or requires the user to manually load the service. Another key piece of information found on the **General** tab is the location of the executable file for the service. Most Windows services run from the c:\windows\system32 folder. Sometimes malware will try to appear as if it is a Microsoft service. However, the malware is often being run from a folder other than c:\windows\system32.

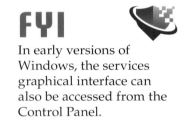

FYI

In early versions of Windows, the services graphical interface can also be accessed from the Control Panel.

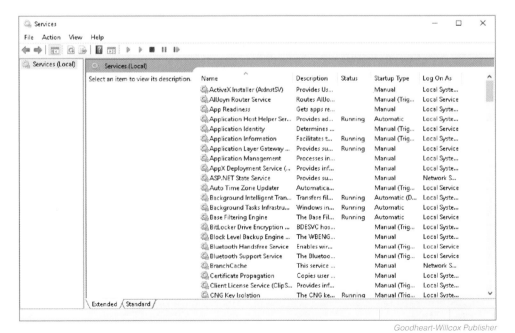

Goodheart-Willcox Publisher

Figure 6-1. Windows has a graphical interface for managing services.

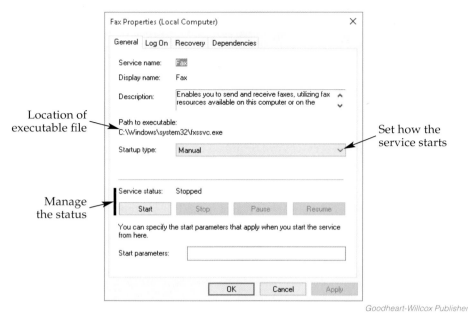

Location of executable file

Set how the service starts

Manage the status

Figure 6-2. A resource can be started or stopped, and it can be set to be manually or automatically launched. Be sure to verify the executable is correct.

The **Dependencies** tab identifies the services that must be running to support this service. It also shows which services will be impacted if you shut down the service. Before shutting down a service, make sure doing so will not negatively impact other services.

Quick Look 6.1.1

Windows Host Services

It is normal to have many services installed and running. There are usually many installed services that are not running as well. It is easy to see all services and which ones are running.

1. Applying what you have learned, launch Windows PowerShell.
2. Enter get-service. All installed services are listed whether they are running or not.
3. To view only the running services, enter: get-service | where-object {$_.status -eq "running"}.
4. You can also look for running services starting with just a specific letter. To find only services beginning with the letter W, enter: get-service w*.

Startup Services and Scheduled Tasks

Some services may be running in memory. It may not be apparent to the user these are being executed. When some software is installed, it is set to launch at system startup. An example of this is Adobe Acrobat Update Service. When Adobe Acrobat Reader is installed, this service is also installed and set to launch at startup. The service runs in the background, but it is active in memory. Monitoring startup programs is one method to help diagnose problems or security issues on a system.

Another area to evaluate is scheduled tasks. A scheduled task is one set to occur at a specific time or interval. A hacker or malware may exploit this by inserting a command that executes only at certain times. For example, a hacker might create a script that turns off the firewall in the evenings. In Windows, the Task Scheduler can be used to set events to occur at a specific time.

Quick Look 6.1.2

Startup Programs and Scheduled Tasks

In Windows, an easy way to locate startup programs is to run a Microsoft utility called msconfig. The Task Scheduler should also be examined for commands set to execute at a specific time.

1. Click the Windows **Start** button, and then enter msconfig in the search bar. Select msconfig.exe or System Configuration in the search results to launch the System Configuration utility.
2. In the System Configuration utility, click the **Startup** tab. In Windows 10, click the **Open Task Manager** link. In older versions of Windows, the startup information is accessed directly in the System Configuration utility.
3. Select a service in the list, and click the **Disable** button to prevent the service from loading, as shown. In older versions of Windows, uncheck the check box for a service to disable it.

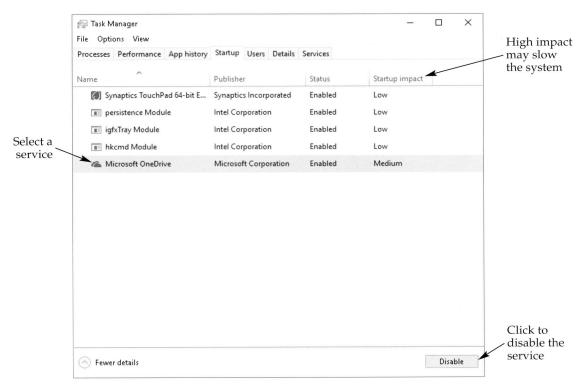

4. Close the Task Manager and the System Configuration utility.
5. Enter task scheduler in the Windows search bar. Select the Task Scheduler application in the search results.
6. The initial view is a dashboard that allows you to view information on tasks, including recently run tasks. How many tasks ran in the last 24 hours? The last hour?
7. Click **Action**>**Display All Running Tasks** in the pull-down menu. A new window is displayed that shows all tasks currently running. Click the **Close** button after viewing the tasks.

Quick Look 6.1.2 Continued

8. In the left-hand pane, expand the Task Scheduler Library tree, as shown. You can view scheduled tasks for various components, such as Microsoft; those scheduled through the event viewer; or other programs, such as Apple.

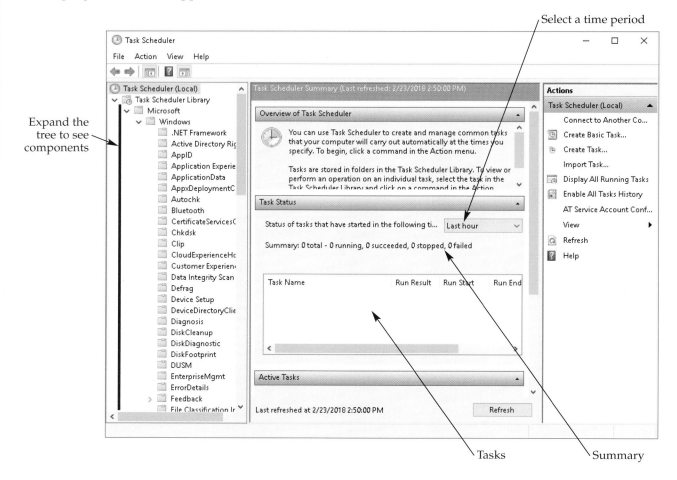

9. Expand the Microsoft branch, and then expand the Windows branch. Scroll down to find the DiskCleanup branch, and select it. Information for this specific component is displayed. When was the last time this program ran?

10. With the DiskCleanup branch selected, click the **Actions** tab in the middle view. The path to the actual executable program is displayed.

11. Click the **General** tab. Can the program run if the user is not logged on? Will it run hidden (not visible to the logged in user)?

12. Close the Task Scheduler.

Best Practices for Hardening Windows

The more privileges and permissions you give users, the potential for vulnerabilities increases. Consider some of the following options for hardening Windows.

- Limit who can install software on the host, and remember that with newer versions of Windows users can find software through the Windows store!

- Set up software-restriction policies, such as disallowing a program to run if it is not stored in a specific location.
- Ensure there are no unapproved shares on the host.
- Disable or remove any unneeded user accounts.
- For Windows 10, disable Live Tiles in the **Start** menu, which accept input from the Internet (right-click the tile, and click **Turn live tile off** in the shortcut menu).
- Set a password for the screen saver.
- Require a password to wake the system from hibernation mode.
- Turn off autoplay to prevent any hacking tools from automatically running in the background if a USB device is connected (autoplay settings are located in the Control Panel or in Settings).
- Enable the host to show hidden files.
- Ensure features of Windows that are not used, such as tablet mode for a desktop and gadgets, are turned off.

Many of these settings can be configured for a Windows-based operating system in a group policy on the network servers. The settings can then be pushed down automatically to all Windows hosts on the network. This means there is no need to configure each host individually.

Baselines and Performance

Another important item to document on a system is the condition of something when it is normal or average. This is known as a baseline. A *baseline* is a starting point from which comparisons can be made. For example, if a system seems very sluggish and slow in responding to requests, you can compare the current amount of network traffic or CPU speed to the baseline. A large difference may indicate a problem.

Establishing Baselines

Baselines should be established for normal usage on various dates and times. Microsoft Windows has some built-in tools that can assist with creating baselines and monitoring systems: Resource Monitor and Performance Monitor. These are shown in **Figure 6-3.** The Resource Monitor is a comprehensive utility that displays real-time data on different hardware elements. The Performance Monitor can be used to track specific data over a wide range of components, such as:

- network traffic;
- memory usage;
- CPU usage; and
- disk space.

Case Study

Performance Management

You are a security technician for the company ACME Quality Auto Parts. This company has a web store for the e-commerce side of its business. The server hosting the web store is very sluggish. Your supervisor asked you to identify what areas are most affected. You are instructed to use Windows Resource Monitor (**resmon**) and the Reliability Monitor (**perfmon /rel**). However, you have never used these utilities. Research these utilities. What data can be gained from these programs? Prepare a report of the types of data you will review. Include screenshots in your report.

Expand the
headings to
show details

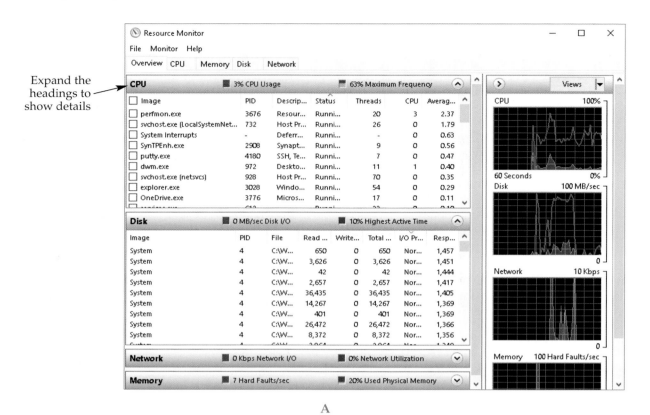

A

Select to display
detailed information

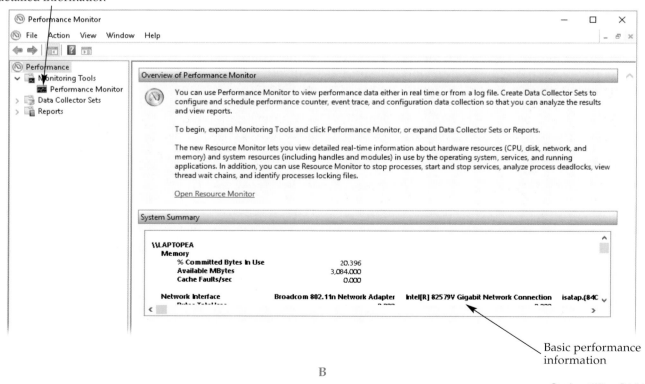

Basic performance
information

B

Figure 6-3. In Microsoft Windows, the Resource Monitor and Performance Monitor can be used to establish baselines and check usage of system resources. A—The Resource Monitor is more detailed overall. B—The Performance Monitor allows you to get very specific on which counters to track.

To establish a baseline, use the Performance Monitor when the system is known to be in normal operating condition. Then, record the data for the elements you wish to track. Save the file in a secure location where it can be easily accessed when needed.

By knowing the baseline data, you could view, for example, if there is an unexpected spike in disk usage. This may indicate a large number of downloads or a high number of files being saved or deleted. Someone downloading a large quantity of files could point to a hacked system or an insider threat, such as what Edward Snowden did when he took data from the NSA. High network traffic may indicate malware or even the presence of a remote user accessing the system.

Performance data may also be used to monitor the condition of hardware. Spikes in disk usage may mean the hard drive is failing. A failed hard drive could result in the loss of critical business data. If the CPU or memory usage is increasing over time or is consistently high, the system may not be meeting the performance goals. An upgrade in processor or RAM may be needed.

FYI

The network-monitoring firm Paessler reports that one of the top five spikes in network traffic is malware outbreaks and hacking attempts.

Monitoring Performance

The default view of the Performance Monitor displays a few key counters, as shown in **Figure 6-3.** These include information related to memory, network interface, the physical disk, and the processor (CPU). To display detailed information and to change counters or other settings, click the Performance Monitor branch in the tree in the left-hand pane. The view changes to display processor utilization in a line graph, as shown in **Figure 6-4.**

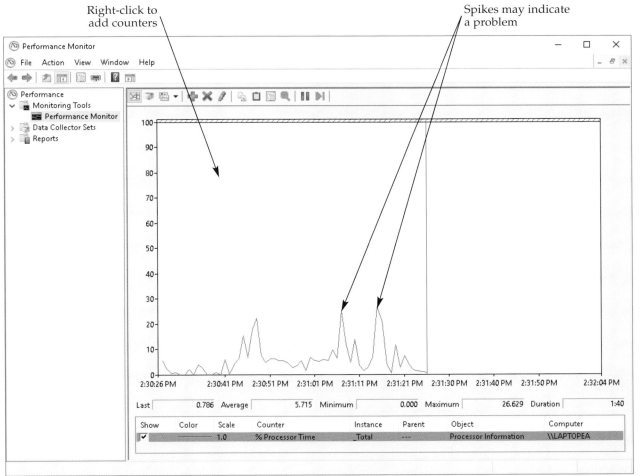

Figure 6-4. The Performance Monitor can be used to display usage data over time.

Another method of monitoring data is to use data collector sets. A *data collector set* gathers information and saves it in a report. The information can then be further studied. Data collectors can be created just as if you were viewing the data in real time. Alerts can also be created with a data collector set. This allows you to know instantly if there is a spike in a performance indicator.

Quick Look 6.1.3

Parameters in Performance Monitor

The Performance Monitor is a versatile tool in Microsoft Windows. It can be used to monitor and collect various information about the system.

1. Click the Windows **Start** menu, and then enter performance monitor in the search box. Select the Performance Monitor application in the search results.

2. In the Performance Monitor, expand the Monitoring Tools branch, and then select the Performance Monitor branch in the left-hand pane. A graph is displayed in the right-hand pane.

Change graph type

3. Click the arrow next to the **Change graph type** button on the toolbar above the chart. Notice the options in the drop-down menu. The view can be changed from the default line graph to bar graphs (histogram) or see the raw data value (report). Change to each type to see the views.

4. Click the **Add** button on the toolbar. This is used to add more counters to monitor. The **Add Counters** dialog box is displayed, which contains a list of available counters.

5. Scroll through the list, and select the down arrow next to Network Adapter. In the expanded list, click Bytes Total/Sec, as shown. Select your network adapter in the **Instances of selected object:** box, and click the **Add** button to add it to the list on the right-hand side. Then, click the **OK** button to add the counter.

Add

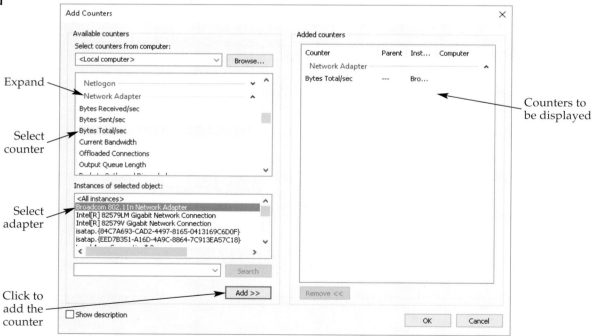

6. Applying what you have learned, display the data as a line graph.

7. Click the **Properties** button on the toolbar. The **Performance Monitor Properties** dialog box is displayed.

Properties

Quick Look 6.1.3 Continued

8. Click the network adapter counter in the list on the **Data** tab, and then click the **Color:** drop-down arrow. Change the color to blue. Also, use the **Width:** drop-down arrow to change the width to the thickest option.

9. Click the **Graph** tab, and then check the **Horizontal Grid** check box. This places horizontal markers on the graph. Click the **OK** button to update the display.

10. Leave the Performance Monitor open, and launch the command prompt.

11. Using the command prompt, use the **ipconfig** command to obtain the default gateway, and then ping your default gateway. Notice how the graph in the Performance Monitor changes.

12. Expand the Data Collection Sets branch in the left-hand pane of the Performance Monitor, and then click the User Defined branch. The right-hand pane is empty as no data collector sets have been defined.

13. Right-click in the right-hand pane, and click **New>Data Collector Set** in the shortcut menu. A wizard appears to guide you through creating a data collector set.

14. On the first page of the wizard, name the data collector set Practice Set, and click the **Create from a template** radio button. Then, click the **Next** button.

15. On the next page of the wizard, select the Basic template, and click the **Next** button.

16. On the next page of the wizard, click the **Finish** button to accept the default location for saving the file. The Practice Set data collector set appears in the right-hand pane, as shown. Notice that by default it is not running.

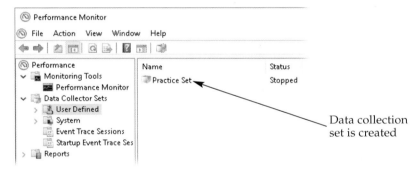

17. Double-click Practice Set in the right-hand pane to expand this branch. Notice the options now available in the right-hand pane.

18. Double-click Performance Counter in the right-hand pane to display the **Performance Counter Properties** dialog box. By default, a processor counter is included. Other counters can be added.

19. Click the **Add...** button in the dialog box. The same dialog box used earlier to add counters is displayed.

20. Applying what you have learned, add a bytes received per second counter for the network adapter. Then click the **OK** button to close the **Performance Counter Properties** dialog box.

21. Right-click on Practice Set in the left-hand pane, and click **Start** in the shortcut menu. Notice the icon for Practice Set changes to indicate it is running.

22. Leave the Performance Monitor open, launch a web browser, and navigate to a few web pages.

23. Return to the Performance Monitor. Right-click on Practice Set in the left-hand pane, and click **Stop** in the shortcut menu.

Quick Look 6.1.3 Continued

24. Expand the Reports branch in the left-hand pane, and then the User Defined branch. Select the Practice Set branch to see the report that was generated, as shown.

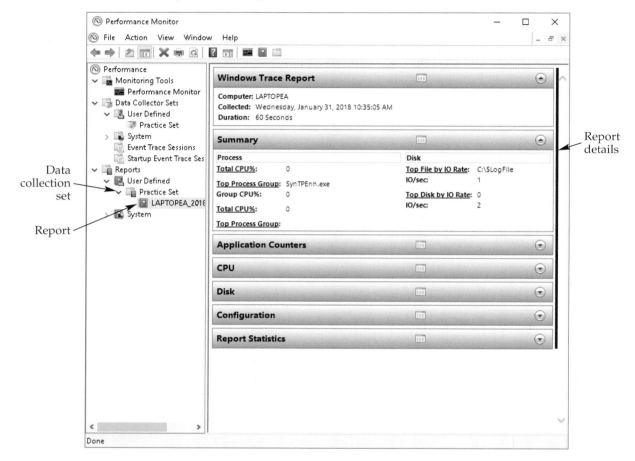

25. Double-click the report in either the left- or right-hand pane. The details are displayed in the right-hand pane.
26. Investigate the data that were saved to the data collection set.
27. Close the Performance Monitor and any other open windows.

Event Logging

Event logging is a function of the operating system or an application that records events or situations in a file. These events can indicate informational announcements and serious or critical errors. Logs provide vital information for security professionals. They can reveal clues of potential security issues. They also can be used after an incident to pinpoint the user or computer involved. Many hackers attempt to clear the logs and cover their tracks. Clearing a log is an event. You can monitor for this as well.

There are many different types of logs, depending on which services are installed. In Windows, the most common logs are system, application, security, and PowerShell. The system log records events that are generated from the operating system or related components. For example, if a server is restarted, this event would be recorded in the system log. The application log records events triggered by applications, such as an update to Windows Defender. The security log is used to track events related to auditing established configurations. For example, this log can audit the failed attempts of logging in as a specific user. PowerShell logs allow administrators to view which providers are accessed. In some cases, the cmdlets that are used are also logged.

Security professionals can use these logs to monitor events that could indicate a potential security breach. Event logs in Windows are categorized by codes. **Figure 6-5** shows some event codes that may indicate a security incident.

Viewing the Windows event logs is done with the Event Viewer. This is a versatile program. It allows for viewing of the different logs, saving and backing up logs, and creating alerts. Alerts can notify administrators of potential concerns as a problem occurs. Multiple logs from different machines can even be forwarded into a combined log. When the Event Viewer is first opened, the main screen provides a dashboard for quick analysis. Windows event logs are categorized by type, as shown in **Figure 6-6.** They include:

- critical;
- error;
- warning;
- information;
- audit success; and
- audit failure.

Service accounts are special accounts used for services or programs to log in and run instead of providing a user's credentials.

Logs can be saved as comma separated value (CSV) files. CSV files are a great way to share data with other programs, such as Excel or Access!

Event Code	Description	Potential Security Concern
1102	Deletion of the security log	This could be a normal administrative task, but it could mean someone tried to cover his or her tracks by deleting the contents of this log.
4663	An attempt to access an object	If a large number of files are being deleted, this event will be recorded. This may indicate someone is trying to remove critical company information.
4724	Password reset (a privileged user changed this user's password)	While this is a normal function of networking, it could be tracked for administrative accounts or service accounts.
4704, 4717	Change to user's rights or permissions assignments	This could indicate a hacker has given an account more rights than it should have.
4740	User account locked out	This is normal; users do forget their passwords. However, frequent occurrences of this event, or it occurring on service, administrative, or manager accounts, should be investigated.

Goodheart-Willcox Publisher

Figure 6-5. In Windows, events are coded. These codes may indicate a security issue.

Type	Meaning
Critical	A serious error. It indicates something is broken. An example of when this entry may appear is if the system is powered off without a clean shutdown.
Error	Indicates a significant problem that could include a loss of functionality or data. For example, if a service failed to start as instructed, this entry may be created.
Warning	Indicates a potential problem or possible future problem. For example, a warning can be logged if the system is low on disk space.
Information	Describes a successful operation of an application, driver, or service. For example, an event will be recorded for downloading and installing a Windows update.
Audit Success	An audited security access that was successful. A common example is a user's successful attempt at logging in.
Audit Failure	An audited security event that fails. For example, an unsuccessful logon attempt is recorded as a failure.

Goodheart-Willcox Publisher

Figure 6-6. Event codes in Windows are classified by a type that indicates their potential severity.

Ethical Issue

Governmental Obligations

One of the issues raised in the aftermath of the WannaCry ransomware was the revelation that the US government, through the National Security Agency, was aware of this vulnerability and did not publicly disclose it. Instead, the government used the information as part of its intelligence-gathering processes. The US government has a process called VEP. This stands for *vulnerabilities equities process*. VEP determines when and whether governmental agencies must disclose what they have discovered.

Investigate VEP, and write a report explaining it. Specifically discuss what happened with the WannaCry malware. As part of your report, defend one of these two statements:

A. You believe the NSA had an obligation to disclose this vulnerability to Microsoft and other key software vendors and was at fault for not doing so.

B. You believe the NSA had an obligation to collect intelligence information and was correct in not disclosing the vulnerabilities.

Quick Look 6.1.4

Event Logs

Event logs can provide much information on the operation of a system. In Windows, the Event Viewer is used to not only view logs, but also manage or export them.

1. Click the Windows **Start** button, and enter event viewer in the search bar. Select the Event Viewer application in the search results.

2. The left-hand pane of the Event Viewer contains items organized in a tree format. Click the Windows Logs branch. The middle pane displays the different logs for the machine. The logs listed will depend on the machine and its installed services. How many logs are listed (in the Name column)?

3. Expand the Windows Logs branch. Notice the branches listed below it match the logs listed in the middle pane. Select the System branch, as shown. The system log is displayed in the middle pane.

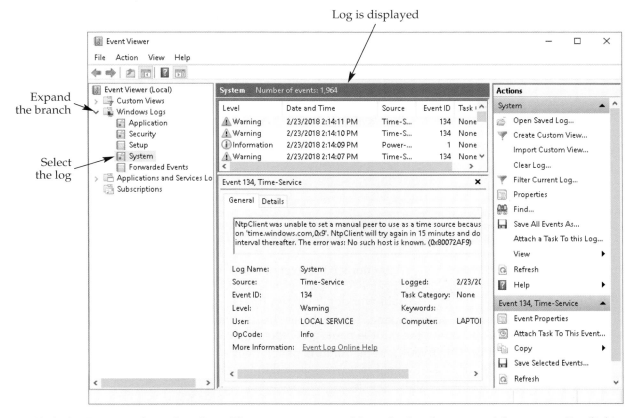

4. Click the Source column heading. The events are sorted in order by the name of the source. By clicking any of the column headings, the view can be sorted in ascending or descending order by column. The default order of events is by date and time with the most recent event at the top.

5. Double-click any event in the list. Additional information about that event is displayed in a dialog box. Click the **Close** button to exit the information.

6. The right-hand pane is the **Actions** pane. This is where you can perform additional tasks, such as searching, filtering, and saving. Click **Find...** to display a search box, and enter DHCP. The first event that references DHCP is selected in the list (it may take a few seconds to find). Click the **Find Next** button to jump to the next related event, and then click the **Cancel** button to end the search function.

Quick Look 6.1.4 Continued

7. Click **Filter Current Log...** in the **Actions** pane. The **Filter Current Log** dialog box is displayed, as shown. This dialog box allows you to define multiple parameters to filter the search, such as looking for any warnings and DHCP or disk.

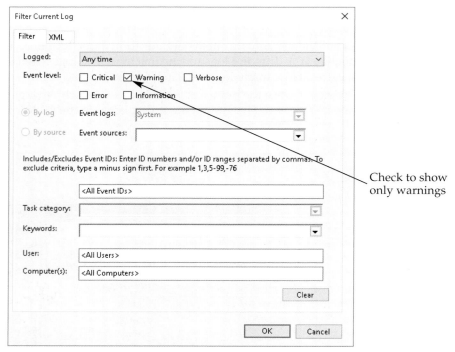

Check to show only warnings

8. Check the **Warning** check box, and then click the **OK** button. The logs are filtered to show only those categorized as warnings.

9. Click **Save filtered log as...** in the **Actions** pane. A standard save-type dialog box is displayed. The log can be saved in comma separated value (CSV), extensible markup language (XML), text (TXT), or event log (EVTx) format. Navigate to your working folder for this class, and save the file as LogTest.csv.

10. Click **Clear Filter** in the **Actions** pane. This removes the filter you just applied, and the full list of events is again displayed in the middle pane. Note: do *not* click **Clear Log...** in the **Actions** pane!

11. Click **Attach Task To This Event...** in the **Actions** pane. A wizard is launched to guide you through setting an alert for the specific event that was selected in the middle pane. Click the **Cancel** button to close the wizard without adding an alert.

CompTIA Security+
2.2

Analyzing Log Events

Event logs can provide evidence of inappropriate activity, suspicious behavior or actions, and even forewarning of system failures. Event logs can become cluttered with a great deal of events. Many events provide information that is not critical. For example, Windows group policy being successfully processed or the DHCP client starting are common events. If auditing is enabled, you may see many entries that indicate a successful event. Whenever a user completes the login process is a successful event.

In Windows, security events can be audited for success, failure, or both. For example, to find everyone who edited a file, audit that event for success. To see unsuccessful attempts to log in as a specific user, then audit that event for failure.

To help in the analysis of event log data, there are some best practices that should be performed to help with this analysis:

- Set up alerts for events that notify of a specific event.
- Plan to review logs on a frequent basis, not just when there is a problem.
- Define only the audit policies that you wish to record.
- Entries in logs that are indicated by critical or error levels are usually more serious than information or warning levels.
- Warnings can be indicative of a larger problem; analyze how often the warning occurs, and look at other events that occurred around the same time.
- Identify key events that could be of security concern and cross-reference against approved actions; for example, an event detailing the creating of a new user should be verified against an approved user account.
- Consider using PowerShell cmdlets or scripts to easily query logs for specific events.

Quick Look 6.1.5

Event Log Data

There are many ways to view an event log. Once a log is created, it can be queried for specific data. PowerShell can be used to quickly query an event log to search for specific events and levels.

1. Applying what you have learned, open PowerShell with administrative access.
2. Enter get-eventlog -list to view the available event logs.
3. Enter get-eventlog -logname system -newest 5. The five most recent entries in the event log of any level or type will be displayed. Specific event IDs are shown as an instance ID in PowerShell.
4. Enter get-eventlog -logname system -instanceid *xx*, where *xx* is the number of an instance ID displayed in the previous step. For example, perhaps you wish to search the installation of a Windows update. This event has an instance ID of 19.
5. Repeat the command from step 4, and add -newest 10. The last ten times this event occurred are displayed.
6. Enter get-eventlog -logname system -entrytype error to display entries with errors.
7. You can search for keywords in the message. Enter get-eventlog -logname system -message "*failed*". Any entry that contains the word *failed* in the message is displayed. Notice that you must use both quotation marks and asterisks around the word.
8. Exit PowerShell.

Log File Management

Every Windows desktop and server maintains various log files. Certain software programs use log files. There are log files for network switches and routers. Therefore, evaluating and managing logs can be challenging. Administrators must develop a plan on log management, which includes the answers to these questions:

- Which logs should be prioritized?
- Which alerts should be implemented?
- How shall logs be viewed and by whom?
- Where and for how long should logs be stored?

The answers to these questions should be decided with executive management. Some decisions may have to take into account governmental regulations. Rules and procedures should be established in the form of log-file policies.

With Event Viewer, other hosts can be set up to forward entire logs or specific events to a single source log, and you can back up your log data. A forwarded events log can be set up on a single machine to allow the events of logs from other systems to be tracked, as shown in **Figure 6-7**. To gather data, you create a subscription to the events on the remote computer. All data can be gathered or the data can be customized to specific events. The data can even be limited to specific events, such as errors or warnings.

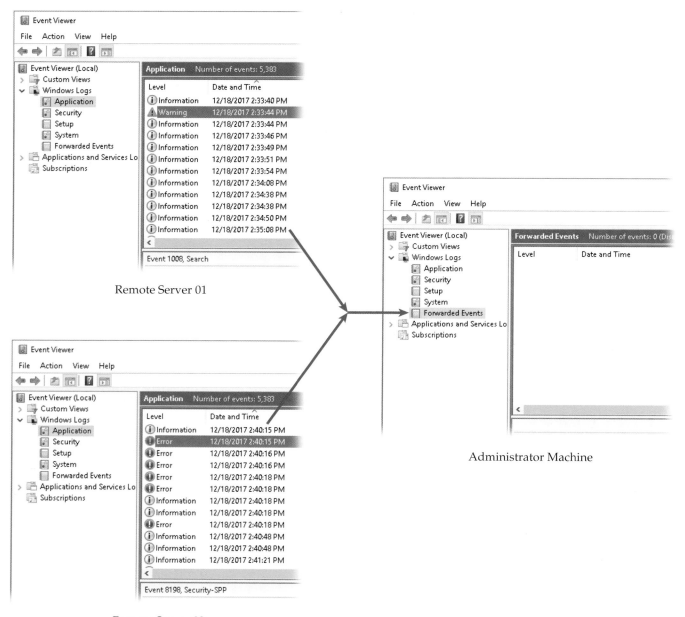

Remote Server 01

Administrator Machine

Remote Server 02

Figure 6-7. Logs can be forwarded from individual machines into a single location on an administrator's machine.

Quick Look 6.1.6

Event Log Backup

The ability to manage logs is a skill important to IT professionals. Part of log management is creating backups of logs.

1. Applying what you have learned, launch the Windows Event Viewer.
2. Expand the tree in the left-hand pane, and select the branch for the log you wish to back up.
3. Click **Save All Events As…** in the **Actions** pane. A standard save-type dialog box is displayed.
4. Navigate to your working folder for this class, name the file *LogName_Year_Month* (such as System_2019_June), and select **Event Files (.evtx)** in the **Save as type:** drop-down list. Click the **Save** button to save the file. The **Display Information** dialog box is displayed. Click the **OK** button to accept the default setting and close the dialog box. The backup file is created.
5. Click **Open Saved Log…** in the **Actions** pane. A standard open-type dialog box is displayed. Navigate to your working folder, and open the EVTX file you just saved. The **Open Saved Log** dialog box is displayed, as shown.

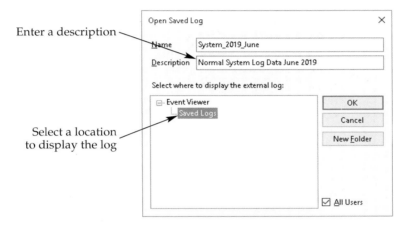

6. Click in the **Description** text box, and enter a brief statement of the log file. For example, you may enter Normal System Log Data June 2019. Also, notice you can choose where the log will be displayed. By default, opened logs are displayed in the Saved Logs branch.
7. Click the **OK** button to finish opening the log. The log is automatically selected in the tree, and the events it contains are displayed in the middle pane. Notice the log name appears above the events, and it also is the name of the branch in the left-hand pane.

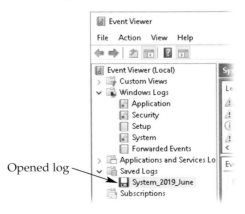

8. Close the Event Viewer.

CompTIA Security+
4.4

MTA Security Fundamentals
2.4

Auditing

Auditing is the process of tracking the actions of an individual using a resource. This may include tracking such tasks as:

- creating users;
- making changes to files;
- printing documents;
- deleting files;
- software installations;
- specific database access; and
- changes to switches and routers.

There are many other areas that can be audited as well. The administrator must configure the systems to determine what will be logged. Logged events can provide critical information. This information may reveal security issues. Auditing needs are driven by the type of business and a company's risk-management strategy. Audits may also be needed for civil or criminal litigation.

Security administrators spend a great deal of time on prevention and real-time monitoring. However, it is essential to also track and view what has been done. Audits can identify potential problems, but they are especially useful in tracking what has been done, when it occurred, and what user or host system was involved.

Consider the case of Reality Leigh Winner. She worked for Pluribus International, which was a contractor for a governmental facility. In June of 2017, she was charged with revealing a classified document to a news outlet. In May of that year, the news outlet went to the NSA to verify the information in the document. When a copy of the document was examined, creases were noted in the document. After deciding the creases indicated the document had been printed, the NSA looked at its event logs, specifically those that tracked usage, such as the security log. It discovered Winner was one of only a few individuals who had printed this document. Further investigation showed she was the only employee who had e-mail contact with the news outlet.

Another consideration in auditing is determining who has the rights to the auditing data. In many instances, the auditor of the information should be an independent person. An independent person is one who has no connection to the systems being examined. When an independent person handles the information, the integrity of the logged data is preserved.

On a Windows host, a *group policy* determines the events that will be logged for auditing. The group policy is an essential tool in Windows. It allows you to implement configuration settings on the local host. If it is running on a server using the Active Directory, it can be used to configure multiple hosts or users.

To configure auditing, open the Group Policy Editor, as shown in **Figure 6-8.** This is accessed from the Administrative Tools. Expand the Computer Configuration branch, then the Windows Settings, Security Settings, and Local Policies branches. Select the Audit Policy branch to see the available option. By default, nothing is enabled for auditing. When an option is configured, it is first enabled to audit either successes or failures. Then, the individual objects to audit are selected.

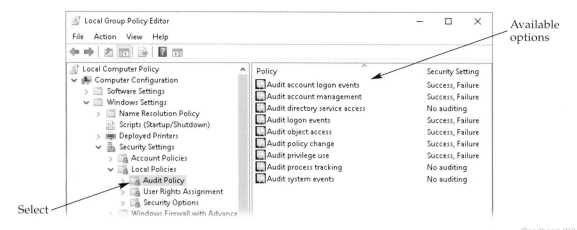

Available options

Select

Goodheart-Willcox Publisher

Figure 6-8. In Windows, the Group Policy Editor is used to create and manage group policies.

Quick Look 6.1.7

Audit Policy

Suppose your sales manager is working on a bid proposal and wants to track everyone who opens the file or changes its content. These events can be audited to help protect the integrity of the data in the bid proposal. Note: this exercise is based on Windows 10, and you will need administrative access to the system.

1. Create a new document in Microsoft Word, and add your name to the file.
2. Save the file as SalesBid in your working folder for this class, and exit Word. You will audit for users who are able to view and make changes to the file.
3. Click the Windows **Start** button, and enter group policy in the search box. Select **Edit group policy** in the results to open the Group Policy Editor application.
4. In the left-hand pane, expand the tree Computer Configuration>Windows Settings>Security Settings>Local Policies and select the Audit Policy branch.
5. In the right-hand pane, double-click Audit object access. The **Audit Object Access Properties** dialog box is displayed, as shown.

Check

6. Check the **Success** check box, and then click the **OK** button. Editing and saving the word-processing file is a "success event."
7. Close the Group Policy Editor.
8. Launch File Explorer, navigate to your working folder, right-click on the SalesBid document, and click **Properties** in the shortcut menu.
9. In the **Properties** dialog box, click the **Security** tab, and then click the **Advanced** button.

Quick Look 6.1.7 Continued

10. In the **Advanced Security Settings** dialog box, click the **Auditing** tab. Click the **Continue** button in the middle of the tab to acknowledge the warning.

11. Click the **Add** button at the bottom of the tab. A new dialog box is displayed for adding an auditing entry. You first need to select the principal, which is the user to audit.

12. Click the **Select a principal** link. In the new dialog box that is displayed, click in the **Enter the object name to select:** text box, enter everyone, and click the **OK** button.

13. Click the **Type:** drop-down arrow, and click **Success** in the list. Also, check **Modify**, **Read & execute**, and **Write** check boxes, as shown. Then, click the **OK** button. If you get any errors regarding enumeration, just click through them.

Set to audit for success

Select what to monitor

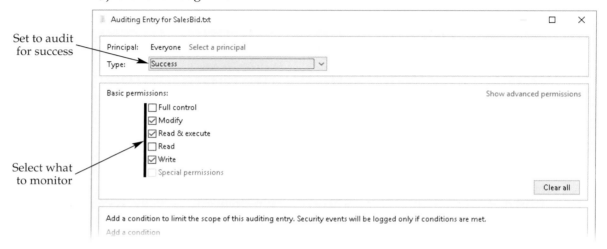

14. Click the **OK** button to exit the **Advanced Security Settings** dialog box, and then the **OK** button to exit the **Properties** dialog box.

15. Open the SalesBid document in a word processor. Add today's date, and save and close the file.

16. Applying what you have learned, open the Event Viewer, and display the security log.

17. Applying what you have learned, open the **Filter Current Log** dialog box.

18. Enter the event ID 4660, as shown. Then, click the **OK** button to show only those events with this code.

Enter the ID by which to filter

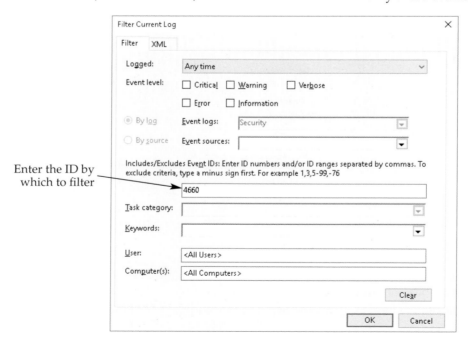

Quick Look 6.1.7 Continued

19. Select the event in the middle pane of the Event Viewer. Look at the details for the event in the **General** tab at the bottom of the middle pane. The **Security ID:** entry is the user who changed the file. The program used to access the file is also listed. For example, if Microsoft Word was used to modify the file, the path to winword.exe will be given.

20. Close the Event Viewer.

SECTION REVIEW 6.1

Check Your Understanding

1. A service in Linux is known by what name?
2. In which folder are most Windows services located?
3. What type of account is a service account?
4. Which Windows program allows you to monitor specific resources such as printers or hard disks?
5. Auditing information is stored in which log file?

Build Your Key Terms Vocabulary

As you progress through this course, develop a personal cybersecurity glossary. This will help you build your vocabulary and prepare you for a career. Write a definition for each of the following terms, and add it to your cybersecurity glossary.

attack surface	event logging
auditing	group policy
baseline	hardening
daemon	service

System Vulnerabilities

Why is open-source software an appropriate choice for security monitoring?

Malware that can infiltrate a computer is a clear vulnerability. In addition, computers can have many other vulnerabilities. Some examples include misconfigured services and programs, unpatched systems, users who have more permissions or rights to the system, and open network ports. There are measures that can be taken to eliminate or minimize the threat of these vulnerabilities. Special programs known as vulnerability scanners can be run. Firewalls can block traffic from entering or exiting a system. This section explores vulnerability scanners and how to protect a system with other preventative measures. Patching, firewalls, and tracking changes are all covered.

Key Terms 🔗

asset tag
botnet
change-management system
credentialed scan
false negative
false positive

firewall
intrusive scan
IT asset management (ITAM) system
noncredentialed scan
nonintrusive scan

out-of-band
packet-filtering firewall
patch
proxy server firewall
stateful-inspection firewall
vulnerability scanner

Learning Goals

- Discuss patch management.
- Use appropriate tools to conduct vulnerability assessments.
- Illustrate host-based firewalls.
- Compare change-management systems.

System Patching

CompTIA Security+
3.3

MTA Security Fundamentals
4.1

The goal of hardening software is to eliminate system vulnerabilities. Regularly patching systems is an integral part of eliminating vulnerabilities. A *patch* is an update provided by the vendor to correct errors or bugs. Often, these errors or bugs are security vulnerabilities. The operating system should have the latest patches applied. However, do not forget about programs such as web browsers, office-productivity suites, and other applications. Unpatched systems present a major vulnerability that could easily be exploited by malware or direct user access. This was evident in the WannaCry ransomware attack referenced earlier.

Patch Tuesday

Most people in IT are familiar with "Patch Tuesday." In October of 2003, Microsoft announced it would only release updates, including patches, on the second Tuesday of each month, as shown in **Figure 6-9.** Prior to this change, Microsoft released security updates on an as-needed basis. Often, there was little or no warning provided. This resulted in IT departments scrambling to test and deploy patches as soon as possible. Patch Tuesday allows IT departments to schedule patching as a regular part of their security routines. Other companies, such as Adobe and Oracle, have also followed this scheduled plan of action.

In 2008, Microsoft discovered a significant flaw in its server service. The flaw could allow remote code execution if the affected system received a specifically crafted remote procedure call (RPC) request. Microsoft was so concerned it issued the patch for this out-of-band. *Out-of-band* means released without waiting until the next regularly scheduled date for patches. This patch was called MS08-067 (Microsoft 2008 – Patch 67). By releasing the patch immediately, Microsoft provided the fix to remove the vulnerability. However, this also alerted hackers to the significant vulnerability. Hackers could potentially perform exploits before the patch was applied. The computer worm Conficker did exactly this. It was able to infect between 10 and 15 million computers.

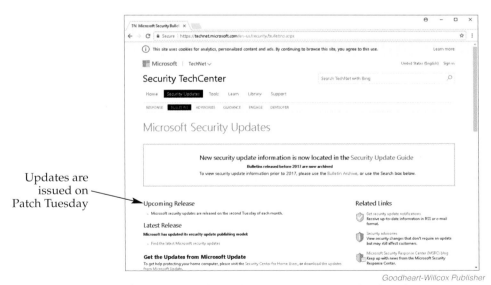

Updates are issued on Patch Tuesday

Goodheart-Willcox Publisher

Figure 6-9. Microsoft has adopted Patch Tuesday as a standardized way to release patches and updates.

Quick Look 6.2.1

Out-of-Band Patches

Releasing patches on a regular schedule allows IT departments to easily manage updates. Sometimes, a vulnerability may be serious enough to release an out-of-band patch. However, this advertises not only the vulnerability, but its seriousness.

1. Launch a web browser, and navigate to a search engine.
2. Search for history of MS08-067, and select the article titled *The Inside Story Behind MS08-067* from the blogs.technet.microsoft.com site.
3. Read the article. Take note of key actions by the security team.
4. Do you agree with the decision to release this patch out-of-band? Discuss your thoughts with your class.

Update Check

In most businesses, system updates are automated through a group policy. However, mobile devices such as laptops or some standalone systems may not be fully updated with this method. It is important that all systems are configured to check for updates.

Windows

In Windows 10, updates are automatically downloaded and installed by default. However, the system may be configured otherwise. To view the settings for updates, click the **Start** button. Then, click **Settings** in the menu. Finally, click the **Update and Security** link. In the window that is displayed, click **Windows Update** in the menu on the left. To see specifics of the current settings, click the **Advanced options** link on the right.

In Windows 7, click **Start>Control Panel**. Then, click the **System and Security** link. In the window that is displayed, click the **Windows Update** link on the right. In the next window, click **Change settings** in the menu on the left. To change how updates are installed, click the drop-down arrow in the **Important updates** area, and click an option in the list. The default option is **Install updates automatically**. This is the recommended setting.

There are times when reviewing updates that have been installed is beneficial. Updates are intended to fix bugs. However, an update could cause a problem. In that case, it must be uninstalled. In Control Panel, click **Programs>Programs and Features>View installed updates**. A list of the updates that have been installed is displayed, as shown in **Figure 6-10**. To uninstall an update, select it in the list, and click the Uninstall link on the toolbar. Note that not all updates can be uninstalled.

Linux

In a Linux system such as Ubuntu, updates can be installed from the command line or through the graphical interface. In the graphical interface, **Edit>Software sources...** to display the **Software Sources** dialog box. Click the **Updates** tab in the dialog box. In the **Automatic updates** area of the tab, check the **Check for updates** check box, and then select how often in the corresponding drop-down list. Finally, below the drop-down list, choose which option to use for how updates should be installed.

The **apt-get** command is used for installing updates on the command line. The *apt* stands for advanced packaging tool. This command must be run as an administrator. To run the command as an administrator, use the **sudo** command with it. Enter sudo apt-get update to install updates.

Click to uninstall

Select an update

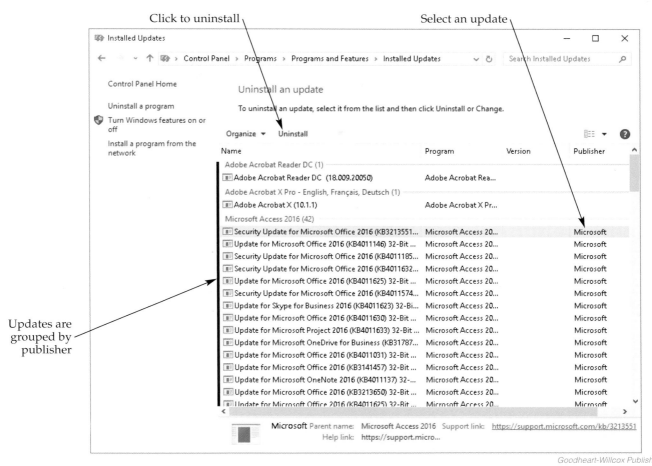

Updates are grouped by publisher

Figure 6-10. The updates that have been installed on Windows can be viewed and, if needed, removed.

Vulnerability Scanners

It can be a lot of work to manually scan systems for potential vulnerabilities. Even with care, it can be easy to miss a vulnerability. Fortunately, there are software programs to do this, as shown in **Figure 6-11.** A *vulnerability scanner* is software that automates the process of scanning systems for potential weaknesses in software, configurations, and other settings. This type of software can scan for many different vulnerabilities. It can also help prioritize the results. Some versions can automatically fix vulnerabilities that are found.

Types of Vulnerability Scanners

There are many different vulnerability scanners on the market. They may be platform specific, such as Windows only or Linux hosts. They may be free, open source, or commercial editions. Commercial editions are versions that must be purchased. Some of the more popular choices include:

- Microsoft Baseline Security Analyzer (MBSA), which is for Windows systems and is free;
- Nessus, which is for Windows and Linux platforms with free-trial and commercial versions; and
- OpenVAS, which is for Windows and Linux platforms and is open source.

The Microsoft Baseline Security Analyzer is an excellent free program to discover vulnerabilities. However, there are limits to what it can discover. Its key features include the ability to scan one host or a range of hosts, look for accounts

CompTIA Security+
2.2

FYI There is a saying, "you often get what you pay for." This is generally true when considering vulnerability scanners. Commercial products often provide deeper scans and better reporting systems than free or open-source options.

MTA Security Fundamentals
4.3

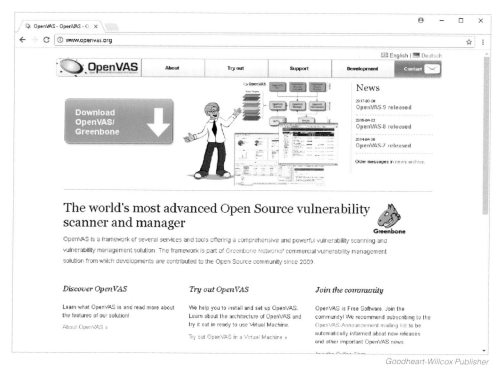

Figure 6-11. Vulnerability scanners are an integral part of system security. There are many available.

with administrator access, and identify weak passwords or even accounts with no passwords. It also analyzes Microsoft's current software patches and advises you if you are missing any critical security updates.

Nessus is another excellent utility. It goes far beyond MBSA. In addition to locating vulnerabilities, it can scan for viruses or other malware. It can also scan for any communication with a botnet. A *botnet* is a loosely connected network of infected computers that are being managed by an unknown host. Most botnets conduct coordinated attacks on other systems. Nessus comes with many templates that can be used to scan for compliance with regulations, such as those from HIPAA.

OpenVAS stands for Open Vulnerability Assessment System. It was forked from Nessus's last free version. OpenVAS is popular among many IT professionals since it is free and builds on the same type of scanning that is offered in the for-purchase Nessus scanner. You can scan specific targets, open ports, or choose from a variety of preconfigured templates of scanning options. It comes preloaded on some Linux distributions, such as Kali Linux.

Quick Look 6.2.2

Vulnerability Scanners

There are many options for vulnerability scanners. While most have some similar capabilities, there are usually differences between each. Knowing the differences is important when selecting a vulnerability scanner for a particular situation.

1. Research vulnerability scanners. Use the Internet, magazines, newspapers, and other sources to gather information.

2. Select three products, and identify common and different features.

Quick Look 6.2.2 Continued

3. Create a document listing each product, where the product can be obtained, and for or five key features of each. Be sure to include which operating systems are compatible for each product.
4. How often do you think a vulnerability scanner should be run? Share your thoughts and reasoning with your classmates.

Vulnerability Scanning Concepts

CompTIA Security+
2.1

As with any scanning software, such as antivirus scanners, the results may not always be accurate. When reviewing scanning reports, you need to analyze and take actions to correct any identified problems. Unfortunately, you may not realize if the reported vulnerability is actually an error. There are two common inaccurate results: false positive and false negative.

A *false positive* is when something is identified as harmful when it really is not. An example is a scan showing that an update did not contain a specific security patch, but the patch was actually installed. A false positive wastes time. The security technician tries to track down why the error occurred. However, since the vulnerability did not exist, there is no higher security concern.

On the other hand, a false negative is more problematic. A *false negative* is when something is not identified as harmful when it really is. For example, the vulnerability scanner may not report a misconfiguration in a program. This is potentially very serious. Security personnel are operating on the assumption that this vulnerability does not exist when it actually does.

To help reduce the number of false returns, ensure the vulnerability scanner is up to date. Also, make sure it is using the most current threat databases. Additionally, compare reporting rates of false positives and false negatives for the vulnerability scanner. If the rates are too high, you may need to consider using a different scanner.

Another concept related to vulnerability scanning deals with intrusive and nonintrusive scanning. A vulnerability scanner takes one of these approaches to search for vulnerabilities. Most commercial vulnerability scanners provide options to select the level of intrusiveness that is desired in a scan. A *nonintrusive scan* is generally a simple scan of the target. This could involve searching for keys in the registry, open ports, missing software patches, and similar vulnerabilities. During this type of scan, the scanner reads and records the requested information. An intrusive scan is a major step further. In an *intrusive scan,* the scanner tries to exploit vulnerabilities. A script automates the attack to prove the target is vulnerable. Intrusive scanning could have a major impact on the system or network that is being scanned. For example, business functions could be disabled during the scan. Even worse, the target could be left more vulnerable if the attack is successful.

CompTIA Security+
1.5

A scan may be noncredentialed or credentialed. A *noncredentialed scan* is not authenticated. The scan is conducted to provide a quick view of vulnerabilities. This type of scan is faster than a credentialed scan. However, it may not provide enough information. It may also not discover all vulnerabilities. Think of it this way: you can look in a window of a store, but you did not actually enter the premises for an accurate scan of what is inside.

CompTIA Security+
1.5

A *credentialed scan* uses appropriate authentication to provide accurate and comprehensive feedback. These scans take longer than noncredentialed scans. They may be more difficult to do if you lack access to all the areas and programs that need to be scanned. However, the greater level of detail and accuracy of information make them a better choice.

MTA Security Fundamentals
3.1

Firewalls

A *firewall* is a security tool that acts as a barrier or protection against an unwanted data transfer. Firewalls can block or filter data coming into the host or leaving the host. Data coming into the host is called inbound or ingress data. An inbound rule would control this type of data. Data leaving the host is called outbound or egress data. An outbound rule would control this type of data. Firewalls can be both hardware and software solutions, as shown in **Figure 6-12.** A firewall may offer extensive reporting on its activity. This may include summary data of the type of traffic processed by the firewall.

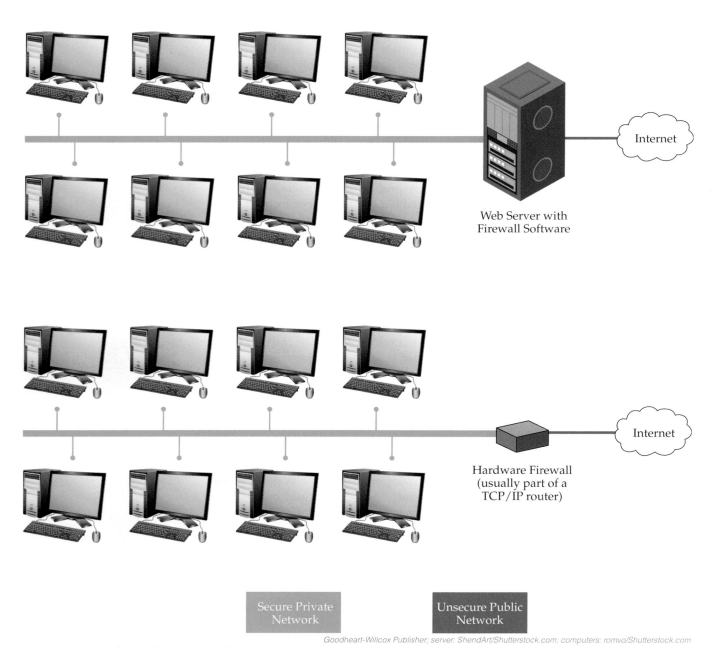

Web Server with
Firewall Software

Internet

Hardware Firewall
(usually part of a
TCP/IP router)

Internet

Secure Private
Network

Unsecure Public
Network

Goodheart-Willcox Publisher; server: ShendArt/Shutterstock.com; computers: romvo/Shutterstock.com

Figure 6-12. A firewall may be software or hardware based.

A firewall designed to protect just a single host is called a *local-* or *host-based firewall*. Those that protect a network are *network firewalls*. Firewalls are often configured at the network level. In this case, the firewall usually sits between private and public networks. However, firewalls can be implemented on segments of a single network. One may also be used to add another defensive layer on key hosts, such as servers, or other critical assets.

According to the National Institute of Standards and Technology (NIST), there are generally three types of firewalls:

- packet filtering
- stateful inspection
- proxy server

Packet-Filtering Firewall

A *packet-filtering firewall* can either allow or block traffic entering or exiting the firewall by evaluating network addresses, ports, or protocols (such as Internet Control Message Protocol, or ICMP). Packet-filtering firewalls often run at the network layer (layer 3) of the OSI model. This is due to the data in the header that is examined by the firewall. In the OSI model, the network layer is concerned about information in the packet's header. This includes source and destination IP addresses.

This type of firewall works by reading the header of the packet. After evaluating the header content, it will either allow (accept) or deny (drop) the packet. **Figure 6-13** shows a packet with a destination port of 23 being examined at the firewall. Since the firewall has a rule to block data to port 23, the packet is dropped. Recall from your understanding of the OSI model, packets will either be TCP or UDP packets. You will need to identify which protocol you are blocking or allowing. For example, to block Trivial File Transfer Protocol (TFTP), block UDP on port 69. To block a DNS zone transfer, block TCP on port 53.

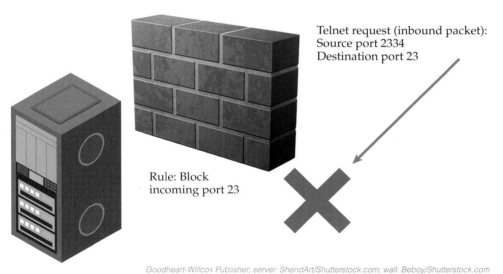

Telnet request (inbound packet):
Source port 2334
Destination port 23

Rule: Block
incoming port 23

Figure 6-13. A packet-filtering firewall controls data traffic based on the header of each packet.

Stateful-Inspection Firewall

Hackers can manipulate a packet's header and add the word *reply*. Packet-filtering firewalls often automatically allow replies through the firewall. Stateful-inspection firewalls can do a better job of blocking unwanted traffic than a packet-filtering firewall. A *stateful-inspection firewall* works by monitoring packets over a period of time and accepting only packets that were previously tracked. Each packet that enters or exits the firewall is analyzed. If a packet matches an active connection that was previously tracked, it is allowed through the firewall. This prevents a packet from being manipulated to appear as if it were part of a larger transmission. It does not stop the packets that originate a conversation.

This type of firewall does not limit its analysis to just the packet header. It also inspects the state of the traffic entering and exiting the firewall. Stateful-inspection firewalls maintain a *state table* of previous packets. In **Figure 6-14,** a packet is inbound for port 80, which is not blocked. However, since the packet is a reply, the firewall searches the state table. It does not find the source IP address (192.168.101.55) in the state table. This means the packet has not previously been through the firewall. Therefore, the packet is dropped.

Proxy Server Firewall

The third type of firewall is known as a proxy server firewall. This is the most advanced firewall. A *proxy server firewall* analyzes the packet's data as well as its header. This includes OSI application layer (layer 7) protocol information such as HTTP or FTP. The firewall acts as a proxy, which is an intermediary agent. It is linked to the client with one connection and to the server with another connection.

Whether or not you realize it, you may be familiar with proxy server firewalls. They are often used in schools to block websites based on the URL or content. For example, if you try to navigate to www.facebook.com on your school's system, the website may be blocked. This is due to a proxy server firewall that is reading the content you requested.

Proxy server firewalls are more common on network segments. These are covered in more depth in the chapter on network security.

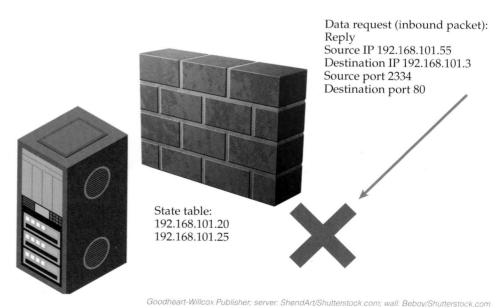

Data request (inbound packet):
Reply
Source IP 192.168.101.55
Destination IP 192.168.101.3
Source port 2334
Destination port 80

State table:
192.168.101.20
192.168.101.25

Figure 6-14. A state-inspection firewall allows only data that has been previously tracked.

Quick Look 6.2.3

Windows Firewall

Microsoft Windows desktop and server operating systems have a built-in firewall. This is a software firewall that can be very useful.

1. Click the Windows **Start** button, and launch the Control Panel.
2. In the Control Panel, click **Windows Firewall** to display the firewall.
3. On the left, click **Turn Windows Firewall on or off**. On the new page, turn on the firewall for all types of network settings. Depending on your system, there may be two or three types.
4. Click the back button at the top of the Control Panel, and then click **Advanced settings** on the left. The **Windows Firewall with Advanced Security** window is opened, as shown.

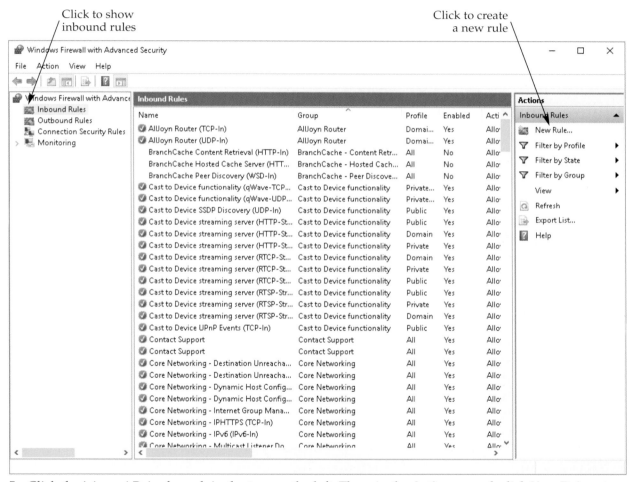

5. Click the Inbound Rules branch in the tree on the left. Then, in the **Actions** panel, click **New Rule…** to launch the **New Inbound Rule Wizard**.
6. On the first page of the wizard, click the **Port** radio button. This rule will control connections to a port. Click the **Next** button.
7. On the next page of the wizard, click the **TCP** radio button. Then, click the **Specific local ports:** radio button, and enter 23 in the corresponding text box. Click the **Next** button.
8. On the next page of the wizard, click the **Block the connection** radio button. This will prevent any inbound data from being sent to port 23. Click the **Next** button.
9. On the next page of the wizard, accept the default settings with the **Domain**, **Private**, and **Public** check boxes checked. Click the **Next** button.

Quick Look 6.2.3 Continued

10. On the final page of the wizard, enter **No Telnet** as the name. Click the **Finish** button. After finishing, you will notice the port now blocked in the inbound rules list, as shown.

New rule is created

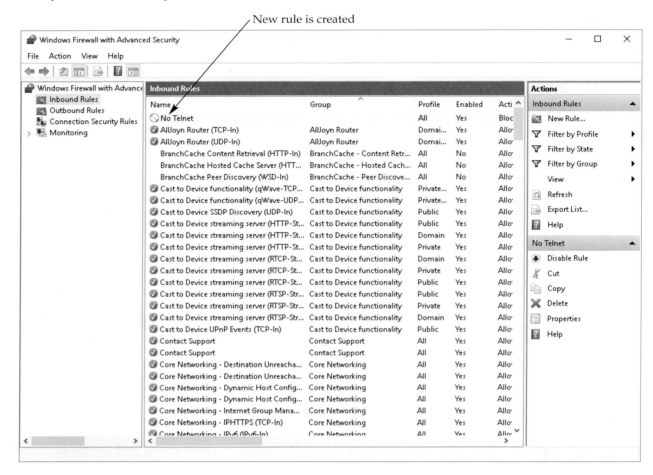

11. Click the Windows Firewall with Advanced Security branch in the left-hand pane.
12. Click **Properties** in the **Actions** pane. The dialog box that is displayed can be used to view or change the logging options.
13. On the **Domain Profile** tab, click the **Customize...** button in the **Logging** area of the tab.
14. In the **Customize Logging Setting for the Domain Profile** dialog box that is displayed, click the **Log dropped packets:** drop-down arrow, and click **Yes** in the list, as shown.

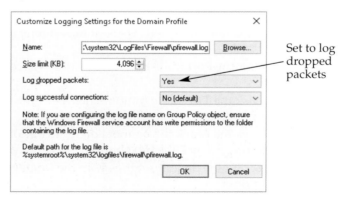

Set to log dropped packets

Quick Look 6.2.3 Continued

15. Click the **OK** button to close the **Customize Logging Setting for the Domain Profile** dialog box, and then click the **OK** button to save the settings and return to the **Windows Firewall with Advanced Security** window.

16. Close the **Windows Firewall with Advanced Security** window, and close the Windows Firewall.

Managing Changes and Assets

The pace of operations in a business can be swift. IT personnel often must react quickly when resolving problems and requests. It is easy to fix a problem and move on to the next one without documenting what happened and what was done to resolve it. While this may allow for quicker responses to problems, failing to document requests and responses could lead to potential problems. For example, one IT staff member might add a new user, but another administrator might not recognize the account and remove the user's credentials. Documenting issues also provides long-term data for recognizing trends or vulnerabilities in the systems.

Change-Management Systems

A *change-management system* is a means of documenting issues and their solutions. It allows a business to create an efficient and systematic approach to managing changes on the network. This type of software allows for a standardization in documenting requests and resolutions. It also provides an audit trail to determine who requested the change and who performed the requested operation. Consider these examples on how a change-management system protects a network from a security angle:

- New users can only be added or removed when requests are made through a controlled system.
- Password changes to key accounts are noted.
- Configuration requests to routers are identified, and the changes made are documented.

The change-management system is part of security. Therefore, it should be set up with controlled access. This helps to protect the integrity of changes to the network.

As with vulnerability scanners, there are commercial products along with open-source solutions. An example of an open-source product is Spiceworks Help Desk, as shown in **Figure 6-15.** Spiceworks has many features. It includes help desk ticketing and change-management functionalities. It can monitor networks. Tickets can be prioritized. Reporting is simple and offers analysis of data.

Asset Management

One of the biggest challenges in maintaining a network is managing the hardware and software assets. All assets need to be accounted for. Their configurations must be up to date. Unknown assets should be identified and addressed. An *IT asset management (ITAM) system* is software that assists in maintaining the assets on a network. A good ITAM system will allow a company to manage inventory. The information it holds can help the company make the best decisions for purchases of new assets or repurposing assets within the company.

IT management may be as simple as a spreadsheet or database containing each asset name, type, and serial number. It may also be very comprehensive. Some software will automatically query the system to track installed software, hardware, and configurations. The software can also assist managers in ensuring

CompTIA Security+
3.6

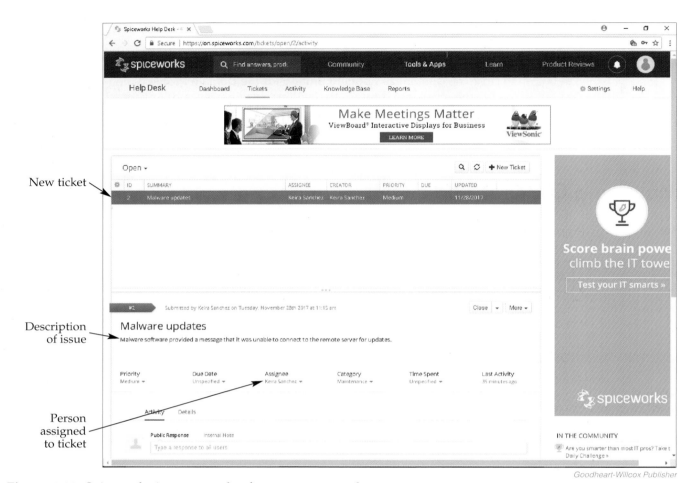

New ticket

Description
of issue

Person
assigned
to ticket

Goodheart-Willcox Publisher

Figure 6-15. Spiceworks is an example of an open-source change-management system.

the correct licensing is being used. This helps the company to be compliant with software-licensing requirements. If a computer is stolen or lost, the ITAM software is a record of what information is on the machine. It also provides specifics of the equipment so law enforcement can be given the details.

A common practice is to place asset tags on devices. An *asset tag* provides information about the device, such as the owner of the equipment and any other relevant information. This information may be contained in a bar code. A bar-code scanner can then be used to log the device into the ITAM system.

Quick Look 6.2.4

ITAM Systems

ITAM systems assist IT managers with keeping track of assets. There are many systems available, from commercial software to freeware and open-source solutions.

1. Launch a web browser, and navigate to a search engine. Research the different types of IT asset management programs available.
2. What are some paid products available? What features do they provide?
3. What are some open source or freeware products?
4. How do asset tags aid in asset management?
5. Which product did you like best? Share your findings with your class.

SECTION REVIEW 6.2

Check Your Understanding

1. A software patch released by a software vendor before its next scheduled update is called what type of update?

2. What is the basic purpose of a vulnerability scanner?

3. A firewall that is blocking TFTP traffic through port 69 is known as what type of firewall?

4. A control on data entering a system is using which type of rule?

5. Alterations to system configuration should be documented in what type of program?

Build Your Key Terms Vocabulary

As you progress through this course, develop a personal cybersecurity glossary. This will help you build your vocabulary and prepare you for a career. Write a definition for each of the following terms, and add it to your cybersecurity glossary.

asset tag

botnet

change-management system

credentialed scan

false negative

false positive

firewall

intrusive scan

IT asset management (ITAM) system

noncredentialed scan

nonintrusive scan

out-of-band

packet-filtering firewall

patch

proxy server firewall

stateful-inspection firewall

vulnerability scanner

Review and Assessment

Summary

Section 6.1 Operating System Services

- Hardening is closing or locking down any unnecessary paths on an operating system that can be used for unapproved access, including services and scheduled tasks.
- A baseline is a starting point from which comparisons can be made to analyze a system for potential issues or problems.
- Event logs provide vital information for security professionals, such as revealing clues of potential security issues or being used after an incident to pinpoint the user or computer involved.

Section 6.2 System Vulnerabilities

- Regularly updating systems by applying patches provided by the vendor to correct errors or bugs is an integral part of eliminating vulnerabilities.
- A vulnerability scanner automates the process of scanning systems for potential attack vectors and helps prioritize the results.
- A firewall is a security tool that acts as a barrier or protection against an unwanted data transfer and may be a packet-filtering, stateful-inspection, or proxy server firewall.
- A change-management system is a means of documenting issues and their solutions in a standardized way and also provides an audit trail.

Check Your Cybersecurity IQ 📱

Now that you have completed this chapter, see what you have learned about cybersecurity by visiting the student companion website (www.g-wlearning.com) and taking the chapter posttest.

Review Questions 📱

For each question, select the answer that is the best response.

1. Which statement *best* describes operating system hardening?
   A. Uninstalling older programs.
   B. Removing potential vulnerabilities in the operating system.
   C. Only allowing one user with administrative privileges.
   D. Viewing vulnerability scanner reports.

2. Before shutting down a service, you should ensure:
   A. the service startup-type is set to manual.
   B. which services are dependent on this service running.
   C. which components are needed for this service to run.
   D. if the service is located in the c:\windows\system32 directory.

3. What security benefit does performance monitoring offer administrators?
   A. The CPU is fast enough to keep up with requests.
   B. The server's hard disk can be monitored before it runs out of space.
   C. Shows an unusual amount of traffic is being recorded on the network adapters.
   D. Maintains the status of antivirus and vulnerability software.

4. An administrator notices a high amount of disk activity. What would the administrator use to determine if this is an unusual occurrence?
   A. Baseline
   B. System event log
   C. Stateful firewall
   D. Vulnerability scanner

5. A security administrator needs to review auditing results. Where will this information be found?
   A. Security log
   B. Properties of the object being audited
   C. Group policy
   D. Forwarded events filter

6. In reviewing a system log, which of the following events should have the highest priority in a security investigation?
    A. A warning message that the DHCP server failed to start on first attempt.
    B. The most recent event in the file.
    C. The Google updater service terminated with an error.
    D. The computer entered sleep mode.

7. What part of the CIA triad does auditing support?
    A. Confidentiality
    B. Integrity
    C. Availability
    D. Reliability

8. MBSA can scan for all of the following except:
    A. Weak passwords
    B. Missing critical security updates
    C. Viruses
    D. Accounts with administrator access

9. A packet-filtering firewall is unable to do which of the following?
    A. Allow a packet based on a destination port.
    B. Block outgoing packets.
    C. Read the data content of a packet.
    D. Block packets based on the source IP address.

10. Stateful-inspection firewalls are more advanced because they:
    A. use commercial programs with more features.
    B. can read the content of each packet.
    C. can determine if a packet is part of a sequencing of previous transactions.
    D. can be incorporated on hosts and network subnets.

Application and Extension of Knowledge

1. Collect performance data, such as CPU usage, current memory usage, or network traffic, for one week. Collect the data at approximately the same time each day. Enter the data in a spreadsheet, and create a line graph. Are the data consistent, or do you notice any anomalies?

2. There are many personal firewall software programs that could be used in place of the built-in Windows firewall. Investigate personal firewalls, including free and for-purchase versions. Summarize two different programs, comparing features and prices, in a slideshow. Be sure to cite your sources.

3. Look into best practices for configuring auditing in a Windows environment. What are some of the recommended items that should be audited for security reasons? Summarize your research in a one- or two-page document. Be sure to cite your sources.

4. Manually managing event logs can be a time-consuming task. It also leads to possibly missing critical information. Investigate programs that offer automated event-log management. Look for a product that would be appropriate for a small business that has about 100 computers and users. Detail your recommendation in a memo to the owner. Include your justification for using your selection.

5. Start Linux, either on a standalone system or as a virtual machine. View the logs in default log folder /var/log. What type of data do you find in the messages or auth log files? View the logs on your system graphically by using the GUI tool System Log Viewer. Create a frequently asked questions (FAQ) document for a new administrator. The FAQ should detail how to view key logs and explain the type of entries and what they contain. Include screenshots and detailed instructions on viewing.

Research Project
Spiceworks

The ACME Quality Auto Parts Company currently does not have help desk ticketing software or the ability to track requests. One of the reasons for this is because the company is on a tight budget. Management has stated it cannot justify spending money on this software for the current fiscal year, but does believe the company needs a ticketing system. The IT manager has proposed implementing the open-source help desk product of Spiceworks. However, to gain approval, upper management requires details about the product and how using it will benefit the company. The IT manager has assigned you the task of researching the help desk software from Spiceworks. Investigate the various features it offers, and examine how the ticket system works.

Deliverables. Create a one- to two-page report detailing the various elements of Spiceworks and how it could help track help desk requests. What other benefits could Spiceworks provide to the company? Format the report following accepted guidelines for a professional report.

Online Activities

Complete the following activities, which will help you learn, practice, and expand your knowledge and skills.

Vocabulary. Practice vocabulary for this chapter using the e-flash cards, matching activity, and vocabulary game until you are able to recognize their meanings.

Communication Skills

College and Career Readiness

Reading. Active readers read groups of words, rather than individual words. Reading word by word is slow, reduces concentration, and reduces the ability to connect concepts to form meaning. If you find that you do not already read in phrases, practice this technique as you read this chapter. This change in the way you read will help you read faster and improve understanding at the same time.

Writing. Objective writing is free of personal feelings, prejudices, and interpretations. Write a paragraph about the importance of protecting host systems using only objective statements and language.

Speaking. Participate in a collaborative classroom discussion about system patching. Pose questions to participants, connecting your ideas to the relevant evidence presented. Use inductive reasoning to formulate an argument regarding system patching. Use deductive reasoning to draw conclusions about your classmates' arguments.

Listening. Passive listening is casually listening to someone speak. This type of listening is appropriate when you do not have to interact with the speaker. Active listening is fully participating as you process what others are saying. Actively listen to a classmate as he or she is having a conversation with you. Focus your attention on the message. Ask for clarification about anything you do not understand. Provide verbal and nonverbal feedback while the person is talking.

Portfolio Development

College and Career Readiness

Digital File Formats. A portfolio will contain documents you created electronically as well as documents that you have in hardcopy format that will be scanned. It will be necessary to decide file formats to use for both types of documents. Consider the technology that you might use for creating and scanning documents. You will need access to desktop publishing software, scanners, cameras, and other digital equipment or software.

For documents that you create, consider using the default format to save the files. For example, you could save letters and essays created in Microsoft Word in DOCx format. You could save worksheets created in Microsoft Excel in XLSx format. If your presentation will include graphics or video, confirm the file formats that are necessary for each item. Use the appropriate formats as you create the documents.

Hardcopy items will need to be converted to digital format. Portable document format (PDF) is a good choice for scanned items, such as awards and certificates.

Keep in mind that the person reviewing your digital portfolio will need programs capable of opening these formats to view your files. An option is to save all documents as PDF files. Having all of the files in the same format can make viewing them easier for others who need to review your portfolio.

1. Decide the strategy you will use for saving documents. Make note of where the technology is available for your use, such as your home computer or the school lab.

2. Document any special instructions needed to use the software or equipment. This will save time when you are ready to create or save files.

CTSO Event Prep

Ethics. Many competitive career and technical student organization (CTSO) events include an ethics component that covers multiple topics. The ethics component of an event may be part of an objective test. However, ethics may also be a part of the competition in which teams participate to defend a given position on an ethical dilemma or topic. To prepare for an ethics event, complete the following activities.

1. Read the guidelines provided by your organization.

2. Make notes on index cards about important points to remember. Use these notes to study.

3. To get an overview of various ethical situations that individuals encounter, read each of the Ethical Issue features that appear throughout this text.

4. Ask someone to practice role-playing with you by asking questions or taking the other side of an argument.

5. Use the Internet to find more information about ethical issues. Find and review ethics cases that involve computer security situations.

Chapter 7

Security Vulnerabilities and Protection of Nontraditional Hosts

Traditional computer networks consisting of servers and personal computers have long been the norm for businesses. IT departments have naturally focused much of their security endeavors on protecting these devices. As technology changes, so do the devices that are used on networks. A new generation of devices has come to be known as the Internet of Things (IoT). The term IoT was originally used in a presentation by Kevin Ashto, during a presentation on RFID chips at his company, Proctor and Gamble. It took years for this term to be widely used. Once IoT devices started gaining widespread attention and their development exploded, the term became common.

There are many other nontraditional hosts in addition to IoT devices. Mobile devices are easily recognized hosts, but other hosts may not be as obvious. The point of sale device that scans your credit card when you buy something is a non-traditional host. Critical infrastructure such as electrical grids and water systems are computerized, so they are nontraditional hosts. Even output devices such as printers and copiers present security vulnerabilities. Regardless where the embedded technology is located, the need for strong security planning, implementation and monitoring is a crucial and necessary component of a cybersecurity strategy.

Chapter Preview

Section 7.1   Mobile Devices
Section 7.2   Nontraditional Hosts

While studying, look for the activity icon for:

- Pretests and posttests
- Vocabulary terms with e-flash cards and matching activities
- Self-assessment

G-WLEARNING.com

Reading Prep

Scan this chapter, and look for information presented as fact. As you read this chapter, try to determine which topics are fact and which are the author's opinion. After reading the chapter, research the topics, and verify which are facts and which are opinions.

College and Career Readiness

Check Your Cybersecurity IQ ➡

Certification Objectives

CompTIA Security+

1.6   Explain the impact associated with types of vulnerabilities.
2.5   Given a scenario, deploy mobile devices securely.
3.3   Given a scenario, implement secure system design.
3.5   Explain the security implications of embedded systems.
5.2   Summarize business impact analysis concepts.

Microsoft MTA Security Fundamentals

2.5   Understand encryption.
2.6   Understand malware.
3.2   Understand network isolation.

Mobile Devices

Essential Question

How is the Internet of Things impacting decisions related to information security?

Desktop computers remain a core computing choice. However, operating systems for desktops are no longer the most used within the United States, per data from StatCounter. It researched and tracked the operating systems of the devices connecting to the Internet. The data reveal that Android devices led over Windows machines by about 4 percent (40 percent to 36 percent), and Apple iOS has about 13 percent of the market. These data reflect the challenges that must be met by security professionals as they adapt to new business practices. IT security professionals must identify risks associated with mobile computing. They must devise strategies to implement data protection.

Key Terms 🔗

BitLocker
bring your own device (BYOD)
choose your own device (CYOD)
company owned, personal enabled (COPE)
drive encryption

Exif data
firmware
geotagging
Internet of Things (IoT)
jailbreaking
kill switch

metadata
quick response (QR) code
rooting
sideloading
Trusted Platform Module (TPM)
wearable technology

Learning Goals

- Illustrate IoT and its impact on system security.
- Set up device and full-drive encryption.
- Describe geotagging.

Changing Network Landscape

Dyn is an Internet-infrastructure company that provides critical technology services to some very large companies. In October of 2016, it was the target of a cyberattack. The attack affected some well-known companies, including Twitter, Amazon, Reddit, Netflix, and Spotify. What made this attack different from other cyberattacks was the majority of the infected hosts that were used in this attack were not traditional computers. Most were other types of Internet-enabled devices, such as CCTV, digital video recorders, and baby cameras.

This attack became known as the Mirai botnet. The name is based on the strain of malware that was used to conduct the attack. This cyberattack had a wide impact, as shown in **Figure 7-1**. It also exposed the vulnerabilities of devices known collectively as the Internet of Things.

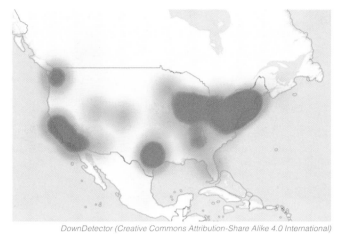

Figure 7-1. This visual illustration shows the extent of the impact of the attack against Dyn had in North America.

Internet of Things

Traditionally, the term *pervasive computing* was used to describe devices that have embedded microprocessors and allowed for continuous connection to networks. The *Internet of Things (IoT)* revolves around incorporating computing technology into nontypical devices to allow communication with other devices and the Internet. These devices are also called *smart devices* or *connected devices*. They are being rapidly developed and implemented.

It is possible now to have Internet-connected appliances, such as refrigerators and stoves. Thermostats and lights can be controlled from your smartphone. There are even medication-monitoring devices, from pills to glowing bottle caps. Smart devices are becoming quite popular in business. In a 2017 survey by Tech Pro Research, 38 percent of businesses have adopted some IoT devices. About 16 percent are planning a rollout of IoT devices in the coming year. Another 24 percent are considering adoption of the technology.

Wearable technology is a type of IoT device worn by a person that is basically a minicomputer performing specific functions. Wearable technology includes smartwatches, such as the Apple Watch and Samsung Gear; glasses, such as Google Glass; and even some medical devices. Fitbit is a commonly used wearable-technology device. It monitors the wearer's activity levels. Another example of wearable technology is the Disney MagicBand, as shown in **Figure 7-2**. This device is a wristband worn by guests that contains sensors and a transmitter. It allows guests to check into their rooms, purchase meals, and enter rides at scheduled times.

There are other examples of IoT. UPS has incorporated sensors into its vehicles. These sensors capture over 200 points of data each day. The data help the company to reduce vehicle emissions, fuel consumption, idle time, and more.

Amazon is also contributing to the expansion of IoT use. It launched a new model of retail store, Amazon Go, as shown in **Figure 7-3**. This store will allow consumers to purchase products via the Amazon Go app. Products are automatically identified as they are placed in the cart. When customers are finished shopping, they simply leave the store. No checkout is required.

Today, the IoT market is booming. The global media company Forbes predicts business will be spending $267 billion on IoT by the year 2020. Most consumers are familiar with IoT devices such as smart doorbells, appliances, and fitness trackers. However, there are even more devices embedded in areas that are not

Goodheart-Willcox Publisher

Figure 7-2. The Disney MagicBand is an IoT device worn by guests to enhance their visits to the theme park.

CompTIA Security+
3.5

FYI

A wearable technology device is often simply called a wearable.

Figure 7-3. The Amazon Go store uses IoT technology to eliminate the checkout line.

consumer-focused. These devices are called *Industrial Internet of Things (IIoT)*. This term, coined by GE, has seen its focus on connecting devices in health-care, transportation, and energy firms. Some areas where IIoT has been used include smart farms, industrial heating and air conditioning equipment, sensors in manufacturing, and environmental monitoring.

IoT devices have brought changes to the field of information technology. Data and data access are evolving from the traditional norm based on desktop computers and servers. Security professionals must adapt and respond to these new business models in their efforts to protect assets and data. The Mirai botnet attack shed new urgency on the need to evaluate nontraditional attack vectors. These vectors pose vulnerabilities that could lead to exploits.

Quick Look 7.1.1

Mobile Malware Threats

CompTIA Security+ 1.6

MTA Security Fundamentals 2.6

About 75 percent of Americans own a smartphone, up from only 35 percent in 2011. About 50 percent of Americans own a tablet computer. These devices present new security threats.

1. Launch a web browser, and navigate to a search engine. Enter the search phrase Xavier malware. Select an article from a reliable source, and read about this malware. What is the intent of this malware? What mobile platform is most infected with this threat?
2. Using the search engine, enter the phrase xCodeHost malware. Select an article from a reliable source, and read about this malware. What were some of the apps in the App store infected by this threat?
3. Malvertising is a problem across all platforms. It is increasingly being targeted against mobile devices. Using the search engine and reliable sources, investigate this threat. What is it?
4. What are some protections users can perform to protect their mobile apps? Share your research and ideas with your class.

BYOD

One of the biggest changes to many workplaces is the introduction of BYOD, as shown in **Figure 7-4.** *Bring your own device (BYOD)* is a strategy that allows employees, partners, and others to use their personal devices, such as tablets and smartphones, to conduct business and connect to an organization's networks. According to Gartner, Inc., BYOD programs represent the single most radical shift in client computing for businesses since personal computers became commonplace. Many schools are also adopting BYOD strategies. This is changing how students access information.

When a business allows the use of personal devices on its networks, there are some unique challenges. This is due to the fact the devices are not owned by the business and, therefore, it cannot control the configuration, content, and updates. There are also many legal and ethical questions that must be addressed as well. For example:

- Can an employer ask to see the data stored on a personal device if it feels there is a security risk?

FYI

Gartner, Inc., is a widely respected business-research firm that provides data for businesses to make informed business decisions.

- If the device is infected with malware, how will it be detected and removed?
- Can a company prohibit the use of unapproved apps if they access its network?

In many IT security circles, threats presented by mobile devices are referred to as *bring your own malware* or *mobile malware.*

Consider these serious mobile malware threats. Carberb can steal online banking credentials. It works by monitoring SMS transactions from financial institutions that validate banking transactions. SMS is used primarily by mobile devices. FinSpy steals contact information, text messages, photos, and more. Mobile malware is not limited to just Android devices. Apple has had its share of apps infected by malware as well.

For an IT administrator, the first line of defense against mobile malware is a BYOD policy. Often, the vulnerabilities related to mobile devices are the result of users unknowingly making uninformed decisions. Many users do not even realize that their devices can be infected with malware. It is important to set policies and provide education and awareness to employees on potential vulnerabilities and best practices.

There are other defenses against mobile malware. It may be required that any personal device used for business purposes or connected to the network have up-to-date antimalware software. This would be covered in the BYOD policy. Also, a specific wireless network could be set up for personal devices. This ensures the devices can connect to the Internet, but not to the business's network. A firewall could be placed between this network and the main network to keep it further isolated.

Another choice management can make regarding mobile devices is CYOD and COPE policies. In *choose your own device (CYOD)*, the company selects which type of devices are approved for connection, but the customer owns the device. The alternative is for the company to provide the device for the employee's work and personal use. This is known as a *company owned, personal enabled (COPE)* device.

MTA Security Fundamentals
2.6

CompTIA Security+
2.5

MTA Security Fundamentals
3.2

Monkey Business Images/Shutterstock.com

Figure 7-4. Many businesses have adopted a BYOD strategy, which allows employees to use their own devices, such as tablets, on the company network.

Quick Look 7.1.2

BYOD Policies

One way many schools are increasing access to digital data is through BYOD strategies. As part of this strategy, the school should have a clearly defined BYOD policy.

1. Does your school allow personal devices to be used? If so, is there a BYOD policy, and where is it located?
2. Read the BYOD policy for your school. If your school does not have a policy, locate one from another school. What are some of the key requirements of this policy?
3. Research a business's BYOD policy. Compare it to the one at your school. Are there any similarities or differences?
4. Discuss with your class some of the security issues you feel could arise if a company does not have a BYOD policy.

Threats to Data on Mobile Platforms

While most people consider smartphones to be the emphasis of BYOD, companies must consider all locations where data reside. This may include devices that are personally owned in addition to corporate assets. The advent of tablets along with decreasing costs of laptops and hybrid laptops (tablet-laptop combination) has increased the number of mobile devices used in business. These devices can be used to store and access data from many locations, not just in a controlled work setting.

There have been many reports of security issues resulting from lost or stolen laptops. A significant data breach pushed this threat to the top of awareness for many professionals. This breach occurred when a laptop stolen from a data analyst for the Veterans Administration was stolen from an automobile. This laptop contained the personal information of up to 26.5 million veterans, their spouses, and active duty personnel. Social Security numbers were included in the data. This incident was projected to cost the United States government between $100 and $500 million to prevent and cover any losses that were the result of this theft.

In another incident, a laptop was stolen from a Secret Service agent in New York City. The laptop contained floor plans for Trump Tower. It also contained details of the investigation into the private e-mail server of Hilary Clinton. It even contained confidential information about Pope Francis.

It is not just laptops that represent vulnerabilities. Any device that holds data must be considered, as shown in **Figure 7-5.** For example, Bank of America misplaced backup tapes that held confidential information. The data included financial information of around 1.2 million governmental employees, including members of Congress. In another example, names, addresses, and Social Security numbers were compromised when a flash drive was stolen from the Florida Department of Revenue.

Antonio Guillem/Shutterstock.com

Figure 7-5. Flash drives can be easily lost or stolen. This represents a vulnerability that must be addressed.

CompTIA Security+
2.5

MTA Security Fundamentals
2.5

Protecting Data on a Mobile Platform

Protecting data on mobile devices can be done in many ways. Password protecting mobile devices is a common practice. This provides only minimal protection. Most passwords are easily guessed or can be hacked with little effort. The flash drive stolen from the Florida Department of Revenue required a password for access. Although encryption had been recommended, it was not used. Once the password was cracked, the information could be accessed.

One of the most significant protections that can be put in place is full-drive encryption. Essentially, *drive encryption* renders data unreadable without the encryption key to unlock it. Encryption is discussed in detail in a later chapter. Encryption is not intended only for mobile devices. However, it is particularly important on mobile devices. They are more likely to be stolen or lost than a traditional desktop computer.

Encrypting disk systems is the best defense in protecting the confidentiality of data. A recent example of how this works involves NASCAR–champion racer Jimmy Johnson. Prior to a 2017 race, his crew chief, Chad Knaus, had his laptop stolen from a rental car. On this laptop were his notes for the upcoming race. Although it is inconvenient to lose the computer, his laptop was encrypted. The data contained on the system could not be accessed by the thief.

There are different programs that can provide device encryption. Which ones can be used depends on the mobile device and operating system. A popular program for Microsoft Windows devices is BitLocker.

BitLocker

BitLocker is software that encrypts data to protect against attacks and theft. It is included with the Microsoft Windows operating system and is available on many versions, from Windows Vista on up, as shown in **Figure 7-6.** To run Bit-Locker on a PC (or laptop), these conditions must exist:

- compatible Windows version
- storage drive with at least two partitions
- Trusted Platform Module microchip and supported computer BIOS

A *Trusted Platform Module (TPM)* is a special chip located in the computer's hardware that runs authentication checks on hardware, software, and firmware. TPM chips provide security to systems by detecting unapproved changes and forcing the computer to start in a restricted mode. *Firmware* is special software embedded on hardware devices to control the system. The most recognizable firmware is the system's BIOS. This is the firmware used to initialize hardware and control some system settings at computer startup.

Once BitLocker is enabled, *all* files on the drive are encrypted, not just personal documents. When you add files to the drive, they are automatically encrypted. Any files copied from the drive to another location are automatically decrypted.

When BitLocker is configured on a computer, the first partition is known as the *system partition.* It contains the boot files. These are the files instructing the computer's BIOS how to locate the operating system. The second partition contains the operating system and related data. Once the drive containing the operating system is encrypted, the BIOS will scan during startup for any changes or configurations that pose a security risk. If any are found, BitLocker locks the operating system.

During the setup of BitLocker, you will be asked to provide a recovery password and create a recovery key. The recovery password must be entered to unlock

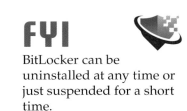

FYI BitLocker can be uninstalled at any time or just suspended for a short time.

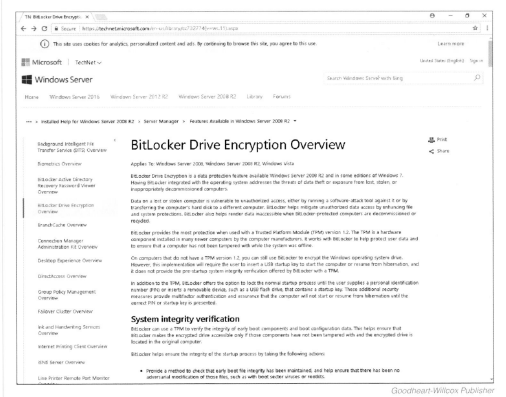

Goodheart-Willcox Publisher

Figure 7-6. BitLocker is a Microsoft program used to encrypt data on storage devices.

the system. If you forget the password, the recovery key is used to access the data being encrypted by BitLocker. The key is the *only* way to access the data if you forget the password. A best practice is to save the recovery key in multiple locations. You may even wish to print it and lock it away.

Removable media, especially flash drives, are easy to misplace. This makes these devices especially vulnerable to data theft. Microsoft has a portable version of BitLocker called BitLocker To Go. Encrypting the portable drive is a simple process. During the encryption, you will be asked to create a password. The password should be a combination of letters, symbols, and numbers. BitLocker To Go will also create a recovery key. This key can be used in the event the password is forgotten.

To use an encrypted flash drive, insert the drive as normal in a computer that supports BitLocker To Go. Once the portable device is recognized by the operating system, a lock is displayed in the drive icon in file explorer. When accessing the drive, you will be asked for the password.

Quick Look 7.1.3

TPM Compatibility

To use BitLocker, the computer must be TPM compatible. There is an easy way in Windows to check if the device is TPM compatible.

1. Click the Windows **Start** button, enter run in the search box, and select the **Run** application in the results.
2. In the **Run** dialog box, enter tpm.msc, and click the **OK** button. The TPM management utility is displayed.
3. Look at the message in the middle pane, as shown. If the message states Compatible TPM cannot be found, then the computer either does not support TPM or it has not been enabled in BIOS of the computer. If the middle pane contains a description and options, TPM is enabled.

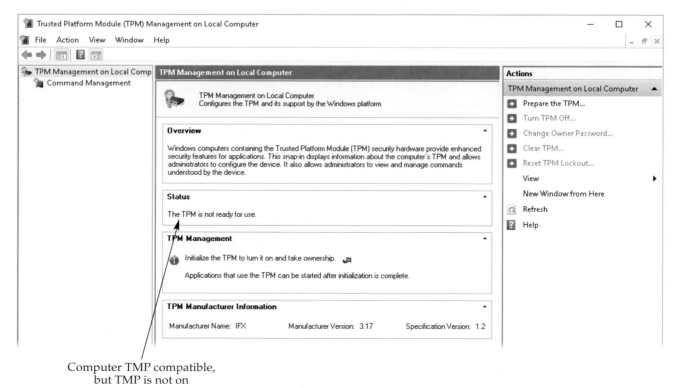

Computer TMP compatible, but TMP is not on

Quick Look 7.1.3 Continued

4. If you have permission to access your computer's BIOS, reboot the system and access the BIOS to view the TPM information.

5. Using a web browser, search for TPM add-on modules that can be purchased. Most motherboards equipped with TPM include the chip as a permanent soldered edition to the board. However, some motherboards do support the ability to add this on as a module.

Security Issues

In addition to the locational data and potential loss of data through loss or theft of the device, there are other security considerations related to mobile devices. These are of special concern if the device is used on the company network or for company business. IoT devices also have security concerns unique to them.

Mobile Device Security Issues

On their personal devices, users control which apps are installed. Apps can be purchased, many for a small fee. Many other apps are free to download and use. Apps can be found in stores. The App Store is for apps for iOS devices. Google Play is for apps for Android devices. Sometimes users unknowingly install unsecure applications. Even though Apple screens apps that are placed in its store, risky apps can still be installed. Android users can also use unofficial stores to obtain apps. Installing unofficial apps is called *sideloading* apps to the device.

Another concern is related to QR codes. QR codes can be found nearly everywhere you look, as shown in **Figure 7-7**. A *quick response (QR) code* is a two-dimensional bar code that can store information such as a URL, phone number, e-mail address, or any other textual data up to 4296 characters. Most mobile devices can read QR codes if an app is installed. The security concerns about QR codes is an attacker can create a QR code that links to a malicious website. A user scanning this code could be directed to the hacker's website and have malware immediately download onto the device. The site may also be used for pharming.

Mobile devices can be configured to bypass built-in limitations. This is a process called *rooting* on an Android device and *jailbreaking* on an iOS device. This is usually done to allow the user to add functionality and features to the device. However, the security measures are often disabled during the process. This creates a security vulnerability.

Often, users lack awareness of security controls. For example, they fail to turn off unneeded services such as Bluetooth. Many users do not regularly lock their phones with a strong code of numbers or a pattern. Also, encryption may not be installed and used. This is a particular concern if the user is storing data for his or her employer.

Goodheart-Willcox Publisher

Figure 7-7. QR codes can be found seemingly everywhere. This QR code contains the word *Cybersecurity*. If you scan it with a QR code reader, the text will be displayed on your device.

CompTIA Security+
2.5

FYI

Developers in Japan invented the QR code in 1994. QR codes were first implemented in the auto-manufacturing industry to improve management efficiency.

Quick Look 7.1.4

QR Codes

QR codes are easy to create and use. There are many websites that can be used to create the codes for free. There are also many QR code reader apps, and many of these are free.

1. Launch a web browser, and navigate to a search engine. Enter the search phrase **QR code generator**, and evaluate the search results for a reputable site.

2. Navigate to the site you choose, and run the code-generator function on that site.

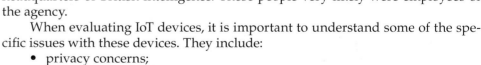

Quick Look 7.1.4 Continued

3. Enter your full name as the text, and generate the QR code.
4. Save the code, and display it on your computer screen or print it out.
5. Ask a classmate to scan the code with a QR reader on his or her mobile device to test the code.

Internet of Things (IoT) Security

The Internet of Things has ushered in a new technological revolution. There are exciting products and innovations that allow connection to other devices and the Internet. Gartner, Inc., predicts that by the year 2020 there will be almost 21 billion IoT devices. Of course, IoT has made businesses and consumers more dependent on the technology. With this dependency comes increased security risks.

Consider Samsung's SmartThings line of products. SmartThings takes home automation to a new level. SmartThings devices can turn on the lights, adjust the thermostat, and even turn on the radio to start your day. SmartThings devices can lock the doors, activate the security alarm, and monitor the home for water leaks or other threats. All this automation can have a positive effect on your daily routine. However, researchers from the University of Michigan tested these devices. They demonstrated how hackers can use vulnerabilities in the system to take over these smart devices.

Some other challenges are related to wearable technologies. In many secure facilities, wearables are prohibited. Testing centers, military facilities, and other places have sensitive data. This information could be captured or photographed with some wearable technologies, such as a Samsung Gear 2 smartwatch, as shown in **Figure 7-8**.

Military leaders and intelligence officials may have been slow to realize the security impact of wearable devices. In 2018, a potential breach of military security was linked to a fitness app. The Strava app collected data from its users' fitness apps. This included GPS information on the paths users jogged, biked, or walked. Although Strava users had the option to opt-out of data sharing, many did not do so. Strava published a global heat map of the data. On this map, several known US military bases could be identified, both at home and abroad in Syria and Afghanistan. In many cases, starting with Strava's data, it was even possible to identify the users and the times they were running their routes. A Berlin-based security analyst was able to identify 573 people who jogged around the parking lot of the headquarters of British intelligence. These people very likely were employees of the agency.

When evaluating IoT devices, it is important to understand some of the specific issues with these devices. They include:

- privacy concerns;
- inadequate security controls;
- inadequate web interface security; and
- infrequent or unencrypted software or firmware updates.

Figure 7-8. The Samsung Gear 2 smartwatch includes a camera. The ability to capture data is why many secure facilities do not allow wearable technology.

How much personal information is being collected, and what is done with that data? Is the data encrypted when sent across the network, or is it easy to intercept and read? These are concerns related to privacy. Also, many devices do not have adequate security controls, such as requiring secure passwords. Additionally, the web interface for the device may not have adequate security measures. Some users do not update the software or firmware, so there may be unpatched vulnerabilities. Another concern related to updates is if the update is encrypted.

Many network devices either do not get updated firmware or users are unaware they need to upgrade the systems. An example of how this vulnerability can be exploited occurred in late 2016. Around 900,000 German customers of Deutsche Telekom were affected by a massive Internet outage. The outage lasted nearly an entire day. Hackers targeted home web routers issued by the provider that had not been upgraded with the latest firmware.

Quick Look 7.1.5

IoT Security Risks

There are always security risks that come with new technology. However, one IoT device made big news and stirred controversy not long after it was introduced. This was the Amazon Echo.

1. Launch a web browser, and navigate to a search engine.
2. Enter the search phrase **amazon echo murder case**. Evaluate the search results, and select an article from a reliable source.
3. What is the controversy of this type of voice assistant with this specific case?
4. Do you think Amazon's argument of First Amendment applies in this case?
5. What are the possible future ramifications of smart devices and future court cases?
6. How can a business protect themselves from security concerns such as those raised in this case?
7. Debate your views with your classmates.

GPS Metadata

A popular feature of mobile devices is logging of geographical information. Smartphones and other mobile devices have a global position system (GPS) built in. Cameras and video recorders may also have GPS. *Geotagging* is the process of identifying a person's location by tagging documents, such as photographs or videos, with GPS data. This can be considered as both a security threat and security asset.

Metadata is data that provides information about other data. This is often stated as *data about data.* There are many types of metadata. Document metadata can include the author's name, storage location, and important dates and times. With a GPS-enabled device, GPS data can also be included in the metadata. This is geotagging. It is done by recording latitude and longitude values in the file's metadata.

Cameras and phones store a great deal of metadata called Exif data. *Exif data* is metadata attached to an image or audio file. This may include date, time, camera settings, and GPS data. Exif stands for exchangeable image file format. You can search for the location of the file, the manufacturer of the device, and other information.

To determine where a photograph was taken, the latitude and longitude coordinates can be entered into a website. There are many websites that can be used for this, such as www.findlatitudeandlongitude.com. For example, if the latitude value is 35, this represents a circle around Earth that is 35 degrees north of the equator.

FYI

Metadata is not always easily found in a file. Some programs, such as Microsoft Word, have a utility for inspecting a document for metadata.

GPS Metadata as a Security Concern

Metadata is usually created automatically without the user knowing. The user may then share a document with someone not realizing he or she is also sharing hidden data. This can lead to embarrassing situations. However, it can also be a security risk. Consider the following two examples.

In 2003, Tony Blair, then the Prime Minister of the United Kingdom, used evidence supposedly obtained by British intelligence to justify Britain's

CompTIA Security+
2.5

```
Rev. #1: "cic22" edited file "C:\DOCUME~1\phamill\LOCALS~1\Temp\AutoRecovery save of Iraq - security.asd"
Rev. #2: "cic22" edited file "C:\DOCUME~1\phamill\LOCALS~1\Temp\AutoRecovery save of Iraq - security.asd"
Rev. #3: "cic22" edited file "C:\DOCUME~1\phamill\LOCALS~1\Temp\AutoRecovery save of Iraq - security.asd"
Rev. #4: "JPratt" edited file "C:\TEMP\Iraq - security.doc"
Rev. #5: "JPratt" edited file "A:\Iraq - security.doc"
Rev. #6: "ablackshaw" edited file "C:\ABlackshaw\Iraq - security.doc"
Rev. #7: "ablackshaw" edited file "C:\ABlackshaw\A;Iraq - security.doc"
Rev. #8: "ablackshaw" edited file "A:\Iraq - security.doc"
Rev. #9: "MKhan" edited file "C:\TEMP\Iraq - security.doc"
Rev. #10: "MKhan" edited file "C:\WINNT\Profiles\mkhan\Desktop\Iraq.doc"
```

Figure 7-9. This metadata on a document used by the British government to support military action against Iraq and Saddam Hussein showed the last several edits had been made by members of the British government.

involvement in the war against Iraq. The documents were also cited by Colin Powell, then the Secretary of State of the United States, as evidence of weapons of mass destruction. However, a researcher named Richard Smith discovered the metadata on the documents, which had been posted on a British governmental website. Subsequent research showed most of the information came from plagiarizing a US researcher in Iraq. It also showed that the last few edits were done by members of the British government, as shown in **Figure 7-9.** This raised questions about the validity of the information in the file.

A second incident involving metadata and Iraq occurred in 2007. In this incident, a new fleet of helicopters arrived at a base in Iraq. Photographs of the helicopters were taken and posted on the Internet. The enemy used the metadata in these photographs to determine the location. It then launched a mortar attack against the base. Four of the AH-64 Apache helicopters were destroyed in the attack.

Location tracking can be a privacy concern as well as a security issue. In June of 2017, the popular social media app Snapchat unveiled a new tool called Snap Map, as shown in **Figure 7-10.** It allows users to see where other people are posting on a map. This new interactive tool has raised privacy and security concerns. One concern for parents is that their children could be targeted and located by their postings.

Ethical Issue

Medical IoT Devices

A person has a heart-related event, an alert is sent from a wearable medical device to the doctor. The doctor promptly calls the person and prescribes medication to deal with the situation. A week later, the person receives notice from the insurance provider that the medication is not being taken every day as directed, and it will not continue paying claims related to the incident. Where should the line be drawn on data sharing? What are your thoughts on data and personal privacy related to IoT? Research how ethics impact the development of IoT devices and what organizations are taking the lead. Prepare a one- to two-page paper that addresses the need for ethical contracts, possible regulation, and your own opinions on this topic.

Goodheart-Willcox Publisher

Figure 7-10. The Snap Map tool in SnapChat has raised privacy concerns because it can be used to track a person's location.

In 2011, an uproar was created over the revelation that Apple was tracking locations and storing the data in a file called consolidated.db in the iOS. Of course, this tracking is not limited to iPhones. Android phones also have the same capabilities and can track locations as well. Both devices can have this setting turned off by the user.

Quick Look 7.1.6

Metadata

In this activity, you will view the metadata in a Microsoft Word document and delete the information. You will also use an iPhone in this activity to view locational data. If you do not have an iPhone, partner with someone who does. You may also use an Android device, but you will need to adapt the instructions to the device.

1. Open a previously saved document in Microsoft Word.
2. Click the **File** tab (or **Office** button) to display the backstage view.
3. Click **Info** on the left-hand side of the backstage view. The file metadata is displayed on the far right under the **Properties** heading.

Quick Look 7.1.6 Continued

4. Click the **Check for Issues** button in the **Inspect Document** section, and click **Inspect Document** in the drop-down menu, as shown. If the file is not saved, you will be asked if you want to save the file.

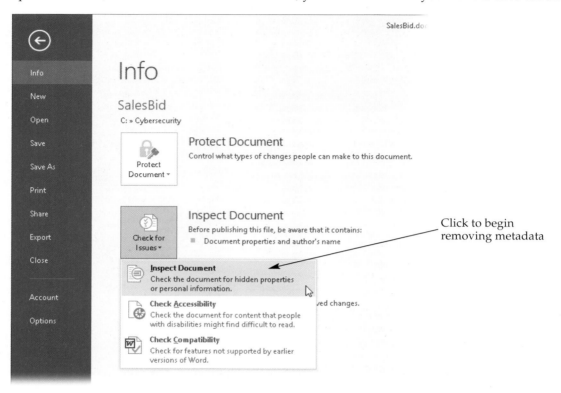

Click to begin removing metadata

5. In the dialog box that is displayed, uncheck all check boxes except for the **Document Properties and Personal Information** check box. This option will look for metadata. Click the **Inspect** button.
6. If metadata is found, as shown, click the **Remove All** button. Then, click the **Close** button.

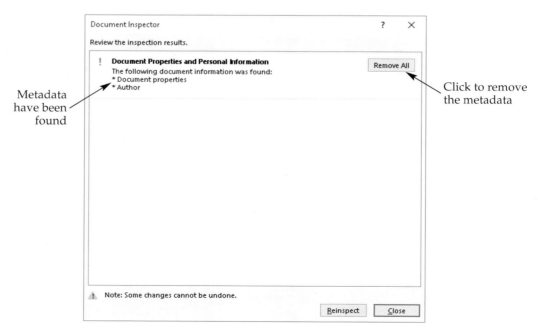

Metadata have been found

Click to remove the metadata

Quick Look 7.1.6 Continued

7. Close Word. Save the changes if you want the metadata permanently removed.
8. On your hard drive, locate an image file of a photograph taken with a smartphone.
9. Right-click on the file, and click **Properties** in the shortcut menu.
10. Click the **Details** tab in the **Properties** dialog box, and scroll down until you reach the **GPS** section, as shown. Note the data provided. If this section is not present, then the image file does not contain GPS data.

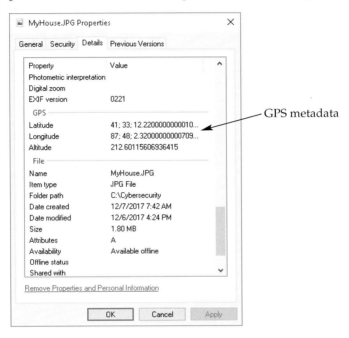

GPS metadata

11. On your iPhone, tap **Settings**. In the next menu, select the **Privacy** option.
12. In the **Privacy** menu, tap **Location Services**.
13. At the bottom of the list, tap **System Services**.
14. Scroll down to **Frequent Locations**, and tap to select.
15. Tap an item in the history to see the map.

GPS Metadata as a Security Aid

GPS metadata can be used as a security tool as well. If a device goes missing, whether it is lost or stolen, the device might be able to be tracked and located. GPS needs to be enabled on the device and tracking software must be available in order to do this. A highly useful app on Apple devices is called Find My Phone. While it is called find my *phone,* it works on other Apple devices, including iPads, Apple Watches, and iPod touch. With this app, an authorized user can locate the device using GPS, make the device play a sound, or enable "lost mode" to display a custom message on a locked screen.

Even more useful from a security standpoint is the "remote erase mode". When this feature is activated, the device is returned to the original factory settings. This means *all* data on the device are deleted. Together, the ability to remotely erase and lock the device are known as a *kill switch.* This has had a positive effect on reducing phone thefts. In fact, in the 12 months following when Apple added this feature, the number of phones stolen dropped 40 percent in San Francisco and

25 percent in New York City. Minnesota was the first state to mandate that phone providers provide a kill switch in all phones sold in the state. Other states have followed suit.

Quick Look 7.1.7

Tracking Software

There are many ways to track a mobile device. One useful tool is a product called Prey. This software allows you to track all your major devices with one account.

1. Launch a web browser, and navigate to the Prey website (www.preyproject.com).
2. Review the features of Prey. What are some key security benefits that you could use to protect your assets and data?
3. What is your overall impression of this product?
4. Search the Internet for similar programs. Share your findings with your classmates.

SECTION REVIEW 7.1

Check Your Understanding

1. What is firmware?
2. What can you do if you forget your password for BitLocker?
3. An unofficial installation of an app is known as what term?
4. Since the actual URL is not visible, this technology could be used to send malicious software.
5. The author of the file or the GPS coordinates of a picture are known by what term?

Build Your Key Terms Vocabulary

As you progress through this course, develop a personal cybersecurity glossary. This will help you build your vocabulary and prepare you for a career. Write a definition for each of the following terms, and add it to your cybersecurity glossary.

BitLocker

bring your own device (BYOD)

choose your own device (CYOD)

company owned, personal enabled (COPE)

drive encryption

Exif data

firmware

geotagging

Internet of Things (IoT)

jailbreaking

kill switch

metadata

quick response (QR) code

rooting

sideloading

Trusted Platform Module (TPM)

wearable technology

Nontraditional Hosts

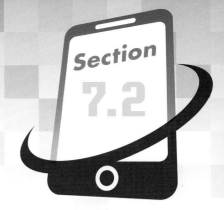

Network security involves more than just protecting hosts and servers. Other devices could also affect network security. These include devices that have been business mainstays such as printers and copiers. Other devices connected to networks, such as point-of-sale devices, present security challenges. Smart boards, televisions, and even gaming consoles may be present on a network. Many self-service kiosks, such as those used by the United States Postal Service, provide convenience and services, but also become another vector that could be exploited by hackers. In addition, highly industrial businesses often have platforms called SCADA that must be protected.

Essential Question

Why are industrial-control systems of particular concern related to cybersecurity?

Key Terms 🔗

critical infrastructure
embedded operating system
multifunction peripheral (MFP)

point-of-sale (PoS) device
RAM scraper
skimmer

supervisory control and data acquisition (SCADA) system
zero-level formatting

Learning Goals

- Identify security risks for point of sale devices.
- Assess security risks of multifunction peripherals.
- Appraise the significance of threats to critical infrastructure.
- Identify security vulnerabilities of industrial-control systems.

Point-of-Sale Devices

A *point-of-sale (PoS) device* is used to record transactions and process payments. These devices are an integral part of most retail establishments. In addition to processing payments, many devices also manage inventory and include customer-relationship-management software.

PoS systems use an embedded operating system to manage their functions. An *embedded operating system* provides only the functionality needed to run a specific

CompTIA Security+
3.3, 5.2

CompTIA Security+
5.2

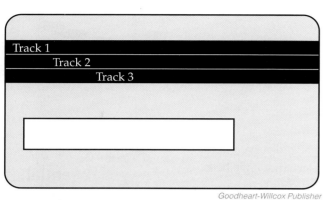

Figure 7-11. The magnetic strip on the back of a credit card contains three tracks of data. Tracks 1 and 2 are used to process transactions.

hardware configuration. It is lightweight to adapt to the hardware limitations typical of embedded computers, such as those in PoS devices. An embedded operating system is sometimes referred to as a *real-time operating system (RTOS)*. Examples of embedded operating systems include Windows Embedded OS (Windows IoT), Symbian (used on Nokia phones), and embedded Linux (such as used on Android devices).

It is important to understand how credit cards interact with PoS devices. When a user swipes a credit card using the magnetic strip, the information is read from tracks in the strip, as shown in **Figure 7-11.** Data are stored on the magnetic strip by modifying the magnetism of tiny iron particles located in the strip. When the card is swiped through a reader, the data are read by a device called a magnetic reading head. The magnetic strip may have three tracks. Only two of these tracks are used for credit card processing. Track 1 stores the customer information including account name and account number. Track 2 contains the credit card number and the expiration date. Track 3 is not used by any worldwide networks. Some cards do not even contain the third track anymore.

Chip-Based Cards

The data on a card's magnetic strip is not very secure. It can be easily read or intercepted. To combat these threats, most credit card companies are moving to chip-based cards called *EMV cards.* EMV stands for Europay, Mastercard, and Visa. It is considered the global standard for chip-based transactions. An EMV card has a microchip embedded in it that interacts with the PoS device. The chip can be seen as a metallic square on the card, as shown in **Figure 7-12.** With a magnetic-strip card, the data in the strip are never changed. Thus, copying the card provides a working card. An EMV card uses a unique code for every transaction. Once a code is used, it cannot be used again. If a hacker were to obtain the chip information and place it on another card, the faked card will be denied. The stolen transaction number would be unusable. Moving to a chip-based transaction system is making a difference on stolen data in the United States. In 2017, Visa reported a 58 percent drop in credit card fraud from one year earlier.

Figure 7-12. The newest credit cards contain an embedded chip. These cards are more secure than the older strip-based cards.

Many retailers have not adopted or implemented EMV-enabled PoS devices yet. In fact, the United States is the last major market to make the conversion to EMV-based cards. While there is no legislation that forces vendors to make this switch, there is liability to consider in not switching. Brick-and-mortar stores (physical stores) had a due date of October 1, 2015, to incorporate the chip machines. If a store continues to use magnetic-strip readers after that date and the financial institution has issued EMV cards, the store assumes the financial liability for a fraudulent purchase made with the card. The reverse is also true. If a retailer has the chip reader, but the credit card is still only available with a magnetic strip, the credit card company assumes the liability. For ATMs, the liability shift began in October 2017. This was the original target date for fuel pumps as well, but the date was extended to October 2020.

Many EMV-enabled cards still carry the magnetic strip. This allows the cards to be used where a chip reader has yet to be installed. If an EMV card is processed with the magnetic strip, the vulnerabilities with that technology still exist.

PoS Device Vulnerabilities

PoS devices represent a security vulnerability faced by many retailers. Hackers aim to get the information from the magnetic strips by accessing the data at the PoS location. This can be done by attaching a unit called a skimmer to the PoS device. A *skimmer* reads the credit card data at the same time as the PoS device, and then sends it to the hacker. Skimmers have become quite sophisticated. In many cases, it is difficult to notice the device is attached to the reader. As an example, in January 2018, two Aldi grocery stores in Montgomery County, Pennsylvania, had their credit card readers in the checkout lines compromised. The skimmers were installed while the cashiers were focused on scanning the groceries. The devices went undetected for two weeks.

Protecting against threats to PoS devices is critical to retail organizations. Many of these systems use Windows or Linux as the underlying operating system. This makes the systems vulnerable to malware just as all other computers are. Because these systems have to communicate with external credit card processors, they are connected to a network. This provides another way for malware to spread.

In many cases, the malware uses a technique called a RAM scraper. A *RAM scraper* scans the memory in the PoS system and reports the findings. When a magnetic-strip card is swiped, there is a very brief period when the credit card information is in clear-text memory before it is encrypted. A RAM scraper searches for patterns that match credit card numbers. When found, the data are copied into a text file. Most hackers remotely access the device to retrieve the text file.

Hackers have found RAM scrapers to be an effective technique, as evidenced by some notable hacks of retail chains. Target stores were subject to this type of attack. Hackers were able to gain access to Target's retail systems by stealing credentials from one of its heating and air conditioning vendors. Data from 40 million credit cards were stolen by infecting the PoS terminals in almost 2,000 stores. Target is not the only retailer to be hit with this type of attack. Home Depot and Niemen Marcus also had significant data breaches as the result of RAM scrapers. Protecting against these threats involves designing network subnets that separate areas of the network, using firewalls, and installing updated antimalware programs.

MTA Security Fundamentals
2.6

MTA Security Fundamentals
3.2

FYI

In the Target hack, the vendor did not need access to the retail network to do its job. This illustrates the importance of allowing only the access needed to complete the job at hand.

Quick Look 7.2.1

Retail Data Breaches

News stories of data breaches at retail stores seem to be a weekly occurrence. When it happens at a large retail chain, hundreds of thousands or even millions of customers can be affected.

1. Launch a web browser, and navigate to a search engine. Search for retailers that suffered breaches of their networks within the past year. Share your findings with the class.
2. Research chip-based credit card security. Why is the replacement of magnetic-strip credit cards with chip-based systems been so slowly adopted in the United States?
3. Research credit card skimmers. What are some steps consumers can take to avoid using a compromised system?

Output Devices

One of the most overlooked areas that data can be at risk are output devices. Output devices include printers, copiers, and fax machines. Printers today can perform multiple functions: printing, faxing, scanning, and e-mailing. They are often called *multifunction peripherals (MFPs)* or multifunction devices (MFDs). Most people do not consider the damage that can be done by these seemingly safe devices.

A common problem is to place the devices in open areas where anyone has access to the printed output, as shown in **Figure 7-13.** Someone near the printer

CompTIA Security+
3.3, 3.5

FYI

Most copy machines and other MFPs sold today have the ability to be networked so they can be used from any point on the network.

may be able to see the output or grab a printout without anyone realizing it. Most users will simply print again if the printout is missing. They think the document is lost in the network not realizing someone has taken the printout.

A possible solution to limit which printers each employee can use. For example, suppose one of the company printers is in a secure area. Limit printing to this device to only those employees who are authorized to be in that area. This prevents other employees from using a print job as an excuse to go into the restricted area. Also, sensitive employee information, such as payroll, should not be printed to a device located in a common area. Personnel who need to print this type of information should not be given access to devices shared by all employees.

In Windows, there are two options for configuring a guest user's access to print: manage documents and manage this printer. These are security settings. They should be checked for excessive permissions. Keep these options in mind when giving these additional permissions to users:

- Manage documents allows the user to pause, stop print jobs, and change options, which may include the number of copies.
- Manage printers allows the user to make settings on the printer such as changing permissions, starting and stopping the printer, and changing the printer properties.

Anutin/Shutterstock.com

Figure 7-13. A shared printer in an unsecured area can be a security risk.

Another security issue related to output devices that is often overlooked is internal storage. Internal storage is a great feature. It allows jobs to be stored and prioritized or stored until a PIN code is entered at the printer. The use of PIN codes ensures the print job is only accessed by the sender. However, by storing print jobs, copies may be retained on the internal storage. Is this far fetched? A CBS news group purchased used copiers from a copier reseller. From them, it was able to retrieve crucial police information on drug raids, information related to other crimes, and sensitive personal information from a health-care company and a construction company.

Before discarding an MFP, take steps to remove or wipe the hard drive. There are reputable vendors who can assist in this process. When purchasing an MFP, consider what security options are available. Some machines offer the ability to encrypt stored data or can perform zero-level formatting. *Zero-level formatting* is process in which new data are written over the top of existing data to destroy the existing data.

Quick Look 7.2.2

Printer Security

You can set security measures to prevent users from printing to network printers. Manufacturers of MFPs have offered various options to offer security for their devices.

1. Click the Windows **Start** button, and enter devices and printers in the search box. Select the **Devices and Printers** application in the list of results.
2. Click **Add a printer** at the top of the **Devices and Printers** window. A wizard is launched to guide you through the process of adding a printer.
3. In Windows 10, click **The printer I want isn't listed**, and in the new window, click the **Add a local printer or network printer with manual settings** radio button followed by clicking the **Next** button.
4. In the next screen on the wizard, click the **Use an existing port:** radio button, and select **LPT1: (Printer Port)** in the corresponding drop-down list. Click the **Next** button to continue.

Quick Look 7.2.2 Continued

5. Scroll through the list of printers, and select **Generic** in the **Manufacturer** column and **Generic/Text Only** in the **Printers** column, as shown. Click the **Next** button to continue.

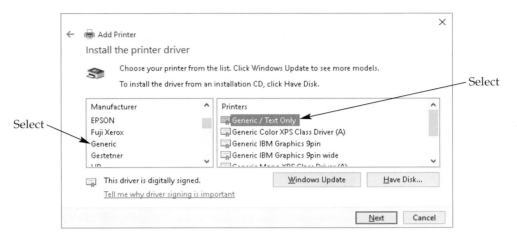

6. On the next screen of the wizard, accept the default printer name by clicking the **Next** button.
7. On the next screen of the wizard, click the **Do not share this printer** radio button, and then click the **Next** button.
8. On the final page of the wizard, uncheck the **Set as the default printer** check box, and then click the **Finish** button. The printer is installed and appears in the **Devices and Printers** window.
9. Right-click on the printer in the **Devices and Printers** window, and click **Printer properties** in the shortcut menu.
10. Click the **Security** tab in the **Properties** dialog box. A list of authorized users and their printing privileges appears here. By default, what is the default printing privileges for all users? Suppose you do not want guest users to print to this printer. The Everyone special identity includes the Guest user. Therefore, the permissions for Guest need to be changed.
11. Click the **Add...** button. In the dialog box that is displayed, enter Guest in the **Enter the object names to select** text box, and then click the **OK** button. If a dialog box appears asking you to select one of several guest users, select the one named Guest. The Guest user is added.
12. Click **Guest** in the list in the **Properties** dialog box, and check the **Deny** check box for **Print** in the **Permissions for Guest** area, as shown. Remember, an explicit deny always takes precedence over an explicit allow.

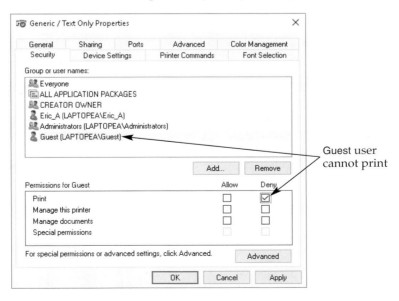

Quick Look 7.2.2 Continued

13. Click the **OK** button to save the changes. Anyone logged in as the Guest user will now not be able to print to the Generic printer.

14. Launch a web browser, and navigate to a search engine. Research MFPs to discover built-in security options that are offered. Do you feel one product superior than others from a security standpoint? Share your findings with your class.

CompTIA Security+
5.2

Critical Infrastructure

It is not just computers and printers that can be hacked. Internet-enabled technology is used for many critical services across the country. *Critical infrastructure* is the physical or virtual assets that are vital to the health and safety of citizens. The Department of Homeland Security (DHS) defines critical infrastructure as "assets, systems, and networks, whether physical or virtual, so vital to the United States that their incapacitation or destruction would have a debilitating effect on security, national economic security, national public health or safety, or any combination thereof." DHS organizes critical infrastructure into 16 areas, as shown in **Figure 7-14.** It is a serious concern to protect these vital areas.

An example of critical infrastructure being hacked occurred in April of 2017. The outdoor warning system for the City of Dallas went off around 11:40 p.m. on a Friday night. Sirens from all 156 of the city's warning alarm systems sounded. These sirens are used for severe weather or other emergencies. They blared until 1:20 a.m. The 911 system was flooded with phone calls by panicked residents unsure of what was happening. It was determined later to be a hack against the radio signals controlling the system. It is thought this was possibly a replay attack of the monthly test of the emergency sirens.

Critical infrastructure is considered a high-value target. State-sponsored hackers and those working for terrorist or criminal organizations could damage infrastructure. The damage could be so severe that loss of life may result. In 2015, there was an attack on the power grid in the Ukraine. Power was out for several hours. This outage had the potential to cause harm to many people. Several cybersecurity industry leaders believed this was a test or trial run for more extreme events. Some of the key players implicated in the Ukrainian attack were behind some attempts in the United States. Another example of an infrastructure attack that had the potential to harm many people was reported by Verizon. In this attack, hackers were able to alter settings related to water flow and the amount of chemicals used to treat the water.

Attacks against critical infrastructure are often performed the same way attacks against business networks are conducted. A common vector is spear-phishing attacks. In fact, in 2014 it was revealed a steel firm in Germany suffered physical damage to its equipment due to attacks originating from spear phishing and social engineering. When the potential outcome from a successful attack against a critical infrastructure is considered, it is vital that IT security personnel deploy strong security measures and use best practices and guidance.

The United States Computer Emergency Readiness Team (US-CERT) created a program called the Critical Infrastructure Cyber Community Voluntary Program. Known as C^3, or C cubed, this program helps businesses manage their critical infrastructure by providing a cybersecurity framework on specific critical areas. The framework consists of lists and recommended guidelines. It supports the five key functional areas, as shown in **Figure 7-15:**
- identify
- protect

- detect
- respond
- recover

C³ is a voluntary program. Not all critical infrastructure areas are owned by the government. In this case, the government is taking an advisory approach. It works with the various industries closely to assist in the protection of assets.

Sector	Description
Chemical	Includes businesses that manufacture, store, use, and transport potentially dangerous chemicals needed by other critical infrastructure sectors.
Commercial Facilities	Includes a diverse range of sites that draw large crowds of people for shopping, business, entertainment, or lodging.
Communication	Includes businesses using terrestrial, satellite, and wireless transmission systems to provide transmission of information.
Critical Manufacturing	Includes industries crucial to the economic prosperity and continuity of the United States a disruption of which would affect essential functions at the national level and across multiple critical infrastructure sectors.
Dams	Includes dam projects, navigation locks, levees, hurricane barriers, mine tailings impounds, and other similar water retention or control facilities.
Defense Industrial Base	Includes industries that enable research, development, design, production, delivery, and maintenance of military weapons systems, subsystems, and components or parts to meet US military requirements.
Emergency Services	Includes industries that provide a wide range of prevention, preparedness, response, and recovery services during both day-to-day operations and incident response.
Energy	Includes businesses supplying fuels to the transportation industry, electricity to households and businesses, and other sources of energy that are integral to growth and production across the nation.
Financial Services	Includes depository institutions, providers of investment products, insurance companies, other credit and financing organizations, and the providers of the critical financial utilities and services that support these functions.
Food and Agriculture	Includes industries involved in food manufacturing, processing, and storage.
Governmental Facilities	Includes buildings that are owned or leased by federal, state, local, and tribal governments either within the United States or overseas.
Health Care and Public Health	Includes industries that protect from hazards such as terrorism, infectious disease outbreaks, and natural disasters.
Information Technology	Includes industries that produce and provide hardware, software, and information technology systems and services together with the Internet.
Nuclear Reactors, Materials, and Waste	Includes businesses that create, use, and maintain power reactors, research reactors, and medical isotopes.
Transportation Systems	Includes industries involved in transporting goods and people domestically and overseas.
Water and Wastewater Systems	Includes industries involved in ensuring the safe supply of drinking water and treatment and service of wastewater.

Goodheart-Willcox Publisher

Figure 7-14. Critical infrastructure is divided into 16 areas by the Department of Homeland Security.

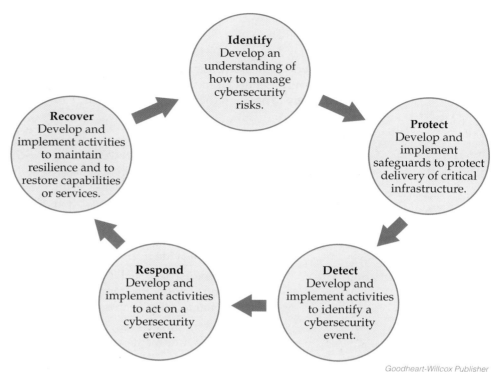

Figure 7-15. The C³ framework supports these five functional areas.

Industrial-Control Systems

One area that is facing increasing threats and attacks is industrial-control systems. According to the Industrial Control System Cyber Emergency Response Team (ICS-CERT), control systems in the United States were threatened by attacks over 245 times from October 2013 to September 2014. The two largest targets were the energy sector (32 percent) and critical manufacturing (27 percent). One of the types of systems often found to be a target are SCADA systems.

A *supervisory control and data acquisition (SCADA) system* is hardware and software used to monitor and interface with the controls for machines and equipment in an industrial process. SCADA systems are the core of many critical infrastructure systems, including energy, water, and transportation. SCADA systems can be simple installations or used to manage complex environments, as shown in **Figure 7-16.** SCADA systems rose from the need to manage systems that were spread out over distances. Remote data gathering and automated controls became critical to managing and monitoring these systems.

SCADA systems have undergone many changes as technology has evolved. Today, these systems provide real-time data that allow management to make information-driven decisions. SCADA systems rely on databases, such as Structured Query Language (SQL), and web interfaces. These technologies present potential vulnerabilities for SCADA systems that must be monitored and managed. Something as simple as malware on a USB stick inserted into a system connected to the SCADA network could launch an attack in seconds with serious or even deadly effects.

Figure 7-16. This is the control room for a power-generation plant. Industrial-control systems can be vulnerable to cyberattacks.

Case Study

Critical Infrastructure

Critical infrastructure presents many unique vulnerabilities and threats due to the nature of the services provided. Additionally, most of these systems are managed by private companies that may not fall under the same security requirements as governmental agencies. To illustrate how a cyberattack could potentially cripple a system, the Idaho National Laboratory conducted a test. It simulated an attack on the physical systems of an electrical grid. Investigate this simulated cybersecurity attack. Then, summarize the facts, from how the "hackers" were able to gain access to the outcome of the attack.

1. What lessons can be learned on attacks from this simulated exercise?
2. Have there been any more recent simulations or actual attacks?

SECTION REVIEW 7.2

Check Your Understanding

1. What are skimmers?
2. To delegate management of print jobs, which permission should be assigned to the user?
3. Which type of formatting should be performed to remove data on an MFP?
4. What did the US-CERT develop to help companies manage their critical infrastructure?
5. Critical infrastructure often uses complex technical systems known as what?

Build Your Key Terms Vocabulary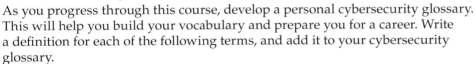

As you progress through this course, develop a personal cybersecurity glossary. This will help you build your vocabulary and prepare you for a career. Write a definition for each of the following terms, and add it to your cybersecurity glossary.

critical infrastructure

embedded operating system

multifunction peripheral (MFP)

point-of-sale (PoS) device

RAM scraper

skimmer

supervisory control and data
    acquisition (SCADA) system

zero-level formatting

Review and Assessment

Summary

Section 7.1 Mobile Devices

- The changing nature of computer networks involving Internet of Things (IoT) and bring your own device (BYOD) has impacted how IT security is applied.
- The increase in use of mobile devices, from smartphones to laptops and tablets, has placed an emphasis on protecting data on mobile platforms, which may include encrypting the data.
- Metadata, such as GPS metadata, is often included in documents without the user being aware of it, which can lead to security issues, but also can be a security aid.
- Security issues on mobile devices and IoT devices present unique challenges to the IT professional.

Section 7.2 Nontraditional Hosts

- Point-of-sale (PoS) devices are used to read customer information from a credit card and are targets for cyberattacks, from skimmers to RAM scrapers.
- Multifunction peripherals (MFPs) can present security concerns, from access to printouts to information retained on the internal storage.
- Critical infrastructure is vital to health and safety and extra steps must be taken to ensure security, such as following the C^3 framework.
- Industrial-control systems, such as supervisory control and data acquisition (SCADA) systems, are increasingly the target of cyberattacks, and successful attacks could have serious or even deadly effects.

Check Your Cybersecurity IQ

Now that you have completed this chapter, see what you have learned about cybersecurity by visiting the student companion website (www.g-wlearning.com) and taking the chapter posttest.

Review Questions

For each question, select the answer that is the best response.

1. What describes computing technology incorporated into nontraditional devices?
   - A. BYOD
   - B. Point of sale
   - C. Internet of Things
   - D. Wearable technology

2. Which of the following is the best way to protect data on a stolen laptop?
   - A. Ensure a TPM chip is included with the motherboard.
   - B. A strong password be placed on the BIOS.
   - C. GPS tracking should be enabled.
   - D. Full drive encryption should be in place on the laptop.

3. A user has used BitLocker to Go on a flash drive. On attempting to use the system, the incorrect password is used. What can this user do?
   - A. Temporarily suspend the encryption.
   - B. Click the **Forgot my password** link, and check his or her e-mail for the password.
   - C. Use the recovery key to change the password.
   - D. The user will have to format the drive to use it again.

4. How can a security administrator find who created a file?
   - A. Check the file properties and view the owner.
   - B. Review the metadata of the file.
   - C. Verify the logged-in user information.
   - D. Process the file through BitLocker.

5. Which of the following is not a concern regarding a smartphone used as BYOD?
   - A. The user engaged in jailbreaking or rooting the device.
   - B. The user accessing confidential information on the device.
   - C. Sideloaded apps have been installed.
   - D. A skimmer has been installed.

6. Which of the following will help with security issues regarding IoT devices?
   A. Ensure device firmware is regularly updated.
   B. Only purchase devices from reputable vendors.
   C. Do not allow the devices access to the Internet.
   D. Only allow administrators to use IoT devices.

7. A retail flower shop is updating its cash register to a PoS system. What is the most likely threat to this system?
   A. Customers using EMV cards only.
   B. Inventory management.
   C. Malware.
   D. Internal storage failure.

8. In a busy accounting office, the administrator wants to delegate a junior IT technician to manage the documents on the shared printers. What should the administrator do?
   A. Allow the junior admin to manage documents.
   B. Allow the junior admin to manage printers.
   C. Make sure the junior admin has the printers in question installed.
   D. Purchase MFP devices and set up security at the printer level.

9. Which is not likely considered critical infrastructure?
   A. A nuclear reactor.
   B. Hoover Dam.
   C. A local newspaper office.
   D. A hospital network.

10. What is not true about SCADA systems?
    A. They collect and report real-time data.
    B. They are the core of many critical infrastructure systems.
    C. They are used exclusively with infrastructure of the United States government.
    D. Their reliance on databases and web interfaces present vulnerabilities.

Application and Extension of Knowledge

1. Consider the future of IoT. Locate some sources that discuss what is on the horizon for this technology. What are some of the products and devices expected to be introduced? Do you think these are likely or far-fetched? Summarize your findings and opinions in a one-page paper. Be sure to cite your sources.

2. Create a one-page flyer that a store may use to warn customers about skimmers. Include photographs or illustrations showing how to identify skimmers. Provide text to describe the dangers of skimmers.

3. BitLocker is used for drive encryption, but there are also for-purchase products that do the same thing. Investigate what for-purchase products are available to protect a laptop running Microsoft Windows. Identify pricing and features of each. Summarize three options that could be used in a one-page paper. What advantages do these for-purchase software have over BitLocker?

4. Many social media sites, such as Facebook and LinkedIn, strip GPS and other Exif data from uploaded pictures. Find out why these companies remove this type of metadata. If you have access to a social media account, take a photograph and view the Exif data. Then, upload it to the site. Finally, download the photograph from the site, save it as a different name, and review the properties of the file. Compare the before and after properties. Create a brief slideshow presentation to illustrate your findings.

5. Assume you have a $2,000 budget. You need to recommend a copier or MFP that has features to protect the confidentiality and integrity of data. Visit a local business-supply store, and ask about the products they offer. Be sure to tell them you are a student conducting research for a class project. Take notes, and ask for copies of sales literature. Then, review the information you gathered and write a paragraph to recommend a product. Include your justification.

Research Project
Drive Encryption

You are a security analyst for a law firm. There are 20 laptops used by staff in and out of the office. The office manager is quite concerned about data and security breaches. Her primary concern is with data on the laptops in case one is lost or stolen. She wants to encrypt the hard drives on the laptops. She is familiar with BitLocker, but wants to know what other choices are available. In addition, she wants to recommend to the attorneys they encrypt their mobile devices. She needs to know what options are available for doing this on mobile devices. The attorneys may have different brands of mobile devices.

Deliverables. Write a memo to the manager highlighting other program choices, their prices, and available features. Which of the options would you recommend and why? What choices would you recommend for Android and iOS devices? Justify your choices for those devices.

Online Activities

Complete the following activities, which will help you learn, practice, and expand your knowledge and skills.

 Vocabulary. Practice vocabulary for this chapter using the e-flash cards, matching activity, and vocabulary game until you are able to recognize their meanings.

Communication Skills

College and Career Readiness

Reading. When engaging in active reading, it is important to relate what you are reading to your prior knowledge, or what you already know. This helps readers evaluate information as they read to ensure understanding and form judgments about what is read. Select one of the sections of this chapter to read again.

As you read, make notes about your prior knowledge relating to the content. Evaluate whether or not your prior knowledge helped you understand the content.

Writing. It is important for an employee to apply both technical and academic skills in the workplace. Writing is an academic skill applied each day in a person's personal and work lives. Write a paragraph describing why writing is considered an academic skill. How do you think good writing skills will help you in your career?

Speaking. Etiquette is the art of using good manners in any situation. Etiquette is especially important when meeting someone for the first time. Create a script you might use to introduce yourself to the president of a cybersecurity firm. Practice your script by making the introduction to a classmate. How do you rate your use of good manners? How does your classmate rate your speech?

Listening. Engage in a conversation with someone to whom you have not spoken before. Ask the person about the importance of cybersecurity to the average consumer. Actively listen to what he or she shares. Build on his or her ideas by sharing your own. Next, summarize and retell what the person conveyed to you in the conversation. Did you really hear what was being said? Try this again with other people to whom you have not spoken before. How clearly were the different people able to articulate themselves? How is having a conversation with someone to whom you do not normally speak different from having a conversation with a familiar friend or family member?

Portfolio Development

College and Career Readiness

File Structure. After you have chosen a file format for your documents, determine a strategy for storing and organizing the materials. The file structure for storing digital documents is similar to storing hardcopy documents.

First, you need a place to store each item. Ask your instructor where to save your documents. This could be on the school's network or a flash drive of your own. Next, decide how to organize related files into categories. For example, Certificates might be the name of a folder with a subfolder named Community Service Certificates and a subfolder named School Certificates. Appropriate certificates would be saved in each subfolder. The names for folders and files should be descriptive, but not too long.

1. Decide on the file structure for your documents.
2. Create folders and subfolders on the school's network drive or flash drive on which you will save your files.

CTSO Event Prep

Parliamentary Procedures. In the parliamentary procedure competitive event, participants must demonstrate understanding of parliamentary procedures such as Roberts Rules of Order. This is a team event in which the group will demonstrate how to conduct an effective meeting. An objective test may be administered to each person on the team that will be evaluated and included in the overall team score. To prepare for the parliamentary procedure, complete the following activities.

1. Read the guidelines provided by your organization.
2. Study parliamentary procedure principles by reviewing Roberts Rules of Order.
3. Practice proper procedures for conducting a meeting. Assign each team member a role for the presentation.
4. Visit the organization's website and look for the evaluation criteria or rubric for the event. This will help you determine what the judges will be looking for in your presentation.

Chapter 8

Overview of Network Security and Network Threats

In 2016, Director of National Intelligence James Clapper warned Congress that the next biggest threats to businesses would be hackers getting into networks and changing data. These actions would destroy the integrity of the data. Thus far, most cyberattacks have not been focused on data sabotage. Attacks that steal data, such as sensitive customer information, affect the confidentiality of the information. Denial of service attacks make data unavailable. However, attacks that sabotage data have occurred. Some businesses have reported their data have been altered, and management made business decisions based on the faulty data.

Security professionals must take all precautions and actively explore all possible threats to prevent attacks against networks. To do this, you must be able to understand networking addresses and know how to view the content, such as the headers of network packets. You must also understand specific aspects of the TCP/IP protocol suite. This chapter explores security threats that involve the network traffic and threats involving the TCP/IP protocol.

Chapter Preview

While studying, look for the activity icon **for:**

- Pretests and posttests
- Vocabulary terms with e-flash cards and matching activities
- Self-assessment

G-WLEARNING.com

Reading Prep

As you read this chapter, determine the point of view or purpose of the author. What aspects of the text help to establish this purpose or point of view?

College and Career Readiness

Check Your Cybersecurity IQ ↗

Before you begin this chapter, see what you already know about cybersecurity by visiting the student companion website (www.g-wlearning.com) and taking the chapter pretest.

Certification Objectives

CompTIA Security+

1.2 Compare and contrast types of attacks.
2.2 Given a scenario, use appropriate software tools to assess the security posture of an organization.
2.6 Given a scenario, implement secure protocols.
3.2 Given a scenario, implement secure network architecture concepts.

Microsoft MTA Security Fundamentals

3.3 Understand protocol security.

Network Basics

A computer network is basically two or more devices talking to each other. Information that is transmitted is contained in a packet. Computer networking has evolved since its beginnings in the early part of the 20th century. Over the years, there have been several popular networking protocols, such as Netbeui, IPX/SPX, and Appletalk. Now, the industry uses a single, standardized protocol for network transmissions called Transmission Control Protocol/Internet Protocol (TCP/IP).

Networks are complex systems that connect a variety of devices from computers, printers, and servers to the infrastructure equipment that ties everything together. As the data travel through these systems, they will be converted into other forms. Transport information such as addressing and error checking is added. Threats to data could occur at any point in the transmission process.

Key Terms

ANDing

Classless Internet Domain Resolution (CIDR)

cyclical redundancy check (CRC)

de facto standard

global unicast address

initial sequence number (ISN)

Internet Assigned Numbers Authority (IANA)

Internet Control Message Protocol (ICMP)

Internet Corporation for Assigned Names and Numbers (ICANN)

link-local address

local host

Media Access Control (MAC) address

Network Address Translation (NAT)

octet

packet sniffer

proprietary

protocol

Regional Internet Registrars (RIRs)

site-local address

socket

subnet mask

three-way handshake

time to live (TTL)

WHOIS

Learning Goals

- Discuss the evolution of networking protocols.
- Identify the components of an IPv4 address.
- Compare and contrast IPv4 and IPv6 protocols.
- Explain TCP and UDP packets.

TCP/IP Review

A *protocol* is an industry-accepted standardized format that allows communication between devices. It is like a rule that everyone must follow. In order for devices to communicate, they must use a standard set of protocols. Networking protocols allow that communication to take place. If devices do not use the same protocol for traffic, the messages will be unreadable. Early protocols were proprietary. *Proprietary* means owned by someone, and it cannot be used without permission. Proprietary protocols were used only for those vendors and their systems.

Once the Internet started to gain popularity, use of the network protocol Transmission Control Protocol/Internet Protocol (TCP/IP) became necessary. It became the de facto standard of networking protocols. A *de facto standard* is one that is generally accepted over time and adopted for use, but not required. Nearly every system that accesses a network today uses TCP/IP as its communication method. TCP/IP is actually a suite of protocols. In fact, the name is composed of two of the most fundamental protocols: TCP and IP. Some of the other protocols in the TCP/IP suite include DNS, DHCP, HTTP, FTP, ARP, ICMP, IGMP, and UDP.

There are two current versions of TCP/IP: IPv4 and IPv6. There are significant differences between the versions. Both are used extensively on Internet hosts. Therefore, security professionals need to have a solid understanding of each version.

FYI

TCP/IP was developed as part of research by the United States agency called DARPA for a network called ARPAnet. This network is the origin of today's Internet.

IPv4 Basics

The IPv4 protocol has long been the predominant network protocol. It has some limitations. Even with its limitations, it is still heavily used on most network systems. It is critical to be able to read network addresses, identify information such as the difference between the host and network portion of an address, and to dissect the IPv4 packet sections.

IPv4 Addresses

An address is a unique value that is assigned to host on a computer network. If you think of the computer network as an apartment building, which has its own address, then each apartment also has a unique address. In TCP/IP IPv4, this address is in a dot-decimal format. It is composed of four sections, and each section is called an *octet*. Each octet consists of 8 bits. The largest number possible in any octet is the value 255. **Figure 8-1** shows a network address that uses the IPv4 protocol. The octets are separated by periods. The entire address is always 32 bits long.

Goodheart-Willcox Publisher

Figure 8-1. This address format follows the IPv4 protocol.

A network host obtains its address through manual assignment or automatically. A manual assignment is called a static IP address. If assigned automatically, the unique address is received from a server that holds a range of available addresses. The IP address serves two purposes. Part of the address identifies the network to which the host is assigned. The remaining portion is the unique ID of the host on that network. As an example, think of your street address. There may be many houses on the same street, but each one has a unique address. So, the street is similar to the network address. The house number is the unique host address.

IPv4 Host vs. Network

It is not possible to look at just the IP address and determine which part of it refers to the network and which part is unique to each host. To determine that information, the subnet mask assigned to the address must be considered.

A *subnet mask* is a value that, when mathematically compared to the network address, can identify which portion of the IP address is part of the network and which portion identifies the unique host value. Thinking of houses on a street, a subnet mask is similar to a ZIP code. A ZIP code identifies a geographic area, and the subnet mask identifies an area on a network.

Subnet Mask

To understand how a subnet mask is used, examine the IPv4 address in its binary form. *Binary* is a numbering system that only uses the values of 0 and 1. This is how computer data are transmitted. Each binary digit represents one bit of information. **Figure 8-2** shows the IPv4 address from **Figure 8-1** represented in binary. As you can see, each octet contains eight bits, or one byte, of information.

A quick review of binary conversion is in order. Each octet in an IPv4 address contains 8 bits, and each of those bits has a numeric value. The numbers are assigned right to left. Values start with 1 and double for each next position to the left, as shown in **Figure 8-2.** When a binary value (0 or 1) is assigned to a position, the binary positional value is multiplied by the binary value. The sums of those calculations are added together, and the answer is the decimal value. This is also shown in **Figure 8-2.**

Humans are comfortable reading values in decimal. However, the computer converts those numbers to binary. In a subnet mask, the number of on, or 1, bits represents the number of bits in the 32 bits that is the network. For example, if you want the network address of a subnet, such as 192.168.100.0, to be the first three octets, then you need to set the subnet mask to turn the first 24 bits to on. Remember, one octet is 8 bits, three octets is 24 bits, and so on. In binary, this address will be 11111111.11111111.11111111.00000000. The last octet is for the unique hosts on the network, so that section is composed of 0 bits.

Before seeing how to use the subnet mask to find the network portion of an IP address, look at the two methods that can represent a subnet mask. A subnet mask is expressed in one of two ways, decimal or CIDR.

In a decimal format, the numbers will be in the four octets, which is the same form as an IP address. Using the same example of 192.168.100 as the network, the

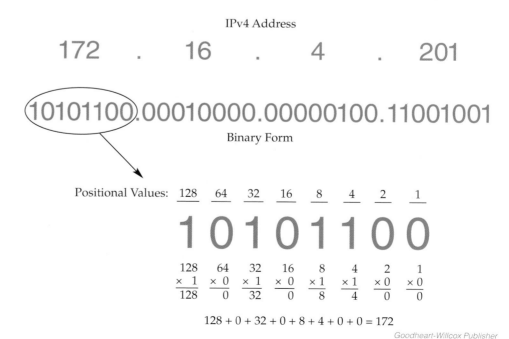

Figure 8-2. The IPv4 address has been converted to binary.

binary representation of 11111111.11111111.11111111.00000000 will be converted to decimal in each octet. The Windows calculator or a programmer's calculator can be used to convert these numbers. The table shown in **Figure 8-3** can also be used as a reference. So, a subnet mask of 11111111.11111111.11111111.00000000 will be written as 255.255.255.0 when using a decimal format.

Classless Internet Domain Resolution (CIDR) is a way to represent IP addresses in compressed form. With CIDR, the subnet mask is written as a total number of the on, or 1, bits in the subnet mask. This is an easier way to visualize the subnet mask. Using the same example, a total of 24 bits are turned on. In decimal, the subnet mask is 255.255.255.0, but in CIDR format it is written as /24. The number 24 identifies the first 24 binary bits of this address as the network portion. The remaining eight bits of the address are the unique address on the host.

For the IPv4 address shown in **Figure 8-1,** the network address is 172.16.4. The unique host address is 201. The subnet mask for this example is either 255.255.255.0 in decimal or /24 in CIDR format. To calculate the network address portion, follow these steps.

1. Convert the decimal numbers to binary. This includes the IP address and the subnet mask. **Figure 8-2** shows the IP address in binary.
2. Use a mathematical function called ANDing to compare the original address to the host. The result of this comparison is the network address.

ANDing is a process of comparing two binary digits and creating a value based on the comparison. Consider the example shown in **Figure 8-4.** When ANDing, the network portion of the subnet mask binary address is represented

Binary Octet for Subnet Mask	Decimal Equivalent of Octet
10000000	128
11000000	192
11100000	224
11110000	240
11111000	248
11111100	252
11111110	254
11111111	255

Goodheart-Willcox Publisher

Figure 8-3. This table can be used to convert between binary and decimal.

In some cases, the result of ANDing looks like the original address in binary form with just the local address represented as zero. However, in many cases with subnets, the network portion cannot be determined without ANDing.

Rules for ANDing
1 AND 1 = 1
1 AND 0 = 0
0 AND 0 = 0
In other words, everything equals 0 *except* 1 AND 1.

IPv4 Address in Decimal

172 . 16 . 4 . 0

IPv4 Address in Binary

10101100.00010000.00000100.11001001

ANDing Values

11111111.11111111.11111111.00000000

Network Address

10101100.00010000.00000100.00000000

Both values are 1, so the result is 1

One value is 1 and the other is 0, so the result is 0

Both values are 0, so the result is 0

Goodheart-Willcox Publisher

Figure 8-4. Using ANDing to find the network portion of the address in the subnet mask. When represented in decimal, the final result is 172.16.4.0, which is the network address.

with the number 1. The unique host address is represented with 0s. Then, the original full binary address is compared to this new string place by place. If both values are 1, then the result is 1. If both values are 0, the result is 0. If one value is 1 and the other value is 0, the result is 0. The final result is a string representing the network portion of the full address in binary form. *Remember:* 1 AND 1 = 1, while everything else equals 0.

The result of the ANDing process has identified the network address of the host. In this example, if the binary result is converted back to decimal, the network address of 172.16.4.0 is revealed. The 201 is the unique portion that represents this host.

Quick Look 8.1.1

Decimal and CIDR Address Formats

The ability to convert addresses between decimal and CIDR formats is an important skill to master. Practice converting the following examples of subnet masks to their equivalent decimal or CIDR formats.

1. The CIDR format of 255.255.192.0 is _____.
2. The CIDR format of 255.255.255.224 is _____.
3. The CIDR format of 255.255.255.128 is _____.
4. Subnet mask in decimal for CIDR format of /17 is _____.
5. Subnet mask in decimal for CIDR format of /28 is _____.
6. Subnet mask in decimal for CIDR format of /20 is _____.

Private, Public, and Special Addresses

Another aspect of IPv4 addresses is the concept of a private and public address and some of the special addresses used. The IPv4 protocol uses an address of 127.0.0.1 to represent the local host, or home address. The *local host* is the device on which you are working. Therefore, regardless of the device, the host can be referenced with this address.

A *private address* is for use on the internal network only. It cannot be used on the Internet. Private addresses are necessary in IPv4, as the pool of available IPv4 public addresses has been exhausted. In this version, if an IPv4 address starts with any of the following octets, it is considered a private address. The lowercase X in the address represents the host portion by default.

FYI

There is no place like 127.0.0.1!

Class	Private Range
A	10.x.x.x
B	172.16.x.x–172.31.x.x
C	192.168.x.x

Since private addresses cannot be placed on the Internet, they must be converted to public addresses. Many private addresses can share a single public address through a device called NAT. *Network Address Translation (NAT)* is a network service that converts an internal private number to a number for a public network, such as the Internet. When the packet is returned, NAT finds the internal reference to the private address in its table and converts the public address back to a private network address. NAT uses the unique port number for each local host to create a unique entry in its table. This is how the same public address can be used for many different private addresses. Thus, NAT is often called *PNAT* (port-based NAT).

NAT often runs on a router to handle the conversion from private to public address, as shown in **Figure 8-5.** The source port for each private Internet protocol (IP) address is appended to the address. This is called the *socket,* which is the IP address and the port together. Think of a socket as a person's name on a package. It is a unique address for the host. When the IP address is converted, NAT uses the unique port number. The router then sends the packet out through the public IP address. When a packet returns to the router, this port is used as the destination. The router checks the NAT table for the port number to locate the correct private IP address.

A business gets its public IP address from an Internet Service Provider (ISP). They can use any private IP address range of their choice. Because public IP addresses cannot be duplicated on the Internet, there is some regulatory control over these addresses. The organization *Internet Assigned Numbers Authority (IANA)* is responsible for the control of IP addresses. To make this more efficient, IANA divided all possible public IP addresses and assigned them to five different registrars, as shown in **Figure 8-6.** These registrars are called *Regional Internet Registrars (RIRs).*

IP Address Owner

Another important ability is identifying who is behind an IP address. When a company sets up a web, e-mail, or other public server, the server names are registered globally so there are no duplicates on the Internet or any network. The nonprofit organization *Internet Corporation for Assigned Names and Numbers (ICANN)* maintains the responsibility for managing and coordinating the maintenance of the databases that store this information. These databases can provide information about the owner of the website, including contact information. Perhaps you are getting a great deal of denial-of-service traffic or e-mail spam. There is a variety of free tools widely available on the Internet to begin tracking down the sender of the packet. There are many sites where you can access reverse IP data and WHOIS data for both IPv4 and IPv6 addresses. *WHOIS* is a system that

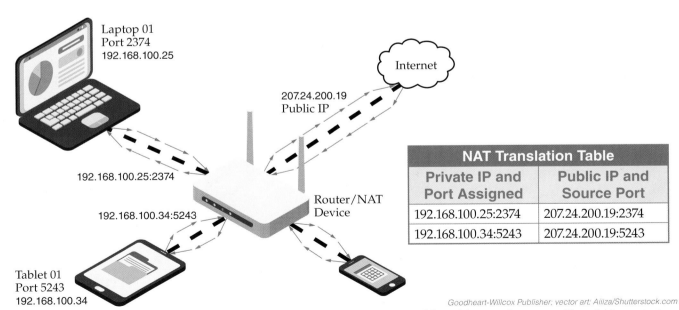

NAT Translation Table	
Private IP and Port Assigned	**Public IP and Source Port**
192.168.100.25:2374	207.24.200.19:2374
192.168.100.34:5243	207.24.200.19:5243

Figure 8-5. Private addresses in the IPv4 protocol are converted into public addresses by appending their ports to the private address using NAT. Each private IP address receives a random (dynamic) port number from NAT. That will become the source port on the public IP address so when a packet returns it can find the correct IP address.

Canada, USA, and
some Caribbean Islands
ARIN

Europe, the Middle East,
and Central Asia
RIPE NCC

APNIC
Asia/Pacific Region

LACNIC
Latin America and
some Caribbean Islands

AFRINIC
Africa Region

Figure 8-6. The world is broken down into five Regional Internet Registrars for IP addresses.

FYI

Oops, not a hack! It happens; big companies can forget to renew domain names. The Dallas Cowboys organization forgot in 2010, and its website went blank. A message was displayed on the domain offering the domain for sale!

provides the owner of a domain and a contact person for the domain by querying the ICANN databases. WHOIS lookups are useful to provide the name and company information of a registered domain name. ICANN and IANA, along with others, provide the management, technical support, and standards behind many of the services and protocols used on the Internet.

It is common to say a company or person owns a domain name. However, domain names are not owned, rather leased for a period of time. You have the right to renew your lease before it can be offered again for sale. If you forget to renew your domain name, there is a mandatory grace period set by ICANN that works with your registration agent so you can still renew the domain if you miss the deadline. If you fail to renew the domain, it becomes available for others to lease.

Quick Look 8.1.2

IPv4 Address Exploration

The Internet Protocol (IP) address can be used to provide much information, such as finding the owner. Additionally, the allocation IPv4 addresses can be determined.

1. Applying what you have learned, launch the command prompt, and enter the **ipconfig** command. Note your IP address, particularly the first two octets. Is it private?

2. Launch a web browser, and navigate to the site www.whatsmyip.com. This is a great site for finding your public IP address, and it provides other tools as well. Note the public IP address reported by this site. Compare this to the ones your classmates are seeing. Are they the same? If so, how are they differentiated from each other?

Quick Look 8.1.2 Continued

3. Navigate to the site ip-lookup.net. This is one of the many reverse–IP–lookup tools available on the Internet.

4. Enter 152.152.31.120 in the IP address search box, as shown. What is the name of the host? What country is this located in?

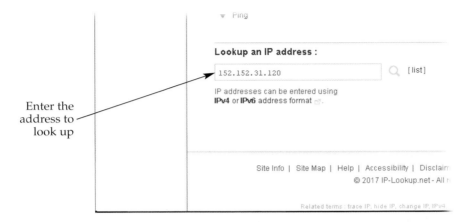

Enter the address to look up

5. Click the **Domain** tab at the top of the web page. Enter the domain name (host) you found in the previous step. What is the IP address registered to that domain?

6. Navigate to the site whois.icann.org. This is the WHOIS lookup tool.

7. Enter the address chicagobears.com in the domain lookup text box. If you were getting malicious packets from this domain, what e-mail address would you use to get assistance from this organization?

8. Scroll down the page. When was the last time this organization updated the registration? When does it expire?

9. Look up the domain of your school system. Review the information about your school's registration.

10. Navigate to the IANA website (www.iana.org).

11. Click the Number Resources link on the home page.

12. Scroll down to the IP Address Allocations area of the page, and click the IPv4 Address Space link.

13. Suppose you receive a malicious packet with the address of 186.17.200.45. Which RIR handled that IP address?

14. Apple Computer was an early adopter of TCP/IP. It has been given a legacy assignment. What is the first octet it was given? Hint: use the browser's find function to search the list.

15. A company in Mexico wants to become an ISP. Which RIR handles this request?

IPv6 Basics

The IPv6 protocol was developed with many goals in mind. Two goals were improved security and an increased number of IP addresses. These requirements meant a completely new format of IP address was needed.

IPv6 Addresses

With IPv4, there are 4.3 billion (4,300,000,000) possible addresses. This number is equal to 2 raised to the power 32 (2^{32}). However, IPv6 offers 2^{128} (340,282,366,920,938,463,463,374,607,431,768,211,456) possible addresses. IPv6 uses addresses based on the hexadecimal, or Base 16, numbering system. This numbering system includes the value 0–9 and A–F, as shown in **Figure 8-7.**

FYI

What happened to IPv5? IPv5 was originally developed as a protocol for streaming video, but it still used the 32-bit–octet formula for addresses. Due to the limited number of available addresses, the IPv5 standard was abandoned before it ever got adopted.

Numbering System	Number															
Decimal	0	1	2	3	4	5	6	7	8	9	10	11	12	13	14	15
Hexadecimal	0	1	2	3	4	5	6	7	8	9	A	B	C	D	E	F

Examples

Decimal	Hexadecimal
77	4D
101	65
1966	7AE

Figure 8-7. The hexadecimal numbering system has values of 0–9 and A–F.

Address Meaning

The length of the address is increased from 32 bits in IPv4 to 128 bits. IPv6 also has eight sections of hexadecimal quartets. Quartets are often called *hextets.* Each quartet, or hextet, represents 16 binary bits. The sections are separated by a colon (:) in IPv6 as opposed to a period (.) separating the octets in IPv4. An IPv6 address looks something like this:

    2001:203A:0000:0000:5300:0000:0027:8A9C

At first glance, it might seem an address in this format would be hard to remember. However, there are some key things to know about an IPv6 address:

- Portions of the address indicate the network address and the host address.
- The first quartet in the address identifies the type of IPv6 address, such as public or private.
- The address possibly can be shortened.

An IPv6 address is shortened by removing consecutive sections of zeros. These sections can be shortened to two colons (::), but only once in an address hextet or quartet. A single section of 0000 can be shortened to a single 0. Leading zeros in a quartet can be removed. Using the above example, the address can be shortened:

    2001:203A:0000:0000:5300:0000:0027:8A9C (unshortened address)
    2001:203A::5300:0:27:8A9C (same address in shortened form)

Notice the two consecutive sections of zeros have been removed (::), and the single section of zeros has been reduced to a single zero.

Hexadecimal Conversion

With the help of conversion calculators and basic math principles, you can convert data from hexadecimal, or *hex,* to decimal. Look at **Figure 8-8.** This shows the properties of a packet as reported by the packet sniffer Wireshark, which is discussed later in this chapter. The **Time to live:** value of 64 is represented as 40 in hexadecimal.

Consider a hexadecimal value of 40 and refer to **Figure 8-9.** Each digit in the hexadecimal value is a placeholder. The 0 is equivalent to 16^0. The 4 is equivalent to 16^1. Taking 16 to the power of 0 is the decimal value of 1. Taking 16 to the power of 1 is the decimal value of 16. To compute the value, multiply each value by the placeholder and add them together. $(0 \times 1) + (4 \times 16) = 64$. The decimal equivalent of the hexadecimal value 40 is 64.

FYI

Hexidecimal conversion is covered in detail in Chapter 17.

IPv6 Host vs. Network

In the IPv6 protocol, the first 64 bits of an address identify the network, as shown in **Figure 8-10.** The last 64 bits identify the host. The first 48 bits represent

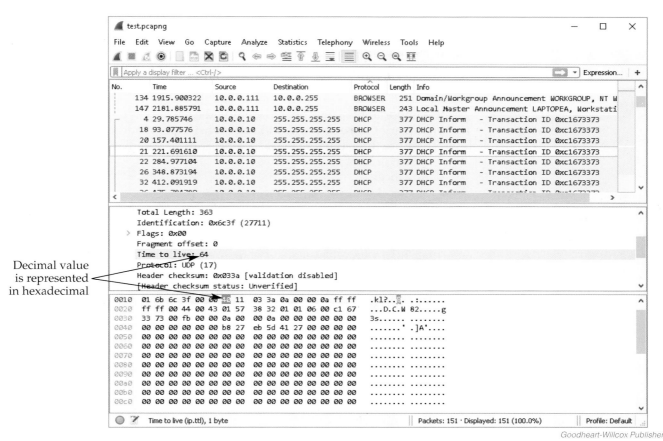

Decimal value is represented in hexadecimal

Figure 8-8. The packet sniffer Wireshark provides data in hexadecimal format at the bottom of the properties page.

Hex Character	4	0
Positional Value	$16^1 = 16$	$16^0 = 1$
Result of Multiplication	$4 \times 16 = 64$	$0 \times 1 = 0$
Add the values to find the decimal equivalent.	\multicolumn{2}{c} $64 + 0 = 64$

Hexadecimal Letter	Decimal Number
A	10
B	11
C	12
D	13
E	14
F	15

Figure 8-9. Converting a hexadecimal value of 40 into its decimal equivalent of 64. Also, be aware of the decimal equivalents for the letters used in hexadecimal.

Position	First 48 bits	Next 16 bits	Last 64 bits
Meaning	Global Routing Prefix	Subnet Mask	Host Interface ID
Example	2000:0000:0000	0000	0000:2A33:4545:002B

Figure 8-10. In the IPv6 protocol, the first 64 bits of an address identify the network, while the last 64 bits identify the host.

the actual network address. The second 16 bits are the subnet mask. However, unlike the IPv4 protocol, there are so many addresses available it is unlikely a subnet mask address will ever need to be assigned.

Often, an IPv6 address will have a network prefix that is similar to the CIDR notation. The address in the previous example may be expressed as 2001:203A:0000:0000::/64 or even shorter as 2001:203A::/64.

It is important to know how to identify the network type for an IPv6 address. The first quartet in section one indicates what type of address is being used in IPv6. There are three types of network addresses, as summarized in **Figure 8-11:**

- global unicast
- link local
- site local

A *global unicast address* is a public IPv6 address. Packets with global unicast addresses can be routed and sent on the Internet. They are called unicast because each address must be globally unique. No other host may use a given address. As with IPv4, the IANA controls the designation of these addresses. There are many prefixes that are used globally, but the most common addresses begin with 2001.

A *link-local address* can be used only on the link (subnet) or broadcast domain. It is new to TCP/IP version 6. This type of address is not forwarded through routers. The interesting fact about these addresses is they are automatically assigned when IPv6 is turned on in the properties of the network interface card.

Consider this situation. Your DHCP server is unavailable. In IPv4, you would receive an APIPA address beginning with 169.254.x.x. However, unless other devices on your network also had an APIPA address, you could not communicate

Case Study

Subnet Masks

You have been hired as an IT consultant to Great Graphic Designs, a small business focusing on marketing and graphic design. You have determined that this network will need two subnets so the traffic is separated by high-bandwidth needs and general administrative work. These subnets will each have one server, one router, and one dedicated printer. All of these devices will receive a static IP address. Create a report for this customer detailing the network address of each network along with each subnet mask.

1. What private range will you use?
2. Identify the static addresses you will assign to these devices.

Summary of IPv6 Address Types			
Type	**Public or Private**	**Routing**	**Example**
Global Unicast	A public address.	Can be routed outside of the subnet.	Any address beginning with 2001 or higher in the first quartet.
Link Local	A special address; automatically created on IPv6 installation.	Cannot be routed outside of the subnet.	Any address beginning with Fe80, Fe90, FeA0, or FeB0 in the first quartet.
Site Local	A private address.	Can be routed outside of the subnet, but only within the local organization.	Any address beginning with FeC0 in the first quartet.

Figure 8-11. There are three types of addresses in the IPv6 protocol.

with them. Essentially, in IPv4, APIPA addresses are rendered useless. A link-local address begins with either FE80, FE90, FEA0, FEB0. All devices, including printers, servers, and computers, obtain a link-local address automatically. They will all be using the same local network if they need to communicate.

A link-local address may contain a percent sign (%) followed by numbers. This occurs if the system has multiple network adapters. The number after the percent sign represents a zone IP. This is done to differentiate the different link-local addresses from each other.

A *site-local address* is similar to a private address in IPv4, such as 10, 172.16 through 172.31, or 192.168. Since there are so many global unicast addresses available, you may not even use this address type. A site-local address begins with FEC0.

IPv6 also has a special address that designates the local host (the one you are working on). This address is 0000:0000:0000:0000:0000:0000:0000:0001, or ::1. This is the "home" address for IPv6, just as 127.0.0.1 is the "home" address for IPv4.

Quick Look 8.1.3

IPv6 Address Exploration

The IPv6 protocol offers many more addresses than the IPv4 protocol. Recall that IPv6 addresses are formatted differently from IPv4 addresses.

1. Launch a web browser, and navigate to the IANA's website (www.iana.org).
2. Click the Number Resources link on the home page.
3. Scroll down to the IP Address Allocations area of the page, and click the IPv6 Address Space link. This shows the allocation of all IPv6 addresses, regardless of type. The forward slash (/) and a number referenced here represents the number of bits in the global routing prefix called the Top Level Aggregator ID (TLA ID).
4. What is FC00::/7 quartet used for?
5. On a Windows computer, open Control Panel, and click the **Network and Sharing Center** link.
6. Click the **Change adapter settings** link on the left of the new screen.
7. Right-click on the primary network adapter, and click **Properties** in the shortcut menu. In the **Properties** dialog box, ensure the **Internet Protocol Version 6 (TCP/IPv6)** check box is checked, as shown.

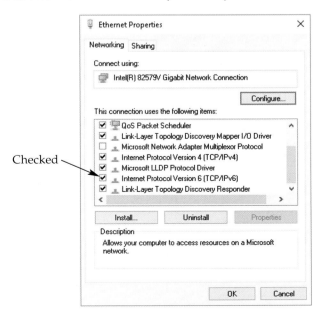

Quick Look 8.1.3 Continued

8. Close the **Properties** dialog box and the Control Panel.

9. Open the Command Line.

10. Enter the **ipconfig** command. Locate the network adapter in the list, and make note of the IP addresses assigned. In addition to an IPv4 address, you should see a link-local IPv6 address.

11. If there are double colons (::) in the address, how many sections of zeros were omitted?

12. Compare your link-local address to that of your classmates. Everyone should have the same network address.

13. Enter ping ::1 on the command line to test a connection to the local host.

14. Get a link-local address from a classmate. Ping that computer. Omit any % entries.

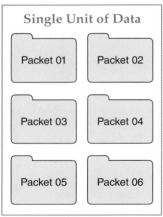

Goodheart-Willcox Publisher

Figure 8-12. A single unit of data is broken into multiple packets for transmission, but all of the packets are considered part of the same transmission.

Packets

Recall from the OSI model that information is often too large to travel as one unit of data. The data are separated into multiple pieces and encapsulated inside packets and frames. Refer to **Figure 8-12.** This is similar to how an online order you placed is shipped in multiple packages. Generally, as data travel across the network, they are usually referred to as *packets* of data. It is important to understand the type of data contained in the packets. It is also important to know which packets are part of the same transmission. This knowledge could help identify packets that have been modified or placed on the network by malware or hackers.

Dissecting IP Packets

It is important to understand the construction of IPv4 and IPv6 packets, including header information. There is much information contained in a packet. This can be used by administrators to analyze traffic, track packets, and search for unusual activity. Packets will be constructed with either Transmission Control Protocol (TCP) or User Datagram Protocol (UDP). There are significant differences in the amount and type of information found in each of these packets.

TCP packets are called *connection-oriented* packets. They contain information that helps ensure reliability of the transmission. These are the most common types of packets used on the Internet. The data are broken up into a series of transmissions and identified by tracking properties, such as a checksum. Checksum is a value computed based on the data in the transmission that is verified when the packets are received at the destination. This allows TCP packets to track various pieces of information to ensure data are received at the client.

UDP packets are known as *connectionless protocol* packets. UDP packets can be transmitted much faster than TCP packets. Part of the reason for this is that UDP does not acknowledge receipt of packets. There is less emphasis placed on reliability and more on speed. A common example of UDP transmissions occurs with streaming media, such as video or audio.

When data are sent, they are packaged or encapsulated into layers, as shown in **Figure 8-13.** Initially, the data are packaged into either a TCP or UDP packet. The appropriate settings in the header are created. This is called a segment. The segment is then placed into an IP packet. The IP packet handles the network addressing. Finally, the encapsulated packet is placed into a frame. This is where MAC addresses are identified and other information, such as a cyclical redundancy check (CRC) value, is established. *Media Access Control (MAC) addresses* are physical addresses embedded into the hardware of network cards. The *cyclical redundancy check (CRC)* is for error checking of the frame. CRC is used on the

MAC addresses are unique and assigned to manufacturers by the Institute of Electrical and Electronics Engineers (IEEE) for setting in the network interface controller.

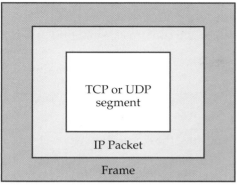

Goodheart-Willcox Publisher; photo: lbreakstock/Shutterstock.com

Figure 8-13. A packet is constructed by encapsulating data in layers. To understand this, it can help to picture Russian stacking dolls.

destination machine to ensure the frame has not been corrupted or damaged during transit. Think of the CRC as a packing slip for your online order. It identifies everything that should be in the package, such as which DVDs you purchased or the number of shirts included in the shipment. If the CRC is not what is expected, the frame is refused.

To use a protocol analyzer and similar tools, you must be able to decipher the information being transmitted. To understand this, first compare the TCP and UDP segment information.

TCP

Figure 8-14 shows the detailed information that will be found in a TCP segment. This segment is created at the Transport layer of the OSI model (layer 4). The ports are important. They show where the data are entering and exiting the system. For example, a data request asking for a specific web page will show the destination port of 80 or 443. The source port will be dynamically assigned. The sequence number is a 32-bit number used to track how much data are sent. During transmissions, the Acknowledgement field will reflect a value indicating the data were successfully received. **Figure 8-15** explains the meaning of flags that are found in the TCP segment. Flags are 1-bit fields that may signal special conditions in the header. The checksum value is used to detect if there was any corruption of the data sent. It is important that the data integrity be maintained. This is a 16-bit field in which data bytes are added together. It is computed on the receiving host to verify they are the same.

FYI

To help understand the layers in a packet, think of the Russian stacking or nesting dolls. Each doll fits inside the next larger doll.

Source Port				Destination Port				
Sequence Number								
Acknowledgement								
Header Length	Reserved	URG	ACK	PSH	RST	SYN	FIN	Sliding window size
Checksum				Urgent Pointer				
Options							Padding	
Data								

Goodheart-Willcox Publisher

Figure 8-14. This is how header information of a TCP segment is assembled.

Flag	Meaning
URG	(urgent) If set to 1, the Urgent Pointer cell contains special info. If 0, it is ignored.
ACK	(acknowledgement) If set to 1, the Acknowledgement cell contains special info. If 0, it is ignored.
PSH	(push) If set to 1, the data should be sent without buffering. If 0, buffering is okay.
RST	(reset) If set to 1, the sender is requesting the connection be reset. If 0, it is ignored.
SYN	(synchronize) If set to 1, the sender is requesting a synchronization of the sequence numbers between two nodes. This is used on the initial request to establish the connection.
FIN	(finished) If set to 1, the segment is the last transaction in a sequence.

Goodheart-Willcox Publisher

Figure 8-15. Flags may appear in a TCP packet header to indicate certain meanings.

UDP

Because UDP is connectionless, there is less information that needs to be sent along with the data. **Figure 8-16** shows the information that will be found in a UDP segment. Data integrity is still important, so the checksum value is computed.

Additional Header Information

Once the TCP or UDP segment is created, the Network layer of the OSI model (layer 3) takes the segment and encapsulates it into an IP packet. This packet contains some important information, as shown in **Figure 8-17.** Especially important are the source and destination network addresses.

Another key value in the IPv4 header is the time to live (TTL) value. The *time to live (TTL)* value controls how long the packet will search for a destination address before it is deleted. Packets cannot be left to wander aimlessly on networks forever if the host cannot be found. The TTL value is reduced in two ways. First, every time a packet goes through a router, the value is decreased. Second, the value decreases after a set period of time. The *Internet Control Message Protocol (ICMP)* is the component of the TCP/IP protocol responsible for transmitting messages across networks. Once the TTL value reaches 1, ICMP sends a message back to the source IP address indicating the packet did not reach the destination. The original packet is then deleted.

The header information with IPv6 packets differs from IPv4 packets. The header is the first 40 bytes and contains the fields shown in **Figure 8-17.** The *hop limit* is the renamed TTL field. Traffic class is the same as the Type of Service field in IPv4. Flow Label is unique to IPv6 headers. It enables the ability to track specific traffic flows.

The last layer of encapsulation occurs at the Data Link layer of the OSI model (layer 2). In this packaging, the segment/packet is now placed in a frame. In the Data Link layer, the destination and source MAC addresses are assigned along with a CRC.

Source Port	Destination Port
Length	Checksum
Data	

Goodheart-Willcox Publisher

Figure 8-16. This is how header information of a UDP segment is assembled.

IPv6 Packet Header Information

Version (IPv6)	Traffic Class	Flow Label
Payload Length	Next Header	Hop Limit
Source Address		
Destination Address		

Figure 8-17. There are differences in the packet header information between IPv4 and IPv6 packets.

Packet Sniffer

CompTIA Security+
2.2

MTA Security Fundamentals
3.3

FYI

Is packet sniffing legal? In most cases, you may not use a packet sniffer on a network that you do not own or have written permission to monitor.

With an understanding of header content, you can start to view the data in a packet sniffer. A *packet sniffer* is a tool that intercepts raw data traveling on the network media. It uses a network interface card (NIC) to capture data. The sniffer must be configured to use a specific NIC.

The tool may only see the traffic coming to and from the host computer or it may see all traffic on the network segment. This depends on the type of sniffer and its configuration. Wireless traffic can be sniffed as well. Wireless traffic can only be viewed one channel at a time. To sniff multiple channels, additional network cards must be configured to see the different channels.

Once the traffic is found, the sniffer reads the header information along with time and sequencing. It analyzes the traffic and presents it in a more logical view of the data.

Packet sniffers can only read data that is not encrypted. Encrypting data is the best defense against a hacker who may be using a sniffer to view data transmitted on the network. As a security administrator, a sniffer can be used to uncover a great deal of information that will also allow you to check for potential security threats and vulnerabilities. Some of this information is covered throughout this chapter.

One of the best-known packet sniffers is a free, open-source program called Wireshark. This has been around a long time. It used to be called Ethereal. Wireshark can be downloaded from its website (www.wireshark.org). For Linux hosts, a text-based solution called tcpdump is often used. This program is included in many Linux distributions.

Quick Look 8.1.4

Wireshark Basics

This activity requires Wireshark to be installed on your computer. When installing it, if prompted to install Winpcap, install that as well. Wireshark offers viewing in legacy mode, but for this activity, the normal mode will be used.

1. Launch Wireshark.
2. Once Wireshark launches, you can open a previous Wireshark capture (.pcap file), or you can double-click a network interface card (NIC) in the list at the bottom of the screen to begin capturing. The graph you see next to an NIC is depicting the network traffic.
3. After double-clicking an NIC, data are immediately displayed as they are captured. If you do not see data, and you are on a wired connection, minimize Wireshark, open a web browser, and ping your default gateway. If you are on a wireless connection, the wireless NIC has to support promiscuous mode (sees all packets transmitted).

Quick Look 8.1.4 Continued

Stop capturing packets

4. Once you see data being captured, let it run for a few minutes. Then, click the **Stop capturing packets** button on the toolbar.

5. By default, information is listed sequentially, which is in the order it is seen. You can sort the view using the column headers. For example, to view all packets by a network source address, click the Source column heading.

6. Another very helpful feature is filtering out. For example, you may only want to see packets from a specific source address or protocol. To view packets by certain criteria, click in the display filter on the toolbar and enter the filter, as shown. For example, to see all DHCPv6 traffic, enter dhcpv6 in the display filter bar. Notice as you begin entering the filter, the text is red. Once you have entered enough for the filter to be recognized, the text turns green. To clear the filter, click the X on the right-hand side of the filter.

Enter the filter

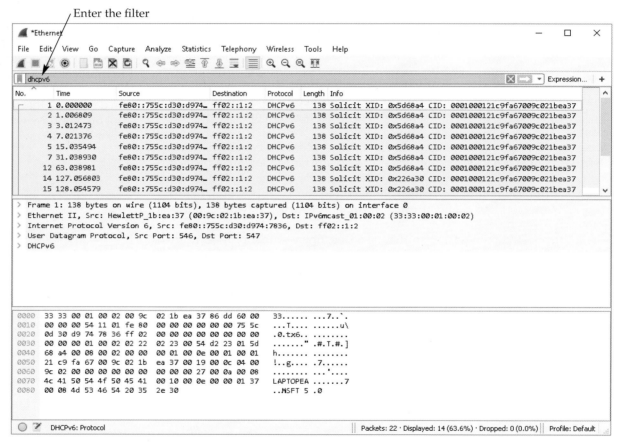

7. Clear any filters, and then enter a TCP filter. Find any packet with TCP in the Protocol column, and select it. Details for the packet are displayed in the middle and bottom areas of the Wireshark window. Notice the different lines displayed in the middle area. What is listed depends on what details are available for the selected packet. Click the triangle to the left of a line to show expanded information about that line. The details in the Frame line are just basic information such as the size of the packet. The Ethernet II line identifies data you would see placed in a frame, such as MAC addresses. The Internet Protocol Version 4 line shows addressing and TTL information. The Transmission Control Protocol line lists the detailed TCP information.

8. Expand the Transmission Control Protocol line, scroll down, and expand the Flags line. What flags are set in your example?

Quick Look 8.1.4 Continued

9. With the filter still set, look at the status bar in the lower right-hand corner of the Wireshark screen. The **Packets:** label shows the total number of packets in the capture. The **Displayed:** label shows how many packets are available with the current filter.

10. To save the capture, click **File>Save As...** to display a standard save-type dialog box. Name the file TestCapture, and save it in your working folder for this class.

11. Close Wireshark.

Three-Way Handshake

An important concept with TCP transmissions is what is known as the three-way handshake. In the *three-way handshake,* the sending host and receiving client complete a three-step process to verify the successful transmission of a data exchange. This process is important. It helps prevent man-in-the-middle (MITM) attacks and spoofing attacks. This is because the packets must know some of the information exchanged in this three-way process. The three steps in the process are as follows.

1. SYN connection (from Host A to Host B)
2. SYN/ACK connection (from Host B to Host A)
3. ACK connection (from Host A to Host B)

Step 1 SYN Connection

Host A wants to set up a connection with Host B. The sending host (A) will transmit a request to the receiving host (B) to establish the connection. The initial sequence number will be randomly generated. The *initial sequence number (ISN)* is used as part of the transmission process to manage packets within a transmission session. It is a random number between 0 and 4,294,967,295. For simplicity, Wireshark displays a relative number, usually a small value.

In the example in **Figure 8-18,** the relevant portion is shown. In this transmission, the initial sequence number is 0. This is the first transmission in the process, so no acknowledgements have been given. The receiving client will expect to see this sequence number. The SYN flag is turned on.

Step 2 SYN/ACK Connection

In the second step, the receiving host needs to acknowledge the SYN from the sending host. Host B sends an acknowledgement of the SYN to Host A. The acknowledgment value increases by 1. Both the SYN and ACK flags are turned on, as shown in **Figure 8-19.**

Source Port				Destination Port				
Sequence Number 0								
Acknowledgement 0								
Header Length	Reserved	URG	ACK 0	PSH	RST	SYN 1	FIN	Sliding window size
Checksum				Urgent Pointer				
Options							Padding	
Data								

Goodheart-Willcox Publisher

Figure 8-18. Header information for step 1 in the three-way handshake.

Source Port				Destination Port				
Sequence Number 0								
Acknowledgement 1								
Header Length	Reserved	URG	ACK 1	PSH	RST	SYN 1	FIN	Sliding window size
Checksum				Urgent Pointer				
Options							Padding	
Data								

Goodheart-Willcox Publisher

Figure 8-19. Header information for step 2 in the three-way handshake.

Step 3 ACK Connection

The third step in the handshake is the ACK connection. Here, the connection is validating receipt of previous steps and acknowledging the transmission. The resulting return transmission will turn on the ACK flag and increment the sequence number by 1, as shown in **Figure 8-20.**

Source Port				Destination Port				
Sequence Number 1								
Acknowledgement 1								
Header Length	Reserved	URG	ACK 1	PSH	RST	SYN 0	FIN	Sliding window size
Checksum				Urgent Pointer				
Options							Padding	
Data								

Goodheart-Willcox Publisher

Figure 8-20. Header information for step 3 in the three-way handshake.

Quick Look 8.1.5

UDP and TCP Information in Wireshark

Wireshark can be used to view the flags in TCP transmissions. Wireshark uses relative ISNs for simplicity. However, this can be changed to view the absolute ISN instead.

1. Applying what you have learned, launch Wireshark.
2. Click **File>Open…**, navigate to your working folder, and open the capture you created earlier.
3. Sort the view by protocol. Scroll down to entries using the TCP protocol. Look for one that shows a SYN transaction in the Info column. When you find one, double-click the entry to see the details.
4. In the top part of the details window, click the arrow next to Transmission Control Protocol to expand that section. What is the sequence number? What flags are set? Note the frame number for this transaction.
5. Close the details window to return to the main Wireshark window. Search for a SYN/ACK response. In terms of frame numbers, the response should be very close to the SYN packet.
6. Double-click the response that corresponds to the SYN packet you opened. Expand the Transmission Control Protocol section. What are the sequence and acknowledgement numbers? Note the frame number. Close the details window.

Quick Look 8.1.5 Continued

7. In the main Wireshark window, find the third part of the handshake. This should be the ACK packet. What do you expect the sequence and acknowledgement numbers to be? Which flags will be set to on (1)? Open the ACK transaction, and see if you were correct.

8. Choose **Edit>Preferences...** from the menu in the main Wireshark window. In the Preferences dialog box that is displayed, double-click **Protocols** on the left-hand side to expand it. Wireshark makes it easier to view the sequence and acknowledgement numbers since they can be quite large. You can change the default view to show the actual numbers, not the relative numbers.

9. Scroll down to find TCP, and click it. Note the default setting is to use relative numbers, as shown.

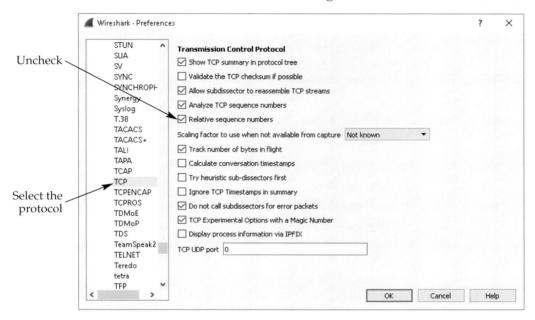

10. Uncheck the **Relative sequence numbers** check box, and then click the **OK** button to save and close preferences.

11. Return to the first frame you identified (the SYN). What is the sequence number now?

12. Change to the SYN/ACK option. What are the sequence and acknowledgement numbers?

13. What do you believe the numbers will be for the ACK transaction? Open the ACK transaction to see if you were correct.

14. In the details window for the ACK transaction, scroll down further under Transmission Control Protocol. Notice the SYN/ACK sequence of events is displayed. RTT stands for round-trip time. Close the details window.

15. Select the first frame (SYN) in the main Wireshark window, but do not open it. Then, click **Statistics>Flow Graph** in the menu. A window is displayed that shows the entire conversation exchanged in this network request. It includes the transfer of data and possibly other transactions such as encryption. The top shows the IP addresses involved in the transaction; the left side indicates the times of each transaction. You can view this in other ways as well. If you see a FIN packet, that indicates the final transmission in the sequence.

16. At the bottom of the window, click the **Flow type:** drop-down arrow, and click **TCP Flows** in the drop-down list. This view makes it easier to see the sequence and acknowledgement numbers in the far right Comment column. Do you understand now why Wireshark shows relative numbers?

17. Click the **Save As...** button at the bottom of the graph window. A standard save-type dialog box is displayed that allows the graph to be saved as a PDF, PNG, BMP, JPEG, or TXT file. Save the graph as a PDF using your name as the file name.

18. Applying what you have learned, reset the TCP display to relative numbers.

19. Close Wireshark.

SECTION REVIEW 8.1

Check Your Understanding

1. Convert the subnet mask of /26 to decimal.
2. Which network service converts a private IP address to a public IP address?
3. What can be used to find out the owner of a website?
4. What function creates a value to ensure a frame is not corrupted or damaged?
5. Which flags are set in the second stage of the three-way handshake?

Build Your Key Terms Vocabulary

As you progress through this course, develop a personal cybersecurity glossary. This will help you build your vocabulary and prepare you for a career. Write a definition for each of the following terms, and add it to your cybersecurity glossary.

ANDing

Classless Internet Domain Resolution (CIDR)

cyclical redundancy check (CRC)

de facto standard

global unicast address

initial sequence number (ISN)

Internet Assigned Numbers Authority (IANA)

Internet Control Message Protocol (ICMP)

Internet Corporation for Assigned Names and Numbers (ICANN)

link-local address

local host

Media Access Control (MAC) address

Network Address Translation (NAT)

octet

packet sniffer

proprietary

protocol

Regional Internet Registrars (RIRs)

site-local address

socket

subnet mask

three-way handshake

time to live (TTL)

WHOIS

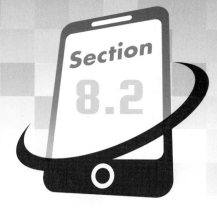

Network Threats

A notable attack occurred in 2013. Syrian hackers were able to access the Twitter network and take over the account of the Associated Press. The hackers tweeted that there were explosions at the White House and President Obama was injured. Although this was not true, it greatly affected the stock market for a brief period of time. The Dow dropped by about 150 points as traders saw the fake tweet. About $136 billion in equity value were lost. While the market quickly recovered, this incident showed how much impact hackers can have.

Companies also are open to these hacks. The Wyndham hotel chain was the victim of network breeches in 2008 and 2009 in which credit card and other information for more than 619,000 customers was stolen. As a result, customers were exposed to over $10.6 million in fraudulent charges. The company was sued by the Federal Trade Commission (FTC). The FTC claimed Wyndham did not have adequate cybersecurity controls in place to protect customer data. Wyndham agreed to settle the case by establishing a comprehensive cybersecurity program.

Essential Question

Why would sniffing a network be considered a black-hat activity?

Key Terms 📩

denial of service (DoS) attack
distributed denial of service (DDoS) attack
File Transfer Protocol/SSL (FTPS)
flood guard

netstat
ping sweep
secure copy protocol (SCP)
Secure File Transfer Protocol (SFTP)

secure shell (SSH)
Smurf attack
SYN flood
Telnet

Learning Goals

- Identify preventative measures for denial of service attacks.
- Explain the role of ICMP in ping sweeps.
- Describe the function of the **netstat** command.
- Discuss security challenges for remote connections.

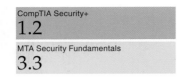

CompTIA Security+
1.2

MTA Security Fundamentals
3.3

FYI

Want to see attacks in real time? Check out the Norse website (www.norsecorp.com) and use the Live Attacks link to see a map of attacks as they happen.

Denial of Service Attacks

Denial of service (DoS) attacks are hacks against the availability of data. DoS attacks do not steal or destroy data. Rather, they are intended to prevent rightful users from accessing systems. Recall the CIA triad. Sadly, DoS attacks happen quite frequently. Some are severe, such as the one described in Chapter 1 that targeted Estonia. If a company has the right preventative plan in place, DoS attacks can be resolved quickly. This was the case in the attack against several bitcoin exchanges in June 2017. One of those companies, Bitfinex.com, was the largest US provider of bitcoin currencies. It tweeted it was under a DDoS attack, but resumed operations within an hour.

The most common DoS attack is a DDoS attack. In a *distributed denial of service (DDoS) attack,* many hosts are contributing in attacking the victim, as shown in **Figure 8-21.** Most often, those hosts are under the control of malware. The hosts, then, are known as bots. *Bot* is a shortened form of *robot.* Hosts are considered bots when their actions are being controlled by another device. There are two types of denial of service attack: Smurf attack and SYN flood.

Smurf Attack

A *Smurf attack* involves overwhelming the victim's computer with ICMP requests. When a target host is pinged, by default, it essentially asks "Hey, are you there?" several times. Each question generates a response from the target host. In a Smurf attack, the victim is overwhelmed attempting to reply to all of the "Are you there?" questions. For this reason, this type of attack is also known as a *ping flood.*

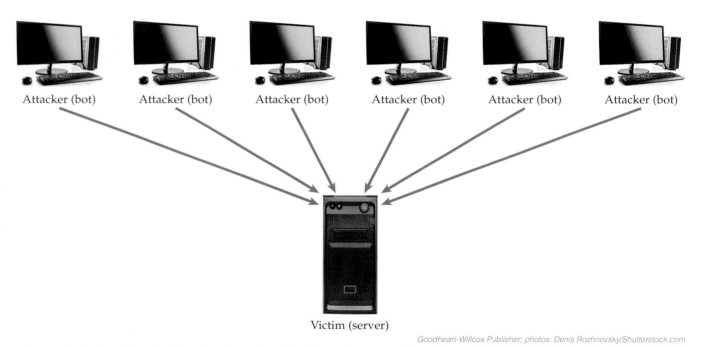

Attacker (bot)   Attacker (bot)   Attacker (bot)   Attacker (bot)   Attacker (bot)   Attacker (bot)

Victim (server)

Figure 8-21. A distributed denial of service attack involves many hosts, usually infected with malware, attacking a single server.

SYN Flood

The other type of DoS attack is called a SYN flood. A *SYN flood* involves the hacker exploiting a vulnerability in the three-way handshake by not closing the handshake. Recall, the normal process is as follows.

1. SYN by sender
2. SYN/ACK by receiver
3. ACK by initial sender

In a SYN flood, the attacker sends a SYN, which the target answers with a SYN/ACK. Instead of closing the handshake with an ACK, the hacker sends another SYN, to which the target again replies, as shown in **Figure 8-22.** This cycle repeats over and over throughout the attack.

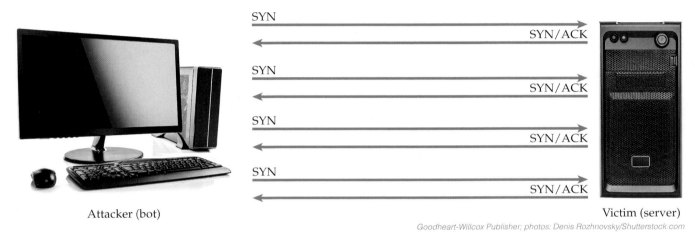

Attacker (bot)

Victim (server)

Goodheart-Willcox Publisher; photos: Denis Rozhnovsky/Shutterstock.com

Figure 8-22. In a SYN flood, the three-way handshake is never completed with ACK.

Quick Look 8.2.1

Ping and ICMP

CompTIA Security+
2.2

The **ping** command is used to check for a valid network address. It requires the target computer to respond. Wireshark can log ping requests.

1. Applying what you have learned, open the Windows Command Prompt.
2. Applying what you have learned, determine your IP address, and then exchange it with a classmate.
3. Enter the **ping** command and your classmate's IP address. Notice how many times the IP address is pinged. In Windows, the default number of ping attempts is four.
4. Enter ping /? to show the options for the **ping** command. Notice that the -n switch is used to set the number of pings.
5. Enter ping followed by your classmate's IP address and the switch -n 2. Notice the IP address is pinged only twice.
6. Open Wireshark. Start a new capture. Minimize Wireshark and return to the command prompt. Ping your neighbor with ten attempts. After verifying your classmate's ping against your target is finished, return to Wireshark and stop the capture.
7. Applying what you have learned, filter the display by ICMP.
8. Look at the ICMP packets. You should find the ten you sent, and the ten replies sent to your classmate, as shown.

Quick Look 8.2.1 Continued

9. Double-click a reply frame to open it. Expand the Internet Control Message Protocol area in the top of the details window, and then expand Data under that. Notice that Windows sends an alphanumeric sequence for the data during ping requests, as shown. The Linux version of the **ping** command uses numerical values for the padding. This will be helpful in revealing the operating system being used in the ping transmissions.

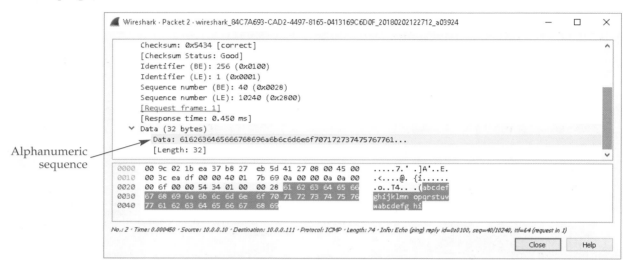

Alphanumeric sequence

CompTIA Security+
3.2

Protecting Against DoS Attacks

Much of the protection against DoS attacks takes place on the edge routers or other security appliances using special configurations and access-control lists. An edge router is a router that separates the internal network from the public network. One such option is the use of flood guards. A *flood guard* can drop the packets or apply filters in place on switches or routers if a denial of service attack is detected. It is either a standalone device installed on the network or a component of a firewall.

During a normal three-way handshake, when the target receives a SYN packet, the transmission control block (TCB) functionality in TCP/IP stores a TCB SYN-RECEIVED state. This indicates the session is only halfway performed. Since a SYN flood never completes this process, the TCB cannot change the status to ESTABLISHED, as shown in **Figure 8-23.** If a SYN flood occurs, so many of these TCB statuses can exhaust the memory of the target.

If the source IP is not faked, or *spoofed,* the IP can be blocked in the firewall. Many DoS attacks occur with spoofed IP addresses. A way to overcome this is to limit the total number of sessions. This prevents the system from being overloaded with traffic.

There are other preventative measures that can be taken. The client can be configured with antimalware to prevent the host from running programs as part of a larger botnet. It is also possible to turn off ICMP at the host through a host firewall. This prevents the host from responding to ICMP requests. However, turning off ICMP prevents legitimate uses of the **ping** and **tracert** commands.

Ping Sweeps

Hackers can often use common networking tools to exploit inherent vulnerabilities. One such tool is a ping sweep. A *ping sweep* scans a subnet using ICMP requests to map out valid IP addresses. This is helpful to network administrators

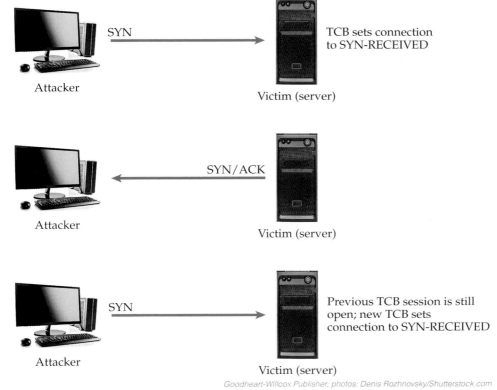

Figure 8-23. In a SYN flood, the TCB is never closed since no ACK is received.

to validate IP addresses in use. However, hackers can use the same information to probe a subnet and find potential targets.

Special software is not needed to do ping sweeps. A simple batch file can be created to perform this task. However, there are many open-source tools to provide this functionality, as shown in **Figure 8-24.** Two popular programs include Advanced IP Scanner and Angry IP Scanner. Both of these programs offer features such as remote administration, cross-platform capability, MAC address identification, and more.

Hackers also do not need access to a computer to install one of these programs. Due to the many portable apps that are available, they just need access to the network and unblocked ICMP connections on the hosts.

Ethical Issue

Ping Sweeps

Your company provides IT services to other businesses. A customer has recently experienced some malware attacks. It is looking for solutions that will reduce the possibility of unknown devices connected to its network. You propose doing a ping sweep to search for all devices on the customer's subnets. The customer is unaware of this reconnaissance method and is a little unsure of this plan of action. In a report to the customer, explain how a ping sweep uses the ICMP protocol to obtain this information on connected hosts such as computers and tablets. Explain how a ping sweep can be used to identify devices on a subnet. Explain why this an ethical action. Also, describe how hackers could unethically use this tool to scout for vulnerabilities.

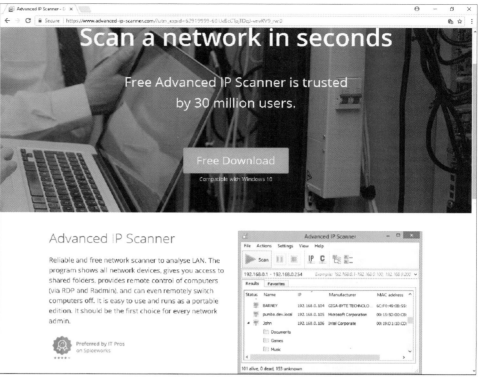

Goodheart-Willcox Publisher

Figure 8-24. Advanced IP Scanner is one of several open-source solutions for conducting ping sweeps.

Quick Look 8.2.2

Ping Sweep Software

A ping sweep can be done without using any special software. In this exercise, you will conduct a ping sweep of your current subnet. This exercise assumes a /24 subnet.

1. Applying what you have learned, open the Windows Command Prompt, run the **ipconfig** command, and note the network address of your subnet.

2. Enter the following command (all this is one command), substituting your network address for x.x.x.%x. For example, if your network address is 192.168.1.0, then enter 192.168.1.%x in place of x.x.x.%x.

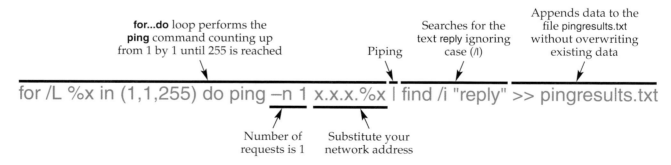

3. This command runs for a while as all hosts on the network are pinged. When the command is finished, open the pingresult.txt file with Notepad or other word processor. Review the valid addresses on your subnet.

Quick Look 8.2.2 Continued

4. Launch a web browser, and navigate to a search engine. Enter the search phrase portable apps ping sweep software. Compare some of the software features between the different programs.
5. Discuss with your classmates the benefits of using some of these programs as a security technician and the potential hacking risks they represent.

Netstat Command

A helpful utility for displaying networking connection information with other computers is the **netstat** command. *Netstat* allows you to view TCP and UDP connections and to further filter the view to ICMP, IPv4 and IPv6. With this command, you can see statistics and which ports are open, closed, or listening to incoming sessions. This may provide clues to the source if you are under attack. The Windows version of the **netstat** command has the switches shown in **Figure 8-25.**

CompTIA Security+
2.2

The syntax for the netstat command is to preface each switch with a dash (–). However, the interval value is not preceded by a dash. Multiple switches can be combined. For example:

netstat –a –n 20

Switch	Definition
a	Active: this switch lists all active connections, which includes the listening ports. netstat –a
e	Ethernet statistics: this switch lists statistics of the Internet connection, which includes the number of packets that were sent, received, errors, etc. netstat –e
n	This switch lists the connections in numerical or IP form; instead of seeing a web address by name, it is listed by its IP address. netstat –n
o	Owning process: this switch shows the active connection along with the process identification (PID) number. netstat –o
p	Protocols: this switch allows you to filter through the different protocols. netstat –p tcp (in place of TCP can be any of the protocols: IP, IPv6, ICMP, ICMPv6, TCP, TCPv6, UDP, UDPv6)
r	Routing table: this switch is the same as the **route print** command. netstat –r
s	Statistics: this switch lists statistics for each protocol (differs from the e switch). netstat –s This switch can be combined with the p switch to identify a specific protocol. netstat –sp udp
f	Fully qualified domain name: this switch displays the entire name of a foreign address. netstat –f
Interval	Use this value to give the computer a specific amount of time (in seconds) between the probing of active connections. netstat –an 20

Goodheart-Willcox Publisher

Figure 8-25. Command switches for the **netstat** command. Multiple switches can be used.

The output screen will list data in columns: Proto (name of protocol), Local Address (the IP address and the port number), Foreign Address (the IP address and port number of the remote computer), and State. **Figure 8-26** explains the different values that may be listed in the State column. There will be different states of connections on the output. Due to the way TCP/IP communicates with other hosts, connections cannot be immediately closed. Packets may arrive out of order or be transmitted after the connection has been closed. This can result in a delay in closing the session.

Connection State	Definition
Established	Both hosts are connected.
Closing	The remote host has agreed to close its connection.
Listening	The local host is waiting to handle an incoming connection.
Syn_rcvd	A remote host has asked to start a connection.
Syn_sent	The local host has accepted to start a connection.
Last_ack	The local host needs to obliterate (erase from memory) the packets before closing the connection.
Timed_wait	The local host has closed the connection, but it is being kept around so any delayed packets can be matched to the connection and handled appropriately; they will time out within four minutes.
Close_wait	The remote host is closing its connection with the local host, but it is being kept around so any delayed packets can be matched to the connection and handled appropriately; they will time out within four minutes.
Fin_Wait 1	A client is closing its connection.
Fin_Wait 2	Both hosts have agreed to close the connection.

Goodheart-Willcox Publisher

Figure 8-26. There are various states that may be listed with the netstat command.

Quick Look 8.2.3

Netstat Command

The **netstat** command is useful in examining network connections. There are much data that the command can provide.

1. Applying what you have learned, launch the Windows Command Prompt, and enter the **netstat** command. It will take a few minutes to collect and view the active connections.
2. Enter netstat –e to see a snapshot of statistics.
3. Enter netstat –a. How does the output with this switch differ from the command with no switches?

Remote Connections

A remote connection allows a person to use another computer or host, such as a router or switch, as if he or she is sitting in front of it. There are a couple of ways to establish remote connections across a network, such as Telnet and SSH. Remote connections present some security challenges since physical access to the machine cannot be controlled.

Telnet

Telnet is a component of the TCP/IP protocol suite that allows a person to remotely log in to another host on the network. Telnet is short for terminal network. It is a text-based interface that uses port 23 and allows for remote configuration and management. When using Telnet, you log in to the remote server or host. Then, you can use the system as if you are directly attached.

Telnet has been around for quite some time. However, it is seldom used today. It has security vulnerabilities. One of the biggest issues is the fact that nothing is encrypted during transfer. Windows operating systems still support Telnet, but it is not enabled by default.

SSH

If you need a terminal-emulation program, it is better to use secure shell. *Secure shell (SSH)* is an encrypted interface that uses port 22 for transactions. SSH was developed with security in mind. It uses a public key encryption to authenticate the source of the data.

Another aspect of SSH that is a helpful security feature is secure copy. *Secure copy protocol (SCP)* is based on SSH to allow the secure copying of files from the local host to the remote host. Like SSH, it also uses port 22. SCP supports the principle of confidentiality due to its encryption and authentication features.

FYI

SCP is a feature used more often on Linux distributions than on Windows platforms.

Quick Look 8.2.4

Exploring the Telnet Interface

Telnet is not installed by default on Windows clients anymore. However, it is still available. To use Telnet, it must first be enabled. Since Telnet is a security risk, it is important to uninstall it once you are done using it.

1. Applying what you have learned, display the Windows Control Panel. Then, click **Programs and Features**.
2. On the left-hand side of the screen, click the **Turn Windows features on or off** link. The **Windows Features** dialog box is displayed, as shown.

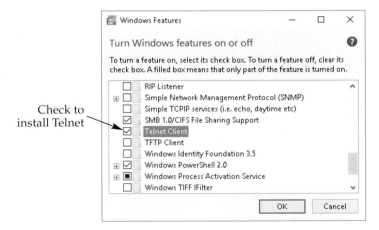

Check to install Telnet

3. Scroll down, and check the **Telnet Client** check box. Click the **OK** button to update the setting. It may take a few seconds for the changes to be applied. Then, close the **Windows Features** dialog box and the Control Panel. After Telnet is installed, it can be accessed in the Windows **Start** menu or by using the command prompt.
4. Applying what you have learned, launch the Windows command prompt, and enter telnet. The prompt changes to reflect that you are in the Telnet interface.

Quick Look 8.2.4 Continued

5. Enter a question mark (?) to see a list of Telnet commands. What do you enter to get additional help? To exit Telnet?

6. At the prompt, enter open telehack.com.

7. There are lots of fun things to try on this site. Enter qr Cyber!, and watch a QR code be created in ASCII characters for the text Cyber!, as shown. If you have a smartphone with a QR code reader, test your code!

8. Enter cal. Calendars for the next three months are displayed.

9. Enter areacode, and then enter 740. Where is this area code found?

10. Enter ipaddr. Did this return your private or public IP address?

11. Press the [Ctrl][C] key combination to go back to the main Telnet interface.

12. Try another site: open rainmaker.wunderground.com.

13. Press the [Enter] key twice to reach the main menu, then enter 1 to view the weather forecast for selected cities.

Quick Look 8.2.4 Continued

14. Try entering the codes for New York City (NYC) and Chicago (CHI).
15. Enter m to return to the main menu, and then x to exit the site.
16. At the main Telnet prompt, enter q to quit Telnet.
17. Return to the Control Panel, and click **Programs and Features**.
18. On the left-hand side of the screen, click the **Turn Windows features on or off** link. The **Windows Features** dialog box is displayed.
19. Scroll down, and uncheck the **Telnet Client** check box. Click the **OK** button to update the setting. It may take a few seconds for the changes to be applied.
20. Applying what you have learned, close the **Windows Features** dialog box, the Control Panel, and the command prompt.

File Transfer Protocol

Any time data can be transferred across network media, it must be protected. A common practice is transferring files or connecting to remote connections from a host. Some web servers offer the ability to download files instead of providing HTTP services. The protocol used in this transmission is File Transfer Protocol (FTP). There are two variations of securing FTP: SFTP and FTPS. *Secure File Transfer Protocol (SFTP)* uses a single channel to transmit and receive data. *File Transfer Protocol/SSL (FTPS)* has SSH functionality with an added second channel for secure transmissions. SFTP is more secure of the two, but FTPS is more widely known.

CompTIA Security+
2.6

SECTION REVIEW 8.2

Check Your Understanding

1. What security principle is violated in a DoS attack?
2. Which type of DoS attack exploits the ICMP protocol?
3. Give the command entry to view all Ethernet statistics on the network interface.
4. Which part of the three-way handshake is not conducted in a SYN flood?
5. Which port should be blocked to prevent Telnet traffic?

Build Your Key Terms Vocabulary

As you progress through this course, develop a personal cybersecurity glossary. This will help you build your vocabulary and prepare you for a career. Write a definition for each of the following terms, and add it to your cybersecurity glossary.

denial of service (DoS) attack

distributed denial of service (DDoS) attack

File Transfer Protocol/SSL (FTPS)

flood guard

netstat

ping sweep

secure copy protocol (SCP)

Secure File Transfer Protocol (SFTP)

secure shell (SSH)

Smurf attack

SYN flood

Telnet

Review and Assessment

Summary

Section 8.1 Network Basics

- Transmission Control Protocol/Internet Protocol (TCP/IP) is a nonproprietary protocol that is the de facto standard for networking.
- The IPv4 protocol has long been the predominant network protocol, and addresses are composed in four sections in dot-decimal format.
- The IPv6 protocol provides improved security over IPv4 and offers more IP addresses due to the use of 128-bit format for addresses.
- IP packets contain much information, including header information, that can be used to analyze traffic, track packets, and search for security anomalies.

Section 8.2 Network Threats

- A denial of service (DoS) attack, including Smurf attacks and SYN floods, does not destroy data, but prevents users from accessing data.
- A ping sweep maps out valid IP addresses on a network and can be used by hackers to find potential targets.
- The **netstat** command is used to view TCP and UDP connections and can also filter the data.
- Remote connections, such as those made with Telnet or secure shell (SSH), present security challenges, however SSH is designed to provide a secure connection.

Check Your Cybersecurity IQ ➦

Now that you have completed this chapter, see what you have learned about cybersecurity by visiting the student companion website (www.g-wlearning.com) and taking the chapter posttest.

Review Questions ➦

For each question, select the answer that is the best response.

1. What is the decimal equivalent of /28?
   A. 255.255.255.240
   B. 255.255.240.0
   C. 255.255.255.248
   D. 255.255.255.224

2. Which service is needed on a network using private IP addresses?
   A. NAT
   B. DNS
   C. UDP
   D. ICMP

3. While reviewing network traffic entries, you do not recognize an IP address. How can you find who was issued this IP address?
   A. Use the WHOIS tool.
   B. Run netstat –f to show foreign addresses.
   C. Contact the IANA.
   D. Use the **nslookup** command to query DNS.

4. Which is the shortest acceptable form of this IPv6 address?
   Fe80:0000:0000:2B2A:0000:0000:023C:1120
   A. Fe80::2b2A::023C:1120
   B. Fe80::2B2A:0:0:23C:1120
   C. Fe80:0:0:2B2A:0:0:023C:1120
   D. Fe80::2b2A:0:0:023C:112

5. While running a packet capturing program, you notice this IPv6 address: 2001::23AA:12CD. What can you determine from this address?
   A. Nothing, the subnet mask is not visible.
   B. The address is a site-local and originated on your own network.
   C. The address was automatically generated with the TCP/IP protocol as it is a link-local address.
   D. This address is a global unicast and is considered a public IP address.

6. Which is true about a denial of service (DoS) attack?
   A. Data can be stolen in transit.
   B. You can prevent this by blocking port 23.
   C. Its objective is to prevent legitimate access to network services.
   D. Encryption of data is necessary to prevent data loss.

7. A Smurf attack is done by:
   A. conducting a ping sweep.
   B. flooding the victim with ICMP requests.
   C. failing to close the three-way handshake connection.
   D. sending malformed packets to the victim.

8. Which defense would help against a SYN flood?
   A. Run netstat –a.
   B. Block ICMP at the firewall.
   C. Prevent incoming packets at the firewall.
   D. Implement a flood guard.

9. Why would a hacker conduct a ping sweep?
   A. To find open ports on the network.
   B. To view data in transit.
   C. To identify known hosts on the network.
   D. To conduct a denial of service attack.

10. What should an administrator use to remote into another host such as a router?
    A. SCP
    B. SSH
    C. Telnet
    D. Netstat

Application and Extension of Knowledge

1. Take a closer look at IANA. Discover its responsibilities and role in IP addresses and domain names. Create a presentation outlining what additional information you learn about IANA. Be prepared to deliver your presentation to the class.

2. Consider this scenario: your organization needs to subnet its existing Class C private network (192.168.100.0) into three networks. Identify the three networks you would create and their corresponding subnet masks in both decimal and CIDR format.

3. On your own home network or the home network of a friend or relative, run a ping sweep. Do you recognize all devices found? Prepare a report describing your results. Include a summary.

4. Using the website whois.domaintools.com, look up Verizon.com. Review the information provided by this site. What IP address was it assigned? Locate the hosting history. Perform the same tasks on your school system's website. Summarize the data in a one-page report that you believe is useful if you suspect an IP address is part of a cyberattack.

5. Prepare for a roundtable discussion with your classmates on the threats of DoS attacks. Consider measures that can be taken to identify an attack in progress. Also consider preventative measures that be taken. Participate in the class roundtable discussion.

Research Project
Packet Sniffers

Wireshark has gained a great deal of popularity as the de facto standard for packet sniffing programs. However, there are other programs available. Packet sniffers are also known as *packet analyzers*. Depending on the software, you may have access to other features including alerts and monitoring multiple addresses. Research other packet sniffing programs and identify three other free packet analyzers. Do not include Wireshark as one of the three. Identify the key features of each program. Also, compare and contrast each to Wireshark. Note which features are not available in Wireshark.

Deliverables. Summarize your research in a memo. Detail the different programs you found. Include screenshots, if possible, and the URLs where the programs can be found. Write the memo as though it is to your IT supervisor. Follow the writing and formatting standards used by your school.

Online Activities

Complete the following activities, which will help you learn, practice, and expand your knowledge and skills.

Vocabulary. Practice vocabulary for this chapter using the e-flash cards, matching activity, and vocabulary game until you are able to recognize their meanings.

Communication Skills

College and Career Readiness

Reading. In order to retain information you read, it is necessary to focus and read with a purpose. The Ethical Issue feature in this chapter discusses ping sweeps. Read the feature with the intention of focusing on each word written. After you have finished, close the book. Can you remember what you read?

Writing. To become career ready, it is important to learn how to communicate clearly and effectively by using reasoning. Create an outline that includes information about packet sniffers. Consider your audience as you prepare the information. Using the outline, make a presentation to your class.

Speaking. The way in which you communicate with others has a significant impact on the success of the relationships you build with them. There are formal and informal ways of communicating a message. Write a speech explaining the three-way handshake. Deliver the speech to your class. How did the style, words, phrases, and tone you used influence the way the audience responded to the speech?

Listening. Reflective listening occurs when the listener demonstrates an understanding of what was said. Engage in a conversation with a classmate about a topic covered in this chapter. After the conversation, use active-listening skills to restate what your classmate said to him or her. How much did you recall?

Portfolio Development

College and Career Readiness

Certificates. Exhibiting in your portfolio certificates you have received reflects your accomplishments. For example, a certificate might show that you have completed a training class. Another one might show that you have obtained CompTIA or Microsoft certification.

Include any certificates that show tasks completed or your skills or talents. Remember that this is an ongoing project. Plan to update when you have new certificates to add.

1. Scan the certificates that will be in your portfolio.
2. Give each document an appropriate name and save in a folder or subfolder.
3. Place the hardcopy certificates in a container for future reference.
4. Record these documents on your master spreadsheet that you started earlier to record hardcopy items. You may list each document alphabetically, by category, date, or other convention that helps you keep track of each document that you are including.

CTSO Event Prep

Extemporaneous Speaking. Extemporaneous speaking is a competitive event you might enter with your career and technical student organization (CTSO). This event allows you to display your communication skills, specifically your ability to organize and deliver an oral presentation. At the competition, you will be given several topics from which to choose. You will also be given a time limit to create and deliver the speech. You will be evaluated on your verbal and nonverbal skills as well as the tone and projection of your voice. To prepare for an extemporaneous speaking event, complete the following activities.

1. Ask your instructor for several sample topics so you can practice making impromptu speeches.
2. Once you have a topic, jot down the ideas and points to cover. An important part of making this type of presentation is that you will have only a few minutes to prepare. Being able to write down your main ideas quickly will enable you to focus on what you will actually say in the presentation.
3. Practice the presentation. Introduce yourself, review the topic that is being presented, defend the topic being presented, and end with a summary.
4. Ask your instructor to play the role of competition judge as you give the presentation. Afterward, ask for feedback from your instructor. You may also consider having a student audience listen and give feedback.
5. For the event, bring paper and pencils to record notes. Supplies may or may not be provided.

Chapter 9

Protecting Network Services and Infrastructure from Attacks

In May of 2017, Target paid $18.7 million to settle claims against it due to a data breach. The massive 2013 hack illustrates how a network design flaw can lead to attacks. The attackers targeted credentials from a vendor, Fazio Mechanical Services. Target allowed the vendor access to its network for monitoring of HVAC systems. With the vendor's credentials, hackers launched the attack on Target's network. Unfortunately, Target did not isolate the portion of its network where credit card transactions are collected from point of sale (PoS) machines. Brian Krebs is a notable security blogger (www.krebsonsecurity.com) who offers current in-depth security news and analysis. He says the attack on Target could have been preventative if the proper preventative steps had been taken.

Network threats are not sure to happen. Many network attacks and threats can be minimized or even eliminated with an efficient network design and by incorporating tools and controls to be proactive in detection of potential threats. This chapter explores options for designing a network with security in mind. Vulnerable areas such as the Domain Name Servers (DNS) and Address Resolution Protocol (ARP) are looked at in detail. Tools and hardware to prevent and react to network threats are also explored along with best practices for securing network hardware such as routers and switches.

Chapter Preview

While studying, look for the activity icon **for:**

- Pretests and posttests
- Vocabulary terms with e-flash cards and matching activities
- Self-assessment

G-WLEARNING.com

College and Career Readiness

Reading Prep

Arrange a study session to read this chapter with a classmate. After you read each section independently, stop, and tell each other what you think the main points are in the section. Continue with each section until you finish the chapter.

Check Your Cybersecurity IQ

Before you begin this chapter, see what you already know about cybersecurity by visiting the student companion website (www.g-wlearning.com) and taking the chapter pretest.

Certification Objectives

CompTIA Security+

1.2 Compare and contrast the types of attacks.
2.1 Install and configure network components, both hardware and software based, to support organizational security.
2.2 Given a scenario, use appropriate software tools to assess the security posture of an organization.
2.4 Given a scenario, analyze and interpret output from security technologies.
2.6 Given a scenario, implement secure protocols.
3.2 Given a scenario, implement secure network architecture concepts.

Microsoft MTA Security Fundamentals

3.2 Understand network isolation.
3.3 Understand protocol security.

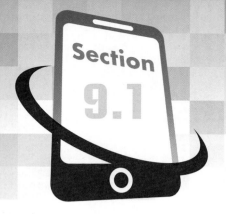

Section 9.1

Network Design

Essential Question

What is the best course of action to prevent systems with outdated security protection from connecting to a network?

The attack surface of a network is large due to the nature of many different hardware and software products in use. Vulnerabilities exist at many levels, including the underlying infrastructure of computer networks and the TCP/IP protocol. Networks connected to the Internet have drastically increased the potential for threats. Considering the many threats associated with networks, it is important to design the network with security in mind. There is not a single solution that can prevent a network from all threats. Implementing smart design principles and incorporating security solutions and additional hardware or software solutions can go a long way to creating strong preventative measures for protecting data and the network.

Key Terms 📑

authoritative DNS server

Challenge Handshake
    Authentication Protocol
    (CHAP)

demilitarized zone (DMZ)

DNS local cache

DNS poisoning

DNS Security Extensions
    (DNSSEC)

Domain Name System (DNS)

Extensible Authentication
    Protocol (EAP)

extranet

Internet Key Exchange Protocol
    version 2 (IKEv2)

intranet

Layer 2 Tunneling Protocol
    (L2TP)

MS-CHAP

nonauthoritative DNS server

Password Authentication
    Protocol (PAP)

perimeter network

Point-to-Point Protocol (PPTP)

Protected EAP (PEAP)

screened subnet

Secure Socket Tunneling Protocol
    (SSTP)

tunneling

virtual local area network
    (VLAN)

virtual private network (VPN)

VLAN access control list (VACL)

VPN concentrator

Learning Goals

- Evaluate threats to DNS.
- Assess network design techniques for isolating segments and improving security.

DNS Review

The *Domain Name System (DNS)* is the network service that resolves names on a network, such as web servers or host computer names, to their IP addresses. It is the user's guide to the Internet. DNS allows a user to communicate with websites or network servers without having to know IP addresses.

The user must trust that when a name is entered, DNS is pointing to the correct, valid site. One of the threats to DNS is DNS spoofing or DNS poisoning. In *DNS poisoning,* a valid DNS name is redirected to another site. This other site is likely malicious. DNS poisoning can be a threat to the DNS. DNS poisoning is introduced in Chapter 5. There are several attack points for DNS poisoning that must be guarded against. Before looking at them, a review of the concept of DNS on a network is worthwhile.

On the client, Windows and some Linux distributions allow for the storing of DNS requests and resolutions in a cache. The *DNS local cache* is a temporary storage location on the local computer. This is a great technique for improving computer performance. It allows the client to resolve the name to the IP address from locally stored data.

The local DNS cache is also known as the DNS resolver cache. It is populated two ways:

- requests made at the client
- entries in the local hosts file

The local hosts file in Windows is located here:

c:\windows\system32\drivers\etc\hosts

In Linux, the file is located here:

/etc/hosts

By default, the local hosts file does not contain any information other than comments. However, anything placed in it will automatically load in the local DNS cache when the operating system starts up. You can review the local DNS cache, flush its contents, and even prevent a local cache from being kept.

An administrator may place information in the local hosts file, but so may a hacker, as shown in **Figure 9-1.** It is highly possible that malware can corrupt the local DNS cache. It is also possible if a hacker had the correct permissions, entries could be written into the hosts file.

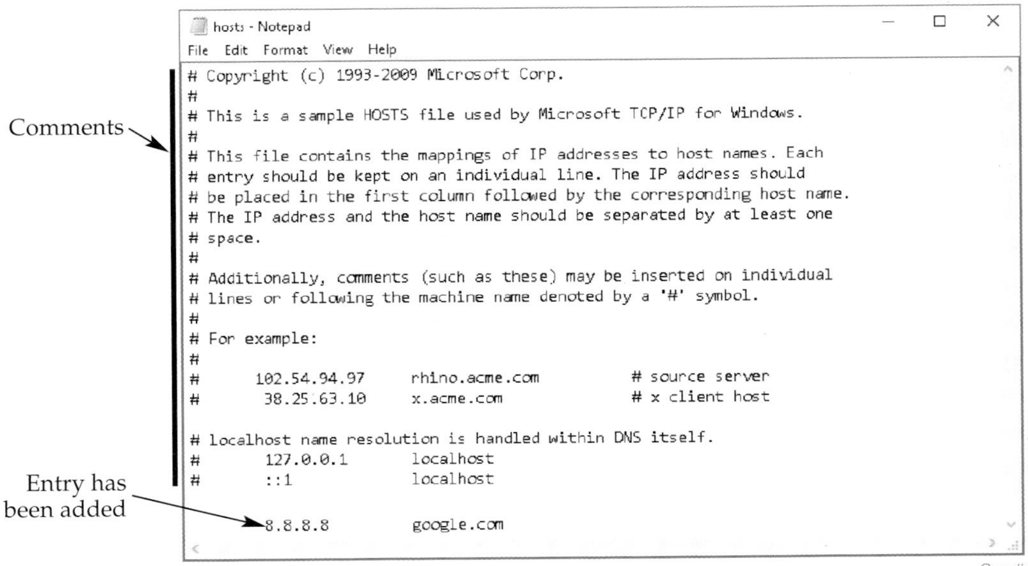

Goodheart-Willcox Publisher

Figure 9-1. Entries in the local hosts file will automatically load into the DNS local cache. This can be an attack vector for hackers.

Quick Look 9.1.1

DNS Cache and Settings

The DNS local cache can provide performance benefits. However, it can also be an attack surface for hackers. It is important to understand how it works.

1. Launch Windows File Explorer, and navigate to this folder: c:\windows\system32\drivers\etc. You should see the hosts file, as shown. Be sure your system is set up to show hidden and system files.

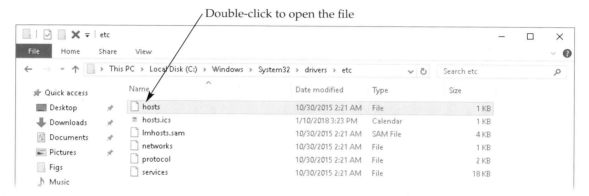

2. Double-click on the hosts file to open it. If prompted, choose Notepad to open the file. This is just a simple text file. The pound sign (#) is used to indicate a comment. Any line starting with a pound sign is ignored and not processed. Are there any lines that do not begin with a pound sign? If so, these have been added by someone.

3. Close the file without saving any changes.

4. Applying what you have learned, launch the command prompt with administrator access.

5. To see the local cache, enter ipconfig /displaydns. DNS stores information in records of different types. An A (Host) Record represents an entry using IPv4 and an AAAA (Host) Record represents an entry using IPv6. An example is shown here.

Quick Look 9.1.1 Continued

6. Enter **ipconfig /flushdns**. This clears, or flushes, the DNS local cache. A message should be displayed indicating the DNS resolver cache has been flushed.

7. Enter **net stop dnscache**. This prevents the local host from storing a cache at all. A message should be displayed indicating the DNS client service was stopped.

8. Without closing the command prompt, launch a web browser, and navigate to a website.

9. Return to the command prompt, and enter **ipconfig /displaydns**. What happened?

10. Enter **net start dnscache**. This restarts DNS caching.

11. Return to the web browser, and navigate to another web page.

12. Applying what you have learned, return to the command prompt, and display the DNS cache. Did it work?

Local-Network DNS Cache

Network servers also store DNS information for the local network. They can also temporarily store DNS entries for websites. This is done to speed up subsequent requests for those sites. The entries in the DNS database are the records that represent the hosts on the database. When DNS resolves these addresses, the response is considered authoritative, as shown in **Figure 9-2.** An *authoritative DNS server* controls the records in the database. It provides answers that have been configured by an original source.

The DNS server cache holds requests from clients for a period of time to speed up subsequent requests. Answers to these requests are said to be nonauthoritative. The server's DNS cache is a *nonauthoritative DNS server.* It does not contain copies of any domains. As with the local cache, the DNS cache could also be compromised or poisoned. When invalid entries are placed in the cache, this corrupts, or poisons, the cache.

> CompTIA Security+
> 1.2
>
> MTA Security Fundamentals
> 3.3

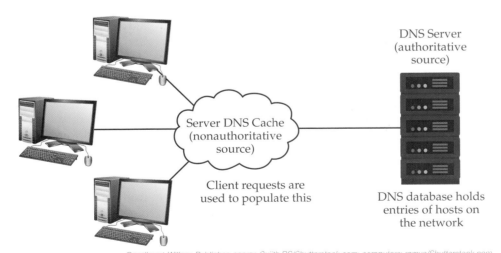

Goodheart-Willcox Publisher; server: Sujith RS/Shutterstock.com; computers: romvo/Shutterstock.com

Figure 9-2. Answers provided from the DNS cache are nonauthoritative, while answers provided by the DNS server are authoritative.

Quick Look 9.1.2

DNS Response Resolution

DNS responses may be authoritative or nonauthoritative. It is important to understand the difference between the two types. When using the **NSLOOKUP** command, the result will tell you if the response is nonauthoritative.

1. Applying what you have learned, open the command prompt.
2. Enter nslookup www.google.com. In this response, the server resolves the address, but the response is coming from the DNS server cache since the answer is nonauthoritative, as shown.
3. Enter nslookup *hostname* using the name of a host on your network. In your classroom lab, this could be the name of another computer or server. The DNS server should respond with the answer. The absence of the nonauthoritative indicator means the response is from the server's DNS database.

CompTIA Security+
1.2

Shared DNS Information

DNS servers get their information from other DNS servers. The validity of the data is only as good as the data themselves. If a DNS server's information is corrupted, especially one from an ISP, the data can be sent to other DNS servers. The data may be corrupted through hacking or a mistake. Sometimes this could have significant impact. The cache is an easier target to compromise than the DNS server. However, if the DNS server is not adequately protected with appropriate security controls, it can be compromised as well.

An incident in 2016 involving a bitcoin wallet provider occurred when the DNS server was hijacked or redirected. For a period of time, the provider's Internet properties were under control of a hacker. The DNS was changed by the hacker. As a result, users were sent to the wrong server. Nearly eight million customers were affected. Eventually, proper service was restored.

In another example, the issue was due to faulty DNS data. An Internet Service Provider (ISP) mistakenly configured its DNS servers to obtain DNS information from Chinese servers. In this example, other ISPs obtained data from the first ISP. Ultimately, some of these records were provided to hosts in the United States. Users suddenly found sites such as Facebook, Twitter, and YouTube were blocked. China is known to block many websites, including these. Even though this was not the result of a malicious hacking attack, the result was the same. Poisoned DNS entries were spread across the Internet.

There are several things you can do to protect a system from DNS poisoning:

FYI

Is it blocked in China? If you want to know if a site is blocked in China, go to the site: www.greatfirewallofchina.org, and enter the web address.

- Install antimalware programs on clients to help prevent *DNS cache hijacking,* which occurs when malicious or invalid entries are inserted into the cache.
- If using Microsoft Server, store the DNS database in the Active Directory to gain additional security protections.
- Limit who has privileges to configure the DNS environment and DNS records.
- Consider not hosting the local DNS client cache.
- Consider configuring *DNS Security Extensions (DNSSEC),* which requires that all responses from a DNS server are digitally signed to ensure they come from an authorized source.

CompTIA Security+
2.6

Network Design Techniques

The physical design of the network can help or hinder protection. The network should be designed to be as efficient as possible. However, the most efficient design may not be the most secure. Often, IT personnel must balance security with efficiency when designing a network. There are several basic network designs or techniques that can be put into practice, including:

- VLAN;
- DMZ; and
- VPN.

Keep in mind, there must be a balance between security and productivity. Recall the CIA triad. The services and data must be available to the users when needed. If security controls prevent users from accessing what they need, then that part of the triad is not fulfilled.

VLAN

CompTIA Security+
3.2

MTA Security Fundamentals
3.2

One method for designing a network is to incorporate virtual local area networks. A *virtual local area network (VLAN)* is a logical grouping of hosts that treats them as if they were physically connected. **Figure 9-3** shows an example of how a VLAN may be organized in an office. Hosts can be located anywhere on the local area network. VLANs are created on network switches.

One of the security benefits of a VLAN is that it limits the broadcast of packets to just that network. This allows traffic from different groups to be separated. For example, in **Figure 9-3,** the research department traffic is separated from the administration traffic on the network. The executive traffic is also isolated from the other two departments. Another security benefit of a VLAN is it can separate

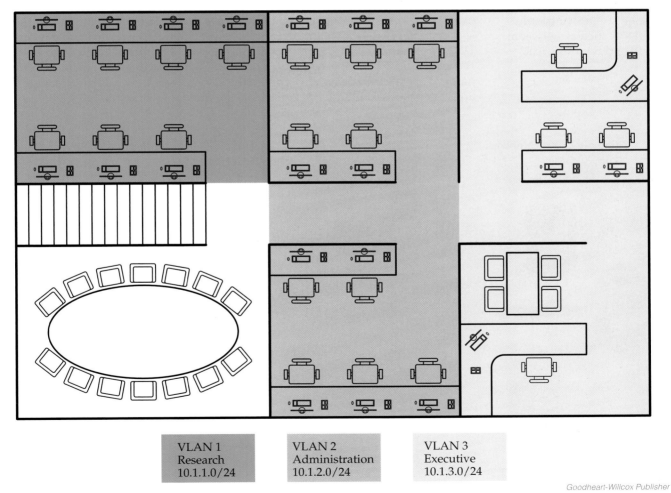

| VLAN 1 Research 10.1.1.0/24 | VLAN 2 Administration 10.1.2.0/24 | VLAN 3 Executive 10.1.3.0/24 |

Goodheart-Willcox Publisher

Figure 9-3. Virtual local area networks (VLANs) can be used to isolate different areas of an organization.

voice traffic from data traffic. VLANs are usually created by assigning devices based on the port or the MAC address. The port is the physical port on the switch.

Another method of VLAN creation is using the host's MAC address. When assigned by MAC address, the VLAN membership is associated with the host's MAC address. This is more secure than assigning by port. It allows the host to connect from any Ethernet port, and VLAN membership is automatically configured. Because cables may be swapped at the switch port, the VLAN assignment could be physically changed. If assigned by MAC address, however, this would not affect the traffic.

VLANs create virtual subnets. This allows the VLAN to be further secured with VLAN access control lists. A *VLAN access control list (VACL)* allows traffic to be filtered within the VLAN. The different VLANs can be configured with unique VACLs.

DMZ

A *demilitarized zone (DMZ)* is a segment of a network that allows some public access and borders the private network where the public access is blocked. A DMZ may also be called a *screened subnet* or a *perimeter network.* A DMZ is typically used for public-facing servers. These may include web servers, FTP servers, or any other server that needs public access. Be sure to place only those servers that need public access in the DMZ. Anything in the DMZ is exposed to the Internet.

DMZs are created by developing borders between the different networks. These borders are established with firewalls, as shown in **Figure 9-4.** In that example, users in the public domain can have access to the web and e-commerce servers. These are located in the DMZ. The type of traffic and hosts that enter the DMZ are filtered with the public-facing firewall. Another firewall then borders the DMZ and the company private network. This firewall locks down the limited amount of traffic that was allowed into the DMZ. Servers such as directory servers and databases should not be accessible from the public domain.

CompTIA Security+
3.2

MTA Security Fundamentals
3.2

FYI

The term DMZ was adapted from the military term describing a buffer zone between two hostile locations, such as between North and South Korea.

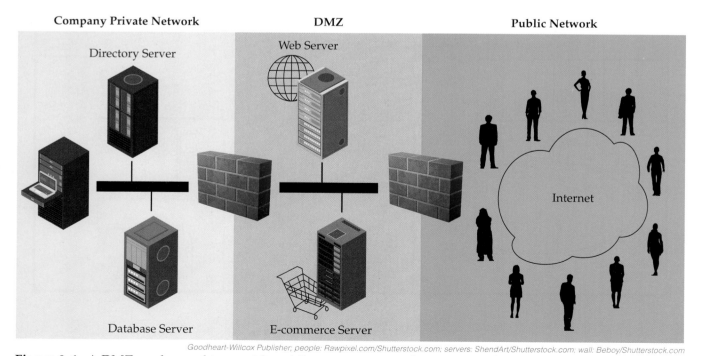

Goodheart-Willcox Publisher; people: Rawpixel.com/Shutterstock.com; servers: ShendArt/Shutterstock.com; wall: Beboy/Shutterstock.com

Figure 9-4. A DMZ can be used to provide public access to network resources while still keeping most of the network isolated from the public.

Case Study

VLAN in Business

Creative Web Masters is a web-development and Internet-hosting company that has about 50 employees. While most users are issued a company laptop and have their own work centers, they sometimes collaborate on projects by moving to one of the two conference rooms in the building. Management wants the users to connect to the same subnet, regardless of which network port they attach to with a network patch cable. Currently the company has two physical subnets, one where the developers and graphic designers are connected and the other for management and support staff. To accommodate this business's need, you have recommend two VLANs using MAC addresses for VLAN placement. To illustrate this design, create a presentation that explains the benefits of VLANs and the setup you have proposed. Include network illustrations to emphasize your plan to management at Creative Web Masters.

Intranets and Extranets

CompTIA Security+
3.2
MTA Security Fundamentals
3.2

Intranets and extranets are other ways to segment data to approved users. An *intranet* is essentially a private Internet environment for internal use only. An intranet is a great resource in a business. It provides a secured environment for forms, information, and portals to other tools to be shared among employees. There are many software programs that can be used to set up and secure the environment so it is only accessible by employees. One example is SharePoint from Microsoft. There are quite a few other platforms as well.

An *extranet* is an extension of an intranet. With an extranet, specific third-party users can be allowed access to a secured intranet. An example of when this environment may be useful is to allow an approved vendor, such as a supplier, access to the intranet. There may also be a case where a vendor or other partner needs access to company data. An extranet could be used for this. Collaborating on projects is another potential application for an extranet.

VPN

CompTIA Security+
3.2

Security administrators must also consider the needs of users not working on-site, as shown in **Figure 9-5.** These are called remote users. Remote users include those who casually access the network from home; traveling employees, such as sales and support representatives; and those who work in satellite offices. It is important to determine who needs remote access to the network. Failure to do this can lead to users making security mistakes. Date may be copied to unsecured devices. Unapproved software that could have security flaws may be installed.

Remote User   VPN Server

Goodheart-Willcox Publisher; server: ShendArt/Shutterstock.com; wall: Beboy/Shutterstock.com

Figure 9-5. A VPN can provide secure access for users who are working from remote locations.

A *virtual private network (VPN)* provides a method to secure data traveling through other networks, such as the Internet. The protection used is data encryption, which is discussed in detail in a later chapter. When the data traveling across the remote connection are encrypted with a VPN it is called *tunneling.* There are many solutions available to provide this secured access. If using Microsoft Server operating systems, VPN Server is included. Windows clients also can setup a VPN client with built-in services. Another feature available in Windows 10 clients is called *always-on-VPN.* This feature automatically connects the client to the VPN when it recognizes Internet access. While the security in VPNs is strong, security professionals must still guard against the possibility of a hacked or stolen laptop configured with this option.

There are two common implementations of VPN configurations: remote access and site-to-site. A *remote-access VPN* allows a user to connect to the network using the Internet from a remote client. This is a popular method for allowing users to work from home or wherever they have an Internet connection. A *site-to-site VPN* allows an organization to connect static or fixed sites to each other using the Internet as the communication platform. This type of VPN allows users to securely access resources on the remote location. Site-to-site VPNs are commonly set up with a VPN concentrator. A *VPN concentrator* is a device by adding support for many tunnels of traffic. It also adds the ability to authenticate users, encrypt and decrypt data, and ensure delivery of data from one site to the other site. This all adds to the routing capabilities of VPNs.

VPN Protocol

CompTIA Security+
2.1

Data on a VPN connection are encrypted. This protects the data when traveling across the public network. When creating the connection, security parameters are set, such as the security encryption protocol. These protocols include:
- Point-to-Point Protocol (PPTP);
- Layer 2 Tunneling Protocol (L2TP);
- Secure Socket Tunneling Protocol (SSTP); and
- Internet Key Exchange Protocol version 2 (IKEv2).

PPTP. *Point-to-Point Protocol (PPTP)* is the most outdated of the tunneling protocols. It was originally created by Microsoft. It supports many Windows clients. It provides data confidentiality in the form of the encryption, but does not support integrity. That is, there is no guarantee the data were not modified in transit. Authentication, or verifying the sending user, is not supported in this protocol. Ports associated with PPTP include TCP 1723 and 47.

L2TP. *Layer 2 Tunneling Protocol (L2TP)* is a tunneling protocol that was created by Cisco and provides more security than PPTP, but is not as fast. However, it has essentially replaced the use of PPTP. This protocol supports Microsoft clients from Windows 2000 and newer. Unlike PPTP, integrity along with confidentiality and authentication are supported. When using L2TP with Internet key exchange traffic, UDP port 500 must allow inbound traffic.

SSTP. *Secure Socket Tunneling Protocol (SSTP)* is a tunneling protocol that provides support for traffic over an SSL 3.0–encrypted connection. By using port 443, it is easier for traffic to pass through proxy servers and firewalls without having to open any additional ports. This version is supported beginning with Vista Service Pack 1. It supports authentication, integrity, and confidentiality.

MTA Security Fundamentals
3.2

IKEv2. *Internet Key Exchange Protocol version 2 (IKEv2)* is a tunneling protocol that uses the IPSEC tunneling protocol over UDP on port 500. *IPSEC* is a security protocol that can be used to encrypt and secure data traveling over computer networks using the TCP/IP protocol. IPSEC allows for strong encryption and authentication protocols. It cannot be used on clients prior to Windows 7 or Microsoft server operating systems lower than Server 2008R2. In addition to supporting confidentiality, integrity, and authentication, it provides significant support for wireless mobility users who move between access points. The key elements of IPSEC include AH and ESP.

AH stands for authentication header. This security feature is used to authenticate the sender and determine if there are any changes to the data during transmission. If the data must use Network Address Translation (NAT), it cannot use AH.

ESP stands for encapsulating security payload. It is an alternative to AH that also authenticates the header as well as encrypts the data. When selecting ESP, data travel on the network in one of two modes: tunnel mode or transport mode. *Tunnel mode* encrypts the IP header of the original packet. This allows for travel through NAT devices. This makes tunnel mode the common choice when setting up site-to-site VPNs. *Transport mode* only encrypts the data and ESP information, not the original packet. This mode is used more commonly with remote-access VPN.

Quick Look 9.1.3

VPN Client Setup

VPN provides a way to securely connect remote users to the network. A VPN can be easily set up in Windows. The ability to create a VPN is built-in to the operating system. The steps are different in Windows 7 and Windows 10.
Windows 7

1. Applying what you have learned, open Control Panel in Windows 7.
2. Click **Network and Internet** and then **Network and Sharing Center**.
3. On the next page, click **Set up a new connection or network**. The description under this option indicates it is used to set up various types of network connections, including VPN. Once you click the option, the **Set Up a Connection or Network** dialog box is displayed. This is a wizard to guide you through the setup.
4. On the first page of the wizard, click **Connect to a workplace**, and then click the **Next** button.
5. The next page of the wizard asks how you would like to connect. Click **Use my Internet connection (VPN)** to advance to the next page of the wizard.
6. You are only simulating a connection, so enter the IP address of 192.168.10.103 in the Internet address: text box and VPN Server in the **Destination name:** text box, as shown.

7. Check the **Don't connect now** check box. Finally, click the **Create** button.
8. Since this is simulating a connection, enter User as the user name and Password as the password for now. When creating an actual connection, be sure to use a secure password.
9. Click the **Create** button. If asked if you want to connect now, do not connect.
10. Click in the search box at the top of Control Panel, and enter connect to a network. Click the link of the same name in the search results.

Quick Look 9.1.3 Continued

11. Click **VPN** on the left side of the **Network & Internet** window, and then click **VPN Connection** on the right side. This is the name of the VPN you created.

12. Click the **Properties** button under your VPN. View the settings available in the **Properties** dialog box.

13. Click the **Security** tab. Then, click the **VPN Type** drop-down arrow, and click **L2TP/IPsec with certificate** in the list. This sets the type of encryption. Save the changes, and close all open windows.

Windows 10

1. Click **Start>Settings** in Windows 10 to display the **Settings** window.

2. Click **Network & Internet** to display the **Network & Internet** window. Click **VPN** on the left-hand side of this window.

3. Click the **Add a VPN connection** button on the right-hand side of the window. A new window is displayed, as shown.

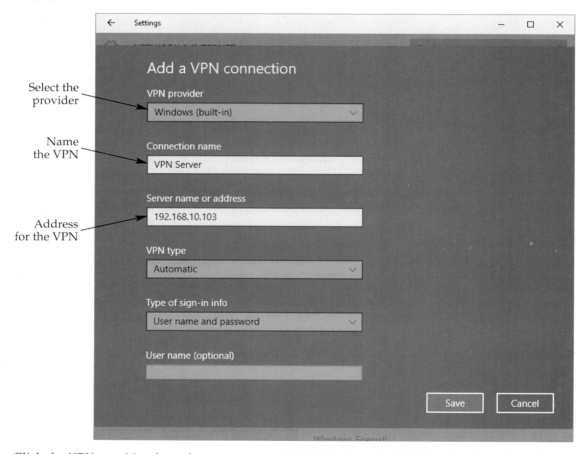

4. Click the **VPN provider** drop-down arrow, and click **Windows (built-in)** in the drop-down list.

5. Click in the **Connection name** text box, and enter VPN Server.

6. Click in the **Server name or address** text box, and enter 192.168.10.103.

7. Click the **VPN type** drop-down arrow. Notice the available options. Click **Automatic** in the drop-down list.

8. Leave the remaining options at the default settings, and click the **Save** button to create the VPN. The new VPN is listed on the right-hand side of the **Network & Internet** window. Click the name of the new VPN, and three buttons appear below it. To delete the VPN, click the **Remove** button. To change the configuration, click the **Advanced options** button.

9. Close all open windows.

VPN Authentication

After choosing a protocol, the next setting to make for the VPN is the method of authentication. Authentication services are used to ensure the user connecting on the VPN is verified as a valid user. There are several choices for authentication, including:

- Password Authentication Protocol (PAP);
- Challenge Handshake Authentication Protocol (CHAP);
- MS-CHAP; and
- Extensible Authentication Protocol (EAP).

PAP. *Password Authentication Protocol (PAP)* is a legacy protocol that is not encrypted. It should not be used. The user name and password will be sent in clear text.

CHAP. *Challenge Handshake Authentication Protocol (CHAP)* is a protocol in which the server sends a challenge to the client after the client establishes a connection to the server. The client converts this to a value. This value is sent to the VPN server where the value must match the value the server calculated. This process is illustrated in **Figure 9-6.**

MS-CHAP. *MS-CHAP* is Microsoft's version of the Challenge Handshake Authentication Protocol. In this protocol, the challenge is a little different than the one used with CHAP. It includes a session ID. The response from the client includes the session ID, the user name, and the user password. **Figure 9-7** shows the MS-CHAP process.

EAP. There are significant vulnerabilities with CHAP. *Extensible Authentication Protocol (EAP)* is needed to transport additional authentication data. This may include data from smart cards and biometric data. EAP was designed as a framework for transporting protocols, *not* the actual authentication protocol itself. It is also designed to work with wireless networks. There are two EAP protocols:

- Lightweight EAP (LEAP)
- Protected EAP (PEAP)

Lightweight EAP (LEAP) was developed by Cisco based on the CHAP protocol. It is designed for use with wireless networking. Windows does not natively support LEAP. Cisco now recommends against its use as it has been found to be cracked.

Protected EAP (PEAP) fully encloses or, encapsulates, EAP. It works with Transport Layer Security (TLS) protocols. PEAP was created by Microsoft, Cisco, and RSA Security.

1. Client establishes a connection

2. Here is a challenge: ABC123

3. My response to your challenge is:
BBF2DED374654CBB32A917AFD236656

4. My computed value is:
BBF2DED374654CBB32A917AFD236656

VPN Client   5. Access is granted   VPN Server

Goodheart-Willcox Publisher; server: Sujith RS/Shutterstock.com; computer: romvo/Shutterstock.com

Figure 9-6. CHAP involves the server challenging the client. The answer the client provides must match what the server has calculated.

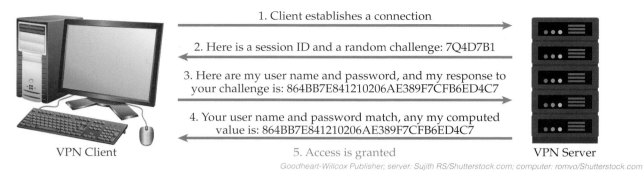

1. Client establishes a connection

2. Here is a session ID and a random challenge: 7Q4D7B1

3. Here are my user name and password, and my response to your challenge is: 864BB7E841210206AE389F7CFB6ED4C7

4. Your user name and password match, any my computed value is: 864BB7E841210206AE389F7CFB6ED4C7

VPN Client   5. Access is granted   VPN Server

Goodheart-Willcox Publisher; server: Sujith RS/Shutterstock.com; computer: romvo/Shutterstock.com

Figure 9-7. MS-CHAP is similar to CHAP with slight differences in the challenge.

Quick Look 9.1.4

VPN Authentication Settings

After a protocol has been set for a VPN, the authentication method must be set. There are several authentication methods that can be used. Choose the best one for the situation at hand.

1. Applying what you have learned, display the **Network & Internet** window, and select the VPN you set up in Quick Look 9.1.3. Then, click the **Change adapter options** link at the bottom of the **Network & Internet** window. The **Network Connections** window is displayed, which shows all network connections.

2. Right-click on your VPN, and click **Properties** in the shortcut menu. The **VPN Connection Properties** dialog box is displayed.

3. Click the **Security** tab, as shown.

Set the authentication method →

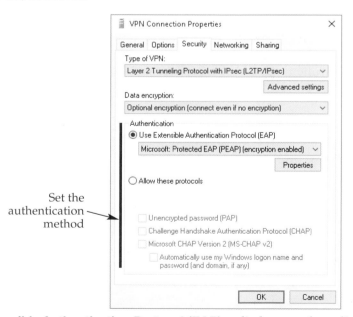

4. Click the **Use Extensible Authentication Protocol (EAP)** radio button, then click the corresponding drop-down list and choose **Microsoft Protected EAP (PEAP)**. Notice the other protocols available in this drop-down list.

5. Click the **Allow these protocols** radio button. Which protocols are not enabled (checked) by default?

6. Click the **Use Extensible Authentication Protocol (EAP)** radio button to restore this setting, and then click the **OK** button to update the VPN.

7. Close all open windows.

Ethical Issue

Workplace VPNs

In many businesses and schools, you may not be able to access certain websites, such as social media sites, using the network. Or, you may need to obtain a file from a computer at your house, but that functionality is not available via your work network. You may also want to privately access a website and not have this request logged through company servers. A VPN can provide a safe means to access these websites without company oversight. Is it ethical to use a VPN on the company network when you are accessing the VPN through your own devices such as a laptop, tablet, or smartphone? State your opinion on this subject and defend your position in two or three paragraphs. Be sure to cite any sources you used in your research, and be prepared to participate in a class debate.

SECTION REVIEW 9.1

Check Your Understanding

1. The DNS server that holds the record mapping the host to its IP address is known as what type of DNS server?

2. What device is used to create a VLAN?

3. A server needing public access should be located in which network location?

4. What UDP port must be open for L2TP traffic?

5. If you are going to send biometric information via a VPN, what authentication security protocol must be used?

Build Your Key Terms Vocabulary

As you progress through this course, develop a personal cybersecurity glossary. This will help you build your vocabulary and prepare you for a career. Write a definition for each of the following terms, and add it to your cybersecurity glossary.

authoritative DNS server

Challenge Handshake Authentication Protocol (CHAP)

demilitarized zone (DMZ)

DNS local cache

DNS poisoning

DNS Security Extensions (DNSSEC)

Domain Name System (DNS)

Extensible Authentication Protocol (EAP)

extranet

Internet Key Exchange Protocol version 2 (IKEv2)

intranet

Layer 2 Tunneling Protocol (L2TP)

MS-CHAP

nonauthoritative DNS server

Password Authentication Protocol (PAP)

perimeter network

Point-to-Point Protocol (PPTP)

Protected EAP (PEAP)

screened subnet

Secure Socket Tunneling Protocol (SSTP)

tunneling

virtual local area network (VLAN)

virtual private network (VPN)

VLAN access control list (VACL)

VPN concentrator

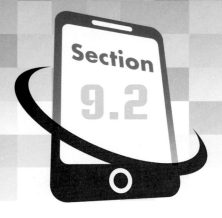

Protecting Network Devices

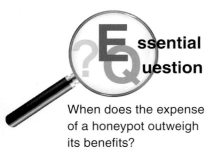

When does the expense of a honeypot outweigh its benefits?

Another key area that must be secured is the devices that are used to manage the data flow within or to and from the network. This includes the routers and switches that are located throughout the network. Misconfigured devices or those that have been hacked can result in network traffic being misdirected or redirected to malicious hosts. They can also prevent the flow of traffic throughout the network. In addition, the network must be protected by incorporating solutions that will assist in protecting it from other threats. These solutions include intrusion-prevention systems that will monitor against live threats, services that protect vulnerable hosts from connecting to the network, and even using a controlled environment to track how the network can be accessed by hackers.

Key Terms

address resolution protocol (ARP)
ARP poisoning
honeynet
honeypot
intrusion-detection system (IDS)

intrusion-prevention
system (IPS)
message of the day (MotD)
network access control (NAC)

Network Access Protection (NAP)
System Health Agent (SHA)
unified threat management
(UTM)

Learning Goals

- Describe securing network switches.
- Discuss securing network routers.
- Explain the operation of intrusion-detection systems.
- Identify benefits of unified threat management.
- Describe access controls on network infrastructure.
- Explain how a honeypot acts as a security device.

Protecting Network Switches

CompTIA Security+
2.1

Network switches are responsible for managing traffic within the subnet. They operate at least on the data link layer of the OSI model. There may also be Layer 3 switches. These provide routing capabilities in addition to normal tasks associated with a network switch. Switches are internal to the network. Therefore, they may be overlooked in security configurations. Some options for securing switches include:

- configure switches so ports can only access specific MAC addresses;
- configure access lists to control traffic in the switch;
- establish secure passwords for console and remote access to the switch; and
- ensure switches are configured with options such as Spanning Tree protocol, which prevents switches from creating a continuous loop of traffic that ultimately floods the switch with needless packets.

A critical area to protect on switches and clients is the address resolution protocol (ARP). The *address resolution protocol (ARP)* handles the process of locating addresses in the MAC address table. Switches maintain a MAC address table. This is used to map an IP address to the physical or MAC address, as shown in **Figure 9-8.** On most switches, these addresses are found dynamically and updated in the table using ARP. Local computers also use an ARP cache to speed up the process of locating a target.

A table entry labeled dynamic means the switch queried the network and discovered the MAC address assigned to the IP address. MAC addresses could also be static, or manually assigned. Hackers can attempt to run programs to redirect the MAC address to another port. This creates a man-in-the-middle attack.

ARP poisoning or spoofing is a man-in-the-middle attack. The hacker intercepts an ARP request and changes its reply. The victim is pointed to the hacker's computer, not the real computer, as shown in **Figure 9-9.** This often happens on routers still using the default settings. The data sent to the router go to the hacker instead of the router.

FYI

MAC addresses are composed of two parts: part 1, the first three sections, represents the vendor; part 2, the last three sections, represents a unique host. There are many sites where you can look up who the manufacturer of the MAC address is by entering those first three sections. That may assist in finding a rogue host.

CompTIA Security+
1.2

MTA Security Fundamentals
3.3

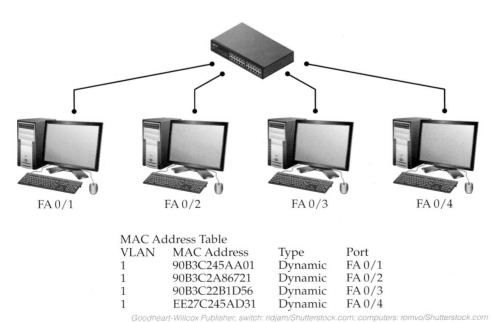

MAC Address Table

VLAN	MAC Address	Type	Port
1	90B3C245AA01	Dynamic	FA 0/1
1	90B3C2A86721	Dynamic	FA 0/2
1	90B3C22B1D56	Dynamic	FA 0/3
1	EE27C245AD31	Dynamic	FA 0/4

Goodheart-Willcox Publisher; switch: ridjam/Shutterstock.com; computers: romvo/Shutterstock.com

Figure 9-8. Switches maintain a MAC address table, and use ARP to access it. The FA 0/x number represents a fast Ethernet port. The second number is the port number.

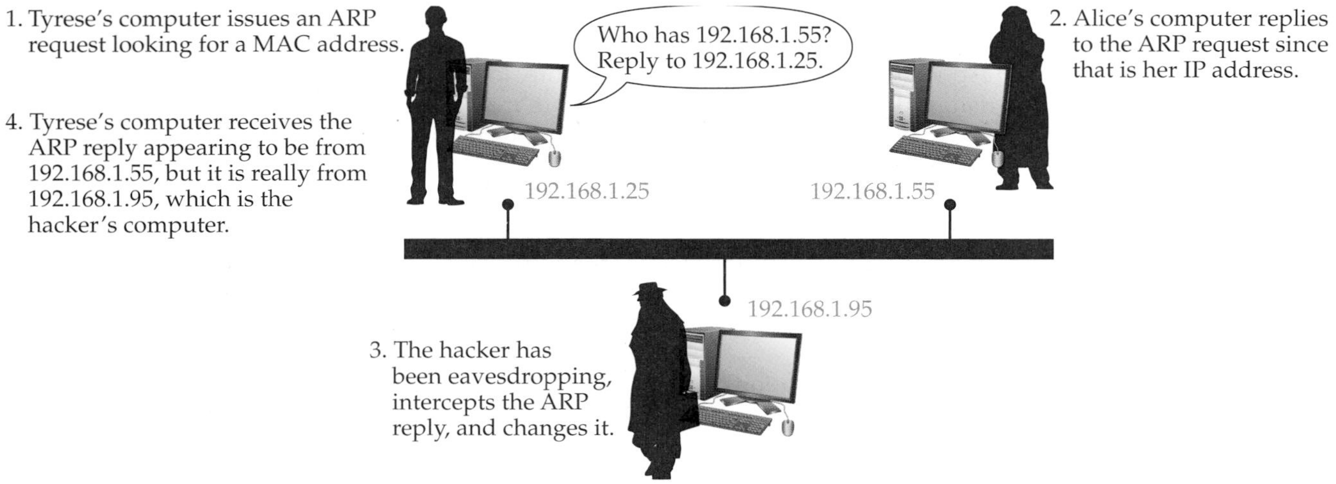
1. Tyrese's computer issues an ARP request looking for a MAC address.
Who has 192.168.1.55? Reply to 192.168.1.25.
2. Alice's computer replies to the ARP request since that is her IP address.
4. Tyrese's computer receives the ARP reply appearing to be from 192.168.1.55, but it is really from 192.168.1.95, which is the hacker's computer.
192.168.1.25
192.168.1.55
192.168.1.95
3. The hacker has been eavesdropping, intercepts the ARP reply, and changes it.

Goodheart-Willcox Publisher; people: Rawpixel.com/Shutterstock.com; computers: romvo/Shutterstock.com

Figure 9-9. An ARP poisoning or spoofing attack is a man-in-the-middle attack. The traffic is intercepted by a hacker and rerouted.

Quick Look 9.2.1

Local ARP Cache and Traffic

The local computer also maintains a cache of ARP requests. Entries in the cache can be easily reviewed. It is also possible to manually add entries, which could be an attack vector for hackers.

1. Applying what you have learned, open the Windows command prompt with administrator privileges.
2. Enter arp –a to display the local cache of ARP entries, or the ARP table, as shown. Depending on your network configuration, you may see entries for other NICs, including virtual adapters.

```
Administrator: Command Prompt
Microsoft Windows [Version 10.0.10586]
(c) 2016 Microsoft Corporation. All rights reserved.

C:\Windows\system32>arp -a

Interface: 192.168.56.1 --- 0x4
  Internet Address      Physical Address      Type
  192.168.56.255        ff-ff-ff-ff-ff-ff     static
  224.0.0.22            01-00-5e-00-00-16     static
  224.0.0.252           01-00-5e-00-00-fc     static

Interface: 10.0.0.111 --- 0x6
  Internet Address      Physical Address      Type
  10.0.0.255            ff-ff-ff-ff-ff-ff     static
  224.0.0.22            01-00-5e-00-00-16     static
  224.0.0.252           01-00-5e-00-00-fc     static

C:\Windows\system32>
```

3. The –s switch is used to add a static entry to the table. Enter arp –s 10.10.10.10 00-AA-11-BB-22-CC to add this fake entry to the table. The prompt returns without displaying a message.

Quick Look 9.2.1 Continued

4. Enter arp –a. The entry you added should be included in the table.

5. To remove the static entry you added, enter arp –d 10.10.10.10.

6. Verify the entry is removed by entering arp –a.

7. Launch Wireshark, and start a capture on your physical adapter. Then minimize Wireshark (leave it open).

8. Return to the command prompt. To create ARP traffic for the capture, delete the ARP cache by entering arp –d *. The asterisk (*) is a wildcard that represents all hosts.

9. Enter arp –a. You should see a smaller ARP cache than before.

10. Ping some of the computers on your network, then return to the Wireshark.

11. Sort the Wireshark display by Protocol. Once you see there is some ARP traffic, stop the capture.

12. Create a filter for just ARP traffic by entering arp in the filter bar.

13. Look for a record that has an entry in the Info column that begins with Who has. Double-click the record to explore it further, as shown. In the Ethernet section, notice the destination MAC address is all Fs. A MAC address of all Fs in hexadecimal represents a broadcast to all nodes on the subnet.

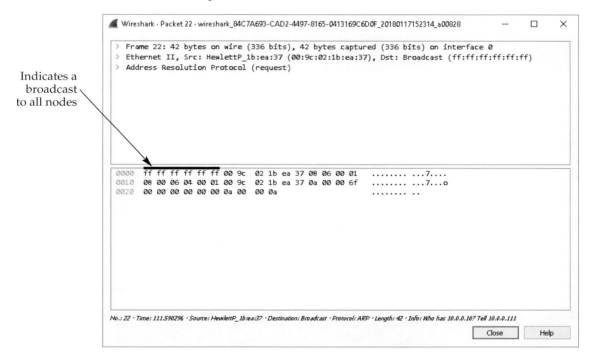

Indicates a broadcast to all nodes

14. Find an ARP reply. The entry in the Info column should contain the text is at.

15. Return to the command prompt.

16. Applying what you have learned, display the ARP cache. Notice that as queries are sent, the local cache is updated.

Protecting Network Routers

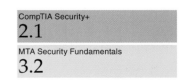

CompTIA Security+
2.1

MTA Security Fundamentals
3.2

Routers are an integral part of the networking environment. Without routers, data would be limited to traveling just the local subnet. Routers play an active role in moving traffic. They continually scan the network. A router searches for updates to routing information and makes adjustments to the information it receives. Routers are used to manage business networks. Wireless routers also manage home networks, as shown in **Figure 9-10.**

Casezy idea/Shutterstock.com

Figure 9-10. Do not forget about the security of home routers. Many home users do not change the password from the factory default, which is a common attack vector for hackers.

As with switches, routers must be protected against network hacks. Home routers especially have been found to be easily hacked. In 2011, 4.5 million Brazilian DSL users fell victim to an unpatched vulnerability in their routers. Hackers exploited this to remotely log in to these routers. Once they had access, the default DNS entries were changed to send data to the hackers. The result was a massive theft of credit card and banking information. There are several steps to take to keep routers safe:

- Regularly patch all router firmware and the router's operating system.
- Secure routers with strong passwords that are hard to guess.
- Back up all router configuration information.
- Ensure that only traffic that should be on the subnet is allowed.
- Remind users about security access and responsibilities with a router banner.
- Have a plan to check for updates to firmware and install only patches directly from the manufacturer as third-party patches may not be reliable.

Passwords on routers should be encrypted if the router software allows this. With commercial routers, limit the access levels to only those who need access. Ensure these changes apply to routers to console and remote access modes.

Make sure router configurations and logs are maintained by using a system log (syslog) server. Ensure change logs are updated anytime a change is made to a router, indicating what was done and by whom.

Routers manage traffic using Access Control Lists (ACLs). This list controls what is allowed on the subnet. Be sure it is accurate so only traffic needed on the subnet is allowed. One of the security concerns associated with routers is IP spoofing. A hacker may fake the IP address of a local IP so the traffic appears to have originated from inside the network. An ACL can be configured to block any inbound traffic into a network that originates from that network's address. For example, if the network is using the 192.168.x.x private IP address range, an entry in the ACL may be:

```
deny ip 192.168.0.0 0.0.255.255 any
```

This will block any inbound traffic using 192.168 in the first two octets from entering your network.

A router banner is displayed to the user before he or she logs in to the router. The banner is often called a *message of the day (MotD).* Use the MotD to provide information on security best practices.

Configuring and securing routers is quite a complex subject. However, the local routing table on a computer can be viewed. In unusual circumstances, it is even possible to configure a Microsoft Server to act as a router. This is called a soft router since it is software driven.

Quick Look 9.2.2

Local Routing Table

This exercise will give you a very basic idea of what routers contain. However, depending on the routing protocol used, routing can be complex.

1. Applying what you have learned, launch the Windows command prompt with administrative access.

Quick Look 9.2.2 Continued

2. Enter route print. There are five sections of the output: interface list, IPv4 route table, IPv4 persistent routes, IPv6 route table, and IPv6 persistent routes, as shown.

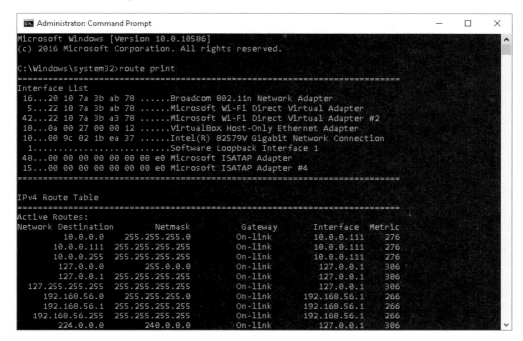

3. Look at the IPv4 route table. The first column indicates the destination network. An address of 0.0.0.0 is used for every network address not specifically on the list. This is done because it is not possible to list every Internet address. The Gateway column indicates where the packet will be sent. This is usually the computer's default gateway. An entry of On-link indicates the packet will be sent through the local NIC to the local subnet. The values in the Metric column only impact the local computer if there are multiple network cards. Essentially, this value indicates the best route to take.

4. Enter route print -4 to only view the interface table and the IPv4 routing information.

5. Enter netstat –r. This is the same as entering route print.

Intrusion-Detection Systems

CompTIA Security+
2.1

It is important to have systems continuously monitoring the network and hosts for anomalies or suspicious actions. There are two basic types of systems to do this. An *intrusion-detection system (IDS)* monitors the system and sends an alert if there is a problem. An extension of the IDS is the IPS. An *intrusion-prevention system (IPS)* not only detects malicious or suspicious behavior, it can take action to stop the problem. An IPS is an extension of an IDS.

Each of these can be located on either a specific host on a network subnet. They are categorized as the following.

- Host Intrusion Detection System (HIDS)
- Network Intrusion Detection System (NIDS)
- Host Intrusion Prevention System (HIPS)
- Network Intrusion Prevention System (NIPS)

A host-based system only protects the actual host where it is installed. A network-based solution will scan the subnet on which it is installed. Network solutions use sensors to detect anomalies. They are usually installed on routers and firewalls.

Snort IPS is the best-known open-source IPS solution. It was developed as a project in 1998. It currently is available for Linux and Windows systems.

For example, a classroom full of students is told to access a specific web page, as shown in **Figure 9-11.** Because the school uses private IPs, each request comes from the same public IP address. The IPS running on the target web server sees all of the requests occurring at almost the same time as a possible attack. It takes immediate action and blocks the IP address. In this case, it is a false alarm, but it could have been an actual attack, such as a DNS attack.

So, how do these intrusion detection systems work? They use a variety of strategies to monitor systems. They search for anomalies. They use signature monitoring. They deploy behavior-based monitoring systems.

Anomalies

Over time, network activity is collected. This establishes a baseline of normal activity. Something that varies from this baseline could be a concern. For example, suppose the baseline shows that around 2 p.m. on most days the network traffic hovers around 30 percent of bandwidth. Then, one day around this time, network traffic is 70 percent utilization. That is a significant deviation from the baseline. It bears further investigation to see if there is a threat.

Signatures

Intrusion detection systems identify traffic or actions that do not match current known examples. This is similar to how antimalware solutions work. Signatures are stored and must be frequently updated so they can be used for comparison. For example, the intrusion detection system may find a pattern of characters in data packets that match known attack patterns. These packets would be flagged as a potential intrusion.

Behavior

There is a problem with signature monitoring. It relies on the signatures and databases being up to date. With a behavior-based monitoring, traffic or actions are examined to see if they are normal. Something that is not considered a normal action will be flagged as a potential risk.

CompTIA Security+
2.4

Unified Threat Management

Consider a small- to medium-size business owner exploring, purchasing, and configuring the security solutions for his or her network. This may involve a great deal of equipment, configuration, time, and money. **Figure 9-12** shows what may

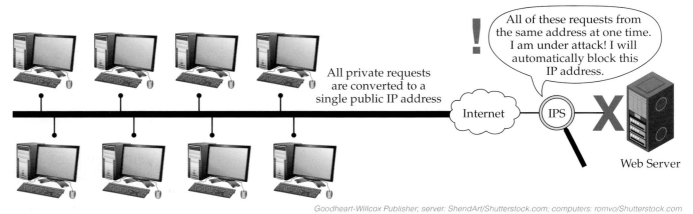

All private requests are converted to a single public IP address

All of these requests from the same address at one time. I am under attack! I will automatically block this IP address.

Internet   IPS   Web Server

Figure 9-11. An intrusion-prevention system (IPS) looks for malicious or suspicious behavior and takes action to stop the problem. Here, multiple requests from the same IP address at the same time are seen as a threat.

Protection of the Network

Goodheart-Willcox Publisher; pikepicture/Shutterstock.com

Figure 9-12. Someone setting up and securing a network may face a long list of tasks. A UTM offers a solution to simplify everything.

be a typical to-do list for getting everything set up. Thankfully, there is an option that will simplify everything. A device called a unified threat management security appliance can be installed.

A *unified threat management (UTM)* appliance is an all-in-one security device that allows the network to be managed from one location. There are a couple of advantages for this type of solution. It reduces the number of devices that must be managed. Administrators do not have to learn how to use multiple systems. This means a shorter learning curve. Overall, it can be a lower-cost solution than purchasing and licensing multiple products.

UTM is not without its disadvantages, however. Because there is one device, it becomes a single point of failure or attack. Also, it may not offer as many features as would be available with multiple devices.

FYI

UTMs are also called next generation firewalls.

Network Access Control

Many pediatrician offices have two entrances, one for healthy children and another for children who are sick. This is done so children who are ill do not infect healthy children. Something similar can be done on networks. There is a way to ensure only machines that meet certain "health standards" are allowed on the network. This is how a network access control system works. In a *network access control (NAC)* environment, standards are set that hosts must meet before they are able to connect to the network. Some examples of these criteria could be:

- host operating system has the latest security patches installed;
- host antivirus signature files are up-to-date;
- host firewall is turned on; and
- not a disapproved device, such as Android or iOS device.

Network Access Protection (NAP) is Microsoft's version of an NAC solution. **Figure 9-13** shows an overview of the general steps for a client attempting to log in using NAP. The *System Health Agent (SHA)* is an agent that performs the self-check on the client.

An *agent* is software or code that searches for vulnerabilities in the client. Some agents may run at system boot, while others can be persistent, constantly checking for vulnerabilities. Most antivirus programs are a type of a persistent

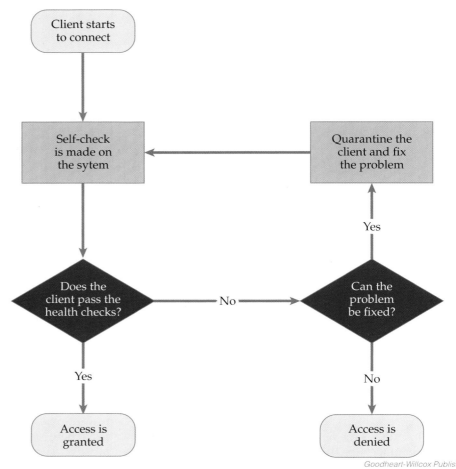

Figure 9-13. This flow diagram shows a simplified view of client access with NAP.

agent. There is also an agentless option, such as with Microsoft and the Active Directory. In this case, when a user logs on or off the domain, NAC runs from the server holding the Active Directory, also known as a domain controller. This eliminates the need to download any software to the host device.

CompTIA Security+
2.2

MTA Security Fundamentals
3.2

Honeypots and Honeynets

You know there are hackers out there, so why not let them hack your system? Well, you do not want to allow them to hack your live system, but why not set a decoy server decoy network to let them hack, as shown in **Figure 9-14**? Hackers are drawn to unprotected systems like flies to honey. A *honeypot* is a decoy server set up to attract hackers. A *honeynet* is a decoy network consisting of two or more honeypots.

There are several reasons for setting up a honeypot. You can learn from the hacking techniques you see on the honeypot. Then, use that information to further protect your live systems. Another reason is the honeypot can distract hackers. They may attack the fake network instead of trying to hack the live network.

A honeypot set up with the intention of attracting hackers is typically known as a *research honeypot*. This is not a lure to attract hackers with the intention of arresting them. Rather, learn from the information and make adjustments.

Setting up a honeypot is more than just plugging in a computer to the network and turning it on. Additional software may need to be installed and configured to gather data and report on statistics.

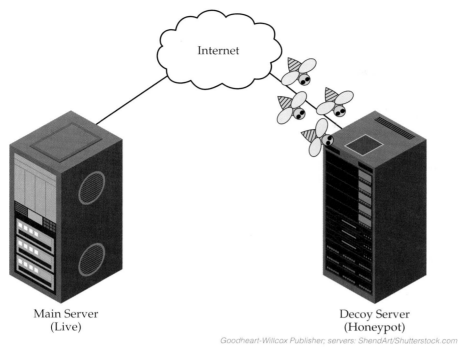

Figure 9-14. A honeypot is a server intentionally unsecured and exposed to attract hackers.

Goodheart-Willcox Publisher; servers: ShendArt/Shutterstock.com

SECTION REVIEW 9.2

Check Your Understanding

1. This protocol resolves an IP address to a MAC address.
2. This type of device can spot problems and take immediate steps to mitigate the threat.
3. This all in one device can offer complete security solutions.
4. What is the basic function of a network access control system?
5. A decoy network designed to watch activity is known as what term?

Build Your Key Terms Vocabulary

As you progress through this course, develop a personal cybersecurity glossary. This will help you build your vocabulary and prepare you for a career. Write a definition for each of the following terms, and add it to your cybersecurity glossary.

address resolution protocol (ARP)

ARP poisoning

honeynet

honeypot

intrusion-detection system (IDS)

intrusion-prevention system (IPS)

message of the day (MotD)

network access control (NAC)

Network Access Protection (NAP)

System Health Agent (SHA)

unified threat management (UTM)

Review and Assessment

Summary

Section 9.1 Threats to DNS

- The Domain Name System (DNS) is the user's guide to the Internet and is vulnerable to threats such as DNS spoofing or poisoning.
- The physical design of the network can help or hinder cybersecurity, and there are several basic designs or techniques such as VLAN, DMZ, and VPN.

Section 9.2 Protecting Network Devices

- Network switches manage traffic within the subnet and should not be overlooked when planning security.
- Routers must be protected against hacks, and home routers often are lacking in proper security.
- An intrusion-detection system monitors the system and alerts when there are problems, while an intrusion-prevention system (IPS) additionally takes action to fix the problem.
- A unified threat management (UTM) security appliance provides a single location for managing network security, which provides many benefits, but not without a downside.
- A network access control (NAC) environment provides certain safety criteria a host must meet before it is allowed on the network.
- A honeypot can be used to attract hackers in an effort to divert them from the live network and to study their actions for areas to improve on the live network.

Check Your Cybersecurity IQ ⤴

Now that you have completed this chapter, see what you have learned about cybersecurity by visiting the student companion website (www.g-wlearning.com) and taking the chapter posttest.

Review Questions ⤴

For each question, select the answer that is the best response.

1. You suspect a bad entry in the local cache. What can be run on a Windows workstation to clear this?
   A. ipconfig /flushdns
   B. net dns flush
   C. arp -a
   D. dns -clearcache

2. When a server can resolve a DNS request from their server cache, the server is called:
   A. poisoned
   B. authoritative
   C. unauthenticated
   D. nonauthoritative

3. You need to isolate certain hosts on a network into one subnet. What solution will you use to create this environment?
   A. VPN
   B. DMZ
   C. VLAN
   D. NAP

4. A company offers online shopping. Which statement about securing this server is true?
   A. The server should be set up for VPN access only.
   B. The server should host it on DNS server for accuracy.
   C. The server should be set up to use PAP authentication.
   D. The server should be placed in a perimeter network.

5. A company wants to allow authorized vendors access to the local intranet. What security measure would protect communication and limit local access on the network?
   A. Incorporate a VPN.
   B. Set up a VLAN.
   C. Create a honeynet.
   D. Use a MAC table.

6. The SSTP uses which port number to send encrypted traffic?
   A. 47
   B. 443
   C. 5001723
   D. 198

7. If an ARP table is changed via a hacker, this is known as:
   A. malware
   B. ARP caching
   C. ARP poisoning
   D. ARP intrusion

8. Which of the following is not an appropriate security practice for hardening a router?
   A. Update the firmware on the router.
   B. Disallow local physical access and use Telnet for management.
   C. Limit access to the router's interface to authorized personnel only.
   D. Encrypt the password to the router.

9. You have a computer programmer who is developing code for a special project. Which defensive tactic should be recommended for this machine?
   A. intrusion-detection system (IDS)
   B. unified threat management (UTM)
   C. intrusion-prevention system (IPS)
   D. honeypot

10. If a system does not have appropriate security settings installed, such as service packs or antivirus updates, you can quarantine the systems using which security strategy?
    A. Quarantine the machines in a separate VLAN.
    B. Configure network access control.
    C. Install the device in a DMZ.
    D. Use a UTM.

Application and Extension of Knowledge

1. Using a drawing program, such as the free online program Draw.io, diagram a business network including identifying a DMZ, the local private network, and a public network. Place a web server, Microsoft Active Directory server, edge router, and inside router in appropriate locations.

2. Compare the output of **NSLOOKUP** command and options from a Windows computer and a Linux host, such as Ubuntu. Create a table comparing the commands. Provide screen shots of the output.

3. Cisco routers have security levels, or privilege levels, for running commands to view and configure systems. Research the default security levels and what levels are used by network administrators IT technicians who are not administrators. Summarize the default configurations, and identify how they are used to aid in router security.

4. Interview a person who uses an intranet at work. What type of data or applications are located on the intranet. Can the intranet be accessed remotely? Ask other questions to find out how a worker uses an intranet. Summarize the responses and share them in a class discussion.

5. Look into the details of using Snort as an IPS solution. Indicate some of the benefits of using this product. Identify which platforms are supported. What is oink code and pulled pork? Write a one- or two-page report detailing aspects of Snort. Follow your school's formatting guidelines.

Research Project
Public DNS Servers

A business owner may want to use a preferred or alternate DNS server other than what is assigned by his or her ISP. There are services such as those offered by Google, OpenDNS, and FreeDNS among others that can provide this. While these may be popular options, there is often mixed reviews on their usage, performance, and security. Research the three options mentioned above, and investigate other options. Identify the features of each. Locate reviews of the services. Investigate the advantages, disadvantages, and potential cybersecurity risks that occur from using one of these services.

Deliverables. Create a one- to two-page report detailing the role of public DNS servers. Summarize three public DNS servers, at least one of which you identified through your own research. Include in your report the IP addresses of the public DNS servers you researched and your opinion on the safety and effectiveness of these services. Cite any sources used in your research, including customer reviews.

Online Activities

Complete the following activities, which will help you learn, practice, and expand your knowledge and skills.

Vocabulary. Practice vocabulary for this chapter using the e-flash cards, matching activity, and vocabulary game until you are able to recognize their meanings.

Communication Skills

College and Career Readiness

Reading. Active reading involves concentration. Select an article from a media source about VPNs. Identify the author's main idea for the article, as well as key supporting details. Draw conclusions about the author's purpose for writing the article. Retell or summarize this information to your classmates.

Writing. Write one or two paragraphs clearly and accurately describing the concept of demilitarized zones for computer networks as you interpret it. Select, organize, and analyze information to support your thoughts and ideas.

Speaking. Career-ready individuals understand that demonstrating leadership qualities is a way to make a positive contribution to a team. Identify leadership characteristics you believe all team members should possess. Use a graphic organizer to record your ideas. Share with the class in an oral presentation.

Listening. Critical listening occurs when specific information or instructions are needed. When your instructor provides instructions to the class, use your critical-listening skills to understand the message. How can critical listening help you follow instructions and accomplish tasks?

Portfolio Development

College and Career Readiness

Community Service. Community service is an important quality to show in a portfolio. Serving the community shows that a candidate is well rounded and socially aware. In this activity, you will create a list of your contributions to nonprofit organizations. Many opportunities are available for young people to serve the community. You might volunteer for a park clean-up project. Perhaps you might enjoy reading to residents in a senior-living facility. Maybe raising money for a pet shelter appeals to you. Whatever your interests, there is sure to be a related service project.

1. Create a Microsoft Word document that lists service projects or volunteer activities in which you have taken part. Use the heading Community Service on the document along with your name. List the name of the organization or person you helped, the date(s) of service, and the activities that you performed. If you received an award related to this service, mention it here.

2. Save the document in an appropriate folder.

3. Update your spreadsheet to reflect the inclusion of this Community Service document.

CTSO Event Prep

Written Events. Many competitive events for career and technical student organizations (CTSOs) require students to write and submit a paper. The paper may need to be submitted before the competition or when the student arrives at the event. Written events can be lengthy and take a lot of time to prepare, so it is important to start early. To prepare for a written event, complete the following activities.

1. Read the guidelines provided by the organization. The topic to be researched will be specified in detail. Also, all final format guidelines will be given, including how to organize and submit the paper. Make certain you ask questions about any points you do not understand.

2. Do your research early. Research may take days or weeks, and you do not want to rush the process.

3. Set a deadline for yourself so that you write at a comfortable pace.

4. After you write the first draft, ask an instructor to review it for you and give feedback.

5. Once you have the final version, go through the checklist for the event to make sure you have covered all of the details. Your score will be penalized if you do not follow instructions.

6. To practice, visit your organization's website and select a written event in which you might be interested. Research the topic and then complete an outline. Create a checklist of guidelines that you must follow for this event. After you have completed these steps, decide if this is the event or topic that interests you. If you are still interested, move forward and start the writing process.

Chapter 10

Wireless Network Security

It is hard to imagine a time when technology kept computer users tethered to network cables or when a bulky desktop computer was needed to access the Internet. Wireless networks offer the ability to have devices communicate without a hardwired connection. This is achieved with radio waves. The use of wireless communication has exploded in recent years. Devices such as tablets, smartphones, laptops, and others offer wireless connections. Today, users are increasingly more mobile. In fact, the number of mobile users has surpassed the number of desktop users for the first time ever.

Wireless and mobile access present significant security challenges for network administrators. There is a wide range of vulnerabilities and avenues of attack on these systems. This chapter explores some of the significant security concerns for wireless networks. Administrators have an ongoing responsibility to balance the needs of user against the security necessary to protect assets and data.

Chapter Preview

While studying, look for the activity icon **for:**

- Pretests and posttests
- Vocabulary terms with e-flash cards and matching activities
- Self-assessment

G-W LEARNING.com

Reading Prep

After you read this chapter, draw a conclusion about what you learned. Did the material cover the information you expected? Do you have additional questions about the material?

College and Career Readiness

Check Your Cybersecurity IQ ➦

Before you begin this chapter, see what you already know about cybersecurity by visiting the student companion website (www.g-wlearning.com) and taking the chapter pretest.

Certification Objectives

CompTIA Security+

1.2 Compare and contrast the types of attacks.
2.1 Install and configure network components, both hardware and software based, to support organizational security.
2.2 Given a scenario, use appropriate software tools to assess the security posture of an organization.
2.3 Given a scenario, troubleshoot common security issues.
2.5 Given a scenario, deploy mobile devices securely.
3.3 Given a scenario, implement secure systems design.
6.3 Given a scenario, install and configure wireless security settings.

Microsoft MTA Security Fundamentals

1.4 Understand wireless security.
2.1 Understand user authentication.

Section 10.1

Wireless Networking Overview

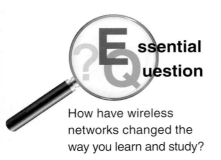

Essential Question

How have wireless networks changed the way you learn and study?

Tablets and laptops are replacing the standard desktop. Cellular telephones evolved into smartphones. Smartphones are used more often for computing, web-based activities, gaming, and social media communication than they are for traditional telephone calls. Mobile technology allows companies to grow their business. They can reach customers on mobile devices anywhere and at anytime. To accommodate mobile users, businesses create responsive web pages that adapt to the smaller screens and multiple platforms of mobile devices. Before wireless security concerns can be addressed, it is important to understand the different types of wireless technologies available.

Key Terms

access point (AP)
ANT
basic service set (BSS)
cell
cellular network

dynamic frequency selection (DFS)
extended service set (ESS)
near-field communication (NFC)
satellite communication (SATCOM)

service set identifier (SSID)
Wi-Fi
wireless client (STA)
wireless NIC
wireless router

Learning Goals

- Discuss the state of wireless technologies.
- Identify components of a wireless network.
- Diagram coverage for a cellular network.
- Describe SATCOM and ANT communication methods.

Review of Wireless Technologies

Businesses are finding that freeing employees from their desks can increase productivity. This, in turn, often leads to higher revenue and profits. Wireless technology allows employees to work from anywhere, as shown in **Figure 10-1.** Schools are also adopting this mobile strategy. Tablets, laptops, and Chromebooks are increasingly used in the classroom.

According to Cisco.com, traffic from wireless and mobile devices will account for about 66 percent of the total IP traffic by the year 2020. By contrast, in 2015 wireless traffic accounted for 48 percent of all traffic.

IT giant Google has invested in wired technology with Google Fiber. However, in 2016, it announced an initiative focused on high-speed wireless connectivity. The need to serve mobile users along with the high costs of installation and regulatory issues related to wired technologies were factors in Google's decision. It is testing this wireless technology in several cities in the United States.

Facebook is also exploring the use of high-speed wireless transmission. It is testing the Terragraph program. This program offers gigabit wireless networking. The goal is to be able to provide this wireless technology in densely populated cities that have poor Internet service.

One of the strongest advocates of wireless networking is the CTIA. This is a trade association representing the wireless-communication industry in the United States. It supports wireless manufacturers and cellular carriers. It also sponsors industry certifications, publishes surveys, and supports many wireless initiatives.

David Gilder/Shutterstock.com

Figure 10-1. Wireless networking allows employees to work from anywhere. This can be especially beneficial for those who travel for work.

CTIA used to be known as the Cellular Telecommunications Industry Association. Since 2015, it is known by just the initials.

Quick Look 10.1.1

CTIA

The CTIA is a well-respected trade association. Its website provides many resources as well and information on the wireless industry.

1. Launch a web browser, and navigate to the CTIA website (www.ctia.org). Be aware this is a .org domain, not a .com domain.
2. Click the menu on the home page, and click **News**. Browse through some of the postings and discuss articles and information of interest with your classmates. You can filter the choices by type using the menu on the left.
3. Click **Facts and Infographics** in the left-hand menu, and deselect any other options. Review some of the research data about wireless and consumer use of wireless technology.
4. From the main menu, click **About CTIA**>**Membership**. Who can become a regular member of this organization?

Wi-Fi Basics

FYI

Wi-Fi is a trademark held by the nonprofit organization Wi-Fi Alliance.

MTA Security Fundamentals
1.4

Wi-Fi is a wireless networking technology that uses radio waves instead of wires or fiber optic cable. It runs on the unlicensed bands of the radio frequency (RF) spectrum. Wi-Fi is defined by the IEEE 802.11 standard released by the Institute of Electrical and Electronics Engineers (IEEE). This standard has evolved over time with technological advances. As a result, there are a number of variations in use, as shown in **Figure 10-2.** It is important to understand the various security issues that exist with Wi-Fi networks. Steps must be taken to reduce these risks.

Setup

Wi-Fi typically runs in infrastructure-mode. In this mode, devices must send data to a central device before the data move on to their destination. Wi-Fi requires some specific hardware:

- *Access point (AP)* is a device that provides a central point of access to enable wireless devices to communicate with each other.
- *Wireless router* has the same capability of an access point, put also adds the functionality of wireless connection to local area networks (LANs) or wide area networks (WANs); a wireless router can be an access point, but a wireless access point cannot be a wireless router.
- *Wireless NIC* is the network interface card used to connect to the wireless network and may be integrated into a system board, such as tablets or laptops, or can be added into a system internally or through a USB wireless NIC.
- *Wireless client (STA),* or station, is the fixed or mobile device that has the ability to communicate as a client using the 802.11 standard.

Devices on a wireless network communicate through access points, as shown in **Figure 10-3.** Smaller networks may have only one AP. A *basic service set (BSS)* is a wireless network with a single access point. Larger networks have multiple APs to allow for continuous coverage over a wider area. An *extended service set (ESS)* is a wireless network with multiple APs. When a network has multiple APs, all APs have the same name. The name of a wireless network is known as its *service set identifier (SSID).* SSIDs are case sensitive. ACME_WiFi is not the same as ACME_WIFI.

Wireless devices, such as printers, can be manually configured to attach to a wireless network. Doing so involves identifying network information and wireless options, such as the SSID. Another option provided by some manufacturers is the use of Wi-Fi–protected setup (WPS). With WPS, a user does not need to provide configuration information. Instead, he or she can set up the device using one of four methods:

- PIN method: the user enters the personal identification number (PIN) on the router that is located on the new device.
- Push method: the user pushes a button on the new device and the access point, and the two devices will discover each other.

IEEE Standard	Year Released	Radio Frequency	Approximate Speed
802.11a	1999	5 GHz	54 Mbps
802.11b	1999	2.4 GHz	11 Mbps
802.11g	2003	2.4 GHz	54 Mbps
802.11n	2009	2.4 GHz or 5 GHz	54–600 Mbps
802.11ac	2013	2.4 Ghz or 5 GHz	450–1300 Mbps

Goodheart-Willcox Publisher

Figure 10-2. The IEEE 802.11 standard has been updated several times over the years. This standard is the basis of Wi-Fi. The standards shown here are the ones that have been most commonly used in consumer products, but there are many more standards.

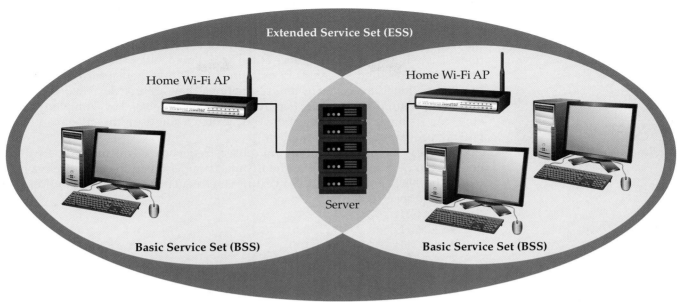

Figure 10-3. Access points are the interface between the client and the network in a wireless network.

- *Near-field communication (NFC)* allows devices to communicate through electromagnetic radio fields as opposed to the radio transmissions used by Wi-Fi; the user must bring the new device close to the access point.
- USB: the user employs a USB flash drive with data to copy information between devices; this is no longer supported on most new routers and access points.

So how does the client (STA) find the AP? Clients and access points can find each other using active or passive scanning. With an active scan, the client issues a probe request. It then listens for a probe response from the AP. With passive scanning, the client listens to the channel on which the AP is broadcasting. It waits for a beacon sent from the access point. A device that can only send signals is called a *transmitter*. An example of a transmitter is an FM radio station. The radios that pick up the signal and play music are called *receivers*. Since wireless devices, such as routers and network cards, need to send and receive, they are usually known as *transceivers*. This term is a combination of *transmitter* and *receiver*.

Interference

Wireless signals are impacted by many things. The surroundings can affect signals. The configuration power capability of the device can also affect signals. Nearby objects and antennae can interfere with signals.

Routers transmit power measured in two scales: milliwatt (mW) and decibel-milliwatt (dBm). Watt is a base unit of measurement for power. It is an absolute measurement. One milliwatt is 1/1000 of one watt. Decibel-milliwatt is a relative measurement. For example, one milliwatt is 0 dBm, and 100 milliwatts is 20 dBm. A low-cost wireless router usually produces around 20 dBm of power.

An antenna may be omnidirectional or unidirectional, as shown in **Figure 10-4.** *Omnidirectional* means it will send and receive in all directions.

Omnidirectional Antenna   **Unidirectional Antenna**

Figure 10-4. An omnidirectional antenna broadcasts in all directions, while a unidirectional antenna broadcasts in only one direction.

CompTIA Security+
2.1

Unidirectional means it will only send and receive from one specific direction. Since a unidirectional antenna is only transmitting in one direction, the power of the transmission will be greater than if the same device transmitted in all directions. There is also less interference at the access point since the receiver only has to listen and respond to signals in one direction. While there are strong benefits to unidirectional antennae, in many situations they are not flexible enough for setting up communication between transmitter and receiver. For example, if there are receivers on opposite sides of the transmitter, a single unidirectional antenna will not provide coverage for both.

Wireless signals transmit on unlicensed frequencies. This means there does not need to be a specific slice of the RF spectrum assigned to each wireless network. The 802.11 workgroup uses five different frequency ranges in the unlicensed areas of the spectrum:

- 2.4 GHz
- 3.6 GHz
- 4.9 GHz
- 5.0 GHz
- 5.9 GHz

With the 802.11n standard, manufacturers began offering wireless access points and routers transmitting on the 2.4 GHz and 5 GHz frequency bands. These devices are known as *dual-band routers*. These devices can be configured to run both frequencies simultaneously. This is an ideal setup for separating data transmissions. For example, normal computer traffic and phones could travel on the 2.4 GHz band. More data-intensive transmissions, such as gaming or video streaming, could be handled more efficiently on the 5 GHz band.

Each of the RF bands is subdivided into slices called *channels.* A device can be set to use a specific channel within each frequency. An issue to consider is the possibility of interference from an overlapping channel. For example, in the 2.4 GHz band, there are 11 possible channels. Channels 1, 6, and 11 are the only channels that do not overlap. A specific problem with the 2.4 GHz channels is many devices operate on this frequency. Examples include cordless telephones, microwave ovens, Bluetooth devices, and even some car alarms. These devices can affect wireless transmissions.

The 5 GHz band has more channels than the 2.4 GHz band. There are 23 channels that do not overlap. This reduces the possibility of using overlapping channels. It also reduces interference from nearby channels. However, the 5 GHz channel is used in the United States by the military and many weather apps. Because of this, the FCC requires any device using the 5.250 to 5.350, 5.470, and 5.725 frequencies to have a feature called DFS. *Dynamic frequency selection (DFS)* detects interference with military and weather radar and automatically shifts the frequency being used by the wireless device. This is needed to ensure critical radar applications are not disrupted.

After the Sept. 11, 2001 terrorist attacks, it was discovered that first responders were not able to communicate due to equipment operating on different frequencies. The military began to use the 5 GHz band, which it had reserved for new safety initiatives. This resulted in disruptions of wireless transmissions. One of the biggest disruptions occurred with garage door openers. Homeowners in Colorado, Virginia, and Maryland found their remotes no longer worked. It was because the military had started transmitting on the bands used by the remotes.

Quick Look 10.1.2

RF Spectrum

In the United States, the RF spectrum is managed by the Federal Communications Commission (FCC). The spectrum can be viewed on its website. Note: the web page used in this activity requires Flash to be enabled. If you cannot enable Flash or it is blocked, skip this activity.

1. Launch a web browser, and navigate to the spectrum dashboard on the FCC website (www.fcc.gov/spectrumdashboard).
2. Click the **Browse Spectrum Bands** link.
3. Scroll on the spectrum to the 2450–2483.5 band, as shown. What are the services used in this band?

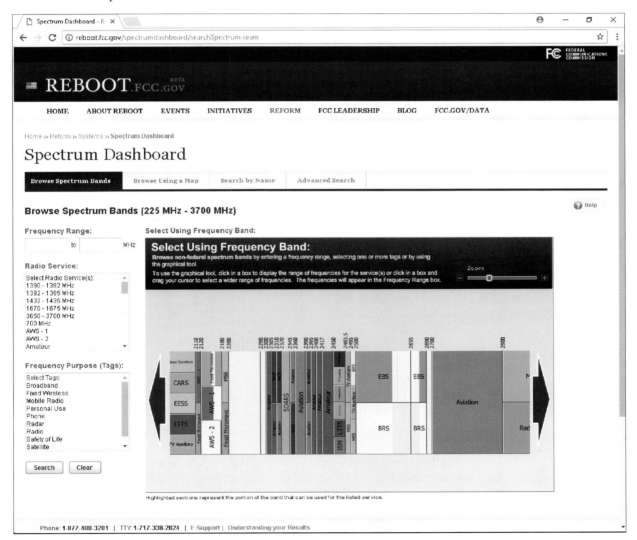

4. On the left side of the page, click **Personal Use** in the **Frequency Purpose (Tags):** area, and then click the **Search** button. Explore the frequencies that are allocated for personal use. What are some of the uses?
5. Click the **Browse Using a Map** button near the top of the page. Locate your county. Note some of the frequencies that are licensed in your area.

CompTIA Security+
2.5

Cellular Wireless Basics

A *cellular network* is a type of wireless network in which transmissions are distributed over groups of geographic areas. While it is a wireless network, the way transmissions are handled differs from a Wi-Fi connection in many ways. A cellular network transmits data from multiple transmitters called base stations. Each base station is given a portion of the overall bandwidth. The coverage provided by the base station is known as a *cell.* **Figure 10-5** shows how cells are arranged to form coverage. When a mobile user moves out of one cell, the base station performs a handoff to the next cell.

Terms such as 4G and LTE are often used when talking about cellular networks. The G stands for *generation.* The specifications are provided by the International Telecommunication Union (ITU). The original Internet connection was 2G. Most users today have a 3G or 4G connection. The 4G standard requires providers to offer certain speeds. Long-Term Evolution (LTE) is the path used to provide 4G speeds. The top wireless providers have standardized on 4G as their communication standard. Testing of the 5G network is ongoing and is expected to be deployed beginning in 2020.

Another way in which cellular networks differ from Wi-Fi networks is in the RF spectrum. Cellular networks operate in licensed areas of the spectrum. Within a given market, mobile carriers cannot transmit or receive data using the same frequencies. Mobile devices can transmit a great deal of data. This means a large spectrum of RF frequencies is desired. With many competing needs, including satellite transmissions, managing the spectrum can be a difficult process. The FCC is tasked with trying to free up additional spectrum. The FCC offers incentives for television broadcasters to use less of the spectrum. It also returns unused spectrum from other governmental agencies.

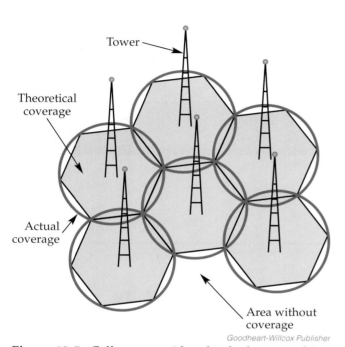

Tower

Theoretical coverage

Actual coverage

Area without coverage

Goodheart-Willcox Publisher

Figure 10-5. Cells are considered to be hexagonal in shape, but in practice each cell is circular.

CompTIA Security+
2.5

Additional Wireless Communication Methods

There are other wireless modes of transmission in addition to radio frequency, cellular, and near-field communication. One of these is SATCOM. *Satellite communication (SATCOM)* is a space-based wireless network in which an orbital satellite provides the connection to the host. It is used for many purposes. Television transmissions, weather data, banking transactions, and even credit card payments may use SATCOM. Satellite services can cover the entire globe using multiple frequencies.

Space-based communication is governed by the International Telecommunication Union (ITU). The ITU assigns radio frequencies to licensed operators and countries. Some of the more popular and heavily used frequencies include the C, L, and Ku bands. Within these bands, there are frequencies allocated for different purposes.

Another wireless communication method is called ANT. *ANT* is a personal area technology similar to Bluetooth that allows devices to communicate with each other wirelessly over short distances. It is designed for low-bit, low-power transmissions of small packets. It is similar to the low-energy version of Bluetooth, but differs from Bluetooth in that it is proprietary. Bluetooth also can handle larger packets. It is owned and managed by ANT Wireless. ANT is ideal for use with sensors. It is used in many products in the sports, fitness, and health-care sectors. For example, the popular Fitbit device uses ANT 2.4 GHz for communication.

SECTION REVIEW 10.1

Check Your Understanding

1. A _____ is a device that allows connections to a wireless network and can send data to another network.
2. What is an SSID?
3. Which channels do not overlap in a 2.4 GHz wireless network?
4. Which governmental agency manages the radio spectrum?
5. What is the coverage area of a base station in a cellular network called?

Build Your Key Terms Vocabulary

As you progress through this course, develop a personal cybersecurity glossary. This will help you build your vocabulary and prepare you for a career. Write a definition for each of the following terms, and add it to your cybersecurity glossary.

access point (AP)	near-field communication (NFC)
ANT	satellite communication (SATCOM)
basic service set (BSS)	service set identifier (SSID)
cell	Wi-Fi
cellular network	wireless client (STA)
dynamic frequency selection (DFS)	wireless NIC
extended service set (ESS)	wireless router

Section
10.2

Wireless Vulnerabilities

Essential Question

How has wireless technology contributed to security issues facing users and businesses?

Wireless networking is reshaping computing choices and access. As its use expands, it is increasingly more exposed and targeted. There are inherent risks that exist in wireless networks and their configurations. A transmission on a wireless network does not follow a set path to and from the destination. Except in a highly secured facility, there is no way to protect the radio signals from interception. Wireless networks are relatively easy to set up and deploy, which is why they seem to be everywhere. This makes them targets for hackers. This section explores vulnerabilities and practices that increase a network's vulnerability.

Key Terms 🔗

attenuation
cantenna
data leakage

dead spot
jamming
piggybacking

warchalking
wardriving
wireless site survey

Learning Goals

- Evaluate the placement of a wireless configuration.
- Discuss the legal and ethical issues of using someone else's wireless signal.
- Identify security vulnerabilities with wireless routers.
- List other peripheral devices that could present vulnerabilities to a wireless network.
- Describe the importance of data sniffing on wireless networks.

Wireless Configuration Placement

Using unlicensed areas of the RF spectrum allows for the easy setup and placement of wireless networks. However, this is an unregulated area of the spectrum. Other activity in the same area may affect the security of these wireless networks. Other issues that arise with RF deal with electromagnetic interference (EMI) and radio frequency interference (RFI). These types of interference could affect a signal's ability to reach the intended destination.

326

Any device that transmits an electromagnetic signal can interfere with RF signals. Cordless phones, microwave ovens, IoT devices, headsets, and even baby monitors can interfere with transmissions. When a client running 802.11 detects or hears another signal on its frequency, the client will pause transmission until the signal ceases. It does not matter if the interference is from a Wi-Fi device or other product. The resulting packet loss requires the devices to resend the transmission. This delays the transaction. The performance throughput of the wireless network will be impacted.

To mitigate interference problems, security professionals should conduct a wireless site survey. This is also known as an RF survey. A *wireless site survey* creates a map of the wireless signal, its strength, and its coverage, as shown in **Figure 10-6.** Once a site survey is complete, appropriate steps can be taken in regard to placement and configuration settings. As a security measure, site surveys should be done on a frequent basis. The area an access point serves is called a cell. *Attenuation* is the weakening of a signal over distance from the access point. One of the goals in setting up devices is to have overlapping cells. This allows a user to roam from cell to cell without signal attenuation or loss.

Another consideration is to identify any obstacles that will affect the signal's ability to reach its destination. Obstacles can be walls, furniture, doors, and windows. These obstacles can limit the ability of a user to reach the network. When a network is unreliable, users often search for other means of communication. They may make poor decisions that could affect the security of their transmissions. For example, they may connect to an unsecured public network.

A site survey that involves more than just identifying RF locations and strength of signals can provide a great deal of helpful information. This type of survey can also identify the types of equipment in use, approximate locations of the equipment, 802.11 standard used, vendor name, and MAC addresses. This site survey can help avoid channel duplication. It can also help identify suspicious wireless networks and devices.

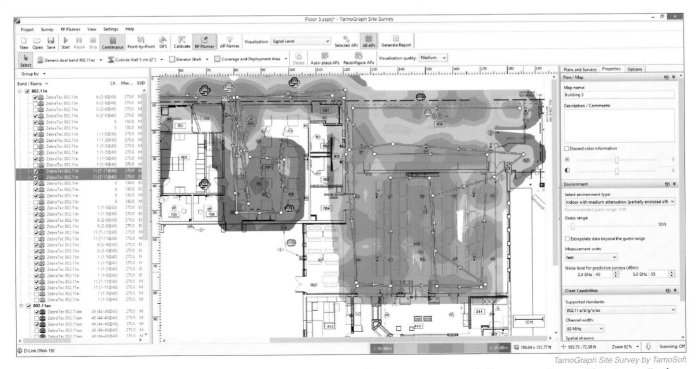

TamoGraph Site Survey by TamoSoft

Figure 10-6. TamoGraph Site Survey is a professional wireless site survey tool. It can produce a "heat map" of wireless coverage.

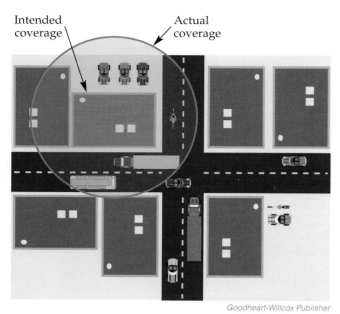

Intended coverage

Actual coverage

Goodheart-Willcox Publisher

Figure 10-7. Wireless signals usually extend beyond the intended area of coverage. This may allow hackers who are outside of the physically secured area access to the network.

A site survey will help identify dead spots for legitimate access. A *dead spot* is a place where there is no Wi-Fi coverage from a nearby cell. A site survey will also indicate the strength of the signal beyond the boundaries of the intended coverage. Wireless signals do not simply stop at the edge of the area the network is designed to cover. They usually extend well beyond, as shown in **Figure 10-7.** Wireless signals travel through the air, not on wires. Anyone in range of the RF signal could attempt to access the wireless network.

Consider the availability of wireless networks after hours. During this time, there is no security personnel on hand to assess potential threats. This can result in a specific vulnerability known as after-hours traffic or wardriving, which is discussed later. Note in **Figure 10-7** that the wireless signal for the building extends to a nearby parking lot and onto the adjacent streets. If individuals linger outside the building using mobile devices, they may be trying to hack into the network. Even if the wireless network appears to be secure, hackers could be trying to crack passwords or exploit known and unknown vulnerabilities.

The placement of access points can help to reduce the amount of coverage outside of the intended area. Use an RF survey to determine the range of access points. Then, locate access points to provide the best coverage with minimal extension outside the building. In addition, it is equally important to identify any access point operating on the property. Look for unauthorized devices that are located on or near the property.

Wardriving

Wardriving is the act of driving around trying to identify wireless networks. This includes the network names, the signal frequencies, and the security encryption used on the networks. Today, wardriving can be done by walking, driving, and even with drones!

The term *wardriving* was derived from the 1980s movie War Games where computers were used for "wardialing". Wardialing was the use of a modem to dial other modems looking for open connections. Peter Shipley, a computer consultant, coined the term wardriving when he created scripts to automate the process.

Warchalking is the act of publicly marking the locations where network connections are found. Symbols are used to alert others to the wireless network. The symbols indicate the type of connection, as shown in **Figure 10-8.**

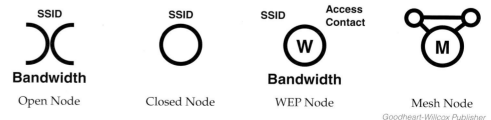

Goodheart-Willcox Publisher

Figure 10-8. These are the standard symbols used in warchalking to indicate wireless access.

Case Study

Wireless Laws and Regulations

The Communications Act of 1934 regulated interstate and foreign commerce in wire and radio communication. The act was amended by the Telecommunications Act of 1996. With the amendment, rules were included to cover Internet communication. The Internet was in its infancy at the time of the amendment. Look into the details of the Communications Act and the Telecommunications Act. Consider how these laws apply to wireless communication. Then research any state or local laws that also deal with wireless communication transmissions and interception of data. Prepare a written report of comparing and contrasting federal, state, and local laws. Follow your school's guidelines for formatting and cite your sources.

There are many tools available for locating networks and their settings. Some of the popular tools include NetStumbler, InSSIDer, and Wi-Fi Analyzer. Most of these are freeware or shareware programs. When using one of these tools, nearby networks are identified as you move around. Reported data include the network name, signal frequency and strength, and encryption.

One of the tricks hackers use to gain access to networks, or conduct wardriving analysis, is to use a high-powered antenna. This can allow the hacker to access the network without being visible to business personnel or the homeowner. A high-powered antenna can be purchased for under a hundred dollars. It can extend the reach of client. This allows a hacker to be physically farther away from the wireless network and less

Goodheart-Willcox Publisher

Figure 10-9. A cantenna is a homemade device for amplifying radio signals.

likely to be caught. A long-reach antenna can even be made with a simple metal can. This is called a cantenna. A *cantenna* is a homemade device used to amplify Wi-Fi signals. It is made out of an open-ended metal can, as shown in **Figure 10-9.** Inside the can is a segment of wire that is connected to a cable on the outside of the can. The cable is then connected to the computer's Wi-Fi card.

A serious problem is unauthorized access to a wireless network. *Piggybacking* is when a user gains access to a wireless network without permission. This is illegal. There are laws in all 50 states as well as federal laws covering unauthorized access to wireless networks. The state laws vary in specifics. Check the laws in your state to see what is covered and the penalties for violating the laws.

Another act that is illegal in the United States is the practice of jamming wireless signals. *Jamming* wireless signals is intentionally interfering with the signals to prevent the transmission from being usable. *Jammers* are RF transmitters that block or scramble other RF signals. The jammer cannot determine which signals are undesirable and which are welcome. It interferes with all signals. This could include Wi-Fi signals, cellular transmissions, and GPS communication. The Communications Act of 1934 amended by the Telecommunications Act of 1996 is the federal law that prohibits the marketing, sale, and use of a transmitter (i.e. jammer) designed to block, interfere, or jam wireless signals.

FYI

The term *cantenna* is a combination of the words *can* and *antenna*. There is an article on WikiHow describing how to make a cantenna.

CompTIA Security+
1.2

Quick Look 10.2.1

Wardriving Tools

Wardriving is not hard to do. There are many tools available that can be used for this activity. Many of these tools have legitimate applications.

1. Launch a web browser, and navigate to a search engine.
2. Enter the search phrase **Wi-Fi analyzers**, and investigate what types of software are available.
3. Enter the search phrase **spectrum analyzers**, and investigate what types of software are available.
4. Enter the search phrase **wardriving**, and investigate what types of software are available.
5. Compare the features of tools you found in the three searches.

Router Vulnerabilities

Routers are not immune to flaws. Even the best manufacturers create products that have vulnerabilities. Often, these vulnerabilities are only discovered after the routers are in use by customers. In 2013, Integrated Security Evaluators (ISE) of Baltimore analyzed some of the most popular off-the-shelf wireless routers. It found that 13 of them had issues that could be exploited by a hacker with just moderate skills. The president and principle security analyst of ISE is quoted as saying, "It's not a safe assumption to make that you are safe," regarding the purchase of well-known routers. The Common Vulnerabilities and Exposures website (www.cve.mitre.org) revealed 274 entries detailing vulnerabilities for wireless routers for 2017 alone.

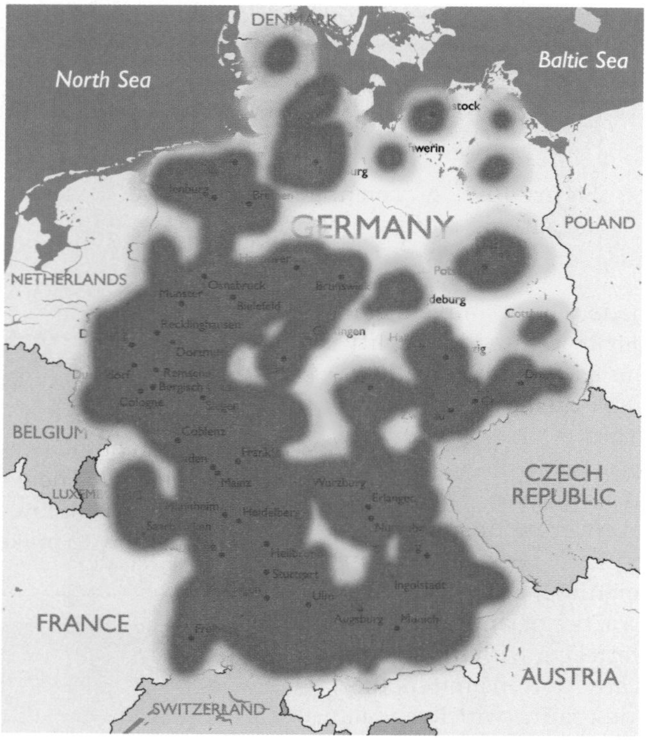

In 2015, the Sunnyvale, California, firm Proofpoint detected a month-long spam campaign that primarily targeted Brazilian Internet users. Users received a phishing e-mail claiming to be from Brazil's largest Internet service provider. The e-mail contained an alert of an unpaid bill. When users clicked a link in the e-mail, malware attempted to enter the router using default credentials.

Changing default SSID and password information are the two most important steps in securing a router. Another important defense against router vulnerabilities is to ensure the firmware is up to date. Also, change the security settings from the defaults. When possible, replace older routers with newer models. Older routers often work quite well. However, they no longer receive manufacturer support. This includes no more important security updates. In 2016, 900,000 routers in Germany fell victim to a cyberattack when routers were attacked through unpatched vulnerabilities. **Figure 10-10** shows a heat map of the attack's impact.

Goodheart-Willcox Publisher; vector art: lynx_v/Shutterstock.com

Figure 10-10. An attack on unpatched routers affected 900,000 routers in Germany.

Quick Look 10.2.2

Router Security Vulnerabilities

Routers are often overlooked in security planning. Many homeowners never change the security settings from the factory defaults. In businesses, routers may continue to be used after manufacturer support has ended.

1. Launch a web browser, and navigate to the Common Vulnerabilities and Exposures website (www.cve.mitre.org).

2. Locate the site's search function, and click it.

3. Enter the name of your router. If you do not know the name of your router, enter a common router name, such as Netgear.

4. Scroll through the list looking at the descriptions. The entry in the Name column contains a number code. The first number is the year the vulnerability was revealed. The second number is an index number assigned to the event. How many reports were returned for the router you entered?

5. Select one of the results to read full information about the reported issue. What is the specific vulnerability?

Other Peripheral Vulnerabilities

Other devices in addition to computers and laptops access wireless networks. These connections could pose vulnerabilities for the network. Many users have a wireless keyboard or mouse. These devices transmit actions using radio frequencies. Cameras, printers, and even microSD cards all have the capability of transmitting to the wireless network.

In 2016, the security firm Bastille discovered that millions of inexpensive wireless keyboards allowed hackers to inject keystrokes into computers from hundreds of yards away. In addition to injecting commands, hackers could read user keystrokes. The firm called the attack keysniffer. It demonstrated the ability to intercept communication between a keyboard and computer from a distance of 250 feet. This vulnerability affected keyboards from dozens of manufacturers, including well-known companies such as HP and Toshiba.

A keysniffer hack can be carried out with a small device that looks like a basic USB charging device, as shown in **Figure 10-11**. However, the internal circuitry can sniff keystrokes on nearby wireless keyboards. It gives the hacker the ability to steal information without touching the computer or injecting malware.

CompTIA Security+
3.3

studio2013/Shutterstock.com

Figure 10-11. A keysweeper can be made to look like a simple USB charger, which usually will not draw attention.

Data Sniffing on Wireless Networks

More and more network communication is done wirelessly. Wireless networks have no borders. As wireless use increases, the amount of data transferred increases. It is imperative that security administrators understand the type of data flowing on the network. The data must remain secure and unaltered. These are two of the principle security goals: confidentiality and integrity.

When data are intercepted and stolen, it is called *data leakage.* Network security administrators face an ethical decision. Should they use intrusion-detection or packet-sniffing software to detect potential security vulnerabilities? The decision to do so may trouble users. Their personal information can be read by company personnel. However, the benefits outweigh the privacy concerns. In short, if security administrators are not doing this, hackers may be. Because a wireless network has no physical boundaries, anyone with a laptop and the right tools could be analyzing the data on the network.

CompTIA Security+
2.2

There are many free or open-source tools for data sniffing. Examples of open-source tools include Wireshark, Ettercap, and Snort, as shown in **Figure 10-12.** For example, with Snort you could run scripts that look for data patterns. Credit card numbers would appear as a data pattern.

Even with networks that are set up with the strongest encryption, a hacker may insert a rogue access point that has no encryption. When a user unknowingly connects to this AP, requests will be transmitted in clear text. A number of scripts have been developed to find unencrypted access points and alert administrators. These work by looking for visible host names that normally would be encrypted in a secure environment.

IoT has also increased the need for oversight of security issues on wireless networks. Many IoT devices use wireless transmission as their means of communication. Ironically, some of the biggest vulnerabilities may exist in the products that are designed to help in home and business security, such as wireless cameras. Some of the notable hacks were on Foscam wireless cameras. Hackers were able to watch live feeds. They also used the systems to send inappropriate messages to the victims. Foscam is not the only vendor to have been hacked. A website based in Russia contained links to 73,011 unsecured cameras located in 256 countries. This problem is not just in homes. Restaurants, stores, and even a US military installation were on the list.

Goodheart-Willcox Publisher

Figure 10-12. Snort is an open-source program that can be used for data sniffing.

Another security concern related to IoT devices is related to the collected data. For example, there are many wireless devices in hospitals. Manufacturing and engineering sectors also collect data from IoT devices. The data may be personal or confidential. Intercepting the data could be a major security breach.

SECTION REVIEW 10.2

Check Your Understanding

1. What is a dead spot when discussing a wireless network?
2. Traveling around searching for Wi-Fi networks is called _____.
3. What is it called if you connect to Wi-Fi of a neighbor or nearby business?
4. What does the warchalking symbol)(mean?
5. List the two most important steps in securing a router.

Build Your Key Terms Vocabulary

As you progress through this course, develop a personal cybersecurity glossary. This will help you build your vocabulary and prepare you for a career. Write a definition for each of the following terms, and add it to your cybersecurity glossary.

attenuation	piggybacking
cantenna	warchalking
data leakage	wardriving
dead spot	wireless site survey
jamming	

Section 10.3

Wireless Access

Essential Question

Is somebody who intentionally leaves his or her Wi-Fi signal unprotected granting permission for anyone to use the signal?

Except in secure facilities where they are not allowed, deploying a wireless network is no longer optional for most businesses. The benefits of wireless networks are enormous, from increased revenue and productivity to meeting the needs of staff and customers alike. Wireless networks have become commonplace in businesses. Internet of Things (IoT) devices have spurred further growth. As the usage of wireless technology increases, wireless networks will begin to surpass wired networks in terms of usage and availability.

Key Terms

authenticator
black listing
Bluejacking
Bluesnarfing
captive portal
censorship

disassociation
enterprise Wi-Fi
evil twin router
initialization vector (IV)
MAC address filtering
man-in-the-middle (MITM) attack

replay attack
rogue router
supplicant
white listing
Wired Equivalent Privacy (WEP)
WPA handshake

Learning Goals

- List the three basic encryption choices for protecting data on a wireless network.
- Explain MAC address filtering.
- Sketch an evil twin router attack.
- Compare the function of various captive portals.
- Identify security threats to data transfer that uses Bluetooth technology.
- Diagram the process for authenticating users under the IEEE 802.1X standard.
- Summarize recommendations for wireless security.

Configuring a Wireless Access Point

A wireless access point is shown on the ceiling in **Figure 10-13.** Wireless access points should be located to provide seamless coverage. Another important aspect of wireless access points is the configure settings. Too often, users simply click through the setup wizard and accept default settings with little thought to the questions being asked. Even when users change settings, they may not choose appropriate options or be aware of other features that may be available during configuration. The first step in securing a wireless network is the configuration settings.

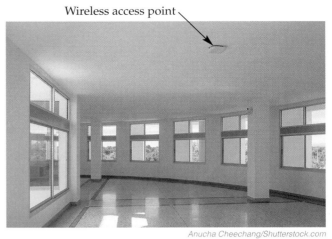

Wireless access point

Anucha Cheechang/Shutterstock.com

Figure 10-13. A wireless access point allows connection to a wireless network.

Default Settings

When a router ships to the consumer, it has a default network name and administrator password. The default network name is called a *service set identifier (SSID).* A potential security issue revolves around these simple settings. The default settings are not unique or confidential. A quick search on the Internet can easily find default settings.

When setting up a router, be sure to change the default settings. Always use a strong password. Failing to change the default settings is a vulnerability. Hackers can quickly and easily gain access to the network.

A homeowner in Buffalo, NY, found out the hard way the perils of not changing the default password on his router. FBI agents with assault weapons raided his home looking for the child pornography images downloaded on his network the night before. After further investigation, the man's neighbor was charged with the crime. He allegedly used the man's Wi-Fi signal to download the illegal images.

Encryption

In a wireless network, there is no set physical path or ability to protect the medium. In this type of network, it is all about protecting the data. Ideally, a wireless network should be set up with the highest level of encryption possible. However, as with every decision, the security administrator must balance the needs of the business against protection of the network. There are three basic choices when it comes to protecting data on a wireless network:
- Leave the network unencrypted.
- Offer minimal protection.
- Set the standards at the highest possible standard.

Unencrypted

An unencrypted network offers no protection at all. However, this may be needed due to a business need. For example, the business may provide open Wi-Fi for customer convenience. In this case, this wireless network must be isolated from the business network. Proper security policies must still be enacted for the wireless network. This may include limiting which websites can be accessed or the type of traffic. *Censorship* is the act of limiting access to information or removing information to prevent it from being seen. A business may not see limiting access to certain information as censorship. It may consider the practice a solid safety principle. There may be legal or ethical ramifications if care is not taken to limit what can be accessed on the network.

CompTIA Security+
2.3

Minimal Protection

An organization may choose to have protection on its wireless network that is not the strongest option available. This is often done to support legacy equipment that cannot use new protections. For example, an older laptop using the 802.11b standard may not be able to support the highest encryption available. However, minimal protection is often easily breakable. Another means that hackers can find their way into a wireless network is through a weak encryption scheme. A network with less than the strongest encryption is more vulnerable to hackers breaking the encryption key.

One of the tools used by hackers is Aircrack-ng, as shown in **Figure 10-14.** It is a versatile program that works on networks running the legacy 802.11a, 802.11b, or 802.11g standard. One of its features is the ability to monitor packets. This is done through packet captures. Another primary feature is the ability to crack passwords in the WPA handshake. The *WPA handshake* is a four-step authentication process used to pass information to and from the WAP and client to set up data encryption. Some of the information exchanged includes the MAC addresses of the devices installed. A security administrator should run this tool as part of setting up a wireless network. Doing so will reveal if a hacker would be able to use this tool to discover the password. Appropriate steps can be taken to harden the wireless networks and access points.

Strongest Encryption

Originally, routers configured to use encryption used WEP. *Wired Equivalent Privacy (WEP)* is a very outdated encryption protocol. It is used with older, legacy wireless equipment. Access points using WEP usually can have their keys cracked in minutes.

FYI

The easiest way to get the MAC address on a Windows computer is to use the **GETMAC** command at the command prompt. In Linux, use the **ifconfig** command.

- -

CompTIA Security+
6.3

MTA Security Fundamentals
1.4

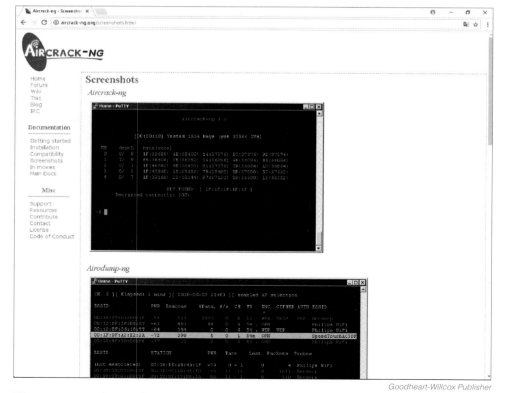

Goodheart-Willcox Publisher

Figure 10-14. Aircrack-ng is a versatile program that hackers can use to crack the password in the WPA handshake.

Ethical Issue

Personal Hotspots

Suppose you are the security administrator for a school. The school has a policy prohibiting the use of personal wireless networks and hotspots. It has come to your attention that a teacher is sharing her cellular plan with two or three other teachers. They are doing this so they can access web pages that are blocked by the school's content-filtering system. These websites contain information the teachers wish to share with their students to complete activities. How does this present a security issue for the school's network? How would you handle this problem to address the needs of the school and the teacher?

One of the concerns of using WEP is the same key (passphrase) is used to encrypt and decrypt data. If a passphrase is weak or could be guessed or discovered during a hacking attempt, the network and data could be accessed. A method to improve on this is to incorporate an initialization vector. An *initialization vector (IV)* adds random information to the key every time there is a transmission. However, this is still not foolproof. In an IV attack, an attacker learns the plain text of a packet. He or she can then compute the encryption key stream used by the IV. Once the key stream is found, any other packet using the same IV can be decrypted. There is a limit to the size of the IV, depending on the length of the WEP key. Therefore, it was possible for hackers to create tables of keys, which could be used to decrypt packets.

Encryption was improved with the introduction of WPA. Wi-Fi Protected Access (WPA) is a protocol that provides stronger encryption than WEP. However, within WPA, there are some insecure versions. Using WPA2 with a preshared key (PSK) is currently used for consumer and small-business wireless networks. PSK verifies users via a password or code. This code is commonly called a *passphrase*. What the client has configured must match the configuration on the access point. WPA encryption offers variations, including TKIP or AES, to generate an encryption key for transmitted data. While TKIP is available with WPA2, it is not secure by current standards. AES is the best option and currently the highest standard of encryption available.

MAC Address Filtering

CompTIA Security+
2.1

MTA Security Fundamentals
1.4

A network open to the public is known as a *public hotspot*. If the network is not a public hotspot, the way to protect against unapproved devices is to use MAC address filtering. MAC addresses are physical addresses embedded into the hardware of network cards. When using the **GETMAC** command at the command prompt, this information will be displayed in the Physical Address column, as shown in **Figure 10-15**. *MAC address filtering* is limiting which MAC addresses are allowed to access the network.

MAC Address Format

All MAC addresses follow the format outlined by the IEEE. A MAC address is composed of a 12-digit hexadecimal number. MAC addresses are usually expressed in the format of two numbers (an octet) separated by either a hyphen or dash (-) or a colon (:). MAC addresses consist of six octets. The first three octets represent the manufacturer. This is called the organizationally unique identifier (OUI). The second three octets represent a unique address within that vendor's identifier. Look at this example:

Organizationally Unique Identifier (OUI)   **Network Specific Device ID**
B4-B5-2F   72-FD-B4

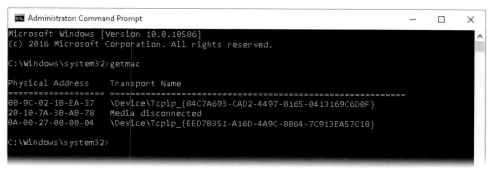

Figure 10-15. A MAC address is physically encoded into the network interface card. It can be reported with the **GETMAC** command.

Quick Look 10.3.1

MAC Addresses

The first three octets of a MAC address indicate the hardware manufacturer. If you have this information, you can use a website to find the name of the manufacturer.

1. Launch the Windows Command Prompt, and enter the **GETMAC** command to find the MAC address on local machine. Note the first three octets.
2. Launch a web browser, and navigate to the What's My IP website (www.whatsmyip.org).
3. Locate the **MAC Address Lookup** menu entry, and click it.
4. In the text box, enter the MAC address of your local machine, as shown. You can enter just the OUI instead of the full address.

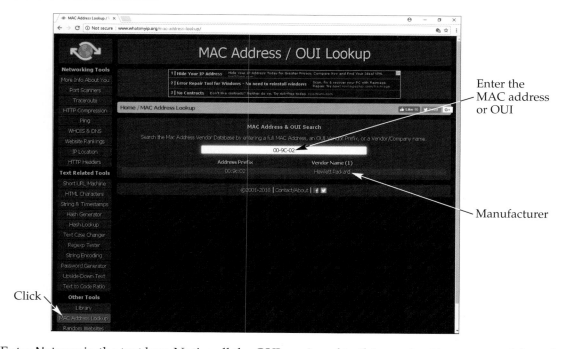

5. Enter Netgear in the text box. Notice all the OUIs assigned to this vendor. You can search by other vendors as well, such as Dell or Intel.

Filtering by MAC Address

MAC filtering is commonly referred to as black listing or white listing. With *black listing,* the MAC addresses you do *not* want connecting to the network are filtered out. Any address on the black list is blocked from accessing the network. White listing is more work, but offers more security. With *white listing,* the MAC addresses you *want* connecting to the network are filtered in. All other addresses are filtered out and blocked. If the address of a device, such as a phone or laptop, is not on the white list, access is not granted. White listing limits the flexibility of someone wanting to use multiple devices. Each device must be registered with the systems administrator to be placed on the white list.

Do not count on MAC filtering to keep out a determined hacker. MAC addresses can be spoofed or faked. This may allow the hacker access through the MAC filter. There are many tools to spoof MAC addresses, including utilities such as Nmap and SMAC, as shown in **Figure 10-16.** In addition, Windows stores MAC addresses in the registry. With the proper permissions, addresses can easily be changed here as well.

User Access Security

Users on a wireless network can potentially experience security issues. In many cases, they are unaware of a hack against them or their data. A serious concern is if the user's attempt to connect to a specific wireless network is intercepted. The data may be redirected to a fake network setup nearby. A hacker may also jump in for an MITM attack. A *man-in-the-middle (MITM) attack* occurs when a hacker intercepts the data transmitted between the client and the WAP.

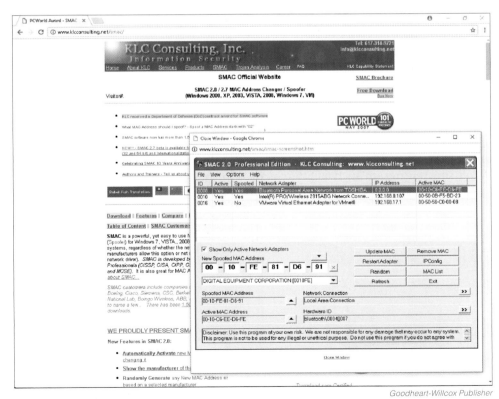

Goodheart-Willcox Publisher

Figure 10-16. SMAC from KLC Consulting is a popular program for spoofing MAC addresses. There is an evaluation version that can be downloaded for free, and several license options for purchasing the software.

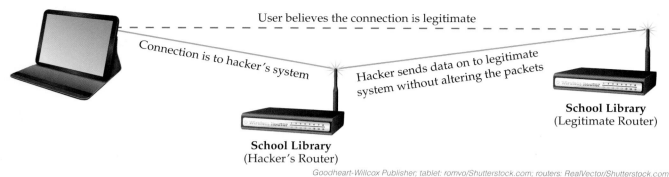

Goodheart-Willcox Publisher; tablet: romvo/Shutterstock.com; routers: RealVector/Shutterstock.com

Figure 10-17. A man-in-the-middle (MITM) attack occurs when a hacker intercepts the data transmitted between two legitimate users. The user thinks the connection is to the legitimate router, but it is to the hacker's router. The hacker can obtain information from the packets the user send, but he or she does not alter the data. The packets are then sent to the legitimate router unaltered, so there is no reason for either legitimate user to suspect a hack.

Figure 10-17 shows what happens during a man-in-the-middle attack. The user is unaware of the attack. The original data are captured, but sent on the legitimate router unaltered. The hacker can gather information such as passwords and user names. However, since the data are sent on unaltered, the user has no reason to suspect a hack.

One way a MITM attack occurs is the use of an evil twin router, as shown in **Figure 10-18.** An *evil twin router* is one that carries the same SSID as the legitimate server, but is in a different ESS. In this case, the rogue router is physically placed near the target. It provides a stronger signal, so the victim connects to evil twin. At this point, all traffic routes through this device. The hacker can intercept and discover all data sent to and from the target. The evil twin is considered a type of rogue router. A *rogue router* is a router that is placed in a business to entice users to connect to it and thus have their credentials stolen. Rogue routers are not just evil twins. Hackers can deploy networks with SSIDs that sound legitimate. One way to do this is to create an SSID that is the same as a legitimate one except for case (ACME_Network vs. ACME_NETWORK).

If the user is already connected to the legitimate router, there are hacking tools to send a disassociation signal. One such tool is aireplay-ng. A *disassociation* signal deactivates the user from the access point. The computer will generally automatically attempt to connect to the current network again. This time, the stronger signal from the evil twin connects the users back to the wireless network. A few clicks later, all traffic between the devices is intercepted. The hacker can capture data using a program such as Ettercap or Wireshark.

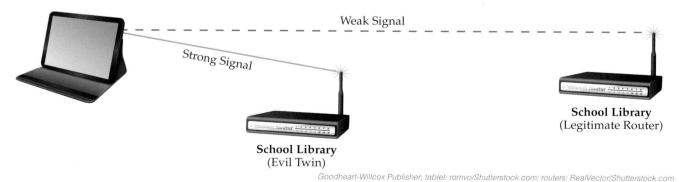

Goodheart-Willcox Publisher; tablet: romvo/Shutterstock.com; routers: RealVector/Shutterstock.com

Figure 10-18. An evil twin router has the same name as the legitimate router. As it provides a stronger signal, it will likely be the one to which the user connects.

Another variation of a MITM attack is a replay attack. A *replay attack* is a hacker capturing login credentials during an initial attack, storing them, and retransmitting them at another time. This may be later the same day or even another day. The hacker could even capture encrypted information and send it later without breaking the encryption on the credentials.

Many public businesses, such as restaurants, offer free Wi-Fi to customers, as shown in **Figure 10-19.** It may be difficult to detect a rogue router in these situations. Customers come and go all the time. A hacker may take advantage of this to hide a rogue router. The best defense when using an open wireless network is a virtual private network (VPN). The data will be protected regardless of the entry point onto the wireless network.

The login process is usually secured and encrypted. However, many websites fail to encrypt session cookies that are set after the user logs in. Firesheep and Faceniff are tools that can be used to exploit unencrypted session cookies. These tools listen in on wireless communication seeking session cookies. When a session cookie is detected, the victim's session can be seized by the hacker. Using a VPN can prevent this type of attack. Ensuring that the session remains encrypted, such as always using the HTTPS protocol, is another way to prevent this attack.

It is good practice for any business to perform a wireless site survey. This will identify all wireless routers broadcasting in or near the facility. Any unauthorized access point can be identified. Then, appropriate action can be taken. This task underscores the need for excellent documentation of the wireless networks, equipment, and their locations in the network.

Sorbis/Shutterstock.com

Figure 10-19. Many restaurants offer free Wi-Fi access points. Using public Wi-Fi presents security challenges.

Quick Look 10.3.2

Free Wi-Fi

It is not difficult to locate free Wi-Fi access. There are websites and apps that can be used to locate these open networks.

1. Launch a browser, navigate to a search engine, and enter the search phrase nearby free Wi-Fi.
2. Review the locations you found.
3. If you have access to Facebook on a smartphone, tap the hamburger button (three horizontal lines), scroll down, and tap **Find Wi-Fi**.
4. Using your phone's web browser, search for apps that can be installed to find Wi-Fi.
5. Discuss your findings with your classmates. Have you used any of these apps? How can you caution friends and families about the risks of using free or open Wi-Fi?

Captive Portals and Acceptable Use Policies

A *captive portal* is a web page that the user is forced to view before being granted further network access. If you have ever used Wi-Fi at a library or restaurant, you likely had to agree to an acceptable use policy before accessing web pages. Essentially, you were "held captive" and could not access the Internet until agreeing to terms. Typically, a captive portal allows the user to connect to the WAP. In order to do anything more, the user must open a browser and accept the terms of service.

There are commercial and open-source products available for creating captive portals. **Figure 10-20** shows an example of a captive portal created with the open-source Wifidog software. Sometimes captive portals are called *landing target pages*.

Landing Target Page

A landing target page provides several benefits to the organization providing the Internet access. The page can be used for marketing purposes. It also is an opportunity to educate users about acceptable use and terms of service access. A landing target page could be used to collect payment for the service. There is also some legal protection. If the user is forced to acknowledge an acceptable use policy, he or she cannot claim ignorance of the rules.

Acceptable Use Policies

As discussed in Chapter 5, an *acceptable use policy (AUP)* is a set of rules that explain what is and is not allowed on the network. Many employers display an AUP on a captive portal whenever an employee logs on to the network. Similarly, public Wi-Fi usually requires the user to acknowledge an AUP before using the service. An AUP may also be called an *acceptable use agreement*.

Bluetooth Security

Bluetooth devices are popular, especially as hands-free earphones, keyboards, and speakers. Bluetooth is a form of wireless networking. However, it is defined by a different standard (IEEE 802.15). Like Wi-Fi, it uses radio waves. The significant difference is that Bluetooth devices must be physically much closer to each

FYI

Bluetooth got its name from King Harald Bluetooth who earned fame for bringing different factions together, the same way Bluetooth devices can communicate!

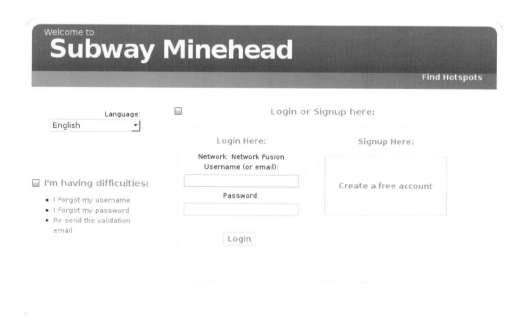

CC-GNU GPL

Figure 10-20. This is an example of a captive portal created with the open-source Wifidog software.

other to communicate. This technology also uses *ad-hoc networking*. This means the devices talk directly to each other instead of going through a router.

Bluetooth devices often can connect to each other with little to no security. However, there are levels of security you can establish to create "trusted devices." There are service-level security and device-level security, encryption options, and the use of PINs and passphrases. For example, the popular AirDrop feature on iPhones and iPads allows users to share images via Bluetooth. The user sets appropriate security levels to allow this sharing, as shown in **Figure 10-21.**

CompTIA Security+
1.2

Security concerns associated with Bluetooth can be minor. *Bluejacking* is when somebody sends you an unsolicited message via Bluetooth, such as an advertisement. You may have had a retailer do this to you as you walked pass the store in the local mall. Bluejacking is usually just annoying, not a serious threat. A more troubling attack is called Bluesnarfing. *Bluesnarfing* occurs when a hacker exploits the Bluetooth connection to steal data from a Bluetooth-enabled device. Hackers may be able to inject viruses and other malware into the device.

Bluetooth hacking is a real threat. There are steps that can be taken to protect the data and device:

- The easiest protection is turning off Bluetooth when it is not in use.
- The risk of data being intercepted or for hijacking is high in public, crowded areas, so the user must be extra vigilant.
- Use the security measures offered on the device, from authentication to encryption.

Enterprise Wi-Fi

Many businesses have a wireless network available. It is not convenient or safe to use the standard connection option of providing users with the passphrase for WLAN access. This information can be easily shared with others who should not be accessing the network. Also, as employees join and leave the company, the security of the passphrase becomes weaker.

CompTIA Security+
2.1

Businesses often use the IEEE 802.1X standard for authenticating users when connecting to the wireless network. The 802.1X standard is known as enterprise

Hadrian/Shutterstock.com

Figure 10-21. The AirDrop feature in the iOS allows users to share images via Bluetooth. Certain security settings are made to allow sharing.

Wi-Fi. With *enterprise Wi-Fi,* users do not need to be given a passphrase for wireless access. Instead, they are authenticated through their network login names and passwords. Recall from Chapter 3, authentication deals with the processing of approving access based on some type of identification. The Extensible Authentication Protocol (EAP), discussed in Chapter 9, was designed to require more than just a user name and password for authentication. With the 802.1X standard, EAP is incorporated into data frames and is used to provide this authentication. In this process, the access point takes the role of security guard. It passes the credentials and information between the client and the authenticating server.

MTA Security Fundamentals
2.1

Figure 10-22 outlines the steps taken for authentication. The computer trying to connect to the WLAN is called the *supplicant.* The *authenticator* is the access point. When the authenticator detects an active link from the supplicant, it sends an EAP request-identity packet to the supplicant. The supplicant replies with an EAP response-identity packet. This is accepted by the authenticator and sent to the server that is responsible for authentication. This server is usually running the Remote Authentication Dial-In User Service (RADIUS) protocol. The server sends a challenge to the authenticator, which then repackages it into EAP over LAN (EAPOL) and sends it to the supplicant. Finally, the supplicant responds to the challenge. If proper identification is provided, the server responds with "success," and the supplicant is allowed access to the network.

Recommendations

Security administrators may feel pressure from upper management to do things quickly. This is a reality in every business. The old adage is *time is money.* Despite this, security administrators must take care when creating, configuring, and securing wireless networks. Plans and policies should be developed with upper management. Wireless networks must meet the needs of the intended audience. Yet, they must be as secure as possible.

Best practices include implementing strong encryption and changing default settings such as names and passwords. In addition, administrators must consider options that may be unpopular or require high ethical standards. Some examples follow.

- Limit the availability of the wireless network to posted working hours only.
- Run scripts or other automated tools to discover potential unencrypted data or unauthorized access points.
- Use MAC filtering to prohibit access by unapproved devices or disable DHCP so devices must receive a static IP address for access.

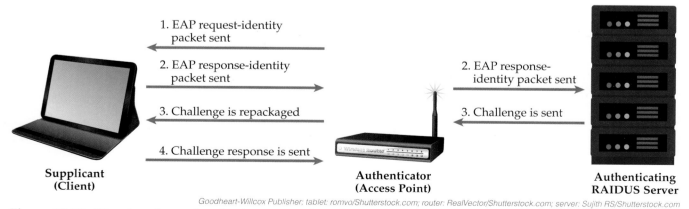

1. EAP request-identity packet sent

2. EAP response-identity packet sent

3. Challenge is repackaged

4. Challenge response is sent

2. EAP response-identity packet sent

3. Challenge is sent

Supplicant (Client)

Authenticator (Access Point)

Authenticating RAIDUS Server

Goodheart-Willcox Publisher; tablet: romvo/Shutterstock.com; router: RealVector/Shutterstock.com; server: Sujith RS/Shutterstock.com

Figure 10-22. The steps for authenticating users when the IEEE 802.1X standard is in place.

- Set up a captive portal with a security agreement and policy statement before allowing access to the wireless network.
- Require confidentiality agreements from security staff.
- Restrict the websites that can be accessed via wireless networks.
- Create strong policies that clearly state acceptable use for users and security staff.
- Require administrators on the wireless network to hold industry certification, such as Certified Wireless Security Professional (CWSP), and to keep it current.
- Have clear procedures for reporting lost or stolen equipment.
- Do not allow use of older devices that do not support the latest in encryption technologies.

SECTION REVIEW 10.3

Check Your Understanding

1. The strongest possible encryption standard is _____.
2. What are the first three sections of a MAC address called?
3. A hacker has placed a router in a business using the same SSID as the business's wireless access point. What type of attack is this?
4. What type of attack has occurred when unwanted text messages are received on your phone?
5. A configuration based on the IEEE 802.1X standard is known as which wireless concept?

Build Your Key Terms Vocabulary

As you progress through this course, develop a personal cybersecurity glossary. This will help you build your vocabulary and prepare you for a career. Write a definition for each of the following terms, and add it to your cybersecurity glossary.

authenticator	initialization vector (IV)
black listing	MAC address filtering
Bluejacking	man-in-the-middle (MITM) attack
Bluesnarfing	replay attack
captive portal	rogue router
censorship	supplicant
disassociation	white listing
enterprise Wi-Fi	Wired Equivalent Privacy (WEP)
evil twin router	WPA handshake

Review and Assessment

Chapter Summary

Section 10.1 Wireless Networking Overview

- Use of wireless technology is increasing in businesses, schools, homes, and everywhere and is projected to account for about 66 percent of IP traffic.
- Wi-Fi is a wireless networking technology that uses radio waves operating on the unlicensed bands of the RF spectrum.
- In a cellular network, transmissions are distributed by base stations over groups of geographic areas called cells.
- Two other methods of conducting wireless communication are SATCOM, which is space based, and ANT, which is similar to Bluetooth, but proprietary.

Section 10.2 Wireless Vulnerabilities

- Issues related to the placement of the wireless network may include interference from other devices, EMI, and RFI.
- Wardriving is traveling around looking for open wireless networks, and warchalking is marking these locations with symbols to indicate access.
- Routers often have security flaws, and not changing the default settings and failing to update firmware are common vulnerabilities.
- Data leakage occurs when data are intercepted and stolen, and packet-sniffing software can be used to detect points in the network that may be weak.

Section 10.3 Wireless Access

- When setting up a wireless access point, be sure to change the default user name and password, and use the strongest encryption that the application allows.
- MAC address filtering is a way to either blacklist (block) or whitelist (allow) certain addresses.
- Wireless networks are especially vulnerable to man-in-the-middle attacks, as well as deception from an evil twin router or other rogue access points.
- A captive portal forces the user to take some action, such as acknowledging an acceptable use policy, before gaining access to the network.
- Bluetooth is a form of wireless networking limited in range compared to Wi-Fi, and security concerns exist such as Bluejacking and Bluesnarfing.

- The standard authentication method of a passphrase is not secure for WLAN access, rather EAP based on the 802.1X standard should be used.
- There is always a balance between providing the most secure wireless network and the needs of the users, and a plan for providing security and access should be developed with upper management.

Check Your Cybersecurity IQ ➮

Now that you have completed this chapter, see what you have learned about cybersecurity by visiting the student companion website (www.g-wlearning.com) and taking the chapter posttest.

Review Questions ➮

For each question, select the answer that is the best response.

1. What is the STA in a wireless network?
   A. The network interface card.
   B. The standard on which the transmissions are based.
   C. The wireless client.
   D. The data packets sent using radio waves.

2. Which of the following would you see if there are any unauthorized devices on your network?
   A. Perform a wireless site survey.
   B. Analyze the network traffic.
   C. Put your Bluetooth device in discovery mode to determine other devices.
   D. Hide all known SSIDs, and search for those that are advertising names.

3. Wardriving is best described as:
   A. Intentionally disrupting wireless signals.
   B. Traveling around trying to identify wireless networks.
   C. Marking locations that have access to an open wireless network.
   D. Intercepting data communication between two users.

4. In addition to changing the SSID and password information, what is the best thing to do to secure a router?
   A. Add shielding to the router.
   B. Install a captive portal.
   C. Use MAC address filtering.
   D. Keep firmware up to date.

5. Which of the following is the weakest form of encryption and should never be used on a WLAN?
   A. WAP
   B. WEP
   C. WPA
   D. EFS

6. Why is MAC filtering not a true security measure?
   A. It is not possible to enter all MAC entries in the wireless router.
   B. MAC address can be spoofed, thus bypassing the configuration.
   C. It is only a temporary measure.
   D. It only applies to Windows and Linux devices, not iOS-based tablets or smartphones.

7. In a situation where two routers have the same SSID, but not the same ESS, the routers are said to be:
   A. Incompatible
   B. Evil twins
   C. BSS devices
   D. Poisoned

8. What benefit is provided by a captive portal from a security standpoint?
   A. It can be used to force a user to acknowledge an AUP.
   B. It can be used to collect payment.
   C. It can be used for marketing purposes.
   D. It can be used to post a company calendar.

9. Which represents an attack of unwanted messages and texts via an open Bluetooth connection?
   A. Bluejacking
   B. Bluetexting
   C. Bluemessaging
   D. Bluesnarfing

10. When using the IEEE 802.1X standard authentication, which of the following is the computer trying to connect to the wireless network?
    A. Authenticator
    B. WNIC
    C. AP
    D. Supplicant

Application and Extension of Knowledge

1. You are consulting with a small business owner. Her business is around 800 square feet and located in a busy strip mall with six other nearby businesses. She wants to offer free Wi-Fi to her customers while they are in her shop or sitting on the reading patio in front of her entrance. She expects anywhere from one to 50 customers in her shop at any given time. Create a business proposal that details what product you would recommend, including price and why you chose the product. Also, indicate what settings you would configure. Include elements such as SSID, passwords, DHCP settings, channel, and so on. Present this proposal to the class in a professional manner.

2. Perform a site survey of your home or, with permission, a relative's home. Map the wireless frequency strengths and the number of wireless networks available. Note the different frequencies and channels in use.

3. Consider applications for near-field communication. Investigate the types of attacks that have occurred or are possible with this technology. Create a slide show explaining near-field communication and your findings.

4. Design and create a poster that could be placed within a business to warn customers about the risks of using open Wi-Fi and best practices for using it safely.

5. You have been asked to present at a meeting of small business owners about the threats to wireless networks. Most of the owners do not maintain an IT staff and have set up wireless networks themselves or with the help of friends or family. Create a slide show to explain some of the threats to consider and best practices that the owners should consider.

Research Project
Wireless Certification

The use of wireless communication has increased dramatically over the past few years. This growth is expected to continue. As more wireless networks are created and more users opt for this service, there is a corresponding increase in the need for security personnel. Obtaining industry certification is one way to demonstrate you have the skills needed to be a security professional. The CWNP organization offers vendor-neutral certification for WLANs. It offers several different certifications for Wi-Fi. Visit the CWNP website (www.cwnp.com), and research the available wireless certifications.

Deliverables. Prepare a written report on wireless certification. Summarize the key objectives of each certification. Include the cost to be certified. Use the salary guide to project an income range for someone who holds each certification. Conclude the report with a paragraph outlining which certification you think you should obtain, if any, and why.

Online Activities

Complete the following activities, which will help you learn, practice, and expand your knowledge and skills.

Vocabulary. Practice vocabulary for this chapter using the e-flash cards, matching activity, and vocabulary game until you are able to recognize their meanings.

Communication Skills

College and Career Readiness

Reading. Reading for detail involves reading all words and phrases, considering their meanings, and determining how they combine with other elements to convey ideas. Using this approach, read the first section in this chapter. Consider the way the author uses the words in each paragraph. After you have finished, determine if you have obtained a grasp of the content by reading for detail.

Writing. To become career ready, it is important to learn how to communicate clearly and effectively by using reasoning. Write several paragraphs clearly communicating your opinion on the importance of wireless security. Consider your audience as you prepare the information.

Speaking. Many careers require individuals to be able to participate in and contribute to group discussions. Developing intrapersonal communication skills is one way to achieve career opportunities. As your instructor lectures on this chapter, participate in the group discussion. Contribute thoughtful comments when participation is invited.

Listening. Empathetic listening occurs when you attempt to put yourself in the speaker's place and understand how he or she feels. How can you demonstrate empathetic listening when a classmate is asking for your feedback or opinion on a situation they are sharing with you?

Portfolio Development

College and Career Readiness

Schoolwork. Academic information is important to include in a portfolio in order to show your accomplishments in school. Include items related to your schoolwork that support your portfolio objective. These items might be report cards, transcripts, or honor roll reports. Diplomas or certificates that show courses or programs you completed should also be included. Other information, such as relevant classes you have taken, can be included as a list.

1. Create a Microsoft Word document that lists notable classes you have taken and activities you have completed. Use the heading Schoolwork on the document along with your name.

2. Scan hardcopy documents related to your schoolwork, such as report cards, to serve as samples. Place each document in an appropriate folder.

3. Place the hardcopy documents in the container for future reference.

4. Update your spreadsheet.

CTSO Event Prep

Public Speaking. Public speaking is a competitive event you might enter with your Career and Technical Student Organization (CTSO). This event allows you to showcase your communication skills of speaking, organizing, and making an oral presentation. This is usually a timed event that you can prepare for prior to the competition. Review the specific guidelines and rules for this event for direction as to topics and props you will be allowed to use. To prepare for a public speaking event, complete the following activities.

1. Read the guidelines provided by your organization. Review the topics from which you may choose to make a speech.

2. Locate a rubric or scoring sheet for the event on your organization's website.

3. Confirm whether visual aids may be used in the presentation and the amount of setup time permitted.

4. Review the rules to confirm if questions will be asked or if you will need to defend a case or situation.

5. Make notes on index cards about important points to remember. Use these notes to study. You may also be able to use these notes during the event.

6. Practice the presentation. You should introduce yourself, review the topic that is being presented, defend the topic being presented, and conclude with a summary.

7. After the presentation is complete, ask for feedback from your instructor. You may consider also having a student audience listen and give feedback.

Chapter 11

Encryption and Cryptography

In 2018, 150 million users of MyFitnessPal from Under Armour had their account information hacked. The number of affected users makes this one of the biggest data breaches. Information that was exposed included user names, e-mail addresses, and passwords. This information exposed customers to potential identity theft. The passwords were hashed using encryption. Under Armour stated that most passwords were encrypted with bcrypt, which is very hard to crack. However, some of the passwords were encrypted with SHA-1. This is a very weak form of encryption that is easy to crack.

Private companies are not the only ones that fail to protect the data in their care. The US Office of Personnel Management fell victim to a hack in 2015 that stole data on more than 25 million former, current, and prospective employees. It is not just databases at risk. Data in transit must be secured. E-mail can and should be encrypted. Portable devices, phones, and wireless transactions all are vulnerable to data theft. Care must be taken to protect the data through encryption. This chapter looks at the different forms of encryption available for various resources. It also explores how to incorporate encryption techniques into security plans.

Chapter Preview

While studying, look for the activity icon for:
- Pretests and posttests
- Vocabulary terms with e-flash cards and matching activities
- Self-assessment

G-WLEARNING.com

Reading Prep

Before reading this chapter, skim the photos and their captions. As you read, determine how these concepts contribute to the ideas presented in the text.

**College
and Career
Readiness**

Check Your Cybersecurity IQ

Before you begin this chapter, see what you already know about cybersecurity by visiting the student companion website (www.g-wlearning.com) and taking the chapter pretest.

Certification Objectives

CompTIA Security+

1.2 Compare and contrast types of attacks.
2.6 Given a scenario, implement secure protocols.
6.1 Compare and contrast basic concepts of cryptography.
6.2 Explain cryptography algorithms and their basic characteristics.
6.4 Given a scenario, implement public key infrastructure.

Microsoft MTA Security Fundamentals

2.5 Understand encryption.

Encryption Overview

Essential Question

What are ethical implications related to hiding data in other objects such as image files?

Two fundamental objectives of cybersecurity are to keep data safe from unauthorized access (confidentiality) and ensure the data remain unchanged (integrity). Data may be vulnerable data at rest or in transit. Since it is not possible to isolate data from unauthorized access, the best protection is to obscure or encrypt the data. This way, the data can be freely stored or transmitted. Only those with the knowledge of translating the data will be able to interpret and convert the data back to a readable format. There are challenges working with encryption systems that must be addressed to ensure confidentiality and integrity.

Key Terms 🔗

Advanced Encryption Standard (AES)
asymmetric encryption
block cipher
Blowfish encryption
cipher
ciphertext
cryptanalysis
cryptogram
cryptology

Data Encryption Standard (DES)
hybrid encryption
IP Security (IPSEC)
key pair
microdot
mutual authentication
polyalphabetic substitution cipher
preshared key
private key

public key
RC4 (Rivest cipher 4) encryption
steganography
stream cipher
substitution cipher
symmetric encryption
transposition cipher
Triple DES (3DES) encryption
Twofish encryption
watermark

Learning Goals

- Differentiate transposition and substitution ciphers.
- Compare and contrast symmetric and asymmetric encryption.
- List types of attacks that are threats to encryption systems.

History of Encryption

The term *encryption* is derived from the Greek word *kryptos,* which means hidden or secret. Encryption is not new. As early as 70 BC, the Spartans used a device called a *scytale* to read a message on a leather or parchment strip that was wrapped around the device. The parchment sent on its own would look just like a bunch of random letters. Once the parchment was tightly wrapped around the *scytale,* the message would appear, as shown in **Figure 11-1.**

A major change in the way messages were coded was the development of ciphers. A *cipher* is a tool used to change normal or plain text into something that is unreadable and then back into readable text. The encoded text is called *ciphertext.* The message as a whole is called a *cryptogram.* There are many types of ciphers. Two common types are transposition and substitution.

A *transposition cipher* is one in which the words are rearranged within the text. For example, *poottrsasniin* is a transposition of the word *transposition.* Deciphering a transposition cipher does not need access to a key. Just use the thought process of rearranging the letters to form a logical word or phrase.

CompTIA Security+
6.2

In a *substitution cipher,* each letter represents a different letter. One of the most popular early substitution ciphers is the Caesar cipher, named for Julius Caesar. He used the cipher to protect military secrets. In the Caesar cipher, each letter is replaced with a letter a fixed number of places away in the alphabet. This is also known as a *monolithic cipher* because the substitution will be the same through the ciphertext. Caesar's initial cipher used a left shift of three, as shown in **Figure 11-2.** With this shift of three, the letter E, for example, will be substituted with a B anywhere in the ciphertext. To decode the message, a right shift of three is used. Try it! Convert the word cybersecurity using the Caesar cipher.

A type of substitution cipher called a polyalphabetic substitution cipher was first documented by Leon Battista Alberti around the year 1467. A *polyalphabetic substitution cipher* mixes a number of cipher alphabets in the cryptogram so each plain text letter is continuously changed. This was considered a very secure cipher and popularized by Blaise de Vigenère. Sometime in the 19th century, the cipher began to be called by his name. The Vigenère cipher uses a table of the alphabet written 26 times in 26 rows. In each row, the alphabet is shifted to the left by one, as shown in **Figure 11-3.** A keyword, or key, determines which row is used to encode a given letter in the message.

Goodheart-Willcox Publisher

Figure 11-1. A *scytale* was used by the ancient Spartans to hide messages. This can be considered an early form of encryption.

Plain Text

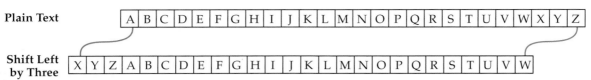

| A | B | C | D | E | F | G | H | I | J | K | L | M | N | O | P | Q | R | S | T | U | V | W | X | Y | Z |

Shift Left by Three

| X | Y | Z | A | B | C | D | E | F | G | H | I | J | K | L | M | N | O | P | Q | R | S | T | U | V | W |

Figure 11-2. The original Caesar cipher used a left shift of three. With this shift, A is always X, Z is always W, and so on.

A	B	C	D	E	F	G	H	I	J	K	L	M	N	O	P	Q	R	S	T	U	V	W	X	Y	Z
B	C	D	E	F	G	H	I	J	K	L	M	N	O	P	Q	R	S	T	U	V	W	X	Y	Z	A
C	D	E	F	G	H	I	J	K	L	M	N	O	P	Q	R	S	T	U	V	W	X	Y	Z	A	B
D	E	F	G	H	I	J	K	L	M	N	O	P	Q	R	S	T	U	V	W	X	Y	Z	A	B	C
E	F	G	H	I	J	K	L	M	N	O	P	Q	R	S	T	U	V	W	X	Y	Z	A	B	C	D
F	G	H	I	J	K	L	M	N	O	P	Q	R	S	T	U	V	W	X	Y	Z	A	B	C	D	E
G	H	I	J	K	L	M	N	O	P	Q	R	S	T	U	V	W	X	Y	Z	A	B	C	D	E	F
H	I	J	K	L	M	N	O	P	Q	R	S	T	U	V	W	X	Y	Z	A	B	C	D	E	F	G
I	J	K	L	M	N	O	P	Q	R	S	T	U	V	W	X	Y	Z	A	B	C	D	E	F	G	H
J	K	L	M	N	O	P	Q	R	S	T	U	V	W	X	Y	Z	A	B	C	D	E	F	G	H	I
K	L	M	N	O	P	Q	R	S	T	U	V	W	X	Y	Z	A	B	C	D	E	F	G	H	I	J
L	M	N	O	P	Q	R	S	T	U	V	W	X	Y	Z	A	B	C	D	E	F	G	H	I	J	K
M	N	O	P	Q	R	S	T	U	V	W	X	Y	Z	A	B	C	D	E	F	G	H	I	J	K	L
N	O	P	Q	R	S	T	U	V	W	X	Y	Z	A	B	C	D	E	F	G	H	I	J	K	L	M
O	P	Q	R	S	T	U	V	W	X	Y	Z	A	B	C	D	E	F	G	H	I	J	K	L	M	N
P	Q	R	S	T	U	V	W	X	Y	Z	A	B	C	D	E	F	G	H	I	J	K	L	M	N	O
Q	R	S	T	U	V	W	X	Y	Z	A	B	C	D	E	F	G	H	I	J	K	L	M	N	O	P
R	S	T	U	V	W	X	Y	Z	A	B	C	D	E	F	G	H	I	J	K	L	M	N	O	P	Q
S	T	U	V	W	X	Y	Z	A	B	C	D	E	F	G	H	I	J	K	L	M	N	O	P	Q	R
T	U	V	W	X	Y	Z	A	B	C	D	E	F	G	H	I	J	K	L	M	N	O	P	Q	R	S
U	V	W	X	Y	Z	A	B	C	D	E	F	G	H	I	J	K	L	M	N	O	P	Q	R	S	T
V	W	X	Y	Z	A	B	C	D	E	F	G	H	I	J	K	L	M	N	O	P	Q	R	S	T	U
W	X	Y	Z	A	B	C	D	E	F	G	H	I	J	K	L	M	N	O	P	Q	R	S	T	U	V
X	Y	Z	A	B	C	D	E	F	G	H	I	J	K	L	M	N	O	P	Q	R	S	T	U	V	W
Y	Z	A	B	C	D	E	F	G	H	I	J	K	L	M	N	O	P	Q	R	S	T	U	V	W	X
Z	A	B	C	D	E	F	G	H	I	J	K	L	M	N	O	P	Q	R	S	T	U	V	W	X	Y

Figure 11-3. The Vigenère square repeats the alphabet 26 times. In each row, the letters are shifted one place to the left. If the letter in the message is M, and the letter in the keyword is P, then the encoded letter is B.

A famous use of the polyalphabetic substitution cipher is the German Enigma machine, as shown in **Figure 11-4.** This machine looks like a form of a typewriter, but it was used strictly for coding and decoding messages in World War II. The operator would turn the rotors to specific settings. Then, the message was entered using the keyboard. The encoded or decoded message was displayed by the lights above the keyboard. Every month, German commanders would receive code-books detailing the month's rotor settings. The Allies were able to crack the code by constructing a machine to break Enigma's encryption process. Alan Turing, Gordon Welchman, and others developed the machine, which was called a *bombe*. Eventually, this machine was called a computer.

Figure 11-4. The Enigma machine used by Germany in World War II created cryptograms based on a polyalphabetic substitution cipher.

Quick Look 11.1.1

Vigenère Cipher

The Vigenère cipher is based on multiple substitution ciphers. A keyword is selected to determine how the message is encrypted and decrypted. Without the keyword, the cryptogram is very difficult to decode.

1. To encrypt a phrase, such as *meet at dawn*, the first step is to remove the spaces: meetatdawn.

2. A keyword needs to be selected that is shorter than the phrase. For this example, use the word *phones*.

3. Write the message. Underneath it, write the keyword. Repeat the keyword until you run out of letters in the message:
   meetatdawn
   phonesphon

4. Match the first letter in the message to the letter below it. This determines which row to use in the cipher matrix. For example, the letter M matches up with the letter P.

5. Using the matrix in **Figure 11-3,** move across the top row to the letter M. Then, move down in that column to the row that begins with the letter P (left-hand column). The letter in the cell at the intersection of the M column and the P row is the encoded letter. In this case, it is the letter B.

6. Repeat the process for the remaining letters. When done, the cryptogram should be: blsgelshka.

7. Decrypt this phrase: j jiiou laerfvs. The key is *beach*. Remember, the message uses the first row, and the key uses the first column. What did you get?

8. Challenge! Decrypt this phrase: b mzrd lxjiit wtar. The key is *hreat*, but it is encrypted with a transposition cipher. You must first decode the key, and then use it to decode the message.

CompTIA Security+
6.1

Cryptology Basics

The work Alan Turing and his fellow analysts did was in the field of cryptology. *Cryptology* is the study of ciphers and ciphertext. There are two distinct specialists in this field: cryptographers and cryptanalysts. A cryptographer develops strong solutions to keep data safe and protected. A cryptanalyst tries to discover the weaknesses and vulnerabilities in the solutions of the cryptographer. *Cryptanalysis* is the process used to discover vulnerabilities in ciphers. As uses of computerized technology increase and cyberthreats increase from nation states, hackers, and terrorists, both areas of cryptology are critical in providing both offensive and defensive responses.

In modern cryptography, a key is used to encrypt and decrypt data. Depending on the form of encryption, this could be the same key, or two different keys could be used. Generally, the longer the key, the more secure the cryptosystem.

Until recently, most encryption techniques were based on mathematical solutions. An emerging field is called quantum cryptology. In *quantum cryptology*, physics is used in place of mathematics as the basis for encryption. Photons are used to encode and transmit cryptograms. A photon is a tiny, massless particle of light. Fiber optic cables are required for transmissions. Encoding based on quantum cryptology is extremely hard to crack. Another benefit is it is impossible to hide eavesdropping on the connection. If somebody eavesdrops, the quantum state of the signal changes. This is due to the *no-cloning theorem* of quantum mechanics. Essentially, this theorem says that a quantum state cannot be copied.

There is a sense of urgency to the development and use of quantum cryptology. Computers in the future are projected to be based on quantum mechanics. These computers will have the capability to very easily discover and break the long keys used in today's mathematical encryption codes. There are already examples where quantum encryption has been used. In 2007, the Swiss government used quantum encryption to protect records in a trial run of voting in the Geneva district.

CompTIA Security+
6.2

MTA Security Fundamentals
2.5

Symmetric Encryption

Symmetric encryption uses a single key to encrypt and decrypt data. In order for this to work, each computer in the exchange must have the same secret key for that transaction. The key used in symmetric encryption is referred to as a *preshared key.*

Symmetric Algorithm Types

There are two types of algorithms used with symmetric encryption: block cipher and stream cipher. A *block cipher* encrypts chunks, or blocks, of data in a fixed size at one time. The fixed size is usually of 64 or 128 bits. This makes this algorithm fast and capable of processing large quantities of data at one time. A *stream cipher* encrypts each bit of data at one time. This method is best for data that are smaller than 64 bits in total. A stream cipher is often found as a hardware solution, such as in the chip of a credit card.

Symmetric Encryption Standards

In the United States, the first major symmetric encryption was DES. The *Data Encryption Standard (DES)* requires keys to be 56 bits in length. This bit depth offers 70 quadrillion possible combinations. Although that sounds like it would be difficult to find the key used, a brute-force attack could break this key. A brute force attack is an intensive attack that tries every possible combination against the key, as shown in **Figure 11-5.** Brute-force attacks are discussed in more detail later in this chapter. As computers became more powerful, it became easier to find keys created with DES.

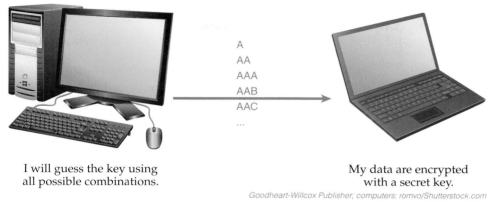

I will guess the key using
all possible combinations.

My data are encrypted
with a secret key.

Goodheart-Willcox Publisher; computers: romvo/Shutterstock.com

Figure 11-5. In a brute-force attack, the attacker tries every possible combination until the key is broken.

In 1998, the Electronic Frontier Foundation responded to a challenge from RSA Security to break the DES encryption. It created a machine nicknamed Deep Crack that was able to break a DES key in 56 hours. Deep Crack contained 1,856 custom chips. It cost around $250,000 to build. The DES encryption is not recommended for use anymore. It has been replaced with AES.

The *Advanced Encryption Standard (AES)* requires 128-, 192-, and 256-bit keys. AES is also known as Rijndael encryption. This name comes from the Rijndael cipher. The cipher was developed by two Belgian cryptographers, Vincent Rijmen and Joan Daemen. They submitted a proposal to the NIST for a new encryption standard. This is the one ultimately selected by NIST.

Today, the official US governmental standard for encryption is AES. However, depending on need, other symmetric encryption techniques may be used. Other forms of symmetric encryption include:

- triple DES (3DES);
- RC4;
- Blowfish; and
- Twofish.

Triple DES (3DES) encryption uses DES encryption, but in this version, the strength of the algorithm uses two or three keys. The encryption function is performed three times on the data. This is a block cipher, as are DES and AES.

The *RC4 (Rivest cipher 4) encryption* is a stream cipher characterized by a variable-size cipher and a random algorithm based on permutation. In mathematics, *permutation* means the order of the digits matters. For example, the combination for a lock is 123. It can only be entered in that order for the lock to be opened. RC4 encryption is named for Ron Rivest, of RSA security, who developed this encryption standard. It is sometimes referred to as the Rivest Cipher 4.

Blowfish encryption is a free symmetric encryption standard created by a security researcher named Bruce Schneier. It is a block cipher originally designed to replace the DES cipher. Only 64 blocks of data are encrypted at a time, which makes it a fast cipher. *Twofish encryption* is a block cipher that encrypts data in 128-bit blocks and is the successor to Blowfish. It was a finalist when NIST conducted a contest to replace the official DES standard.

Asymmetric Encryption

Asymmetric encryption uses two keys, a public key and a private key, to encrypt and decrypt data. The *public key* encrypts the data and can be located anywhere. It is not secret. The public key is used with an associated private key. The *private key* decrypts the data once they are received. This key is only known to the receiver and not shared in any way. The data cannot be decrypted without

FYI

NIST is the National Institute of Standards and Technology, an agency of the US Department of Commerce. Its stated mission is to foster innovation and industrial competitiveness. More information can be found on its website (www.nist.gov).

CompTIA Security+
6.2, 6.4
MTA Security Fundamentals
2.5

both keys. Since only the receiver has the private key, that is the only device able to decrypt the data.

For example, suppose a user is sending encrypted information, such as a password, to a server. When asymmetric encryption is used, the public key is obtained from the receiver (in this case, the server), as shown in **Figure 11-6.** The data are encrypted at the user's machine with that key and sent. The receiver then uses its private key to decrypt the data. The use of both public and private keys in this transaction is known as a *key pair.*

If anyone were to intercept the data, he or she would not be able to read the contents of the transmission. The private key is only found at the remote site. Knowing the public key does not mean the private key can be determined. The

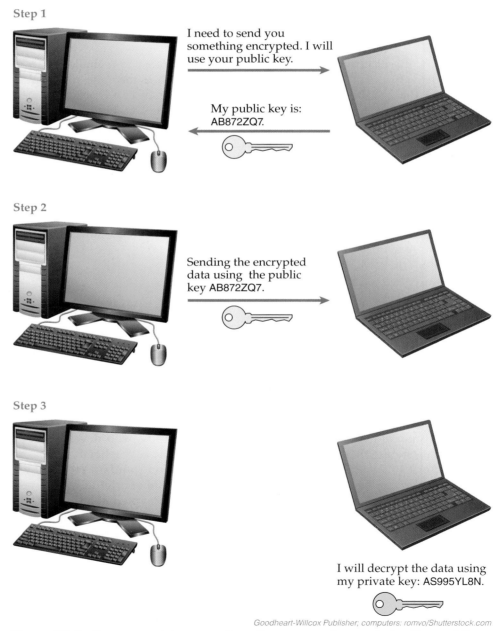

Step 1

I need to send you something encrypted. I will use your public key.

My public key is: AB872ZQ7.

Step 2

Sending the encrypted data using the public key AB872ZQ7.

Step 3

I will decrypt the data using my private key: AS995YL8N.

Goodheart-Willcox Publisher; computers: romvo/Shutterstock.com

Figure 11-6. In asymmetric encryption, the message is encoded with a public key that can be seen by anyone. However, the receiver's private key is needed to decrypt the message.

larger the value is for the private key, the harder it would be to figure out. If the private key is ever exposed or released, the key pair must be replaced.

Asymmetric encryption is used with such security protocols as SSL/TLS, SSH, the VPN transport protocols (PPTP, L2TP, SSTP), and IPSec. There are several asymmetric encryption methods in use:

- Diffie-Hellman
- Elliptical-curve cryptography (ECC)
- Rivest-Shamir-Adleman (RSA)

Diffie-Hellman was the first asymmetric encryption developed. It was created in 1976 by Whitfield Diffie and Martin Hellman. Elliptical-curve cryptography is based on numbers located on an elliptical curve. It was first described in the mid-1980s. By the early 2000s, it was in widespread use. Rivest-Shamir-Adleman (RSA) is based on factoring large numbers into their prime number values. This is a very popular algorithm. It is named after Ron Rivest, Adi Shamir, and Leonard Adleman. They first described the algorithm in 1978.

Hybrid Encryption

Hybrid encryption is a form of encryption that merges symmetric and asymmetric encryption. This takes benefits from both forms of encryption, giving it speed and security. This is commonly implemented in many public key encryptions.

Figure 11-7 shows an example of how it is performed. First, the sender requests the receiver's public key. Then, the sender encrypts the data using its private key *and* encrypts its private key with the receiver's public key. Both are sent to the receiver. The receiver first uses its own private key to decrypt the sender's private key. Then, the sender's private key is used to decrypt the data. This process is used to securely send the private key to a remote site. Once the receiver has this key, he or she can now safely communicate with the preshared symmetric key.

Steganography

CompTIA Security+
6.1

Steganography is the practice of hiding a file, text, image, or even a video inside another file. What makes steganography an interesting security practice over just encryption is that users do not know anything is different about a file. The larger the host file, the easier it is to hide something in it. This is what makes pictures an obvious choice.

Ethical Issue

Encryption Privacy

In December of 2015, two individuals committed a terrorist attack in San Bernardino, California. The FBI found the iPhone 5C from one of the terrorists that was locked with a four-digit code. The phone was set to delete all personal data after ten failed attempts to unlock it. During the investigation, the FBI asked Apple to create new software for their phones that would enable them to get into the devices if the courts issue a warrant. This sparked an outcry from technology users and people concerned about privacy. Law-enforcement officials argued for the need to extract critical information from the phones of criminals and terrorists. Consider the pros and cons of allowing law enforcement personnel the means to decrypt data on smartphones. Do you feel this should be legal or not? Be prepared to defend your position.

Step 1

I need to send you something encrypted. I will use your public key.

My public key is: AB872ZQ7.

Step 2

I will send you data encrypted with my private key. I will send you my private key encrypted with your public key:

AB872ZQ7   RT39WF6

Step 3

I will first decrypt your private key using my private key: S995YL8N.

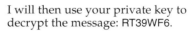

I will then use your private key to decrypt the message: RT39WF6.

Figure 11-7. In hybrid encryption, the sender's private key is used to encrypt the message and then is itself encrypted with the receiver's public key. The receiver must first decrypt the sender's private key, and then use that to decrypt the message.

There are several examples of where steganography can be used. Still images can be embedded into videos. They can only can be viewed by stepping through the video frame by frame. The human brain cannot recognize each still image when the video is played at normal speed. Messages can be hidden in photos by using the last two bits of color. This type of message can only be revealed by special tools. A *watermark* is image or text included in a file often used to prove ownership. Watermarks may be hidden or visible, although a visible watermark does not qualify as steganography. A visible watermark may provide special instruction to the user, like *do not copy*. A *microdot* is an image shrunk to roughly the size of a period. It appears harmless or sometimes not even noticed, yet it can contain much information. Microdots are a popular theme in many spy movies.

Some computer printers place microdots on their printouts without users knowing they are even there. You can see those dots with a blue light!

Quick Look 11.1.2

Steganography in Practice

It is quite easy to hide text in an image file. In this activity, you will visually compare two image files to see if a hidden message can be detected. Then, you will hide a message in an image file.

1. Download the image files provided on the student companion website (www.g-wlearning.com). There are two image files, one containing a hidden message.

2. Open each image file in an image viewer. Can you tell which one contains a hidden message? If so, how?

3. Launch a web browser, and navigate to the Steganography Online website (stylesuxx.github.io/steganography). Google Chrome is recommended for this activity. If this site is not available, search for online steganography tools, and select a website to use. Be aware, however, that you may not be able to decode the hidden message in the file from the student companion website.

4. Click the **Decode** tab on the web page. Then, click the **Browse...** button, navigate to your working folder, and open the Bison01.png image file. Once the image is displayed on the web page, click the **Decode** button. Is there a hidden message in this image? If so, what is it?

5. Applying what you have learned, try decoding the Bison01.png image file. Is there a hidden message in this image? If so, what is it?

6. Click the **Encode** tab on the web page. Then, click the **Browse...** button, and open the Bison01.png image file. You will add a hidden message to this image.

7. Click in the text box that contains the text Enter your message here. Enter This is a top-secret message for *your name* in the text box, and click the **Encode** button. The web page will display a binary representation of the message and two new images. The bottom image contains your hidden message.

8. Right-click on the bottom image, click **Save image as...** in the shortcut menu, and save the image as MyMessage.png in your working folder.

9. Applying what you have learned, use the website to decode the message in the MyMessage.png image file.

Threats Against Encryption Systems

A hacker's ultimate goal is to gain access to data. For encrypted data, the attacks are focused on methods to break the encryption or find a method to use the encrypted information as part of the attack. There are several types of attacks.

Types of Attacks

CompTIA Security+
1.2

As mentioned earlier, brute-force attacks are threats to encryption systems. There are other types of attacks targeted against cryptosystems as well:

- known plain-text attack
- chosen plain-text attack
- replay attack
- chosen ciphertext attack

In the case of a *known plain-text attack,* the attacker has seen the unencrypted plain text and the resulting ciphertext. From these, the attacker can attempt to crack the validation key, which is the cipher.

In a *chosen plain-text attack,* the attacker uses an unattended computer to send a specific plain-text message to the target. He or she captures the session and grabs the ciphertext. By carefully crafting the text message, the attacker can learn characteristics about the algorithm. At that point, the attack is the same as a known plain-text attack. He or she has the information to attempt cracking the validation key.

A *replay attack* occurs when the attacker attempts to retransmit the encryption keys. The attacker hopes to access the encrypted resource while it is decrypted. In this attack, the hacker is not trying to crack the encryption. Instead, he or she is trying to use it again in a transmission to obtain data.

In a *chosen ciphertext attack,* the attacker produces ciphertext. Then, he or she tries to decrypt the text to get the plain-text result.

IP Security

CompTIA Security+
6.1

FYI

What is IETF? The Internet Engineering Task Force (IETF) is an open community of researchers, manufacturers, and professionals who collaborate to ensure the Internet architecture runs smoothly and adapts to changes in technology.

When the IP suite was developed, security of the traffic was not considered necessary. When the need became clear, the IPSEC framework was developed to provide security. *IP Security (IPSEC)* uses cryptographic functions to provide data integrity and confidentiality for IP traffic. It is often used to protect data in transit. IPSEC was developed by the IETF. Specifically, IPSEC has four goals:

- confidentiality: data encryption
- integrity: data have not been changed or tampered with during transit
- data authentication: the sender is verified as who they say they are
- antireplay: ensures each packet is unique and there was no duplication or interception

IPSEC relies on negotiations from the sender to the receiver to establish mutual authentication and encryption keys. Together, senders and receivers are known as *peers. Mutual authentication* is when both peers agree that the other is who they claim to be. They prove their identities to each other before they can transmit data securely between the two hosts.

SECTION REVIEW 11.1

Check Your Understanding

1. Which method of encryption is based on physics principles?
2. How many keys are used with the Blowfish encryption?
3. Hiding text in a picture is known as _____.
4. Which type of encryption combines symmetric and asymmetric encryption?
5. An attack type that does not attempt to break encryption, rather reuse it, is called a(n) _____.

Build Your Key Terms Vocabulary

As you progress through this course, develop a personal cybersecurity glossary. This will help you build your vocabulary and prepare you for a career. Write a definition for each of the following terms, and add it to your cybersecurity glossary.

Advanced Encryption Standard (AES)	mutual authentication
asymmetric encryption	polyalphabetic substitution cipher
block cipher	preshared key
Blowfish encryption	private key
cipher	public key
ciphertext	RC4 (Rivest cipher 4) encryption
cryptanalysis	steganography
cryptogram	stream cipher
cryptology	substitution cipher
Data Encryption Standard (DES)	symmetric encryption
hybrid encryption	transposition cipher
IP Security (IPSEC)	Triple DES (3DES) encryption
key pair	Twofish encryption
microdot	watermark

Validating and Securing Network Transmission

Essential Question

What is the impact of public key infrastructure on digital (online) commerce?

One of the challenges in protecting data traveling over the Internet or any other computer network is ensuring the data will be safely transmitted. Consider logging into an online e-mail provider or online banking service. Have you ever wondered how data can be encrypted and read by the provider, but not by anyone else? Could you be giving your user ID and password to a hacker? Fortunately, there is a secure process used to exchange encrypted information and to ensure connection to a valid site. This process involves the use of digital certificates and security keys. Another important aspect of verifying validity of information is ensuring the information has not been altered from its original state.

Key Terms ➦

certificate authority (CA)
certificate chaining
certificate-signing request (CSR)
Certification Revocation List (CRL)
digital certificate
digital signature
distributed-trust model
hash-based message authentication code (HMAC)
hashing

hierarchical-trust model
key escrow
message digest
path validation
public key infrastructure (PKI)
Secure Sockets Layer (SSL) protocol
Transport Layer Security (TLS)
X.509

Learning Goals

- Describe uses for hashing.
- Diagram how digital certificates are used for authentication.

Hashing

CompTIA Security+
6.1

Hashing is a mathematical function that creates a value based on the data. It is a one-way process uniquely identifying data. Its intended use is to ensure data integrity. It does not ensure confidentiality. Hashing is *not* an encryption function. The value created by hashing is said to be a *hash.*

Uses of Hashing

FYI

Hashing requires *determinism:* for every input, the same value must be created.

An example use of hashing is to ensure that a file has not been tampered with from the original source, as shown in **Figure 11-8.** If the original hash value is known, it can be compared to the hash value computed after the file is downloaded. If both hashes match, the downloaded file is identical to the original. It has not been altered or become corrupted.

The hash value, or output, is called a *message digest.* The larger the digest, the more secure the hash. There are several hashing programs available and used today:

- Message Digest Version 5 (MD5) was developed by RSA and creates a 128-bit hash.
- Secure Hash Algorithm (SHA) was developed by the National Security Agency; SHA-1 produces a 160-bit hash; other variations include SHA-256 and SHA-512.
- RACE Integrity Primitives Evaluation Message Digest (RIPEMD) was developed by Cosic Research of the Catholic University of Leuven in Belgium; RIPEMD-160 produces a 160-bit hash.

Another type of hashing function to be aware of is called HMAC. *Hash-based message authentication code (HMAC)* adds an authentication function as well does creating a hash. HMAC provides the server and client with the same private key that is not used anywhere else. When data are transmitted, the key and message are hashed together and sent. Once the server receives the message, it generates its own HMAC. This HMAC should match the one sent by the client.

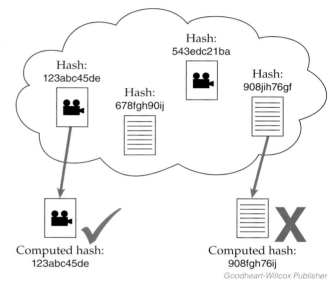

Goodheart-Willcox Publisher

Figure 11-8. Hashing can be used to verify the integrity of the file that is transferred. If the hash calculated on the transferred file matches the hash on the original file, the files are identical.

Quick Look 11.2.1

Hash Output

It is easy to generate hashes using Windows PowerShell. Hashes can be generated with the default algorithm or an algorithm can be specified. Additionally, there are websites that can be used to generate hashes. You need Windows 10 or an updated version of PowerShell in Windows 7 to complete this activity.

1. Create a file using a word processor. Type the following in exactly as written:
   I want a career in cybersecurity.
2. Save the file with the name career in your working folder, and then close the file.
3. Open PowerShell and navigate to your documents folder where you saved the career file.
4. Enter get-filehash career.docx. Be sure to enter the file extension that matches your file. What is the default algorithm used?

5. Compare your hash to a classmate's hash. Is the hash digest the same? If each person entered the text exactly as shown above, you all should have identical hash digests.
6. Enter get-filehash career.docx -algorithm sha1. Compare this digest to the previous one. This time, the command forced the SHA-1 algorithm to be used.
7. Enter get-filehash career.docx -algorithm md5. This forces the MD5 algorithm to be used, as shown. What do you notice about the three different hash digests?

8. Launch a web browser, and navigate to the OnlineMD5 website (www.onlinemd5.com).
9. Click the **Browse...** button on the page, navigate to your working folder, and select the career file.
10. Click the **MD5** radio button, and note the hash (file checksum) that is generated.
11. Repeat the process for SHA-1 and for SHA-256. Write down the SHA-256 hash digest.
12. Open the career document, add your name at the end of the file, and save the file.
13. Reload (refresh) the web page, then generate a new SHA-256 hash digest for the file. What happened?

Hashing Collisions

Hashing relies on the creation of unique, uncrackable hash digests. However, it is possible that a hash is not unique. A *collision* occurs when two different inputs produce the same message digest output. This collision can then be exploited by any application that compares two hashes. Both MD5 and SHA-1 have been found to generate collisions. Neither hashing algorithm is recommended for most applications.

Public Key Infrastructure

Consider the processes involved in the use of public keys. Think how complex this could be for your computer having to contact so many different hosts to get the public keys. *Public key infrastructure (PKI)* is a process in which communication from different entities can occur securely. It combines hardware, software, and trusted third parties to establish ownership and thus integrity of the public key. One of the concerns with getting a public key is how do you know the public key is from the authorized source? If Bob asked Alice for her public key, what confidence does he have that he in fact is using Alice's public key, not one that has been substituted during the exchange? This is where the concepts of digital signatures and digital certificates come into play.

Case Study

Hashing Concerns

The business Kelly Automotive has decided to set up its own CA and sign its own digital certificates since it does not have a lot of web authentication access. Its security administrator has selected MD5 as the hashing algorithm. You are contracted as a security consultant to oversee the security plan and know this algorithm is not recommended. You need to explain to the security administrator why MD5 is not a good choice.

1. How would you convince the administrator MD5 should not be used? Be sure to present your argument in a professional manner.
2. What would you recommend for a hashing algorithm? Support your choice with details.

Digital Signatures

When you get an e-mail from someone, you want to know it came from the person who appears to have sent it. Similarly, you want recipients of e-mail appearing to be from your address to know it actually came from your account. One way to make this happen is to use a digital signature.

A *digital signature* is a computed value used to validate the sender of a digital file, such as an e-mail. Digital signatures use encryption to create the signature. They may use private or public keys to ensure this validation.

Digital signatures can be used for much more than e-mail. They can be used for any file. The signature ensures *integrity* of the file. If a file is digitally signed, no one has tampered with the file from when it was sent to when it was received.

Quick Look 11.2.2

Digital Signature in Microsoft Word

A digital signature is a way to ensure the integrity of a file. It is easy to add a digital signature to a document created in Microsoft Office.

1. Launch Microsoft Word, and begin a new document.
2. Add some text to the document, such as your name, and save the document as D-Sig.docx in your working folder.
3. Click **File>Info** on the ribbon.
4. On the right-hand side of the backstage view, click the **Protect Document** button, and then click **Add a Digital Signature** in the drop-down menu. The **Sign** dialog box is displayed. Note: if you receive a message indicating you need to obtain a digital signature from Microsoft, click the **Yes** button to get one.
5. Click the **Commitment Type:** drop-down arrow, and click **Select Created this Document** in the drop-down list.
6. Click in the **Purpose for signing this document:** text box, and enter Validate the author.
7. Click the **Details...** button, add your information in the dialog box that appears, and click the **OK** button to save the information.
8. Click the **Sign** button in the **Sign** dialog box to complete the signature.
9. Click **File>Info** on the ribbon. Notice that the document is now protected.
10. Click the **View Signatures** button to see the signature you created.
11. Close Microsoft Word.

Digital Certificates

One way to manage public keys is to use organizations that will host the public keys for their customers. Anyone can host a public key. You can host the public key on your own web server or use another company to host your public key. Your web server will tell users where to find the public key. A digital certificate can be used to verify the authenticity of the key.

A *digital certificate* is a digital file used to verify that the public key belongs specifically to a person or entity (like an organization). This certificate is also verified by using a cryptographic function. By using a digitally signed certificate, you can be assured that the public key belongs only to the entity you want, and it has not been tampered. All public certificates must be in the same format so browsers of all types can read their contents. *X.509* is the format for public certificates to ensure consistent formatting.

There are a number of different file extensions associated with digital certificates. These extensions define or restrict the usage of the certificates for specific purposes. Some of the common extensions include PEM, which stands for privacy-enhanced electronic mail; CER; DER; and PFX.

A *certificate authority (CA)* is a trusted third-party source that issues digital certificates. The CA ensures certificates are valid. The CA is an important part of verifying security of the key. Think of it this way, you would not want a ride-share or taxi driver to tell you he or she created his or her own driver's license. Instead, you want to see a license issued by your state. The state is the trusted third party in this scenario.

A CA will perform an identity check to ensure that the person requesting a digital signature is in fact an authorized person of the organization that has requested the service. An organization wishing to apply for a digital certificate sends the CA a *certificate-signing request (CSR)* and includes its public key. Once an organization proves its identity to the CA, a digital certificate is issued in its name that is signed by the private key of the CA.

The purpose of using a digital certificate is to ensure trust or confidence in the information being received. A digital certificate given to Bob by Alice is a personal trust. Bob knows Alice personally and trusts the certificate she has given him. When you start going online, this is a difficult relationship to maintain. PKI uses various trust models to distribute digital signatures. The first is a hierarchical-trust model. In the *hierarchical-trust model,* there is just one master CA, which is known as the root. The root CA signs all digital certificates it issues, as shown in **Figure 11-9.**

In a company that issues its own certificates within the organization, having a single CA sign all the certificates can be acceptable. On a large-scale model, such as the Internet, this can be limiting. All requests for verification would have to go to just one CA. An alternative to the hierarchical model is a distributed-trust model. In the *distributed-trust model,* the workload of signing certificates is distributed among several intermediate CAs, as shown in **Figure 11-10.** The additional CAs are trusted and known as intermediate authorities. Any of the intermediate authorities can validate a signature because it was issued from the higher-level and trusted root CA.

In PKI, the private key stays with the original requesting company, such as your bank. However, in some circumstances, it may be necessary to allow a trusted third party to archive a copy of a private key. This process is known as *key escrow.* If the key is needed to decrypt data and the original holder is unable to do so, it can be retrieved from the key escrow.

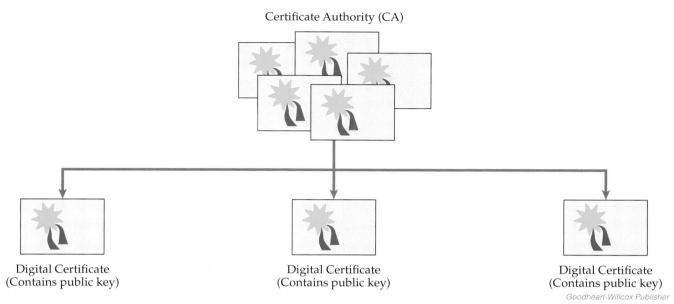

Figure 11-9. The hierarchical-trust model contains only one CA, which signs all digital certificates.

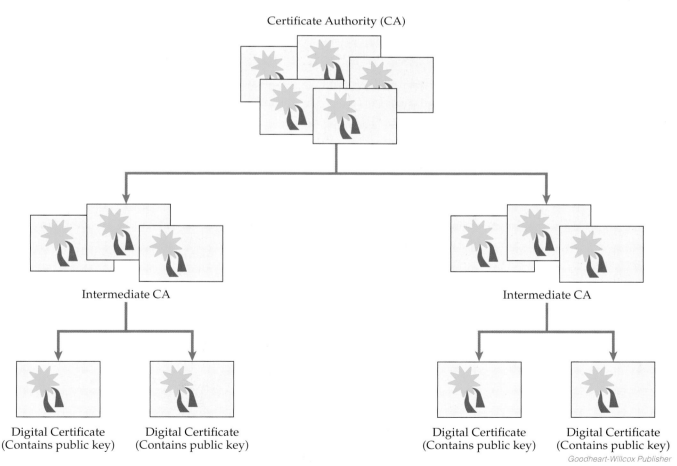

Figure 11-10. The distributed-trust model contains a root CA that allows trusted intermediate authorities to sign and issue digital certificates.

Quick Look 11.2.3

Certificate Authorities

Secure websites are critical to online retail businesses. To ensure customers know a site is secure, most retail websites display a seal or logo of the certificate authority that issued the digital certificate used on the site.

1. Launch a web browser, and navigate to a search engine.
2. Enter the search phrase online certificate authority. What are the names of some of the companies listed? Are there any free resources?
3. Navigate to the Thawte website (www.thawte.com). This is a CA. Notice the address bar in the browser shows the HTTPS protocol in use, and an icon such as a padlock is displayed to reinforce this.
4. Look for the option to buy an SSL certificate, and click the button.
5. How much does this company charge for an SSL certificate with extended validation (EV)?
6. Click the **SSL Web Server with EV** hyperlink (it may be the heading).
7. On the details page, select a two-year certificate. How much does a term of two years cost?
8. Scroll to the bottom of the page to preview how each type of browser will indicate a secure connection.
9. In the main menu of the website, locate the link for **Thawte Trusted Site Seal**, and click it.
10. Read the information on the detail page. How is the Thawte seal helpful for the users of a website displaying it?

CompTIA Security+
2.6

You may notice some secure sites display the HTTPS in green while other sites do not. This does not affect the security. It is merely a visual indicator. A company can purchase an extended validation certificate. One of the benefits of doing so is having additional address information appear in green!

Accessing Secure Data Through Browsers

When a client goes to a website where confidential or personal information must be entered, the site should encrypt the information. A popular secure transport protocol of the public key infrastructure is the SSL protocol. The *Secure Sockets Layer (SSL) protocol* was developed by Netscape to transmit sensitive information with encryption. Today, SSL is implemented as part of the enhanced security protocol of TLS. SSL alone is no longer considered secure and has been upgraded to a new security protocol and the name was changed to *Transport Layer Security (TLS).* TLS uses port 443 for encrypted traffic.

A user should make sure the TLS protocol is in use before entering confidential information. In a web browser, the address bar normally shows the HTTP protocol in use as http:// and the website address. When SSL/TLS is in use, the address bar shows https:// and the website address. The S indicates a secure connection. The browser should also display an icon in or near the address bar to indicate a secure connection, as shown in **Figure 11-11.**

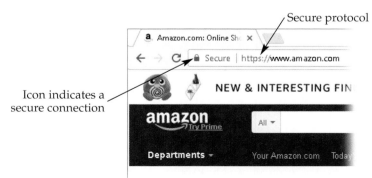

Secure protocol

Icon indicates a secure connection

Goodheart-Willcox Publisher

Figure 11-11. A web browser will display cues to indicate the connection is secure.

Quick Look 11.2.4

Web Page Security

When transmitting confidential information, it is critical to ensure the web page is using SSL/TLS and the certificate is valid. This can be verified from most browser's address bar. This activity uses Google Chrome, but the process for other browsers is similar.

1. Launch Chrome, and navigate to a website where security is important. Any site where a login is used, such as Amazon.com, should work.

2. Look at the browser's address bar. You should see https:// as part of the website's address. To the left of that, you should see the word secure and a closed lock.

3. Click the word Secure once. A dialog box is displayed, as shown. Under the certificate, it should indicate valid. Click the Valid link, and you are directed to the actual certificate used to validate this site. From there you can review details such as issuer, expiration, date, and more.

Click to view the certificate

Validating a Public Key

The web browser trusts a number of certificate authorities. These certificate authorities are called *root certificate stores*. The major root stores include Microsoft, Apple, Android, and Mozilla. The certificates that are trusted and placed in operating systems are decided by the individual certificate store. Although each operating system has its own requirements, all of them require that certificates pass an audited process for verifying identity. This process is called WebTrust for Certification Authorities.

Figure 11-12 outlines how a public key is verified. In this scenario, Trey wants to log in to his Amazon account to do some shopping. His web browser asks Amazon's web server for Amazon's public key so data can be encrypted. Before that can occur, his browser must trust that the certificate from Amazon, which contains the public key, is actually from Amazon. To provide this validation, Amazon's web server returns a certificate signed by a CA, which is itself signed by another certificate. This is known as certificate chaining. *Certificate chaining* is the linking of one certificate to another. This certificate should be present on Trey's computer. If the certificate is present in the local operating system, Trey's computer can trust the public key provided in the certificate from Amazon.

The certificate presented by Amazon that includes the public key contains information about the issuer of the certificate (the CA). The request is sent to the CA. Before the CA validates the key, it must make sure the certificate that Trey presented has not been revoked by Amazon. The CA will check a list called the CRL. The *Certification Revocation List (CRL)* contains all digital certificates that have been canceled. A certificate may be revoked if there was a security concern. For example, the private key held by Amazon may have been exposed. This would be reason to revoke the digital certificate. In Windows, *path validation* is the process of verifying a digital certificate has not been revoked.

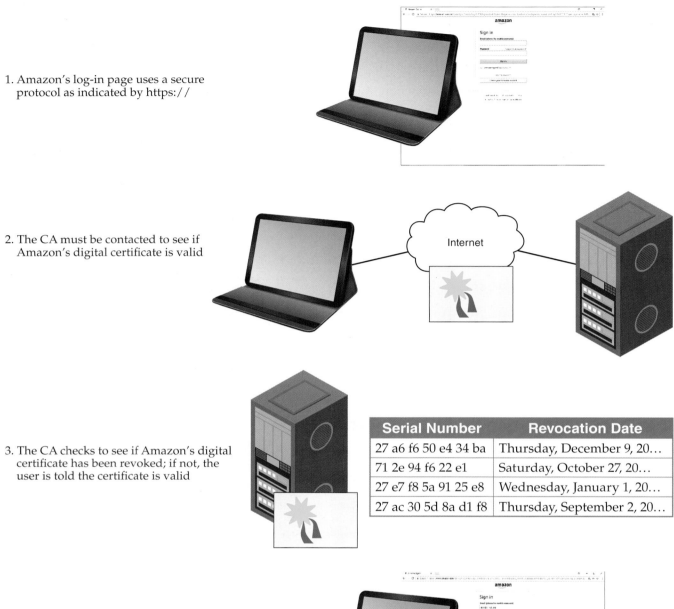

1. Amazon's log-in page uses a secure protocol as indicated by https://

2. The CA must be contacted to see if Amazon's digital certificate is valid

3. The CA checks to see if Amazon's digital certificate has been revoked; if not, the user is told the certificate is valid

Serial Number	Revocation Date
27 a6 f6 50 e4 34 ba	Thursday, December 9, 20…
71 2e 94 f6 22 e1	Saturday, October 27, 20…
27 e7 f8 5a 91 25 e8	Wednesday, January 1, 20…
27 ac 30 5d 8a d1 f8	Thursday, September 2, 20…

4. The user can securely enter the log-in information

Goodheart-Willcox Publisher; servers: ShendArt/Shutterstock.com; computers: romvo/Shutterstock.com

Figure 11-12. When a secure website is used, the digital certificate must be verified before the user enters confidential information.

Once the CA verifies the certificate, Trey's browser is notified it is valid. The browser is also told it should find the certificate in its own store. Trey can begin to exchange information safely and securely with Amazon.

Browsers such as Chrome and Internet Explorer are among those that get the list of certificate authorities from Microsoft. Changes to this list are handled using Microsoft's update program. There are daily checks.

Quick Look 11.2.5

Viewing a Certificate

Operating systems are populated with many certificates from the CAs. These are seen in the browser as intermediate authorities. Which certificates an operating system has along with the contents of the certificates can be viewed using a web browser. This activity uses the Chrome web browser.

Customize and Control Google Chrome

Main Menu

1. Launch Chrome.
2. Click the **Customize and Control Google Chrome** button in the upper-right corner of the window, and click **Settings** in the drop-down menu.
3. In the upper-left corner of the new screen, click the **Main Menu** button, and then click **Advanced** to expand this section.
4. In the expanded **Advanced** area, click the **Privacy and Security** link.
5. On the new screen, scroll down, and click **Manage Certificates**. The **Certificates** dialog box is displayed.
6. Click the **Intermediate Certification Authorities** tab in the dialog box. This tab displays the certificates that are loaded into Chrome. The column headers can be used to sort the certificates. For example, to view the certificates by expiration date, click on the **Expiration Date** header.
7. Locate a certificate that has **CA** in its name, and double-click it to display information about the certificate in a new dialog box.
8. The **General** tab in the dialog box displays basic information including purpose of the certificate and dates it is valid.
9. Click the **Details** tab, as shown.

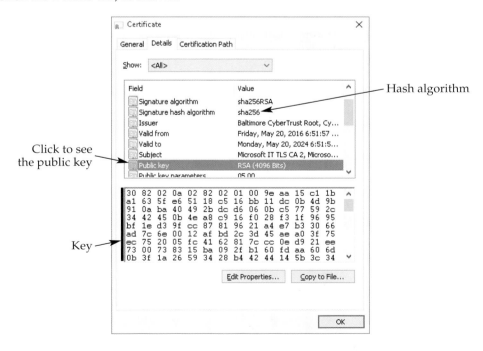

Quick Look 11.2.5 Continued

10. Which hashing algorithm is being used?
11. Click Public Key in the list. The key is displayed in the lower part of the dialog box. Look how long this key is!
12. Click the **Certification Path** tab. Who issued this certificate?
13. Close all open dialog boxes and Chrome.

SECTION REVIEW 11.2

Check Your Understanding ⤤

1. What do you call a mathematical computation of a file?
2. The goal of signing a certificate is to provide which core security principle?
3. When a company wants to create a new certificate it contacts which type of company?
4. A browser running a secure connection will be using which transport protocol?
5. If compromised, a digital certificate will be identified in what location?

Build Your Key Terms Vocabulary ⤤

As you progress through this course, develop a personal cybersecurity glossary. This will help you build your vocabulary and prepare you for a career. Write a definition for each of the following terms, and add it to your cybersecurity glossary.

certificate authority (CA)

certificate chaining

certificate-signing request (CSR)

Certification Revocation List (CRL)

digital certificate

digital signature

distributed-trust model

hash-based message authentication code (HMAC)

hashing

hierarchical-trust model

key escrow

message digest

path validation

public key infrastructure (PKI)

Secure Sockets Layer (SSL) protocol

Transport Layer Security (TLS)

X.509

Other Uses of Computer Encryption

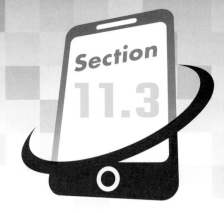

Encryption is not necessary just for exchanges of data through websites. Anywhere data need to be protected is an ideal candidate for data encryption. For example, mobile devices should have full drive encryption in the event they are lost or stolen. It may not be necessary to encrypt an entire volume of a desktop computer, but perhaps just some files in a folder. Encryption occurs in many places, including on the new credit cards with chips, ATM machines, secure e-mail transmissions, and password usage. This section explores some of these uses of encryption and the processes associated securing the relevant data.

Essential Question

Is it better to fully encrypt a local drive or to selectively encrypt files and folders?

Key Terms ☞

bcrypt
brute-force attack
cryptographic salt
dictionary attack
Encrypting File System (EFS)
gpg
hash table

key stretching
LM hash
nonce
NT hash
Password-Based Key Derivation Function 2 (PBKDF2)

Pretty Good Privacy (PGP)
rainbow table
recovery agent
Security Account Manager (SAM)
shadow file

Learning Goals

- Encrypt local folders and files.
- Examine e-mail encryption options.
- Describe methods for encrypting passwords.

MTA Security Fundamentals
2.5

File and Folder Encryption

Another way to protect data in an operating system is to encrypt local files and folders. When using the Windows operating system, this can be done to the entire drive with BitLocker, which was discussed in an earlier chapter. However, it can also be done to only select files or folders. This is done with a built-in feature of Windows called EFS. *Encrypting File System (EFS)* encrypts the files or folders you select. It protects data against unauthorized access by someone who has physical access to the drive. Even if the hacker is able to see the folder or files, without having the key, he or she will not be able to read the data.

By backing up the key, you can ensure that you can restore access to the data in the event the user cannot decrypt the data. You can also create a special account called a *recovery agent* to restore access.

To use EFS, the data must be stored on an NTFS formatted volume. Some Windows versions, such as the Home Editions, do not support EFS.

A document can be encrypted directly in Microsoft Office. A password is entered that acts as the key. To encrypt a file through Office, click **File>Info** on the ribbon. Then, click the **Protect Document** button in the backstage view, and click **Encrypt with Password** in the drop-down menu, as shown in **Figure 11-13.** The **Encrypt Document** dialog box is displayed in which a password is entered. Be warned! There is no recovery if the password is lost or forgotten.

Specific files can be encrypted in a Linux distribution as well. Most Linux distributions use the command called **gpg**. The **gpg** command stands for GnuPG or GNU Privacy Guard. In addition to encrypting or decrypting files, the command can be used to create a digital certificate. To use the tool, the appropriate package for your Linux distro must be installed. For example, if using Ubuntu, enter sudo apt-get install gnupg. Then, to encrypt a file, enter gpg -c *file name*. A password must be provided and confirmed. The **-d** switch removes the encryption.

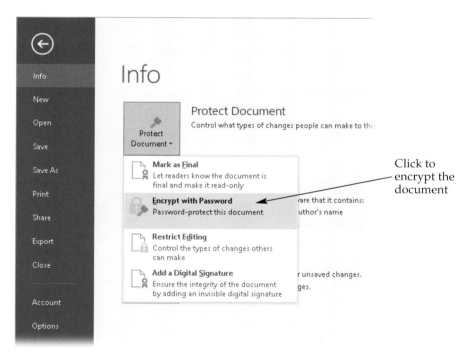

Goodheart-Willcox Publisher

Figure 11-13. A Microsoft Office document can be quickly encrypted with a password. Be sure not to lose the password as there is no way to recover it.

Quick Look 11.3.1

EFS File Encryption

It is easy to encrypt a folder using EFS. The folder will be accessible to you because you are the user who encrypted it. If another person logs on and tries to use the folder, he or she will not have access to the private key.

1. Launch Windows file explorer.
2. In your working folder, create a subfolder named Payroll.
3. Right-click on the Payroll folder, and click **Properties** in the shortcut menu.
4. On the **General** tab of the **Properties** dialog box, click the **Advanced...** button. The **Advanced Attributes** dialog box is displayed, as shown.

Check

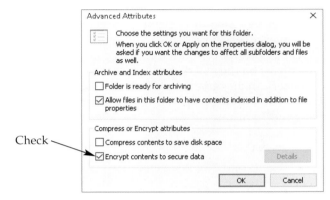

5. Check the **Encrypt contents to secure data** check box, and then click the **OK** button.
6. Click the **OK** button in the **Properties** dialog box to apply the encryption. In Windows 7, the folder name is displayed in green to indicate it is encrypted. In Windows 10, this display option can be enabled.
7. Open Windows Control Panel, and click the **User Accounts** link.
8. On the User Accounts page, click the **Manage your file encryption certificates** link to launch a wizard. The wizard will step you through the process of creating a backup of the recovery key. It can also be used for managing certificates. Click the **Next** button to continue.
9. On the second page of the wizard, click the **Use this certificate** radio button. There should be a certificate listed below it that was issued by you. Click the **Next** button to continue.
10. On the next page of the wizard, make sure the **Back up the certificate and key now** radio button is on, and then click the **Browse...** button. Navigate to your working folder, and enter a descriptive name such as PayrollPrivateKey.
11. In the wizard, enter a secure password in the **Password:** text box, and reenter it in the **Confirm password:** text box. Then, click the **Next** button. The file is saved as soon as you click this button.
12. On the next page of the wizard, click the **Cancel** button. If you wanted to update previously encrypted files, you could continue with the wizard.
13. Using Windows file explorer, navigate to your working folder to verify the backup file was created. The file will have a .pfx file extension.
14. Close all open windows.

E-mail Encryption

There have been many stories in the news about leaked e-mail. Leaked e-mail was a frequent topic in the 2016 presidential campaign. If the e-mail had been encrypted, the damage caused by the leaks may have been minimized. Without the private key, the e-mail would not have been able to be read. The only individuals who could leak the e-mail would be those holding the private key.

CompTIA Security+
6.2

One of the most popular encryption techniques for e-mail is a protocol called PGP. *Pretty Good Privacy (PGP)* is an encryption protocol and program for creating secure data communication. PGP began as an open-source e-mail–encryption algorithm, but it is now proprietary. There is, however, a new open source e-mail protocol derived from PGP called Open PGP. Open PGP works on Windows, Linux, and Apple operating systems and even smartphone operating systems from Android and Apple. It uses asymmetric encryption.

Another tool that can be used to encrypt and digitally sign e-mail is to use the S/MIME protocol. Secure Multipurpose Internet Mail Extensions (S/MIME) is used for encrypting public keys and Multipurpose Internet Mail Extensions (MIME) data.

Password Encryption

In addition to the data stored in files and traffic transmitted over networks, another key area of encryption involves passwords. A hacker's goal is often to uncover a password. This may involve breaking the password encryption. On a local Windows computer, user accounts and passwords are stored in the SAM database on the machine. *Security Account Manager (SAM)* is the local database of users and groups on a Windows system.

The Windows operating system encrypts passwords using one of two hashing mechanisms:

- LM
- NT

LM hash, or LAN Manager hash, is an older (pre-Windows NT) method of encrypting local passwords. One of the encryption methods used to create the hash is DES, which is weak and not difficult to break. There are many issues with LM hash, as shown in **Figure 11-14:**

- Password-length limitation.
- Longer passwords are divided into two halves.
- Does not use a cryptographic salt.

An LM hash is considered much weaker than an NT hash. An *NT hash* is created simply by using one of the hashing algorithms. Like an LM hash, an NT hash does not support the use of cryptographic salt.

Cryptographic salt, or a cryptographic nonce, is a random value that can be applied to the algorithm to make the resulting hash unique. A *nonce* is a random value only used once that can help disguise a password. Adding a nonce to the password is often referred to as key stretching. *Key stretching* is the process of salting the passwords to make them longer and more complex, thus harder to crack.

Consider the password 2@taT1ME. Adding salt includes random numerical values, such as 742B. The resulting stored password in this example would be 2@taT1ME742B. The user does not need to know the salt. It is only added for additional protection against hacking.

The Linux operating system stores passwords separate from the user account information. They are stored in a file called shadow in the etc folder (/etc/shadow).

FYI

When a cryptographic salt is applied, this is often referred to as *salting the hash!*

CompTIA Security+
6.2

Condition	Security Issue
Uses DES encryption.	Easily cracked.
Password limited to 14 characters.	Since there are 95 printable ASCII characters, there is a finite number of possible password combinations, which is 95^{14}.
Passwords longer than seven characters are divided into two halves.	Each half can be attacked on its own, which reduces the possible combinations to 95^7.
Does not use a cryptographic salt.	Lacks security of additional random value on the password.

Figure 11-14. There are several security issues with the Windows LM hash.

As in Windows, the passwords are hashed. Hashing can be done with MD5-crypt, bcrypt and sha256, or sha512 crypt. However, unlike the Windows operating system, Linux distros use cryptographic salt. The encryption algorithm varies based on which distro is in use, but most use bcrypt. *Bcrypt* is a cipher based on the Blowfish block cipher with a nonce added to the password.

Linux is not the only operating system to use salt. Salt is also used with Apple's IOS mobile operating system and Cisco operating systems. The wireless encryption WPA2 uses salt as well. These systems use a process called PBKDF2. *Password-Based Key Derivation Function 2 (PBKDF2)* is a key-stretching technique based on public key cryptography standards (PKCS).

Quick Look 11.3.2

Linux Passwords and Hashes

The file containing Linux passwords can be easily viewed by the root user. It is also easy to see the hash Linux creates for a file based on the algorithm used.

1. Sign in to Linux as the root user.
2. Enter cd /etc to change to the etc directory.
3. Enter ls shadow to list the file containing the user passwords. The nano text editor can be used to open this file and view its contents.
4. Enter nano shadow to open the shadow file.
5. Scroll through the file to see the user accounts that are in this system. Notice the hash of each password is not displayed. Instead, an * appears in place of the hash. To view file hashes, use the Linux command appropriate to the hash you want to calculate.
6. Press [Ctrl][X] to exit the file. If prompted, do not save any changes.
7. Enter cd ~ to move to the home directory.
8. Enter nano to create a new, blank file.
9. In the file, enter cybersecurity as the text, press [Ctrl][X], and when prompted press [Y] to save the file. Name the file MyFile.
10. Enter md5sum MyFile to view the MD5 hash of this file.
11. Enter sha256sum MyFile to view the SHA256 hash.

Password-Cracking Methods

CompTIA Security+
1.2

There are many tools hackers can find online to allow them to crack passwords. One of the methods used by these tools is called a dictionary attack. In a *dictionary attack,* the password-cracking software uses a list of words and their precomputed hash values to determine a password. Most of the words can be found in a dictionary, which is where the name originates. The program compares a user's password hash to the ones found in the dictionary list. If there is a match, the plain text password of the hash is revealed.

Another method that is more time-consuming, but ultimately more successful, is a brute-force attack. In a *brute-force attack,* the password-cracking software tries every possible keystroke in every possible position, as shown in **Figure 11-15.** On an average computer, the process could take years, depending on the size and complexity of the stored passwords. This also requires many CPU processing cycles.

To speed up the process of brute-force attacks, hackers have created hash tables. A *hash table* contains cracked passwords with preconstructed hashes for every password entered into the table. The passwords are more complex than those found in a dictionary. This allows a password-cracking program to quickly

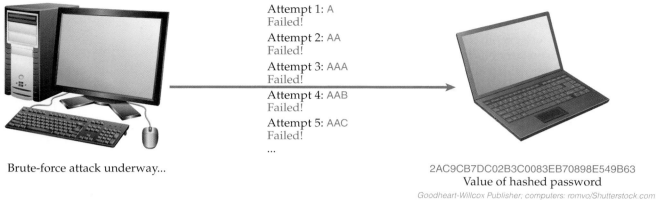

Brute-force attack underway...

2AC9CB7DC02B3C0083EB70898E549B63
Value of hashed password

Figure 11-15. An effective method hackers use to crack passwords is the brute-force attack. The best defense against this type of attack is a long and strong password.

CompTIA Security+
1.2

FYI

A rainbow table is called such because it contains the entire spectrum of possibilities!

search through the list for a password that has already been cracked. A hash table can lead to fast cracking. However, the trade-off is the creation of an exceptionally large file for the hash table.

A rainbow table is another tool for cracking passwords. It is more complex than a hash table. A *rainbow table* is a precomputed table of calculations that can be used to speed up the process by using two functions to crack a password, a hashing function and a reduction function. A rainbow table is needed for each hashing method. For example, one rainbow table is needed for Windows passwords and another for the database program MySQL. Rainbow tables are often bought and sold between hackers.

Password-Cracking Tools

There are many different programs for cracking passwords, as shown in **Figure 11-16.** Some may be for Windows, others for Linux. Some have variants for

Figure 11-16. Hash Suite is one of the many tools available that can be used to validate the security of passwords by attempting to crack them.

both operating systems. Common programs include John the Ripper, Cain & Abel, Hash Suite, and hashcat. Each tool offers different features, some include speed, hybrid accounts, the number of algorithms supported and more.

Cracking passwords is not just for logon accounts. For example, a hacker may be running Aircrack-ng. This is a Wi-Fi password-cracking tool that targets WEP and WPA passwords.

Best Password Defenses

Selection of strong passwords is one of the best defenses against password-cracking tools. Also, create and enforce policies for users to ensure passwords meet minimum requirements and change them often. Where possible, salt passwords to further protect against cracking attacks.

SECTION REVIEW 11.3

Check Your Understanding 🗘

1. If you encrypt a folder in Windows and forget the password, what is needed to access the data?

2. What is OpenPGP?

3. Which method used by Windows to encrypt passwords is older and considered less secure?

4. Random characters added to a password are called _____ or _____.

5. Which type of attack involves trying all combinations of characters to crack a password?

Build Your Key Terms Vocabulary 🗘

As you progress through this course, develop a personal cybersecurity glossary. This will help you build your vocabulary and prepare you for a career. Write a definition for each of the following terms, and add it to your cybersecurity glossary.

bcrypt
brute-force attack
cryptographic salt
dictionary attack
Encrypting File System (EFS)
gpg
hash table
key stretching
LM hash

nonce
NT hash
Password-Based Key Derivation
    Function 2 (PBKDF2)
Pretty Good Privacy (PGP)
rainbow table
recovery agent
Security Account Manager (SAM)
shadow file

Review and Assessment

Summary

Section 11.1 Encryption Overview

- Data encryption goes back thousands of years when the ancients used various ciphers to create cryptograms, and common ciphers include transposition and substitution ciphers.
- Symmetric encryption, such as block or stream ciphers, uses a single key for both encryption and decryption, while asymmetric encryption uses a key pair of a public and a private key; hybrid encryption is a combination of symmetric and asymmetric encryption.
- Threats against encryption systems include known plain-text, chosen plain-text, and replay attacks, and IPSEC is a framework developed to provide IP security.

Section 11.2 Validating and Securing Network Transmission

- Hashing creates a value based on data and can be used for verifying integrity of a downloaded file or to securely transmit a password, but there is the possibility that two separate pieces of data may generate the same hash, which can then be exploited.
- Security of public key infrastructure can be verified with the use of digital certificates and digital signatures to ensure data are not tampered with from sender to receiver.

Section 11.3 Other Uses of Computer Encryption

- A built-in Windows function called EFS can be used to selectively encrypt files and folders on a local machine.
- If e-mail is encrypted, it cannot be read by anyone who does not have the correct key; PGP and Open PGP are two popular encryption protocols for e-mail.
- Encryption may be applied to individual files or folders, e-mail messages, and passwords to increase the security of these elements.

Check Your Cybersecurity IQ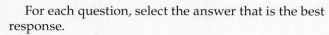

Now that you have completed this chapter, see what you have learned about cybersecurity by visiting the student companion website (www.g-wlearning.com) and taking the chapter posttest.

Review Questions

For each question, select the answer that is the best response.

1. If *PLACSPUEEA* is *APPLESAUCE*, this is considered a:
   A. Caesar cipher
   B. Transposition cipher
   C. Monolithic cipher
   D. Polyalphabetic cipher

2. What is the Vigenère cipher for *do your homework* using the key *school*?
   A. X7FBIBQTSMJZKS
   B. VMQJFCDTQIFZS
   C. MJZKSTQZCICFQV
   D. VQFCICZQTSKZJM

3. You are employed as a security analyst whose job it is to test encryption schemes for vulnerabilities. What is your job position?
   A. Cryptanalyst
   B. Cryptogram
   C. Cryptographer
   D. White hat hacker

4. Which encryption method would you select to send secure information that does not involve knowing any information prior to the encryption?
   A. Asymmetric encryption
   B. Block symmetric encryption
   C. Stream symmetric encryption
   D. SHA-1

5. Which of the following is an asymmetric encryption standard?
   A. RC4
   B. 3DES
   C. Diffie-Hellman
   D. ECC

6. If you have the unencrypted text and the encrypted text, what type of hack could be performed?
   A. Chosen plain-text attack
   B. Replay attack
   C. Known plain-text attack
   D. Chosen-cipher attack

7. Which statement is not true about hashing?
   A. The same algorithm must be used by sender and receiver.
   B. A hash digest can be reverse engineered.
   C. MD5 is no longer considered secure.
   D. A hash that can be duplicated is called a collision.

8. Where is an invalid digital certificate listed?
   A. shadow file
   B. NSA
   C. CRL
   D. PKI

9. Which feature allows you to selectively encrypt files and folders?
   A. Digital certificate
   B. BitLocker
   C. PGP
   D. EFS

10. What is the best way to protect e-mail from snooping?
    A. Implement quantum encryption.
    B. Use Open PGP.
    C. Hash the e-mail content with SHA-256.
    D. Use hybrid encryption.

Application and Extension of Knowledge

1. The Enigma machine is a famous example of cryptography. It was used with much success by the German armed forces during World War II. However, there was a so-called flaw in the design that increased the probability the code could be broken. Investigate the Enigma machine and the flaw. Summarize your findings in a two- to three-page paper. Follow your school's formatting guidelines, and cite your sources.

2. Create a series of clues using some of the legacy ciphers including transposition, Caesar, or Vigenère ciphers. Ask a classmate to solve or decode your secret messages.

3. Create a how-to document comparing the process of encrypting files in Windows and Linux. The purpose of the document is to allow a user to encrypt files. Include screenshots in your document.

4. George Mason University developed a program called Kryptos to demonstrate the use of public and private keys and digital certificates. With a partner, download the program, which can be found on the SourceForge website (www.sourceforge.net). Taking turns, one of you create a public-private key pair. Share the public key with your partner who will then use this file to send you a private message. Only you can open the message by using your private key. Document your results, and be prepared to discuss them with your classmates.

5. Consider encrypting a Microsoft Office file. In what situations would this be an acceptable form of protection? When would using this be considered inappropriate or unethical? Write a one- to two-page paper discussing your views. Be sure to justify your positions.

Research Project Steganography

Steganography is not a new technology. It extends back thousands of years. Research the history behind steganography. Locate examples from different time periods. Identify some of the cases where steganography has been used and its purpose. Can you identify any major historical events in which steganography played a role? Consider how steganography is used in the digital world. Include some of the software that is available to embed information in files. Also, identify what software can be used to detect files with embedded text or images. Some computer printers use steganography to hide identifiers in printouts. Identify some printers known to do this. Do you feel the user should be able to turn this feature off, and why or why not?

Deliverables. Prepare a detailed presentation that provides an overview of steganography, its history, and how it may be used today. Create the presentation as if you will be giving an informative presentation to introduce steganography to security professionals. Be prepared to deliver the presentation to your classmates.

Online Activities

Complete the following activities, which will help you learn, practice, and expand your knowledge and skills.

Vocabulary. Practice vocabulary for this chapter using the e-flash cards, matching activity, and vocabulary game until you are able to recognize their meanings.

Communication Skills

College and Career Readiness

Reading. Analyze the quality of the information presented in the visuals you find in this chapter. Is the information coherent? Is concrete evidence presented? Note any changes you would make to specific figures. Report your findings to the class.

Writing. Generate your own ideas to support the need for and importance of data encryption. Write an argument to support your reasoning.

Speaking. Create an outline that includes information about the importance of data encryption. Consider your audience as you prepare the information. Using the outline, make a presentation to your class.

Listening. When a person speaks literally, he or she means exactly what the words indicate. Ask a classmate to verbally summarize one of the topics presented in this chapter. Carefully listen to the statements he or she makes. Did your classmate speak literally?

Portfolio Development

College and Career Readiness

Talents. You have collected documents that show your skills and talents. Select a book report, essay, or poem that you have written that demonstrates your writing talents. If you are an artist, include copies of your completed works. If you are a musician, create a video with segments from your performances.

1. Create a Microsoft Word document that lists your talents. Use the heading Talents along with your name. Next to each talent listed, write a description of an assignment or performance and explain how your talent is shown in it. If there is a video, state that it will be made available on request or identify where it can be viewed online. Indicate that sample screenshots are attached.

2. Scan hardcopy documents related to your talents to serve as samples. Save screenshots from a video, if appropriate. Place hardcopies in the container for future reference.

3. Place the video file in an appropriate subfolder for your digital portfolio.

4. Update your master spreadsheet.

CTSO Event Prep

Case Study. A case study presentation may be part of a career and technical student organization (CTSO) competitive event. The activity may be a decision-making scenario for which your team will provide a solution. The presentation will be interactive with the judges. To prepare for a case study event, complete the following activities.

1. Conduct an Internet search for case studies. Your team should select a case that seems appropriate to use as a practice activity. Look for a case that is no more than one page long. Read the case and discuss it with your team members. What are the important points of the case?

2. Make notes on index cards about important points to remember. Team members should exchange note cards so that each evaluates the other person's notes. Use these notes to study. You may also be able to use these notes during the event.

3. Assign each team member a role for the presentation. Ask your instructor to play the role of competition judge as your team reviews the case.

4. Each team member should introduce himself or herself, review the case, make suggestions for the case, and conclude with a summary.

5. After the presentation is complete, ask for feedback from your instructor. You may also consider having a student audience to listen and give feedback.

Chapter 12

Threats to Data

Poor or inefficient software design is a problem for many attacks on data, from insecure handling of data to poorly written instructions or the lack of in-depth testing on systems and programs before they are released. Software programs that run on operating systems, web pages, or apps on phones all are potential attack vectors for hackers. Databases are treasure troves of vast amounts of information stored in one place that are often the target of hackers. These are the cyberattacks most often heard about. An example of this was the attack on Verizon Wireless in 2017 that revealed information for millions of accounts. Hacked data included subscriber names, telephone numbers, and PINs.

The massive database hacks are the cyberattacks that get the most attention in the media. However, any data, software, or web page could be vulnerable. Previous chapters have focused on threats to networks and hosts. Now, the areas of most concern regarding data protection need to be looked at more closely. These include software programs; web server security, including client and browser security; and database systems. There is much discussion and development over changes that will come as software and other technology continue to advance. However, if they build it, hackers will come!

Chapter Preview

While studying, look for the activity icon **for:**

- Pretests and posttests
- Vocabulary terms with e-flash cards and matching activities
- Self-assessment

G-WLEARNING.com

College and Career Readiness

Reading Prep

Before reading this chapter, review the objectives. Based on this information, write down two or three items you think are important to note while you are reading.

Check Your Cybersecurity IQ ⟳

Before you begin this chapter, see what you already know about cybersecurity by visiting the student companion website (www.g-wlearning.com) and taking the chapter pretest.

Certification Objectives

CompTIA Security+

1.2   Compare and contrast types of attacks.
1.6   Explain the impact associated with types of vulnerabilities.
2.4   Given a scenario, analyze and interpret output from security technologies.
3.4   Explain the importance of secure staging deployment concepts.
3.6   Summarize secure application development and deployment concepts.

Threats to Software

Which stage of the system design life cycle is the most critical to security?

Software and hardware work together in computer systems. Both are needed for a functioning system. Even if you are not a programmer, as a cybersecurity professional, you need to have a basic understanding of software, including the intended functionality of programs. A significant number of threats come from software attack vectors. It is important to be aware of the most common vulnerabilities of a program. Even if you are not a software developer, knowing the various ways in which software is designed can aid in providing security. Often, the workflow or design process itself may lead to vulnerabilities in the software. Hackers may be able to exploit these vulnerabilities. This section explores some of these models and potential vulnerabilities in software.

Key Terms ➦

agile model
application programming
   interface (API)
buffer-overflow attack
compiler
data canary

DevOps
immutable server
infrastructure as code
injection attack
input validation

library
programming language
systems development life cycle
   (SDLC)
waterfall model

Learning Goals

- Discuss software programming.
- Explain software-development models.
- Compare and contrast threats to software.

Software Programming

Do an Internet search for the phrase *programming languages,* and you will find many articles. Some articles will discuss which ones are in demand by employers. There will be offers for software training. Other links will lead to pages that discuss many varied topics on programming. Some of these topics include different programming languages and different platforms. Software programming is not just for PCs. There are many different platforms, including traditional computers, mobile devices, web interfaces, and embedded systems. A business could be using software produced for a number of different platforms.

A survey was conducted in 2017 by the Institute of Electronic & Electrical Engineers (IEEE). It revealed that Python, C and its related languages, and Java are the most popular programming languages, as shown in **Figure 12-1.**

To have an overall understanding of software, it is important to know the terminology associated with programming languages. First, consider the term *language* itself. A *programming language* is the interface and structure used by the programmer to develop code to create a meaningful application. Examples of programming languages include Java, Ruby, Python, and Visual Basic as well as the others shown in **Figure 12-1.**

Two other important terms are *library* and *application programming interface.* These features allow sharing of commonly used commands and functionality. A *library* is generally used to share commands within the program itself. This allows the programmer not to have to keep rewriting the same code. An *application programming interface (API)* allows the program to share functionality with other modules, such as products or services in other programs. An API can save a programmer hours of coding by using modules that already provide functionality he or she needs in code. Examples of when APIs are used include incorporating Google Maps on web pages or printing functionality through Microsoft APIs.

Machine language is the language the computer CPU can use. Programs must be translated, or compiled, into machine language for the computer to use. A *compiler* is a function that takes the code the programmer writes and converts it into machine language. Compiling could be a big process for an application program suite or a web application. Compiling is often faster when the program is compiled as it is run. This is known as *just-in-time compilation.* Other programs are known as *interpreted programs.* These programs are run on another program that is called the interpreter. The interpreter sits between the computer and the program and handles the requests between these two entities. This program is not compiled to run directly from the operating system. For example, programs created in Python are interpreted programs.

You can learn more about APIs and view tutorials, research, and other information regarding APIs on the ProgrammableWeb website (www. programmableweb.com).

Rank	Programming Language	Platforms
1	Python	computers, web
2	C	computers, embedded, mobile
3	Java	computers, mobile, web
4	C++	computers, embedded, mobile
5	C#	computers, mobile, web
6	R	computers
7	JavaScript	mobile, web
8	PHP	web
9	Go	computers, web
10	Swift	computers, mobile

Figure 12-1. The top ten most popular programming languages as reported by a 2017 IEEE survey.

Software Design

Application development should follow the standards set forth in an SDLC. A *systems development life cycle (SDLC)* is the process used to create, deploy, and maintain a software program. In the traditional model of the SDLC, the phases begin with planning and end with maintaining the software.

CompTIA Security+
3.4

SDLC Stages

The six stages in the traditional SDLC model are shown in **Figure 12-2.** The model is shown as a linear set of stages. However, the stages are often represented in a circular fashion with maintenance leading back to the beginning.

Stage 1 is gathering and analyzing the requirements for the program. You have to know what the program must accomplish. What output is needed? Who are the users of the system? Once the requirements are established, they serve as the model as you move forward. This is the most important step in the process to achieve success.

Stage 2 is designing the software. In this phase, the system requirements are identified and documented. This serves as the blueprint for the remainder of the process.

Stage 3 is writing the code. Coding the program should not be done until the first two phases are complete. These instructions help the programmer stay on target and only develop the code necessary to support the project requirements.

Stage 4 is testing the code. The application should be thoroughly tested. Any problems should be identified and fixed before the next phase begins.

Stage 5 is deploying the program. The tested and corrected program is released. This means it is in the user's hands.

Stage 6 is maintaining the program. Programs should be evaluated, problems corrected, and patches and updates delivered as necessary. This is a part of the overall process of developing a program.

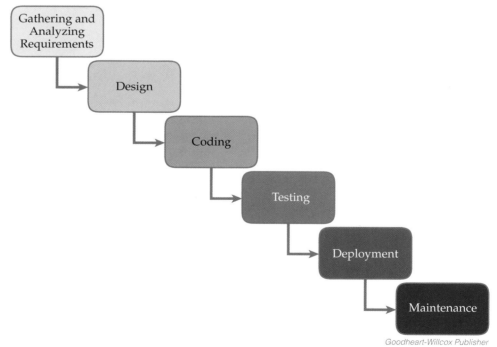

Figure 12-2. The traditional software design life cycle consists of six linear stages. This model is often shown in a circle with maintenance leading back to the beginning.

Types of SDLCs

CompTIA Security+
3.6

There are two popular SDLCs: waterfall and agile. The *waterfall model* is a sequential process. Each step is completed before moving to the next phase of the cycle. Each phase is dependent on the previous phase. This is the traditional model shown in **Figure 12-2.** With the waterfall method, each group on the developmental team tends to work independently of each other. Programmers do not always participate in the process until the actual coding occurs. Programmers then must resolve any problems that arise.

The agile SDLC is different. In the *agile model,* everyone stays involved in the process through all stages. This is done through cycles, called *iterations*, as shown in **Figure 12-3.** Each iteration of the project is cooperatively reviewed and critiqued. The project continues to go through iterations until everyone involved agrees the goals have been met. Then, the software is deployed.

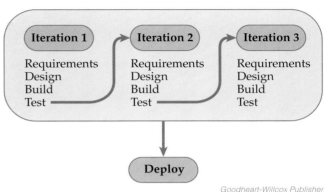

Goodheart-Willcox Publisher

Figure 12-3. An agile SDLC has iterations, and everyone remains involved throughout the process.

DevOps

A new trend in software development is called DevOps. DevOps is short for developer operations. DevOps is focused on moving applications from the development and testing phases to deployment in as quick a manner as possible. Agile SDLC fits neatly into this business model. In fact, DevOps is often referred to as *agile operations.*

DevOps is a business philosophy that encourages collaboration between developers, managers, and other IT and operational staff from development through production and support, as shown in **Figure 12-4.** This differs from a model in which each department independently works on its own piece of the project. In typical developmental models, programmers only code the project and have some interaction with the testing phase. The operations group is then responsible for maintaining the infrastructure and integration. DevOps eliminates these divisions to foster a collaborative environment from the beginning. One of the goals with DevOps is for the developers to be able to release code more rapidly while the operations group works on the maintenance of the system. This continuous integration allows developers to release potentially multiple updates in a single day.

DevOps often follows a principle known as infrastructure as code. In *infrastructure as code,* the operations team uses a system starting point as a baseline. It then creates scripts that will make configuration changes from the baseline. The scripts are used to automate the process. This removes the need to manually configure the system. Here is how infrastructure as code may work:

1. A business creates a baseline configuration for a server operating system.
2. A need for a specific type of server is identified in the business. Instead of starting to build the server from scratch, the operations team creates a script that works from the baseline configuration already in place.
3. Once this new server is configured with the specific changes, testing can be done quickly as all that needs to be tested are the new changes identified in the script.
4. This new server can quickly be deployed, and the older server (if in place) can be discarded.

This type of approach creates what is called an immutable server. The term *immutable* means unchanging over time or unable to be changed. With an *immutable server,*

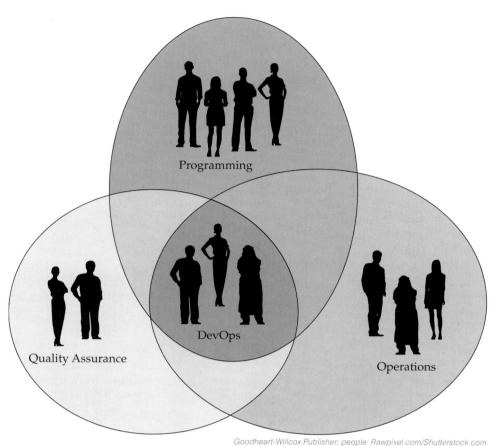

Figure 12-4. DevOps is a philosophy for developing software in which all areas are involved throughout the process instead of individually working on their own parts.

the server configuration is made from the baseline, not by directly configuring a live production server. Cybersecurity engineers can follow this same philosophy for making security configurations on servers.

Security Threats to Software

The best defense against threats to software is development of secure programs following a detailed plan. This includes code written by staff members. In some cases, code may be written by third-party vendors. Code from vendors must be checked. Do not assume that vendors follow the plans and protocols put in place. The Pentagon experienced a serious security breach in 2011 related to vendors. Vendors had been hired to write code for sensitive US military systems. The vendor turned out to be Russian programmers, and hiring them was illegal. More importantly, the code was written to allow the Pentagon's system to be infected with viruses.

One of the biggest areas of vulnerabilities to software is when a user is allowed to input data. A majority of the attacks occur at this point during execution. One of these types of attacks is called a buffer-overflow attack. In a *buffer-overflow attack,* the hacker exploits a programming flaw in which more data can be entered than the program can accept, and the extra data are written to memory outside of the buffer. In some cases, the overflow may just crash the program. However, a hacker could have the extra input include executable instructions in this location, as shown in **Figure 12-5.** When that entry is written into RAM, the computer executes the command.

CompTIA Security+
1.6

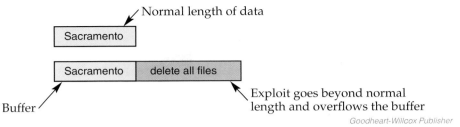

Figure 12-5. A buffer-overflow attack exploits a vulnerability of being able to enter more data than the program can accept.

Programmers have different options to protect against a buffer overflow. For example, a limit can be set for the data-entry box. Another interesting method is for the programmer to use a data canary. A *data canary* is a known value placed at the end of the assigned buffer space. If this value remains the same, a buffer overflow has not occurred.

Other issues related to input need to be addressed. For example, you may want the user to enter numbers only. In this case, the input field should be programmed to reject letters and other characters that are not numbers. This is called *input validation.* Performing input validation on content is critical. Input validation is implementing safeguards to control the type and amount of data entered into an input field. It also helps prevent other injection attacks. An *injection attack* is malicious code inserted into a web application to cause an unexpected outcome. There are different types of injection attacks. Two of the most common are discussed later in this chapter: cross-site scripting and SQL injection attacks.

The error message generated by improper user input can disclose information to hackers. For example, suppose the user enters an incorrect username or password. The error message should not tell the user the password is incorrect or that the username is incorrect. Doing so tells a hacker that the other entry *is* correct. Instead, the error message should tell the user that either the username or the password is incorrect. Better yet, simply tell the user the login information was incorrect. This does not allow a hacker to know which part was correct. Notice on the Bank of America website shown in **Figure 12-6** that an incorrect entry does not indicate which part of the entry was invalid.

FYI

Why is it called a data canary? Canaries were used in coal mines to determine when toxic gases reached a dangerous level for humans. Data canaries are also used to test for a dangerous situation.

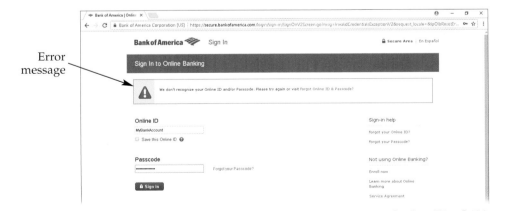

Figure 12-6. A properly formatted error message will not provide clues to a hacker. Here, the message does not tell a hacker the username or the password is incorrect, simply that at least one of them is incorrect.

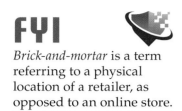

Another coding problem not often addressed by programmers is the data left over after a process completes. This could include data in RAM, cookies, or similar data. Any data in RAM is vulnerable. Consider how most credit card numbers are stolen from brick-and-mortar retailers. One of the biggest threats against point of sale (PoS) devices is data stored in RAM, which can be extracted using a *RAM scraper.* This is discussed in detail in Chapter 7.

Quick Look 12.1.1

Buffer-Overflow Attack

Richard Enbody of Michigan State University has posted an article providing an overview of a buffer-overflow attack in which the hacker does not need to know the password to log in. Note: if this article is no longer available, search for a different buffer-overflow simulation and share with your classmates.

1. Launch a web browser, and navigate to a search engine.
2. Enter the search phrase michigan state university buffer overflow. In the list of results, select the article entitled *Security in CS1: Buffer Overflow.* This is a brief article that includes a simulation on how a buffer-overflow attack works.
3. Read the article. Take note of the comparison between a normal login process and a buffer-overflow attack.
4. Download the demonstration. This is a PowerPoint file.
5. Once the PowerPoint file is downloaded, open it and run the slide show. You may be asked to enable content in order for the slide show to run.

SECTION REVIEW 12.1

Check Your Understanding

1. A programmer uses what resource to share functionality with other programming modules?
2. What converts program code into machine language?
3. Which development model involves a sequential process to develop a program?
4. Ensuring text cannot be entered into a form where only decimal numbers are expected is called what?
5. A hacker entered a malicious command into a user ID entry on a form. What type of attack was performed?

Build Your Key Terms Vocabulary

As you progress through this course, develop a personal cybersecurity glossary. This will help you build your vocabulary and prepare you for a career. Write a definition for each of the following terms, and add it to your cybersecurity glossary.

agile model	infrastructure as code
application programming interface (API)	injection attack
buffer-overflow attack	input validation
compiler	library
data canary	programming language
DevOps	systems development life cycle (SDLC)
immutable server	waterfall model

Threats to Web Applications

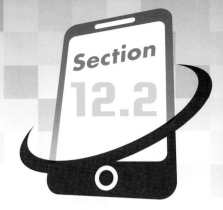

The World Wide Web launched a global revolution. Since its beginnings, many changes have come along leading to a more interactive environment. Web pages originally were static things to be viewed. Now, there is active participation through blogging, social media, online shopping, posting comments, video sharing, and much more. This evolution became known as Web 2.0. Innovation continues today as Web 3.0 develops to tailor the online experience to the specific user. Web searches will return results of web pages, video programming, entertainment, and much more based on the user's profile.

Protecting the web server and hosted web pages should be a top priority for security administrators. Simply putting a web server in a DMZ behind a firewall is not enough to stop many of the attacks against web servers and web pages.

Essential Question

Should scripts be forbidden on web pages?

Key Terms 🖝

Apache
clickjacking
client-side script
code repository
code signature
cross-site request forgery (CSRF)
cross-site scripting (XSS) attack
dead code
directory traversal

dynamic analysis
Easter egg
fuzzing
Hypertext Markup Language (HTML)
Hypertext Transfer Protocol (HTTP)
Internet Information Service (IIS)

Open Web Application Security Project (OWASP)
server-side script
software development kit (SDK)
static-code analysis
typosquatting
Uniform Resource Identifier (URI)
web application firewall (WAF)

Learning Goals

- Appraise web-application scanners.
- Identify security threats to web applications.
- Differentiate methods for protecting source code.

Web-Server Protection

Tim Berners-Lee is a British computer scientist who has a lifelong interest in computers and how they work. While Berners-Lee was employed at CERN in Switzerland during the late 20th century, he realized his coworkers often had difficulty accessing data on the multiple computers connected to the Internet. This was because they stored data differently and often had different methods to access the computer and the data. He believed there was a better, more consistent means of sharing information across systems. He looked to a technology called hypertext. *Hypertext* is text displayed on a computer interface that contains a link to other information.

Berners-Lee received little enthusiasm for his idea from his bosses. However, he began research on how to improve access to data. By 1990, he had created three key elements of his process that remain the basis of the web today: HTML, HTTP, and URI.

- *Hypertext Markup Language (HTML)* is the format used by the web to exchange information.
- *Hypertext Transfer Protocol (HTTP)* is the protocol that allows all the hosts to exchange information across the web.
- *Uniform Resource Identifier (URI)* is the address of each resource on the web; each must be unique.

It was not enough that Berners-Lee created a means for accessing data, the process needed to be accepted by users at large. He convinced his bosses at CERN to make these tools available free of charge. Making the standards open allowed anyone to use them. Eventually Berners-Lee moved on to MIT and founded the World Wide Web Consortium (W3C). The W3C took over the open standards and continues development of the standards for the World Wide Web.

When a user requests a web page, this is done by entering an address into a web browser. The address is a URI or URL. Each part of the address has a specific meaning, as shown in **Figure 12-7.** When a client requests a web page, the request is sent to the web server where the page is located. The web server then fetches the specific HTML page and sends that to the client's web browser.

Web servers are servers that use special software to share web pages or other web services, such as access via File Transfer Protocol (FTP). In Microsoft Server operating systems, the web-server software is *Internet Information Service (IIS).* On Linux machines, the open-source program *Apache* is often used as the web-server software. Regardless of the software, web servers must be hardened and locked down as much as possible:

- Remove any services that should not be running on the system.
- Consider turning off remote access, and log in locally whenever possible.
- Practice the Principle of Least Privilege by making sure accounts on the machine only have the rights they need and disabling any unused accounts.

FYI

Today, most people refer to a web address as a URL. The L stands for locator. URI and URL are technically different with URL a subset of URI.

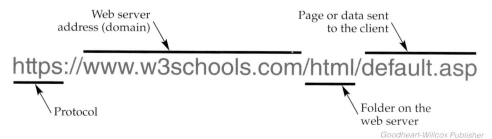

Goodheart-Willcox Publisher

Figure 12-7. A web address consists of several parts that together direct data to the correct location.

- Keep everything on the web server up-to-date with patches, from applications to the operating system.
- Test new applications in a virtual environment or on a server not connected to the network, and only deploy applications and web pages proven safe and secure.

Web servers should be protected with a firewall specific to web traffic. This type of firewall is known as a *web application firewall (WAF)*. Its purpose is to monitor, filter, and block HTTP traffic coming from a web client to the web server. It offers deep inspection of the packet looking for threats such as XSS and SQL injection.

A serious threat that affects web servers is an exploit called directory traversal. In *directory traversal,* hackers are able to get beyond the web server's root directory and execute commands. For example, the root directory for a web server running IIS is Inetpub\wwwroot. It is critical to lock web users into this environment. This will keep them out of sensitive directories, such as the Windows directory. The best way to check for the directory traversal threat is to use a web-application scanner.

CompTIA Security+
2.4

Quick Look 12.2.1

Web-Application Scanner

A web-application scanner looks for vulnerabilities in a website. This software tool should be used to fully test a website before it goes live to the public.

1. Launch a web browser, and navigate to a search engine.
2. Enter the search phrase burp suite, and select the site for the software. Is this a free or commercial product?
3. On the Burp Suite web page, tools are offered to automate custom attacks on a web server. What is the advantage of a tool like this having the capability of offensive hacks?
4. Investigate other features offered by Burp Suite. What are some features you find interesting?
5. Navigate to a search engine, enter the search phrase netsparker, and select the site for this software.
6. View the pricing for the desktop version. Do you feel this pricing is worth the money to protect your web servers?
7. Click **Desktop Scanners** in the page's menu, and view the video for the product tour.

Web-Application Protection

The open nature of web development has led to remarkable success. Web pages have moved from static-page designs intended only to provide information to interactive pages that can be uniquely customized in seconds. Much has changed due to web applications. These are programs that can be run dynamically on request at the client without requiring software to be installed. Instead, the programs are run directly through web browsers as scripts. The first scripting language was JavaScript. It was introduced in 1995 by Netscape. Since then, many other products have been developed and included in a user's web experience. Today, many applications, including traditional software programs, use these features in their interfaces. While the changes have made using the web and applications an exciting and productive experience, they have also increased the number of vulnerabilities and attack vectors against systems.

Web-Based Vulnerabilities

There are many challenges faced in protecting against web attacks. Some challenges can be controlled by the programmers and developers. Creating

CompTIA Security+
3.6

quality code and conducting comprehensive testing can reduce threats, but vulnerabilities exist on the client. This is especially true in regard to security settings in the browser. Users often unknowingly contribute to their own attacks. Users may click on links from unknown sources, change browser security settings, and even make simple mistakes using the keyboard.

It is important to thoroughly test programs and web applications in a protected environment before implementation. A test that should be done regardless of project development is known as fuzzing. *Fuzzing,* or *dynamic analysis,* is an extensive testing process in which a program is tested for all types of actions. It is often an automated process. In a fuzz test, for example, a name-input field would be tested by entering numbers, special characters, and large values; pressing function keys; and so on. Does pressing a function key during the program expose any vulnerabilities? Testing should also try to introduce buffer-overflow problems or other types of command injection. This type of testing is sometimes called *stress testing*. The system is pushed to respond, or stressed. Then, any flaws and vulnerabilities found are fixed.

CompTIA Security+
1.2

Scripts

Scripts are essentially "mini-programs." They run on either the web server or the client's computer. A *server-side script* runs on the web server. A *client-side script* runs on the client's computer. In general, scripts are a necessary part of the web experience for users. A web page dynamically responds to user actions through scripts.

XSS attacks are one of the top ten threats to websites. XSS stands for cross-site scripting. It is a very widespread attack method. In a *cross-site scripting (XSS) attack,* hackers are able to inject client-side scripts into web pages that are viewed by other people, as shown in **Figure 12-8.** A user can be the victim of an XSS attack by clicking on a malicious link created by an attacker, or visiting a page that has injected code. Once on the fake site, scripts are downloaded into the user's computer without his or her knowledge. At this point, the attacker can gain control of the user data being entered. Protecting against an XSS attack must be done in the web application itself. Programmers and web developers must thoroughly test and inspect their applications before making them available.

Another script-based threat is a cross-site request forgery (CSRF) attack. Sometimes this is referred to as an XSRF attack. This attack is not as common as an XSS attack, but has the potential to cause serious damage.

A *cross-site request forgery (CSRF)* attack takes advantage of the trust relationship between a website and the client's browser to run malicious commands.

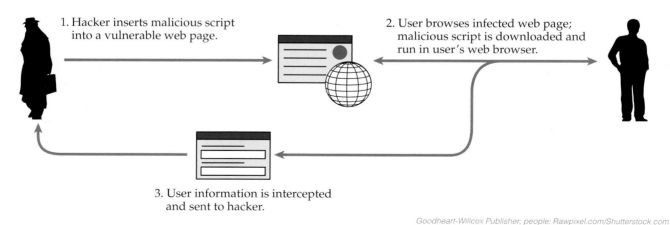

1. Hacker inserts malicious script into a vulnerable web page.

2. User browses infected web page; malicious script is downloaded and run in user's web browser.

3. User information is intercepted and sent to hacker.

Figure 12-8. In a cross-site scripting (XSS) attack, the hacker injects a client-side script into a web page. This script intercepts user information and sends it to the hacker.

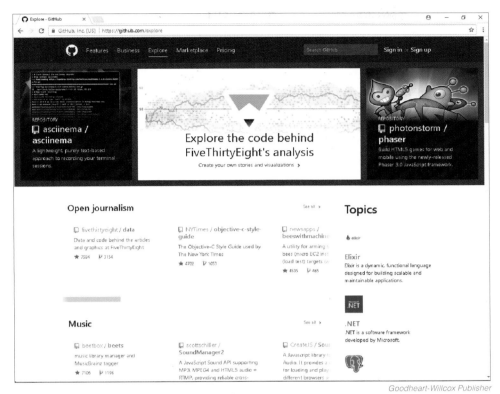

Goodheart-Willcox Publisher

Figure 12-11. GitHub is a popular way to track revisions to software as well as share code with other developers.

Quick Look 12.2.4

GitHub

GitHub is a collaborative environment for managing projects. It offers many features. Depending on how it is used, there may or may not be a fee.

1. Launch a web browser, and navigate to the GitHub website (www.github.com).
2. What are some of the benefits given for managing a project with GitHub?
3. Click **Business** in the menu, then scroll down, and click on the **Customers** link.
4. Review some of the videos on how customers have used GitHub for their projects. Share your comments on these reflections with your classmates.
5. Click **Pricing** in the menu, and review the pricing options. If you were working on an open-source product, what would you pay? If it were a business project and you had a team of ten members, what is the monthly cost?

SDK

It is common for programmers to use code written by others. This is known as using third-party libraries. These code libraries are often made available to outside developers by packaging them into an SDK. A *software development kit (SDK)* is a collection of tools, such as libraries, that help programmers create applications for specific software.

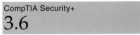

CompTIA Security+
3.6

For example, a company like Facebook or Twitter provides an SDK to Apple iOS developers. In the SDK are common utilities found on the platform, such as login abilities and ad deployment. In this way, developers do not have to rewrite common functions. Instead, they can spend their time on the specific functionality of the app they are creating.

Security personnel must document their use of SDKs. If there is a flaw or vulnerability revealed in the code of an SDK, the IT team will need to make necessary updates. If which SDKs were used are not recorded, it would be impossible to apply the updates.

Another consideration for security personnel is assuring that the code obtained from others is legitimate. Is the code actually from the person or organization where it supposedly originated? This can be checked by testing the code signature. A *code signature* is a digital signature placed on the code to verify its authenticity and integrity. It is created like other types of digital signatures, as discussed in Chapter 11. The developer obtains a digital certificate from a trusted CA. A private key is then used to create the digital signature. Once that is done, the code can then be validated by anyone.

SECTION REVIEW 12.2

Check Your Understanding

1. Name the web server software used by Microsoft Server.
2. Which vulnerability would allow a hacker to search the entire drive containing the web server?
3. What is an automated process used to test applications?
4. A program that runs in the local browser is called a(n) _____?
5. A(n) _____ is a programming package written by a company for use by other companies in developing programs.

Build Your Key Terms Vocabulary

As you progress through this course, develop a personal cybersecurity glossary. This will help you build your vocabulary and prepare you for a career. Write a definition for each of the following terms, and add it to your cybersecurity glossary.

Apache
clickjacking
client-side script
code repository
code signature
cross-site request forgery (CSRF)
cross-site scripting (XSS) attack
dead code
directory traversal
dynamic analysis
Easter egg
fuzzing

Hypertext Markup Language (HTML)
Hypertext Transfer Protocol (HTTP)
Internet Information Service (IIS)
Open Web Application Security Project (OWASP)
server-side script
software development kit (SDK)
static-code analysis
typosquatting
Uniform Resource Identifier (URI)
web application firewall (WAF)

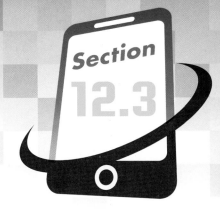

Threats to Databases

Information, or data, is the heart and soul of a business. Consider the many uses of data, from collecting customer information and employee records to managing and maintaining product inventory, sales statistics, and research records. In addition to collected data, other data are dynamically produced. For example, the total dollar amount for a shopping cart is data. Since data drive decisions, a critical IT function is protecting data from unauthorized access or unapproved changes. There are many ways to store data, such as in many separate files. However, data are often stored in large tables and managed by specialized software. This section explores some basic elements of data design and common threats against data systems.

Essential Question

What is the importance of a DBMS to database security?

Key Terms ✍

database
database management system
   (DBMS)
field

field value
NoSQL
query
record

relational database
SQL injection attack
Structured Query Language
   (SQL)

Learning Goals

- Diagram the construction of a database.
- Identify security risks associated with an SQL–enabled database.

Overview of Databases

Information technology is driven by data. Data are the raw inputs that become useful information when given context. To give context to data, data must be stored in a format that users are able to add to, edit, and query. This is done with a database. A *database* is an organized collection of data. This includes more than just the tables holding the data, but the reports, data-entry views, queries, and other elements.

In a database, the data are stored in a table, as shown in **Figure 12-12.** Each row of the table represents a unique record. A *record* is a collection of related information. The columns, which are called *fields,* contain data about one aspect of the table. A *field value* is the specific information. It is contained in a cell, like in Excel, where the record and field intersect. For example, a record may be for a specific student. A field may be the student's first name. In this case, the field value would be the first name of one specific student.

A *database management system (DBMS)* provides the interface and functionality for working with a database. This includes storing, retrieving, adding, and deleting data. Microsoft Access is an example of a DBMS you may have used. Other common DBMSs include Oracle, MySQL, Microsoft SQL server, and File-Maker Pro. Microsoft Access is a database program that is part of the Office suite. It allows you to create many elements, including custom queries and reporting. It also includes some performance and analysis features.

Relational Database

A concept often used with a database is that of a relational database. A *relational database* contains multiple tables that are linked together. In this way, information does not need to be repeated. In a nonrelational database, information may be repeated in multiple tables. When this occurs, it is easy to forget to update every instance when the data change. If the data do not match, data integrity is lost.

Consider this scenario. Your school has over 2,000 students. The administration wants to track each student along with the standardized and advanced placement tests taken. It would be very difficult to predict how many tests each student will take over the course of his or her years in high school. Instead, it is easier to create two tables, one with student information and the other with student testing information only. The only commonality between the two tables is the student ID number, as shown in **Figure 12-13.** This is a relational database. The Student ID field can then be used to *query,* or draw data from, both tables.

A report can take data from one table matched with the Student ID field in the next table to link additional data. There would be a single report, but it takes data from multiple, linked tables. **Figure 12-14** shows an example of this type of output.

SQL

Although Microsoft Access and other similar programs offer great capabilities, working with extremely large amounts of data requires other methods. Large

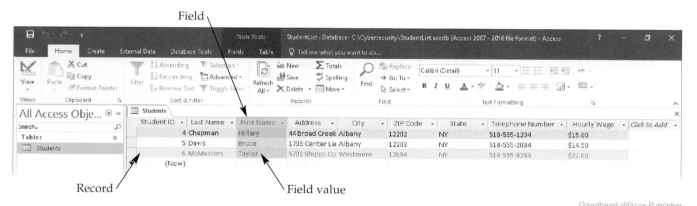

Figure 12-12.   A table in a database consists of records (rows) and fields (columns). The intersection of a record and a field contains the field value, which is a specific piece of information.

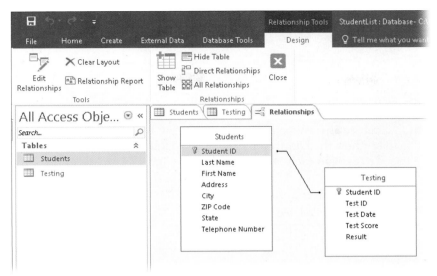

Figure 12-13. The Student ID records in these two tables are linked to create a relational database.

databases often require the use of SQL. *Structured Query Language (SQL)* is a programming language for managing a relational database. The commands in SQL are close to English. This makes the language easy to learn.

Consider the student tables discussed earlier. A query of all the testing and scores for one student can be created. The SQL statements may look like this:

```
SELECT Students.FirstName, Students.LastName, Testing.[TestID],
    Testing.[TestScore]
FROM Students INNER JOIN Testing ON Students.[StudentID] =
    Testing.[StudentID]
WHERE (((Students.[StudentID])=110));
```

There are many SQL solutions, including Oracle from Sun Microsystems, Microsoft has SQL Server, and MYSQL. MYSQL is a very popular open-source version of SQL. Microsoft Access also has SQL capabilities.

FYI SQL is pronounced *see-kwill*.

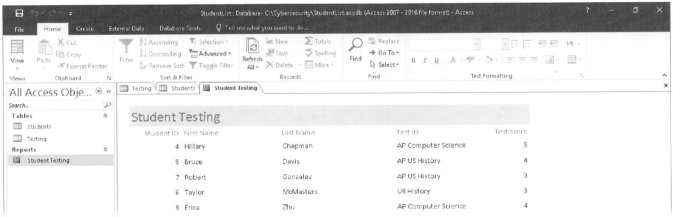

Figure 12-14. A report created in a relational database can draw data from multiple, linked tables.

Case Study

DBMSs

Database management systems use an ACID model to ensure data integrity. ACID stands for atomic, consistency, isolation, and durability. Your company is moving to an SQL database environment. Investigate the ACID model so you can explain to your manager how the DBMS you have selected follows the ACID model. You will also need to explain each of the four elements and why each is important to database management.

1. How will you explain the atomic aspect of ACID?
2. What is durability as related to a database?

Quick Look 12.3.1

SQL Use

SQL is a powerful, yet easy-to-use, means of managing a database. For example, a table can be accessed using SQL commands. This can be done using the SQL functions in Microsoft Access.

1. Launch Microsoft Access. On the startup screen, click the **Blank desktop database** button to create a new database.

Browse

2. In the **Blank desktop database** dialog box, click the **Browse** button, navigate to your working folder, and name the database Practice. All elements of the database, such as tables, reports, and queries, will be stored in this file.

3. Click the **Create** button in the **Blank desktop database** dialog box to begin the database. The database begins with an empty, unnamed table.

Create

4. Right-click on the tab for the table, which is currently named Table1, and click **Design View** in the shortcut menu. You are first asked to save the table. Enter the name Students, and click the **OK** button. The design view is displayed, which can be used to set up the layout of the table, as shown.

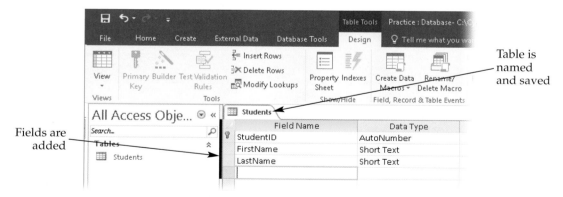

5. For the first field name, enter StudentID (no space). Field names should be descriptive, but simple.
6. Press the [Tab] key to move to the Data Type column.
7. Accept the default data type of AutoNumber by pressing the [Tab] key. Press the [Tab] key a second time to move to the next row.
8. Applying what you have learned, create a second field named FirstName (no space) and a data type of Short Text. Create a third field named LastName with the Short Text data type.
9. Right-click on the table's tab, which now displays Students, and click **Save** in the shortcut menu.

Quick Look 12.3.1 Continued

10. Right-click on the table's tab again, and click **Datasheet View** in the shortcut menu. This is the view in which data are entered into the table.

11. Click in the cell in the first record for the first field (First Name), and enter a fictional name. Add a fictitious last name as well.

12. Add two more fictional students to the table, and save the table. Notice as you enter additional records, the StudentID field is automatically populated. This is because the data type for this field is AutoNumber.

13. Click **Create>Queries>Query Design** on the ribbon. The query design view is displayed, which is used to create a query of the database. The **Show Table** dialog box is also open. Close this dialog box. Notice that the query appears as a separate tab and is currently unnamed (Query 1).

Query Design

14. Right-click the query's tab, and click **SQL View** in the shortcut menu. The view changes to a text editor for writing the SQL commands, as shown. The command SELECT; appears by default.

15. Enter these SQL commands:
    SELECT Students.FirstName, Students.LastName
    FROM Students

16. Click **Design>Results>Run** on the ribbon. Your three students should appear!

17. Applying what you have learned, display the SQL view. Add this to the line after FROM Students:
    Where (((Students.StudentID)=xx));
    Enter a student ID from your table in place of *xx*.

Run

18. Applying what you have learned, run the query again. Now, only one student should be displayed.

NoSQL

Another type of database is created with NoSQL. Originally meaning non-SQL, this refers to the structure and data access methods. Unlike SQL databases, NoSQL is not a relational database. A *NoSQL* database is nonstructured and does not rely on tables or accessing data through SQL commands.

NoSQL databases are often used for performance purposes, especially in cloud storage. These types of databases are able to provide quick responses. They offer high availability. *High availability* refers to the ability of a system to run continuously for a long period of time. NoSQL systems also have the ability to store vast quantities of data and the ability to store a variety of data.

NoSQL was created in the open-source community, but there are commercial products available. There are over a hundred NoSQL database choices available. Some of the more well-known products include Hadoop, MongoDB, and Cassandra.

NoSQL is growing in popularity, but it is not as mature as SQL. There is no commonality or standardization between offerings. This poses a challenge for security personnel. Always use the recommended security procedures for the NoSQL solution in place. Also, ensure the host systems are fully protected.

CompTIA Security+
1.2

Threats to Databases

One of the biggest threats against SQL databases is an attack called an SQL injection attack. In an *SQL injection attack,* instead of data, the hacker injects SQL–formatted commands as the input. The hacker enters commands to perform actions, as shown in **Figure 12-15.** For example, commands could be injected that tell the database to show all tables, the fields in the tables, and the data values stored in the tables.

Some notable hacks using SQL injection includes the 2011 hack against HB Gary Federal by members of the group Anonymous. This resulted in the theft of all company accounts and passwords. It also resulted in the dumping of 60,000 e-mails online. Another SQL–injection hack was against 7-11 stores in which credit and debit card numbers were accessed.

Just having a SQL–enabled database is not enough to allow an SQL injection attack. Two conditions must exist to allow the hack:

- the database must be relational using SQL
- the query the hacker will attempt to exploit must be user-controllable input

An example of user-controllable input is a username and password. SQL can be used to query these items.

Preventing SQL hacks through data and input validation is critical. In one method of accessing the data, the hacker will purposely enter data of the wrong type. For example, if a string (text) is expected, a number would be entered. The resulting error message may provide information about the database, including table structures.

Quick Look 12.3.2

SQL Injection

A poorly programmed website can be vulnerable to SQL–injection attacks. The company Acunetix produces a vulnerability scanner to check for security risks in web applications. It maintains a website for testing its scanner, which can be used to simulate attacks.

1. Launch a web browser, and navigate to the Acunetix test website (www.vulnweb.com).
2. On the main page, click the link for the Acuart test (testphp.vulnweb.com). The test page is formatted to look like a normal web page.
3. Click the **Browse artists** link in the menu on the left, and then click the link for the artist **Blad3**, as shown. Look at the address bar in your browser. Notice that the website has run a PHP–based SQL query of the database: artists.php?artist=2.

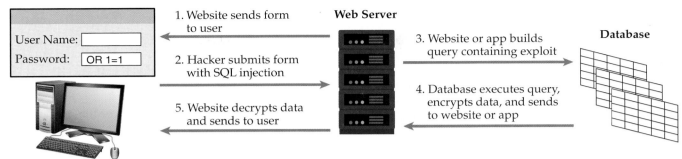

1. Website sends form to user
2. Hacker submits form with SQL injection
5. Website decrypts data and sends to user

Web Server

3. Website or app builds query containing exploit
4. Database executes query, encrypts data, and sends to website or app

Database

User Name:
Password: OR 1=1

Figure 12-15. In an SQL injection attack, the hacker enters SQL commands into user forms. In this case, since 1=1 is always true, the database will return data to the hacker.

Quick Look 12.3.2 Continued

4. Click in the browser address bar, and change the query to artists.php?artist=−1 UNION SELECT 1,pass,cc FROM users WHERE uname='test'. This looks for an artist record that does not exist (−1) as database records usually do not have negative numbering and extracts data from the database. The **UNION** command is used to join the attack (SELECT 1,pass,cc FROM users WHERE uname='test') with the original query(artists.php?artist=−1). The resulting data are displayed on the web page. In this way, hackers can extract data from the website's database.

5. Navigate to a search engine, and enter the search phrase sql injection test site. See if you can locate another simulator that demonstrates SQL–injection attacks. Experiment with the simulator, and discuss your findings with your classmates.

SECTION REVIEW 12.3

Check Your Understanding

1. A unique element of a table that contains one aspect of the data is called what?
2. A database consisting of tables that are linked by a common element is which type of database?
3. What programming language is used for managing relational databases?
4. Which type of database typically consists of large tables containing vast amounts of data and are often stored in the cloud?
5. If a hacker inserts commands in user-controllable input fields in a website, what type of attack is being committed?

Build Your Key Terms Vocabulary

As you progress through this course, develop a personal cybersecurity glossary. This will help you build your vocabulary and prepare you for a career. Write a definition for each of the following terms, and add it to your cybersecurity glossary.

database	query
database management system (DBMS)	record
field	relational database
field value	SQL injection attack
NoSQL	Structured Query Language (SQL)

Review and Assessment

Summary

Section 12.1 Threats to Software

- A programming language is interface and structure used to create software and often includes libraries or an API to allow sharing between modules.
- Software should be designed with the six-stage system design life cycle, which may follow a waterfall, agile, or NoDev model.
- There are various security threats to software, including buffer-overflow attacks.

Section 12.2 Threats to Web Applications

- The World Wide Web consists of interconnected web servers, which are vulnerable to a directory traversal attack if users are not locked into the root directory of the server.
- Fuzzing, or dynamic analysis, can be used to conduct extensive testing of web applications for vulnerabilities, such as cross-site scripting and cross-site request forgery attacks.
- A code repository is a secure location for storing code and can help reduce dead code, which can consume computer resources.

Section 12.3 Threats to Databases

- A database is a collection of related information in records and fields composing tables, which may be linked to create a relational database, and SQL is often used to query a database.
- SQL injection attacks are a serious threat to databases, which result when a hacker enters SQL commands into a user-controllable input, such as a username or password.

Check Your Cybersecurity IQ ↪

Now that you have completed this chapter, see what you have learned about cybersecurity by visiting the student companion website (www.g-wlearning.com) and taking the chapter posttest.

Review Questions ↪

For each question, select the answer that is the best response.

1. Which of the following is used to reuse code within an application?
   A. SDK
   B. Library
   C. Compiler
   D. SDLC

2. In the waterfall SDLC, which stage details the blueprint for the project?
   A. Requirements gathering
   B. Design
   C. Coding
   D. Testing

3. What is an exploit in which more data can be entered than the program can accept?
   A. Data canary
   B. RAM scraper
   C. Buffer-overflow attack
   D. Immutable server

4. A hacker was able to remotely access your web server and explore folders on the server. Which of the following is likely the type of attack being attempted?
   A. SQL injection
   B. Directory traversal
   C. CSRF
   D. Buffer overflow

5. Which of the following is a specific testing method on web applications?
   A. Probing
   B. Input validation
   C. Fuzzing
   D. Deep analysis

6. Which attack method exploits the trust relationship between the web server and the client?
   A. SQL injection
   B. Directory traversal
   C. CSRF
   D. Buffer overflow

7. GitHub is an example of:
   A. Backdoor to other code
   B. Code repository
   C. Certificate authority
   D. Linux server

8. What is needed for a code signature?
   A. Digital certificate from a trusted CA
   B. Data canary
   C. Software development kit (SDK)
   D. Cross-site scripting

9. What provides the interface and functionality for working with a database?
   A. Software development kit (SDK)
   B. Open Web Application Security Project (OWASP)
   C. System design life cycle (SDLC)
   D. Database management system (DBMS)

10. Which of the following is a threat to databases?
    A. Buffer-overflow attack
    B. SQL–injection attack
    C. Directory traversal
    D. Cross-site scripting (XSS) attack

Application and Extension of Knowledge

1. Create and design a simple database containing two tables using Microsoft Access. Make up five student names and data for the tables. In the first table, list student information, including a unique student ID. In the second table, list scores for standardized tests, including PSAT, SAT, and ones specific to your state and school. Create a relationship between the two tables based on student ID. Demonstrate your result with a query that lists student name (first and last), test date, test name, and test score.

2. You are tasked with creating a mobile app for students in your school. Create an SDLC chart using the waterfall method. List three to four tasks that would be accomplished in this section.

3. Microsoft Excel allows you to perform input validation. Create a simple workbook. In the first row, enter First Name in column A, Last Name in column B, Hourly Wage in column C, and Start Date in column D. The data in the Hourly Wage column should be numerical and between the values of 8.00 and 15.00. The date should be from March 1 of the current year to May 31 of the current year. For any incorrect entry, the error alert should read You have entered incorrect data, try again. To add data validation, click **Data**>**Data Tools**>**Data Validation** on the ribbon. After completing the setup, demonstrate your design with five records (rows). Show the test conditions you set. Write a one-page paper describing how you added data validation. Include screenshots to illustrate your work. Turn in the paper and Excel workbook.

4. Buffer overflow is a very common and widespread vulnerability. Investigate why this is the case and solutions to prevent buffer-overflow attacks. Create a one- to two-page report explaining the buffer-overflow vulnerability and reasons why this attack is still so common. List some solutions a company can take to prevent this type of exploit from occurring in its applications.

5. Codecademy (www.codecademy.com) provides online instruction in writing computer code. It offers free courses in languages such as Python, Java, and SQL. There are also options to upgrade for greater content for a fee. Take the first free course on SQL named Learn SQL. This course will take between 10 and 15 hours, so plan to complete the course over the next two or three weeks. When finished, demonstrate your completion of the course to your instructor.

Research Project
SQL Vulnerabilities

There have been cases involving knowledgeable people discovering SQL vulnerabilities as a probe, but not actually using this knowledge for personal gain. Two cases involving this type of action have sparked controversy. These are the cases of David Levins, a Florida-based white-hat hacker, and Robert Baptiste, a French white-hat hacker.

In the case of Levins, he found the vulnerability in the Lee County, Florida state elections website in late 2015 and early 2016. He revealed the vulnerabilities to a candidate in the election in order to show the vulnerabilities and help publicize the current problems.

In the case of Baptiste, in early 2018, he found vulnerabilities in the Telangana government's portal for NREGA, which is a social-aid program. Telangana is a south-Indian state. He claimed he contacted the site owners about the security issue and only published his results online after receiving no responses from Indian officials. The Indian government claims the Indian Information Technology Act 2000 prevents Indian researchers from looking into source codes of governmental digital services to find flaws, and it relies on foreign researchers to conduct security scans.

Research these two cases. Levins was charged with criminal activity, but Baptiste was not. Would you categorize either of these cases as a crime? The Indian government has downplayed the seriousness of Baptiste's attack. Do you feel either attack had criminal intent or was a genuine threat to data security?

Deliverables. Write a paper outlining and comparing the two cases. Present your opinion on whether you believe either case was a criminal act. Cite all sources you use following your school's accepted guidelines.

Online Activities

Complete the following activities, which will help you learn, practice, and expand your knowledge and skills.

Vocabulary. Practice vocabulary for this chapter using the e-flash cards, matching activity, and vocabulary game until you are able to recognize their meanings.

Communication Skills

College and Career Readiness

Reading. After you read this chapter, analyze how the author unfolds a series of ideas, including the order in which the points are made, how they are introduced and developed, and the connections drawn among them.

Writing. Interview a cybersecurity professional in your area. Ask this person what he or she likes best and least about the job, as well as several other questions of your own. Write a one-page paper describing what you learned from the interview. Follow your school's style guide for proper formatting.

Speaking. Read the Ethical Issue feature in this chapter. Think of a time when you used your ideals and principles to make a decision involving ethics. In retrospect, do you think you made the correct decision? Did your decision have any consequences? Participate in a conversation with your classmates in which you share your opinions on this subject.

Listening. Watch a television news broadcast. Listen to what the reports are saying. Are you able to determine the message each reporter is communicating? Are the reporters trying to persuade you to adopt a position?

Portfolio Development

College and Career Readiness

Diversity Skills. As part of an interview with an organization, you may be asked about your travels or experiences with people from other cultures. Many different organizations serve people from a variety of geographic locations and cultures. Some have offices or other types of facilities in more than one region or country. You may need to interact with people from diverse cultures. You may travel to facilities in different countries. Speaking more than one language and having traveled, studied, or worked in other countries can be valuable assets. You may be able to help an organization understand the needs and wants of diverse people. You may also be better able to communicate and get along with others.

1. Identify travel or other educational experiences that helped you learn about another culture, such as foreign languages studied or trips taken abroad.

2. Create a Microsoft Word document that describes the experience. Use the heading Diversity Experience and your name. Explain how the information you learned might help you better understand classmates, customers, or coworkers from this culture. Save the document in an appropriate folder.

3. Place a printed copy in your portfolio container for future reference.

4. Update your checklist to reflect the file format and location of the document.

CTSO Event Prep

Communications Skills. Communications skills may be judged as part of competitive events. Presenters must be able to exchange information with the judges in a clear, concise manner. This requirement is in keeping with the mission of CTSOs: to prepare students for professional careers in business. Communication skills will be judged for both the written and oral presentation. The evaluation will include all aspects of effective writing, speaking, and listening skills. To prepare for the communications portion of an event, complete the following activities.

1. Visit the organization's website, and look for specific communication skills that will be judged as a part of a competitive event.

2. Spend time to review the essential principles of communication, such as grammar, spelling, proofreading, capitalization, and punctuation.

3. If you are making a written presentation, ask an instructor to evaluate your writing. Review and apply the feedback so that your writing sample appears professional and correct.

4. If you are making an oral presentation, ask an instructor to review and listen for errors in grammar or sentence structure. After you have received comments, adjust and make the presentation several times until you are comfortable with your presentation.

5. Review the Communication Skills activities that appear at the end of each chapter of this text as a way to practice your reading, writing, listening, and speaking skills.

6. To practice listening skills, ask your instructor to give you a set of directions. Then, without assistance, repeat those directions to your instructor. Did you listen closely enough to be able to do what was instructed?

Chapter 13

Penetration Testing

Help wanted, Hacking skills required. This is not just a recruiting ad from some foreign government or the group Anonymous, but a desired skill set for many organizations. These businesses are not looking to hire hackers to steal competitors' secrets or obtain personal information from strangers. They are looking for those individuals literally to hack the company itself. A company hacking itself is not as uncommon as you might think. Companies do it to find where their defenses are weak, where unknown problems exist, and to ensure adequate protections are in place. This form of hacking is referred to as penetration testing.

A company may choose to use its own staff to probe the network's infrastructure and assets. Alternatively, it may choose to hire an outside resource. There are advantages and disadvantages to performing the testing as well as what degree of testing and information is provided. This chapter covers the types of penetration, the legality and ethics of conducting the testing, and some of the tools that are available to these security professionals.

Chapter Preview

While studying, look for the activity icon for:

- Pretests and posttests
- Vocabulary terms with e-flash cards and matching activities
- Self-assessment

G-W**LEARNING**.com

Reading Prep

Examine the visuals in this chapter before you read it. Write down questions you have about them. Try to answer the questions as you read.

College and Career Readiness

Check Your Cybersecurity IQ ➦

Before you begin this chapter, see what you already know about cybersecurity by visiting the student companion website (www.g-wlearning.com) and taking the chapter pretest.

Certification Objectives

CompTIA Security+

1.2 Compare and contrast types of attacks.
1.4 Explain penetration testing concepts.
3.1 Explain use cases and purpose for frameworks, best practices and secure configuration guides.
5.1 Explain the importance of policies, plans and procedures related to organizational security.
5.3 Explain risk management processes and concepts.

Microsoft MTA Security Fundamentals

1.1 Understand core security principles.
1.2 Understand physical security.

Overview of Penetration Testing

Essential Question

When should the actions of a penetration tester result in criminal charges?

Much of the time spent as an IT security professional is responding to threats. Much time is also spent on creating and instituting preventative measures to reduce or remove the risk of security threats. Another way to prepare, institute, or modify defensive security measures is to assess the security configurations in place on your network. These tests, or vulnerability assessments, are carried out with the objective of discovering where a network or systems are vulnerable to threats and exploits. They look for ways hackers can penetrate defenses.

Before just jumping in and conducting these tests, the process must be carefully planned. Are the testers doing a blind test where they know little to nothing about your organization? Or, do you want to give them known data, such as what type of equipment and software you use, and have them focus on these areas? Other considerations include determining the impact on operations this test could have and prewarning existing staff. This section reviews the elements of penetration testing.

Key Terms 📇

active information gathering

banner grabbing

black box test

Electronic Data Gathering Analysis and Retrieval System (EDGAR)

ethical hacking

executive summary

gray box test

National Institute of Standards and Technology (NIST)

nondisclosure agreement (NDA)

Open Source Intelligence (OSINT)

OS fingerprinting

passive information gathering

penetration testing

Penetration Testing Execution Standard

port scanning

pretext

scope

scope creep

semipassive information gathering

STRIDE

technical report

testing time line

threat modeling

Visual, Agile, and Simple Threat (VAST)

vulnerability analysis

white box test

Learning Goals

- Describe penetration testing and its use in ethical hacking.
- Design a penetration test covering the standard test procedures.
- Assess legal issues related to penetration testing.

Penetration Testing Basics

As you learned in Chapter 1, *penetration testing* is a process in which security personnel attempt to penetrate a network to locate vulnerabilities. Penetration testing is often referred to as *pen testing.* Another term for penetration testing is *ethical hacking.*

A penetration tester has a very important job. He or she must have expertise in the areas that are being tested. Many firms use a team approach to the penetration testing. A methodical approach is used. This means each step and task is carefully documented, as shown in **Figure 13-1.** This documentation allows the team to provide solid reporting and to remove any files and changes left in the system.

Penetration testers, or pen testers, must continually update and improve their skills. One way to prove your skills is through industry certification. Expertise in both Windows and Linux operating systems is essential. It is also important to be skilled in other areas, including web services, databases, and networking. Certifications for penetration testing are discussed in more detail later in this chapter.

A penetration test is much more than just sitting down and running hacking tools and methods to see if you can access sensitive data. Consider the five Ws of penetration testing:

- why
- who
- what
- where
- when

Roman Samborskyi/Shutterstock.com

Figure 13-1. A penetration tester has a very important job, and the steps taken during testing must be carefully documented.

Why

The first W is *why.* As the security tester, you need to know what the objectives of the testing are for the customer. What does the customer expect from the test? In other words, why does the customer want the test completed? Knowing the why will help guide the testing.

Who

The second W is *who.* A company should consider who likely wants to attack it. This can help the security tester focus on specific testing areas. For example, if the company has high-value and desired assets, these might be targeted. Depending on what these assets are may help determine who will be the most likely attacker.

What

The third W is *what.* What does the customer want tested? Does the physical security need to be tested? Are the wireless networks and routers to be tested? The what tells the tester the boundaries of testing. This needs to be clearly defined in the scope, which is discussed later in this chapter.

Where

The fourth W is *where.* Where will the security testing take place? If there is more than one location, this needs to be clarified for the pen tester. Is physical access to the facility required? In some cases, testing can be done remotely. In other cases, the testing must be done on-site.

FYI

If penetration testing is conducted internally within a company, the "customer" is the company itself.

When

The last W is *when*. When will the security testing be conducted? Often, an annual test should be performed. In some cases, it is better to conduct several smaller tests throughout the year. Smaller tests can focus on specific areas. Smaller tests may also be less disruptive to the company's daily operations.

Standard Test Procedures

A group of security practitioners from many different backgrounds has developed the Penetration Testing Execution Standard. The goal of the *Penetration Testing Execution Standard* is to provide a minimum set of standards that all penetration tests should address. The main standards are shown in **Figure 13-2.**

Preengagement Interactions

Before penetration testing can be conducted, there must be discussions and agreements that cover topics such as:

- scope of the testing;
- time lines;
- payment of fees;
- third-party individuals or businesses impacted by the testing; and
- white box, black box, or gray box testing.

This happens before engaging in the test, which is why this standard is called preengagement interactions.

During the course of testing, the pen tester may uncover private information about users or devices. The target company's acceptable use policy is the guide if this information can be used. This must be discussed with the target during the first phase of the project. Employees may not be aware their access of the network could expose this information or be used to gain additional information. There could be some legal implications. Legal implications are discussed later in this section.

Penetration Testing Execution Standard

The sections or standards are sequential in nature. They should be performed in order.

1. **Preengagement interactions**
   Conducted before the testing begins.
2. **Intelligence gathering**
   Collecting information about the target before trying to penetrate it.
3. **Threat modeling**
   Creating a plan of attack.
4. **Vulnerability analysis**
   Discovering flaws in the system being tested.
5. **Exploitation**
   Actually penetrating the system being tested.
6. **Post exploitation**
   Evaluating each penetration for its value and holding the asset for further exploitation.
7. **Reporting**
   Providing the customer with the results of the testing and recommendations.

Goodheart-Willcox Publisher

Figure 13-2.   The Penetration Testing Execution Standard consists of seven overall sections or standards for penetration testing.

Scope

Many areas can be tested. It is important to identify each area in the test to protect the tester and to fulfill the needs of the customer. The *scope* defines exactly what will be tested. If what is to be tested is not clearly identified, it is very possible that things arise. You could find other areas that need testing. The customer also may request additional testing. Without a clearly written scope, the penetration tester might find he or she is doing more work for no additional money. *Scope creep* occurs when changes or additional requests are made after the project begins.

Be sure the scope is clearly stated in the contract. For example, suppose the customer is only concerned about access to its server room. The scope should clearly state the penetration testing will only cover physical access to that area. Then, when the testing is conducted, the tester should test only the physical access. If the customer requests additional testing, that should be handled with a new contract. The scope of the new contract should clearly state the additional testing required.

There are many questions to ask the customer when establishing the scope. Use a questionnaire to cover all possibilities for each type of testing. Some common areas for testing are physical, web, network, and social engineering.

Physical Testing. If the company has multiple locations, specify which location will be tested. Are there certain rooms that need to be accessed? Are there security guards on staff? If so, are they armed? Should locks be picked?

Web Testing. Ask the customer which web applications will be tested. Does this include databases? Should stress testing be done? Stress testing likely involves a DoS attack.

Network Testing. Ask the customer if testing will include both the physical and the wireless networks. What IP addresses will be included in the penetration test? Should the tester set up a rogue wireless router to perform man-in-the-middle attacks? This type of test may be set up as shown in **Figure 13-3.** Another important question deals with the security appliances in place, such as firewalls and intrusion-prevention systems. How far should the tester attempt to exploit these devices? When should active scanning or DoS attacks be done? If done during regular hours, the business may be impacted. If this is not okay, the tests will need to be conducted after-hours. After-hours work may be billed at a higher rate than other work.

Social Engineering Testing. Phishing and spear phishing are common social engineering attacks. Many of these attacks include a pretext in the e-mail. A *pretext* is a fabricated scenario or story that entices the recipient to click on a link. The pretext that will be used in testing should be approved by the customer. This is to ensure it does not contain anything considered offensive to the customer and employees.

MTA Security Fundamentals
1.2

MTA Security Fundamentals
1.1

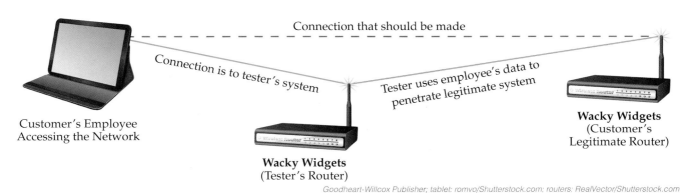

Connection that should be made

Connection is to tester's system

Tester uses employee's data to penetrate legitimate system

Customer's Employee Accessing the Network

Wacky Widgets (Tester's Router)

Wacky Widgets (Customer's Legitimate Router)

Goodheart-Willcox Publisher; tablet: romvo/Shutterstock.com; routers: RealVector/Shutterstock.com

Figure 13-3. Penetration testing may involve setting up a rogue router to look for vulnerabilities in a wireless network.

Quick Look 13.1.1

Social Engineering Pretext

You have been asked to be a penetration tester for your school district. The scope of the testing is to conduct a spear phishing attack against the teachers and administrative staff of the school. The first task is to draft an e-mail to be used in the attack.

1. Using a word processor, create an e-mail that includes a pretext for the target. Remember, consider the victim! What would make the victim click a link?

2. Share your word-processing document with your classmates. Do *not* send the e-mail to anyone.

3. In pairs or small groups, discuss the various pretexts. Which ones do you feel would be the most effective? Why?

Time line

A *testing time line* states when the stages of testing will happen. It ensures the testing will occur within the dates specified by the contract, as shown in **Figure 13-4.** The skills and background of the pen tester should be considered when setting the time line. An experienced tester may be able to complete the required tasks in a short time frame. On the other hand, a new tester may need more time.

A common practice is to cushion the time. This gives the tester more time than you believe is needed. Adding a cushion to the time line is commonly referred to as *padding.* Padding can help keep a project on time if something unexpected comes up.

Fees

Most security firms have set fees for different types of penetration testing. The fees charged should always refer to the scope of the job. This is why having a clearly defined scope is so important. Every company has unique needs, situations, and network configurations. Fees should be based on the actual work required to complete the testing.

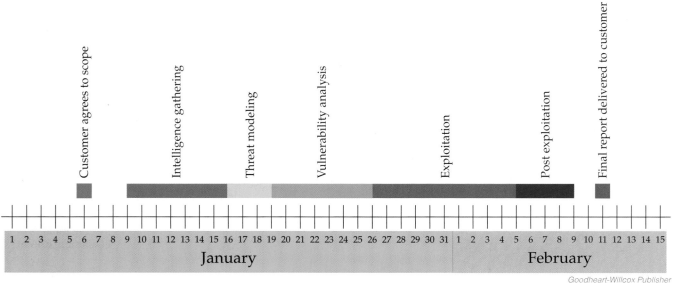

Figure 13-4. The testing time line shows dates for completing the stages of penetration testing.

Third-Party Vendors

Another critical aspect of preengagement interactions is considering any third parties that will be involved. For example, a company's assets may be stored with a cloud vendor. Some common cloud vendors include Microsoft, Amazon, and Rackspace. If the testing is to involve third-party vendors, written permission must be obtained from these companies allowing the testing. Also be aware of and follow the policies of the vendors.

White, Black, or Gray Box

CompTIA Security+
1.4

As you learned in Chapter 1, penetration testing will be conducted under one of the following conditions.

- no previous knowledge of the system
- some knowledge of the system
- overview of system provided before testing

A *black box test* is when the pen tester has no knowledge of the system. A *gray box test* is when the tester has some knowledge of the system. A *white box test* is when the pen tester has been given full knowledge of the system.

There are merits to all three types of test. Having advanced knowledge of the system allows the tester to focus on the system and its configurations. On the other hand, if the tester has no knowledge of the system, the tester can approach the test just as a hacker may. This can show information that may lead to an actual hack.

Intelligence Gathering

Gathering information about a target can provide clues to gaining entry into the building or network. This will help the tester reach the ultimate target. The more information that can be obtained before an attack, the easier it will be for the tester to penetrate the systems.

The vulnerabilities exposed by social engineering are explored in Chapter 2. Social engineering is one way preliminary intelligence can be obtained. There are other sources often used to find information. One of these sources is online job-posting websites, such as CareerBuilder and Indeed. When companies post open positions, they often reveal what type of infrastructure they have. This can be discovered by looking at the skills or certifications desired. For example, a post may say the job requires skill in specific software programs or programming languages.

Another source is called EDGAR. The *Electronic Data Gathering Analysis and Retrieval System (EDGAR)* is a database found on the United States Security and Exchange Commission (SEC) website for electronic SEC filings. Many companies are periodically required to file forms and reports with the SEC. This may include quarterly reports, annual reports, and other required disclosure information. This information is located on EDGAR. It is available at no charge. EDGAR includes a search engine, as shown in **Figure 13-5.** Using this database, a pen tester or hacker can find out about a company and its financial dealings.

The use of job posting sites, EDGAR, and other similar resources is a method of intelligence gathering called OSINT. *Open Source Intelligence (OSINT)* involves obtaining information that is freely available online. There are three levels or methods of OSINT:

- passive information gathering
- semipassive information gathering
- active information gathering

Search for a company

Goodheart-Willcox Publisher

Figure 13-5. The Securities and Exchange Commission website contains EDGAR, which can be used to search for information on companies that are required to file with the SEC.

CompTIA Security+
1.4

Passive Information Gathering

In *passive information gathering,* the target is not aware of the reconnaissance. Using job sites and EDGAR are examples of passive information gathering. Other sources of passive information gathering include LinkedIN and ZoomInfo. Company press releases can yield information as well. Searching for WhoIs data for the organization can provide more information. As discussed in Chapter 2, court records can be potentially used to find information on employees. Looking at the digital footprint of an individual is another passive means of finding information.

The problem with this method is the information often comes from third-party sources. The data are only as reliable as the source and the date of the information.

Semipassive Information Gathering

Semipassive information gathering involves using the target's resources just as any normal customer would, but collecting data at the same time. Nothing is done that may alert the target. Only normal traffic is generated. The goal is to gather data without drawing attention.

Semipassive information gathering could involve using the company's website to view information. Documents may be downloaded to get information. These documents may also contain metadata that could provide additional information. A company's annual report may also be requested. This provides financial information for the fiscal year. It may also yield other information that can be used in an attack.

Observing the physical location and actions of employees may yield information. War driving may allow information to be detected on the wireless network, including which RF signals are used. Again, the key is to do this without making your behavior and actions appear suspicious.

Active Information Gathering

With *active information gathering,* actions are taken that may be noticed by the target. This type of activity includes port scanning. It also includes banner grabbing and SMTP querying, which are discussed later. These actions all will likely be noticed by the company's defenses. This will alert the company that someone is attempting to gather information.

A fiscal year is the 12-month period the business uses for budgetary purposes. Many companies do not follow a traditional January to December calendar for business and accounting purposes.

Quick Look 13.1.2

Intelligence Gathering

There are many ways to gather information on a target. Passive information gathering is often based on the digital footprint left by the target.

1. Launch a web browser, and navigate to the Indeed website (www.indeed.com).

2. Enter network engineer in the search text box. For the location, select either your hometown or nearby larger city. Then, click the **Find Jobs** button to conduct the search.

3. Look through some of the positions. What types of hardware and software are listed as required knowledge for these positions?

4. Conduct another search using the phrase programmer. What types of programming languages or skills did you find were desired?

5. Conduct another search using the phrase help desk. What types of skills are required for this position? Help desk personnel often need to have a variety of skills to support the different aspects of a company. The skills needed for this position often reveal internal systems in use.

6. Navigate to the EDGAR page on the SEC website (www.sec.gov/edgar.shtml).

7. Click **Company Filings Search** in the menu or look for the option to search for companies.

8. On the search page, enter chipotle as the company name to search. On the results page, general company information appears at the top. A listing of available documents appears at the bottom.

9. Scroll through the list of documents to find the one dated July 25, 2017 (2017-07-25). Click the Documents button for this entry to display a new page containing links to the related documents.

10. On the new page, click the link for the EX-99.1 document, as shown. Look through the information. The document talks about revenue information, comparable sales, and other information. This particular document also addressed the cyberattack at the restaurants. Think about how this information could be used in a spear phishing attack.

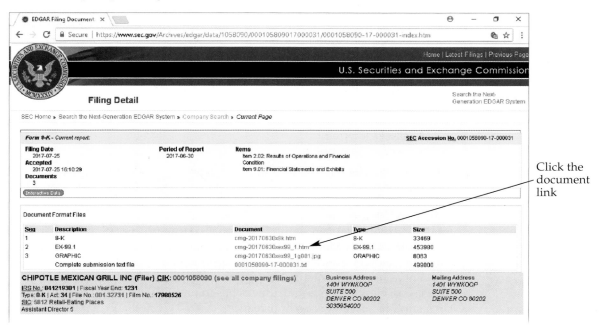

Figure 13-6. Just as a burglar will steal items that have the most value, such as computers, hackers will focus on the assets that have the most value. Part of threat modeling is determining which assets are high-value targets.

Threat Modeling

A critical step of a penetration test is threat modeling. *Threat modeling* is identifying the potential threats and determining which ones are high-value assets. A high-value asset is one that a hacker would most likely want or that will be most damaging to the company. For example, a burglar will not likely break into a house to steal a toaster if he or she can steal a new computer, as shown in **Figure 13-6.** Hackers will want to get the most out of their attacks. They will likely focus on assets that provide the biggest return.

When creating a threat model, take relevant information about the target, and determine the primary and secondary targets. In the example of a burglar, he or she wants to steal the computer. However, once in the house, a smartphone is seen on the shelf. The computer is the primary target. The smartphone is the secondary target. Both have value to the burglar.

A hacker's primary target may be to steal a customer database and the credit card information it contains. However, once on the server, he or she may see an employee database. This database contains Social Security numbers and other private information. While the primary target is the credit card information, the Social Security numbers are a secondary target. Consider other assets that may be the target of hackers:

- upcoming (not released) marketing plans or product rollout
- confidential documents relating to the research of products, patents, trade secrets, or software source code
- internal policies
- financial information for the company, including pay, credit information, or bank account information

The pen tester may work with their customer to identify what targets may be of interest to potential hackers.

Threat modeling typically defines three ways to view the security threats against a system:

- attacker viewpoint
- asset viewpoint
- system viewpoint

The attacker's viewpoint is why the hacker is conducting this attack. Hacker motivations are covered in Chapter 1. The asset viewpoint is the assets that have value to a hacker. How can they be accessed? The system viewpoint is the entry points. What are the vulnerable areas that can be targeted? There are threat-modeling tools that can be used to assist in this process. Some are free, such as Microsoft's Threat Modeling tool. Others may apply to the IT infrastructure with computer-aided design (CAD)–based approaches.

There are some distinctive approaches. The model designed by Microsoft focuses on viewing potential attacks based on STRIDE. *STRIDE* is a threat model consisting of six categories of threats:

- spoofing identity
- tampering
- repudiation
- information disclosure
- denial of service (DoS)
- elevation of privilege

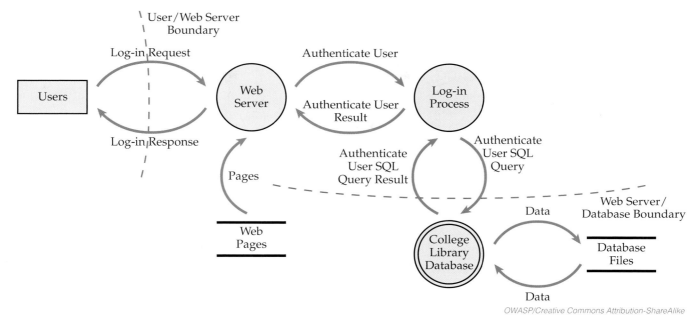

Figure 13-7. A data-flow diagram (DFD) is a visual representation of the infrastructure or application.

Some threat models, including STRIDE, use a data-flow diagram (DFD). This is a visual representation of the infrastructure or application, as shown in **Figure 13-7.**

Another popular approach is VAST. *Visual, Agile, and Simple Threat (VAST)* is a threat model based on scaling the model across the infrastructure. Scalability is one of the biggest benefits of VAST. It is a combination of two model types: operational and application. The application threat model is not the typical DFD output. It use a process-flow model, as shown in **Figure 13-8.** The process-flow model helps understand the interdependency of activities and operations. It does not necessarily present as a sequential process. The operational model provides an end-to-end view of the business, including users and all components of the operation.

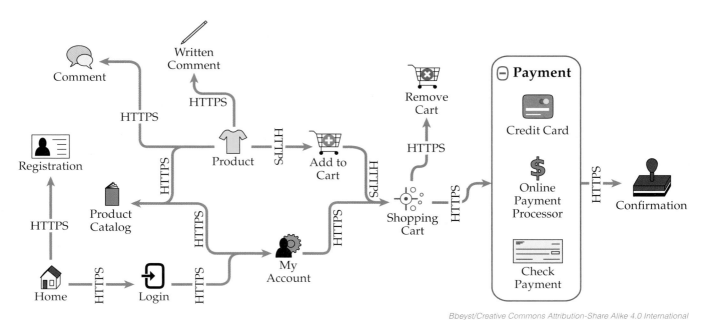

Figure 13-8. A process-flow model shows how data move through the system.

Quick Look 13.1.3

Microsoft Threat Modeling Tool

There are many threat modeling tools available. Some are free, but many are commercial solutions. One free option is the Threat Modeling Tool from Microsoft.

1. Launch a web browser, and navigate to the Microsoft website (www.microsoft.com).
2. Using the search tool, enter the phrase threat modeling tool. In the list of results, select the article entitled *SDL Threat Modeling Tool.*
3. On the overview page, watch the short video that describes the tool. As you watch the video, consider these questions:
   A. When should the problems be found?
   B. What makes this tool a good option for a software engineer?
   C. Do you feel programmers could effectively use this?
   D. Should a tool like this be mandated when developing software?

Vulnerability Analysis

The *vulnerability analysis* stage of penetration testing involves attempting to discover flaws that may be exploited by a hacker. This stage is typically when active intelligence gathering techniques occur. As part of that, the pen tester may conduct port scanning and banner grabbing.

Port Scanning

Port scanning involves actively probing a system to discover ports that are open on a system. Recall a service uses a system port as a means of entering or exiting the system. Think of a port as a doorway that can have traffic enter or exit. By conducting a port scan, you are seeing not only which ports are open, but also which service is using that port.

A well-known port scanning software is Nmap (network mapper), as shown in **Figure 13-9.** Nmap is an open-source tool. It runs on Windows, Linux, and Mac operating systems. It can rapidly scan thousands of machines or just a single host. The software can be downloaded free at Nmap.org. The standard version has command-line entry. There are versions with a graphical interface, such as Zenmap.

In addition to scanning ports, Nmap can attempt OS fingerprinting. *OS fingerprinting* is identifying the operating system of the network being tested. This can even include version numbers of services in use.

Quick Look 13.1.4

Nmap

Nmap is a widely used, open-source tool for conducting security scans. These instructions are for the Windows-based, graphical version of Nmap.

1. Launch a web browser, and navigate to the Nmap website (www.nmap.org).
2. Locate and click the **Download** link in the menu.
3. Follow your instructor's directions as to which version to download and install. Install the Zenmap option if prompted.
4. Once installation is complete, open Nmap –Zenmap GUI using the **Start** menu.

```
$ nmap -A scanme.nmap.org

Starting Nmap 6.47 ( http://nmap.org ) at 2014-12-29 20:02 CET
Nmap scan report for scanme.nmap.org (74.207.244.221)
Host is up (0.16s latency).
Not shown: 997 filtered ports
PORT      STATE SERVICE   VERSION
22/tcp    open  ssh       OpenSSH 5.3p1 Debian 3ubuntu7.1 (Ubuntu Linux; protocol 2.0)
| ssh-hostkey:
|   1024 8d:60:f1:7c:ca:b7:3d:0a:d6:67:54:9d:69:d9:b9:dd (DSA)
|_  2048 79:f8:09:ac:d4:e2:32:42:10:49:d3:bd:20:82:85:ec (RSA)
80/tcp    open  http      Apache httpd 2.2.14 ((Ubuntu))
|_http-title: Go ahead and ScanMe!
9929/tcp  open  nping-echo Nping echo
Warning: OSScan results may be unreliable because we could not find at least 1 open and 1 closed port
Device type: general purpose|phone|storage-misc|WAP
Running (JUST GUESSING): Linux 2.6.X|3.X|2.4.X (94%), Netgear RAIDiator 4.X (86%)
OS CPE: cpe:/o:linux:linux_kernel:2.6.38 cpe:/o:linux:linux_kernel:3 cpe:/o:netgear:raidiator:4 cpe:/o:linux:linux_kernel:2.4
Aggressive OS guesses: Linux 2.6.38 (94%), Linux 3.0 (92%), Linux 2.6.32 - 3.0 (91%), Linux 2.6.18 (91%), Linux 2.6.39 (90%), Linux 2.6.32 - 2.6.39 (90%), Linux 2.6.38
- 3.0 (90%), Linux 2.6.38 - 2.6.39 (89%), Linux 2.6.35 (88%), Linux 2.6.37 (88%)
No exact OS matches for host (test conditions non-ideal).
Network Distance: 13 hops
Service Info: OS: Linux; CPE: cpe:/o:linux:linux_kernel

TRACEROUTE (using port 80/tcp)
HOP RTT      ADDRESS
1   14.21 ms  151.217.192.1
2   5.27 ms   ae10-0.mx240-iphh.network (94.45.224.129)
3   13.16 ms  hmb-s2-rou-1102.DE.eurorings.net (134.222.120.121)
4   6.83 ms   blnb-s1-rou-1041.DE.eurorings.net (134.222.229.78)
5   8.30 ms   blnb-s3-rou-1041.DE.eurorings.net (134.222.229.82)
6   9.42 ms   as6939.bcix.de (193.178.185.34)
7   24.56 ms  10ge10-6.core1.ams1.he.net (184.105.213.229)
8   30.60 ms  100ge9-1.core1.lon2.he.net (72.52.92.213)
9   93.54 ms  100ge1-1.core1.nyc4.he.net (72.52.92.166)
10  181.14 ms 10ge9-6.core1.sjc2.he.net (184.105.213.173)
11  169.54 ms 10ge3-2.core3.fmt2.he.net (184.105.222.13)
12  164.58 ms router4-fmt.linode.com (64.71.132.138)
13  164.32 ms scanme.nmap.org (74.207.244.221)

OS and Service detection performed. Please report any incorrect results at http://nmap.org/submit/ .
Nmap done: 1 IP address (1 host up) scanned in 28.98 seconds
```

Roman Samborskyi/Shutterstock.com

Figure 13-1. A penetration tester has a very important job, and the steps taken during testing must be carefully documented.

Quick Look 13.1.4 Continued

5. In the **Target:** text box, enter the IP address of your default gateway. Click the **Profile:** drop-down arrow, and click **Intense scan** in the drop-down list. Notice that as you make these selections, the **Command:** text box displays the command-line equivalent. Click the **Scan** button to begin scanning.

6. When finished, review the information on the **Output** tab. How many ports were scanned? Did the scan identify the operating system of your target?

7. Click the **Ports** tab, and review information. Do the same for the **Hosts** tab. Then, review the other tabs.

8. In the **Target:** text box, enter a range of ten IP addresses in your subnet. For example, if your network address is 192.168.2.0, you can enter 192.168.2.1-10.

9. Applying what you have learned, change the **Profile:** setting to **Quick scan**, and then start the scan. How many hosts are identified as being up?

10. Click the **Topology** tab. Review your output with the **Fish Eye** view. To the top right of the screen, choose **Legend** to identify the colors of the targets. Which hosts could be most vulnerable? After using this view, explore the **Host Viewer** tab.

Banner Grabbing

A *banner* is a message transmitted to the sender from the target host. *Banner grabbing* is used to determine what services are running on a remote system. It is done by using Telnet or some other utility to send a request to the target. The target responds with a *banner message* that can be used to obtain information about the host. The banner will contain service information, including a version number.

A utility commonly used for banner grabbing is called Netcat. It can be downloaded for Linux and Microsoft operating systems. Some Linux distros include it. A version of Netcat was created as part of the Nmap project and is included with the Nmap download. This version is called Ncat.

Exploitation

Once vulnerabilities are found, the pen tester will see if those can be exploited to successfully access the target. The tester should still try to remain unnoticed to evade detection. For example, if doing a physical test, avoid being seen by security guards. Also, make sure not to be captured by surveillance cameras.

At this stage, defenses need to be tested. The results must be enumerated. *Enumerate* means to list and identify. In this case, each defense would be listed and identified. Some of the defenses likely to be encountered include:

- antivirus programs;
- firewalls; and
- intrusion-detection and prevention systems.

For example, to bypass antivirus or intrusion-detection systems, package the data to avoid being flagged as dangerous. This is known as obfuscating the data. *Obfuscate* means to bewilder or make unclear. Encryption is one way to obfuscate the data, as shown in **Figure 13-10**.

There may be other potential vulnerabilities. The pen tester can attempt to exploit buffer overflows and SQL injections. Monitoring and analyzing traffic to identify what is being sent and received potentially allows the pen tester to manipulate this traffic. If a wireless system is in place, wireless hacks are done. These could be creating rogue access points or attacks against WEP, WPA, WPA2. Searching through DNS and ARP caches could provide additional information that can be exploited.

The pen tester may use the old tried-and-true hack of USB injection. USB injection is when content on a flash drive, such as malware, is automatically loaded when a user inserts the drive into a computer. This was done in 2013 by the Department of Homeland Security. It ran a test in which staffers dropped flash drives in parking lots of governmental and contractor buildings. Despite warnings that unapproved devices should never be used, 60 percent of the drives were plugged into the governmental network. Some of the flash drives were labeled with governmental logos. The insertion rate for those drives was 90 percent.

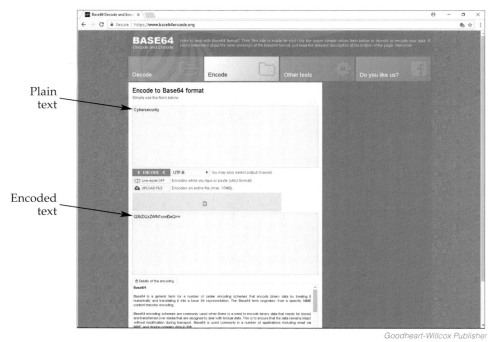

Figure 13-10. Encrypting text obfuscates its meaning. Here, plain text is converted into Base-64.

The pen tester may use social engineering to attempt a hack. For example, he or she may pretend to be a vendor sending literature for a new program. As part of this, a "Thank you in advance" gift of a flash drive is included in the mailing. This flash drive could be embedded with a root kit. When the target inserts the device in a computer, the root kit launches.

Quick Look 13.1.5

Encoded Data

A way to obfuscate data is to encode it. Doing this makes it less likely the data sent by the pen tester will be flagged by security measures in place on the target.

1. Launch a web browser, and navigate to the Base64 Encode website (www.base64encode.org). Base-64 coding is a coding mechanism that represents binary data as ASCII using a radix, or base, of 64 digits.
2. Click **Encode** at the top of the page. Note there is also an option for decoding.
3. Click in the top text box, and enter the word Dog.
4. Click the **Encode** button below the text box. The resulting encoded text is RG9n. The value of *Dog* in binary is 01000100 01101111 01100111. This binary value is then encoded with the Base-64 coding to give the result of RG9n.
5. Applying what you have learned, decode this: RG9scGhpbg. Case matters! What is the plain-text version of this? Do you notice any similarities between these two examples?

Post Exploitation

When exploits are successful, the pen tester attempts to keep the connection alive. One way to do this may be to place tools on key devices in the network so the tester can still obtain data. Other examples include installing key loggers and root kits. The tester may escalate account privileges to gain additional resources. The tester may even run a denial-of-service attack against the target.

The pen tester is not a black-hat hacker. He or she is just testing the security defenses. Therefore, it is *critical* to document everything that was done. Throughout penetration testing, activities should be logged. The log should include dates and times of activities as well as what was done. This includes every trap that was set.

Reporting

Once all objectives of the testing have been met, including targets and time lines, the pen tester compiles his or her documentation for the customer. The final responsibility to the customer is a detailed report. This is submitted following completion of the penetration testing. A report on penetration testing generally includes two key areas: an executive summary and the technical report. There is not a set format for the report. Companies that are contracted to do the penetration testing will usually have a standard presentation based on their own business practices.

Once the report is submitted to the customer, all data and information collected during the test must be destroyed. This includes paper and electronic copies of the data. The customer should be given verification of the method and date of destruction.

Also at the end of the testing period, all files must be removed from the customer's site. This includes files such as scripts, executable programs, and temporary files. If any configuration files were changed, these must be restored to the original values. If key loggers, rootkits, or backdoor accounts were inserted, they need to be deleted and removed at this time.

Executive Summary

The *executive summary* states in plain language the high-value targets that were identified and the impact breaches of these targets will have. It should be brief and to the point. Information should be easy to read and understand for even readers who are not cybersecurity experts. This includes management and executives who may have little or no technical background.

Graphs and infographics help present information. Infographics go a long way in making data more understandable. They easily attract the reader's attention and simplify data, as shown in **Figure 13-11.** Infographics can also be used to promote brand awareness for your business as well.

This section should include a security-risk-rating scale. Using color for this provides easy visual cues. For example, problems classified as extreme or critical could be identified with red. Green is generally associated with errors and problems that are not urgent. Whatever rating scale used, the scale should explain the risk. For example, an extreme or critical rating might indicate a catastrophic event.

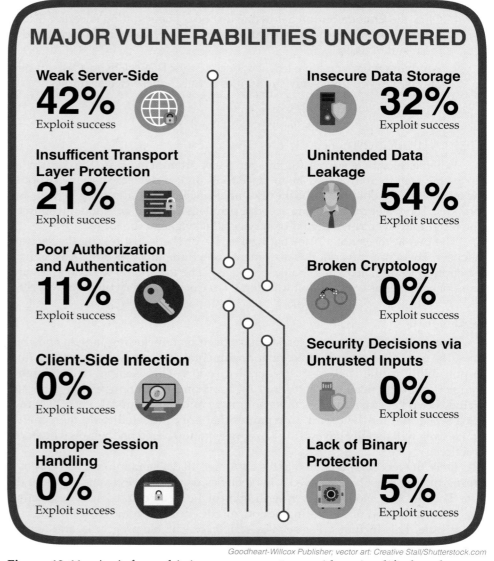

Goodheart-Willcox Publisher; vector art: Creative Stall/Shutterstock.com

Figure 13-11.   An infographic is an easy way to provide a simplified explanation of data. These may be used in the executive summary.

Technical Report

The *technical report* details the specific vulnerabilities found during the pen test. This section should provide specific details on why the issues are vulnerabilities. Include an analysis of the vulnerability. Explain why each should be a concern to the customer. This will allow the security staff to use this information to verify accuracy and correct any information. The technical report's target audience is the IT staff who will be tasked with correcting these vulnerabilities. It is okay to use technical language to describe the vulnerabilities.

This report may include screenshots of details. For example, a screenshot may be used to show which users are members of the administrators group. A screenshot may also be used to show a port scan on a web server.

The technical report can be organized by the scope of the project. This may be identifying vulnerabilities by physical security or network testing. The report may also be organized by the degree of the vulnerabilities identified. In this case, the highest-risk vulnerabilities are presented first.

Quick Look 13.1.6

Penetration Test Report

You have been hired to do a gray box penetration test on a company's wireless network. The wireless network has ten routers with the same SSID and is using Radius to authenticate users. The company uses half of the first-floor offices in a building. It has only Windows computers.

1. Work with a partner to come up with the following. Your instructor is the customer.
   A. Questions to ask the customer before creating the testing proposal.
   B. Time line for the test.
   C. Fees to charge the customer.
2. After gathering information from the customer, identify the following.
   A. Scope of the test.
   B. Specific tests to be conducted.
3. Identify some specific examples that would be included in the executive summary and the technical summary.
4. Share your team's responses with the class. Compare and contrast the approaches taken by the teams.

Additional Report Terminology

There are some key terms and documents you should be familiar with for testing and reporting. The *National Institute of Standards and Technology (NIST)* is a governmental organization for standardizing measurement, technology, and industrial standards. It is part of the US Department of Commerce and maintains its own website (www.nist.gov). There are many publications that can be used freely by anyone to help manage their IT and security cultures. Use the document-search function on its website (instead of the general search function) to locate a specific document.

For example, there is a series of documents numbered NIST SP 800-xx, where *xx* is a number. The 800 series all deal in some manner with computer security. SP stands for *special publications*. The series of numbers is a report number. Consider the report NIST SP 800-15. This document provides recommendations and guidelines for organizations wishing to conduct a security assessment. All computer security NIST documents can be found on the NIST website (csrc.nist.gov).

CompTIA Security+
3.1

CompTIA Security+
5.3

Legal Considerations

The first and most important step a pen tester must take before conducting any type of security testing is to obtain *written permission* from the customer. The permission must come from an authorized person within the company. This is usually a manager or executive. This must be part of a contract that details the scope of the testing. The contract must state what will be tested and who is responsible for the testing. It should also clearly outline immunity from prosecution or repercussions due to performing the agreed-on tests. If other networks will be used to reach the customer, additional permission is needed from those vendors to access the customer's resources. For example, a customer may have infrastructure located in the cloud. The customer cannot grant permission to use the cloud vendor's networks. That permission must come from the cloud vendor itself.

CompTIA Security+
5.1

A pen tester often must sign a nondisclosure agreement. A *nondisclosure agreement (NDA)* forbids revealing any of the information discussed or discovered. This protects the confidentiality of any data viewed or recovered by the tester. Most NDAs specify that all data, notes, and records remain the property of the organization. Most also state everything must be returned at the conclusion of the investigation. Failure to abide by the terms of the agreement could result in loss of employment or litigation. An NDA may be written by an attorney. Generic NDAs can be found online for free.

The tester must also check for applicable laws. There are federal laws covering computer crime, as shown in **Figure 13-12.** Some states and localities have their own laws beyond federal laws. It is possible testing could expose or discover unintended information. Extra care should be taken to ensure no laws are broken.

Even if it is ethical hacking, pen testing is still hacking. Therefore, there is some exposure to legal ramifications. If a pen tester is not careful to get advance

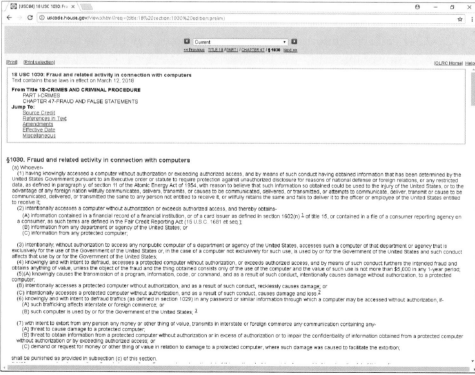

Goodheart-Willcox Publisher

Figure 13-12.   The United States has laws governing computer crime. The United States Code is available on the Office of the Law Revision Counsel website (uscode.house.gov).

Case Study

Penetration Test Executive Summary

You recently conducted a penetration test for a company, R&K Financial Services. During the course of this test, you performed these tasks: ping sweep using Advanced IP scanner, port scanning using Nmap, enumeration of accounts on the ten workstations using DumpSec, and a brute-force attack on the user database on the company's web server. You also sent a simulated phishing e-mail to the 28 employees. Of these, 11 responded, including two in management. During the course of this testing, you discovered 23 hosts responding to the ping sweep. The web server had open ports for 22, 23, 80, 443, and 53. You were able to discover the password of the admin account (RKFinance$$).

1. Based on this information, what would you include in the executive summary of your penetration test?

2. Speculate who would be the audience for the executive summary at R&K Financial Services, and what type of language would you use for this audience?

permission and stay within the scope of the test, he or she may be charged with any number of criminal penalties, from criminal trespass to electronic fraud. In addition to criminal charges, accessing personal or business information could lead to a civil lawsuit against the pen tester. Even if there is no criminal intent or malice, the tester still may be exposed to these charges. However, a written contract can help provide some legal protection. This contract must include permission from the customer granting access to its resources.

In addition to written permission granting access to resources, what the pen tester is being asked to test must be specifically stated. For example, during a pen test reviewing open ports, the tester discovers an unrelated vulnerability. Is this a crime? The answer is not necessarily clear. If probing for ports was not part of the scope stated in the contract, computer crime laws may apply. One federal law in particular, 18 USC 1030, is important in this area. This law makes it a crime to access or even attempt to access a computer or network without proper authorization. It also makes access *in excess* of authorization a crime. This may mean the discovery of an unrelated vulnerability would be considered a crime.

Consider the case of a city in Georgia. It wanted to hook up to the county's 911 system. A security consultant working for the county ran a port scan and throughput test to see if the city's computers were vulnerable for exploits. The pen tester proceeded no further after discovering vulnerabilities. The vulnerabilities were reported to the county. The county then alerted the city. The city in turn contacted the Georgia Bureau of Investigation. The GBI launched an investigation to see if any laws were violated, including Georgia's computer crime laws. Ultimately, there were no criminal charges.

FYI

USC stands for United States Code. It indicates a federal law.

Quick Look 13.1.7

US Code for Computer Crime

Federal law related to computer crime is contained within the United States Code. The United States Code is the official compilation of federal laws in the United States. It is prepared by the Office of the Law Revision Counsel of the United States House of Representatives.

1. Launch a web browser, and navigate to the Office of the Law Revision Counsel website (uscode.house.gov).

Quick Look 13.1.7 Continued

2. Look through the listing of titles in the code. Notice this is set up as a tree. Each branch can be expanded to show more detail in additional branches. Which main branch do you think contains the laws related to computer crime?

3. The law 18 USC 1030 is important to pen testing. Click **Title 18** on the web page to expand that area. Notice how the subentries are broken down into sections, and each section indicates which statute numbers are in it. Click **Part I—Crimes** since 1030 falls in the range 1–2725.

4. Applying what you have learned, locate 18 UCS 1030, and click the link to display the law. What is the name of this statute?

5. Scroll down on the statute page to the Amendments section. What is the date of the most recent amendment?

SECTION REVIEW 13.1

Check Your Understanding

1. In a penetration test, the _____ identifies what is to be tested.

2. What public database would a pen tester use to locate information about a company's financial data?

3. Which type of port scanning during a pen test may be noticed by the customer's security?

4. What is used in pen testing to help determine high-value assets in a company?

5. A message sent to the target contains service information. This message is called a(n) _____.

Build Your Key Terms Vocabulary

As you progress through this course, develop a personal cybersecurity glossary. This will help you build your vocabulary and prepare you for a career. Write a definition for each of the following terms, and add it to your cybersecurity glossary.

active information gathering

banner grabbing

black box test

Electronic Data Gathering Analysis and Retrieval System (EDGAR)

ethical hacking

executive summary

gray box test

National Institute of Standards and Technology (NIST)

nondisclosure agreement (NDA)

Open Source Intelligence (OSINT)

OS fingerprinting

passive information gathering

penetration testing

Penetration Testing Execution Standard

port scanning

pretext

scope

scope creep

semipassive information gathering

STRIDE

technical report

testing time line

threat modeling

Visual, Agile, and Simple Threat (VAST)

vulnerability analysis

white box test

Certifications for Penetration Testing

It is important that individuals involved in penetration testing are highly skilled. The tester must have the technical skills necessary to perform the vulnerability scanning. There are several industry certifications related to penetration testing. Anyone pursuing a career in ethical hacking should consider these as a way to prove he or she has the needed skills. They will add credibility to your experience and ability to conduct testing. In the case of court proceedings, they will help in your understanding of the legal requirements for evidence collection. The International Council of E-Commerce Consultants (EC-Council) has several ethical hacking certifications. These are well respected for security penetration testers. They include Certified Ethical Hacker (CEH), Certified Hacking Forensics Investigator (CHFI), Certified Security Analyst (ECSA), and Licensed Penetration Tester (LPT).

Essential Question

Should penetrations have governmental regulation and be required to hold a license or certification?

Key Terms

Certified Ethical Hacker (CEH)
Certified Hacking Forensics Investigator (CHFI)
Certified Security Analyst (ECSA)
CompTIA Penetration Tester (CPT+)

computer forensics
cyber range
Cybersecurity Analyst (CySA+)
enumeration
GIAC Penetration Tester (GPEN)

Licensed Penetration Tester (LPT)
metasploit
pass-the-hash attack
password spraying

Learning Goals

- Describe what is measured by Certified Ethical Hacker (CEH) certification.
- Explain the use of frameworks in the Cybersecurity Analyst (CySA+) certification.
- Identify unique aspects of CompTIA Penetration Tester (CPT+) certification.
- Evaluate computer forensic topics related to Certified Hacking Forensics Investigator (CHFI) certification.
- Differentiate Certified Security Analyst (ECSA) certification from CEH certification.
- Appraise the requirements to obtain Licensed Penetration Tester (LPT) certification.
- Discuss GIAC Penetration Tester (GPEN) certification.

Certified Ethical Hacker

The *Certified Ethical Hacker (CEH)* certification tests your ability to conduct, analyze, and assess the security of a system. This includes penetration testing. CEH certification is offered by the International Council of E-Commerce Consultants (EC-Council). EC-Council is a member-based organization. It provides industry certification for e-business and cybersecurity.

Some specific tasks that a candidate for this certification needs to perform include:
- vulnerability scanning;
- network sniffing;
- web server attacks including SQL injection; and
- show skill in wired and wireless networks.

The CEH certification requires skills in a wide array of hardware and software. A pen tester needs to be well versed in Windows and Linux operating systems. He or she must also have a detailed understanding of the different types of malware and how threats can bypass existing security measures.

The tester will need to enumerate to the customer information found during a test. *Enumeration* is the process of extracting information, such as user and computer names, running services, and permissions. Once a hacker gains access to this type of data, he or she can discover potential attack vectors or additional vulnerabilities in the system. Enumeration is also used to gather information on IP and routing tables, DNS information, SMTP, LDAP, and more.

While the technical skills are critical, ethical behavior cannot be overlooked. The tester may have access to or uncover confidential information through the course of the test. A company that hires or contracts with a pen tester or firm will expect the tester to be honest and ethical. The EC-Council promotes the use of high ethical standards. It has created a code of ethics for individuals in the cybersecurity field. The list of 19 standards can be found on the EC-Council website (www.eccouncil.org), as shown in **Figure 13-13.**

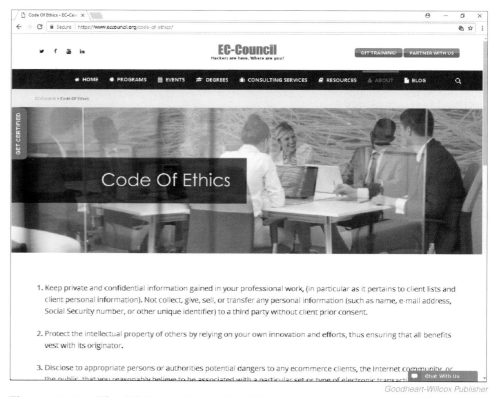

Figure 13-13. The EC-Council provides 19 standards in its code of ethics.

Quick Look 13.2.1

Enumeration in Windows

DumpSec by SomarSoft is a security-auditing program for Microsoft Windows. It can be used to discover permissions, audit settings, registry settings, printers, and shares. This is the type of information that would be enumerated for a customer during a pen test.

1. Launch a web browser, navigate to the SomarSoft website (www.somarsoft.com). You will be transported to the DumpSec download page on the SystemTools website, which is the distributor for DumpSec.
2. Download and install DumpSec. You must have permission to install software on the computer you are using.
3. Once DumpSec is installed, launch it. Its icon looks like a dump truck.
4. Click **Report**.
5. Click **Select computer**, and enter the IP address of your host computer.
6. Click **Report**, and click **Dump Users as a column**.
7. Choose these fields: UserName, FullName, AccountType, and PswdExpires. Then, click the **OK** button.
8. Record your results. Do you see any vulnerabilities with these accounts?
9. Go back, add the AcctDisabled field, and choose **Dump users as a table**.
10. Applying what you have learned, dump the groups (the group, comment, and members).
11. Applying what you have learned, dump the permissions for shares.
12. Applying what you have learned, dump the services. How might a hacker use the information in this dump?

Cybersecurity Analyst

CySA+ is one of the certifications from CompTIA in its cybersecurity pathway. The *Cybersecurity Analyst (CySA+)* certification has the candidate apply the fundamental issues defined in the Security+ certification. The candidate must analyze threats and vulnerabilities, interpret incident response actions, perform data analysis, and provide recommendations for securing systems. The exam will test your ability to understand data. This includes reading and interpreting information from logs, packet sniffing captures, and port scanning. A strong understanding of popular tools for protecting hosts and systems is essential. The exam's competencies are based on four key domains, shown in **Figure 13-14.**

One of the key aspects of this exam is understanding the use of industry-standard frameworks. As discussed in Chapter 2, frameworks help break down the aspects of a business and security domains into manageable task areas and tasks. In cybersecurity, a framework is a structured document that provides guidance for IT staff. It helps assess security threats. It also helps improve the ability to prevent, detect, and respond to threats. There are many available frameworks, some for no cost.

A popular framework comes from NIST. This is known as the Cybersecurity Framework (CSF). The document can be downloaded from the NIST website (www.nist.gov/cyberframework). The NIST CSF is based around a framework core that is based around four key areas:

- functions
- categories
- subcategories
- informative references

There are five functions: identify, protect, detect, respond, and recover. This document is not a checklist. Rather, it is designed around outcomes that are beneficial in managing cybersecurity risk.

The CySA+ certification used to be called the CSA+, but due to copyright issues, it was renamed in 2018.

CySA+ Domain Coverage

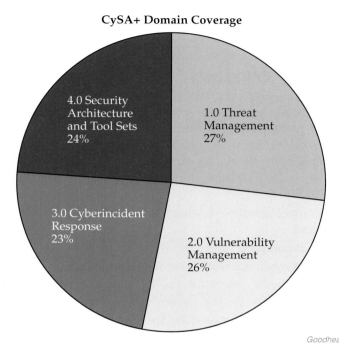

Figure 13-14. The CompTIA Cybersecurity Analyst (CySA+) certification covers four domains.

Quick Look 13.2.2

NIST CSF Framework

The NIST Cybersecurity Framework is a free resource provided by the National Institute of Standards and Technology (NIST). In this exercise, you will review some of the elements and information in the framework.

1. Launch a web browser, and navigate to the Cybersecurity Framework page on the NIST website (www.nist.gov/cyberframework).

2. Using the menu on the website, locate and open the PDF of the framework. Open the PDF in a new window or tab so the Cybersecurity Framework page remains open.

3. Review the executive summary. What was the justification of creating this framework, and what size of businesses is it designed to help?

4. Locate Table 1. This table highlights the overall framework, including identifier information and categories. Did you notice how the colors subtly reflect the urgency of each function?

5. Locate Table 2. This table deals with asset management. The category of asset management is broken down further to help identify assets. The informative references column displays a number of abbreviations. These reflect other frameworks and documents that can assist in the functionality.

6. Locate the subcategory ID.AM-1. This deals with physical devices and inventory of these assets. To see how the informative reference can help, take a look at the NIST document referenced here: NIST SP 800-53 Rev 4. CM-8. SP stands for special publication, 800-53 is the publication series and specific document, Rev 4 means the fourth revision of the document, and CM means it is a control in that document (Configuration Management #8).

7. Return to the Cybersecurity Framework page. Using the search function, search for the NIST SP 800-53 Rev 4. CM-8 document. A direct link is nvd.nist.gov/800-53/Rev4/control/CM-8. Look over the supporting documentation of this informative reference.

8. Return to the framework PDF. Scroll through the document to find another subcategory that is of interest to you. Research some of the informative references. Share with your classmates how you feel this specific category and its related resources can be helpful in a business.

Penetration Tester

The *CompTIA Penetration Tester (CPT+)* certification tests your ability to conduct penetration testing, including vulnerability assessment and management skills. It is from CompTIA and similar to the CEH certification. A diverse set of skills is needed to pass the exam. This includes skills in Windows and Linux. Also, a clear understanding of attack vectors is needed. You will need to use a variety of open-source penetration testing and vulnerability tools. You must also demonstrate working as a member of a team to conduct an assessment. The exam consists of multiple-choice questions along with hands-on simulations.

A unique aspect of this certification involves exploiting vulnerabilities as a malicious hacker might do. Some of the areas focused on include attacks such as those against wireless technologies. These include bluejacking, using evil twin routers, and other network vulnerabilities including those in DNS and FTP. One of the interesting exploits is one called pass-the-hash. A *pass-the-hash attack* involves obtaining the hash of an object, such as a user's password, and submitting the hash as if it were the real data.

CompTIA Security+
1.2

Certified Hacking Forensics Investigator

The *Certified Hacking Forensics Investigator (CHFI)* certification from the EC-Council demonstrates knowledge of properly extracting evidence from data gathering and ensuring this evidence can be submitted in a court of law. *Computer forensics* refers to finding evidence in computers and digital media, as shown in **Figure 13-15.** This can include cell phones, hard drives, the cloud, or anywhere digital data may be found. It may even include extracting data from automobiles, trains, or airplanes. The evidence must be collected in a way that will preserve, identify, recover, analyze, and present the data.

The field of computer forensics is in high demand and requires specific skills. A computer forensic technician may be asked to respond to a potential hack for criminal prosecution. He or she may also be asked to investigate situations where trade secrets or intellectual property may be at risk or stolen.

A technician may examine an attack called password spraying. In *password spraying,* a hacker tries the same password on every account in a system. In most cases, the hacker's efforts will fail, but the system will still be logging the station information from where the attacker is conducting its attack. On a Windows computer, the technician will search Windows event logs for ID 4625.

Currently, the CHFI exam is 150 multiple-choice questions. However, more is involved than just signing up and taking the exam. The candidate must prove one of two things. You can attend training from EC-Council. If you have not done this, you must prove at least two years of work experience in the information security field.

Figure 13-15. A computer forensics technician locates evidence in computers and digital media.

Certified Security Analyst

The *Certified Security Analyst (ECSA)* certification tests the candidate's ability to incorporate testing methodologies in a variety of testing. It is an advanced certification from the EC-Council taken after completing the requirements for CEH. Covered are many of the topics discussed in this course. However, advanced subjects are also covered. This includes voice over IP (VoIP) systems, broadband communication testing, e-mail security, cell phones, and surveillance systems.

One of the unique elements of the official course is the use of a cyber range. A *cyber range* is a virtual environment used to train for cyberwarfare and malicious hacks. Originally, cyber ranges were used extensively by the military. Now, many universities and some states have created their own practice ranges. They are becoming popular methods for learning about threats and testing and experimenting in closed systems.

Quick Look 13.2.3

Cyber Ranges

There are many online cyber ranges. Some are associated with specific organizations or universities, but others support a broader range.

1. Launch a web browser, and navigate to Virginia's cyber range website (www. virginiacyberrange.org).
2. Browse this site. Who is the intended audience?
3. Review the information about the courses offered here. What are some of the advantages of using a cyber range such as this one?
4. Click the **About** link. Under Leadership, there are two designations that a college or university can earn to demonstrate its commitment and ability to deliver quality cybersecurity education. Choose the options for the NSA/DHS Cybersecurity Centers of Academic Excellence. Review the information about these sites and then review the list of accredited universities. Is your favorite or intended college on the list?
5. Navigate to Michigan's cyber range (www.merit.edu/cyberrange).
6. View some of the videos on the main page. Discuss with your classmates some of the information you viewed.
7. Navigate to a search engine, and search for other cyber ranges. Is there one in your state? Do you think states have a responsibility to create sites for high schools or colleges in the state? Discuss with your classmates.

Licensed Penetration Tester

FYI

The US Army encourages its soldiers to explore the connection between their training and these high-end certifications. The LPT certification and others are mapped to their jobs. Check out the matrix on the Army's website (www.cool.army.mil).

The *Licensed Penetration Tester (LPT)* certification is a hands-on demonstration of the candidate's ability to successfully test a target. It is considered the highest certification for pen testing from the EC-Council, as shown in **Figure 13-16**. As its website states, the purpose of this certification is to "differentiate the experts from the novices in penetration testing." It consists of three levels with three challenges each. The test takes 18 hours to complete. While you are performing and testing against the challenges, the masters at the EC-Council are watching your activities and actions live.

To prepare for this process, the EC-Council provides a four-day intense course. It requires the candidate demonstrate an ability to conduct tests and perform various tasks. In addition to learning some advanced skills, participants will conduct attacks on multiple cyber ranges with a variety of configurations and operating systems. The goal of the course is to encourage out-of-the-box thinking. It also forces the user to react to dynamically changing settings and scenarios. The user must determine attack surfaces without being provided any starting points.

To apply for LPT certification, you must have already completed the CEH and CSA certifications. In the application, you must provide references. You must

The LPT (Master) Training Program:
Advanced Penetration Testing Course

Figure 13-16. The Licensed Penetration Tester (LPT) certification from the EC-Council is considered the highest certification for pen testing.

submit documentation for a criminal background check. US residents are also required to obtain FBI clearance.

GIAC Penetration Tester

Another highly respected certification for penetration testing is GPEN certification. Candidates wishing to pass the *GIAC Penetration Tester (GPEN)* certification need to demonstrate skill in pen testing methods, conducting pen tests, and understanding legal issues related to pen testing. Some skills include advanced password cracking, port and target scanning, and using the command line and

Ethical Issue

DEF CON and Candidate Employment

You are interviewing candidates for a pen tester for your security firm. One of the candidates has the background and certifications you require. However, during the interview, the candidate disclosed he is an avid attendee of DEF CON. This is one of the world's largest hacking conventions. It is annual and is customarily held in Las Vegas, NV. Although DEF CON attracts many professionals and governmental officials, it also attract many individuals with dubious backgrounds. Many of the projects and breakout sessions demonstrate hacking techniques, lock picking, and other questionable activities. Do you feel this candidate is a better choice because he learns of new tools and techniques? Or, is he a risk due to the questionable attendees and activities promoted by DEF CON? Why?

GIAC stands for Global Information Assurance Certification.

PowerShell. Proper reporting must also be demonstrated. Certification consists of passing a single test of 115 questions. The GPEN certification was created by the SANS Institute in 1999. The SANS Institute is a widely respected information and cybersecurity-training company.

One of the interesting competencies of this GPEN certification is the ability to use Metasploit at an intermediate level. *Metasploit* is an open-source computer security project that provides information and tools for pen testers. It has a wide following from novice to advanced users. Metasploit was purchased by Rapid7. This is a highly renowned security company. It has created multiple versions of Metasploit, including a free version called Metasploit community.

Metasploit has many tools. It has the ability to use prewritten exploits to target known vulnerabilities in systems, including browsers. You can scan systems to search for buffer overflows, extract password hashes from systems, and conduct session hijacks (MitM attacks). This program offers penetration testers a variety of options to use on target systems to identify vulnerabilities. However, as with any useful penetration-testing tool, it can also be used maliciously. This is another reason why many pen testers want to use this program. They want to defend against those who would use it against a company.

Quick Look 13.2.4

EC-Council Certification

There are a number of highly desired advanced certifications. This exercise will look at some of the questions and scenarios you would be expected to understand for the basic Certified Ethical Hacker certification. You can review your results and determine your strengths and areas you can explore for future growth.

1. Launch a web browser, and navigate to the EC-Council website (www.eccouncil.org).
2. Using the site's search function, search for ceh assessment. In the search results, click **CEH Assessment**. You will be transported to a starting page for Certified Ethical Hacker practice.
3. Click the **Start** button to begin the 50-question, multiple-choice exam.
4. Complete all questions to obtain your score. Do this without looking up any answers.
5. Review the questions after you get your score. You can see both correct and incorrect questions.
6. Record new terms and concepts you would like to research further.
7. Once your classmates have all finished, discuss the test and scores with each other.

SECTION REVIEW 13.2

Check Your Understanding

1. Which organization promotes many penetration testing certifications of different levels, including the Certified Ethical Hacker?

2. The process of extracting information such as user names is called _____.

3. Which CompTIA certification tests vulnerability assessment and management skills and is similar to CEH?

4. What is password spraying?

5. A(n) _____ is a virtual environment to test cyberwarfare and security skills.

Build Your Key Terms Vocabulary

As you progress through this course, develop a personal cybersecurity glossary. This will help you build your vocabulary and prepare you for a career. Write a definition for each of the following terms, and add it to your cybersecurity glossary.

Certified Ethical Hacker (CEH)

Certified Hacking Forensics Investigator (CHFI)

Certified Security Analyst (ECSA)

CompTIA Penetration Tester (CPT+)

computer forensics

cyber range

Cybersecurity Analyst (CySA+)

enumeration

GIAC Penetration Tester (GPEN)

Licensed Penetration Tester (LPT)

metasploit

pass-the-hash attack

password spraying

Review and Assessment

Summary

Section 13.1 Overview of Penetration Testing

- Penetration testing, or ethical hacking, is a process in which security personnel attempt to penetrate a network to locate vulnerabilities, and the five Ws of penetration testing should be considered when planning a test.
- The standard test procedures for a penetration test include preengagement interactions, intelligence gathering, threat modeling, vulnerability analysis, exploitation, post exploitation, and reporting.
- Penetration testers must be careful not to break any laws, and having a comprehensive and clearly stated contract containing the necessary written permissions is an important protection the tester must have.

Section 13.2 Certifications for Penetration Testing

- Certified Ethical Hacker (CEH) certification from EC-Council measures the ability to conduct, analyze, and assess the security of a system.
- Cybersecurity Analyst (CySA+) certification from CompTIA has the candidate apply the fundamental issues defined in the Security+ certification.
- Penetration Tester (CPT+) certification from CompTIA tests measures the ability to conduct penetration testing, including vulnerability assessment and management skills.
- Certified Hacking Forensics Investigator (CHFI) certification from the EC-Council demonstrates knowledge of properly extracting evidence from data gathering and ensuring this evidence can be submitted in a court of law.
- Certified Security Analyst (ECSA) certification from the EC-Council measures the candidate's ability to incorporate testing methodologies in a variety of testing and is obtained after obtaining CHE certification.
- Licensed Penetration Tester (LPT) certification is a hands-on demonstration of the candidate's ability to successfully test a target and is the highest certification for pen testing from the EC-Council.
- GIAC Penetration Tester (GPEN) certification from SANS Institute measures skill in pen testing methods, conducting pen tests, and understanding legal issues related to pen testing.

Check Your Cybersecurity IQ ⤤

Now that you have completed this chapter, see what you have learned about cybersecurity by visiting the student companion website (www.g-wlearning.com) and taking the chapter posttest.

Review Questions ⤤

For each question, select the answer that is the best response.

1. Which of these terms is not included in the five Ws of penetration testing?
   A. Who
   B. When
   C. Which
   D. Where

2. A pen tester is hired and given the range of IP addresses, brand of computers, routers, etc. and operating system versions. This type of testing is known as a(n):
   A. white box test
   B. OSINT test
   C. gray box test
   D. black box test

3. A threat model designed by Microsoft focuses on viewing potential attacks. Its threat model is called:
   A. Process-flow
   B. STRIDE
   C. VAST
   D. Agile

4. During a port scan, Nmap can also attempt to reveal other system information through:
   A. intense scanning
   B. obfuscation
   C. banner grabbing
   D. OS fingerprinting

5. This part of a pen tester's contract states what is to be tested:
   A. executive summary
   B. technical summary
   C. scope
   D. time line

6. A story or made-up scenario used in a social engineering attack:
   A. ploy
   B. ruse
   C. con
   D. pretext

7. Which of the following would not have been obtained from OSINT?
   A. The type of network infrastructure used by a job posting description.
   B. Vulnerable systems to buffer overflows.
   C. A company's annual financial report.
   D. Press releases.

8. Which certification requires 18 hours of testing against virtualized systems?
   A. CySA+
   B. LPT
   C. CHFI
   D. GPEN

9. A person certified in CHFI would be typically focusing on which of the following?
   A. Injection attacks.
   B. Using Metasploit tools.
   C. Stealing of trade secrets.
   D. Password cracking.

10. The SANS Institute created this certification for pen testers:
    A. ECSA
    B. CEH
    C. CPT+
    D. GPEN

Application and Extension of Knowledge

1. On your home network, practice using the Nmap command with OS fingerprinting. Analyze the results. Did you have any machines with open ports that was unexpected? Summarize your scan.

2. Assume you have been hired to conduct a physical security scan for your school. Using the five Ws of penetration testing as a guide, compile a list of questions that you would ask before you create your contract.

3. Using a job-search website, look for jobs with Penetration Testing in the title. Identify at least 15 different job postings. Compile a list of some of the topics and certifications you saw introduced in this unit. Create another list of new skills or terms unfamiliar to you.

4. Assume a customer hosts its business in one of the cloud companies, such as Amazon, Google, Microsoft, or Rackspace. Choose one of these companies, and research the rules they have before a customer can have a pen test performed on their systems. Summarize your research in a report.

5. Using OSINT tools only, no active scanning, compile a list of information regarding a local or regional company. Summarize your findings in a brief report.

Research Project
Pen-Testing Tools

You are preparing for a career as a penetration tester. Once you earn your Security+ certification, you want to begin pursuing certifications in penetration testing. On the GPEN list of required competencies, you are expected to use Metasploit and its tools to demonstrate your ability to conduct testing. You realize there are many tools that can be used during a pen-testing project. Excluding Wireshark, Nmap, and DumpSec, identify programs and tools that are used by penetration testers. Identify some of the outcomes of these tools. Begin your research with Metasploit, as this is a comprehensive program. Next, find at least two other tools and identify those programs and their features.

Deliverables. Write a report of your findings. Summarize each tool you identified. Follow your school's guidelines for formatting and citing sources.

Online Activities

Complete the following activities, which will help you learn, practice, and expand your knowledge and skills.

Vocabulary. Practice vocabulary for this chapter using the e-flash cards, matching activity, and vocabulary game until you are able to recognize their meanings.

Communication Skills

College and Career Readiness

Reading. Imagery is descriptive language describing how something looks, feels, smells, sounds, or tastes. Using this text, find an example of how the author uses imagery to describe a concept. List the page number and paragraph where you found the example. Why do you think this is a good example? How does learning about imagery improve your vocabulary?

Writing. Many college applications require an essay as part of the application process. Write a 500-word essay explaining why cybersecurity is the perfect career for you. Identify the audience, and determine an effective approach and technique clearly stating your purpose.

Speaking. A presentation is usually a speech given to a group of people. This chapter discusses different ways to conduct penetration testing. Plan and deliver a speech to your class about an idea you have for ensuring the pen tester is legally protected. Be clear in your perspective of the idea, and demonstrate solid reasoning.

Listening. Ask a classmate to give you directions on how to walk to the school's guidance office. Take notes as the directions are given. Evaluate and summarize your notes. If necessary, ask the speaker to slow down or repeat a point. Use prior knowledge of the school's layout to follow the directions given.

Portfolio Development

College and Career Readiness

Hard and Soft Skills. Employers review candidates for various positions, and colleges are always looking for qualified applicants. When listing your qualifications, illustrate both hard and soft skills. For example, you might discuss software programs you know or machines you can operate. These abilities are often called hard skills. The ability to communicate effectively, get along with customers or coworkers, and solve problems are examples of soft skills. These are also important skills for many jobs. Make an effort to learn about and develop the hard and soft skills needed for your chosen career field.

1. Conduct research about hard and soft skills and their value in helping people succeed.

2. Create a Microsoft Word document and list the hard skills you possess that are important for a job or career that interests you. Use the heading Hard Skills and your name. Next to each skill, write a paragraph that describes the skill and give examples to illustrate it. Save the document.

3. Create a Microsoft Word document and list the soft skills you possess that are important for a job or career that interests you. Use the heading Soft Skills and your name. Next to each skill, write a paragraph that describes the skill and give examples to illustrate it. Save the document.

4. Update your master spreadsheet.

CTSO Event Prep

Community-Service Project. Many competitive events for career and technical student organizations (CTSOs) include a community-service project. This project is usually carried out by the entire CTSO chapter and will take several months to complete. It will probably span the school year. There will be two parts of the event, written and oral. The chapter will designate several members to represent the team at the competitive event. To prepare for a community-service project, complete the following activities.

1. Read the guidelines provided by your organization.

2. Contact the association immediately at the end of the state conference to prepare for next year's event.

3. As a team, select a theme for your chapter's community-service project.

4. Decide which roles are needed for the team. There may be one person who is the captain, one person who is the secretary, and other roles that will be necessary to create the plan. Ask your instructor for guidance in assigning roles to team members.

5. Identify your target audience, which may include business, school, and community groups.

6. Brainstorm with members of your chapter. List the benefits and opportunities of supporting a community-service project.

Chapter 14

Cloud Computing

Anytime, anywhere. That is the simplest lure most companies hear when they consider how cloud computing can improve their business models and their bottom lines. Cloud computing is no longer a novelty or an IT strategy used by large businesses. Businesses of all sizes can benefit from a cloud-based approach to storing data or offering features and services. The cloud is a symbolic reference for using the Internet for storage and services instead of from locally managed systems. Cloud-based services can be managed by third-party companies. A firm can also choose to create and manage its own cloud systems.

Cloud services include providing access to application software or to the underlying hardware or system software. These are some of the fastest growing cloud services. The success of cloud computing will depend on many factors. Not the least of these factors are consistent Internet access and better connection speeds. The implementation of 5G cellular networks will assist in this development. However, for companies and other users to embrace the cloud, issues surrounding cybersecurity must be addressed. Many local cybersecurity risks can be removed by using a cloud-based environment. The cloud presents new security challenges that need to be identified and addressed.

Chapter Preview

Section 14.1   Cloud Basics
Section 14.2   Cloud Services
Section 14.3   Other Cloud Considerations

While studying, look for the activity icon for:

- Pretests and posttests
- Vocabulary terms with e-flash cards and matching activities
- Self-assessment

G-WLEARNING.com

Reading Prep

Arrange a study session to read this chapter aloud with a classmate. At the end of each section, discuss any words you do not know. Take notes of words you would like to discuss in class.

College and Career Readiness

Check Your Cybersecurity IQ ⤷

Before you begin this chapter, see what you already know about cybersecurity by visiting the student companion website (www.g-wlearning.com) and taking the chapter pretest.

Certification Objectives

CompTIA Security+

3.7 Summarize cloud and virtualization concepts.
3.8 Explain how resiliency and automation strategies reduce risk.
5.6 Explain disaster recovery and continuity of operation concepts.

Section 14.1

Cloud Basics

Essential Question

Are data safer or more at risk in the cloud?

The evolution of Internet technologies has changed how people live, shop, work, and learn in many ways. Have you shopped online in the last few days or weeks? How about listen to or download new music using your smartphone? Have you streamed Netflix or played games against other people on Xbox Live? All of these actions are possible due to cloud computing solutions. While the Internet has made access to data possible, it is the role of cloud computing that has revolutionized how people use data located online.

Key Terms 🖒

cloud computing
cloud-deployment model
community cloud

hybrid cloud
network neutrality
personal cloud

private cloud
public cloud
terms of service (ToS)

Learning Goals

- Describe cloud computing.
- Compare and contrast the four cloud-deployment models.
- Appraise the advantages and disadvantages of cloud storage.

Introduction to Cloud Computing

A basic definition of *cloud computing* is the use of resources such as servers that are running from a remote location instead of located locally at a business or home. However, it is much more than using remote resources. An important aspect of cloud computing is collaboration and sharing of data. These are what make cloud computing such an essential component of increasingly digitally connected lives.

One of the first cloud successes was the iTunes Store from Apple, as shown in **Figure 14-1**. It showed the potential of the cloud beyond storage. Apple launched the first-ever digital music store in 2003 with just 200,000 songs that could be

Figure 14-1. Apple's iTunes was one of the first to show how powerful cloud computing can be. Apple has continued to expand cloud services since iTunes was introduced.

purchased and downloaded to a customer's iPod. Within the first 18 hours of operation, Apple sold around 275,000 song tracks. That is over 15,000 songs per hour!

As the success of iTunes continued to grow, Apple extended the base product to its iCloud service. This is a service used to keep devices in sync. Did you take a picture on your iPhone? The iCloud service allows you to pull it up automatically on your iPad. If you purchase a new song from iTunes, you can listen to it on any of your Apple-connected devices. You no longer have to keep a personal address book. Now, your contacts are shared across your Apple devices. All of this is done automatically in the background without you having to initiate the process. Best of all, a loss of your phone, does not mean a loss of your photos and contact information. Other companies offer cloud services similar to these Apple services, including Google and Amazon.

Why is it called the "cloud"? The general consensus is that when network engineers were designing systems, they needed a conceptual way to identify a network for which they did not know all details. They settled on a cloud as a symbol to represent the unknown network design elements. Today, most cloud-based services use a cloud symbol to illustrate their cloud connection to customers.

Cloud computing is not without security concerns and vulnerabilities. For example, moving the data to the cloud increases the exposure of the systems. Additionally, if using a third-party vendor, companies are placing their trust in the vendor and its security practices. Aspects of cloud computing are explored in this chapter. This includes vulnerabilities and the impact cloud computing has on business and IT decisions.

Cloud Types

A *cloud-deployment model* describes how the cloud environment is created and operated, as shown in **Figure 14-2**. The method in which the resources are shared describes the model type. There are five common deployment models:

- private
- public
- hybrid
- community
- personal

A *private cloud* is owned and managed by its own organization. The services are typically only provided to the employees and members of the organization. This model provides the most security and control. However, it is costly to set up and use this model. Costs include startup, maintenance, staffing, and upgrades.

A *public cloud* offers services to anyone. These services can be free or paid. Google cloud services such as Google Drive are free. An example of a paid service is Carbonite backup solutions. Since the data are located in a shared space, security is a concern. However, this model can provide a cheaper solution than creating and using a private cloud.

A *community cloud* is shared by everyone within affiliated organizations, but is not available to anyone outside of these organizations. For example, a community college system in a state might create a community cloud. This allows resources to be shared among the different campus locations within the state. However, only faculty, staff, and students of the community college are allowed access. This could help reduce the costs of offering the same information in multiple places. There is one master location for information and services. However, expanding system usage increases the attack surface. Management of the community cloud and its security must be coordinated.

A *hybrid cloud* uses features from public, private, or community clouds. The advantages and disadvantages of those models exist with the hybrid cloud. Hybrid clouds are very popular. For example, many schools use their own storage systems, but Google for e-mail. This combines a private cloud (the storage) with a public cloud (Gmail). It often makes sense for businesses to incorporate multiple public cloud services with private services in this manner.

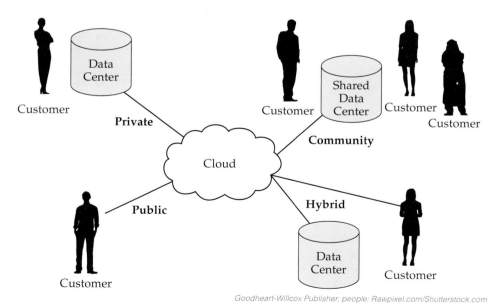

Figure 14-2. There are four basic models of deployment used in cloud computing.

A *personal cloud,* or *home cloud*, is becoming a popular option for many consumers. Even though public clouds exist, it may make sense to manage your own cloud service to store files or offer services within your household. There are many software choices you can use to create a personal cloud. You can also purchase a hardware and software solution from a reputable vendor. Once a home cloud is created, it can be connected to the home Wi-Fi and accessed from any Internet connection.

Cloud Storage

Cloud storage is a popular type of cloud service. It is of particular interest to businesses, security professionals, home users, and hackers alike. By storing data in the cloud, the information is away from your primary location. This offers many advantages, which are discussed later. However, there are very important issues to consider before storing your data outside of your physical premises:

- Will you use a private or public cloud service?
- How will your data be secured, both in storage and transit?
- Will your data be available when you need access?

Public or Private

CompTIA Security+
3.7

The first decision to make is which cloud deployment model will be used. Should a business create its own private cloud so employees can access data at anytime and anywhere? Or, will it be okay to use a public cloud, such as Google Drive? **Figure 14-3** compares the two cloud options. The good news is there are a great deal of cloud vendors that offer data storage.

There are several public cloud solutions. Examples include Google Drive and Amazon Drive. These are free options. Dropbox is another option, which has both free and paid solutions. Microsoft OneDrive is another option. Like Dropbox, it has free and paid solutions.

There are many solutions available to create a private cloud environment. The Azure product from Microsoft is one option. Cisco has options as well. Other options are better suited for smaller organizations and personal use. OwnCloud and Nextcloud are two examples. These are free and open-source solutions. If you decide to go with established vendors, then you pay a service fee to use their products and storage space. Some examples include Amazon Web Services (AWS),

FYI Microsoft OneDrive is included in the Office suite, but it can be accessed directly on the web.

Cloud Features	Private Cloud	Public Cloud
Control	It's your cloud! Your employees manage the service, and all decisions are yours.	Managed by the cloud vendor. Unless specified in agreements, the vendor can make changes to delivery, such as utilization and support.
Storage Capacity	You are limited by your hardware and infrastructure. Not as easy to quickly scale.	More resources available. Easier to scale with limited notice.
Cost	In addition to hardware and cloud software, you must also pay personnel to manage the cloud. However, costs can be more stable and predictable.	Depending on contracts, payment may be based on storage, access, or usage. Costs could vary depending on those options.
Security	Your data remain under your control and decision-making. However, your employees may not have advanced skills in cloud data security.	The data is managed by third-party organizations. Their staffs are usually more skilled in cloud solutions, including security. However, these staffs are not your employees.

Goodheart-Willcox Publisher

Figure 14-3. Private and public clouds have different characteristics for control, storage capacity, cost, and security.

HP, IBM, AT&T, and Rackspace. Many of these are fee-based services. The services often charge on a pay-as-you-go model. For example, if you use more resources one month, you may pay a higher fee than in a month when there was not as much activity.

Quick Look 14.1.1

Private Cloud

Personal clouds allow you to store files, including photos, videos, and music. You can then access these files from any Internet connection. There are many options for creating a personal cloud.

1. Launch a web browser, and navigate to the Amazon website (www.amazon.com).
2. Search for **seagate personal cloud**. What are some of the storages sizes available? Select one of these products, and review the product details. What are some of the other options or features of this product?
3. Navigate to a search engine, and enter the search phrase **western digital my cloud home**. Select a review of this product, and read the details. How does it compare in features and price to the Seagate product?
4. You do not need to buy specialized hardware to create a personal cloud. Navigate to the Tonido Server website (www.tonido.com). What platforms can be used to access this software?
5. Navigate to the FuguHub website (fuguhub.com). What are some of the unique features of this product? Compare this product to the Tonido product.
6. Using a search engine, look for other products or solutions for personal clouds. Discuss your findings with your classmates.

Data Security

There is always a great deal of concern when a business entrusts its data to another company. Control is lost to management of the data. The business also does not know the individuals who are the gatekeepers of the data. Will the data be available when needed? Can anyone else, either the public or other cloud employees, read or steal data? These concerns go directly back to main security principles of CIA. However, you can make decisions to keep your data as secure as possible in the cloud.

First, choose a cloud vendor that provides encryption of data both at rest and in transit. This protects the data and allows only authorized users to access the data. Second, make sure you read and understand the terms of service from the cloud provider. The *terms of service (ToS)* is a legal agreement outlining what services are and are not provided by the vendor and your responsibilities toward fulfilling the agreement. The ToS is closely related to the acceptable use policy (AUP), which is discussed in Chapters 1 and 10. The AUP may be part of the ToS. The AUP may also be a separate document.

Quick Look 14.1.2

Cloud Vendor Terms of Service

All cloud vendors should have a terms of service agreement and most will also have an acceptable use policy. Dropbox is a popular provider of data storage. It has both a ToS and an AUP.

1. Launch a web browser, and navigate to the Dropbox website (www.dropbox.com).
2. Scroll to the bottom of the page, and click the **Privacy & Terms** link.
3. On the next page, click the **Terms of Service** tab to display the ToS. Notice there is also a tab for the acceptable use policy.
4. Read the ToS. For what reason would Dropbox view your content?
5. If you want to sue Dropbox over a ToS issue, and you live in Austin, TX, where will the case be heard?
6. Can you belong to a class-action lawsuit against Dropbox? A class-action lawsuit involves many users suing over the same claim.
7. Click the **Privacy Policy** tab at the top of the page, and read the policy. Dropbox states it uses cookies and pixel tags. Click the **cookies and pixel tags** link within the document to learn how a pixel tag is used.
8. Scroll down in the privacy policy to locate the **Transparency Report** link, and click it. How does Dropbox respond to requests from law enforcement and governmental agencies?
9. Dropbox may store your data on servers located in foreign countries. Scroll down in the privacy policy to locate the link to www.privacyshield.gov, and click it. What is the Privacy Shield? Have you ever considered that your data may be stored in foreign locations? Does this concern you? Discuss your thoughts with your classmates.

Data Availability

Availability is one of the core fundamentals of any security policy. What makes this security principle more challenging are the variables of using the cloud. The cloud user depends on the reliability of the Internet provider. Additionally, your employees or customers must also have an Internet connection. Even though it may seem everyone has Internet access, this is not true. Some people do not have access. In other cases, their access is not reliable.

One of the other concerns deals with the concept of network neutrality. *Network neutrality,* or *net neutrality,* is a concept that states all traffic on the Internet should receive equal consideration. Net neutrality ensures companies and users have the same access to the Internet without being charged more. Without net neutrality, a user may be given reduced access speeds compared to a user who pays a higher usage fee. Reduced speeds could affect access to data on the cloud.

There is a great deal of uncertainty and debate over net neutrality. It has been championed by many users. However, Internet providers have argued against it. In December 2017, the Federal Communications Commission (FCC) voted to roll back network neutrality rules. This allowed telecommunication companies to charge providers based on usage. Many lawsuits and state legislatures have challenged this rollback. The uncertainty related to Internet speeds could affect a business's decision to use cloud services.

SECTION REVIEW 14.1

Check Your Understanding ↪

1. Which cloud-deployment model is established and managed by a single organization?
2. Microsoft Office 365 accessed on the cloud is an example of which cloud-deployment model?
3. Which IT company publishes the Azure cloud platform?
4. A(n) _____ is a document from a cloud vendor that specifies what level of service it will provide.
5. Network neutrality rules are enforced by which governmental entity?

Build Your Key Terms Vocabulary ↪

As you progress through this course, develop a personal cybersecurity glossary. This will help you build your vocabulary and prepare you for a career. Write a definition for each of the following terms, and add it to your cybersecurity glossary.

cloud computing

cloud-deployment model

community cloud

hybrid cloud

network neutrality

personal cloud

private cloud

public cloud

terms of service (ToS)

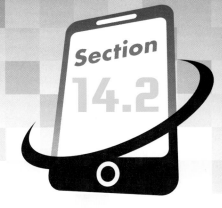

Section 14.2

Cloud Services

When you consider what cloud computing can provide, you are looking at the type of services offered by the cloud model. The three most well-known cloud services are software as a service (SaaS), infrastructure as a service (IaaS), and platform as a service (PaaS). There are also many new and emerging services, including security as service. These services deliver a variety of offerings. You may be familiar with some of these as a consumer. They include music and video streaming services such as Spotify and Netflix and online data storage including Google Drive or Dropbox. Many educational platforms are cloud services that allow grades and other student services to be hosted online.

Essential Question

How are cloud-based services improving society?

Key Terms

infrastructure as a service (IaaS)
load balancing
managed security service (MSS)
platform as a service (PaaS)
resilience
sandbox
scalability
security as a service (SECaaS)
software as a service (SaaS)

Learning Goals

- Differentiate SaaS from locally installed applications.
- Identify advantages of PaaS.
- Evaluate the benefits of using IaaS.
- Discuss the application of SECaaS.

Software as a Service

Software as a service (SaaS) is a complete software solution from the cloud without needing to install resources locally. Software as a service is probably the most well-known and visible of the services to most end users. The Google Apps suite of software is an example of SaaS. When using Google Docs, for example, the word-processing software is not installed on your local machine. The software is installed on a remote server. You access the software through a web portal, as shown in **Figure 14-4.**

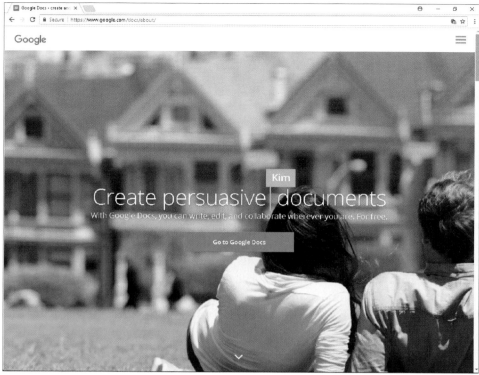

Figure 14-4. Google Docs is a well-known example of software as a service (SaaS).

CompTIA Security+
3.8

Google is not the only company offering SaaS. Microsoft extended its popular Office suite products to an online-based service with Office 365. It is delivered through the cloud, and storage is provided in the cloud as well. Office 365 can be installed locally, yet is managed through the cloud. It can be used offline, but if you do not regularly connect to the Internet, the software may go into a reduced-function mode.

ThinkFree Cloud is another example of SaaS for office-type applications. It can be used to spread the applications across desktop, mobile, or any operating system platform. This is an interesting solution. It allows a business to create its own ThinkFree cloud on its own equipment. This allows the business to avoid using a third-party cloud provider.

There are many advantages to using software provided over the Internet. It eliminates the need to install, configure, and maintain a local application. Security patches are applied by the cloud vendor. They are immediately applied to all instances of the application. Upgrades to new versions are easily implemented. Users with an Internet connection can have access to the software from any location at any time.

Another advantage is resilience. *Resilience* is the capacity to recover quickly from a situation. This may be a system failure or natural disaster. Cloud-based data and services are available without any delay. All that is needed is an Internet connection.

There are disadvantages in using SaaS solutions as well. An active and reliable connection to the Internet must be maintained to use the cloud services. The user must also rely on the vendor to maintain the hardware and software. Data stored in the cloud must be done in a way that complies with regulations or policies governing the physical storage locations.

It is important to keep in mind that just because an application is running from the cloud, any licensing rules for software usage still apply. This can be confusing. Most everyone is familiar with paying for a license per installed seat of software. In the case of the cloud, the software is not installed. If the software is not free or open source, it is important to review the vendor's EULA for permitted usage.

Quick Look 14.2.1

Google SaaS Offerings

Most people are familiar with Gmail, which is Google's e-mail product. Google Docs is its free online equivalent to the Microsoft Word product and also well known. However, Google has quite a few of SaaS offerings available.

Google apps

1. Launch a web browser, and navigate to the Google home page (www.google.com).
2. Click the **Google apps** button located next to the **Sign in** button. A drop-down menu appears containing the applications that are popular.
3. Click **More** at the bottom of the menu. The menu expands to show more apps.
4. Click **Finance** in the expanded menu. The finance page offers an overview of markets, currencies, and top stories affecting the markets and finance.
5. Click the **Google apps** button, then click More, and finally click Even More. A page is displayed that shows a complete set of services Google offers.
6. Scroll down on the page until you see the complete list of icons representing all the Google services. What is Cardboard?
7. On the Google Cardboard page, click the menu, and then click **TiltBrush**. On the TiltBrush page, watch the introductory video. What do you think of this service?
8. Return to the page showing the expanded services from Google. Explore additional SaaS offerings. What else is of interest to you?

Platform as a Service

Deploying web pages has become quite a complex operation. It is often more work than just installing a web server, securing it, and copying some HTML files to it. Today, there are many programming languages, apps, databases and the related configurations, and updates and settings that must be applied. High-demand servers also need more processing power and high-speed bandwidth. All of this may make hosting your own servers very costly.

Many companies turn to platform as a service solutions. *Platform as a service (PaaS)* allows a customer to develop applications and to run and manage them without creating the underlying platform. PaaS allows a company to provide efficient design. It also allows web developers to focus on the apps and not the environment. Think of a platform as something on which you build. That is what PaaS providers do. They allow the development team to focus on the actual product. The web development platform is left to the provider.

There are many different PaaS providers. **Figure 14-5** shows just a few of the popular PaaS providers and the type of platform they provide to their customers. Some offer specific platforms, others are more versatile. Examples include Engine Yard, Google App Engine, Windows Azure, and AppFog. There are many others as well.

Engine Yard is designed for developers who use node.js, Ruby on Rails, and PHP to create their web applications. It runs on the Amazon Web Services.

Users who select the Google App Engine are developing web applications with languages such as Java, Python, PHP, and Go. An interesting feature of this

PaaS Provider	Services Offered
Engine Yard	For Node.js, Ruby on Rails, and PHP. Runs on the AWS cloud. www.engineyard.com
Google App Engine	For languages such as Java, Python, PHP and Go. Runs in a sandbox. cloud.Google.com/appengine/
Microsoft Azure	Supports a number of languages including .NET, Ruby on Rails, PHP, Java, Node.js, and Python. Can mix components to create a dynamic environment. azure.microsoft.com
AppFog	Supports Java, Ruby, PHP, Python, Node.js, Scala, MySQL, and other languages. Can be installed on a private cloud. www.ctl.io/appfog/

Figure 14-5. These are some common examples of platform as a service (PaaS), but there are others as well.

PaaS is it runs the web applications in a sandbox. A *sandbox* is a virtual environment that separates running programs and processes from the main computer system. This prevents the physical machine from having rogue processes disrupt or harm it.

Microsoft Azure is a special PaaS in that it also has an IaaS environment. You can mix components to create a dynamic environment. It supports a number of languages including .NET, Ruby on Rails, PHP, Java, Node.js, and Python.

AppFog can be installed on a private cloud. It is based on the open-source platform from Cloud Foundry. AppFog supports Java, Ruby, PHP, Python, Node.js, Scala, MySQL, and other languages.

Infrastructure as a Service

The third most popular cloud service is known as infrastructure as a service. *Infrastructure as a service (IaaS)* is a cloud-computing solution where the vendor provides the customer with virtualized computing resources over the Internet. This is more complex than a SaaS or PaaS environment, but offers enormous benefits. With this environment, a business does not need to host any IT technology at its location. The servers, related hardware, and infrastructure can be outsourced to the IaaS provider. There are many advantages for this feature:
- load balancing
- scalability
- hardware investment

CompTIA Security+
3.8

Load Balancing and Scalability

Some businesses may have a consistently high or low demand on their equipment. Hardware needs are easy to predict and manage in this scenario. However, other businesses experience unexpected spikes in demand. When this happens to an online retailer and its hardware cannot adapt, customers may be unable to shop, as shown in **Figure 14-6.** *Scalability* is the ability of the hardware to accommodate based on demand of the system as a business's needs grow or shrink. Load balancing is an important part of scalability. *Load balancing* spreads the processing needs over multiple servers.

Goodheart-Willcox Publisher; vector art: Happymay/Shutterstock.com

Figure 14-6. If the hardware for a website is unable to handle unexpected spikes in demand, customers may be faced with an error message.

Target experienced unexpected high demand in 2014 when it launched its Missoni label and Lily Pulitzer products. Target's servers were unable to handle the high load. Many online customers were faced with a message indicating the site was down due to high traffic. Similarly, Best Buy lost the ability to provide customers online shopping on Black Friday in 2014 due to performance and other problems.

A public IaaS provider has vast hardware resources it can use to meet immediate needs. This includes more hard disk space, memory, processing power, and bandwidth. When the demand drops, the IaaS can scale back these resources from that one customer. The resources are returned to the "pool" for other customer needs.

Consider this example. An IaaS provider has a great deal of hardware available for its customers. One of its customers is an online toy store. In December, the toy store finds it needs more resources to meet the demands of holiday business. The IaaS provider shifts resources from its pool to the toy store through January. In February, another customer, a flower store, needs extra power for a few weeks for Valentine's Day. Since the toy store no longer has high demand, the resources it had been using can be shifted to the flower store.

Hardware Investment

Another advantage to using an IaaS is letting another company handle the investment in hardware. This includes the hardware itself, as shown in **Figure 14-7.** However, it also includes maintenance, upgrades, and patching. The cloud vendor

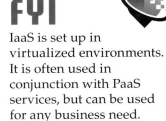

FYI

IaaS is set up in virtualized environments. It is often used in conjunction with PaaS services, but can be used for any business need.

- - - - - - - - - - - - - - - - - - - -

wavebreakmedia/Shutterstock.com

Figure 14-7. An IaaS provider takes on the cost of purchasing and maintaining equipment instead of the IaaS customer.

takes care of all the infrastructure needs. It also owns the hardware and is responsible for the upkeep. On the other hand, the customer is responsible for licensing of the operating systems and applications in use. Typically, a customer pays for this service by any combination of these options:

- resource utilization by time (usually per hour)
- resource utilization by storage (gigabit)
- resource utilization by bandwidth usage

There are many ways to obtain cost savings by outsourcing the hardware. There are no purchases for hardware, cabling, racks, and so on. There is no cost for the electricity needed to run the equipment. An IT staff is not needed to set up, test, configure, patch, and monitor the hardware, so there are not the associated employee costs. No costs are involved for spare parts needed for hardware failures. Naturally, these savings are offset by the costs involved from usage at the IaaS. All of the data must be evaluated and factored into a company's *total cost of ownership (TCO)*.

Quick Look 14.2.2

IaaS Vendors

There are many websites that compare cloud vendors. As you look through these sites, take note of the strengths, costs, and any potential disadvantages of using IaaS.

1. Launch a web browser, and enter the search phrase cloud wars bob evans. Bob Evans has created a weekly Cloud Wars ranking. Evaluate the search results for a reputable source, and read one of his Cloud Wars articles. Which vendors are within the top ten?
2. Navigate to the Rackspace website (www.rackspace.com). Rackspace is an IaaS provider.
3. Locate the **About** link, and click it. Read about some of the strengths and features of Rackspace, its employees, and its product offerings. Take particular note about the certifications possessed by its staff.
4. Navigate to the Google Compute Engine website (cloud.google.com/compute/).
5. Search the site for pricing information. How does Google price this cloud product? How much is provided in the free plan?

CompTIA Security+
3.7

Security as a Service

Another cloud service that is gaining in popularity in light of the multitude of cybersecurity threats is security as a service. In 2016, this market was worth $3 billion and expected to grow $8 billion by 2020! *Security as a service (SECaaS)* is cloud-based malware, firewall, and intrusion protection. An SECaaS vendor acts as a type of off-site gatekeeper for your network, as shown in **Figure 14-8.** It can scan e-mail for viruses. It hosts the network's firewall. It looks for intruders and prevents their access to the network. It uses analytics to detect patterns to develop early warnings to potential threats.

SECaaS systems can also analyze web applications for vulnerabilities. Vulnerabilities to web applications include SQL injection and cross-site scripting problems. These are discussed in Chapter 13. SECaaS systems can also provide encryption services, e-mail archiving, and even log retention storage.

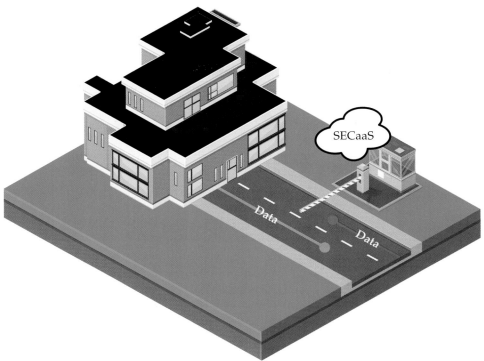

Figure 14-8. An SECaaS is a cloud-based service that acts as an off-site gate-keeper for an organization's network.

SECaaS vendors are usually highly regarded security firms. Some vendors include SonicWall, FireEye, Alien Vault, and Alert Logic. They provide customers with highly skilled and trained professionals in the areas of cybersecurity. Many of their customers do not have this type of expertise in-house, so it makes sense to use an outside service.

Using a SECaaS product makes sense for many businesses. With new cyber-threats appearing on an almost daily basis, it can be very difficult for a business to keep employees trained and well-versed on the latest threats. It may not have the correct tools in place. A variety of products may need to be used to achieve better protection. SECaaS products offer the expertise of the vendor and its employees to create dynamic and strong security solutions.

Case Study

SaaS-based LMS

The Johnson County Public School system has three high schools, four middle schools, and eight elementary schools. It is evaluating a move to an SaaS-based learning management system (LMS) platform. The LMSs being considered are Schoology, Blackboard, and Google Classroom. Evaluate these offerings for features. Based on features only, not pricing, make a recommendation as to which LMS is the best fit.

1. Which LMS do you feel is the best match for Johnson County Pubic School system?
2. Why did you choose this LMS over the other two LMSs?

A SECaaS solution is often offered as a managed security service. A *managed security service (MSS)* is an outsourced firm that oversees the security aspect of a customer's business. These firms often promote three key benefits: cost savings, off-loading busywork, and compliance. As discussed in Chapter 1, there are certain regulations or standards that a company must follow. This may include HIPAA or PCI DSS. The MMS can assist with ensuring the proper security measures are enacted to comply with these regulations.

Quick Look 14.2.3

SECaaS Solutions

SECaaS has become a good option for companies and organizations who do not have in-house security experts. There are many solutions for SECaaS.

1. Launch a web browser, and navigate to the FireEye website (www.fireeye.com). Review the features and pricing for this SECaaS.
2. Navigate to the Sonicwall website (www.sonicwall.com). Review the features and pricing for this SECaaS.
3. Navigate to the Alert Logic website (www.alertlogic.com). Review the features and pricing for this SECaaS.
4. Navigate to the Qualys website (www.qualys.com). Review the features and pricing for this SECaaS.
5. Create a table to compare and contrast these four SECaaS. Which ones are specialized? Which ones are more generalized? What features does each offer? What pricing models are used?
6. Compare your findings with those of your classmates.

SECTION REVIEW 14.2

Check Your Understanding

1. A system that can respond quickly to a catastrophic event is said to be _____.
2. Using this service, you can focus on app development, not the software necessary to run the apps.
3. Virtualized systems are the norm for this cloud service.
4. When using IaaS, it is easy to even out the processing demands among multiple machines. This is known as _____.
5. Running a virus from the cloud can be provided through which service?

Build Your Key Terms Vocabulary

As you progress through this course, develop a personal cybersecurity glossary. This will help you build your vocabulary and prepare you for a career. Write a definition for each of the following terms, and add it to your cybersecurity glossary.

infrastructure as a service (IaaS)	sandbox
load balancing	scalability
managed security service (MSS)	security as a service (SECaaS)
platform as a service (PaaS)	software as a service (SaaS)
resilience	

Other Cloud Considerations

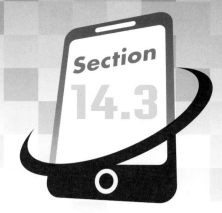

The implementation of cloud solutions continues to increase and expand. The global cloud computing market is expected to gross $1 trillion by 2024 for SaaS, PaaS, and IaaS. In North America alone, through the year 2020, market revenue is forecasted to exceed $410 billion. This growth reflects the opportunities and validity of the cloud-computing environment. When adopting cloud computing, there are many aspects to consider. These include how the cloud can be used to leverage increased computing power, such as with grid computing. Threats to the cloud, including data security and privacy, are increasingly important as more data are stored off-site and managed by other companies. The need for qualified individuals to configure and manage clouds will continue to grow. Certification is a way for IT professionals to prove their skills.

Essential Question

What implications exist for a business that entrusts its data to a cloud provider?

Key Terms ✍

Clarifying Lawful Overseas
   Use of Data (CLOUD) Act
cluster network

data sovereignty
grid computing

multitenant computing
noisy neighbor issue

Learning Goals

- Diagram the function of grid computing.
- Interpret issues with cloud computing.
- Describe functions of a cloud access security broker.
- Compare and contrast cloud computing certifications.

Grid Computing

The Internet has made possible another network feature with a large positive impact on the evolution of technology. *Grid computing* involves using resources from multiple computers to spread out a workload. This allows services to run in a distributed model, as shown in **Figure 14-9.** The result is high-performance

Job Assigned

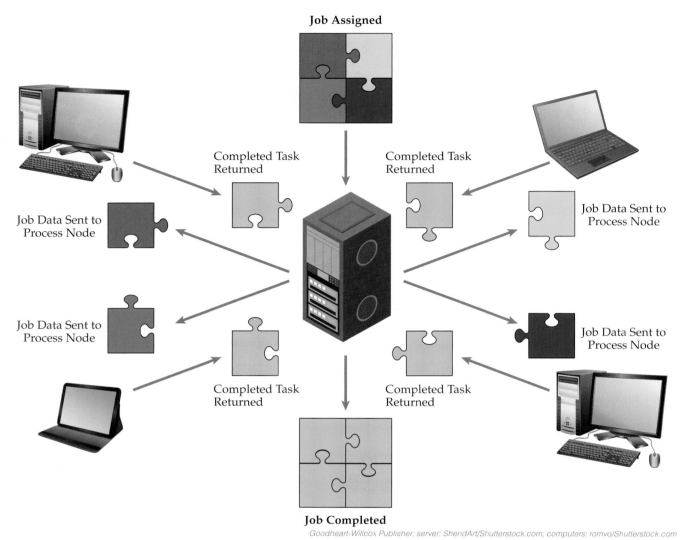

Completed Task Returned

Completed Task Returned

Job Data Sent to Process Node

Job Data Sent to Process Node

Job Data Sent to Process Node

Job Data Sent to Process Node

Completed Task Returned

Completed Task Returned

Job Completed

Figure 14-9. In a grid-computing environment, a given workload is distributed between resources located on multiple computers.

operations. Applications in mathematics and science often need high-powered systems. Grid computing offers a solution. A grid-computing environment is also known as a *cluster network.*

Consider the idle time for your computer's CPU. In Windows, this can be seen as CPU usage in the Performance Monitor. If the CPU usage is 10 percent, for example, the remaining capability can be shared. The unused CPU capability of your computer can be combined with potentially thousands of other machines, each working on a small part of a task to create a grid or distributed network. If a computer in the grid needs more resources locally, the CPU cycling returns to the local machine. That machine then contributes less to the task on the grid. Not just CPU resources can be shared. Grid computing can utilize hard drive storage and computer memory.

Many people confuse grid computing with network clusters or load balancing. In those cases, the systems are managed by a centralized resource manager. With grid computing, there is not a centralized resource manager. Each device or node in the grid manages itself. That allows a machine participating in a grid project to join or disconnect at any time.

Managing the security is an essential aspect of grid computing. Some of the key factors to be considered include integrity, privacy, and least privilege. Integrity will ensure the resources provided by a node machine cannot be modified. To address privacy concerns, it is important that any sensitive information is kept confidential. Encryption techniques are often implemented to ensure this. The principle of least privilege ensures that the process or resource submitted by the grid to the node is the only feature that can be accessed by the grid. Of course, a properly configured grid environment should also provide accountability. This will ensure compliance with the security measures can be audited.

The possible applications for grid computing are endless. Of course, there are other considerations to consider. The data in the grid must still be protected. For example, every computer in the grid is using the same software. If there is a vulnerability in that code, all computers in the grid would be vulnerable as well.

Quick Look 14.3.1

Grid Computing Applications

Scientists believe that harvesting the power of the grid can help with finding cures for diseases. The calculations required in much of the research can be distributed with grid computing. One such application is the World Community Grid.

1. Launch a web browser, and navigate to the World Community Grid website (www.worldcommunitygrid.org).
2. Review the page to see what types of projects with which the organization is involved. Which of the projects would you consider supporting?
3. Click the **Join** or **Join Now** button, but do not complete the process of joining.
4. On the join page, click the **end user license agreement** link. Are you able to join this initiative based on the EULA? Why or why not?
5. What company is behind this initiative?

Other Considerations for Cloud Computing

There are many benefits to cloud computing. Convenience, reduced cost and overhead, and distributing workloads are just a few benefits. However, cloud computing has issues as well. Resources are shared with others. There are concerns related to which laws apply and how. A level of uncertainty exists, and data privacy is a concern.

Sharing with Others

When a business chooses to use a public cloud, it is sharing the hardware resources of the cloud vendor with other customers. This is often referred to as *multitenant computing.* Think of this like the cloud being an apartment building. In that building live several people who share heat and hot water. One of the concerns of sharing these resources is an occurrence or situation known as the noisy neighbor issue. The *noisy neighbor issue* is when one customer of the cloud uses most of the resources. This causes other customers to have degraded performance or bandwidth.

Noisy neighbor problems can exist if the cloud vendor does not deploy strategies for maintaining performance. Most public cloud vendors use a scalable virtualized platform that adjusts for on-demand computing. This makes it difficult for one organization to monopolize resources of the cloud. Another strategy is balancing loads across servers to improve performance. A storage quality of service (QoS)

CompTIA Security+
3.7

FYI Some cloud experts consider the noisy neighbor issue to be a myth.

policy can be implemented on the virtual machines. This is used to control inputs and output operations.

Legal Concerns

Another serious issue concerns the laws related to where data are stored. Cloud vendors can store data on servers located in different states or even different countries. This sets the stage for differing laws and cross-jurisdictional issues to come into play. *Where* the data are actually stored may make this a difficult situation, as shown in **Figure 14-10.** *Data sovereignty* is a concept that digital data are subject to the jurisdiction and laws of the country where the storage device is located. Many states and countries have laws that regulate the storage and transfer of data. These laws likely will be different from one location to another. This could affect the privacy of and access to your data.

Suppose a business is located in the United States, but the cloud it uses is based on a server located in Norway. Do US laws take precedence over Norwegian laws? This is the type of question that can arise in the event of a jurisdictional dispute. Some of this can be addressed in the contract or ToS with the cloud vendor. However, laws regulating data and business may prevail.

An example of cross-jurisdictional issues arose when the US Department of Justice served Microsoft with a subpoena for user content, including e-mail. The subpoena was related to a criminal narcotics case. The data sought by the government were stored on servers in Dublin, Ireland. However, the data could be accessed and retrieved from within the United States. The US government argued that Microsoft must turn over the data. It cited the Electronics Communication Privacy Act (ECPA) of 1986. Two US court rulings favored the government's position. However, in 2016 an appeals court sided with Microsoft. It ruled that the United States could not seize data stored only on servers located in foreign countries. The case at present is pending a hearing with the United States Supreme Court.

In March of 2018, the United States Congress passed the CLOUD Act. The *Clarifying Lawful Overseas Use of Data (CLOUD) Act* provides more oversight into data storage on cloud providers. Essentially, the CLOUD Act allows federal law enforcement to compel any US–based service provider to turn over requested

CompTIA Security+
5.6

Sergey Nivens/Shutterstock.com

Figure 14-10. Data in the cloud may be stored anywhere in the United States or around the world. This complicates legal issues related to the data.

Ethical Issue

Data Storage Locations

The Chinese government has been accused of many state-sponsored hacks and has repressive Internet policies for its citizens. In July of 2017, Apple announced it would open a data center in China. Apple is reacting to a law in China that requires companies to store their users' data in China and the cloud service must be operated by Chinese companies. Apple has stated that data from customers who are not in China will be stored outside of China and that encryption keys would not be shared with China. Do you believe there is a long-term implication of data privacy to iCloud data for non-Chinese customers? Considering the privacy implications, potential security issues, and growth of the market share for Apple, do you feel Apple made a smart decision?

data stored from any location. The location may be within the United States or in another country. A subpoena or warrant is required for this request. The CLOUD Act modified the existing Stored Communications Act (SCA). The SCA was written and passed in 1986.

Uncertainty

Uncertainty is a consideration that businesses must understand when they use a cloud. Creating a cloud platform can cause uncertainty in demand and costs. Zynga is an excellent example of how cloud computing worked and failed. Zynga makes games such as FarmVille and CityVille. It spotlighted the initial success of using a cloud solution. Instead of extending existing business into the cloud, it launched products from cloud sites. In particular, it used Amazon Web Services. Once Zynga understood the hardware demands, it moved the products to its own private cloud. This was called zCloud. Due to the fluctuation of the game market, in particular mobile app games, Zynga found its business did not grow as expected. In 2015, it decided to shut down its private cloud and move the resources back to AWS. Fortunately for Zynga, the cloud business grew. AWS was also able to offer more pricing flexibility to Zynga and other companies.

Of course, using the cloud depends on access to the Internet. It also depends on the reliability of the connection. This is true for not only a business, but its customers as well. Suppose your cloud vendor advertises a 99 percent reliability and availability. While that sounds great, it means 1 percent of the time you would not have access, as shown in **Figure 14-11.** How much would that cost your firm? There are 43,200 minutes in 30 days. One percent of that is 432 minutes. That means for 432 minutes each month, on average, you and your customers have no access to data or services. That is close to one full business day.

Cloud outages can be the result of the vendor or the ISP. In 2012, Microsoft and its Azure product were impacted by a software bug that caused a significant disruption and downtime for customers. The outage affected customers in Western Europe for over two and a half hours. Outages can come from other failures. For example, an attack may be carried out against an ISP. Or, the ISP's infrastructure could fail. In another example, a DDoS attack on the Internet service provider DYN in October of 2016 took down many popular websites. Some of the websites affected included Netflix and Twitter.

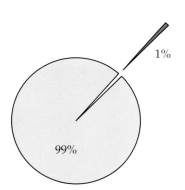

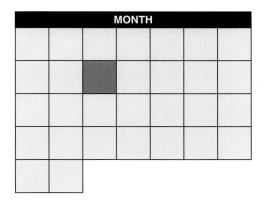

60 minutes per hour × 24 hours per day × 30 days per month = 43,200 minutes per month

43,200 × 1 percent = 432 minutes per month

432 minutes ÷ 60 minutes per hour = 7.2 hours

Figure 14-11. Downtime of one percent may not seem like much, but over the course of one month, that is close to one full business day without cloud access.

Data Privacy

An important concern for many cloud users is data privacy. This is particularly true when it comes to what the government can and cannot access. Where the data storage is physically located can influence the extent to which governments can view the stored data. A government may be able to access data not located within its borders due to mutual legal assistance treaties (MLATs). These are agreements between countries to gather and exchange data in efforts to enforce the laws of those countries.

The Society for Computers and Law (www.scl.org) did a comprehensive research of governmental access to data in the cloud. It looked at ten major countries. These were Australia, Germany, United States, Canada, Denmark, France, Ireland, Japan, United Kingdom, and Spain. Here are some findings:

- All ten countries must provide data in the course of a governmental investigation.
- Only Germany and the United States require customers to be notified if their data are provided to the government, and both countries make exceptions to this, such as if a search warrant was issued.
- Only Germany and Japan require cooperation from a foreign government to obtain data from a cloud vendor when the data are located in the other country.
- All ten countries allow the government to monitor data and electronic communication through the systems of the cloud vendor.

There is proposed legislation in the United States called the Law Enforcement Access to Data Stored Abroad (LEADS) Act. This would push back against agencies in the US government seeking to gain access to data in the cloud. It would require a court-issued warrant for the government to request such data. There are many in favor of tightening these disclosures. For example, many news organizations worry their research may be subject to governmental intrusion. The protections offered by the LEADS Act may also remove some uncertainty of companies that may be wary of placing their data on a cloud vendor.

Cloud Access Security Broker

CompTIA Security+
3.7

A cloud access security broker (CASB) allows CIOs the ability to provide enterprise security policies across multiple cloud platforms. The CASB is located between the users and the cloud, as shown in **Figure 14-12.** It may be cloud based or hosted at the customer's location. Cloud access security broker is a term coined by Gartner, Inc. It describes a set of security solutions organized around four main areas. These areas are visibility, compliance, data security, and threat protection.

Visibility allows you to see which users are accessing data and the type of device used to access the data. You can view which apps users are running from the cloud and when. This information gives more insight into how the cloud services are being used.

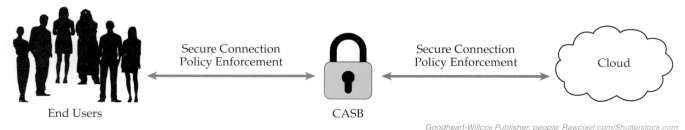

End Users

Secure Connection
Policy Enforcement

CASB

Secure Connection
Policy Enforcement

Cloud

Figure 14-12. A CASB sits between the cloud and the users to provide secure connection and enforcement of policies.

Compliance with laws, such as HIPAA or SOX, is essential. Even internal policies must be followed by users. A CASB helps ensure a business is compliant with rules and regulations.

Data security is essential. A CASB can ensure monitoring and securing of sensitive data occurs. This includes encryption. Data being accessed and shared will be examined to determine if the use is proper. This helps with data loss protection (DLP).

A CASB will help with threat protection. It helps ensure an organization remains vigilant against threats. This includes not only external threats, but also internal threats.

In 2015, only 15 percent of large enterprises used a CASB solution. Gartner believes this market will rapidly increase. It expects the market to grow to 85 percent of large enterprises by the year 2020.

Cloud security is a shared responsibility between the cloud vendor and its customers. The cloud vendor handles the security of the infrastructure. The customers are responsible for the user layer. This includes user behavior, apps, and data.

Cloud Computing Certifications

For many organizations, the cloud has become an essential component of delivery and storage of data. Therefore, it is critical IT staff are well-trained in cloud solutions and services. There are several industry certifications in cloud computing, as shown in **Figure 14-13.** Certifications are a good way to demonstrate your skill in cloud management.

Microsoft has a cloud certification within its Microsoft Technology Associate (MTA) line of certifications. This certification is called Cloud Fundamentals. The exam number is 98-369. The exam covers these areas:

- understand the cloud (20–25%)
- enable Microsoft cloud services (20–25%)
- administer Office 365 and Microsoft Intune (15–20%)
- use and configure Microsoft cloud services (20–25%)
- support cloud users (15–20%)

FYI

Microsoft Intune is a cloud platform that allows a business to deliver apps and manage mobile devices. This allows a unified and seamless experience regardless of the device being used, while providing security for the business.

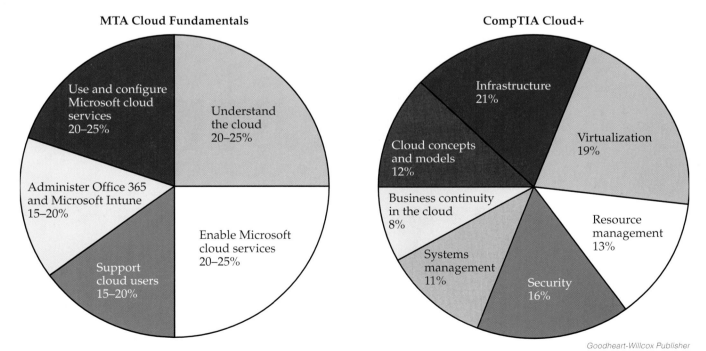

Figure 14-13. MTA Cloud Fundamentals and CompTIA Cloud+ are two popular certifications to demonstrate skill in cloud computing. These graphs show the percentages of coverage on each exam.

Another popular cloud certification is from CompTIA. This certification is called Cloud+. The certification exam covers these areas:

- cloud concepts and models (12%)
- virtualization (19%)
- infrastructure (21%)
- resource management (13%)
- security (16%)
- systems management (11%)
- business continuity in the cloud (8%)

There are other, specialized certifications in cloud computing. There are five different levels for Amazon Web Services (AWS). There are also many certifications from HP, IBM, Rackspace, and VMWare.

Quick Look 14.3.2

Cloud+ Certification

Certification is a good way to demonstrate your skills to a potential employer. There are many certifications related to cloud computing. The Cloud+ certification from CompTIA is popular for showing skill in cloud computing.

1. Launch a web browser, and navigate to the CompTIA website (www.comptia.org).

2. Locate the **Certifications** button or link, and click it to navigate to the certification portion of the website.

3. Once in the certifications portion of the website, click **Certifications** at the top of the screen. You are transported to a page listing all of the available certifications, as shown. Notice there are two options for cloud certification: Cloud+ and Cloud Essentials.

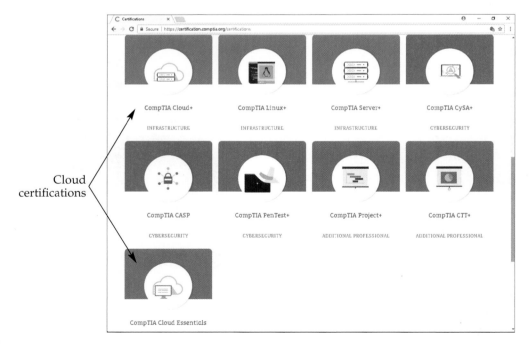

Quick Look 14.3.2 Continued

4. Click the Cloud+ icon, and then click the **Click for Details** button. You are transported to a page showing detailed information about this certification.
5. Review the general information on Cloud+, including the types of jobs available for people with this certification.
6. In the Exam Details section of the page, look for the exam format. How many questions are on the exam? How is the exam scored? What does the exam cost?
7. With your instructor's permission, fill out the form to download the practice questions and exam objectives.
8. Return to the main certifications page, click the Cloud Essentials icon, and click for details.
9. What is the primary difference between the Cloud+ and Cloud Essentials certifications?
10. With your instructor's permission, download the practice questions and exam objectives for this certification.
11. Review the downloaded material for both certifications. Discuss with your class.

SECTION REVIEW 14.3

Check Your Understanding

1. A cluster network in the cloud is also known as _____.
2. A cloud vendor usually has many customers using its equipment. This is known as _____ computing.
3. _____ means companies must understand that a cloud service could be unavailable when needed.
4. Which term describes what an enterprise uses to provide security services across multiple cloud platforms?
5. What is the cloud platform from Microsoft used to deliver apps and manage mobile devices?

Build Your Key Terms Vocabulary

As you progress through this course, develop a personal cybersecurity glossary. This will help you build your vocabulary and prepare you for a career. Write a definition for each of the following terms, and add it to your cybersecurity glossary.

Clarifying Lawful Overseas Use of Data (CLOUD) Act

cluster network

data sovereignty

grid computing

multitenant computing

noisy neighbor issue

Review and Assessment

Summary

Section 14.1 Cloud Basics

- Cloud computing is the use of resources running from a remote location instead locally, but an important aspect is collaboration and sharing of data.
- The four cloud-deployment models are private, public, community, and hybrid and each has advantages and disadvantages.
- Cloud storage is popular, but several issues must be considered including the type of service, how data will be secured, and if data will be available when needed.

Section 14.2 Cloud Services

- Software as a service (SaaS) is a complete software solution from the cloud without needing to install resources locally, such as the Google Apps suite.
- Platform as a service (PaaS) allows a customer to develop applications without creating the underlying platform and allows web developers to focus on the apps and not the environment.
- Infrastructure as a service (IaaS) is a cloud-computing solution where the vendor provides the customer with virtualized computing resources over the Internet.
- Security as a service (SECaaS) is cloud-based malware, firewall, and intrusion protection that acts as an off-site gatekeeper for a network.

Section 14.3 Other Cloud Considerations

- Grid computing involves using resources from multiple computers to spread out a workload, which offers high performance for applications in fields such as mathematics and science.
- There are several issues with cloud computing, including sharing resources with others, concern over which laws apply, the uncertainty with the cloud, and privacy of data.
- A cloud access security broker (CASB) is located between the users and the cloud and is a set of security solutions organized around visibility, compliance, data security, and threat protection.

Check Your Cybersecurity IQ

Now that you have completed this chapter, see what you have learned about cybersecurity by visiting the student companion website (www.g-wlearning.com) and taking the chapter posttest.

Review Questions

For each question, select the answer that is the best response.

1. Woodland Electric is a regional electricity supplier serving a 200-square-mile area. A great many of the service technicians need access to data on a regular basis. Security of the information is important. What should Woodland Electric incorporate?
   A. A multitenant solution
   B. A private cloud
   C. Grid computing
   D. SaaS

2. Barbara's Bookstore has many locations in the San Francisco area. Barbara decides on a public cloud for her data storage. Which of the following is not a benefit of using this solution?
   A. As Barbara's business grows, the cloud is easier to scale.
   B. The owner of the bookstore is not responsible for hardware and maintenance.
   C. Access to the data is dependent on reliable Internet connections.
   D. Skilled professionals will manage the system.

3. What do mobile app developers use to allow them to focus completely on the product, not the development environment?
   A. Community cloud
   B. Load balancing
   C. Sandbox
   D. PaaS solution

4. An IaaS vendor typically charges the customer by:
   A. How much time they are on the system.
   B. The software licenses installed.
   C. The amount of hardware they install.
   D. All of these are typical charges.

5. By having a SECaaS solution, which of the following do you not have to do?
   A. Use an IaaS.
   B. Use encryption.
   C. Hire your own cybersecurity professionals.
   D. Use host-based antivirus programs.

6. The ToS provide instructions for:
   A. The SaaS vendor only.
   B. The customer only.
   C. The SaaS vendor and the customer.
   D. The ISP and the customer.

7. What is the benefit of grid computing?
   A. The workload is distributed over many computers.
   B. The computer in the grid share security resources.
   C. A flaw in the grid software cannot affect the node computers.
   D. The grid decreases performance of the node computers.

8. Which is a true statement regarding the noisy neighbors issue in cloud computing?
   A. It occurs when the cloud vendor does not virtualize servers.
   B. The problem is more common if the cloud vendor incorporates QoS on a server.
   C. A scalable, virtualized platform can minimize the problem.
   D. Multitenant computing eliminates the problem.

9. Which is not a feature provided by CASB?
   A. Ensures a business meets the requirements of governmental mandates such as HIPAA.
   B. Enables grid computing.
   C. Ensures only authorized users access data.
   D. Integrates security with existing security solutions.

10. Which certification from CompTIA will test the skills necessary to manage a cloud environment?
    A. Cloud Fundamentals
    B. Cloud+
    C. Cloud Management+
    D. Cloud Deployment

Application and Extension of Knowledge

1. Google and Amazon have many different cloud certifications. Identify one certification from each vendor. Summarize the skills measured and benefits from obtaining this certification. Which one interests you more? Why?

2. As cloud platforms evolve, more services are being offered. One of the intriguing new offerings is artificial intelligence as a service (AIaaS). Investigate this emerging technology. Prepare a presentation on its application, intended benefits, and other interesting facets.

3. Explore how cloud models can be used for scanning systems for malware as opposed to installing antimalware programs locally and updating the definitions. Compare and contrast two different online scanners. Summarize functionality, pricing, advantages, and disadvantages of using this type of protection.

4. RightScale (www.rightscale.com) is an industry leader in cloud management. It periodically produces a State of the Cloud Report. Locate this report, and review the facts it contains. Assume you are making a pitch to an organization about adopting cloud services. Which facts and data did you find most interesting that you would include in your presentation? What did you find interesting on a personal level?

5. Some companies worry that shifting to the cloud makes their data more vulnerable than if storage is at their local locations. Analyze both aspects of that statement. Create a chart to show advantages and disadvantages for each option. If possible, interview business managers who have adopted or are not adopting the cloud model.

Research Project
SaaS Backup Solutions

A best practice in computing is to always back up data. This allows recovery from an accidental deletion, a hardware failure, malware infections, and many other issues. A common SaaS solution is a service that backs up data on the cloud. There are several advantages to doing this, including the backup being in a different location and redundancy in the data storage. Several companies offer cloud-based backup programs. Some of the available options include Carbonite, Mozy, Spider Oak, Sugar Sync, SOS Online Backup, and Zoolz. Select two of these options, and research what functions and features are offered. Compare and contrast the choices. Which would you recommend to your parents and why?

Deliverables. Write a one- to two-page paper detailing your findings and recommendations. Include a table to compare and contrast the features and options of the two solutions you selected. If possible, include screenshots of the software in your paper.

Online Activities

Complete the following activities, which will help you learn, practice, and expand your knowledge and skills.

Vocabulary. Practice vocabulary for this chapter using the e-flash cards, matching activity, and vocabulary game until you are able to recognize their meanings.

Communication Skills

College and Career Readiness

Reading. Select several chapters of this textbook. Identify two generic features used in each chapter you selected. Compare and contrast how each feature is used. Why do you think the author chose these particular features to apply to multiple chapters?

Writing. Generate ideas relating to the importance of accurate information. Make a list of reasons you would provide a business owner when explaining why it is important to read carefully the terms of service for a cloud vendor. After your list is complete, write a paragraph summarizing your reasoning.

Speaking. Select a member of your class to whom you will present the information you learned from Quick Look 14.3.2. Make use of displays or demonstrations to enhance the presentation.

Listening. Your purpose for listening varies, depending on where you are—in a personal conversation, group discussion, or large audience. What was your purpose for listening to your instructor present this lesson today? Did you listen because you had to, because you needed to learn the material for a test, or for other reasons? When you listen with purpose, you get more out of the information being presented.

Portfolio Development

College and Career Readiness

Technical Skills. Your portfolio must also showcase the technical skills you have. Are you exceptionally good working with computer hardware? Do you have a talent for programming software? Can you build a website? Technical skills are very important for succeeding in school or at work.

1. Create a Microsoft Word document that describes the technical skills you have acquired. Use the heading Technical Skills and your name. Describe the skill, your level of competence, and any other information that will showcase your skill level. Save the document file.

2. Update your master spreadsheet.

CTSO Event Prep

Proper Attire. Some career and technical student organizations (CTSOs) require appropriate business attire from all entrants and those attending the competition. This requirement is in keeping with the mission of CTSOs: to prepare students for professional careers. To be sure the attire you have chosen to wear at the competition is in accordance with event requirements, complete the following activities.

1. Visit the organization's website, and look for the most current dress code.

2. The dress code requirements are very detailed and gender specific. Some CTSOs may require a chapter blazer to be worn during the competition.

3. Do a dress rehearsal when practicing for your event. Are you comfortable in the clothes you have chosen? Do you present a professional appearance?

4. In addition to the kinds of clothes you can wear, be sure the clothes are clean and pressed. You do not want to undermine your appearance or event performance with wrinkled clothes that may distract judges.

5. Make sure your hair is neat and worn in a conservative style. If you are a male, you should be clean shaven. Again, you do not want anything about your appearance detracting from your performance.

6. As far in advance of the event as is possible, share your clothing choice with your organization's advisor to make sure you are appropriately dressed.

Chapter 15

Risk Management

In a business or organization, risk is a natural consequence of the actions and decisions taken by the business and its employees. Just opening a business is a risk: will your company be profitable, and will it grow? Risk occurs on many levels and in many areas. If a decision or product could present a problem, how do you resolve the possibility of risk? Ignoring the risk could result in significant problems if you are not prepared to respond to the situation. How susceptible are your business computers to a virus? Can your employees spot a phishing e-mail? This is where risk management comes into play.

Risk management is a detailed process. There are guidelines you can follow. These guidelines are typically called frameworks. Ultimately, decisions that are made depend on how much risk a business or organization is able to accept. This chapter introduces the processes of managing risk with a structured approach. This approach views the responses to risk and analyzes the risk factors that contribute to risk. There are also choices to make in identifying the accepted level of risk.

Chapter Preview

While studying, look for the activity icon for:

- Pretests and posttests
- Vocabulary terms with e-flash cards and matching activities
- Self-assessment

G-WLEARNING.com

Reading Prep

Before reading this chapter, look at the chapter title. Write a paragraph describing what you already know about the topic. After reading the chapter, write a paragraph to summarize what you have learned. How do the two paragraphs compare?

Check Your Cybersecurity IQ ⤴

Before you begin this chapter, see what you already know about cybersecurity by visiting the student companion website (www.g-wlearning.com) and taking the chapter pretest.

Certification Objectives

CompTIA Security+

5.2   Summarize business impact analysis concepts.
5.3   Explain risk management processes and concepts.

Microsoft MTA Security Fundamentals

1.1   Understand core security principles.

Section 15.1

Overview of Risk

Essential Question

Why are users the most important risk faced by IT staff?

IT security professionals must always be aware of the issues surrounding the protection of a business and its data. Previous chapters have identified many potential vulnerabilities and threats that could affect a business's operations and security. It is important to analyze these threat vectors. However, it is equally important to prepare a comprehensive strategy to deal with threats. The plan should take into account the likely threats and the response to each risk.

Risk management helps an organization understand the areas of potential harm and likelihood harm may occur. It also can outline the financial costs of these risks. Risk management allows professionals to identify and prioritize risks and create a risk-response plan. This may include preventative actions to reduce the possibility of risk. These strategies allow security practitioners to focus on the most common or intrusive threats that their organization faces.

Key Terms

annual loss expectancy (ALE)
annual rate of occurrence (ARO)
asset
IT Infrastructure Library (ITIL)

qualitative risk assessment
quantitative risk assessment
risk
risk assessment

risk management
semiqualitative values
single loss expectancy (SLE)
threat agent

Learning Goals

- Define risk.
- Identify IT assets.
- Differentiate vulnerabilities and threats.
- Construct a risk-management model.
- Assess risks.

Risk

MTA Security Fundamentals
1.1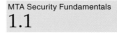

Risk can be defined as a situation that could cause harm, create a hazard, or otherwise cause problems that need to be addressed. There are varying degrees of risk. For example, suppose you are driving to the store. If there is heavy traffic, the risk of being involved in an accident is greater than if there is light traffic. However, even in light traffic, there is a risk of an accident. This is why you carry auto insurance. The insurance industry is built around protecting people against the potential loss from specific risks.

A business, organization, or individual faces many types of risk. There are the risks from physical and natural disasters, as shown in **Figure 15-1.** These risks include events such as floods, fires, or other unexpected catastrophes. Severe weather, such as tornadoes or hurricanes, may not be common, but if they do occur, they can be very destructive. The risk of fires is always present, but steps can be taken to reduce the risk. The risk of flooding exists anywhere there is water, such as near a river or lake. However, this risk is present anywhere that may experience heavy rain.

The IT field faces its own set of risks. Computers are hardware and software. These both present risks. A hardware or software problem might prevent access to data. A hardware failure may even permanently destroy data. Additionally, there are risks due to security breaches.

Users represent the weakest link in the IT security chain. Therefore, they represent a risk. As you have learned, there are ways to manage users. For example, policies can be created to limit a user's access to only the data he or she needs. This is one way to limit the risk presented by users.

There must be a balance between handling risk and usability. For example, you can mostly avoid the risk of getting into a traffic accident by not driving or taking a bus. However, you would have to walk everywhere. You would still be exposed to some risk of being in a traffic accident because a car may strike you while you are walking.

FEMA News Photo

Figure 15-1. Severe weather, such as tornadoes, poses a risk. Tornadoes can be devastating when they occur, as demonstrated by this house.

IT Assets

You have been learning about the many areas that pose a threat to IT assets. Threats are risks. It is important to view IT assets in the context of risk.

An *asset* is something that has value. Most people think of IT assets as hardware, such as servers, printers, and copiers. These are tangible items. They can be seen and felt. The building you are located in is a tangible asset. However, assets may be intangible. For example, the company's reputation is an intangible asset. Employees represent another asset that most people do not consider.

For the sake of risk management, IT assets need to be assigned a value and level of importance to the organization. For example, if an employee notifies IT that his or her laptop computer is missing, you need to respond to that event. However, if a company server is missing, that is a high priority. The server has a higher value and level of importance than an individual laptop. Something like a broken mouse is a minor issue and would not be part of a risk assessment. For each asset, assign a numeric value, such as a dollar amount, or a description such as essential or nonessential. Also, assign a priority impact to indicate the level of importance. For example, an asset may be assigned a priority such as critical, high, medium, low, or very low.

The *IT Infrastructure Library (ITIL)* is a framework that offers best practices for IT. It was developed in Great Britain in the 1980s as a means to achieve better quality of IT services for reduced costs. Today, the ITIL is a globally recognized organization that produces many frameworks and standards for IT services. Included in their documents are guidelines for incident urgency. For example, **Figure 15-2** shows a priority list offered by the ITIL framework. You can use this or modify it to suit your needs. The ITIL is hosted by AXELOS (www.axelos.com) under Best Practices.

Category	Description
High (H)	A large number of staff are affected or not able to do their job.
	A large number of customers are affected or acutely disadvantaged in some way.
	The financial impact of the incident is, for example, likely to exceed $10,000.
	The damage to the reputation of the business is likely to be high.
	Someone has been injured.
Medium (M)	A moderate number of staff are affected or not able to do their jobs properly.
	A moderate number of customers are affected or inconvenienced in some way.
	The financial impact of the incident is, for example, likely to exceed $1,000, but will not be more than $10,000.
	The damage to the reputation of the business is likely to be moderate.
Low (L)	A minimal number of staff are affected or are able to deliver an acceptable service, but doing so requires extra effort.
	A minimal number of customers are affected or inconvenienced, but not in a significant way.
	The financial impact of the incident is, for example, likely to be less than $1,000.
	The damage to the reputation of the business is likely to be minimal.

Figure 15-2. This priority list from ITIL offers guidance on how to assign levels of importance to IT assets.

Quick Look 15.1.1

Assets at Risk

An important task for the IT staff is to identify assets. After identifying assets, a value and level of importance need to be assigned to each.

1. Form teams of two to three student as directed by your instructor.
2. Select one person to record your observations in a spreadsheet.
3. Launch a spreadsheet program, and create the following columns.

Asset	Tangible or Intangible	Value	Priority Impact

4. Look around your classroom for IT assets. This includes services and resources. If you have 20 classroom computers, for example, count those as one asset since they are all used by students.
5. List each asset in the first column.
6. Identify each asset as tangible or intangible in the second column.

Quick Look 15.1.1 Continued

7. Assign an estimated value for each asset in the third column. You may choose to use descriptive terms instead of a value.

8. Discuss with your team what you believe the priority impact would be if there is a loss of the asset. Use the examples in **Figure 15-2.** Enter the impact in the fourth column.

9. Share your team's findings with the class. Each team should then create one master list from the class findings.

10. Save the file. Your team will use it again later in this chapter.

Causes and Likelihood of Risk

Once assets are identified, determine some of the problems that could cause risk to each asset. You must look at the vulnerabilities, threats, and the threat agents that could pose risk. In order to do this, consider the concept of vulnerabilities and threats in the context with risk.

As discussed in Chapter 2, a *vulnerability* is a flaw or potential for harm. This may be something inherent (built-in) or some other type of weakness in the asset. A vulnerability could be the result of a design, or something that just could naturally occur by its makeup. For example, you may have the best laptop with encryption set up. However, it is still vulnerable to being lost or stolen.

Also discussed in Chapter 2, a *threat* is something that takes the vulnerability to a level that the flaws can be exploited. This is an actual occurrence that can cause damage. A hurricane heading for your town is a threat. Just living in a coastal town along the Gulf Coast makes your home vulnerable to hurricanes. Threats exploit vulnerabilities. A weak password is vulnerable. The threat in this case is an attack that obtains the password.

A *threat agent* is the source, or *actor,* that causes a threat to occur. Refer to **Figure 15-3.** A threat agent could be an employee shoulder surfing to determine another employee's password. The vulnerability is the visible keyboard. The threat is the actor actually obtaining the password and then using it for access.

An important aspect when considering risk is how likely the event is. For example, a tornado is more likely to occur in Alabama than in Maine. Sometimes, likelihood can be determined from data. Data from the Storm Prediction Center show that Alabama has an average of 47.1 tornadoes annually. Maine's average is 2, on the other hand. Other times, hard data like these are not available. In these cases, estimate the likelihood based on related research or on common sense.

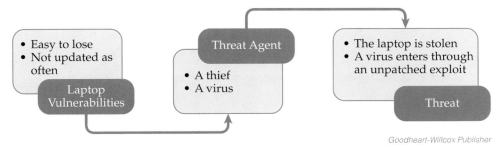

Goodheart-Willcox Publisher

Figure 15-3. This illustration shows the relationship between vulnerabilities, threat agents, and threats.

Quick Look 15.1.2

Risk Factors

Knowing the causes of risks is important to identifying a risk. It is not enough just to identify a risk. You must also determine how likely the risk is to occur. For this activity, work in the same group as the last activity.

1. Open your group's vulnerability spreadsheet.
2. Add columns for vulnerability and likelihood.

Asset	Tangible or Intangible	Value	Priority Impact	Vulnerability	Likelihood

3. For each asset, identify one vulnerability that could occur and its likelihood of occurring. Use these ratings for likelihood: seldom, occasionally, or frequently.
4. Share the results with your classmates.
5. Make any changes based on the work of other teams, and save your work.

Risk Management

Risk management is identifying the areas that could result in risk and then planning solutions and methods to reduce, eliminate, or respond to the situation. It is a structured approach. Analyzing risk is a normal task for any business-management team. Many businesses heavily rely on technology. Therefore, it is critical the IT staff is an active participant with upper management in a risk-management plan.

A risk-management model provides steps to follow. Use these steps to identify assets, determine the extent of vulnerability, come up with a response plan, and long-term monitoring. The NIST SP 800-39 document provides a framework to set up a risk-management program. This framework recognizes four steps, as shown in **Figure 15-4.** The document can be found by searching the NIST website (www.nist.gov).

Frame the Risk

To frame the risk, the environment in which risk decisions are made is described. This step asks, what is your plan for assessing, responding to, and monitoring risk? The answer is the *risk management strategy.* Tools that will be used are identified. Methods of evaluation and procedures for risk evaluation are

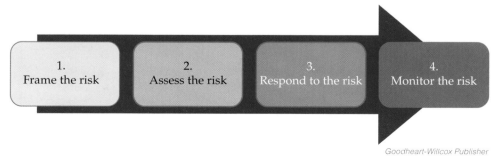

1. Frame the risk   2. Assess the risk   3. Respond to the risk   4. Monitor the risk

Figure 15-4. The NIST SP 800-39 document identifies four components or steps of risk management.

established. Management also makes other decisions, such as what level of tolerance will the company support.

Assess the Risk

With protocols and procedures identified, a risk assessment is performed. An analysis of the risk to the assets must be addressed. This includes threats, vulnerabilities, and the likelihood of these threats and vulnerabilities. Also, the potential harm should the risk be realized is calculated. Risk assessment is discussed in detail later in this chapter.

Respond to the Risk

The organization must decide on the types of responses or courses of action to a risk. For example, should there be an attempt to reduce the risk or avoid the issue that is causing the risk? For example, if you are worried about stolen data on laptops, you can decide to ban the use of laptops. That would eliminate that risk. Strategies for responding to the risk are discussed later in this chapter.

Monitor the Risk

Once the response is established and implemented, you need to determine if it is effective and acceptable. For example, suppose you choose to use a specific antimalware to reduce the possibility of malware and viruses. Over time, you find a number of infections are not being caught and cleaned. This may indicate the response is not effective. If that is the case, you may decide to use different antimalware.

Risk Assessment

In a risk-management strategy, there must be a complete understanding of the types of risks faced. A complete inventory of the potential risk factors must be identified. This is done through a risk assessment. A *risk assessment* involves identifying risks and ranking them with the most critical risks listed first. This is also called a *risk analysis*. For example, data loss from a server failure is a more critical risk than data loss from a flash drive.

Risk assessment is a comprehensive approach to identifying the IT assets. The first step is to list all assets. Then, look at what could happen to each of these. In other words, what are the vulnerabilities and threats? Finally, identify safeguards or controls to handle the risks. Risk assessments are generally conducted by one of two methods: quantitative or qualitative.

Ethical Issue

Employee Responsibility in Risk Management

It is often said that employees are an organization's greatest asset. From an IT perspective, people are also the weakest link in the security chain. Everyone in the organization must help manage risks and minimize the damage that could occur. Ethical responsibility is an important consideration. Consider this scenario: Tony often takes a laptop home and uses his home Internet service. What is the risk in this scenario? Another employee, Kara, is aware of this situation, but she has not said anything to Tony, IT staff, or management. Does Kara share responsibility for exposing the company to the risk? Should she report Tony's use of his home Internet service on the company laptop? Why or why not?

CompTIA Security+
5.3

Quantitative Method

Quantitative risk assessment is a method based on actual data that uses numbers or monetary values. It is an objective method. This means it is not based on personal beliefs or opinions. This type of assessment requires data to support your claim. A specific value on an item is a piece of objective data. For example, suppose you know a replacement computer costs $400, as shown in **Figure 15-5.** Then, the quantitative method can be used to determine loss from the risk. Since the quantitative method assigns an objective value, such as monetary value, it is easier to compute loss. There are several key terms that are associated with a quantitative method:

- single loss expectancy
- annual rate of occurrence
- annual loss expectancy

Phovoir/Shutterstock.com

Figure 15-5. When assigning a value for a loss, include not only the physical items, but also intangible items such as software and labor costs.

Single Loss Expectancy (SLE)

The *single loss expectancy (SLE)* is the amount of value that will be lost from one incident. For example, if a laptop is stolen, you would compute the cost for a replacement laptop. This cost would include software and any data that need to be recreated or restored.

Annual Rate of Occurrence (ARO)

The *annual rate of occurrence (ARO)* is the number of times an incident will happen in one year. How many times a year do you expect this incident to occur? If over the course of a year you expect four laptops will be lost or stolen, the ARO is 4. If a problem happens only once every two years, the ARO is 0.5.

Annual Loss Expectancy (ALE)

The *annual loss expectancy (ALE)* is the amount of value anticipated to be lost from one type of incident in one year. This is calculation. Multiply the SLE by the ARO to find the ALE (SLE × ARO = ALE). For example, you determine the SLE of a lost or stolen laptop is $650.00. You also project there will be four incidents related to this risk over the course of one year (ARO). Then, the ALE is $2,600 ($650.00 × 4 = $2,600).

Quick Look 15.1.3

SLE, ARO, and ALE

The quantitative method relies on factual data. Using objective information, the SLE, ARO, and ALE can be set. For this activity, work in the same group as the last activity.

1. Open your group's vulnerability spreadsheet. It should include a classroom computer, either desktop, laptop, or tablet.
2. Research by the type of device you have and software installed. Determine what it would cost to replace this computer. This is the SLE for the loss of one of these devices.
3. Add a column to the spreadsheet for SLE, and enter your data.
4. Assume the device will fail twice each year.
5. What is the ALE for one of these devices?

Qualitative Method

CompTIA Security+
5.3

A *qualitative risk assessment* is used when there are not actual data or values to back up a claim. It is a subjective method. This means the values are based on opinions, research, and probability of risk.

In the qualitative method, there may not be exact values to assign to a particular loss. Instead, a descriptive analysis can be assigned to a loss. For example, rating values of high, moderate, or low may be used. Each level can be further divided into value ranges. Those value ranges are known as *semiqualitative values.*

The qualitative method should be familiar to you. It is how some rubrics are created. **Figure 15-6** shows an example of a rating sheet. In this example, the instructor decides how well the student did. This is subjective. Two different instructors could draw different conclusions.

You can determine your own qualitative and semiqualitative values and scales. You can choose to be as detailed, or granular, as your plans allow.

Component	Strong	Average	Weak
Demonstrates understanding of problem to be solved			
Identifies pros and cons of each conclusion			
Identifies logical solution			

Goodheart-Willcox Publisher

Figure 15-6. A letter-based grading system is an example of qualitative data, while the range of scores for each letter are examples of semiqualitative data.

SECTION REVIEW 15.1

Check Your Understanding ↱

1. What is a built-in weakness in a software program called?
2. A fire delivers a threat, so the fire is known as a(n) _____.
3. Per the NIST framework, after you frame the risk, what do you do next?
4. Printers fail every two years. What is the ARO of printer failures?
5. An assessment that uses objective data is which type of risk assessment?

Build Your Key Terms Vocabulary ↱

As you progress through this course, develop a personal cybersecurity glossary. This will help you build your vocabulary and prepare you for a career. Write a definition for each of the following terms, and add it to your cybersecurity glossary.

annual loss expectancy (ALE)

annual rate of occurrence (ARO)

asset

IT Infrastructure Library (ITIL)

qualitative risk assessment

quantitative risk assessment

risk

risk assessment

risk management

semiqualitative values

single loss expectancy (SLE)

threat agent

Handling Risk

?**E**ssential **Q**uestion

What is the best response to risk?

Decisions and choices have risk. Risk is an inevitable outcome of all decisions. Humans will make mistakes. They may leave a work laptop in a car overnight only to return in the morning and find it stolen. A programmer may not properly validate data entries, which left an application vulnerable to injection attacks. A 2018 fire at Trump Tower in New York City was the result of someone connecting too many power strips together.

Once the risks involved are recognized, planning the risk response is the next step. There are many ways to approach the risk, from eliminating the possibility altogether to pushing the risk to a third party. In many cases, a multiple-response approach may have the best outcome. For example, reduce the likelihood of the risk and then create a response for remaining risk. In the case of the fire at Trump Tower, only allowing one surge protector per electrical socket will reduce the risk. Smoke alarms and sprinklers may be follow-up responses.

Key Terms 🔗

Common Vulnerabilities and
   Exposures (CVE)
CVE numbering authorities
   (CNAs)
data loss prevention (DLP)
head crash

mean time between failures
   (MTBF)
mean time to failure (MTTF)
mean time to repair (MTTR)
physical controls
procedural controls

residual risk
risk acceptance
risk avoidance
risk mitigation
risk transfer
technical controls

Learning Goals

- Compare and contrast responses to risk.
- Prepare information for reducing risk.
- List best practices for risk management.

Risk-Response Methods

So, there is risk, now what do you do? How do you respond to this risk? These are the generally accepted responses to risk:

CompTIA Security+
5.3

- risk mitigation
- risk avoidance
- risk transfer
- risk acceptance

Risk Mitigation

Risk mitigation is taking steps to reduce the likelihood or the impact of the risk. *Mitigating* means to make something less severe. For example, running an antivirus program reduces the likelihood of infection from viruses or other malware. Having backup or redundant hardware is another example of mitigating risk. This does not eliminate the risk, but reduces the impact if the risk occurs. The backup can be immediately used in the event of a failure. The risk that remains after the mitigation controls are implemented is known as *residual risk.*

Risk Avoidance

Risk avoidance is eliminating the risk. By avoiding agents that cause the risk, then the risk does not exist. For example, a business chose to be a cash-only establishment. This eliminates the risk of hacked credit card transactions and stolen credit card data. It will also eliminate the problem of dealing with PCI DSS regulations and the possibility of customer data being revealed. However, accepting only cash may not be convenient or popular for customers. Therefore, it may not be the best business decision. With risk avoidance, there are often tradeoffs. These must be considered before choosing avoidance.

Risk Transfer

Risk transfer is assigning the responsibility for the risk to a third party. The insurance industry is built around risk transfer. For example, if you drive a car, there is no way to avoid the risk of an accident, as shown in **Figure 15-7.** To handle that risk, you purchase automobile insurance. In doing so, you have transferred the risk to the insurance company in return for a payment. If there is an accident or other damage to your car, the insurance covers the loss.

Businesses often purchase insurance for risks such as fire or theft. However, there are also cyberinsurance policies as well. Most people are not aware this type of insurance has been around for quite some time. Coverage is usually determined by the risks faced by an organization factored against the potential loss of data and corporate revenue. An insurance underwriter will look closely at the potential for risks to a company. He or she will then balance those risks against the company's risk-management plan. From this examination, the rate charged for the insurance is determined.

For IT, risk can be transferred from an internal program to a third-party company in many situations. Suppose you do not want to manage a web server to host your company's web page. This can be outsourced to a third-party web-service provider. One example of a provider is GoDaddy. The third party is then responsible for the upkeep and management of the web services. The risks associated with doing this are transferred to the third party.

Carolyn Franks/Shutterstock.com

Figure 15-7. Automobile insurance is an example of transferring risk. The insurance company takes on the risks associated with driving in return for a payment from the customer.

Risk Acceptance

Risk acceptance is making the decision to assume the risk. This is an informed decision based on the likelihood and impact of the risk. It is not ignoring the issue. Risk acceptance usually happens after an attempt has been made to minimize the risk to an acceptable level. Often, you will deploy other strategies, such as risk mitigation and risk transfer, but ultimately, you accept the risk.

Risk acceptance in which the financial cost is accepted instead of transferring it to a third party is known as *risk retention*. Suppose you buy a smartphone, but do not purchase insurance for it. You have retained risk of the replacement cost for a damaged or stolen phone.

For example, a company is located in Tulsa, Oklahoma. This area is prone to severe weather such as tornadoes. In this example, management evaluates if doing business in Tulsa is worth the risks of property damage and other destruction if a tornado should strike. After thoughtful deliberation, management decides the company must be located in Tulsa. The business has accepted the risk of severe weather and its related ramifications. Of course, the risk can be mitigated with sturdier construction and locating IT services off-site. The risk can also be transferred with insurance. The costs could also be assumed by the business through risk retention.

Quick Look 15.2.1

Risk Response

There are four basic ways to respond to risk. Each risk is different. A risk-response method may or may not be better than the others for a given risk. For this activity, work in the same group as the last activity.

1. Open your group's vulnerability spreadsheet.
2. Select two items from the list.
3. In a blank area in the spreadsheet under the list of assets, add the following information.

Risk Response			
Asset	Risk-Response Strategy	Rationale	Comments

4. For each asset, discuss with your group which risk-response method you would choose. Then, enter the method in the Risk-Response Strategy column. At least one of the assets should use the mitigation method.
5. In the Rationale column, describe why your group selected the method.
6. For the mitigation method, identify all factors you could perform to mitigate the risk. Enter these in the Comments column.
7. If you select risk avoidance, identify some of the issues that will result from this choice. Enter these in the Comments column.
8. If you select risk transfer, identify where you will transfer this risk. Enter this in the Comments column.
9. If you select risk acceptance, list the possible losses. Enter these in the Comments column.
10. Share your selections and options with your classmates. Compare and contrast the various choices made. Collaborate to see if more mitigation options can be implemented.

Reducing Risk

Throughout this course, you have learned how to prevent cybersecurity incidents from happening. Some of these topics include:

- hardening systems;
- using firewalls;
- setting security measures, such as using the Principle of Least Privilege; and
- using appropriate permissions.

These are all methods to reduce the vulnerabilities or threats that are risks of a security violation. Another area that should be managed is the possibility of hardware failures.

System Vulnerability

To reduce the risk of vulnerabilities to a system, always install the latest patches and updates. You can also check a database for posted information. *Common Vulnerabilities and Exposures (CVE)* is a centralized location for listing and uniformly identifying publicly known cybersecurity vulnerabilities. Its website (cve.mitre.org) provides a list of vulnerabilities, as shown in **Figure 15-8**. Other information is also provided. This includes descriptions of the vulnerabilities and references or advisories issued regarding each problem.

Each vulnerability has a unique identifier known as the CVE ID. The ID will be formatted as follows.

CVE-*YYYY-NNNN*

The *YYYY* portion represents the year CVE assigned the ID or the vulnerability was made public. The *NNNN* portion is a sequence number. For example, a CVE ID may look like this: CVE-2013-12345.

FYI CVE is sponsored by US-CERT in the Department of Homeland Security, specifically the office of Cybersecurity and Communications. MITRE is the not-for-profit company that manages this federally funded project.

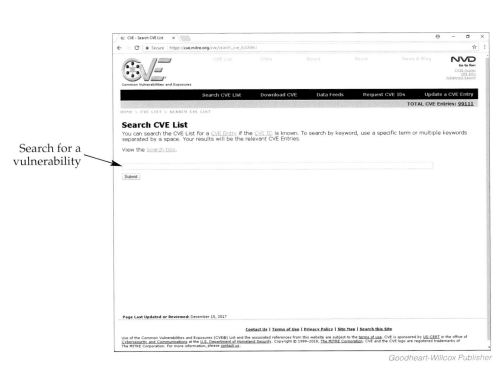

Goodheart-Willcox Publisher

Figure 15-8. CVE is a valuable resource for researching known cybersecurity vulnerabilities. You can search by CVE ID or keyword.

The CVE reports are issued by organizations from around the world. These organizations have been authorized by MITRE to assign CVE IDs to vulnerabilities that may affect their products. They are known as *CVE numbering authorities (CNAs).* Notifying CVE of a vulnerability is not a requirement. However, doing so does allow businesses to get the word out about potential problems.

Quick Look 15.2.2

CVE Information

CVE is a valuable resource for researching known cybersecurity vulnerabilities. It provides detailed information on each known issue.

1. Launch a web browser, and navigate to the CVE website (cve.mitre.org).
2. Locate the CVE list. This may be in the menu on the page or it may be given as a hyperlink somewhere on the page. Click to go to the list.
3. On the list page, there is a function to search by CVE ID or keyword. Click this option.
4. Enter CVE-2017-10677, and click the **Submit** or **Search** button.
5. In the search results, click the link for this document to view the detailed information. To what product does this vulnerability apply? What is the vulnerability?
6. Use your browser's **Back** button to return to the search page.
7. Enter the keyword firefox. How many entries match your search? How many are from this year?
8. Find the most recent entry, and click to display that document. Who is the CNA that issued this advisory?

Hardware Failure

Hardware failures occur. Hardware can experience wear and tear. This can cause mechanical elements to give out. You cannot prevent hardware failures from occurring. However, you can better prepare for them by analyzing failure rates to predict when hardware might need to be replaced.

An example to compare this to is buying tires. Look at the tire advertisement shown in **Figure 15-9.** Notice the tread wear information. The warranty is 45,000 miles. Based on that information, car owners can reasonably predict the

Case Study

Responding to Risk

Accurate Financial Services Corporation (AFSC) is located in Sarasota, Florida. This is the location where it can best serve its customers. Sarasota is located on the Gulf Coast. For this reason, it is vulnerable to hurricanes and other severe weather. AFSC is concerned about possible physical losses of structure, equipment, and data due to weather-related incidents. Any of these losses would affect the company's ability to continue serving its customers. In the event of a weather-related incident, AFSC would need to resume customer services within two days. What risk response strategies would you recommend? Provide a detailed justification for your recommendation.

Quick Look 15.2.3

Security Policy Types

Security controls are based on the company's security policy. It makes more sense to create security policies specific to the topic at hand. The SANS Institute has created a detailed list of security policy templates that are free.

1. Form teams of two or three. You may form the same teams used throughout this chapter.
2. Launch a web browser, and navigate to the SANS Institute website (www.sans.org). Note this is an ORG domain, not a COM domain.
3. Locate the free security resources, and then select the security policy samples or templates.
4. With your team, choose a policy. Each team must select a different policy, so check with the other teams. If there are more teams than policies, it is okay to repeat policies.
5. Download the policy template your team selected, and review its purpose.
6. Prepare a class presentation on the purpose and overview of the policy. Include information on how to check for compliance with the policy.
7. As a class, discuss the policies covered by each team. Should any be used in your classroom?

SECTION REVIEW 15.2

Check Your Understanding

1. Installing an intrusion-protection system (IPS) is an example of which risk-response method?
2. The risk that remains after mitigation efforts have been incorporated is called _____.
3. What statistic identifies how long a hard drive is expected to last under normal conditions?
4. Keeping spare hard drives for servers on hand will reduce this statistic.
5. Conducting annual training for e-mail security and other threats is what type of control?

Build Your Key Terms Vocabulary

As you progress through this course, develop a personal cybersecurity glossary. This will help you build your vocabulary and prepare you for a career. Write a definition for each of the following terms, and add it to your cybersecurity glossary.

Common Vulnerabilities and Exposures (CVE)

CVE numbering authorities (CNAs)

data loss prevention (DLP)

head crash

mean time between failures (MTBF)

mean time to failure (MTTF)

mean time to repair (MTTR)

physical controls

procedural controls

residual risk

risk acceptance

risk avoidance

risk mitigation

risk transfer

technical controls

Review and Assessment

Summary

Section 15.1 Overview of Risk

- Risk is a situation that could cause harm, create a hazard, or otherwise cause problems that need to be addressed, and there must be a balance between handling risk and usability.
- It is important to view both tangible and intangible IT assets in the context of risk.
- A threat agent is the source, or actor, that causes a threat to occur, and it is important to consider how likely the agent is.
- Risk management is a structured approach to identifying risk and planning solutions and methods to reduce, eliminate, or respond to the risk.
- Risk assessment, or risk analysis, involves identifying risks and ranking them with the most critical risks listed first, which may be done using a quantitative or qualitative method.

Section 15.2 Handling Risk

- The four generally accepted responses to risk are risk mitigation, risk avoidance, risk transfer, and risk acceptance.
- Reducing risk involves several things, from hardening systems to using firewalls, setting security measures, and using appropriate permissions as well as managing possible hardware failures.
- Best practices in risk management include extending risk management beyond IT, looking for weaknesses, and implementing physical, procedural, and technical security controls.

Check Your Cybersecurity IQ 📇

Now that you have completed this chapter, see what you have learned about cybersecurity by visiting the student companion website (www.g-wlearning.com) and taking the chapter posttest.

Review Questions 📇

For each question, select the answer that is the best response.

1. Risk can be defined as:
   A. The chance something will happen.
   B. A situation that could cause harm or create a hazard.
   C. The loss from harm or a hazard.
   D. The ability to avoid damage.

2. Which of the following is not considered an IT asset that should be included in a risk assessment?
   A. Web server
   B. Employee who develops apps
   C. Standard keyboard
   D. HVAC system

3. What is considered a natural weakness in a system or product?
   A. Threat agent
   B. Vulnerability
   C. Risk
   D. Threat

4. The NIST SP 800-39 document provides a four-step framework for a risk-management program that includes all of the following except:
   A. Frame the risk
   B. Assess the risk
   C. Define the risk
   D. Monitor the risk

5. A local library has reported it experiences a failure of a $600 laser printer every other year. What is the ALE for this printer?
   A. $300.00
   B. $600.00
   C. $900.00
   D. $1200.00

6. Management has conducted a risk assessment and decided that a third-party company should provide functions for a specific service. What risk-response method did the company choose to use?
   A. Risk acceptance
   B. Risk avoidance
   C. Risk mitigation
   D. Risk transfer

7. What information does a CVE document provide?
   A. Description of the vulnerability and related references.
   B. Average time until device failure.
   C. Financial impact of a system flaw.
   D. Plan for defense in depth for security issues.

8. Your business has a complex fire-suppression system. It wants to be prepared in the event a critical part fails. Which of the following provides management with a time line for part replacement?
   A. MTBF
   B. AFR
   C. MTTR
   D. MTTP

9. In which situation is a hard drive most likely to experience a failure due to manufacturing?
   A. Shortly after the drive is installed and in use.
   B. When the machine is jostled while the drive is in use.
   C. If the water sprinklers are deployed.
   D. During routine operation about a year after installation.

10. Which *procedural* control can be implemented regarding a data backup?
    A. A copy of a weekly backup should be stored off-site every Friday.
    B. Backups are configured to occur automatically at 2 a.m.
    C. Critical data are instantly backed up to cloud storage on changes.
    D. Backup personnel require read access to files that are to be backed up.

Application and Extension of Knowledge

1. Determine the SLE of the computing electronics in your house. Include all tablets, desktop computers, laptops, phones, and printers. Create a spreadsheet of your results.

2. Contact an insurance company, and explain that you are a student conducting research for a class project. Politely ask permission to discuss insurance topics. Then, find out what cyberinsurance offerings are available. What are the types of considerations when a policy is issued? Prepare a report of your findings.

3. Look for 1 TB hard drive from four different manufacturers. Compare the AFR or MTBF statistics among the drives. Create a table comparing the drives for price, performance, and reliability.

4. Create a presentation that lists five different procedural controls a company could implement for cybersecurity awareness training of employees. Provide a specific example for each control.

5. There is risk-management software tailored for cybersecurity. Investigate this type of software. Create a presentation that details how this software helps with prevention, its key features, and costs to use it on an annual basis.

Research Project
Risk-Management Framework

Griffith University in Australia has created an excellent risk-management framework. It is published with its policies on the university's policies web page (policies.griffith.edu.au). Navigate to this web page, and use the search function to search for risk-management framework. Then, open the document of the same name. Review this document. Locate the section on risk appetite. What is meant by this term? Review the risk-ranking matrix. Think of an example that could fit into this chart. Remember, this is a university. The appendix may provide information to help put this into perspective. Where would you place it and why? Do you think it is helpful to break out the consequences on the different likelihood of outcomes?

Deliverables. Write a one- to two-page summary of the risk-management framework. Provide answers to the questions above. What are your impressions or questions about this using this policy template? Include your own thoughts and opinions on the information in the template.

Online Activities

Complete the following activities, which will help you learn, practice, and expand your knowledge and skills.

 Vocabulary. Practice vocabulary for this chapter using the e-flash cards, matching activity, and vocabulary game until you are able to recognize their meanings.

Communication Skills

College and Career Readiness

Reading. After you have read this chapter, determine the central ideas, and analyze their development over the course of the chapter. How do details shape or refine the chapter? Review the major arguments or points the author makes, and provide an objective summary of the chapter.

Writing. Interview someone in your city's planning department or office of emergency management. Ask this person to describe various strategies the city has for managing risk. Write a one-page paper describing what you learned from the interview. Edit your draft, and refine the information to create an effective report. Focus on the interviewee's important quotes or information provided.

Speaking. There are many situations in which you are required to persuade a listener. When you persuade, you convince a person to take a course of action or adopt a viewpoint you propose. Write a persuasive message about risk-response methods. Deliver your message to a classmate. Ask your classmate for feedback about whether your persuasive message was successful or not.

Listening. Deliberative listening is determining the quality or validity of what is being said. Listen to a classmate's presentation from an activity in this chapter. Listen carefully, using deliberative listening. Cite which points the person made that would convince you to accept the speaker's position.

Portfolio Development

College and Career Readiness

Clubs and Organizations. Being involved in academic clubs or professional organizations will help you make a good impression. You can also learn a lot that will help you with your studies or your career. While in school, you may belong to clubs, such as National Honor Society and Future Business Leaders of America. When you are employed, you may belong to professional organizations related to your career area, such as the Information Systems Security Association (ISSA).

1. Identify clubs or organizations to which you belong. Create a Microsoft Word document to list the name of each organization. Use the heading Clubs and Organizations and your name. Briefly describe the organization, your level of involvement, and how long you have been a member. Save the document.

2. Update your master spreadsheet.

CTSO Event Prep

Job Interview. Interviewing for a job is an event you might enter with your career and technical student organization (CTSO). By participating in the job interview, you will be able to showcase your presentation skills, communication talents, and ability to actively listen to the questions asked by the interviewers. For this event, you will be expected to write a letter of application, create a résumé, and complete a job application. You will also be interviewed by an individual or panel. To prepare for a job interview event, complete the following activities.

1. Use the Internet or textbooks to research the job application process and interviewing techniques.

2. Write your letter of application and résumé, and complete the application form (if provided for this event). You may be required to submit this before the event or present the information at the event.

3. Make certain that each piece of communication is complete and free of errors.

4. Solicit feedback from your peers, instructor, and parents.

Chapter 16

Business Continuity and Disaster Recovery

Consider this scenario: four days before the start of the school year, a school catches fire and burns over one-third of the building. Essentially, the building and its contents were destroyed. How does the school district respond? Does it have a plan to relocate the students and provide essential services such as transportation, meals, and technology? If this sounds like a fictional scenario, it is not. This happened to Princess Anne High School in Virginia Beach, VA. An arsonist set fire to the school in the middle of the night.

Within just a few weeks, Princess Anne High School was holding classes. Students were attending a nearby vacant mall that was transformed into a temporary school. This quick response did not happen by chance. It involved a risk assessment analyzing the possibility a catastrophic event could occur and then determining a plan to provide continuity of essential services. Many events are beyond the control of a business or organization. These include natural disasters, terrorist attacks, and extreme weather. However, evaluating and planning for the resulting actions is a responsibility of management. In order to manage potential risks, a business or organization must develop continuity and disaster recovery plans.

Chapter Preview

While studying, look for the activity icon for:

- Pretests and posttests
- Vocabulary terms with e-flash cards and matching activities
- Self-assessment

G-WLEARNING.com

Reading Prep

Before reading this chapter, preview the section heads and key terms lists. Make a list of questions you have before reading the chapter. Search for answers to your questions as you read the chapter.

College and Career Readiness

Check Your Cybersecurity IQ 🔗

Before you begin this chapter, see what you already know about cybersecurity by visiting the student companion website (www.g-wlearning.com) and taking the chapter pretest.

Certification Objectives

CompTIA Security+

5.1   Explain the importance of policies, plans and procedures related to organizational security.

5.2   Summarize business impact analysis concepts.

5.6   Explain disaster recovery and continuity of operation concepts.

5.8   Given a scenario, carry out data security and privacy practices.

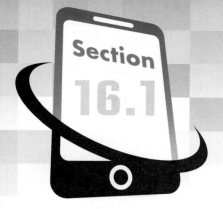

Business Continuity and Disaster Recovery

Essential Question

Why would a company choose not to develop a business-continuity plan?

Many potential issues could threaten the functionality and operations of a business. Some are natural disasters. This includes weather situations and earthquakes. Others are the result of failed hardware components, unintended errors, and damage caused by hackers. It is essential an organization have a detailed and comprehensive plan to follow when these events occur. This plan should allow the business to resume normal operations as soon as possible. The steps and processes that should be done need to be determined before disaster strikes. Fault-tolerant and redundant systems will minimize the risk of data loss. Additionally, policies need to be set for backups and media disposal to prevent loss of data.

Key Terms 🔗

after-action report
business-continuity plan (BCP)
business-impact analysis (BIA)
disaster-recovery plan (DRP)

IT contingency plan
memorandum of understandings (MOU)
recovery point objective (RPO)

recovery team
recovery time objective (RTO)
service level agreement (SLA)
tabletop exercise

Learning Goals

- Design a business-continuity plan.
- Illustrate the sections of a disaster-recovery plan.

CompTIA Security+
5.1

Business Continuity

What is business continuity? *Business continuity* is the ability of a business to continue operations when an event occurs that could be disruptive. It is costly when a business is unable to open or provide services. Revenue and profit are reduced. Employees may not be able to work. This may mean they are not paid. This could have a significant ripple effect. Reduced wages means less money is added to the economy. A *business-continuity plan (BCP)* provides the steps needed to keep a business operational after an incident. The Federal Emergency Management Agency (FEMA) states all businesses have an obligation to plan for disasters. This applies even to small businesses.

FEMA/Dominick Del Vecchio

Figure 16-1. Hurricane Harvey affected many areas across Texas. Storm damage was severe, which included flooding such as shown here in the city of Houston.

In August of 2017, Hurricane Harvey hit the state of Texas, as shown in **Figure 16-1.** It affected other states as well and proved to be deadly. It also hurt businesses, especially in the city of Houston. In Houston, record floods displaced tens of thousands of people from their homes. Employees were not able to return to work, in some cases due to being relocated. Many businesses found critical assets such as buildings and IT infrastructure had been damaged. These businesses had to rely on their continuity plans to remain operational or to return the business to an operational state.

Business continuity planning is not just for disasters such as floods and fires. Businesses need to plan for continued operations from *any* disruptive event. This may be malware or a ransomware attack. It could be failure of critical hardware. A disruptive event could even be an outbreak of disease. The influenza season was unusually severe in the winter of 2017–2018. This prevented many employees from going to work.

Business continuity planning goes beyond the concept of risk management. It identifies the impact threats may have on the business. It also outlines actions for prevention and recovery to ensure continuity of operations.

FYI

Did you know the US government formally identifies a designated survivor during presidential inaugurations and State of the Union addresses? This provides for governmental continuity in the event of a catastrophic event. The practice began during the Cold War due to the risk of nuclear attack.

Quick Look 16.1.1

FEMA Resources

FEMA has created many resources for businesses to use to plan for emergency preparedness. These are available for free on its website.

1. Launch a web browser, and navigate to the FEMA website (www.fema.gov).
2. Using the site's search function, enter the search phrase every business should have a plan. In the search results, locate the 12-page booklet of the same name, and click the link to go to that page.
3. On the next page, open the PDF file.
4. Scroll through the document. In the section Continuity Planning, what are the four items a company needs to identify to stay operational?
5. The Continuity Planning section talks about succession of management. Why is this important?

Quick Look 16.1.1 Continued

6. Review additional tips in the document, including identifying business suppliers, calling trees, and planning for employees with disabilities. Discuss these tips with your classmates.

7. The document also mentions the www.ready.gov website. Navigate to this site.

8. Click the **Be Informed** link. The page that is displayed contains a list of different disasters. Each item is a link to a new page. Divide the list among the class. Take turns discussing the key items from each of these disaster types.

Business-Impact Analysis

To assist in establishing a BCP, a business-impact analysis should be performed as the first step. A *business-impact analysis (BIA)* determines the potential effects of an event that disrupts critical business operations. It is a detailed process. The BIA identifies mission-critical and essential business functions. It also quantifies these items to identify the financial and operational affect on an organization. Once this information is identified, the next step is to build the continuity plan. This includes a disaster-recovery plan. Disaster-recovery plans are discussed later in this chapter.

A BIA can be developed by asking questions. Using descriptive incident examples helps the respondents answer questions more accurately. These are some questions that may be used in a BIA:

- What happens if there is a catastrophic event and the CEO is unavailable to make decisions?
- What would you do if your IT operations room, including the server, is destroyed?
- What are your next steps if your system is hit with a ransomware attack?
- What happens if your e-commerce server crashes the day before Thanksgiving and Black Friday sales?

The answers to these and many other questions must be addressed in order to plan for the prevention and mitigation of risks and eventual recovery.

Look at the sample BIA template shown in **Figure 16-2.** Consider the example of a fire at a high school. What data would be entered into the BIA template? The business unit is the department offering a given service at the school. Some examples include:

- cafeteria;
- science department; and
- guidance counseling.

The staff count is the number of employees in the business unit. Principle activities are the key and essential services delivered by the unit. There are two other very important items here: recovery time objective and recovery point objective.

The *recovery time objective (RTO)* is the target date by which services must be restored after a disaster to avoid unacceptable consequences. In the school

CompTIA Security+
5.2

Business-Impact Analysis				
Business Unit	**Staff Count**	**Principal Activities**	**Recovery Time Objective**	**Recovery Point Objective**

Figure 16-2. This template is an example of how a BIA may be set up.

Rating	Description
Extremely Critical (1 to 3 days)	These are essential services needed to fulfill operational, legal, or safety issues.
Critical (4 to 14 days)	These services are critical to the organization's ability to operate. Failure to restore them within 14 days could cause significant issues.
Important (15 to 30 days)	These services or resources support the critical applications. If they are not functioning, there will be minimal impact on the organization's operation.
Noncritical (Over 30 days)	If these applications or resources are not restored, they will have little to no impact on normal business operations.

Goodheart-Willcox Publisher

Figure 16-3. This rating system can be used in a BIA to identify the recovery time objective.

example, perhaps the longest amount of time students can be out of school is three weeks (15 days). After that, dual-enrollment, graduation, or other requirements may be affected. A rating system should be used to define the *maximum* amount of time that can be lost. **Figure 16-3** shows an example of a rating system. It can be customized to a given organization.

The *recovery point objective (RPO)* is the maximum amount of data that can be afforded to lose. One hour's worth? Two hours' worth? One day's worth? A backup strategy must take into account this time. If you can lose one day's worth of data, then restoring a previous day's backup would likely be acceptable. If one hour is your benchmark, you will need to consider options that automatically moves data to other storage locations.

There are no set standards for how a BIA should look or the data it must contain. The template shown in **Figure 16-2** just provides a few of the items that may need to be identified. Other data can be added as appropriate. For example, Parent Process For is a common category. This would identify who relies on a given business unit. Recovery Strategy is another category that may be found in a BIA. **Figure 16-4** shows the sample template from **Figure 16-2** updated and with data from the school example.

Testing Continuity of Operations

Your school regularly conducts fire drills. This is to ensure all students and staff know what to do in the event there is a fire. Businesses must also regularly conduct tests to ensure their BCPs are effective. Of course, it would be highly disruptive to cease operations to conduct a full-scale test. Therefore, most organizations conduct what is known as a tabletop exercise.

In a *tabletop exercise,* the individuals involved in the process are led through the BCP process by a facilitator. Focus is on the steps involved in the BCP.

CompTIA Security+
5.6

Business-Impact Analysis						
Business Unit	Staff Count	Principal Activities	Recovery Time Objective	Recovery Point Objective	Parent Process For	Recovery Strategy
Cafeteria	8	Provide breakfast and lunch	3 weeks	1 day	Students	Deliver premade meals from nearby schools
Administration	14	Manage school activities	4 days	2 days	School	Use technology and other resources at district office

Goodheart-Willcox Publisher

Figure 16-4. This sample BIA includes columns for Parent Process For and Recovery Strategy.

Executive management and all leadership positions are included in the exercise. The facilitator may be an independent consultant. The exercise is often acted out based on a hypothetical disaster or event. The steps in the BCP are carried out. Open discussion is encouraged. If there are concerns or unexpected issues, they can be addressed and documented at this time.

There are several disasters that should be practiced in tabletop exercises. Recovering from malware infections or hacks are examples. However, there are other examples. As previously mentioned, fire drills should be conducted. Also, practice what to do in case of severe weather. A tabletop exercise should be conducted for unauthorized personnel on the premises. This should include an active-shooter drill.

It is important to document what the organization did during and after an event. This is often known as an after-action report. An *after-action report* identifies what worked well and where problems arose. These reports are critical to evaluating a BCP and disaster-recovery plan. They allow for modification and correction of those plans.

Disaster-Recovery Plan

Once the goals, objectives, and recovery methods needed for business continuity are identified, how services will be restored must be outlined. This is where the disaster-recovery plan comes into play. A *disaster-recovery plan (DRP)* is the steps needed to restore services. Some companies may use the terms BCP and DRP interchangeably. However, the BCP is concerned with the overall business. The DRP is a detailed response for regaining functionality in the computer and network systems. An *IT contingency plan* is an outline of *what* must be restored. The DRP tells you *how* to restore services. The DRP should be regularly reviewed. Ensure the most current technologies are being evaluated. Update the vendors in use. Consider other operational issues that may have changed over time.

The DRP is detailed and consists of many sections. There are many templates available that can be used to create a DRP. There are several essential sections that should be included in a detailed DRP:
- Section I Policies and Objectives
- Section II Key Personnel
- Section III External Contacts and Vendors
- Section IV Emergency Procedures
- Section V Media
- Section VI Insurance and Financial Information

Section I Policies and Objectives

The first section of the DRP identifies the critical systems covered by the plan. It also lists the key objectives for response and recovery of the critical systems. This section summarizes the critical service, the previously identified RTO, and RPO for the service. It also outlines what the preventative, response, and recovery strategies for this system include. An example of information found in the first section is shown in **Figure 16-5**.

The DRP often references corporate objectives and other policies. Link or direct readers to these policies as applicable. The DRP should identify the individuals involved in the approval process. Also included in the first section is the company's plan for how often the DRP should be reviewed and updated.

Section II Key Personnel

The Key Personnel section identifies those people who are required for completing a DRP. These people may be called the *recovery team.* Information in this section should include each person's name, title, and contact information.

Critical System	RTO and RPO Information	Preventative Strategy	Initial Response Strategy	Recovery Response Strategy
Network switch for manufacturing department	2 hours; previous day's configuration	Back up switch-configuration files daily; keep a spare switch in inventory	Replace unit with temporary backup switch; verify functionality	Reset or replace switch; restore configuration files; verify functionality

Goodheart-Willcox Publisher

Figure 16-5. Section I Policies and Objectives in a DRP typically includes this type of information.

An organizational chart is often included in the Key Personnel section. This is helpful in determining hierarchy when working with staff. It clearly identifies the line of reporting, as shown in **Figure 16-6.** This is known as the *chain of command.*

Section III External Contacts and Vendors

The External Contacts and Vendors section identifies key individuals from outside the organization who may need to be involved in disaster recover. This may be contractors or suppliers. The ISP, utility companies, and landlord are other examples. However, it could also include important customers who would need to be notified of a disruption. All external contacts should have verified phone numbers, e-mail, and emergency points of contact.

All contracts with vendors should be reviewed, including service level agreements and memorandums of understandings. A *service level agreement (SLA)* specifies the expected responsibilities the vendor must provide. A *memorandum of understandings (MOU)* is an agreement that businesses have in respect to what each party provides. A MOU is a nonbinding agreement.

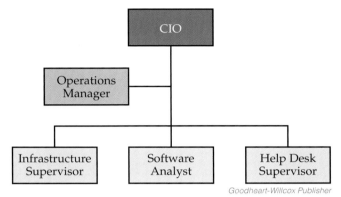

Goodheart-Willcox Publisher

Figure 16-6. An organizational chart clearly identifies a chain of command for an organization.

Section IV Emergency Procedures

The Emergency Procedures section should outline the specific plans and information needed for recovery. This section may be organized into subsections. These may be broken out by specific emergency issues. For example, if organized by type of disaster, sections may be Fire, Flood, Natural Disasters, and so on. Some examples of information included in this section may be:

- procedures to turn off water in the event of a burst pipe;
- use of fire extinguishers and evacuation orders;
- locations of in-house emergency equipment and supplies; and
- contact information of emergency services or agencies that must be notified.

Emergency-response procedures must first focus on the safety of employees and other individuals. The individuals who initially react in an emergency are known as first responders. This section provides the instructions for the first responders. First responders are discussed in more detail in Chapter 17.

Section V Media

The Media section should identify how information should be given to news organizations and the public. Depending on the situation, a spokesperson may need to be designated. This may be a person within the organization or an outside professional. The spokesperson can help control any negative publicity. He or

Case Study

Continuity of Operations

Erika Reich is the owner of a small retail business with two locations. While she was on vacation, the computers at one of the locations were infected with a virus that resulted in the point-of-sale terminals being inoperable. The second site was unaffected. Employees did not know what to do. They ended up telephoning the second location for processing of credit card numbers and creating handwritten receipts for customers. On Erika's return, she contacted her IT services provider, who cleaned the virus. Erika has consulted you for advice. What are your suggestions so her business can function more efficiently in case something like this happens again?

she can also promote positive messaging. Most organizations have a social media presence. This can also be used to keep customers and the public informed.

An example of a well-performed media strategy occurred in the summer of 2017. In North Carolina, a company building a new bridge to connect the mainland to Hatteras Island accidentally severed the main electrical lines that provided power to the island. The island suffered a complete power loss during the heart of its tourist season. Tourists were evacuated. Businesses and residents were greatly affected by the lost revenue and lack of power. While the situation was dire, two of the electricity providers maintained a strong media presence. They provided regular updates, detailed information, and outlets for questions and comments on Facebook, as shown in **Figure 16-7**. Many of the public comments showed satisfaction with the strong and consistent media updates.

Goodheart-Willcox Publisher

Figure 16-7. Social media can be an effective means of providing information to the public when a disaster occurs.

Section VI Insurance and Financial Information

The Insurance and Financial Information section covers issues related to the loss of revenue, credit cards, or other important financial documents. Information regarding banking, key contacts, and monthly expenditures should be documented. Insurance information, including contacts, deductibles, and other critical components, should be recorded. This is a critical section. It should be carefully constructed.

Quick Look 16.1.2

Disaster-Recovery Plans

There is not a single format for a disaster-recovery plan. There are many examples and templates online. These can be used as-is or modified to suit individual needs.

1. Launch a web browser, and navigate to a search engine.
2. Search for examples and templates for DRPs. Evaluate the search results to find reliable sources.
3. You learned about six sections that should be found in a DRP. What other items did you find in your research that may be included in a DRP?
4. Discuss with your class some of the additional elements. Share specific examples or templates that you liked or disliked.

SECTION REVIEW 16.1

Check Your Understanding 🔗

1. Which plan outlines the key elements that an organization should follow to return to operations following a disaster?
2. The process of asking "what if" questions to determine if an asset is a critical function is done in what?
3. This value identifies the target time or date that a service must be restored.
4. What is a tabletop exercise?
5. The detailed steps to recover from a failed web server are located in which document?

Build Your Key Terms Vocabulary 🔗

As you progress through this course, develop a personal cybersecurity glossary. This will help you build your vocabulary and prepare you for a career. Write a definition for each of the following terms, and add it to your cybersecurity glossary.

after-action report

business-continuity plan (BCP)

business-impact analysis (BIA)

disaster-recovery plan (DRP)

IT contingency plan

memorandum of understandings
    (MOU)

recovery point objective (RPO)

recovery team

recovery time objective (RTO)

service level agreement (SLA)

tabletop exercise

Section 16.2

Fault Tolerance and Redundancy

Essential Question

What impact does media sanitization have on the economy?

One of the problems that a business must avoid on a critical asset or service is a single point of failure. For example, if a business has one location and that location cannot be opened, the business will not open. Likewise, if a hard drive in a server fails, any services and data that are not available on another server cannot be provided to the users. Protecting critical assets, including sites, can include building fault tolerance and redundant system solutions.

Key Terms ↪

archive bit
cold site
data backup
degaussing
differential backup
disk mirroring
disk striping
disk striping with parity
failover cluster

fault tolerance
full backup
generator
hot site
incremental backup
media sanitization
mirrored site
power spike
power surge

RAID 0
RAID 1
RAID 1+0
RAID 5
redundancy
snapshot
uninterruptible power supply (UPS)
warm site

Learning Goals

- Explain fault tolerance.
- Compare and contrast methods of providing data redundancy.
- Illustrate methods for protecting against power issues and to prevent data recovery on discarded media.

Fault Tolerance

When working with mechanical and electrical systems, it is common to see components fail. It can be inconvenient and time-consuming to troubleshoot and repair the item. Where possible, a fault-tolerant solution should be considered. *Fault tolerance* allows for the possibility of a failure of a system by having a solution that immediately protects the system while minimizing downtime. For example, many people rely on home automation systems. These systems may include security cameras, light management, and thermostatic controls. These systems are connected by smart hubs. If a smart hub loses power, the devices are unavailable. One of the selling features of the Samsung SmartThings Hub is it includes a battery backup. The batteries provide power to the hub if electrical power to the system is lost.

A fault-tolerant solution does not fix the original cause of the outage. What it does is keep a system operational. For a computer system, this allows the administrator to schedule an appropriate time to take the system down for repairs. One of the aspects of fault tolerance covered later in this chapter is the use of RAID systems. These systems maintain access to data in the event of failure of a single hard drive.

Redundancy

A *single point of failure (SPF)* occurs when there is no redundancy. *Redundancy* in IT is having a backup solution that can immediately be used in the event of a failure. There are many ways to provide redundancy. Examples include maintaining additional sites, using multiple network interface cards, database replication, failover systems, and backups.

Maintaining Additional Sites

Companies must be able to provide those services that have been previously identified as critical or highly critical. One plan a business may choose to continue operations is moving operations to another location. The decision to maintain an additional site will be primarily based on RPO, RTO, and costs. There are several options for maintaining an additional site, as shown in **Figure 16-8.** These include cold site, warm site, and hot site.

A *cold site* is a location that provides the office space needed to move operations, but it contains no equipment. The customer must provide and install equipment and restore backups of data in order to get the site operational. This is the least costly of all the site solutions. However, it takes the longest to restore operations. The Princess Anne High School example described earlier is an example of moving operations to a cold site.

With a *warm site,* the customer maintains equipment in the location, but does not maintain current backups of data. In most cases, the site does not have an active Internet connection. The customer could shift operations to this site faster than with a cold site. However, backups still must be restored and Internet service established.

A hot site is the most expensive of the three solutions. A *hot site* is a duplicate of the currently working site. In some cases, data are automatically synchronized to the site. In other cases, the most current backup may have to be restored at the site. A business that uses a hot site has decided it must drastically reduce or eliminate downtime. If a company cannot afford any downtime, it can create a mirrored site. A *mirrored site* is an operationally active site that is continuously synched with the primary site to maintain current information. An organization can create a hot or mirrored site and manage it on its own. Many companies will use a disaster-recovery firm to maintain and manage this environment.

CompTIA Security+
5.2

CompTIA Security+
5.6

FYI

Companies can share data center facilities in the event of a disaster.

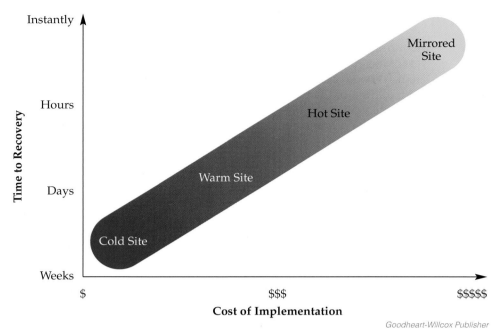

Goodheart-Willcox Publisher

Figure 16-8. Choosing an alternative site for continuity is a balance between cost and time to recovery.

FYI

After the September 11 terrorist attacks, Cantor Fitzgerald had competitors jump in to help with trades until it could become operational.

Some of the lessons for the use of hot or mirrored sites can be illustrated by the aftermath of the terrorist attacks on September 11, 2001. The financial-services company Merrill Lynch was located next to the World Trade Center towers in New York City. It lost its primary data center for six weeks after the attack. The bond-trading company Cantor Fitzgerald lost 658 employees in the attack. Its primary data center was also lost. When planning for disasters, companies must consider the worst-case scenarios.

In some situations, it does not make sense for a business to maintain another site in the same geographic area. Instead, it may create a site in another geographic location. For example, a company with data centers in Florida and Louisiana could face the risk of a single hurricane affecting both locations. Instead, it would be better to locate an additional site where hurricanes are not a threat.

Quick Look 16.2.1

Evaluating Site Choices

Discuss with your classmates which type of site you feel is best in each of the following scenarios and why. Choose from cold, warm, hot, or mirrored sites. Consider some of the environmental factors that could influence your choices. After you choose the alternate site, where would you suggest it be located?

1. An executive jet service with its only headquarters located in Southern California.
2. The data center for a private university located in upstate New York.
3. A hospital network in Baton Rouge, LA, that maintains patient health records and other pertinent medical information in electronic format.

Using RAID

CompTIA Security+
5.6

RAID is an acronym that stands for *redundant array of independent disks.* In many RAID configurations, a company's fault tolerance for a failed hard drive can be improved. In some cases, performance can be improved at the same time. RAID systems are often hardware configurations. However, they can also be created using operating system software. The Disk Management utility in Microsoft Windows is one example of a software implementation. There are several common RAID solutions:

- RAID 0
- RAID 1
- RAID 5
- RAID 1+0

RAID 0

In *RAID 0,* multiple hard drives work in sync with each other when saving or retrieving data. This version is also known as *disk striping.* There must be a minimum of two hard disks to implement this RAID version. It supports a maximum of 32 disks. RAID 0 does not provide any fault tolerance, but does provide increased performance.

Although there are multiple drives, they work together as one drive. Each drive's read-write arm will be located in the same spot on each drive, as shown in **Figure 16-9.** If each drive is 1 TB in size, this RAID array will operate as one logical drive with 2 TB total of disk space. Therefore, one instruction is needed for both drives. For example, the instruction may be "retrieve data from platter 1, location C." This speeds up the reading and writing of data.

Data is written, or striped, across the array in passes, as shown in **Figure 16-10.** In pass 1, part of the data is written on Drive 1 (A1). The next part is written in the same location on Drive 2 (A2). In the second pass, data are written in the next location on Drive 1 (B1). This is followed by and the next part written in the same location on Drive 2 (B2).

Drives operate in unison

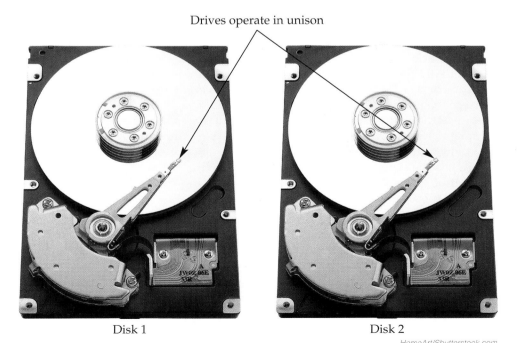

Disk 1   Disk 2

Figure 16-9. In a RAID 0 configuration, multiple hard drives work in synchronized action.

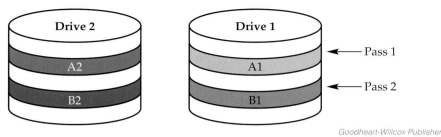

Figure 16-10. In RAID 0, data are written across drives in striped (by row) passes.

RAID 1

RAID 1 uses two hard drives, each a mirror or copy of the other drive. When data are written to one drive, they are automatically written to the second drive, as shown in **Figure 16-11.** This solution is called *disk mirroring.* Unlike RAID 0, the main reason to choose this solution is to increase fault tolerance. Should one of the hard drives fail, the other drive will continue to provide access to the data. However, this would not be a fault tolerant situation until the failed drive is replaced.

Keep in mind, with RAID 1, half of the total disk space is used for mirroring. If Drive 1 is 1 TB and Drive 2 is 1 TB, there is *not* a total of 2 TB. The total amount of disk space available for data is 1 TB.

RAID 5

RAID 5 combines the performance of RAID 0 with fault tolerance. Data are written across at least three drives similar to a striping array (RAID 0). However, on the third drive, a value called parity is created and written. In each pass of writing data, the parity bit is switched to a different drive, as shown in **Figure 16-12.** RAID 5 is known as *disk striping with parity.* It requires a minimum of three drives. It can host up to 32 drives.

Parity is an additional digit of information that helps recover data in the event one of the drives fails. The parity information can be used to recreate the missing data. Assume the third drive in **Figure 16-12** fails. On the first pass, no data loss has occurred. A1 and A2 are still available. On the second pass, the data at B2 is lost. The parity written on Drive 2 will recreate the missing data.

A RAID 5 array can only suffer the loss of a single drive in the array. If more than one drive fails, the array is no longer fault tolerant. Parity can only be used to recreate the missing data on a single physical disk.

Total disk space depends on the number of drives in the array. Assume each of three drives is 1 TB. Only two of the drives can store data because a parity bit must always be written. Therefore, 1/n is the amount of space used for parity, where n is the number of drives in the array. In this example, 1/3, or 1 TB, is the amount of space dedicated to parity. The remaining space is dedicated to data, which in this example is 2 TB.

FYI

Parity in RAID is also known as *even parity.* It uses a binary operator called XOR. How parity works in RAID is beyond the scope of this course.

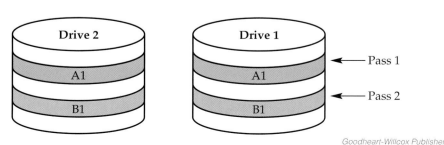

Figure 16-11. In RAID 1, each drive receives the same data.

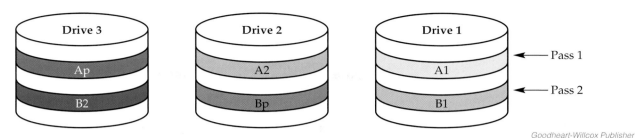

Goodheart-Willcox Publisher

Figure 16-12.   RAID 5 saves data across drives similar to RAID 1, but includes a parity bit to help recover data.

RAID 1+0

RAID 1+0 is a combination of RAID 1 and RAID 0. It is not called "RAID ten," but is often written without the plus symbol. This version of RAID requires four physical disks as a minimum. Since a mirror requires exactly two drives, RAID 1+0 has pairings of mirrored drives, as shown in **Figure 16-13.** These drives are then striped for performance. This provides for fault tolerance with high availability. RAID 1+0 is sometimes called a *stripe of mirrors,* a *nested RAID,* or a *hybrid RAID.*

Database Replication

Another way to achieve fault tolerance is to use replication. A continuously synchronized copy of a database is placed on another server or location. This ensures data remain the same on multiple devices. If one server or computer fails, the database is still available via other locations. As part of the BCP, servers should

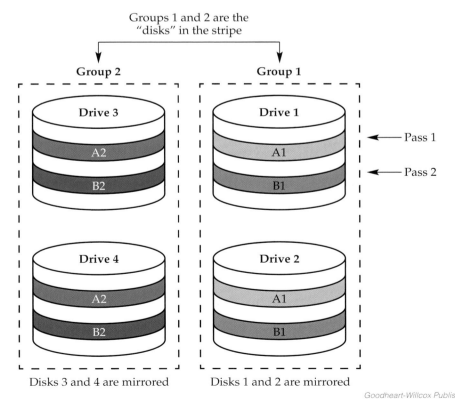

Goodheart-Willcox Publisher

Figure 16-13.   In RAID 1+0, two drives are mirrored to form a group, and there are at least two groups across which data are striped.

be strategically placed in multiple locations, if possible. This will provide redundancy of information and help ensure continued access to data.

A common implementation of database replication is used with servers and their security databases. These security databases are known as directories. Microsoft calls its directory the Active Directory. When using Microsoft Server, a common database is shared between servers configured with the Directory Services role. These servers are known as *domain controllers*. As changes are made to the database, those changes are replicated to the other domain controller servers. Changes may include adding or deleting a user or changing a password, for example. In addition to directory services, other databases can be configured with replication, such as those using SQL.

Failover Systems

Another technique to provide high availability is to create a failover cluster. A *failover cluster* allows servers to be grouped to increase the availability and scalability of resources. These machines are physically connected with cabling and software. They act together as if there is a single server, as shown in **Figure 16-14.** If one of the devices in the cluster fails, the other machines continue to provide resources. The services are rolled over into the remaining nodes. The system remains operational.

Backups

A critical component of a DRP is ensuring that an organization's information is backed up. A *data backup* is the process of copying data from one location and to a separate medium. This allows the data to be restored if something happens to the original source location. In order to be most secure, the backup should be physically stored away from the original location. The plan for creating backups should address these questions:

- What must be backed up?
- How often should data be backed up?
- Where will the data be backed up (to what medium)?
- Who is responsible for backups?
- Where will backup media be stored?
- What program will be used to back up the data?

There is no correct answer to these questions. The decisions will be based on the needs of the organization and key indicators, such as RTO and RPO.

What Must Be Backed Up?

What will be backed up must be set. Does a backup need to include content that does not often change? Applications and the operating system usually can be reinstalled. Therefore, there is likely little need to back up these items. Some of the decisions on what to back up will be based on media storage availability and the time it takes to create a backup.

When you consider what must be backed up, it is important to know where data are stored. That may sound like a strange statement, but you have to consider the work environment. Are users storing data on servers, workstations, the cloud,

Failover cluster acts as a single server

Goodheart-Willcox Publisher; vector art: Sujith RS/Shutterstock.com

Figure 16-14. In a failover cluster, the servers act together as a single unit. If one node fails, services roll over into the remaining nodes.

Ethical Issue

Data Backups

Your company has decided to store its data in a cloud-based solution. The data include employee salaries, performance reviews, and other personal information. Management has not notified employees of this backup choice and has no plans to do so. There is not a legal requirement to notify employees where the data are stored. Is using a cloud-based backup a smart business solution? There are legal considerations for cloud-based storage based on where the servers are located. Is it ethical to choose this solution without making employees aware where their personal data are stored? Write a one-page paper defending your choice.

laptops, or portable storage? All of the above? It is important to identify locations where data are stored and ensure there is a backup strategy in place for saving the data.

There are three types of backups, as shown in **Figure 16-15:**
- full backup
- incremental backup
- differential backup

A *full backup* is a copy of all files. An *incremental backup* is copies of only the files that have changed or been created since the last backup. A *differential backup* is copies of only the files that have changed or been created since the last full backup. Files are flagged for backup by the use of an attribute called the *archive bit,* or *A bit*. When this bit is on, it indicates the file is new or changed and needs to be backed up.

Each backup strategy can be compared by the time it takes to perform backups, as shown in **Figure 16-16.** Full backups are fairly consistent in time during a schedule. However, significant fluctuations in workload will affect this. Incremental backups start with a full backup. During the remainder of the week, only new or changed files are backed up. This significantly reduces the amount of time to create a backup on those days. Differential backups also start with a full backup.

FYI

Linux uses a concept similar to the A bit for backups. Its tool is called tar.

Type	Description	Archive Bit	Restore Information
Full	All files are backed up.	The archive bit is cleared on each file after the file is backed up.	Easiest type to restore; all data are included in the backup.
Incremental	Only files that were changed or created since the last backup will be backed up. A full backup first must be created before the incremental backup cycles can start.	The archive bit is cleared on each file after the file is backed up.	The full backup must be restored first, then the incremental backups are restored in the order they were created.
Differential	Only files that were changed or created since the full backup will be backed up. A full backup first must be created before the differential backup cycles can start.	The archive bit is *not* cleared after backup.	The full backup must be restored first, then the last differential backup is restored.

Goodheart-Willcox Publisher

Figure 16-15. A comparison of the types of backups. Each type has a distinct function.

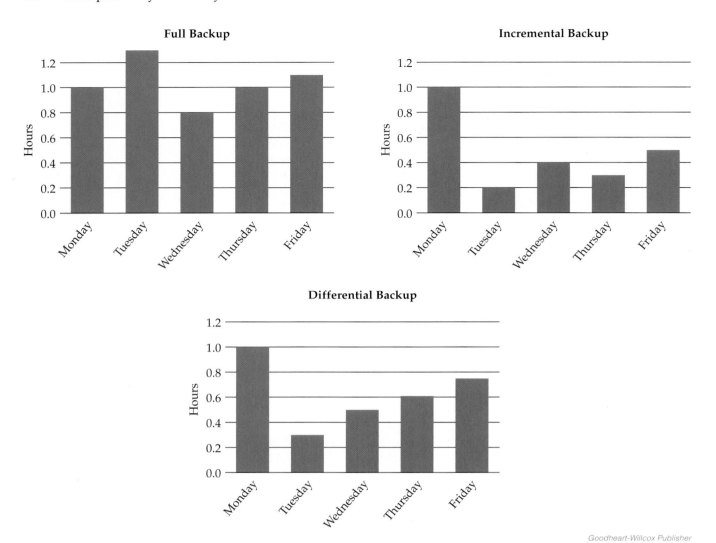

Figure 16-16. The type of backup being created can greatly affect the amount of time needed to complete the process.

However, the archive bit is not cleared on subsequent days. Therefore, the amount of time needed to create a backup will increase during the week. Each backup will include data from any previous days that had the A bit set.

An option is to create a full + incremental backup. A full backup is created at the beginning of the cycle. Then only changed files are backed up. Make sure the daily incremental backups are not overwritten. The daily backups must be stored separately from the full + incremental backup. For example, if you edit a spreadsheet on Tuesday. No changes are made to the spreadsheet the remainder of the week. That file will be located only on Tuesday's incremental backup.

With a full + differential backup, the same media can be used for the differential backups. A full backup is created at the beginning of the cycle. Then only the previous day's files are backed up. Using the spreadsheet example, even if there are no changes after Tuesday, the file's A bit will still be on. Therefore, it will be backed up again on Wednesday, Thursday, and Friday.

There is another option for creating backups on a virtual system. A snapshot can be created. A *snapshot* is a freeze frame of the system image and all its files and configuration. The snapshot can be named. It can then be used to revert to the frozen moment at any time.

Quick Look 16.2.2

Windows Archive Settings

In Microsoft Windows, the A bit can be set or removed using the Command Prompt. You can also use the Command Prompt to view the current setting for files in a folder.

1. Applying what you have learned, open the Windows Command Prompt.
2. Change to your working folder for this class.
3. Enter the **attrib** command. This displays all files and their current attributes. If a file is flagged for backup, the A bit will be listed, as shown. If the A bit is not listed, the file will not be backed up. Hint: If you have too many, enter attrib | more.

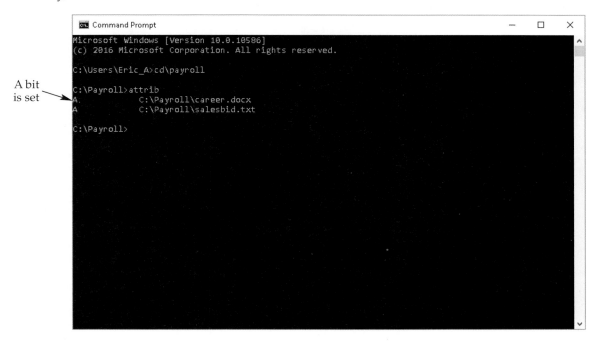

4. Enter the **dir** command and the /aa switch. This is another way to view the files that have the A bit set in the current folder. The /aa switch stands for attribute, archive.
5. Enter attrib –a. This removes the A bit from all files in the current folder.
6. Enter copy con newfile.txt, then enter test as the textual content in the file, and finally press the [Ctrl]+[Z] key combination and press [Enter] to exit editing mode and save the file.
7. Enter attrib newfile.txt. Notice the A bit is set because the file is new.
8. Enter attrib +a. This adds the A bit to all files in the current folder.

How Often Should Data Be Backed Up?

The frequency of backups must be set. The answer to "how often?" lies in the RPO. If you cannot lose yesterday's data, then create backups nightly. However, the frequency of backups needs to be balanced with how long it takes to create a backup. As discussed above, there are several methods to decrease backup times.

Where Will the Data Be Backed Up?

The destination location must be able to store the data being backed up. In the past, the preferred medium for backups was magnetic tape, as shown in **Figure 16-17.** This was similar to the tape that was used in music cassettes. Tape

Figure 16-17. Magnetic tape was the backup medium of choice in the past, but this is now an outdated technology.

was inexpensive and held a great deal of information. However, tape was susceptible to failure. Restoring data from tape was also slow. Tape is now an outdated technology.

Today, backups can be saved to removable media, such as hard drives or flash drives. Recordable DVDs are an option, but they do not have the capacity of hard drives. Backing up to the cloud is a popular option. Keep in mind, when backing up data to the cloud, you have to be aware of data sovereignty. Data sovereignty is discussed in Chapter 14.

Who Is Responsible for Backups?

Specifying who is responsible for backups is an important consideration. The person who will perform the backup must have certain file permissions to see and copy the files. This person must be trustworthy as he or she will have complete access to all data.

Where Will the Backup Media Be Stored?

The backup media must be protected against theft, loss, and adverse environmental conditions. The best practice is to store backups off-site. Use a restricted location, such as a bank vault or other secured location. Storing backups in someone's home is not a recommended strategy. If backups must be stored within the company's building, they should be secured. If possible, keep them in a locked and environmentally safe room.

What Program Will Be Used to Back Up the Data?

There are many products on the market that can be used for backup and restore operations. Some products are commercial. Others are free or open-source software. Operating systems such as Windows also have a built-in tool that provides for backups. However, this tool may lack additional options and features found with stand-alone software. Some users may find the additional features helpful.

Quick Look 16.2.3

Windows Backup Program

In Windows 10, the backup system is located under update and security. This backup system is different from the system in Windows 7. A backup created in the older system can still be used in Windows 10.

1. Click the Windows **Start** button, and then click **Settings**.
2. In the **Settings** window, click **Update & Security**.
3. In the **Update & Security** window, click **Backup** on the left-hand side. You must first add a drive.
4. Click the **Add a drive** button (+). Windows will look for any usable external drives. Once it finds a usable drive, select it.
5. After a drive is selected, click the **More options** link to display the **Backup Options** window, as shown. Scroll through this window to review the options. Several folders will likely be specified for backup. Also notice the settings for how often to create backups and how long to keep backups.

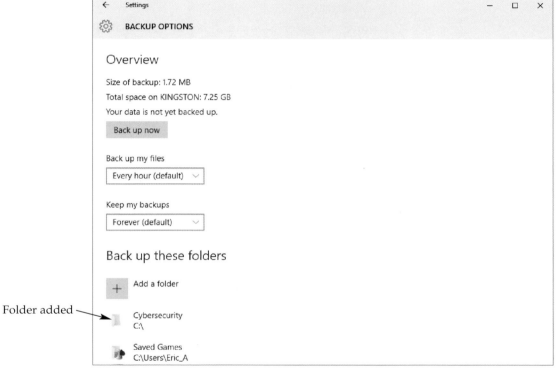

6. Click the **Add a folder** button (+). Then, navigate to your working folder on the local hard drive, and select it. The folder is now listed at the bottom of the **Backup Options** window and will be included in the backup.
7. Click the **Back up my files** drop-down arrow, and click **Daily** in the drop-down list. The backup will be created once each day. This is the longest interval allowed in the Windows 10 backup system.
8. Click the back button at the top of the window to return to the **Update & Security** window. Note: your instructor may tell you to disable the backup at this point.

Considerations Beyond Backups

Security administrators must consider the systems and media used to provide and store data. Servers and essential hosts rely on electrical power. This makes them susceptible to fluctuations in power. Damage may result if systems are left unprotected from this threat.

Another security matter concerns the disposal of media when it will no longer be used. Media includes hard drives, portable storage, and mobile devices. It is important to ensure that data are not left on the media. Any remaining data could result in the recovery of sensitive information from unauthorized sources. The security firm Avast demonstrated this through an experiment. It purchased 20 phones from ebay. Using widely available free tools, it was able to restore photos, text messages, and e-mails from these phones.

Power Issues

A consistent power supply is critical when working with electronic equipment. Even small power fluctuations can have a corrupting effect on data. You cannot control the power coming into a building. For example, a catastrophic event could disrupt power to the building. However, there are steps that can be taken to protect data and critical systems. There are three solutions to consider. These are surge protector, uninterruptible power supply, and generator.

Surge Protector

A *power surge* or a *power spike* is a fluctuation in the supplied voltage. Power fluctuations result in an unstable flow of electricity to a device. In the United States, standard voltage for a wall outlet is 120 volts. If power rises above this voltage, the computer system may not be able to handle it. This could lead to damage. A fluctuation may last only a few nanoseconds. That may not seem like enough time to cause damage, but it is. What is the difference between a power surge and a power spike? Longer than three nanoseconds is a surge. Less than three nanoseconds is a spike.

Fortunately, there is an easy and inexpensive way to protect devices against power surges. Use a device known as a surge protector, as shown in **Figure 16-18.** The computer is plugged into the surge protector. The surge protector is plugged into the wall outlet. The surge protector evens out any fluctuations in the voltage from the wall outlet. This device may also be called a surge suppressor.

Uninterruptible Power Supply

A surge protector guards against fluctuations in power. However, it cannot do anything about a loss of power. An *uninterruptible power supply (UPS)* is a device that can provide power from a battery in the event of a power loss. An

FYI

Be careful to purchase a surge protector, not an ordinary power strip. These devices look nearly identical, but an ordinary power strip does *not* provide surge protection.

FYI

The word *uninterruptible* is in the name because when electricity from the wall outlet is interrupted, or stopped, the UPS instantly switches to the battery to keep electricity flowing to the protected devices.

BW Folsom/Shutterstock.com

Figure 16-18. A surge protector guards against power fluctuations that could damage electronic equipment. Be sure to use a surge protector, not an ordinary power strip.

example of a UPS is shown in **Figure 16-19.** There are outlets on the back of the device to plug in the computer. The UPS is plugged into the wall outlet.

A UPS is not a long-term solution to providing power. The amount of time a UPS can provide power depends on the capacity of its battery and the load (computer) connected to it. It may be able to provide power for several minutes or several hours. Even a few minutes is enough time to save your work and safely shut down the system.

There are many UPSs on the market. Some have software that allow you to manage the system remotely. Others can automatically shut down the system if there is no human intervention. Correctly selecting a UPS is a complex topic beyond the scope of this course. However, most manufacturers provide selection assistance.

nikkytok/Shutterstock.com

Figure 16-19. An uninterruptable power supply will provide electricity for a period of time during a power outage, but it is not a solution for a long-term outage.

Quick Look 16.2.4

Viewing UPS Systems

UPS systems are not just for servers. They can be used for any device that you deem critical to your organization or home. One of the most well-known vendors of UPS systems is APC by Schneider Electric.

1. Launch a web browser, and navigate to the APC website (www.apc.com). If prompted to select your country, choose the United States.
2. Review some of the products and services offered.
3. Click the **How to Buy** menu option, and then on the page that is displayed click the **Try our product selectors** link under the Help Me Choose heading. On the next page, click the **UPS selector** link.
4. Choose the **Home, Home Office, and Small Business** category. You are prompted to choose by load or device. Choose to configure by device.
5. In the **Choose Your Device** area of the web page, click **PC/Workstation**. Use your lab computer or your home computer as the device, enter the computer's specifications, and then click the **Add to Summary** button.
6. On the selector page, set the preference for 10 minutes of additional power.
7. Click the **Save and Continue** button to display the recommended devices.
8. Discuss your results with classmates.

Generator

In some situations, keeping computers running is so critical even a UPS is not enough. Hospitals, emergency centers, and similar organizations must have computers running at all times. For these applications, a generator is necessary. A *generator* is a device that creates electricity. You may be familiar with small, portable generators. Many people use these for temporary power during outages. Standby generators for buildings are similar, but much larger.

A standby generator is permanently installed, usually outside the building, as shown in **Figure 16-20.** It is fueled by natural gas or diesel fuel. It is configured to start automatically whenever there is a loss of electricity from the grid. There is a transfer switch to isolate the building from the electrical grid. This is to prevent electricity from the generator feeding back into the grid. Once electricity in the grid is restored, the generator shuts off and the transfer switch is reset.

FYI

Standby generators require regular monitoring and maintenance. This must be included in the BCP.

Figure 16-20. A standby generator will automatically provide electricity for when a power outage occurs and can do so for a long period of time.

CompTIA Security+
5.8

Media Sanitization

If you are like most Americans, you probably replace your smartphone every two years. Most people will trade in the old phone or sell it for additional cash. A common practice when doing this is to perform a factory reset on the phone. Have you ever asked if your data are really gone? The Purdue University Cyberforensics Lab conducted a test to analyze phones "wiped" by factory resets. In one instance, a researcher was able to extract contacts, text messages, and banking information from a wiped phone. This took less than three minutes! Computers are no less vulnerable to data recovery.

Media sanitization is the process of completely removing data from a computerized device. The US government has a standard for ensuring data are removed. The DOD 5220.22-M standard outlines the number of times a drive must be written with random bits to make data unrecoverable. It specifies seven passes of data overwriting. There are many software programs available to perform this task. Some are free and some are commercial. There is even hardware that allows sanitization to be performed on multiple drives at one time. This is useful if you have a large number of drives.

The most secure method of ensuring data cannot be recovered is by physically destroying the media. For DVDs and CDs, snap the disc in half. Crush flash drives. Hard drives can be pulverized, shredded, or incinerated. With magnetic media, purging the data is another option. *Degaussing* is removing or neutralizing the magnetic property. Degaussing cannot be used on flash storage. This type of device is based on ROM, not magnetic storage.

NIST has created a special publication 800-88 Guidelines for Media Sanitization outlining how to sanitize media. This can be found on the NIST website (www.nist.gov) using the site's search function.

SECTION REVIEW 16.2

Check Your Understanding

1. The company's laser printer failed and there is no backup printer available. This is an example of _____.

2. A location where there is equipment, but no data, is an example of which type of alternate site?

3. Disk mirroring is an example of which type of RAID?

4. Recovery of lost data in RAID 5 is possible due to what type of data?

5. What power solution is best for a server in a small office of four people and one computer?

Build Your Key Terms Vocabulary

As you progress through this course, develop a personal cybersecurity glossary. This will help you build your vocabulary and prepare you for a career. Write a definition for each of the following terms, and add it to your cybersecurity glossary.

archive bit	incremental backup
cold site	media sanitization
data backup	mirrored site
degaussing	power spike
differential backup	power surge
disk mirroring	RAID 0
disk striping	RAID 1
disk striping with parity	RAID 1+0
failover cluster	RAID 5
fault tolerance	redundancy
full backup	snapshot
generator	uninterruptible power supply (UPS)
hot site	warm site

Review and Assessment

Summary

Section 16.1 Business Continuity and Disaster Recovery

- A business-continuity plan (BCP) provides the steps needed to provide business continuity and should include a business-impact analysis and testing of continuity or operations.
- A disaster-recovery plan (DRP) is the steps needed to restore services and covers items such as policies and objectives, key personnel, external contacts and vendors, emergency procedures, media, and insurance and financial information.

Section 16.2 Fault Tolerance and Redundancy

- Fault tolerance is allowing for the possibility of a failure by having a solution that protects the system in that event.
- Redundancy in IT is having a backup solution that can immediately be used in the event of a failure, which may be provided through maintaining additional sites, using RAID, database replication, failover systems, and backups.
- A consistent power supply is critical when working with electronic equipment, and care must be taken to completely remove data from computerized devices when they are discarded.

Check Your Cybersecurity IQ ➦

Now that you have completed this chapter, see what you have learned about cybersecurity by visiting the student companion website (www.g-wlearning.com) and taking the chapter posttest.

Review Questions ➦

For each question, select the answer that is the best response.

1. Which should be done first when creating a BCP?
   A. Designate an order of succession.
   B. Create the steps for a DRP.
   C. Decide on an RPO.
   D. Create a BIA on critical operations.

2. A business will make decisions on how fast it needs to be operational based on this indicator:
   A. RPO
   B. SPF
   C. RTO
   D. BIA

3. The _____ provides the detailed steps to restore services after a catastrophic event.
   A. BIA
   B. DRP
   C. BCP
   D. RPO

4. Which situation best describes a fault-tolerant solution?
   A. Multiple network cards installed in a busy server.
   B. A surge protector attached to a printer.
   C. The use of a RAID 5 array in a file server.
   D. Performing a daily backup.

5. A company has determined it must be very quick in moving to another location following a catastrophic event. It estimates it must be operational within two days in order to prevent significant operational disruption. Which choice should this company select?
   A. Cold site
   B. Warm site
   C. Hot site
   D. Alternate location

6. Which version of RAID provides increased performance, but does not provide any fault tolerance?
   A. RAID 1
   B. Disk mirroring
   C. Disk striping
   D. Disk striping with parity

7. Your company chooses to configure six 1 TB drives for a RAID 5 array. What percentage of the drives will be used for parity?
   A. 17 percent
   B. 20 percent
   C. 83 percent
   D. 100 percent

8. Which is the best choice for a company that is trying to minimize overall backup time during the week?
   A. Full every day.
   B. Full on Monday, incremental the remaining days of the week.
   C. Full on Monday, differential the remaining days of the week.
   D. Full on Monday, switch between incremental and differential the remaining days of the week.

9. A company needs to ensure its computers remain operational for at least 30 minutes during a power outage. Which solution best provides this protection?
   A. Portable generator
   B. Standby generator
   C. Uninterruptable power supply
   D. Surge protector

10. A shipbuilding company does contractual work for the US navy and is upgrading its systems. What is the most secure method of ensuring the data on the drives cannot be recovered?
    A. Degauss the systems.
    B. Run a data wipe on the machines four times each.
    C. Contract with a reputable company to shred the drives.
    D. Discard the drives in a secure dumpster.

Application and Extension of Knowledge

1. Android smartphones and iPhones have a process to return the phone to factory defaults. Investigate the process for both phones. What is deleted? Can data be recovered? Prepare a summary of your findings.

2. Create a text file containing miscellaneous data, and save it in your Documents folder on a Windows system. Using the built-in Windows backup program, create a backup of your Users\Documents folder. Exclude all subfolders. Back up to a USB or network location if available. Then, delete the text file. Using the Windows backup/recovery option, restore the file. Document your successful completion of these steps through screenshots.

3. Contact a local business owner or a member of senior management in a local company. Ask to meet to discuss the concepts of BCP and DRP and how or if they are used in the business. Be courteous and professional in your request. Be sure to explain you are a student completing a school project. Prepare a set of five interview questions. After the interview, summarize the responses in a presentation delivered to your class.

4. Research data-recovery software. Identify one open-source or freeware program and one for-purchase program. Compare and contrast the features of the software.

5. A computer programmer is looking for protection against data loss in the event of a power outage. The solution must provide power for two stand-alone PCs for at least one hour. Identify UPS solutions that would be suitable. Create a memo detailing your selection and justifying your choice. Identify where the item can be purchased.

Research Project
Backup Solutions

Clear View Windows is a small company that installs windows in homes and small offices. It has two servers that run Microsoft Windows Server 2012. It also has six workstation computers running a mix of Windows 7 and Windows 10. Since it does not have an IT staff, the owner, Timo Torres, is looking for a simple, fast solution that offers potential security features. The company has allotted an annual budget of $500 to use for backup software and media. Based on these criteria, research backup solutions that will be suitable. Identify advantages and disadvantages of each solution. Be sure to include the costs of not only purchasing the solution, but running and maintaining it.

Deliverables. Write a memo to the owner with your two top choices. Summarize the benefits and costs of each. Outline additional costs beyond the initial purchase the company may encounter.

Online Activities

Complete the following activities, which will help you learn, practice, and expand your knowledge and skills.

 Vocabulary. Practice vocabulary for this chapter using the e-flash cards, matching activity, and vocabulary game until you are able to recognize their meanings.

Communication Skills

College and Career Readiness

Reading. Now that you have completed reading several chapters in this text about cybersecurity, analyze the themes and structures the author uses. Create a concept map illustrating how the themes of this text are related.

Writing. Record four important things you learned in this chapter. Write a paragraph for each one about how you can use this information to communicate your message as a cybersecurity professional. Share your responses with the rest of the class during open discussion.

Speaking. What do you think the old adage "necessity is the mother of invention" means? Find examples of how the need for various cybersecurity measures has sparked their invention. Identify a need for a new cybersecurity measure. Speaking in front of the class, explain why you think this is needed and give your ideas on how it may be approached.

Listening. Attend a local school board meeting. Listen carefully to what each speaker has to say. Are there common themes between the speakers? Were you able to understand the message each speaker delivered?

Portfolio Development

College and Career Readiness

Professional Networking. Professional networking means talking with others and establishing relationships with people who can help you achieve career, educational, or personal goals. You have probably already begun to build one, even if you have not thought of it in these terms. People in your network include your instructors, employers, coworkers, and counselors who know about your skills and interests. Those who participate with you in volunteer efforts, clubs, or other organizations can also be part of your network. These people may help you learn about open positions and may be able to give you information that will help you get a position.

1. Identify people who are part of your network.

2. Create a spreadsheet that includes information about each person. Include each person's name, contact information, and relationship to you. For example, the person might be a coworker, employer, or fellow club member. Save the file. This will be for your personal use and *not* included in your portfolio.

CTSO Event Prep

Role-Play and Interview. Some competitive events for Career and Technical Student Organizations (CTSOs) require that entrants complete a role-play or interview. Those who participate will be provided information about a situation and given time to practice. A judge or panel of judges will review the presentations or conduct the interview. To prepare for the role-play or interview event, complete the following activities.

1. Read the guidelines provided by your organization.

2. Visit the organization's website, and look for role-play and interview events that were used in previous years. Many organizations post these events for students to use as practice for future competitions. Also, look for the evaluation criteria or rubric for the event. This will help you determine what the judge will be looking for in your presentation.

3. Practice in front of a mirror. Are you comfortable speaking without reading directly from your notes?

4. Ask a friend or an instructor to listen to your presentation or conduct an interview. Give special attention to your posture and how you present yourself. Concentrate on the tone of voice. Be pleasant and loud enough to hear, but do not shout. Make eye contact with the listener. Do not stare, but engage the person's attention.

5. After you have made your presentation, ask for constructive feedback.

Chapter 17

Incident Response and Computer Forensics

Throughout this course, you have learned many techniques to prevent cybersecurity attacks as well as other types of attacks. However, even with the best planning, training, and security configurations, a security event is still likely. A SANS Institute survey showed the most common incident companies had to deal with involved malware. Over 82 percent of the respondents indicated this. Unauthorized access was ranked second at 70 percent of incidents. Planning, respond to, and documenting incidents that occur is an important part of system security.

Another critical area of dealing with incidents involves the use of digital detective work. This is known as computer forensics. In the past decade, television shows from CSI to NCIS have shined the spotlight on computer forensics. These shows have helped excite many people into this ever-growing specialty field. In practice, computer forensics may involve the use of highly specialized software and hardware, advanced training, and knowledge of evidence collection. This is especially true if the incident can result in a criminal or civil case.

Chapter Preview

While studying, look for the activity icon for:

- Pretests and posttests
- Vocabulary terms with e-flash cards and matching activities
- Self-assessment

G-WLEARNING.com

Reading Prep

College and Career Readiness

The summary at the end of the chapter highlights the most important concepts presented in the chapter. Before reading this chapter, go to the end of the chapter, and read the summary. Make sure you understand these concepts as you read the chapter.

Check Your Cybersecurity IQ

Before you begin this chapter, see what you already know about cybersecurity by visiting the student companion website (www.g-wlearning.com) and taking the chapter pretest.

Certification Objectives

CompTIA Security+

5.4　Given a scenario, follow incident response procedures.

5.5　Summarize basic concepts of forensics.

Incident Response

Essential **Q**uestion

What is the importance of an incident-response plan to a company's reputation?

Chapter 16 explored the steps to maintain business operations in the event of catastrophic situations, such as a major cyberattack. Thankfully, businesses do not face major crises that often. However, they do experience frequent security episodes or incidents that must be dealt with and documented. These may be easy to fix or serious attacks that take longer to address. Regardless of the severity of the incident, it is important to follow proper procedures when responding to the situation and documenting the steps taken to resolve the event. Documentation is essential. It can help prevent future incidents, identify procedures that need to be modified, and provide clues of a larger security threat.

Key Terms

computer incident response team (CIRT)

computer security incident response team (CSIRT)

Federal Information Security Modernization Act (FISMA)

first responders

incident response (IR)

incident-response plan (IRP)

jump bag

National Cybersecurity and Communications Integration Center (NCCIC)

United States Computer Emergency Readiness Team (US-CERT)

Learning Goals

- Describe the role of an incident-response plan.
- Illustrate the function of first responders.
- Diagram the phases of an incident.

Incident-Response Plan

Incident response (IR) is acting against and recovering from a specific issue. It involves planning and attention to detail for potential incidents. A structured plan and organized approach will help resolve the situation. The goal is to return the organization to a safe and operational state. Following the resolution of an incident, the lessons learned are documented. If necessary, changes are applied to policies and procedures.

Quick Look 17.1.1

Incident Scoring

US-CERT has created a demonstration page to illustrate the NCCIC cyberincident scoring system. This will give you an idea of how a score is assigned.

1. Launch a web browser, and navigate to the US-CERT website (www.us-cert.gov).
2. Use the site's search function, and search for nciss demo. In the search results, select the link for **NCISS Incident Scoring Demo**.
3. Scroll through the page, and notice the areas that are assessed and scored.
4. Consider this scenario: an employee lost a laptop that held unencrypted employee information, but nothing classified.
5. Make an appropriate selection in each area. Notice how the score is built as you make a selection in each area.

Containment

In some cases, the incident will need to be isolated, or contained. This will limit any damage beyond what has already been affected. Containment allows the team to limit the scope of the incident. For example, if it is a virus, the infected system needs to be quickly isolated. This will prevent the virus from infecting other devices on the network.

In another example, suppose a rootkit is found on a computer. That machine should be removed from the network, as shown in **Figure 17-6.** Doing so helps prevent the problem from spreading. Access to the machine is prohibited. Any potential attacks or threats originating from the machine are prevented from launching.

Eradication

Once the threat is isolated and contained, eradication of the threat can begin. Eradication is removing the issues causing the incident. If the incident is an attack from a worm, containment will stop the spread, but the threat still remains. The worm must be removed. Other machines that were potentially infected need to be analyzed for infection. If found on other machines, they need to be contained and

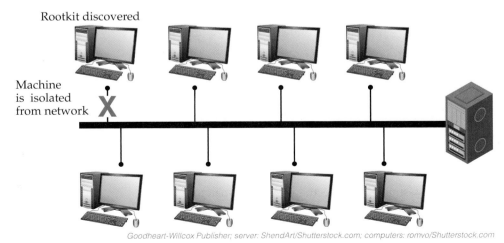

Goodheart-Willcox Publisher; server: ShendArt/Shutterstock.com; computers: romvo/Shutterstock.com

Figure 17-6. The device involved in an incident should be isolated to contain the problem and prevent it from spreading throughout the network.

the worm eradicated there as well. If the problem is too many permissions given to a user, configuring the appropriate security settings would be the next step.

In this phase, the CSIRT will try to find the root cause of the incident. Was it a virus attached to an e-mail or a download? Did infection occur via a portable drive? Discovering how the incident occurred will help prevent similar incidents.

Not all causes can be easily eradicated. A DoS attack on a company's web page may require removing the web server from operation. This would eradicate the cause, but would also prevent legitimate access to the web page. A stolen laptop may contain private or confidential information. Little can be done to eradicate this cause. Instead, the response must focus on preventing the stolen information from being used. There also may be laws that require notification be given to affected individuals.

Recovery

After the issues have been eradicated, the situation is returned to normal operation. This may involve reconnecting devices that were isolated. For example, after a computer is cleaned of a virus, reconnect it to the network. All computer systems should be functioning normally at the completion of the recovery phase.

Lessons Learned

Once the immediate actions of the incident have been dealt with, the next step is the post-incident responses. These are the lessons learned from dealing with the incident. It is important to document how the incident occurred and what steps were needed to resolve it. This allows the IT staff to learn from the incident. Safeguards can be put in place to improve the ability to prevent similar incidents or to respond more quickly and effectively. This final step can have a huge impact on preventing and resolving future incidents.

Part of the post-incident response is to evaluate the risk-assessment plan and its associated policies. Were there policies in place that may have prevented the incident? If so, why were they not followed? Should the risk-assessment plan or policies be modified? For example, consider the Equifax breach discussed at the beginning of this chapter. Equifax confirmed a web-server vulnerability in Apache Struts was the root cause of the breach. A patch was available months before the data breach, as shown in **Figure 17-7.** However, Equifax had not installed it. Was a patching policy not in place? Or was the policy in place, just not followed?

It is critical to analyze why procedures and protocols were not followed. This allows the organization to adjust policies, procedures, or even personnel. The lessons learned could help identify other areas where policies are not being followed. They may even help identify risks in areas that have not been considered or prioritized.

Quick Look 17.1.2

CSIRT Team

A CSIRT is responsible for the incident-response plan. It must address all six phases of an incident. For this exercise, you will act as a member of a CSIRT.

1. Create a team with two or three classmates, as directed by your instructor.
2. Prepare a summary of how you would respond to the discovery of keylogger on the system.
3. Record information on how you might approach the six phases. Be detailed, especially for the last three phases.
4. Discuss and share your team's approach with the class.

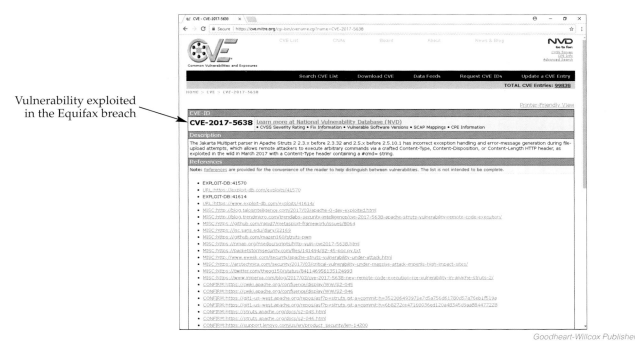

Figure 17-7. A fix for the vulnerability exploited in the Equifax data breach was available before the hack, but it had not been applied by Equifax.

SECTION REVIEW 17.1

Check Your Understanding

1. What is the name of the team that responds to security incidents?
2. What is a first responder?
3. Which act requires federal agencies to document incidents?
4. Determining if an incident is a security threat is done during which phase of the IRP?
5. This agency within the NCCIC documents and tracks incidents across agencies.

Build Your Key Terms Vocabulary

As you progress through this course, develop a personal cybersecurity glossary. This will help you build your vocabulary and prepare you for a career. Write a definition for each of the following terms, and add it to your cybersecurity glossary.

computer incident response team (CIRT)

computer security incident response team (CSIRT)

Federal Information Security Modernization Act (FISMA)

first responders

incident response (IR)

incident-response plan (IRP)

jump bag

National Cybersecurity and Communications Integration Center (NCCIC)

United States Computer Emergency Readiness Team (US-CERT)

Computer Forensics

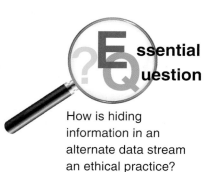

How is hiding
information in an
alternate data stream
an ethical practice?

Forensic investigations are often used in criminal or civil proceedings to gather evidence or document activities. Those involved use science and technology to discover and analyze evidence. Strict procedures of evidence collection must be followed in the collection and processing of data. This is to ensure its integrity admissibility and in any court proceedings. Security professionals need to be aware of procedures and the forensic tools available to discover, extract, and protect evidence. This section explores the field of computer forensics. Some of the industry certifications and potential employment opportunities that exist in this field are also covered.

Key Terms ⟡

alternate data stream (ADS)
American Standard Coded
  Information Interchange
  (ASCII)
Certified Computer Examiner
  (CCE)
Certified Forensic Computer
  Examiner (CFCE)
chain of custody
Computer Analysis Response
  Team (CART)

computer forensics
Cyber Security Forensic
  Analyst (CSFA)
Faraday shielding bag
file signature
GIAC Certified Forensic
  Examiner (GCFE)
hex editor
hexadecimal numbering system
intellectual property

junk science
legal hold
order of volatility
paging
Regional Computer Forensic
  Laboratories (RCFL)
slack space
write-blocker

Learning Goals

- Compare and contrast relevant certifications for careers in computer forensics.
- Discuss the history of computer forensics.
- Differentiate issues related to computer investigation.
- Decode digital evidence in hexadecimal and ASCII format.
- Identify metadata and alternate data streams.

Computer Forensics Careers

Forensics is the process of using science and technology to investigate situations to obtain facts. Forensics plays a role in several popular television shows, such as CSI. There are many fields of forensics. The fields are varied, from medical to criminal and engineering. *Computer forensics* involves using scientific methods to uncover and determine digital evidence on a multitude of computing devices. Someone involved in computer forensics is usually called an *information security analyst*.

According to the Bureau of Labor Statistics (BLS), the job market for information security analysts is expected to grow at a faster rate than most jobs, as shown in **Figure 17-8.** Most analysts have training in advanced computer science concepts along with training in criminal justice. Typical employees will earn a related bachelor degree. Degrees in cybersecurity and other IT fields often lead to careers in computer forensics. At this time, there are not many colleges and universities offering degrees in computer forensics.

However, while there may not be many options for a college degree in computer forensics, industry certifications are available. These are highly desirable for individuals working in the field. Many of the certifications are vendor neutral. This means they are not aligned with specific hardware or software. Other certifications are proprietary. One example of this is EnCase Certified Examiner (EnCE) certification. This certification validates the skills of users of the popular EnCase forensic solutions. Some other popular certifications include:

- Certified Computer Examiner;
- Certified Forensic Computer Examiner;
- GIAC Certified Forensic Examiner; and
- Cyber Security Forensic Analyst.

Goodheart-Willcox Publisher

Figure 17-8.   The BLS projects a much faster than average growth rate for information security analyst jobs.

Certified Computer Examiner (CCE) is a vendor-neutral certification that focuses on knowledge and practical examination skills. It is from the International Society of Forensic Computer Examiners.

Certified Forensic Computer Examiner (CFCE) is a vendor-neutral certification that consists of a peer review, an objective test, and a practical test. It is from the International Association of Computer Investigative Specialists (IACIS). A background check is required to obtain this certification.

GIAC Certified Forensic Examiner (GCFE) is a Windows-based certification that focuses on skills for collecting and analyzing data. It is from the Global Information Assurance Certification (GIAC).

Cyber Security Forensic Analyst (CSFA) is a vendor-neutral certification focused on advanced forensic skills. It is considered a top-level certification for computer forensics. A criminal background check is required for this certification. Anyone with a felony record is disqualified from obtaining this certification. Certain misdemeanors will also disqualify a candidate. CSFA is from the Cybersecurity Institute.

Quick Look 17.2.1

Computer Forensics Certification

The CFCE is one of the popular industry certification in the forensics field. This exercise explores CFCE certification.

1. Launch a web browser, and navigate to the International Association of Computer Investigative Specialists website (www.iacis.com).
2. Click the **Certification** menu, and then click **CFCE** in the menu. The overview page is displayed.
3. What are the two phases that must be completed to obtain this certification? How does this differ from other certifications you are familiar with obtaining?
4. In the **Certification** menu, click **Certification FAQ**. Review the frequently asked questions.
5. In addition to a background check, what is the cost to enroll in the CFCE program?
6. Using the options in the **Training** menu, review some of the available classes. Which ones interest you?

Computer Forensics History

The need for computer forensics grows alongside our ever-increasing reliance on technology. However, computer forensics is not new. Since computers started to provide essential services, there has been a need for expertise in forensics. Tools for computer forensics have existed since the early PCs. At that time, a common need was recovering deleted files. One of the most popular programs for this was XTree, as shown in **Figure 17-9.** It was introduced in 1985 and was a DOS-based program. It offered the ability to restore deleted files as well as manage files.

Eventually, the need to examine computer disks extended to law enforcement. In 1989, the FBI was investigating the Rocky Flats nuclear weapons plant. It discovered much of the evidence was stored on computers. At that time, the FBI did not have a team to handle digital evidence collection. It assembled an ad-hoc team of computer professionals to handle the investigation. Ultimately, this led to creating CART in 1992.

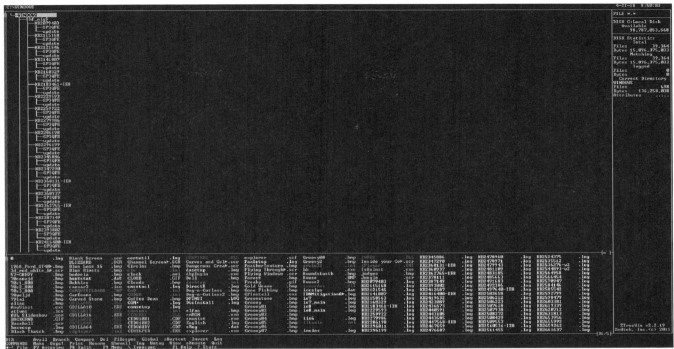

Figure 17-9. XTree was an early software that could recover deleted files.

The FBI's *Computer Analysis Response Team (CART)* is a permanent team of trained specialists for conducting computer forensics, as shown in **Figure 17-10.** It consists of almost 500 highly trained and certified special agents and professionals. This team works in field offices and a network of RCFLs. A *Regional Computer Forensic Laboratories (RCFL)* is a facility dedicated to the examination of digital evidence. RCFLs are located throughout the country. CART also has mobile labs that can be rapidly deployed in response to forensic needs.

FYI

CART handles forensic investigations of all types. Just a few examples include public corruption, the ambush of US Representative Gabby Giffords, and terrorist attacks.

FBI

Figure 17-10. This FBI agent is investigating a cyberintrusion in Jacksonville, Florida.

Computer Investigations

Responding to a forensic incident is not the same as answering a help desk call. A computer investigation requires a methodological process. Most forensic investigations lead to a criminal or civil proceeding. Therefore, preserving evidence and proper handling of equipment are critical. It is helpful for the forensic investigator to have basic training in criminal justice. Some knowledge of legal issues is also needed. For example, can a computer be searched without a subpoena? If evidence is improperly obtained, it may be ruled inadmissible in court proceedings.

There are many standards and organizations involved in computer forensics. These standards help ensure the methods used to acquire and analyze evidence preserve the integrity of investigations. Forensic investigators must follow best and recommended practices. This includes having appropriate and approved tools to gain access to the evidence. If the case goes to court proceedings, the tools used must be acceptable to the courts. If the forensic tool is new or seldom used, the experience and integrity of the examiner comes into play. If uncommon or new tools are used, opponents often attack the methods as junk science. *Junk science* is the use of methods and data that are fraudulent or fake.

There are many tools available for computer forensics. EnCase Forensic is commercial software commonly used by law enforcement and forensic investigators. This forensic tool can find deleted or hidden evidence in files, pictures, Internet history, the registry, and more. The company opentext (formerly Guidance Software) publishes EnCase Forensic. It has many other programs available for security forensics. It even offers industry certification for its products.

Data Integrity

Digital evidence can be retrieved from computers, mobile devices, security cameras, digital media players, and nearly any digital device. Ensuring the integrity of the data is critical. Forensic examiners should use copies of the original devices whenever possible. To prevent accidental changes to data, investigators often use a write-blocker. A *write-blocker* is a tool that permits read-only access to the storage device. Write-blockers are also known as *forensic disk controllers*. These tools allow a copy of the drive to be made without making any changes to the data. This includes retaining access dates from the original device. There are many products available. One example is shown in **Figure 17-11.**

CompTIA Security+
5.5

Case Study

FBI: Victim and Responder

The FBI is the go-to federal law-enforcement agency for computer forensic analysis. However, in one case, the FBI was a victim of the same type of incident it is tasked to investigate. A teenager from the United Kingdom named Kane Gamble was able to hack senior members of the FBI, CIA, and other agencies. He obtained sensitive information on intelligence operations in Afghanistan, data on over 20,000 FBI members, and much more. He was even able to impersonate then CIA director John Brennan. Gamble was fifteen years old when the hacks started, and the hacks resulted in millions of dollars in damage. He was sentenced to two years in a youth-detention center after he pleaded guilty.

1. Do you feel the sentence Gamble received is appropriate for his actions given his age? Why or why not?
2. Should hacking of high-level governmental officials have harsher penalties than hacking of a common person? Defend your position.

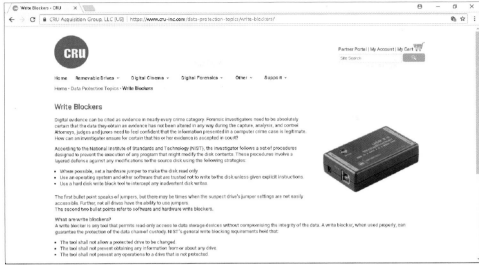

Goodheart-Willcox Publisher

Figure 17-11.   A write-blocker can be used by forensic investigators to preserve the integrity of digital data.

Before beginning any analysis, technicians should take a hash of the drive. Matching hashes ensure the integrity of the investigation. For example, the examiner takes a hash of a file before beginning an examination. Then, the file is duplicated. Before starting the examination, the examiner takes a hash of the duplicated file, as shown in **Figure 17-12**. The two hashes are compared. If the values are the same, the data integrity is intact. Hashing is discussed in detail in Chapter 11.

Communication

In addition to appropriate computer skills, a forensic technician must possess good communication skills. Investigators often must present evidence in court. Therefore, effective oral communication is essential. Investigators also usually need to create reports that are detailed. These reports need to be understood by others who may not have a technical background. Skill in writing is important to communicate technical topics in a simple way.

A report for a digital investigation is not the same as a memo. These reports are similar to the reports for penetration testing discussed in Chapter 13. An executive summary is usually included. A nontechnical description of the investigation and results is provided. The remainder of the report contains the detailed technical results of an investigation. The report may be created based on a template or may follow the step-by-step results of testing.

Goodheart-Willcox Publisher

Figure 17-12.   Compare hashes between the original and the copy to ensure the integrity of the data.

Confidentiality

Forensics investigators will have complete access to equipment when performing an analysis. They may be accessing confidential, proprietary, or sensitive information. In many cases, technicians have access to a business's intellectual property. ***Intellectual property*** is work that comes from a person's mind. This can be an idea, an invention, or a process. Intellectual property can be owned. Forensics investigators must have high ethical standards. This is especially true when dealing with intellectual property.

Evidence Handling

CompTIA Security+
5.5

Before collecting evidence, the investigator may record a video of the scene. This is a way to document the area in an undisturbed state. Photographs may also be taken showing papers on the desk or messages on the monitor. Even papers in a trash can will be photographed.

An important consideration in a forensic investigation is how the evidence is handled. It may be necessary to place a legal hold on potential evidence. A ***legal hold*** forbids destroying data, documents, or other items relevant to an investigation. This is usually done in anticipation of a potential criminal or civil case. All evidence must be preserved and unaltered. This may include computers, hard drives, flash drives, phones, e-mail, and documents. A legal hold helps protect the integrity of the investigation.

All evidence must be documented on an evidence-tracking sheet. This includes data. A ***chain of custody*** is a log that identifies the case, the evidence, and when and who accessed the evidence. The NIST has a sample chain of custody log available on its website, as shown in **Figure 17-13.** This is free to use.

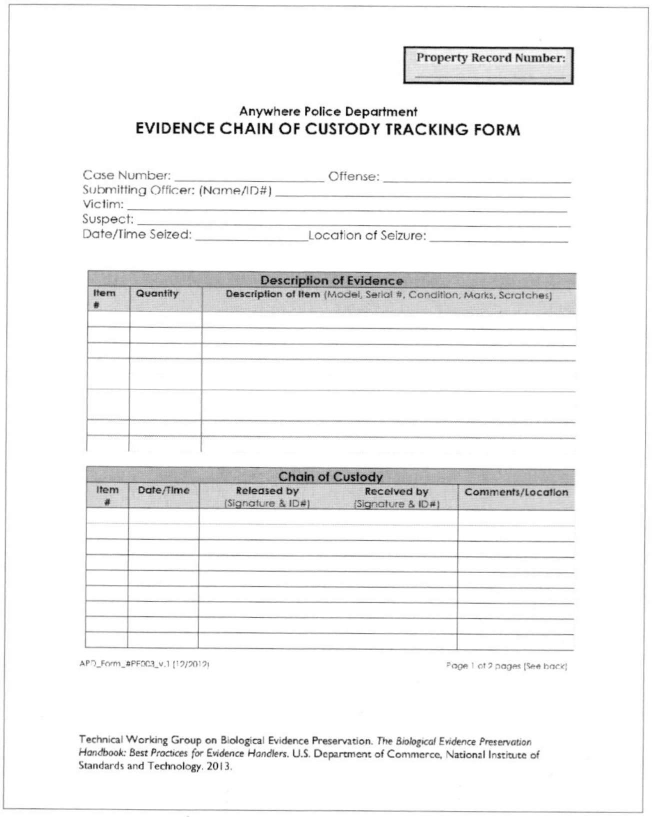

Property Record Number:

Anywhere Police Department
EVIDENCE CHAIN OF CUSTODY TRACKING FORM

Case Number: ____ Offense: ____
Submitting Officer: (Name/ID#) ____
Victim: ____
Suspect: ____
Date/Time Seized: ____ Location of Seizure: ____

Description of Evidence

Item #	Quantity	Description of Item (Model, Serial #, Condition, Marks, Scratches)

Chain of Custody

Item #	Date/Time	Released by (Signature & ID#)	Received by (Signature & ID#)	Comments/Location

APD_Form_#PE003_v.1 (12/2012) Page 1 of 2 pages (See back)

Technical Working Group on Biological Evidence Preservation. *The Biological Evidence Preservation Handbook: Best Practices for Evidence Handlers.* U.S. Department of Commerce, National Institute of Standards and Technology. 2013.

NIST

Figure 17-13. A chain of custody log is used to document evidence and who has handled it and when.

Evidence must also be protected from damage. For electronic devices, this includes protection against static electricity. A *Faraday shielding bag* is an antistatic container. If you have ever purchased a hard drive, RAM, or video card, it was packaged in this type of bag. A Faraday bag should be used for any evidence prone to damage from static electricity. Other evidence should be packaged with appropriate packaging. All evidence bags should be secured with tamper-evident tape.

Another key piece of information to be documented is the time and time zone on the computer. This will be important when reviewing the time files were accessed, created, or deleted. Different operating systems and file systems might record time in different formats. For example, time in NTFS is often stored as Greenwich Mean Time (GMT). Also, document if the system is set to use the Daylight Saving Time feature. The time offset needs to be noted so data can be matched to the time on the local system.

Decoding Digital Evidence

A computer forensics technician must know how to review information stored in hexadecimal format. Hexadecimal, or hex, is introduced in Chapter 8. The *hexadecimal numbering system* has 16 characters to represent numbers. It is also known as the Base 16 numbering system. The character used in hex are the numbers 0–9 and the letters A–F, as shown in **Figure 17-14**.

Examiners must also be able to convert hexadecimal numbers to ASCII format. The *American Standard Coded Information Interchange (ASCII)* is a set of 128 characters and symbols and numerical equivalents for each (0–127). Computers use ASCII to convert text from different programs into a generic format. This allows the text to be read by different computers or programs. A table for standard ASCII conversions is provided in Appendix A.

FYI

ASCII is pronounced *ask-kee.*

Binary Value	Decimal Value	Hexadecimal Value
0000	00	0
0001	01	1
0010	02	2
0011	03	3
0100	04	4
0101	05	5
0110	06	6
0111	07	7
1000	08	8
1001	09	9
1010	10	A
1011	11	B
1100	12	C
1101	13	D
1110	14	E
1111	15	F

Goodheart-Willcox Publisher

Figure 17-14. This table can be used to convert between binary, decimal, and hex values.

Hex to Decimal

To convert a hexadecimal address to decimal, work right to left. Each position of a hex character represents a positional value. For example, consider this address in hex:

A 2 1 B

To convert this to a decimal value, take the value of each character and multiply it by its positional value. From the right, the positional value is 16^0. Working left, the next positional value is 16^1. Then 16^2 followed by 16^3. The positional values keep increasing following this same pattern. Since letters cannot be multiplied, use the table in **Figure 17-14** to see the values. The character A = 10, B = 11, C = 12, and so on. Therefore, to convert the above value:

$$\begin{array}{cccc} B & 1 & 2 & A \end{array}$$
$$(11 \times 16^0) + (1 \times 16^1) + (2 \times 16^2) + (10 \times 16^3) =$$
$$(11 \times 1) + (1 \times 16) + (2 \times 256) + (10 \times 4096) =$$
$$11 + 32 + 512 + 40960 = 41{,}499$$

Quick Look 17.2.2

Hex to Decimal

Information extracted from a file contained an IP address in hexadecimal value: c0 a8 01 01. What is the IP address in decimal format? Approach this as four separate numbers: C0, A8, 01, and 01.

1. First evaluate C0, and begin at the right. Multiply 0 by 16^0. The result of 16^0 equals 1, and $0 \times 1 = 0$.
2. Convert the C to its decimal equivalent (12) using the table in **Figure 17-14.**
3. Multiply 12 by 16^1. The result of 16^1 equals 16, and $12 \times 16 = 192$.
4. Add the two decimal values to find the decimal equivalent of the first octet in the IP address: $0 + 192 = 192$.
5. Applying what you have learned, convert the remainder of the address. What is the full IP address in decimal format?

Hex to ASCII

Converting from hex to ASCII is straightforward. Identify the hex number to convert. Then, use a conversion table to locate the ASCII equivalent. Remember that an uppercase character such, as C, differs from a lowercase character such as c. The uppercase ASCII character C has a hex value of 43. The lowercase ASCII character c has a hex value of 63.

Quick Look 17.2.3

Hex to ASCII

Use the data in the table in Appendix A for this exercise. The word Cyber in hex is: 43 79 62 65 72. The hex value of 73 63 68 6f 6f 6c in ASCII characters is school.

1. Look at the following forensic evidence extracted from a packet. Can you determine what the user accessed?

   77 77 77 2e 66 61 63 65 62 6f 6f 2e 63 6f 6d

2. Take the first number, 77. Using the table in Appendix A, the equivalent ASCII character is a lowercase w.
3. Continue decoding the remaining information from the packet. What did the user access?

File Signatures and Hex Editors

A tool called a hex editor allows an investigator to view contents of a file. A *hex editor* is software that reveals the raw binary data within a file. This strips all the encoding and conversion from the data. For example, when you open a word-processor document, you see the words in the document. Opening the same file in a hex editor will show you the binary data before it is converted into the words you see onscreen. There are many free hex editors available on the Internet. One popular example is Free Hex Editor Neo.

Whenever a file is saved, file signature is applied. A *file signature* is data used to identify or verify what the file contains. Each file type has a unique file signature. If someone changes a file's extension, the file signature is *not* modified. A person may change the file extension in attempt to hide the real content of the file. If the file is opened in a hex editor, the actual file type can be determined.

Look at the example shown in **Figure 17-15.** This shows a file viewed in a hex editor. The file signature in this example is represented by the hex characters of 25 50 44 46. This signature corresponds to a PDF file from Adobe. Suppose the PDF file is renamed as NewFile.docx. Opening NewFile.docx in a hex editor will reveal the file is actually a PDF file. Even though the file name has a different extension, the code for the file signature still reflects a PDF file.

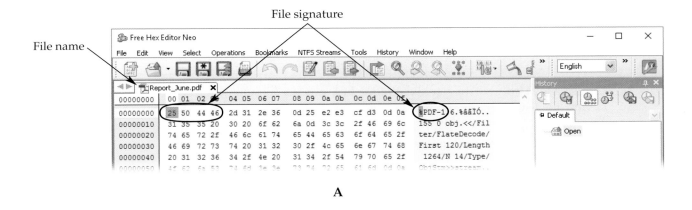

A

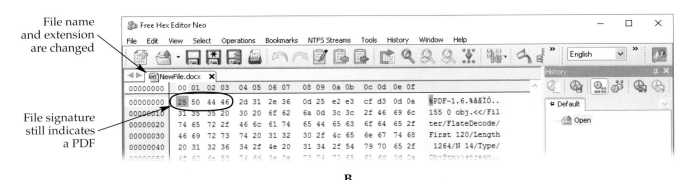

B

Figure 17-15. A hex editor reveals the file signature for a file (A). If the file extension is changed, the file signature is not changed (B).

Quick Look 17.2.4

Hex Editor

This exercise requires Free Hex Editor Neo from HHD Software. Before beginning, download the software (www.hhdsoftware.com/free-hex-editor), and install it. You must have permission to install software.

1. Launch Free Hex Editor Neo.
2. Click **File>New File** in the pull-down menu. A blank file is started, and the cursor (green block) is in the first position.
3. Enter these hex values: 43 79 62 65 72. As you enter values, the ASCII characters displayed in the area on the right will spell Cyber, as shown.

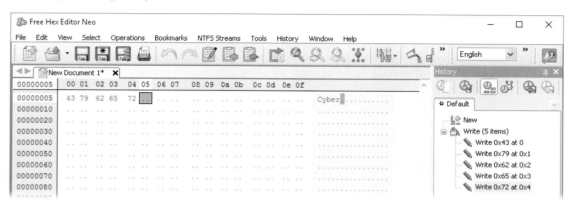

4. Launch a web browser, navigate to Wikipedia (www.wikipedia.org), and search for list of file signatures. Review the list. What file signature would you expect to find in an executable (EXE) file?
5. Switch to the hex editor, and open the file c:\windows\write.exe. What is the file signature?
6. Close all files without saving, and exit the editor.

Additional File Evidence

When a file is saved, it includes areas that may contain data not visible to the user. Also, messages and other data may be hidden within a file. These are concerns for the computer forensic investigator.

Metadata

As described in Chapter 7, metadata is simply data about data. Properties may be included in the internal properties of the data. This may include the author's name. It may also include the date and time a file was created or modified. The folder location may be saved as well as the company name used to register the software. Two prominent cases illustrate how metadata can reveal information.

Between 1974 and 1991, a serial killer was active in the Wichita, Kansas area. The killer came to be known as BTK (bind/torture/kill). The killer taunted law enforcement with letters containing details of the murders. After a long absence of murders and contact, the killer sent another taunt. This time the letter was on a 3.5″ floppy disk. When the forensic examiners searched the disk, they found a deleted Microsoft Word file. They were able to restore and examine this file. The file's metadata revealed the file was created by a user named Dennis and the company was a local church. Investigators reviewed the church's website and found a man named Dennis Rader. He was in charge of the church's congregation council.

After gathering additional physical evidence, Rader was arrested. He was later convicted of his crimes.

A common method of storing metadata is through the use of the Extensible Metadata Platform (XMP) created by Adobe. This standard provides a method of embedding metadata in a variety of file types, including PDF, JPG, and MP3. Without the ability to embed, metadata must be stored in a separate file that is linked to the original file. By allowing other programs the ability to customize the metadata properties directly in a file, a variety of information can be stored and tracked. This may include information such as when a photograph was cropped and who edited the content.

Another common piece of metadata is GPS data. This is discussed in detail in Chapter 7. Most smartphones and digital cameras record Exif data by default. This includes GPS data. GPS data can reveal the exact location and time a photograph was taken. This can prove valuable to forensic investigators.

Quick Look 17.2.5

Exif Data

Many digital documents, including images, may contain hidden information. Metadata can provide forensic investigators with important information. Before beginning this activity, download the image file from the student companion website (www.g-wlearning.com).

1. Open the downloaded image file in an image editor or by double-clicking the file in file explorer. Look at the photograph. It could have been taken at any seaside location.
2. Close the image file.
3. In file explorer, right-click on the image file, and click **Properties** in the shortcut menu. The **Properties** dialog box is displayed.
4. Click the **Details** tab in the **Properties** dialog box, as shown. Review the Exif data. From this data, it is easy to determine what device took the photograph and when it was taken. The GPS data can be used to find the exact location where the photograph was taken.

Quick Look 17.2.5 Continued

5. Latitude and longitude can be used to locate any place on Earth. Both are specified in degrees, minutes, and seconds. The latitude data for this image is 35 degrees, 12 minutes, 30.1699999999… seconds. The seconds value can be rounded to 30. These values can be entered into a geolocator website or converted to a decimal degree value and entered directly into the Google search engine.

6. To convert the latitude to a decimal degree value, take the seconds (30) and divide by 60. There are 60 seconds in one minute. The result is .5.

7. Add .5 to the minutes (12) and divide the result by 60. There are 60 minutes in one degree. The result is .2.

8. Add .2 to the degrees. The final decimal degree equivalent for the latitude of this image is 30.2 degrees.

9. Applying what you have learned, convert the longitude value for the photograph to a decimal degree value. What is the decimal degree value?

10. Launch a web browser, and navigate to Google Maps (maps.google.com). Enter the latitude decimal value, a space, a dash, and the longitude decimal value. The dash indicates the western hemisphere. Where was the photograph taken?

Slack Space

There is another area that could contain nonvisible data. When a file is saved on a computer, it is stored in a unit called a cluster. Files generally are saved among many connected clusters on the storage media, as shown in **Figure 17-16.** When a file is written to the last cluster and not all the space is used, the remaining space is called *slack space.* Slack space is often searched in forensic examinations. It was referenced in a statement from James Comey, then FBI director, regarding the e-mail investigation of Hillary Clinton. A hex editor or other tool can be used to gather slack space and hide data in it.

When a file is deleted, the content is not erased from the disk. Instead, the area where the file was stored is marked as available. If a new file that uses less space than the previous file is written to this area, leftover data could remain in the slack space. In **Figure 17-16,** a file was stored using three clusters. Only one-half of the space in the third cluster was used. Suppose this file is deleted and a new file is saved in the same clusters. However, the new file only needs 768 bytes. The first cluster will be completely overwritten, but only needs 256 bytes are written to the second cluster. The remaining bytes in the second cluster will be slack space. The slack space will contain remnants of the original file, as shown in **Figure 17-17.**

Additional Data Locations

An alternate data stream is another way that data could be hidden on NTFS file systems. An *alternate data stream (ADS)* is a data-hiding technique in which data are inserted behind another file. ADS has been used to hide data, including malware by attaching programs or other files to the source file. Consider a file saved on a system. The file contains the attribute $Data. This is simply a pointer to the content in the file. If another attribute or stream of data is linked to the file, it will have a name. This is where the name alternate data stream originates.

CompTIA Security+
5.5

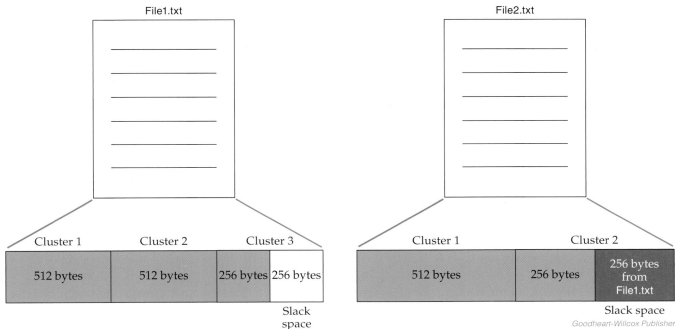

Figure 17-16.   Slack space is the remaining space in a cluster after a file is saved. It may contain hidden data.

Figure 17-17.   When a file is deleted, the space it occupied is marked as available, but the data remain. If a new, smaller file is written to that location, the slack space will contain remnants of the original file.

When searching for data, it is important to understand the concept of order of volatility. *Order of volatility* refers to the sequence in which items should be searched for evidence. *Volatility* is a quality of changing quickly or unpredictably. Generally, the order is from most volatile to least volatile:

1. data in random access memory (RAM), including CPU caches
2. swap files
3. data on hard disk drives
4. log files located on remote systems
5. data located on archive media (CDs, DVDs, etc.)

There are two types of swap files. One is used by the system for paging. The other is used for recovery when a system enters hibernation mode. *Paging* is a process used by the operating system when physical memory becomes low. To temporarily free physical memory, the operating system removes unused processes to a file on the hard disk. When the processes need to run again, they are moved back into memory. This file in Windows is called paging.sys. It is located in the root directory of the primary partition and hidden by default. The hiberfile.sys file in a Windows computer contains the contents of RAM when a computer moves into hibernate mode. The hiberfil.sys file is in the same location as the pagefile.sys file. Data can be extracted from both of these files. While the system is running, these files cannot be opened.

Another area of concern in forensic analysis is the use of hiding data inside another file. A common example is text embedded in an image file. This practice is called steganography. Steganography is discussed in detail in Chapter 11. Watermarks can be a form of steganography. United States currency contains watermarks to ensure the money is not counterfeit. Digital watermarks can be embedded in files. These can be detected through forensic analysis.

Quick Look 17.2.6

Alternate Data Stream

A simple alternate data stream can be easily created. In this exercise, you will create an ADS using a basic text editor and the Windows Command Prompt.

1. Launch Notepad, enter the text This is a file with sample text, and save the file as sample.txt in your working folder.
2. Close the file.
3. Launch the Windows Command Prompt, navigate to your working folder, and enter the **DIR** command prompt. Notice the length of the file.
4. Enter: notepad sample.txt:secret.txt. You will be prompted to create the file. Click the **Yes** button. Notepad is launched with a new text file open.
5. Enter the text This is my secret information, save the file, and exit Notepad.
6. At the command prompt, enter the **DIR** command again. Notice the file size of sample.txt did not change, and you cannot see a file called secret.txt.
7. Enter the **DIR** command again, but this time use the /r switch. This switch allows you to find files that have alternate data streams. Notice how you can now see the secret.txt file, as shown.

```
Command Prompt                                              —   □   ×

C:\Cybersecurity>notepad sampletxt:secret.txt

C:\Cybersecurity>dir
 Volume in drive C has no label.
 Volume Serial Number is CA57-3D5E

 Directory of C:\Cybersecurity

02/06/2018  12:19 PM    <DIR>          .
02/06/2018  12:19 PM    <DIR>          ..
02/06/2018  12:16 PM                32 sample.txt
02/06/2018  12:22 PM                 0 sampletxt
               2 File(s)             32 bytes
               2 Dir(s)  478,846,980,096 bytes free

C:\Cybersecurity>dir /r
 Volume in drive C has no label.
 Volume Serial Number is CA57-3D5E

 Directory of C:\Cybersecurity

02/06/2018  12:19 PM    <DIR>          .
02/06/2018  12:19 PM    <DIR>          ..
02/06/2018  12:16 PM                32 sample.txt
02/06/2018  12:22 PM                 0 sampletxt
                                    30 sampletxt:secret.txt:$DATA
               2 File(s)             32 bytes
               2 Dir(s)  478,846,980,096 bytes free

C:\Cybersecurity>
```

SECTION REVIEW 17.2

Check Your Understanding

1. What device needs to be connected before a forensic technician examines a disk drive?

2. Electronic evidence should be protected from static electricity using what storage medium?

3. This document records all individuals who accessed a particular piece of evidence.

4. What is leftover space in a file-storage cluster called?

5. What is an additional file attached to an original file called?

Build Your Key Terms Vocabulary

As you progress through this course, develop a personal cybersecurity glossary. This will help you build your vocabulary and prepare you for a career. Write a definition for each of the following terms, and add it to your cybersecurity glossary.

alternate data stream (ADS)

American Standard Coded Information Interchange (ASCII)

Certified Computer Examiner (CCE)

Certified Forensic Computer Examiner (CFCE)

chain of custody

Computer Analysis Response Team (CART)

computer forensics

Cyber Security Forensic Analyst (CSFA)

Faraday shielding bag

file signature

GIAC Certified Forensic Examiner (GCFE)

hex editor

hexadecimal numbering system

intellectual property

junk science

legal hold

order of volatility

paging

Regional Computer Forensic Laboratories (RCFL)

slack space

write-blocker

Review and Assessment

Summary

Section 17.1 Incident Response

- An incident-response plan (IRP) is a written document that provides instructions to be followed when an incident occurs and helps prepare employees to handle incidents.
- First responders are the individuals who react to incidents, and are often designated employees known as a computer security incident response team (CSIRT) or computer incident response team (CIRT).
- An incident consists of six distinct phases: preparation, identification, containment, eradication, recovery, and lessons learned.

Section 17.2 Computer Forensics

- Computer forensics involves using scientific methods to uncover and determine digital evidence on computing devices, and there are several certifications relevant to this field including Certified Computer Examiner (CCE), Certified Forensic Computer Examiner (CFCE), GIAC Certified Forensic Examiner (GCFE), and Cyber Security Forensic Analyst (CSFA).
- The need for expertise in computer forensics has existed since computers began providing essential services and has become a comprehensive field that includes a dedicated FBI team known as the Computer Analysis Response Team (CART).
- There are several areas of concern in a computer investigation, including data integrity, communication, confidentiality, and evidence handling.
- Decoding digital evidence in hexadecimal and ASCII formats is a necessary skill for a computer forensic investigator, and a key element is the ability to identify a file signature.
- Digital evidence found in a file may include metadata or an alternate data stream, and the slack space on storage devices may also contain digital evidence.

Check Your Cybersecurity IQ

Now that you have completed this chapter, see what you have learned about cybersecurity by visiting the student companion website (www.g-wlearning.com) and taking the chapter posttest.

Review Questions

For each question, select the answer that is the best response.

1. Which is a written document that provides instructions to be followed when an incident occurs?
   A. File signature
   B. Incident-response plan
   C. Jump bag
   D. CART

2. Which of the following would not be individuals reacting to an incident?
   A. CSIRT
   B. US-CERT
   C. CIRT
   D. First responders

3. This incident would be given the highest priority:
   A. A missing flash drive containing unencrypted spreadsheets of last month's sales projections.
   B. An employee reports information left in a printer.
   C. The guest account is not disabled on a computer.
   D. An unpatched server.

4. The correct order in addressing the security incident of user who is found to have local admin rights on a secure computer is:
   A. Remove the admin rights, and create a policy that details who should have admin rights.
   B. Document why this occurred, and remove the admin rights.
   C. Determine this is a security incident, and remove the admin rights.
   D. Remove the admin rights, and contain any potential issues that may have occurred.

5. Of the following, which is not a vendor-neutral certification?
   A. GCFE
   B. CCE
   C. CFCE
   D. CSFA

6. What is the FBI team dedicated to conducting computer forensics?
   A. RCFL
   B. EnCase
   C. US-CERT
   D. CART

7. A(n) _____ is a device that prevents accidental or intentional changes to a storage device.
   A. NDA
   B. write-blocker
   C. legal hold
   D. Faraday shielding bag

8. Which of the following is not a valid hexadecimal number?
   A. 1F234B5I6K
   B. 2B3CCCD4
   C. FBCA21699
   D. 0C2D4A5B

9. Which statement is true about a file signature?
   A. It is computed from the hash of the file.
   B. It is located at the beginning of a file.
   C. It can be viewed by right-clicking the file and choosing properties.
   D. If you rename the file, the file signature changes.

10. Hiding data behind another file is an example of:
    A. steganography
    B. digital watermarking
    C. alternate data stream
    D. Exif data

Application and Extension of Knowledge

1. Assume you are investigating an incident. Locate a photograph taken with a digital camera or smartphone. Also locate a PDF file. Navigate to the Get-Metadata website (www.get-metadata.com). This is a free Exif viewer. Upload the photograph, and analyze the metadata. Repeat with the PDF. Write a report identifying the metadata you think is relevant. Include screenshots in your report. Format the report following your school's style guidelines.

2. Autopsy is a free, open-source forensic tool. Many security technicians use it to analyze systems and collect information. Research this software. Then, create a presentation on the capabilities and features it offers.

3. Work with a partner for this activity. Locate two files of different types, and rename them with different extensions. Give the files to your partner. Do not tell your partner the original file types. Using Neo Hex Editor, determine the original file signature of the files given to you by your partner. Then, rename the files and open them.

4. Write-blockers are not just for law enforcement. Assume your company is looking for a write-blocker in case it needs to respond to a legal incident. Research different brands of write-blockers. Write a memo to your supervisor (instructor), and recommend two products. Be sure to include the reasons you recommend the products.

5. Explore the types of forensic certifications and skills desired by employers. Use job-search websites such as Indeed.com or CareerBuilder.com. Summarize the skills and certifications most often referenced.

Research Project
Certification Sponsorship

You are a security technician for a medium-size company. There have been some recent high-profile security issues. In the wake of these, the company hired an outside consultant to review its systems. You feel if you were trained and certified in computer forensics, you could help save money by reducing the need for outside consultants. You also feel the company would be able to provide quicker responses to incidents.

After considering the different certifications, you feel GCFA is most appropriate for your situation. To have the company sponsor your certification, you need to prepare a detailed memo requesting the training and outlining the scope of the training and certification. Research the GCFA certification. Identify the skills that will be tested. Describe the courses from the SANS Institute, and determine which ones would be helpful in preparing for the exam. Locate the cost of the exam and the certification. Then, write a memo to the company's CISO (your instructor) requesting sponsorship for the training and certification.

Online Activities

Complete the following activities, which will help you learn, practice, and expand your knowledge and skills.

Vocabulary. Practice vocabulary for this chapter using the e-flash cards, matching activity, and vocabulary game until you are able to recognize their meanings.

Communication Skills

College and Career Readiness

Reading. Determine the meanings of the words and phrases used to explain the concepts discussed in this chapter. Different words and phrases might have figurative, connotative, or technical meanings. Analyze the impact of the author's word choices on the meaning and tone of the chapter.

Writing. To become career ready, it is important to learn how to communicate clearly and effectively using reasoning. Using the information in this chapter, write several paragraphs summarizing your assessment of computer forensics.

Speaking. Select a member of your class to whom you will present the information you learned from the last chapter about business continuity. Make use of displays or demonstrations to enhance the presentation.

Listening. Locate an online video describing computer forensics. Listen carefully to what the video has to say about this topic. Does having a visual aid (the video) help you listen to the message? Do you find it easier to listen without looking at the screen?

Portfolio Development

College and Career Readiness

References. An important part of any portfolio is a list of references. A *reference* is a person who knows your skills, talents, or personal traits and is willing to recommend you. References will probably be someone from your network. These individuals can be someone who you worked for or with who you provided community service. Someone you know from your personal life, such a youth group leader, can also be a reference. However, you should not list relatives as references. Consider which references can best recommend you for the position for which you are applying. Always get permission from the person before using his or her name as a reference.

1. Ask several people from your network if they are willing to serve as a reference for you.
2. Create a Microsoft Word document with the names and contact information for your references. Use the heading References and your name. Save the document.
3. Update your master spreadsheet.

CTSO Event Prep

Event Preparation. No matter what competitive events you will participate in for a career and technical student organization (CTSO), you will have to be well organized and prepared. Study the content exhaustively before the event. Make sure all the tools you need for the event have been secured and travel arrangements to the event have been made. Confirming details well in advance of an event will decrease stress and leave you free to concentrate on the event itself. To prepare for a competition, complete the following activities.

1. Pack appropriate clothing, including comfortable shoes and professional attire.
2. Prepare all technological resources, including anything that you might need to prepare or compete. Double-check that any electronic presentation material is saved in a format that is compatible with the machines that will be available to you at the event.
3. If the event calls for visuals, make sure you have them prepared in advance, packed, and ready to take with you.
4. Bring registration materials, including a valid form of identification.
5. Bring study materials, including the flash cards and other materials you have used to study for the event. If note cards are acceptable when making a presentation, make sure your notes are complete and easy to read. Have a backup set in case of an emergency.
6. At least two weeks before you go to the competition, create a checklist of what you need for the event. Include every detail down to a pencil or pen. Then, use this checklist before you go into the presentation so you do not forget anything.

Chapter 18

Career and Workplace Considerations

After you finish school, the next step in life is to find a job. The courses you take in school prepare you with the skills needed to be successful in your chosen career. It is critical to have the employability skills to help find a job, perform well in the workplace, and gain success in a job or career. In today's workplace, employers look for people who not only have the job-specific hard skills to perform on the job, but also the ability to interact with coworkers and customers. The most qualified person in a field in terms of hard skills who lacks soft skills may face challenges in finding and keeping a job.

In addition to being workplace ready with hard and soft skills, to be successful in a career requires an overall understanding of industries and businesses. Knowing how a workplace is organized helps a person understand how he or she fits into the overall operation. All industries and businesses face issues related to their workforces, from employee happiness to following governmental regulations. Industries and businesses are themselves part of a larger community. Health, safety, and environmental issues affect the community as well as the industries and businesses themselves.

Chapter Preview

While studying, look for the activity icon for:

- Pretests and posttests
- Vocabulary terms with e-flash cards and matching activities
- Self-assessment

G-W LEARNING.com

Reading Prep

Review the chapter headings, and use them to create an outline for taking notes during reading and class discussion. Under each heading, list any key terms. Write two questions you expect the chapter to answer.

College and Career Readiness

Check Your Cybersecurity IQ ⤴

Before you begin this chapter, see what you already know about career skills by visiting the student companion website (www.g-wlearning.com) and taking the chapter pretest.

Section 18.1

Workplace Readiness

?EQ Essential Question

How important are soft skills to a career in cybersecurity?

A career-minded person needs certain manners, talents, and skills in order to communicate well as a professional. To become ready for the workplace, you need the soft skills that will help you find a job and do well at it. In today's workplace, employers look for people who have job-specific skills to perform on the job, as well as the skills to relate to coworkers and clients. Today's employers request social skills. Mastering the art of professionalism for your chosen career will have great value for you.

Key Terms 🔗

active reading
career and technical student
   organizations (CTSOs)
collaboration skills
conflict resolution
critical-thinking skills
customer service
decision-making
diversity awareness
ergonomics

ethics
etiquette
integrity
job-acquisition skills
leadership
lifelong learner
listening
morals
Occupational Safety and Health
   Administration (OSHA)

problem-solving
professional attire
professional communication
résumé
soft skills
teamwork
time management
verbal communication
work ethic
written communication

Learning Goals

- Describe personal qualities and people skills necessary for the workplace.
- Identify professional knowledge and skills needed for the workplace.
- Assess the benefits of career and technical student organizations (CTSOs).

Personal Qualities and People Skills

Successful students and effective team members have strong soft skills. *Soft skills* are the personal skills used to communicate and work well with others. They are also known as *interpersonal skills, people skills,* and *transferrable skills.* Soft skills enable a person to interact with others in a positive manner, as shown in **Figure 18-1.**

Ethics

Students and employees are expected to make good decisions. They are also expected to act ethically. *Ethics* are rules of behavior based on a group's ideas about what is right and wrong. These groups can be society, social groups, or organizations. *Morals* are an individual's ideas of what is right and wrong. Ethical actions result when a person, a business, or an organization applies ethics and moral behavior.

Integrity is the honesty of a person's actions. People show their integrity through their senses of ethics and morals. You can show integrity by following laws and policies. Another way is to respect the property of your employer and coworkers. People with integrity can identify the far-reaching effects of their actions. In addition, they are reliable.

Work ethic is the belief that honest work is a reward on its own. It is a soft skill that can help a person be successful. Coming to school on time and respecting your instructors and classmates are ways to demonstrate a good work ethic. Other ways include taking direction willingly and exhibiting motivation to accomplish a task.

Self-Representation

Each day, ask yourself how you want others to perceive you. Represent yourself in the best way possible. This is especially true when you are on the job. Dress appropriately. Maintain good personal hygiene. Use language and manners suitable for your workplace.

Dress is the type and style of clothing worn. It is the first thing that makes an impression on people you meet. *Professional attire* is the dress your workplace dictates. Appropriate dress for the workplace shows an individual's professionalism. This attire is appropriate for your job. Good grooming complements your dress. It is necessary to practice good personal hygiene. Your employer's human resources department will have a dress code or guidelines for employees.

Etiquette is the art of using good manners in any situation. Examples of etiquette are shown in **Figure 18-2.** *Professional etiquette* is using good manners in a business setting. It means to be courteous, as well to act and speak appropriately in all situations. The way in which you represent yourself can have an effect on others. In a professional situation, it reflects on your employer as well as yourself.

Diversity

Another people skill needed for the workplace is diversity awareness. *Diversity* means having people from unlike demographics come together in a group. Demographics can include age, race, gender, ability, and other qualities. *Diversity awareness* is the ability to embrace the unique traits of others. You can show this

Firma V/Shutterstock.com

Figure 18-1. Have a positive manner when interacting with others.

Ways to Exhibit Etiquette

- Compose a thank-you letter after somebody does something extraordinary for you.
- Show thoughtfulness and politeness to each individual with whom you come in contact.
- Praise those around you when they contribute in a constructive way.
- Wait to speak until it is your turn.
- Arrive on time to each conference and appointment.
- Address each individual with whom you speak by his or her name.
- Turn off your digital devices when in a conference or discussion.
- Shake hands when meeting somebody for the first time.
- Show you are listening when involved in a dialogue.
- Respect the workspaces of your colleagues.
- Do not let your movements or discussions become a disruption.

Goodheart-Willcox Publisher

Figure 18-2. Etiquette is applying the rules of good manners in all situations.

by working in a friendly way with all people. It is vital to respect cultural differences found in the workplace.

A diverse workforce has many benefits. Diverse employees can help a company create products and services that might be new in the marketplace. New ways of thinking are a benefit of hiring people with varied backgrounds. Diversity also increases the pool of potential candidates. This can result in a more effective workforce.

Diversity does not come without challenges. Special training might be required for workers to learn how to communicate in a diverse workplace. Employees may have to adjust their ways of thinking to work with a diverse population.

Quick Look 18.1.1

Diversity Awareness

The value of diversity in the workplace is being recognized by more and more businesses. As companies become more diverse, diversity awareness becomes a critical skill.

1. Launch a web browser, and navigate to a search engine.
2. Enter the search phrase diversity awareness. Evaluate the search results for an article from a valid source, such as a university (.edu domain).
3. Read the article.
4. How did the article define diversity awareness? Is there another term for diversity awareness?
5. Did the article identify why diversity awareness is important? If so, what did it state?
6. List any key points the article provided for being aware of diversity in the workplace.

Teamwork and Conflict Resolution

Demonstrating teamwork skills is vital in the workplace. *Teamwork* is the cooperative efforts of team members to reach a goal. A team consists of two or more people working together to reach a common goal. Effective team members are people who contribute ideas and effort. They contribute to the success of the team by doing things such as brainstorming answers, volunteering, and acting in accordance with their assigned roles. They are cooperative and work well with others on and outside of the team.

People who are positive contributors show leadership qualities, even when they are not in leadership roles. *Leadership* is the ability to influence others to reach a goal. Effective team members also have collaboration skills. *Collaboration skills* are behaviors for working with others. Effective team members help others. They support other team members and their leaders. These people take initiative when appropriate. Another way to demonstrate teamwork skills is to request help when needed.

When people work together, there is likely to be some conflict. A *conflict* is a strong disagreement between two or more people or a difference that prevents agreement. Conflict can be positive when people learn from the disagreements. Positive solutions can result when conflict is handled in a proper manner.

Conflict resolution is the process of resolving disputes. Following a conflict-resolution model can help a team solve differences. See **Figure 18-3.** Conflict resolution requires each party to show *emotional control.* This means each person directs his or her reactions toward a desirable result. You can show conflict-resolution skills by discussing solutions to conflicts in the workplace.

Formal methods of conflict resolution might be required in some cases. *Negotiation* is people coming together in an attempt to reach an agreement. Sometimes, mediation is needed in negotiation. *Mediation* is the inclusion of a neutral person to help the parties resolve their dispute. This person is called a *mediator.*

Creativity and Resourcefulness

Creativity is another quality helpful for success at school and in the workplace. Creative people are not afraid to contribute new ideas. They show ingenuity freely.

A quality linked to creativity is resourcefulness. Resourcefulness is the ability to come up with new ways to do things. When a new situation present itself, resourceful people deal with it promptly. They also work to develop measures that use resources in a sustainable way.

Communication Skills

What does communication mean to you? Sending an e-mail? Using your cell phone? *Communication* is the process of using words, sounds, signs, or actions to exchange information or express thoughts. Communication skills affect your basic ability to understand others, establish positive relationships, and perform in most situations. Being able to communicate skillfully is essential to succeeding in a career.

Professional communication is communication associated with technology or business. It incorporates written, verbal, visual, and digital communication to provide factual information. Professional communication uses visuals, such as charts, design elements, and illustrations, to convey data. The language is simple and descriptive. It does *not* focus on creative writing techniques.

Written communication is recording words through writing to communicate. This may be done with pen and paper or a digital device, as shown in **Figure 18-4.** Written communication is used to record and convey information of varying levels of importance. It can have an enormous impact on how a business functions. In a business situation, your writing represents you and your company.

Professional writing requires use of Standard English. *Standard English* refers to English language usage that follows accepted rules for spelling, grammar, and punctuation. This is true of all documents, including digital communication. In a business situation, the use of texting language is not appropriate.

Reading is something many people take for granted. However, it is a learned skill. When reading skillfully, you get meaning from written words and symbols.

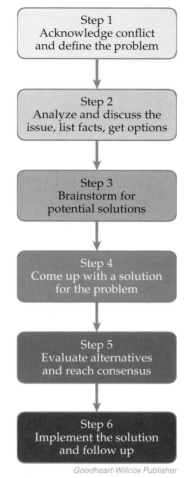

Goodheart-Willcox Publisher

Figure 18-3. Conflict-resolution skills are the skills required to resolve a situation in which a difference can lead to hostile conduct. Hostile conduct can include shouting and fighting.

Fizkes/Shutterstock.com

Figure 18-4. Writing may be done with a pen and paper or it may be done using a digital device such as a laptop computer.

At the same time, you evaluate the accuracy and validity of the words. *Active reading* is processing the words, phrases, and sentences you read. It is a complex task involving concentration. You must be involved and do something in response to the words. To actively read, you must:

- consider the writer's purpose for writing;
- consider your purpose for reading;
- relate what you read to your prior knowledge; and
- evaluate information both as you read and after you read to ensure understanding and form judgments.

Verbal communication is speaking words to communicate. It is also known as *oral communication*. Most people spend at least some portion of time talking with coworkers, supervisors, managers, or customers. This communication involves a variety of situations. There may be conversations about work tasks. You may need to ask and answer questions. Requests may be made verbally. Participating in meetings requires verbal communication. It is important to learn to speak fluently and with confidence.

Hearing is a physical process. *Listening* is an intellectual process that combines hearing with evaluating. In addition, listening often leads to follow up. Just because you can hear a person speak does not mean you are listening to what is said. When you *listen*, you make an effort to process what you *hear*. To process what you hear, consider why the person is speaking, relate what you already know, and show attention.

Few people would argue against the importance of listening. Yet, listening skills are often ignored. To develop listening skills takes time, patience, and practice. Children are expected to listen, but are not always taught to listen as they are taught to read, write, or speak. Listening skills are difficult to observe and measure. In most cases, listening is assumed. How effectively someone is listening is often unknown.

Customer service is an important part of many jobs. Communication skills are an important part of customer service. *Customer service* is the way a business interacts with its customers before, during, and after the sale of a product or

Case Study

Workplace Dress Code

Employee dress codes are constantly evolving. Suppose a company decides it wants to promote a more professional look. The company says it will continue to supply its signature red vests to its employees. Employees will be required, however, to wear button-down shirts and black pants with the vests. The cost for the new attire will be the employees' expense. Suggest a strategy employees should use to discuss conflict with management. Discuss the importance of employee participation or nonparticipation in a decision to change a dress code.

1. Why do you think a company would prefer a dress code?
2. When should the company pay for clothing required by a dress code? Justify your answer.

service. It may involve sending and receiving e-mail. This is written communication. Online chats, social media, and discussion boards are other examples where written communication is used. Verbal communication is used when speaking with a customer. This may be in person or on the phone, as shown in **Figure 18-5.** The ability to listen is important to verbal communication.

Professional Knowledge and Skills

Along with soft skills, professional knowledge and skills are needed to be effective in the workplace. Problem-solving and critical-thinking skills are needed in most any profession. Being aware of healthy and safe behaviors is also important in any career. Successful professionals are good managers of their time, tasks, and resources. In addition, good workers realize they are never really done learning. Continuing your education and staying current in your field will help you advance in your career.

There are some job-specific skills needed in the IT field. Skill in working with spreadsheets is needed. You should be able to enter data and create formulas. Also, know how to take data from one system to another. This is often done with a comma separated values (CSV) file format. Skill in using databases is also needed. This includes the abilities to create queries and reports. You should also be able to create and use relational tables. Skill in creating technical drawings is also useful. You should be able to sketch network layouts and flowcharts. Having knowledge of drawing software is helpful to create a permanent document from a sketch. Visio and draw.io are two common software applications used for drawing.

Luis Camargo/Shutterstock.com

Figure 18-5. Customer service is an important aspect of many careers. Good customer service reflects well on you as an employee and your employer.

Quick Look 18.1.2

CVS File Format

Excel can be used to work with comma separated values (CSV) files. The file can be opened directly in Excel, but a wizard is used to format the data.

1. Launch Windows Notepad or any other plain-text editor.
2. Add this text: First Name, Last Name, Title. Be sure to include the commas.
3. Press the [Enter] key to start a new line.
4. Enter a first name, last name, and a title for someone you know. You may choose to create a fictitious person. Be sure to include commas.
5. Continue adding names until there are five entries, as shown. Place each person on a new line.

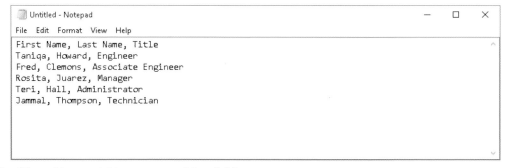

6. Save the file as Names.txt in your working folder.
7. Launch Microsoft Excel, and on the opening screen, click **Open Other Workbooks**.
8. On the next screen, click **Browse** to display the **Open** dialog box.

Quick Look 18.1.2 Continued

9. Navigate to your working folder, and change the file type to **All Files (*.*)**. This needs to be done so you can see the TXT file.

10. Select the **Names.txt file** you created, and click the **Open** button. A wizard is displayed to guide you through importing the CSV data.

11. On the first page of the wizard, click the **Delimited** radio button. The data in a CSV file are separated, or delimited, by commas.

12. Check the **My data has headers** check box. The first line in your text file is the header for the table. Click the **Next** button to continue.

13. On the next page of the wizard, check the **Comma** check box in the **Delimiters** area. Also, uncheck all other check boxes.

14. Click the **Finish** button. The CSV file is opened in Excel. To save the file as an Excel workbook, click **File>Save As**, and change the file type to the Excel format.

Mathematical Skills

Math skills are needed in everyday life. You will need to be able to estimate your purchases at a grocery store, calculate sales tax, or divide a lunch recipe between friends. Math skills are also important to most jobs. You may need to plan budgets or estimate time. Computer programmers must have a strong background in math. Some jobs require advanced math skills. For example, someone working in the financial sector needs to know how compound interest is calculated.

Many math functions can be performed on a calculator or with a computer program. However, it is still important to know how the calculations are done. You should be able to look at the answer and know if it is correct.

The job-specific math skills will vary from one job to the next. Some jobs may require skill in basic algebra, such as addition, subtraction, multiplication, and division. Other jobs may require skill in geometry. For example, an IT technician may need to calculate the square footage of a room to see if a wireless router will provide sufficient coverage. Converting between the US Customary and metric systems is also an important skill for some jobs. For example, networking cable may be sold by the meter. An IT technician needs to know how many feet are in a meter.

It is important to research the careers that interest you. Identify which math skills are needed for those careers. Then, be sure to develop strong skills in those areas.

Problem-Solving and Critical Thinking

Problem-solving is the process used to evaluate a situation and find a solution. Closely related to problem-solving is decision-making. *Decision-making* is the process of taking a course of action after weighing the benefits and costs of alternate actions. In this process, the outcome can be an action or opinion. Decision-making is a logical process that always ends up with a choice. There are five general steps to the decision-making process, as shown in **Figure 18-6.**

A clear idea of the problem first must be formulated in order to find the best approach. Then, potential solutions to the challenge should be listed and analyzed. After considering all potential solutions, the one that best fits the situation can be selected. The solution can be a single alternative or some blend of alternatives. Once a decision is made, it should be executed. After time has passed, the solution can be analyzed to determine if it was the correct course of action.

Decision-making and problem-solving involve critical-thinking skills. *Critical-thinking skills* provide the ability to make sound judgments. Critical-thinking skills involve being unbiased about the possibilities. Applying

Decision-Making Process

Goodheart-Willcox Publisher

Figure 18-6. Problem-solving is the process of choosing a course of action after assessing existing information and weighing the costs and benefits of different actions.

critical-thinking skills is an important part of problem-solving. You can also show critical-thinking and problem-solving skills by identifying resources that might help solve a problem.

Healthy and Safe Behaviors

Successful students and employees show healthy and safe behaviors. It is important to manage your personal health. You can do this by setting physical-fitness goals. Striving to eat unprocessed or minimally processed foods is another way to stay well. The following are some hints for keeping yourself well.

- Rest is crucial, as fatigue can keep you from being productive at school, at your job, or in your personal life.
- Hydration is necessary and can be accomplished by drinking water and limiting sugar and caffeine.
- Balanced meals are important, and excessive snacking should be avoided to keep your body healthy and your mind sharp instead of feeling hyperactive, sluggish, or distracted.

Ergonomics is the science concerned with placing things people use so they can safely interact with them. Applying ergonomic principles results in a healthy and safe environment. **Figure 18-7** identifies actions that can be taken to help prevent strain on a person's body.

Following safety rules is another vital skill for success. This includes following all instructor and company rules. You and your company must also adhere to any applicable OSHA regulations. The *Occupational Safety and Health Administration (OSHA)* is a federal agency that sets and enforces standards related to safe and healthy working conditions. It also provides training and assistance.

FYI

Proper physical fitness is a particular concern in the IT field. Many IT jobs involve little physical activity throughout the day. Take care to be physically fit.

Quick Look 18.1.3

OSHA

OSHA was established in 1970 with the Occupational Safety and Health Act of 1970. The agency covers most private-sector employees as well as public-sector employees.

1. Launch a web browser, and navigate to the Occupational Safety and Health Administration website (www.osha.gov).
2. In which federal department is OSHA?
3. How many regional offices does OSHA have?
4. Using the office locator, find the office nearest to your town or city.
5. Review other information on the site. How valuable do you feel this agency is to the welfare of workers in the United States?

Ergonomic Workstation

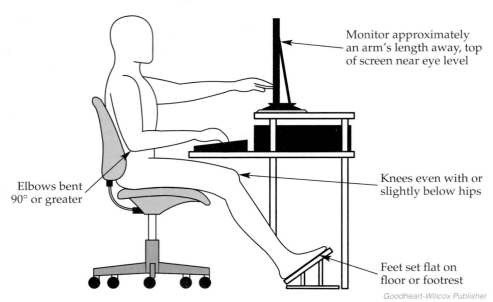

Monitor approximately an arm's length away, top of screen near eye level

Elbows bent 90° or greater

Knees even with or slightly below hips

Feet set flat on floor or footrest

Goodheart-Willcox Publisher

Figure 18-7. Ergonomics help prevent muscle pain and eyestrain caused by improper placement of screens, desks, and chairs.

Time, Task, and Resource Management

Good time-management skills are needed to be productive and accomplish your goals. *Time management* is the practice of organizing your time and tasks to be most efficient. Tasks must be prioritized by determining which ones should be completed before others. The difference between average and excellent students and workers is often not how hard they work, but how well they prioritize tasks. Creating a list of tasks to do each day is one simple way to manage your time. It is also important to schedule your lunch and breaks. Leaving your desk, even for just a few minutes, can help you relax and avoid feeling trapped. This can lead you to be more productive when you return to your desk.

Time-management skills help people meet goals and keep to schedules. Disruptions and unplanned events are inevitable, though. A customer may call you. A coworker may stop in to discuss a project. Time management helps balance these unscheduled events with other tasks demanding attention.

Resource-management skills are also important. Resources include items such as equipment and office supplies. Resources also include people and time. The strengths of each person should be identified. Then, put these strengths to best use. At the same time, a person's professional desires should be respected. Equipment should be maintained to ensure its efficiency. Balance the cost of maintenance with purchasing new equipment. When purchasing equipment, consider the environmental impact. Seek options that use natural resources in a sustainable way.

Job Acquisition and Advancement

Job-acquisition skills are those skills used to obtain employment, such as writing a résumé and filling out an application. These are vital as you move into the workplace. You will need to prepare to apply for a job. It will be necessary to create a résumé. A *résumé* is a document profiling your career goals, education, and work history, as shown in **Figure 18-8.** Write and format this document so it appears professional. It will be the first impression you make on an employer.

Robert Jefferies
123 Eastwood Terrace
Saratoga Springs, NY 60123
123-555-9715
rjefferies@e-mail.edu

OBJECTIVE
A mature and responsible high school senior seeks an entry-level job as an information technology assistant.

EXPERIENCE
Saratoga Computers
January 2019 to present
Retail Sales

- Assist customers with selection of computers and peripherals.
- Set up new purchases for customers.
- Train customers as needed on use of new purchases.
- Write repair tickets for customer devices.

JFK High School
August 2018 to June 2019
Computer Lab Assistant

- Performed maintenance on lab computers and peripherals.
- Installed new software and hardware as needed.
- Assisted students with using devices.

EDUCATION
JFK High School, Saratoga Springs, NY
Expected graduation date: June 2020
Relevant coursework: Computer Service and Repair (A+ certification)

HONORS, AWARDS, AND CERTIFICATIONS

- CompTIA A+ Certification
- JFK High School Honor Roll, eight quarters

Goodheart-Willcox Publisher

Figure 18-8. A résumé may present information in chronological order. The sections shown are standard, and employers expect to see this information.

An employer will screen all résumés it receives. If your résumé passes the screening process, you may be asked to interview. To prepare for a job interview, learn as much as you can about the position. Also, learn about the company. People in your network might be able to help you find this information.

Networking means talking with people you know and making new contacts. The more contacts you make, the greater your opportunities for finding career ideas. Talking with people you know can help you evaluate career opportunities. It also may lead to potential jobs. Many people use LinkedIn to create a professional network and look for career opportunities. As with all social media sites, take care in what you post.

In order to be successful in getting a job, it is vital to have the skills required to cooperate. It is also vital to have the technical skills necessary to complete the tasks. Obtaining certifications is one way to prove you have the requisite technical skills.

Getting a job is only the first step in building a career. As you gain experience, strive to advance in your career. *Promotion* is advancing to the next level in a company's hierarchy. Promotions must be earned. They are not automatically given. Identify what is needed to seek promotion. These steps include taking advantage of professional development opportunities, offering to take on extra assignments, and learning new skills. Show you can follow company rules. Prove you have the skills needed for the higher position. Demonstrate the soft skills required to work with coworkers.

Lifelong Learning

A good attitude about learning includes a sense of responsibility for your own education. Strive to be a lifelong learner. A *lifelong learner* looks for chances to acquire information throughout his or her life. This may be for personal or professional use. Some of your learning will come from formal schooling. Other learning will come from life experiences and a desire to improve your mind. You can always improve your professional skills to stay current in your field and promote personal progress.

Student Organizations

Career and technical student organizations (CTSOs) are national groups related to career and technical education (CTE) programs. These organizations have local chapters in many schools. There are many different CTSOs. However, most share the same general purposes and goals. Students in these groups have responsibilities that will benefit them in many ways. One of the biggest benefits of belonging to a CTSO is gaining leadership skills.

Purposes and Goals

CTSOs provide opportunities for personal growth and training for adult life. These groups can help prepare high school graduates for their next steps, whether they are going to college or a looking for a job. They provide opportunities for making choices and assuming duties. These groups inspire democracy through cooperation. They prepare students for many nontraditional roles in society. In addition, these groups promote understanding between youth and adults.

The main goal of CTSOs is to help students gain knowledge and skills in diverse career and technical areas. Other goals include promoting personal growth and leadership development. Another goal of these groups is to help students develop life skills. Life skills include character growth and ethical conduct. They also include creative and critical thinking. Social communication, applied knowledge, and job training are additional life skills CTSOs help students develop.

Benefits and Responsibilities

There are many benefits of student groups. These benefits include the development of leadership and other life skills. Social communication is another skill that CTSOs develop. CTSOs provide opportunities for school and community service, as shown in **Figure 18-9.** They help develop social connections and provide chances for practical learning.

CTSOs offer access to professional information. They also offer chances for career development. Often, professionals volunteer their time to CTSOs. This provides an opportunity to build a professional network. In your career, you can find these same benefits in professional groups. Other professional-development opportunities might include the following.

- completing a school or community project related to the field of study
- training in the field
- supporting a local or national philanthropic organization
- attending CTSO state meetings
- participating in leadership conferences

Competitive events are a main feature of most CTSOs. Contributing and competing are the key duties of membership in a student group. Competing in events allows students to show mastery of specific content. Events also measure the use of leadership skills. Members are responsible for displaying good conduct in all events related to the group. Students might receive awards for partaking in events. Scholarships might be given if the students win at state- and national-level competitions.

Rawpixel.com/Shutterstock.com

Figure 18-9. CTSOs provide students with opportunities to perform community service. Community service is a chance to demonstrate your interest in and caring for the community.

Leadership

CTSOs help students develop the skills needed to be good leaders. Honesty and competence are common characteristics of leaders. Other examples are reliability and poise. Communication and problem-solving skills are also characteristics of good leaders. The ability to set goals is a key behavior of a leader. Leaders also follow through on tasks. They are forward thinking. People who have leadership skills influence others. They have ideas and solutions for challenges. These people also set examples for conduct. You can show these skills through involvement in student group activities. These activities might include meetings, programs, and projects.

Quick Look 18.1.4

CTSOs

There are many CTSOs. Each has a focus in a particular area, such as agriculture, business, or trade skills. The NCC-CTSO is an organization that promotes CTSOs.

1. Launch a web browser, and navigate to the National Coordinating Council for Career and Technical Student Organizations website (www.ctsos.org).
2. How many CTSOs are listed on this website?
3. Select the link for one of the CTSOs that interests you.

Quick Look 18.1.4 Continued

4. What information is provided about the organization?
5. Click the link to navigate to the specific CTSO website. The link may be the logo for the CTSO.
6. Locate information about competitive events for the CTSO. Are there any events for cybersecurity?

SECTION REVIEW 18.1

Check Your Understanding

1. The personal skills used to communicate and work well with others are known as what?
2. How are ethics and morals different?
3. Identify the steps for successful decision-making.
4. What is the purpose of a résumé?
5. What type of national group is related to CTE and has local chapters in schools?

Build Your Key Terms Vocabulary

As you progress through this course, develop a personal cybersecurity glossary. This will help you build your vocabulary and prepare you for a career. Write a definition for each of the following terms, and add it to your cybersecurity glossary.

active reading

career and technical student
   organizations (CTSOs)

collaboration skills

conflict resolution

critical-thinking skills

customer service

decision-making

diversity awareness

ergonomics

ethics

etiquette

integrity

job-acquisition skills

leadership

lifelong learner

listening

morals

Occupational Safety and Health
   Administration (OSHA)

problem-solving

professional attire

professional communication

résumé

soft skills

teamwork

time management

verbal communication

work ethic

written communication

Understanding Industries

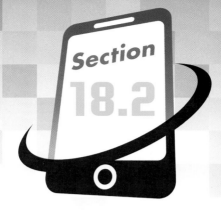

Having an understanding of the business or industry in which you work should help you be a better employee. Knowing how your company is structured is important. It is also important to understand how the company makes and carries out plans to meet its financial responsibilities. Managers in the company have many responsibilities, from maintaining good communication to ensuring employee rights, health, and safety. All businesses face issues. There are issues related to labor, such as the legal aspects of employment. There are also issues related to the community and the environment.

?Essential **Q**uestion

What importance should a business place on addressing community and environmental issues?

Key Terms 👉

budget
digital citizenship
discrimination
Fair Labor Standards Act (FLSA)

Form I-9 Employment Eligibility
   Verification
Form W-4 Employee's
   Withholding Allowance
   Certificate

green energy source
harassment
mission statement
organizational chart

Learning Goals

- Diagram the organizational structure of a business.
- Discuss labor, community, and environmental issues facing businesses.

Knowing the Workplace

The workplace is where your job activities and those of others take place. It can be a complex environment. There are rules and responsibilities to which everyone must adhere. Additionally, each company has its own culture. A business's *culture* is how those in the company think, feel, and act. This starts with the top managers and carries down to all employees. It is important to know how a workplace is organized. It is also important to understand how planning fits into the workplace. Managers have various responsibilities, both to the company and to its employees. The company as a whole has various financial responsibilities as well.

Organization

A business will have structure. It will be organized by different levels and departments. Some employees work in entry-level positions. Some employees are managers. Some employees focus on the overall business operations and goals. A large business will have many levels. However, even a small business will have some form of organization. A business organization should support the functions of a business.

An *organizational chart* shows the line of authority in a business. See **Figure 18-10.** Lines are used to show who reports to whom in the organization. This is known as the chain of command. Those at the top of the chain of command have a broader view of the business. Those lower in the chain of command focus on the specific tasks in a certain area of the business.

Planning

To plan is to set goals and decide how to meet them. A business will have a mission statement. A *mission statement* is a single sentence stating why the company exists. It is the most basic goal for a company. All other plans are made to fulfill the mission statement.

There are four basic types of plans for a business. A strategic plan focuses on the major goals of the company. It covers long-term goals. A tactical plan covers short-term goals that need to be met within a few weeks or months. An operational plan outlines what to do on a day-to-day basis. A contingency plan covers what to do if other plans do not work out. This is "plan B." The business-continuity plan discussed in Chapter 16 is a type of contingency plan.

Quick Look 18.2.1

Mission Statement

A mission statement is the foundation on which a business is built. Public companies often include the mission statement as part of the annual report.

1. Launch a web browser, and navigate to a search engine.
2. Search for a mission statement from a large corporation. For example, you may search cisco mission statement.
3. Read the mission statement. What does it tell you about the company?
4. Search for a mission statement from another corporation. Read the statement, and compare it to the previous statement you read. Are there similarities or differences?
5. Does your school have a mission statement? If so, does it reflect the values and goals of the students and staff?

Managerial Responsibilities

Management is making decisions about the business. There are three basic types of management. Top management is focused on the major goals and objectives of the company. Middle management is responsible for ensuring the direction set by top management is carried out. First-line management supervises the day-to-day activities of employees who are completing tasks to fulfill company objectives.

Among the many responsibilities of managers is setting norms in projects. Norms are what is and is not expected. This can be a broad category. For example,

Company Organizational Chart

Goodheart-Willcox Publisher

Figure 18-10. Organizational charts show channels of authority and reporting.

telling employees when it is okay to check personal cell phones is a norm. The proper times to take breaks and lunches are also norms.

Managers must also be aware of how employees interact. They must be able to recognize a monopolizer. A *monopolizer* is someone who requires more attention than others or who tries to control a group. Managers also need to recognize underachievers. An *underachiever* is someone who is capable of performing at a higher level.

Communication

A key function of management is to ensure open communication channels. This is true for both within the company and outside the company. There are various channels of communication. These include telephone, e-mail, social media, and intranets.

Businesses generally have policies for using e-mail, as well as disclaimers and other guidelines for sending e-mail correspondence. **Figure 18-11** shows an example of an e-mail completed in business style. Use Standard English. Always spell-check an e-mail before sending it. Also, include a subject line. The subject line allows the receiver to know what the message is about before opening it.

The COPY: line is for names of those who are receiving the information as secondary recipients. This line is sometimes called the CARBON COPY: or CC: line. Normally, a reply is not expected from those who are copied. You can opt to send blind copies (BCC). However, use this option sparingly. In most business situations, it is courteous to let the reader know all who are receiving the e-mail. For an e-mail sent to a large number of people outside of an organization, however, it is courteous to use the blind copy function to ensure the e-mail addresses of the recipients remain private.

Digital citizenship is the standard of proper conduct when using technology. Good digital citizenship focuses on using technology in a positive way. Companies use social media to build their personal brands, develop a community, and communicate with others. If you are representing your business on social media, professional etiquette is required. Most organizations have guidelines for posting information about the company. You are expected to follow proper writing and grammar and general rules of appropriateness. Careful consideration should be given to what is posted. Anything posted on the Internet creates a digital footprint. Online communication will never really go away.

As discussed in Chapter 9, an intranet is a private website for internal use. Many companies maintain an intranet as a way to provide information to their employees. Company notices can be posted on the intranet. For example, if there

FYI

Remember, you are in a professional environment, and your e-mail can be forwarded to others who might make judgments about what you have written.

- -

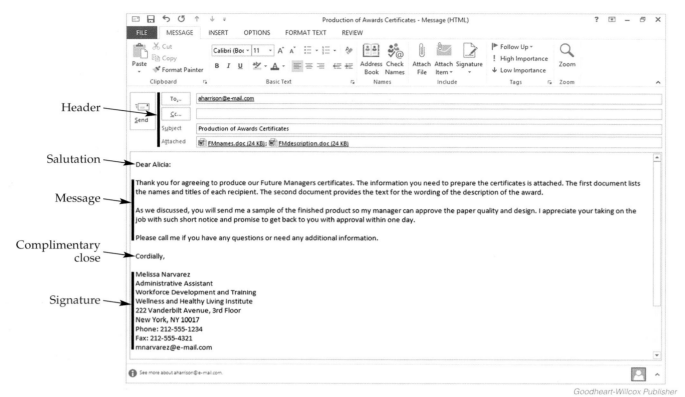

Goodheart-Willcox Publisher

Figure 18-11. When sending e-mail, use Standard English and properly format the e-mail. This shows professionalism and reflects positively on you and your company.

is an upcoming social event, such as a cookout, a reminder may be posted. The intranet can also be a place to communicate company policies. Often, human resource information, such as the company handbook, is placed on an intranet. This allows employees to access it at their convenience. Other information that may be communicated via the intranet includes company holidays, phone extensions, and resources for tasks such as templates or forms.

Employee Evaluations

An important part of a manager's job is evaluating the employees who report to him or her. Performance evaluations are key to career growth. Evaluations are a way to identify those who are excelling and should be promoted. They are also a way to identify employees who need to improve. Careful thought is required. The performance evaluation is very personal to the employee. It should be considered just as personal to the manager.

Most companies use a performance-rating sheet. The manager takes time to consider an employee's performance throughout the year when completing the sheet. A rating scale is typically used on the sheet. This may be a numerical scale, such as 1 to 5 or 1 to 10. Some companies may use a letter scale similar to grades in school. Other companies may use a simple exceeds-pass-fail system.

In the cybersecurity field, a performance evaluation may consider technical aspects of a person's job. Were security issues correctly identified? Were issues solved in a timely manner? However, as with all jobs, soft skills will be evaluated as well. Did the employee work well with others? Is the employee an effective communicator?

Some companies conduct performance evaluations on the anniversary of when an employee started. Other companies conduct all performance evaluations at the same time each year. The performance evaluation is also an opportunity to adjust an employee's wages. Some companies offer raises each year. However, this is not always the case. Most companies offer raises only when the employee has shown merit to justify an increase.

Employee Rights

In the United States, employees are guaranteed certain rights, as shown in **Figure 18-12.** For example, discrimination is illegal. *Discrimination* is treating a person differently due to race, gender, religion, national origin, disability, or age. In many cases, harassment is also illegal. *Harassment* is uninvited conduct toward a person based on a protected characteristic, such as race. This includes sexual harassment. Even when not specifically prohibited by law, harassment is inappropriate. Most companies have a written policy covering discrimination and harassment. Managers should ensure every employee understands the policy. Managers should also go over how to report violations.

Quick Look 18.2.2

Bullying

Harassment includes bullying. Many states have or are considering antibullying laws. In this activity, you will investigate antibullying laws.

1. Launch a web browser, and navigate to the Cyberbullying Research Center website (www.cyberbullying.org).
2. Click the **Laws** tab to display a map of the United States.
3. Hover the cursor over a state in the map. Does the state have criminal sanctions for bullying?
4. Click on your state to display detailed information.
5. What laws does your state have related to bullying?

Health and Safety

A key managerial responsibility is ensuring a safe and healthful working environment. However, maintaining a safe workplace is the joint responsibility of the employer and employee. Individuals should be aware of workplace safety for themselves, as well as for those with whom they work. Employers, schools, and other organizations are responsible for providing a safe environment for everyone on the premises. The employer makes sure the facility and working conditions are such that accidents are unlikely to occur. The employee uses common sense and care while at the office.

Managers should ensure all employees understand the hazards that exist in the workplace. Employees should understand what to do in case of a fire. Conducting fire drills is one way to help ensure this. IT technicians may be required to use ladders. Managers should provide training on the proper and safe use of ladders. IT technicians also work around electricity and electrical devices. Managers should discuss the dangers of working around electricity. Cover the proper safety equipment that must be used. Also cover the correct way to protect electrical equipment, such as wearing a ground strap.

FYI

OSHA is the governmental agency tasked with assuring safe and healthful working conditions for employees.

Financial Responsibility

A business has a financial responsibility. This includes earning money. Even a nonprofit organization has to earn money to cover its expenses. Completing a budget is a way to ensure financial responsibilities are met. A *budget* is a plan for projecting earnings and how they will be used.

Figure 18-12. The Equal Employment Opportunity Commission (EEOC) is responsible for enforcing federal laws that make it illegal to discriminate against a job applicant or an employee.

A chief financial officer (CFO) is the person responsible for a company's finances. Smaller companies may not have this specific position. However, there will be someone in the company responsible for finances. A small-business owner may have this responsibility along with many other responsibilities. A large corporation may have a vice president of finance above the CFO.

There are many aspects to financial responsibility. Making financial plans is one area. A budget is part of financial planning. Financial responsibility also extends to purchase orders, RMAs, accounts payable, and accounts receivable. A *purchase order (PO)* is an agreement to buy a specific product or service. It is a numbered document. The seller references the PO number when sending the bill to the company. A *return merchandise authorization (RMA)* is permission from a seller for a customer to return a product. The customer must reference the RMA number when sending the product back to the seller. The seller uses the RMA number to track the return process through accounting. Accounts payable is a list of businesses to who the company owes money. This is the money going out. Accounts receivable is a list of businesses who owe the company money. This is the money coming in.

Issues Facing Businesses

There are many aspects of business. There are the details of creating a product or providing a service. However, there are many issues beyond this. Businesses face labor issues, community issues, and environmental issues.

Labor Issues

Labor is the employees of a company. The Department of Labor (DOL) enforces workplace laws and regulations. Among the labor laws are laws covering fair wages and work hours.

Labor Laws

The *Fair Labor Standards Act (FLSA)* sets minimum wage, overtime, and minimum-age requirements for employees, as shown in **Figure 18-13.** Under the FLSA, there are two types of employees: exempt and nonexempt. These classifications are used for minimum wage and overtime purposes. An exempt employee is not legally entitled to overtime pay. These employees are paid a salary and perform exempt job duties as outlined by FLSA. There is also a minimum salary requirement. A salary is a wage paid for a period of time, such as per year. Nonexempt employees are paid on an hourly basis. An hourly wage is a set amount paid for each hour worked.

In addition to federal labor laws, each state has its own laws. Federal laws take precedence, but states can enact their own laws to supplement federal laws. Each state maintains a labor department. This agency enforces state laws and regulations related to labor issues.

Employment Agreements

As a condition of employment, an employee may be asked to sign certain agreements. An example is a nondisclosure agreement, which is discussed in Chapter 13. Similar agreements include nondisparagement, nonsolicitation, and noncompete. A nondisparagement agreement is a contract in which an employee agrees not to make negative statements about the company. This is often included as part of a severance package when an employee is terminated. A nonsolicitation agreement is a contract in which an employee agrees not to pursue the company's customers for business after he or she leaves the company. This agreement may also cover trying to get other employees to leave the company. A noncompete agreement is a contract in which an employee agrees not to work for a competing

FYI

The technical definition of an exempt employee is complex. For example, certain jobs are exempt even if the employee is paid hourly. Consult the Fair Labor Standards Act page on the Department of Labor website (www. dol.gov) for detailed information.

Goodheart-Willcox Publisher

Figure 18-13. Information regarding the Fair Labor Standards Act (FLSA) can be found on the Department of Labor website (www.dol.gov).

Ethical Issue

Employment Eligibility

Form I-9 Employment Eligibility Verification is used to verify a person's eligibility to work in the United States. The form has many questions. Among the questions, it asks if the person is a United States citizen, a noncitizen national, a lawful permanent resident, or an alien authorized to work until a specified date. Do you think this is a question a person should be required to answer in order to be employed? Why or why not?

The form clearly states it is illegal to discriminate against work-authorized individuals. It also states the employer cannot specify which of the allowed documents can be used for verification. Do you feel this statement will deter discrimination against somebody seeking employment? If not, what do you suggest to ensure no discrimination occurs?

business. This agreement may be in place while the employee is working for the company. However, it often extends for a period of time after the employee has left the company.

Employment will be offered on either a contractual or at-will basis. *Contractual employment* involves a document that specifies what the employee is guaranteed. A contract is often used for employment of temporary workers. In this case, the contract may specify when the employment will end. However, a company may enter into an employment contract with permanent employees. Executives often have contracts that guarantee them certain compensation even if their employment is terminated. Most people are employed on an *at-will* basis. This means there is no legal requirement the person remain employed by the company. The individual can leave whenever he or she chooses and for whatever reason. It also means the company can terminate the person whenever it chooses and without a reason. However, most states have what is called an *implied contract exemption*. The specific definition of this varies by state. In general, it means an employment contract exists even though there is not a written document. For example, if a company's handbook states an employee cannot be fired without cause, this could be seen as an implied contract.

Compensation guaranteed to someone after employment is terminated is often called a golden parachute. This is usually used in reference to someone guaranteed a very large sum of money.

Employment Documents

As part of beginning employment, you will need to fill out *Form W-4 Employee's Withholding Allowance Certificate.* This form gives the employer the information needed to withhold the appropriate tax from your paycheck. At the end of the year, the employer gives you Form W-2 Wage and Tax Statement. This form summarizes all of your wages and deductions for the year. It is used when filing income tax returns.

You will also need to complete *Form I-9 Employment Eligibility Verification,* as shown in **Figure 18-14.** This form is used to verify a person's identity. It is also used to confirm the person can legally work in the United States. Photo identification must be provided when completing this form. Commonly used are a valid driver's license, a state-issued ID, and a passport.

The human resources department will provide a variety of forms specific to the compensation package the employer offers. This often comes in the form of an offer of employment. The wages to be paid will be stated along with additional benefits. Benefits may include health insurance, retirement savings, and reimbursement for the cost of obtaining certification.

Employment Eligibility Verification

Department of Homeland Security

U.S. Citizenship and Immigration Services

**USCIS
Form I-9**

OMB No. 1615-0047

▶**START HERE.** Read instructions carefully before completing this form. The instructions must be available during completion of this form.

ANTI-DISCRIMINATION NOTICE. It is illegal to discriminate against work-authorized individuals. Employers **CANNOT** specify which document(s) they will accept from an employee. The refusal to hire an individual because the documentation presented has a future expiration date may also constitute illegal discrimination.

Section 1. Employee Information and Attestation *(Employees must complete and sign Section 1 of Form I-9 no later than the **first day of employment**, but not before accepting a job offer)*

Last Name *(Family Name)* | First Name (Given Name) | Middle Initial | Other Names Used *(if any)*

Address *(Street Number and Name)* | Apt. Number | City or Town | State | Zip Code

Date of Birth *(mm/dd/yyyy)* | U.S. Social Security Number | E-mail Address | Telephone Number

I am aware that federal law provides for imprisonment and/or fines for false statements or use of false documents in connection with the completion of this form.

I attest, under penalty of perjury, that I am (check one of the following):

☐ A citizen of the United States

☐ A noncitizen national of the United States *(See instructions)*

☐ A lawful permanent resident (Alien Registration Number/USCIS Number): _____

☐ An alien authorized to work until (expiration date, if applicable, mm/dd/yy) _____. Some aliens may write "NA" in this field.
(See instructions)

*For aliens authorized to work, provide your Alien Registration Number/USCIS Number **OR** Form I-94 Admission Number:*

Goodheart-Willcox Publisher

Figure 18-14. A new employee is required to complete Form I-9 to confirm his or her identity and eligibility to work in the United States.

Many companies offer group health insurance as a benefit. In some cases, the employer may pay the entire premium. However, more commonly the employer pays a portion of the premium. The employee must pay the remainder. Some companies also offer dental or vision insurance. Wellness programs that focus on preventative health care are also common.

Many companies also offer a retirement-savings plan. The 401K plan is the most common. In a 401K plan, the employee contributes a portion of his or her paycheck to the plan. This money is usually not taxed until it is taken out of the plan. In many cases, the employer will match the contribution. However, there is usually a limit to the employer match. There is also a maximum annual contribution amount. Another company-sponsored savings plan is ESOP. With an employee stock ownership plan (ESOP), the employer provides company stock as a benefit. In some plans, the employee can purchase additional stock. Like 401K, ESOP is a tax-deferred plan.

As discussed throughout this text, there are many certifications available in the IT field. Many employers will pay the cost of obtaining certification. In some cases, the employer will also pay for any education related to pursuing certification. The employer may pay the cost up front. However, more commonly, the employer reimburses the employee after he or she has obtained the certification. Certifications are usually only valid for a specific period of time. Other certifications may only be valid for a certain version of software. This is the case with many Microsoft certifications. An employer that pays for obtaining certification usually also pays for recertifying.

Quick Look 18.2.3

Form W-4

Every employee must fill out Form W-4 when starting a new job. This is just one of the forms you will need to complete as a new employee.

1. Launch a web browser, and navigate to the Internal Revenue Service website (www.irs.gov).
2. Locate the link for Form W-4. If you cannot find the link, use the site's search function.
3. Locate the current form, and open it. The form is a fillable PDF.
4. Complete the form using a fictitious person. Do not use any of your own personal information.
5. Save the form to your working folder.

Community Issues

Businesses have a responsibility to the communities they serve. This responsibility is not a legal one or based on profit. Instead, it is related to the good of the community. Giving back to the community helps the community prosper. Employees live in the community and benefit as well.

One way in which a business can help the community is by using local resources. If there is a local vendor, choose that over one located elsewhere. This helps the local vendor prosper. Family members of your company may be employed by the vendor. As the vendor prospers, so do they.

Another way a business can give back to the community is to encourage its employees to engage in volunteer work. The business may also provide supplies for its employees to use. For example, it may donate trash bags for a park cleanup day. The business may allow those volunteering to leave work early on the day of the event.

An employee can be involved in giving back to the community without the company being involved. For example, a member of the IT department may volunteer to teach computer skills to children in a park district workshop.

Environmental Issues

A business may face many environmental issues. Some of these may be legal. For example, there are certain laws that govern the use of chemicals and proper waste disposal. Manufacturing processes may produce toxic by-products. These must be handled in a legal manner.

Other environmental issues may be part of the corporate culture. A company may want to support environmentalism by choosing a green energy source. A *green energy source* is renewable. Renewable energy sources include wind, sunlight, plants, algae, biomass, tidal, and geothermal. Many power companies offer customers the option of purchasing green electricity. This is electricity generated from wind or solar sources, as shown in **Figure 18-15**.

The equipment commonly used in offices today is much more energy-efficient now than even just ten years ago. Upgrading to new equipment can save a business money in energy cost. However, using less energy is also environmentally friendly. Some businesses are replacing desktop computers with laptops. Laptops can be as much as 30 percent more energy-efficient than desktop computers. To get the most out of office equipment, turn off any equipment not in use. The IT department may establish a policy for shutting off computer equipment at night.

Photo by Kathy Eystad, USDA Agricultural Research Service

Figure 18-15. A properly sited wind turbine can provide clean electricity. The turbine shown here provides half of the annual electricity for the University of Minnesota-Morris.

Electronic equipment changes so quickly, it has become a throwaway item. However, electronic equipment should be properly recycled, not just placed in the trash. Electronic waste includes computers, cell phones, and batteries of all kinds. Before discarding electronic waste, research proper disposal of the item.

Out-of-use electronic equipment can also be donated. Often, charities and community groups in need of equipment can refurbish and use older equipment. Some charities accept these donations to reclaim the precious metals in the equipment. Electronic equipment may contain gold, silver, and platinum. Other valuable metals may include cobalt, aluminum, copper, and nickel. These are not the only metals found in some electronic equipment.

Remember, before donating or discarding storage media, properly destroy data on the device. This ensures recovery of the data is not possible.

FYI

In some states and municipalities, there is a legal requirement to recycle electronics.

Quick Look 18.2.4

Green Energy

There are many options for green energy, or clean energy. The Department of Energy maintains a website dedicated to providing information about energy.

1. Launch a web browser, and navigate to the Energy.gov website.
2. Using the menu or the site's search function, navigate to the Clean Energy page.
3. How many sources of clean energy are listed?
4. Read about each clean energy source. Which one do you feel is the best choice for your area?

SECTION REVIEW 18.2

Check Your Understanding

1. What are the four basic types of business plans?
2. What are the three basic types of management?
3. Which type of account represents the money coming into a business?
4. Compare and contrast how wages are paid between exempt and nonexempt employees.
5. Which employment document is used to verify a person's identity and eligibility for employment in the United States?

Build Your Key Terms Vocabulary

As you progress through this course, develop a personal cybersecurity glossary. This will help you build your vocabulary and prepare you for a career. Write a definition for each of the following terms, and add it to your cybersecurity glossary.

budget

digital citizenship

discrimination

Fair Labor Standards Act (FLSA)

Form I-9 Employment Eligibility Verification

Form W-4 Employee's Withholding Allowance Certificate

green energy source

harassment

mission statement

organizational chart

Review and Assessment

Summary

Section 18.1 Workplace Readiness

- There are many personal qualities and people skills necessary for the workplace, including acting morally, presenting themselves well, and respecting diversity as well as having teamwork and conflict-resolution skills, vision, and creativity.
- Professional knowledge and skills are needed for the workplace, including mathematical skills, problem-solving and critical-thinking skills, knowledge of healthy actions, safety skills, and the ability to manage time, tasks, and resources.
- CTSOs can prepare a student for a career by providing personal-growth opportunities and training for adult life and helping students gain knowledge and skills in diverse career and technical areas.

Section 18.2 Understanding Industries

- The workplace can be a complex environment, but understanding the organizational structure, planning, the responsibilities of management, and the financial responsibilities of the business can help a person be a better employee.
- Businesses face many issues, from labor issues, such as the legalities of employment, to community issues, such as helping the community prosper, and environmental issues, such as selecting green energy and proper disposal of electronic equipment.

Check Your Cybersecurity IQ ➦

Now that you have completed this chapter, see what you have learned about career skills by visiting the student companion website (www.g-wlearning.com) and taking the chapter posttest.

Review Questions ➦

For each question, select the answer that is the best response.

1. Being courteous is an example of _____.
   - A. etiquette
   - B. integrity
   - C. professional attire
   - D. work ethic

2. A special team has been formed to make changes to the dress code. The team consists of individuals from every department with varying positions, from assistants to managers. None of the younger employees in the company, however, has been included on this team. Which of the following may not be reflected by this team?
   - A. collaboration
   - B. diversity
   - C. leadership
   - D. teamwork

3. Which federal agency sets and enforces standards related to safe and healthy working conditions?
   - A. CTSO
   - B. OSHA
   - C. professional group
   - D. social group

4. A _____ is a document profiling a person's career goals, education, and work history.
   - A. lifelong learner's certificate
   - B. promotion
   - C. résumé
   - D. time-management log

5. This is a national organization with local school chapters.
   - A. CTSO
   - B. OSHA
   - C. professional group
   - D. social group

6. What is the purpose of an organizational chart?
   A. It describes how to act in the workplace.
   B. To identify first responders for incidents.
   C. It demonstrates a well-constructed mission statement.
   D. To show the line of authority in a business.

7. Which of the following means treating a person differently due to race, gender, religion, national origin, disability, or age?
   A. ethics
   B. diversity
   C. discrimination
   D. ergonomics

8. What is a plan for projecting earnings and how they will be used?
   A. business résumé
   B. budget
   C. accounts receivable
   D. CFO

9. Which of the following sets minimum wage, overtime, and minimum-age requirements for employees?
   A. Fair Labor Standards Act
   B. Form W-4
   C. Form I-9
   D. OSHA

10. What is a benefit of a business giving back to the community?
    A. It fulfills a legal requirement as outlined by the Fair Labor Standards Act.
    B. It is a way to provide employees with a retirement-savings plan.
    C. It helps the community prosper, and the company's employees benefit from this prosperity.
    D. It demonstrates proper ergonomics.

Application and Extension of Knowledge

1. Participate in a job shadow. Then, summarize some of the workplace behavior you experienced that is related to topics as addressed in this chapter. This may include dress, values, mission, and communication.

2. Identify a professional skill in which you are proficient. Write a paragraph explaining why you think you are proficient in this specific skill. After this paragraph, identify three soft skills that you are not proficient in, and identify one way to improve each skill.

3. Write a one- to two-page paper detailing why you joined a student organization. Highlight your interests and goals. What are your plans for pursuing a career?

4. Contact the human resource department in a local company. Explain that you are a student completing a school project, and ask for a blank copy of the company's employee evaluation form. Inquire about the rating scale or other system used to evaluate an employee's performance. Prepare a class presentation illustrating your findings.

5. There are many types of green or clean energy. Solar and wind are just two examples. Select one of these two sources, and investigate it. Locate a payback calculator. Sales literature often includes this type of information, or it may be available from the local power company. How long would it take your family to see a return on its investment in this clean energy source?

Research Project
Conflict Management

Conflict can be defined as a struggle between people with opposing needs, ideas, beliefs, or goals. The results of a conflict are not necessarily negative. In some cases, conflict can escalate and lead to unproductive results. In other cases, however, conflict can be resolved effectively and lead to a positive outcome. One of the goals of conflict management is to minimize the negative outcomes that conflicts in the workplace can cause. Your task is to conduct research on conflict management. What do you typically do when you disagree with others? Which conflict-management techniques seem the most effective to you? Discuss how you might be able to incorporate these into your next conflict. What have you learned that can help you in your career or personal life?

Deliverables. Create a one- to two-page report detailing various techniques for managing conflict. It should include a title page and be formatted following your school's style guidelines. You must cite multiple references. No Wikipedia references are allowed. Include a summary focusing on the negative aspects of conflict and the positive aspects of conflict management.

Online Activities

Complete the following activities, which will help you learn, practice, and expand your knowledge and skills.

Vocabulary. Practice vocabulary for this chapter using the e-flash cards, matching activity, and vocabulary game until you are able to recognize their meanings.

Communication Skills

College and Career Readiness

Reading. This chapter is about career readiness. After you read the chapter, identify and analyze the audience, purpose, and message of the author's writing.

Writing. The workplace requires employees to adapt to the diversity of the many individuals with whom they come in contact. The interactions can be in formal or informal situations. Make a list of potential barriers that can evolve. Write one paragraph for each barrier identifying possible solutions to eliminate the barrier.

Speaking. Acquiring a cybersecurity job requires an individual to be able to stay driven throughout a job search. Prepare a one- to two-minute speech you might deliver to a friend who is becoming discouraged during the search for a cybersecurity job. Deliver the speech to a peer, using note cards if needed. Practice correct diction and grammar.

Listening. Informative listening is the process of listening to gain specific information from a speaker. Interview a person who is responsible for customer service in a business or another organization. Ask this person to explain how etiquette is applied in his or her job. Make notes as the policies are described. Evaluate the speaker's point of view and reasoning. Select and organize key information the speaker shared. Did you listen closely enough to write accurate facts?

Portfolio Development

College and Career Readiness

Introduction. As you assemble your final portfolio, compose an introduction that gives an overall snapshot of who you are. This will be the first page of the portfolio that sets the stage for your presentation, so you want to make a good impression. Tell the reader who you are, your goals, and any relevant biographical information. You might want to highlight information by making references to sections or page numbers. There might be a website to direct the reader to that contains examples or documents of importance. In addition to the items you have already collected, there are some additional ones you might include:

- résumé;
- letters of recommendation;
- photos; and
- a table of contents.

CTSO Event Prep

Day of the Event. You have practiced all year for this CTSO competition, and now you are ready. Whether it is for an objective test, written test, report, or presentation, you have done your homework and are ready to shine. To prepare for the day of the event, complete the following activities.

1. Get plenty of sleep the night before the event so that you are rested and ready to go.

2. Use your event checklist before you go into the event so you do not forget any of the materials needed.

3. Find the room where the competition will take place, and arrive early. If you are late and the door is closed, you will be disqualified.

4. If you are making a presentation before a panel of judges, practice what you are going to say. State your name, your school, and any other information that will be requested. Be confident, smile, and make eye contact with the judges.

5. When the event is finished, thank the judges for their time.

ASCII Characters

This table shows the ASCII characters along with the binary and hex equivalents. Characters listed as UP are unprintable.

ASCII Character	Binary	Hex
UP	00000000	00
UP	00000001	01
UP	00000010	02
UP	00000011	03
UP	00000100	04
UP	00000101	05
UP	00000110	06
UP	00000111	07
UP	00001000	08
UP	00001001	09
UP	00001010	0A
UP	00001011	0B
UP	00001100	0C
UP	00001101	0D
UP	00001110	0E
UP	00001111	0F
UP	00010000	10
UP	00010001	11
UP	00010010	12
UP	00010011	13
UP	00010100	14
UP	00010101	15
UP	00010110	16
UP	00010111	17
UP	00011000	18
UP	00011001	19
UP	00011010	1A

ASCII Character	Binary	Hex
UP	00011011	1B
UP	00011100	1C
UP	00011101	1D
UP	00011110	1E
UP	00011111	1F
(space)	00100000	20
!	00100001	21
"	00100010	22
#	00100011	23
$	00100100	24
%	00100101	25
&	00100110	26
'	00100111	27
(	00101000	28
)	00101001	29
*	00101010	2A
+	00101011	2B
,	00101100	2C
-	00101101	2D
.	00101110	2E
/	00101111	2F
0	00110000	30
1	00110001	31
2	00110010	32
3	00110011	33
4	00110100	34
5	00110101	35

Continued

Continued

ASCII Character	Binary	Hex
6	00110110	36
7	00110111	37
8	00111000	38
9	00111001	39
:	00111010	3A
;	00111011	3B
<	00111100	3C
=	00111101	3D
>	00111110	3E
?	00111111	3F
@	01000000	40
A	01000001	41
B	01000010	42
C	01000011	43
D	01000100	44
E	01000101	45
F	01000110	46
G	01000111	47
H	01001000	48
I	01001001	49
J	01001010	4A
K	01001011	4B
L	01001100	4C
M	01001101	4D
N	01001110	4E
O	01001111	4F
P	01010000	50
Q	01010001	51
R	01010010	52
S	01010011	53
T	01010100	54
U	01010101	55
V	01010110	56
W	01010111	57
X	01011000	58

ASCII Character	Binary	Hex
Y	01011001	59
Z	01011010	5A
[	01011011	5B
\	01011100	5C
]	01011101	5D
^	01011110	5E
_	01011111	5F
`	01100000	60
a	01100001	61
b	01100010	62
c	01100011	63
d	01100100	64
e	01100101	65
f	01100110	66
g	01100111	67
h	01101000	68
i	01101001	69
j	01101010	6A
k	01101011	6B
l	01101100	6C
m	01101101	6D
n	01101110	6E
o	01101111	6F
p	01110000	70
q	01110001	71
r	01110010	72
s	01110011	73
t	01110100	74
u	01110101	75
v	01110110	76
w	01110111	77
x	01111000	78
y	01111001	79
z	01111010	7A
{	01111011	7B

Continued

Continued

ASCII Character	Binary	Hex
|	01111100	7C
}	01111101	7D
~	01111110	7E
UP	01111111	7F
€	10000000	80
UP	10000001	81
‚	10000010	82
ƒ	10000011	83
„	10000100	84
…	10000101	85
†	10000110	86
‡	10000111	87
ˆ	10001000	88
‰	10001001	89
Š	10001010	8A
‹	10001011	8B
Œ	10001100	8C
UP	10001101	8D
Ž	10001110	8E
UP	10001111	8F
UP	10010000	90
'	10010001	91
'	10010010	92
"	10010011	93
"	10010100	94
•	10010101	95
–	10010110	96
—	10010111	97
~	10011000	98
™	10011001	99
š	10011010	9A
›	10011011	9B
œ	10011100	9C
UP	10011101	9D
ž	10011110	9E

ASCII Character	Binary	Hex
Ÿ	10011111	9F
UP	10100000	A0
¡	10100001	A1
¢	10100010	A2
£	10100011	A3
¤	10100100	A4
¥	10100101	A5
¦	10100110	A6
§	10100111	A7
¨	10101000	A8
©	10101001	A9
ª	10101010	AA
«	10101011	AB
¬	10101100	AC
-	10101101	AD
®	10101110	AE
¯	10101111	AF
°	10110000	B0
±	10110001	B1
²	10110010	B2
³	10110011	B3
´	10110100	B4
µ	10110101	B5
¶	10110110	B6
·	10110111	B7
¸	10111000	B8
¹	10111001	B9
º	10111010	BA
»	10111011	BB
¼	10111100	BC
½	10111101	BD
¾	10111110	BE
¿	10111111	BF
À	11000000	C0
Á	11000001	C1

Continued

Continued

ASCII Character	Binary	Hex	ASCII Character	Binary	Hex
Â	11000010	C2	á	11100001	E1
Ã	11000011	C3	â	11100010	E2
Ä	11000100	C4	ã	11100011	E3
Å	11000101	C5	ä	11100100	E4
Æ	11000110	C6	å	11100101	E5
Ç	11000111	C7	æ	11100110	E6
È	11001000	C8	ç	11100111	E7
É	11001001	C9	è	11101000	E8
Ê	11001010	CA	é	11101001	E9
Ë	11001011	CB	ê	11101010	EA
Ì	11001100	CC	ë	11101011	EB
Í	11001101	CD	ì	11101100	EC
Î	11001110	CE	í	11101101	ED
Ï	11001111	CF	î	11101110	EE
Ð	11010000	D0	ï	11101111	EF
Ñ	11010001	D1	ð	11110000	F0
Ò	11010010	D2	ñ	11110001	F1
Ó	11010011	D3	ò	11110010	F2
Ô	11010100	D4	ó	11110011	F3
Õ	11010101	D5	ô	11110100	F4
Ö	11010110	D6	õ	11110101	F5
×	11010111	D7	ö	11110110	F6
Ø	11011000	D8	÷	11110111	F7
Ù	11011001	D9	ø	11111000	F8
Ú	11011010	DA	ù	11111001	F9
Û	11011011	DB	ú	11111010	FA
Ü	11011100	DC	û	11111011	FB
Ý	11011101	DD	ü	11111100	FC
Þ	11011110	DE	ý	11111101	FD
ß	11011111	DF	þ	11111110	FE
à	11100000	E0	ÿ	11111111	FF

Continued

Note: The number in parentheses following each definition indicates the chapter in which the term can be found.

A

acceptable use policy (AUP). Document created by the owner of the network containing information on proper usage of the network and related assets. (5)

access point (AP). Device that provides a central point of access to enable wireless devices to communicate with each other. (10)

Active Directory. Database of the network resources on a Microsoft network. (3)

active information gathering. Actions are taken that may be noticed by the target. (13)

active reading. Processing the words, phrases, and sentences you read. (18)

address resolution protocol (ARP). Handles the process of locating MAC addresses associated with a specific IP address. (9)

Advanced Encryption Standard (AES). Symmetric encryption standard, requires 128-, 192-, and 256-bit keys; also called *Rijndael encryption.* (11)

adware. Software installed on a computer that collects data on the user and then redirects advertising sites to the web browser. (2)

after-action report. Identifies what worked well in correcting an incident and where problems arose. (16)

agile model. Systems development life cycle in which everyone stays involved in the process through all stages. (12)

alias. A replacement way to enter a command. (4)

alternate data stream (ADS). Data-hiding technique in which data are inserted behind another file. (17)

American Standard Coded Information Interchange (ASCII). Set of 128 characters and symbols and numerical equivalents for each (0–127). (17)

ANDing. Process of comparing two binary digits and creating a value based on the comparison. (8)

annual loss expectancy (ALE.) Amount of value anticipated to be lost from one type of incident in one year. (15)

annual rate of occurrence (ARO). Number of times an incident happens in one year. (15)

ANT. Personal area technology similar to Bluetooth that allows devices to communicate with each other wirelessly over short distances using low-bit, low-power transmissions of small packets. (10)

Apache. Open-source web-server software for Linux machines. (12)

append. To add to an existing data set. (4)

application cell. An individual virtual machine; also called a *container.* (1)

application programming interface (API). Allows a program to share functionality with other modules, such as products or services in other programs. (12)

archive bit. Flag that when turned on indicates the file is new or changed and needs to be backed up; also called *A bit.* (16)

armored virus. Malware designed to prevent security analysts from reading the source code by attempting to prevent access to or disassembly of the code itself. (2)

ARP poisoning. Man-in-the-middle attack in which a hacker intercepts an ARP request and changes its reply to point the victim to the hacker's computer, not the real computer; also called *ARP spoofing.* (9)

asset. Something that has value. (15)

asset tag. Provides information about the device, such as the owner of the equipment and any other relevant information. (6)

asymmetric encryption. Uses two keys, a public key and a private key, to encrypt and decrypt data. (11)

attack surface. All points or areas in a system that could be used or compromised to allow hackers entry into the system. (2, 3, 6)

attack vector. The avenue or path a hacker uses to commit an attack. (1)

attenuation. Weakening of a signal over distance from the data source. (10)

auditing. Process of tracking the actions of an individual using a resource. (6)

authentication. Process of validating a user. (3)

authenticator. Access point in the WLAN. (10)

authoritative DNS server. Controls the records in the DNS database. (9)

B

backdoor. A secret or unknown access point of entry into a system. (2)

banner grabbing. Used to determine what services are running on a remote system. (13)

baseline. Starting point from which comparisons can be made. (6)

basic service set (BSS). Wireless network with a single access point. (10)

batch file. Single file in which a command, series of commands, or set of instructions to be processed in sequence is listed. (4)

Bcrypt. Cipher based on the Blowfish block cipher with a nonce added to the password. (11)

behavioral biometrics. Authentication method identifying measurable patterns in human activities. (3)

biometrics. Authentication method using measurement and analysis of a biological feature. (3)

BitLocker. Software in the Microsoft Windows operating system that encrypts data to protect against attacks and theft. (7)

black box test. Pen test in which the tester has no knowledge of the system. (13)

black listing. MAC addresses not allowed to connect to the network are filtered out. (10)

black-hat hacker. Hacker usually operating outside the law. (1)

block cipher. Encrypts chunks, or blocks, of data in a fixed size, usually of 64 or 128 bits, at one time. (11)

Blowfish encryption. Block cipher in which only 64 blocks of data are encrypted at a time; free symmetric encryption standard. (11)

Bluejacking. Sending an unsolicited message via Bluetooth, such as an advertisement. (10)

Bluesnarfing. Hacker exploits the Bluetooth connection to steal data from a Bluetooth-enabled device. (10)

bollard. Vertical cylinder permanently installed to prevent vehicles from passing; may be retractable to either allow or deny passage. (5)

botnet. Loosely connected network of infected computers that are being managed by an unknown host. (6)

bring your own device (BYOD). A strategy that allows employees, partners, and others to use their personal devices, such as tablets and smartphones, to conduct business and connect to an organization's networks. (7)

brute force attack. Attack in which the password-cracking software tries every possible keystroke in every possible position. (11)

budget. Plan for projecting earnings and how they will be used. (18)

buffer-overflow attack. Hacker exploits a programming flaw in which more data can be entered than the program can accept and the extra data are written to memory outside of the buffer. (12)

bug-bounty program. Initiative by a vendor that offers rewards for finding flaws and vulnerabilities found in its software. (1)

business-continuity plan (BCP). Provides the steps needed to keep a business operational after an incident. (16)

business-impact analysis (BIA). Determines the potential effects of an event that disrupts critical business operations. (16)

C

cantenna. Homemade device constructed from open-ended metal can and used to amplify Wi-Fi signals. (10)

captive portal. Web page that the user is forced to view before being granted further network access. (10)

career and technical student organizations (CTSOs). National groups to related career and technical education (CTE) programs. (18)

cell. Coverage area provided by the base station in a cellular network. (10)

cellular network. Type of wireless network in which transmissions are distributed over groups of geographic areas. (10)

censorship. Act of limiting access to information or removing information to prevent it from being seen. (10)

certificate authority (CA). Trusted third-party source that issues digital certificates. (11)

certificate chaining. Linking of one digital certificate to another. (11)

certificate-signing request (CSR). Sent to the certificate authority by an organization wishing to apply for a digital certificate and includes its public key. (11)

Certification Revocation List (CRL). Contains all digital certificates that have been canceled. (11)

Certified Computer Examiner (CCE). Vendor-neutral certification from the International Society of Forensic Computer Examiners that focuses on knowledge and practical examination skills. (17)

Certified Ethical Hacker (CEH). Professional certification from the EC-Council testing the ability to conduct, analyze, and assess the security of a system. (13)

Certified Forensic Computer Examiner (CFCE). Vendor-neutral certification from the International Association of Computer Investigative Specialists (IACIS) that consists of a peer review, an objective test, and a practical test. (17)

Certified Hacking Forensics Investigator (CHFI). Professional certification from the EC-Council demonstrating knowledge of properly extracting evidence from data gathering and ensuring this evidence can be submitted in a court of law. (13)

Certified Information Systems Security Professional (CISSP). Certification for those with strong managerial background and technical expertise. (1)

Certified Security Analyst (ECSA). Professional certification measuring the ability to incorporate testing methodologies in a variety of tests. (13)

chain of custody. Log that identifies the case, the evidence, and when and who accessed the evidence. (17)

Challenge Handshake Authentication Protocol (CHAP). Protocol in which the server sends a challenge to the client after the client establishes a connection to the server. (9)

change-management system. A means of documenting issues and their solutions. (6)

choose your own device (CYOD). Employees can connect a mobile device that has been approved for connection to the network. (7)

CIA triad. The three underlying principles of data protection: confidentiality, integrity, and availability. (2)

cipher. Mathematical algorithm used to change normal, or plain, text into something that is unreadable and then back into readable text. (11)

ciphertext. Encoded or encrypted text. (11)

Clarifying Lawful Overseas Use of Data (CLOUD) Act. Allows federal law enforcement to compel any United States–based service provider to turn over requested data stored from any location. (14)

Classless Internet Domain Resolution (CIDR). A way to represent IP subnet mask addresses in compressed form. (8)

clickjacking. User is tricked into clicking a concealed link. (12)

client-side script. Script in a web page that runs on the client's computer. (12)

closed-circuit television (CCTV). System in which video cameras transmit signals to a centralized monitoring location, but the signals are not publically broadcast; also known as *video surveillance.* (5)

cloud computing. Use of resources running from a remote location instead of located locally at a business or home. (14)

cloud-deployment model. Describes how the cloud environment is created and operated. (14)

cluster network. Grid computing. (14)

cmdlet. A program inside PowerShell. (4)

code repository. Location where code is stored. (12)

code signature. Digital signature placed on the code to verify its authenticity and integrity. (12)

cold site. Location that provides the office space needed to move operations, but contains no equipment. (16)

collaboration skills. Behaviors for working with others. (18)

command prompt. Command-line interface for manually entering commands in a Windows computer. (4)

command-language interpreter (CLI). Executes the commands from direct keyboard entry or a program. (4)

Common Vulnerabilities and Exposures (CVE). Centralized location for listing and uniformly identifying publically known cybersecurity vulnerabilities. (15)

community cloud. Shared by everyone within affiliated organizations, but is not available to anyone outside of these organizations. (14)

company owned, personal enabled (COPE). Company purchases and issues mobile devices for employee use and connection to work and personal resources. (7)

compiler. Function that takes the code the programmer writes and converts it into machine language. (12)

compliance. Following the rules or standards that have been established. (2)

CompTIA Advanced Security Practitioner (CASP). Focuses on critical thinking, incident response, risk management, and technical integration throughout business. (1)

CompTIA Cybersecurity Analyst (CySA+). Focuses on the skills to assess, combat, and prevent security threats. (1, 13)

CompTIA Security+. The entry-level certification for computer security; focuses on the major aspects of security in a business. (1)

Computer Analysis Response Team (CART). Permanent team of trained specialists within the FBI for conducting computer forensics. (17)

computer forensics. Using scientific methods to uncover and determine digital evidence on a multitude of computing devices. (13, 17)

Computer Fraud and Abuse Act (CFAA). Law dealing with unauthorized access of computers. (2)

computer incident response team (CIRT). Employees designated as first responders; also called *computer security incident response team (CSIRT).* (17)

computer security incident response team (CSIRT). Employees designated as first responders; also called *computer incident response team (CIRT).* (17)

confidentiality. The condition of being private or secret. (2)

conflict resolution. Process of resolving disputes. (18)

container. An individual virtual machine; also called an *application cell.* (1)

cookie policy. Statement of if the site uses cookies and, if so, how. (2)

credentialed scan. Scanner uses appropriate authentication to provide accurate and comprehensive feedback. (6)

critical infrastructure. Physical or virtual assets that are vital to the health and safety of citizens. (7)

critical-thinking skills. Provide the ability to make sound judgments. (18)

crossover error rate (CER). Point where the false acceptance rate and false rejection rate are equal. (3)

cross-site request forgery (CSRF). Attack that takes advantage of the trust relationship between a website and the client's browser to run malicious commands. (12)

cross-site scripting (XSS) attack. Hacker is able to inject client-side scripts into web pages that are viewed by other people. (12)

cryptanalysis. Process used to discover vulnerabilities in ciphers. (11)

cryptogram. An encoded message as a whole. (11)

cryptographic salt. Random value that can be applied to the algorithm to make the resulting hash unique; also called *cryptographic nonce*. (11)

cryptology. Study of ciphers and ciphertext. (11)

cryptomalware. Malware that encrypts the user's data; also called ransomware. (2)

current directory. The directory that is active. (4)

customer service. The way a business interacts with its customers before, during, and after the sale of a product or service. (18)

CVE numbering authorities (CNAs). Organizations that have been authorized by MITRE to assign CVE IDs to vulnerabilities that may affect their products. (15)

cyberattack. Attempt to steal, damage, or destroy data or a computer system. (1)

cyber range. Virtual environment used to train for cyberwarfare and malicious hacks. (13)

Cyber Security Forensic Analyst (CSFA). Vendor-neutral certification from the Cybersecurity Institute focused on advanced forensic skills; considered a top-level certification for computer forensics. (17)

cybersecurity. Process of protecting a system against unintended or malicious changes or use. (1)

cyclical redundancy check (CRC). Error-checking of the frame. (8)

D

daemon. A service on a Linux host. (6)

darknet. Part of the Internet not easily accessible to the average user; also called the *dark web*. (1)

data backup. Process of copying data from one location and to a separate medium. (16)

database. Organized collection of data. (12)

database management system (DBMS). Software that provides the interface and functionality for working with a database. (12)

data canary. A known value placed at the end of the assigned buffer space; if this value remains the same, a buffer overflow has not occurred. (12)

data center. Facility specifically designed to store and manage vast quantities of data; considerably larger than a server room. (5)

Data Encryption Standard (DES). Symmetric encryption that requires keys to be 56 bits in length; offers 70 quadrillion possible combinations. (11)

data leakage. When data are intercepted and stolen from a wireless network. (10)

data loss prevention (DLP). Strategy for ensuring data are not accidentally or intentionally exposed outside of the organization. (15)

data sovereignty. Concept that digital data are subject to the jurisdiction and laws of the country where the storage device is located. (14)

dead code. Programs that are no longer maintained or, in some cases, even used in any fashion. (12)

dead spot. Place where there is no Wi-Fi coverage from a nearby cell. (10)

decision-making. Process of taking a course of action after weighing the benefits and costs of alternate actions. (18)

deep web. Part of the Internet that includes resources not found with a typical search engine. (1)

de facto standard. One that is generally accepted over time and adopted for use, but not required. (8)

defense in depth. Having multiple levels of protection. (2)

degaussing. Removing or neutralizing the magnetic property. (16)

demilitarized zone (DMZ). Segment of a network that allows some public access and borders the private network where the public access is blocked; also called *screened subnet* or *perimeter network*. (9)

denial of service (DoS) attack. Hack against the availability of data by flooding the victim with numerous and continual packets. (8)

device driver. Software program that instructs a piece of hardware how to operate. (4)

DevOps. Business philosophy that encourages collaboration between developers, managers, and other IT and operational staff from development through production and support of software. (12)

dictionary attack. Attack in which password-cracking software uses a list of words and their precomputed hash values to determine a password. (11)

differential backup. Only the files that have changed or been created since the last full backup are copied. (16)

digital certificate. Digital file used to verify that the public key belongs specifically to a person or entity. (11)

digital citizenship. Standard of proper conduct when using technology. (18)

digital footprint. Information about a person left behind by his or her actions on the Internet. (2)

digital signature. Computed value used to validate the sender of a digital file. (11)

directory. Storage location for files and other directories. (4)

directory traversal. Hacker is able to get beyond the web server's root directory and execute commands. (12)

disassociation. When a signal deactivates the user from the access point. (10)

disaster-recovery plan (DRP). Steps needed to restore services after an incident. (16)

Discretionary Access Control (DAC). Security strategy in which a user can be granted additional rights to data beyond what is allowed by his or her assigned access level. (3)

discrimination. Treating a person differently due to race, gender, religion, national origin, disability, or age; is illegal. (18)

disk mirroring. RAID 1 system in which data on one disk drive are automatically written to a second drive. (16)

disk striping. RAID 0 system in which data are written simultaneously across two or more drives for increased performance. (16)

disk striping with parity. RAID 5 system that utilizes disk striping and adds a special parity bit to reconstruct data missing from a single drive failure. (16)

distributed denial of service (DDoS) attack. Many hosts are contributing in a DoS attack. (8)

distributed-trust model. The workload of signing certificates is distributed among several intermediate certificate authorities. (11)

distro. A specific version of Linux; short for *distribution*. (4)

diversity awareness. Ability to embrace the unique traits of others. (18)

DNS local cache. Temporary storage location on the local computer that allows the client to resolve the name to the IP address from locally stored data. (9)

DNS poisoning. An entry is embedded in the victim's local DNS cache that redirects a legitimate URL to an incorrect IP address. (5, 9)

DNS Security Extensions (DNSSEC). Security measure in which authorized DNS servers digitally sign certificates to validate their authenticity. (9)

Domain Name System (DNS). Network service that resolves names on a network to their IP addresses. (9)

dongle. Physical token inserted into a computer's USB port. (3)

drive encryption. Renders data unreadable without the encryption key to unlock it. (7)

drive-by-download. Ransomware automatically downloaded when a user visits a web page that is infected. (2)

dumpster diving. Digging through trash for useful information. (2)

dynamic analysis. Extensive testing process in which a program is tested for all types of actions; also called *fuzzing*. (12)

dynamic frequency selection (DFS). Detects interference with military and weather radar and automatically shifts the frequency being used by the wireless device. (10)

E

Easter egg. Feature or message intentionally placed inside computer code. (12)

electromagnetic radiation (EMR). Electromagnetic signals given off by all electronic equipment. (5)

Electronic Communication Privacy Act (ECPA). Law protecting wire and electronic transmissions of data. (2)

Electronic Data Gathering Analysis and Retrieval System (EDGAR). Database found on the United States Security and Exchange Commission (SEC) website for electronic SEC filings. (13)

electronic health record (EHR). Digital or electronic platform for health records. (2)

embedded operating system. Provides only the functionality needed to run a specific hardware configuration. (7)

EMI shielding. Barrier placed around wires to block electromagnetic interference from affecting the electrical signals in the wires. (5)

Encrypting File System (EFS). Built-in feature of Windows that encrypts selected files or folders. (11)

enterprise Wi-Fi. Users are authenticated for wireless access through their network login names and passwords instead of being given a passphrase. (10)

enumeration. Process of extracting information, such as user and computer names, running services, and permissions. (13)

ergonomics. Science concerned with placing things people use so they can safely interact with them. (18)

ethical hacking. Penetration testing used to identify vulnerabilities in a system. (13)

ethics. Rules of behavior based on a group's ideas about what is right and wrong. (18)

etiquette. The art of using good manners in any situation. (18)

event logging. A function of the operating system or an application that records events or situations in a file. (6)

evil twin router. Carries the same SSID as the legitimate server, but is in a different ESS. (10)

executive summary. In a pen-testing report, states in plain language the high-value targets that were identified and the impact breaches of these targets will have. (13)

explicit permissions. Those a user is given at a specific location, such as a folder or a file. (3)

extended service set (ESS). Wireless network with multiple access points. (10)

Extensible Authentication Protocol (EAP). Needed to transport additional authentication data; a framework for transporting protocols, *not* the actual authentication protocol itself. (9)

extranet. Extension of an intranet that allows specific third-party users access to the secured intranet. (9)

F

failover cluster. Servers are grouped with physical connections to increase the availability and scalability of resources. (16)

Fair Labor Standards Act (FLSA). Sets minimum wage, overtime, and minimum-age requirements for employees. (18)

false acceptance rate (FAR). Ratio of the number of false *acceptances* divided by the number of identification attempts. (3)

false negative. Something not identified as harmful when it really is. (6)

false positive. Something identified as harmful when it really is not. (6)

false rejection rate (FRR). Ratio of the number of false *rejections* divided by the number of identification attempts. (3)

Faraday shielding bag. Antistatic container. (17)

fault tolerance. Allows for the possibility of a failure of a system by having a solution that immediately protects the system while minimizing downtime. (16)

Federal Information Security Modernization Act (FISMA). Requires federal agencies to develop, document, and implement information security safeguards. (17)

federated identity management (FID). Allows semi-independent systems to work together so users of one system can access resources from another system. (3)

field. Columns in a database that contain data about one aspect of the table. (12)

field value. Specific information in a database. (12)

file signature. Data used to identify or verify what the file contains. (17)

Fire Transfer Protocol/SSL (FTPS). Secure method of transferring data using the SSL protocol. (8)

fire class. The type of fire based on the fuel that feeds the fire. (5)

firewall. Security tool that acts as a barrier or protection against an unwanted data transfer. (6)

firmware. Software embedded on hardware devices to control the system. (2, 7)

first responders. Individuals who react to incidents. (17)

flood guard. Can drop the packets or apply filters in place on switches or routers if a denial of service attack is detected (8)

forked. A program that has been modified to create a new development branch as a separate program. (4)

Form I-9 Employment Eligibility Verification. Used to verify a person's identity and to confirm the person can legally work in the United States. (18)

Form W-4 Employee's Withholding Allowance Certificate. Gives the employer the information needed to withhold the appropriate tax from your paycheck. (18)

frameworks. Help break down the aspects of a business and security domains into manageable task areas and tasks to organize protection against cybersecurity threats. (2)

free and open source software (FOSS). Software whose source code is not locked and can be modified by anyone. (4)

full backup. Copy of all files. (16)

fuzzing. Extensive testing process in which a program is tested for all types of actions; also called *dynamic analysis.* (12)

G

generator. Device that creates electricity. (16)

geotagging. Process of identifying a person's location by tagging documents, such as photographs or videos, with GPS data. (7)

GIAC Certified Forensic Examiner (GCFE). Windows-based certification from the Global Information Assurance Certification (GIAC) that focuses on skills for collecting and analyzing data. (17)

GIAC Penetration Tester (GPEN). Professional certification demonstrating skill in pen testing methods, conducting pen tests, and understanding legal issues related to pen testing. (13)

global unicast address. Public IPv6 address; packets with global unicast addresses can be routed and sent on the Internet. (8)

Gramm-Leach-Bliley Act (GLBA). Law ensuring financial businesses protect consumer's private data.

gray box test. Pen test in which the tester has some knowledge of the system. (13)

gray-hat hacker. Hacker whose actions fall somewhere between white hat and black hat. (1)

green energy source. Renewable energy source. (18)

grid computing. Using resources from multiple computers to spread out a workload; also called a *cluster network*. (14)

group policy. Policies set on computers and users that control system privileges. (6)

H

hacker. A person who engages in hacking. (1)

hacking. The act of circumventing or breaking past security boundaries. (1)

hacktivisim. Actions of individuals motivated by ideals or personal beliefs targeting and harming companies or individuals with whom the hackers have a fundamental disagreement. (1)

harassment. Uninvited conduct toward a person based on a protected characteristic, such as race; always inappropriate and may be illegal. (18)

hardening. Closing or locking down any unnecessary paths on an operating system that can be used for unapproved access. (3, 6)

hard link. Points directly to the original data. (4)

hash-based message authentication code (HMAC). Provides the server and client with the same private key that is not used anywhere else; includes authentication function based on a secret key. (11)

hashing. Mathematical function that creates a value based on the data; is a one-way process uniquely identifying data. (11)

hash table. Contains cracked passwords with preconstructed hashes for every password entered into the table. (11)

head crash. The read-write head of the drive comes into physical contact with the drive's platters. (15)

Health Insurance Portability and Accounting Act (HIPAA). Law protecting electronic medical records and personal health information. (2)

heuristic methodology. An approach to finding previously undetected unwanted programs or variants of known viruses through a learning approach. (2)

hexadecimal numbering system. Base 16 numbering system, which uses 16 characters (0–9, A–F) to represent numbers. (17)

hex editor. Software that reveals the raw binary data within a file. (17)

hierarchical-trust model. Model in which there is just one master certificate authority, which is known as the root, that signs all digital certificates it issues. (11)

home directory. Where personal files are stored in Linux. (4)

honeynet. Decoy network consisting of two or more honeypots. (9)

honeypot. Decoy server set up to attract hackers. (9)

host operating system. The operating system located on the physical machine. (1)

hot and cold aisles. Technique in which server racks are placed in rows with cold air entering the room on one side and hot air exiting the room on the other side. (5)

hot site. Duplicate of the currently working site. (16)

hybrid cloud. Uses features from public, private, or community clouds. (14)

hybrid encryption. Form of encryption that merges symmetric and asymmetric encryption. (11)

Hypertext Markup Language (HTML). Format used by the web to exchange information. (12)

Hypertext Transfer Protocol (HTTP). Protocol that allows all the hosts to exchange information across the web. (12)

Hyper-V. Virtualization platform developed by Microsoft for its servers and desktops. (1)

hypervisor. Specific software that handles the responsibilities of running a virtual machine; also called *virtual machine monitor (VMM)*. (1)

I

immutable server. Server configuration is made from the baseline, not by directly configuring a live production server. (12)

implicit permissions. Those a user receives through another object, such as a group. (3)

incident response (IR). Acting against and recovering from a specific issue. (17)

incident-response plan (IRP). Written document that provides instructions to be followed when an incident occurs. (17)

incremental backup. Only the files that have changed or been created since the last backup are copied. (16)

infrastructure as a service (IaaS). Cloud-computing solution where the vendor provides the customer with virtualized computing resources over the Internet. (14)

infrastructure as code. DevOps model in which the operations team uses a system starting point as a baseline, and then creates scripts that will make configuration changes from the baseline. (12)

inherited permissions. Those a user receives by default at a lower level. (3)

initialization vector (IV). Random information added to the key every time there is a wireless transmission. (10)

initial sequence number (ISN). Random number between 0 and 4,294,967,295 used as part of the transmission process to manage packets within a transmission session. (8)

injection attack. Malicious code inserted into a web application to cause an unexpected outcome. (12)

inode number. Corresponds to the location of the file's contents (the data in the file); the file name *links* to the inode number. (4)

input validation. Safeguards implemented to control the type or amount of data entered into an input field. (12)

integrity. The state of data being complete or uncorrupted; also the honesty of a person's actions. (2, 18)

intellectual property. Work that comes from a person's mind. (17)

Internet Assigned Numbers Authority (IANA). Nonprofit organization responsible for the control of IP addresses. (8)

Internet Control Message Protocol (ICMP). Component of the TCP/IP protocol responsible for transmitting messages across networks. (8)

Internet Corporation for Assigned Names and Numbers (ICANN). Nonprofit organization that maintains the responsibility for managing and coordinating the maintenance of the databases that store information about the owner of website, including contact information. (8)

Internet Information Service (IIS). Web-server software in the Microsoft Server operating system. (12)

Internet Key Exchange Protocol version 2 (IKEv2). Tunneling protocol that uses the IPSEC tunneling protocol over UDP on port 500. (9)

Internet of Things (IoT). Computing technology incorporated into nontypical devices to allow communication with other devices and the Internet. (2, 7)

intranet. A private Internet environment for internal use only. (9)

intrusion-detection system (IDS). Monitors the system and sends an alert if there is a problem. (9)

intrusion-prevention system (IPS). Extension of the IDS that not only detects malicious or suspicious behavior, but can take action to stop the problem. (9)

intrusive scan. Scanner tries to exploit vulnerabilities. (6)

IP Security (IPSEC). Uses cryptographic functions to provide data integrity and confidentiality for IP traffic. (11)

IT asset management (ITAM) system. Software that assists in maintaining the assets on a network. (6)

IT contingency plan. Outline of what must be restored after an incident. (16)

IT Infrastructure Library (ITIL). Framework that offers best practices for IT. (15)

J

jailbreaking Bypassing built-in limitations of an iOS mobile device. (7)

jamming. Intentionally interfering with wireless signals to prevent the transmission from being usable; this act is illegal. (10)

Jersey wall. Tee-shaped wall usually made of concrete to prevent vehicles from passing; can be moved into and out of place with heavy equipment. (5)

job-acquisition skills. Skills used to obtain employment, such as writing a résumé and filling out an application. (18)

job rotation. Users cycle through different roles. (3)

jump bag. Includes hardware and software tools that can be used by first responders to help isolate or remove threats. (17)

junk science. Use of methods and data that are fraudulent or fake. (17)

K

Kerberos. Standard authentication protocol on all versions of Microsoft Server when using the Active Directory. (3)

Key Distribution Center (KDC). Service running on a server that has a copy of the Active Directory to manage the main functions of Authentication Service (AS) exchange and Ticket Granting Service (TGS) exchange. (3)

key escrow. Archive of a copy of a private key held by a trusted third party. (11)

keylogger. Technology that tracks a user's keystrokes on the keyboard. (2)

key pair. The use of both public and private keys. (11)

key stretching. Process of salting passwords to make them longer and more complex, thus harder to crack. (11)

kill switch. Together, the ability to remotely erase and lock the mobile device. (7)

L

Layer 2 Tunneling Protocol (L2TP). Tunneling protocol created by Cisco and provides more security than PPTP, but is not as fast. (9)

LDAPS. Secure form of LDAP where transmissions are encrypted for confidentiality. (3)

leadership. Ability to influence others to reach a goal. (18)

legal hold. Forbids destroying data, documents, or other items relevant to an investigation. (17)

library. Used to share commands within the program itself, which allows the programmer not to have to keep rewriting the same code. (12)

Licensed Penetration Tester (LPT). Professional certification that is a hands-on demonstration of the ability to successfully test a target; considered the highest certification for pen testing from the EC-Council. (13)

lifelong learner. Person who looks for chances to acquire information throughout his or her life. (18)

Lightweight Directory Access Protocol (LDAP). Provides standards and ensures that directories or directory services are constructed and used in the same manner. (3)

link-local address. IPv6 address that can be used only on the link (subnet) or broadcast domain; not forwarded through routers. (8)

Linux. Open-source computer operating system that is derived from the UNIX operating system. (4)

listening. Intellectual process that combines hearing with evaluating. (18)

LM hash. Older method of encrypting local passwords (pre-Windows NT); also called *LAN Manager hash.* (11)

load balancing. The processing needs are spread over multiple servers. (14)

local host. The device on which you are working. (8)

logic bomb. Malware deployed when conditions exist that the malware is seeking. (2)

M

MAC address filtering. Limiting which MAC addresses are allowed to access the network. (10)

macro virus. A macro that has been programmed to carry out a malicious intent. (2)

malware. Computer code intentionally written to cause some form of harm; short for *malicious software.* (2)

managed security service (MSS). Outsourced firm that oversees the security aspect of a customer's business. (14)

Mandatory Access Control (MAC). Security strategy that sets a strict level of access to resources based on criteria set by the network administrator. (3)

mandatory vacations. Users are forced to take vacations where they are not on the premises or using the systems. (3)

man-in-the-middle (MITM) attack. A hacker intercepts the data transmitted between the client and the wireless access point. (10)

man page. Formal piece of documentation (manual) in Linux providing help. (4)

mantrap. Physical access control system that uses two sets of interlocking doors; the first set of doors must close before the second set can be opened. (5)

mean time between failures (MTBF). Average time that passes before a failure occurs. (15)

mean time to failure (MTTF). A complex statistic that essentially involves calculating the loss due to failure. (15)

mean time to repair (MTTR). Describes the time it takes to repair or replace a failed component. (15)

Media Access Control (MAC) address. Physical address embedded into the hardware of a network card. (8)

media sanitization. Process of completely removing data from a computerized device. (16)

message digest. The hash value, or output. (11)

message of the day (MotD). Banner displayed to the user before he or she logs in to the router. (9)

metadata. Data that provides information about other data. (7)

metasploit. Open-source computer security project that provides information and tools for pen testers. (13)

microdot. An image shrunk to roughly the size of a period. (11)

mirrored site. Operationally active site that is continuously synchronized with the primary site to maintain current information. (16)

mission statement. Single sentence stating why the company or organization exists. (18)

morals. An individual's ideas of what is right and wrong. (18)

MS-CHAP. Microsoft's version of the Challenge Handshake Authentication Protocol. (9)

multifactor authentication. Combining different forms of authentication to authenticate a user. (3)

multifunction peripheral (MFP). Output device that can perform multiple functions: printing, faxing, scanning, and e-mailing. (7)

multitenant computing. Sharing the hardware resources in a public cloud with other customers. (14)

mutual authentication. When both peers agree that the other is who they claim to be before transmitting data securely between the two hosts. (11)

N

National Cybersecurity and Communications Integration Center (NCCIC). Centralized location within the Department of Homeland Security for sharing and coordinating cybersecurity efforts. (17)

National Institute of Standards and Technology (NIST). Governmental organization for standardizing measurement, technology, and industrial standards. (13)

near-field communication (NFC). Allows devices to communicate through electromagnetic radio fields as opposed to the radio transmissions used by Wi-Fi. (10)

netstat. Command that allows viewing TCP and UDP connections and further filtering the view to ICMP, IPv4 and IPv6; used to see statistics and which ports are open, closed, or listening to incoming sessions. (8)

network access control (NAC). Environment in which standards are set that hosts must meet before they are able to connect to the network. (9)

Network Access Protection (NAP). Microsoft's version of a network access control solution. (9)

Network Address Translation (NAT). Network service that converts an internal private number to a number for a public network such as the Internet. (8)

network neutrality. Concept that states all traffic on the Internet should receive equal consideration; also called *net neutrality.* (14)

New Technology File System (NTFS) permissions. Allow rights to be set for users on a Windows system. (3)

noisy neighbor issue. When one customer of the public cloud uses most of the resources. (14)

nonauthoritative DNS server. Holds requests from clients for a period of time to speed up subsequent requests and does not contain copies of any domains. (9)

nonce. Random value only used once that can help disguise a password. (11)

noncredentialed scan. Scanner is not authenticated; conducted to provide a quick view of vulnerabilities. (6)

nondisclosure agreement (NDA). Forbids revealing any of the information discussed or discovered. (13)

nonintrusive scan. A simple scan of the target not generally detected. (6)

nonrepudiation process. Changes to a system are tracked by which user account made them. (2)

NoSQL. Nonstructured database language that does not rely on tables or accessing data through SQL commands. (12)

NT hash. Created simply by using one of the hashing algorithms; does not support the use of cryptographic salt. (11)

O

object. Self-contained resource that stores information about itself in properties and provides program code that can be used to interact with it. (4)

Occupational Safety and Health Administration (OSHA). Federal agency that sets and enforces standards related to safe and healthy working conditions. (18)

octet. One of the four 8-bit sections in a TCP/IP IPv4 address. (8)

offboarding. Process of closing an employee's accounts and records when he or she leaves the company. (5)

onboarding. Process of providing a new employee with all information he or she needs on the company, business processes, security policies, and other related material. (5)

one-time password (OTP). A password valid for only one login or transaction, often for only a short period. (3)

onion network. A method of rerouting of data through many computers on the Internet before being delivered to the destination. (1)

Open Source Intelligence (OSINT). Involves obtaining information that is freely available online using passive information gathering, semipassive information gathering, or active information gathering. (13)

Open Web Application Security Project (OWASP). Nonprofit, worldwide community effort that focuses on development of secure web environments. (12)

order of volatility. Sequence in which locations should be searched for evidence. (17)

organizational chart. Shows the line of authority in a business. (18)

OS fingerprinting. Identifying the operating system of the network being tested. (13)

out-of-band. Released without waiting until the next regularly scheduled date for patches. (6)

P

packet-filtering firewall. Can either allow or block traffic entering or exiting the firewall by evaluating network addresses, ports, or protocols. (6)

packet sniffer. Tool that intercepts raw data traveling on network media. (8)

paging. Process used by the operating system when physical memory becomes low to temporarily free physical memory by removing unused processes from RAM to a file on the hard disk. (17)

passive information gathering. Target is not aware of the reconnaissance. (13)

pass-the-hash attack. Hacker obtains the hash of an object, such as a user's password, and submits the hash as if it were the real data. (13)

Password Authentication Protocol (PAP). Legacy authentication protocol that is not encrypted and should not be used. (9)

Password-Based Key Derivation Function 2 (PBKDF2). Key-stretching technique based on public key cryptography standards (PKCS). (11)

password spraying. Hacker tries the same password on every account in a system. (13)

patch. Update provided by the vendor to correct errors or bugs. (6)

path validation. Process in Windows of verifying a digital certificate has not been revoked. (11)

payload. The actions of malicious code. (2)

Payment Card Industry Data Security Standard (PCI DSS). Set of regulations from credit card vendors that apply to businesses using their services; an industry standard, not a law. (2)

Penetration Tester (CPT+). Professional certification from CompTIA testing the ability to conduct penetration testing, including vulnerability assessment and management skills. (13)

penetration testing. Process in which security personnel attempt to penetrate a network to locate vulnerabilities; also called *pen testing* or *ethical hacking.* (13)

Penetration Testing Execution Standard. Minimum set of standards that all penetration tests should address. (13)

perimeter network. A demilitarized zone (DMZ). (9)

permission. Specific abilities within a right or with files and folders. (3)

persistent cookie. Cookie that stays on the computer until an expiration date is met. (2)

personal cloud. Cloud service managed by the user to store files or offer services within his or her household; also called *home cloud.* (14)

personally identifiable information (PII). Any data that can be used to pinpoint a specific person. (5)

pharming. Involves setting up a website that looks legitimate and credible, but is used to steal personal information entered by users. (5)

phishing. Attempting to obtain personal information through fake e-mails that appear to be real. (5)

phreaking. Hacking into a phone system. (1)

physical controls. Tangible items installed for security. (15)

piggybacking. Gaining access to a wireless network without permission; this act is illegal. (10)

ping sweep. Scans a subnet using ICMP requests to map out valid IP addresses. (8)

piping. Process of sending output results from one command into another. (4)

platform as a service (PaaS). Cloud-computing solution that allows a customer to develop applications and to run and manage them without creating the underlying platform. (14)

point of sale (PoS) device. Used to record transactions and process payments. (7)

Point-to-Point Protocol (PPTP). Tunneling protocol that provides data confidentiality in the form of the encryption, but does not support integrity; the most outdated of the tunneling protocols. (9)

policy. Set of rules that can automatically control access to resources. (3)

polyalphabetic substitution cipher. Mixes a number of cipher alphabets in the cryptogram so each plain text letter is continuously changed. (11)

polymorphic virus. Malware that changes its characteristics in attempts to avoid detection from antivirus programs. (2)

port scanning. Actively probing a system to discover ports that are open on a system. (13)

power spike. Brief surge of power. (16)

power surge. Fluctuation in the supplied voltage; also called *power spike.* (16)

preshared key. Key used in symmetric encryption that must be shared in advance of use. (11)

pretext. Fabricated scenario or story that entices the recipient to click a link. (13)

pretexting. Using a lie or scam to obtain private information. (2)

Pretty Good Privacy (PGP). One of the most popular encryption protocol and program for creating secure data communication for e-mail. (11)

private cloud. Cloud environment owned and managed by its own organization. (14)

private key. Decrypts data encrypted with its corresponding public key; only known to the receiver and not shared in any way. (11)

problem-solving. Process used to evaluate a situation and find a solution. (18)

procedural controls. Processes and policies put in place for security. (15)

professional attire. The dress a workplace dictates. (18)

professional communication. Communication associated with technology or business. (18)

programming language. The interface and structure used by the programmer to develop code to create a meaningful application. (12)

proprietary. Owned by someone and cannot be used without permission. (8)

Protected EAP (PEAP). Fully encloses or, encapsulates, the Extensible Authentication Protocol. (9)

protected health information (PHI). Individually identifiable health information in the form of electronic data, paper records, or even spoken conversation. (2)

protocol. Industry-accepted standardized format that allows communication between devices. (8)

provider. Environment in PowerShell like a layer that allows managing a specific data store using common commands. (4)

provisioning. In virtual computing, the ability to quickly deploy resources when needed. (1)

proxy server firewall. Analyzes the packet's data as well as its header; the most advanced firewall. (6)

public cloud. Offers services to anyone. (14)

public key. Encrypts the data to be used with an associated private key and can be located anywhere; is not secret. (11)

public key infrastructure (PKI). Process in which communication from different entities can occur securely through the use of security certificates. (11)

Q

qualitative risk assessment. Used when there are not actual data or values to back up a claim. (15)

quantitative risk assessment. Method of assessing risk based on actual data that uses numbers or monetary values. (15)

query. Drawing select data from the tables in a database. (12)

quick response (QR) code. A two-dimensional bar code that can store textual information. (7)

R

RAID 0. Redundant array of independent disks in which multiple hard drives work in sync with each other when saving or retrieving data; also called *disk striping.* (16)

RAID 1. Redundant array of independent disks in which two hard drives are used, each a mirror or copy of the other drive; also called *disk mirroring.* (16)

RAID 1+0. Redundant array of independent disks that is a combination of RAID 1 and RAID 0; also called *stripe of mirrors, nested RAID,* and *hybrid RAID.* (16)

RAID 5. Redundant array of independent disks in which data are written across at least three drives similar to a striping array (RAID 0), however, on the third drive, a value called parity is created and written; also called *disk striping with parity.* (16)

rainbow table. Precomputed table of calculations that can be used to speed up the process of cracking a password by using two functions, a hashing function and a reduction function (11)

RAM scraper. Scans the memory in the PoS system and reports the findings. (7)

ransomware. Encrypts data, rather than stealing or destroying, to prevent user access unless a fee is paid to the hacker; also called *cryptomalware.* (2)

RC4 (Rivest cipher 4) encryption. Stream cipher characterized by a variable-size cipher and a random algorithm based on permutation. (11)

record. Collection of related information in a database. (12)

recovery agent. Special account in Encrypting File System to restore access. (11)

recovery point objective (RPO). Maximum amount of data that can be afforded to lose. (16)

recovery team. Those people who are required for completing a disaster-recovery plan. (16)

recovery time objective (RTO). Target date by which services must be restored after a disaster to avoid unacceptable consequences. (16)

redundancy. In IT, having a backup solution that can immediately be used in the event of a failure. (16)

Regional Computer Forensic Laboratories (RCFL). Computer Analysis Response Team facilities dedicated to the examination of digital evidence. (17)

Regional Internet Registrars (RIRs). Five different registrars for IANA that assign IP addresses. (8)

relational database. Database containing multiple tables that are linked together. (12)

remote access Trojan (RAT). Malware that allows the hacker to use an embedded backdoor to gain administrative control of the victim's computer. (2)

replay attack. Hacker captures login credentials during an initial attack, stores them, and retransmits them at another time. (10)

residual risk. Risk that remains after mitigation controls are implemented. (15)

resilience. Capacity to recover quickly from a situation. (14)

résumé. Document profiling your career goals, education, and work history. (18)

right. Ability to perform a type of action on the computer. (3)

risk. Situation that could cause harm, create a hazard, or otherwise cause problems that need to be addressed. (15)

risk acceptance Making the decision to assume the risk. (15)

risk assessment. Identifying risks and ranking them with the most critical risks listed first; also called a *risk analysis.* (15)

risk avoidance. Eliminating the risk by removing the vulnerability. (15)

risk management. Structured approach to identifying the areas that could result in risk and then planning solutions and methods to reduce, eliminate, or respond to the situation. (15)

risk mitigation. Taking steps to reduce the likelihood or the impact of the risk. (15)

risk transfer. Assigning the responsibility for the risk to a third party. (15)

rogue router. Router that is placed in a business to entice users to connect to it and thus have their credentials stolen. (10)

Role-Based Access Control (RBAC). Security strategy in which rights are assigned to a role instead of manually to each individual user. (3)

rooting. Bypassing built-in limitations of an Android mobile device. (7)

rootkit. A virus that infects a computer before the operating system loads. (2)

rule-based access control. Similar to MAC, DAC, and RBAC except rules are established for various situations. (3)

S

sandbox. Virtual environment separating running programs and processes from the main computer system to provide an isolated place to test and deploy applications and configurations. (1, 14)

Sarbanes-Oxley Act (SOX). Law preventing company executives from hiding or destroying electronic records. (2)

satellite communication (SATCOM). Space-based wireless network in which an orbital satellite provides the connection to the host. (10)

scalability. Ability of hardware to accommodate based on demand of the system as needs grow or shrink. (14)

scope. In a pen test, defines exactly what will be tested. (13)

scope creep. Changes or additional requests are made after the project begins. (13)

screened subnet. A demilitarized zone (DMZ). (9)

script. Single file listing PowerShell commands and options that will be processed in order. (4)

script kiddie. Slang for an individual who uses premade tools to perform attacks. (1)

secondary logon. Allows log in as a standard user, but the ability to run specific programs as an administrator. (3)

secure cookie. Cookie that can only be sent using an encrypted session. (2)

secure copy protocol (SCP). Based on SSH to allow the secure copying of files from the local host to the remote host. (8)

Secure File Transfer Protocol (SFTP). Method of transferring data securely between clients. (8)

secure shell (SSH). An encrypted interface that uses port 22 for transactions and a public key encryption to authenticate the source of the data. (8)

Secure Socket Tunneling Protocol (SSTP). Tunneling protocol that provides support for traffic over an SSL 3.0–encrypted connection. (9)

Secure Sockets Layer (SSL) protocol. Developed by Netscape to transmit sensitive information with encryption; implemented as part of the enhanced security protocol of Transport Layer Security. (11)

Security Assertion Markup Language (SAML). XML framework that ensures transmissions for secure-sign on capabilities are secure. (3)

Security Account Manager (SAM). The local database of users and groups on a Windows system; is nonhierarchical. (3, 11)

security as a service (SECaaS). Cloud-based malware, firewall, and intrusion protection. (14)

semipassive information gathering. Using the target's resources just as any normal customer would, but collecting data at the same time. (13)

semiqualitative values. Descriptive analysis setting ranges assigned to a loss. (15)

sender policy framework (SPF). DNS solution that creates a special DNS record to verify the validity of an e-mail sender. (5)

separation of duty. Responsibilities are divided so no single individual has complete control over a process or task. (5)

server room. Secured room in which servers and networking equipment are installed. (5)

server-side script. Script that runs on the web server. (12)

service. Any program that is run in the background of an operating system to provide specific features and functionality; called a *daemon* on Linux hosts. (6)

service set identifier (SSID). Name of a wireless network when a network has multiple access points and all APs have the same name. (10)

session cookie. Cookie that exists only as long as the web browser is open. (2)

share permissions. Allow users to set folder usage that can be accessed by other users. (3)

Shibboleth. Open-source standard that offers single sign-on capabilities. (3)

sideloading. Installing unofficial apps on a mobile device. (7)

single loss expectancy (SLE). Amount of value that will be lost from one incident. (15)

single sign-on (SSO). Authentication service that allows a user to use one login and password combination to access a set of services. (3)

site-local address. IPv6 address similar to a private address in IPv4; cannot be seen on the Internet. (8)

skimmer. Reads the credit card data at the same time as the PoS device, and then sends the data to the hacker. (7)

slack space. Remaining space in a cluster when a file is written and not all the space is used by the file. (17)

smishing. Use of SMS messages as the means of reaching victims. (5)

Smurf attack. Involves overwhelming the victim's computer with ICMP requests. (8)

snapshot. Freeze frame of the system image and all its files and configuration. (1, 16)

social engineering. Using social tools and techniques to obtain information. (2)

socket. IP address and port together. (8)

soft skills. Personal skills used to communicate and work well with others; also called *interpersonal skills, people skills,* and *transferrable skills.* (1, 18)

software as a service (SaaS). Complete software solution from the cloud without needing to install resources locally. (14)

software development kit (SDK). Collection of tools, such as libraries, that help programmers create applications for specific software. (12)

spear phishing. Phishing attack targeting specific individuals who may not be wealthy or prominent. (5)

SQL injection attack. Hacker injects SQL–formatted commands instead of data as the input. (12)

stateful-inspection firewall. Monitors packets over a period of time and accepts only packets that were previously tracked. (6)

static-code analysis. Tools are used to analyze the code without actually running the program to find possible vulnerabilities. (12)

steganography. Practice of hiding a file, text, image, or even a video inside another file. (11)

stream cipher. Encrypts each bit of data at one time. (11)

STRIDE. Threat model consisting of six categories of threats: spoofing identity, tampering, repudiation, information disclosure, denial of service (DoS), and elevation of privilege. (13)

Structured Query Language (SQL). Programming language for managing a relational database. (12)

subnet mask. A value that, when mathematically compared to the network address, can identify which portion of the IP address is part of the network and which portion identifies the unique host value. (8)

substitution cipher. Cipher in which each letter represents a different letter. (11)

supervisory control and data acquisition (SCADA) system. Hardware and software used to monitor an interface with the controls for machines and equipment in an industrial process. (7)

supplicant. Computer trying to connect to the WLAN for authentication. (10)

switch. Command option or parameter. (4)

symbolic link. Made to *another* link, not directly to the original data. (4)

symmetric encryption. A single key is used to encrypt and decrypt data. (11)

SYN flood. Involves the hacker exploiting a vulnerability in the three-way handshake by not closing the handshake. (8)

System Health Agent (SHA). Software or code that performs the self-check on the client. (9)

systems development life cycle (SDLC). Process used to create, deploy, and maintain a software program. (12)

T

tabletop exercise. Individuals involved in the process are led through the business-continuity plan process by a facilitator. (16)

tailgating. An unauthorized person walking into a facility with or right behind authorized people to appear as if with them. (5)

teamwork. Cooperative efforts of team members to reach a goal. (18)

technical controls. Technology used to automate security functions. (15)

technical report. In a pen-testing report, details the specific vulnerabilities found during the test. (13)

Telnet. A component of the TCP/IP protocol suite that allows a person to remotely login to another host on the network; short for *terminal network*. (8)

TEMPEST. Specification developed by the National Security Agency (NSA) that deals with methods for spying using electromagnetic radiation and methods to prevent such activities. (5)

terms of service (ToS). Legal agreement outlining what services are and are not provided by the vendor and the user's responsibilities toward fulfilling the agreement. (14)

testing timeline. States when the stages of testing will happen. (13)

third-party cookie. Cookie that originates from a visit to a website, but references a different website. (2)

threat. Something that takes a vulnerability to a level where the flaws can be exploited. (2)

threat agent. Source, or *actor,* that causes a threat to occur. (15)

threat modeling. Identifying potential threats and determining which ones are high-value assets. (13)

three-way handshake. The sending host and receiving client complete a three-step process to verify the successful transmission of a data exchange: 1. SYN connection from Host A to Host B; 2. SYN/ACK connection from Host B to Host A; and 3. ACK connection from Host A to Host B. (8)

time bomb. Malware that deploys its payload when a date or time occurs. (2)

time management. Practice of organizing your time and tasks to be most efficient. (18)

time to live (TTL). Value that controls how long a packet will search for a destination address before it is deleted. (8)

Tor browser. Used to access the anonymous websites on the darknet. (1)

transitive trust. Two-way trust relationship; when a user is authenticated in one security domain, he or she is authenticated into the other security domain. (3)

Transport Layer Security (TLS). Upgraded Secure Sockets Layer protocol with a new security protocol. (11)

transposition cipher. Cipher in which the words are rearranged within the text. (11)

Triple DES (3DES) encryption. Symmetric encryption that uses Data Encryption Standard, but with two or three keys. (11)

Trojan horse. Malware hidden inside other software that appears to be harmless. (2)

Trusted Platform Module (TPM). A special chip located in the computer's hardware that runs authentication checks on hardware, software, and firmware. (7)

tunneling. Encrypting the data traveling across the remote connection with a VPN. (9)

turnstile. Device with bars or other obstruction to alternately block an entryway and allow only one person to pass at a time. (5)

Twofish encryption. Block cipher that encrypts data in 128-bit blocks; successor to Blowfish. (11)

Type 1 hypervisor. A hypervisor that interacts directly with the hardware instead of interfacing with the host operating system. (1)

Type 2 hypervisor. A hypervisor that runs on the host operating system. (1)

typosquatting. Hacker registers a web domain name that is similar to a trusted website to take advantage of users making a mistake when entering a web address. (12)

U

unified threat management (UTM). An all-in-one security device that allows the network to be managed from one location. (9)

Uniform Resource Identifier (URI). Address of each resource on the web; each must be unique. (12)

uninterruptible power supply (UPS). Device that can provide power from a battery in the event of a power loss. (16)

United States Computer Emergency Readiness Team (US-CERT). Responsible for analyzing cyberthreats, issuing warnings, and coordinating incident-response activities; a branch of National Cybersecurity and Communications Integration Center. (17)

user account control (UAC). Technology used to govern security by limiting what a standard user is able to do on a system. (3)

V

verbal communication. Speaking words to communicate. (18)

VirtualBox. Open-source virtualization platform from Oracle. (1)

virtual local area network (VLAN). Logical grouping of hosts that treats them as if they were physically connected. (9)

virtual machine (VM). Looks and functions like an actual computer operating system, but is separated from the operating system running on the machine. (1)

virtual machine escape. An exploit in which malicious code is run on the VM that allows the guest operating system to break out of its environment and interact directly with the hypervisor. (1)

virtual machine monitor (VMM). A hypervisor. (1)

virtual machine (VM) sprawl. Occurs with the continuous deployment of virtual machines. (1)

virtual private network (VPN). Provides a method to secure data traveling through other networks, such as the Internet. (9)

virus. Malicious software code that is unleased and attempts to perform its destructive content when it is opened or accessed. (1)

vishing. Voice-based phishing in which the hacker calls the user impersonating someone else. (5)

Visual, Agile, and Simple Threat (VAST). Threat model based on scaling the model across the infrastructure. (13)

VLAN access control list (VACL). Allows traffic to be filtered within the virtual local area network. (9)

VMWare. A line of virtualization products that includes desktop workstation and player versions. (1)

VPN concentrator. Device that adds support for many tunnels of traffic. (9)

vulnerability. A flaw or potential for harm. (2)

vulnerability analysis. Stage of penetration testing attempting to discover flaws that may be exploited by a hacker. (13)

vulnerability scanner. Software that automates the process of scanning systems for potential weaknesses in software, configurations, and other settings. (6)

W

warchalking. Act of publicly marking the locations where wireless network connections are found. (10)

wardriving. Act of driving around trying to identify wireless networks. (10)

warm site. Equipment is maintained in the location, but not current backups of data. (16)

waterfall model. Systems development life cycle that is sequential. (12)

watering hole. Attack in which hackers embed malicious code in websites often visited by specific individuals, departments, or all employees of a company. (5)

watermark. Image or text included in a file often used to prove ownership. (11)

wearable technology. Type of IoT device worn by a person that is basically a minicomputer performing specific functions. (7)

web application firewall (WAF). Firewall designed to specifically monitor and filter HTTP traffic in and out of a web server. (12)

whale phishing. Phishing attack targeting individuals with a high net worth or with high status; also called *whaling.* (5)

white box test. Pen test in which the tester has been given full knowledge of the system. (13)

white-hat hacker. Generally ethical and law-abiding hacker. (1)

white listing. Process in which MAC addresses allowed to connect to the network are filtered in. (10)

WHOIS. System that provides the owner of a domain and a contact person for the domain by querying the ICANN databases. (8)

Wi-Fi. Wireless networking technology that uses radio waves instead of wires or fiber optic cable. (10)

wildcard character. Used to represent one or more unknown characters in a string. (4)

Windows Management Instrumentation (WMI). Infrastructure in Windows for managing data and operations. (4)

Wired Equivalent Privacy (WEP). Very outdated encryption protocol for routers used with older, legacy wireless equipment. (10)

wireless client (STA). Fixed or mobile device that has the ability to communicate as a client using the 802.11 standard; known as the *station.* (10)

wireless NIC. Network interface card used to connect to the wireless network. (10)

wireless router. Has the same capability of an access point, but also adds the functionality of wireless connection to local area networks (LANs) or wide area networks (WANs). (10)

wireless site survey. Creates a map of the wireless signal, its strength, and its coverage. (10)

work ethic. Belief that honest work is a reward on its own. (18)

worm. Malicious software that spreads on its own through computer networks. (1)

WPA handshake. Four-step authentication process used to pass information to and from the WAP and client to set up data encryption. (10)

write-blocker. Tool that permits read-only access to a storage device. (17)

written communication. Recording words through writing to communicate. (18)

X

X.509. Format for public digital certificates to ensure consistent formatting. (11)

Z

zero-day vulnerability. Flaw that exists in software when it was released and remains unknown until it is exploited by hackers. (2)

zero-level formatting. Process in which new data are written over the top of existing data to destroy the existing data. (7)